PARKIN ◆ BADE
ECONOMICS
CANADA IN THE GLOBAL ENVIRONMENT

STUDY GUIDE
THIRD EDITION

AVI J. COHEN
York University

HARVEY B. KING
University of Regina

Addison-Wesley Publishers Limited

Don Mills, Ontario • Reading, Massachusetts • Menlo Park, California
New York • Wokingham, England • Amsterdam • Bonn
Sydney • Singapore • Tokyo • Madrid • San Juan • Paris • Seoul
Milan • Mexico City • Taipei

ISBN 0-201-42958-6

Printed and bound in Canada.

A B C D E -MP- 01 00 99 98 97

Executive Editor:	**Joseph Gladstone**
Managing Editor:	**Linda Scott**
Acquisitions Editor:	**Dawn Lee**
Copy Editor:	**Pamela Erlichman**
Production Coordinator:	**Melanie van Rensburg**
Manufacturing Coordinator:	**Sharon Latta Paterson**
Cover Design:	**Anthony Leung**
Desktop:	**Nelson Gonzalez**

*Dedicated to
Alexis, Madeleine, and Katherine,
who teach me as they learn (AJC)
and to
Tracy (HBK)*

TABLE OF CONTENTS

INTRODUCTION

Before You Begin...

Our experience has taught us that what first-year economics students want most from a study guide is help in mastering course material in order to do well on examinations. We have developed this *Study Guide* to respond specifically to that demand. Using this *Study Guide* alone, however, is not enough to guarantee that you will do well in your course. In order to help you overcome the problems and difficulties that most first-year students encounter, we have some general advice on how to study, as well as some specific advice on how to best use this *Study Guide*.

Some Friendly Advice

The study of economics requires a different style of thinking than what you may encounter in other courses. Economists make extensive use of assumptions to break down complex problems into simple, analytically manageable parts. This analytical style, while not ultimately more demanding than the styles of thinking in other disciplines, feels unfamiliar to most students and requires practice. As a result, it is not as easy to do well in economics simply on the basis of your raw intelligence and high school knowledge as it is in many other first-year courses. Many students who come to our offices are frustrated and puzzled by the fact that they are getting A's and B's in their other courses but only a C or worse in economics. They have not recognized that the study of economics is different and requires practice. In order to avoid a frustrating visit to your instructor after your first test, we suggest you do the following.

Don't rely solely on your high school economics. If you took high school economics, you will have seen the material on supply and demand which your instructor will lecture on in the first few weeks. Don't be lulled into feeling that the course will be easy. Your high school knowledge of economic concepts will be very useful, but it will not be enough to guarantee high marks on exams. Your college or university instructors will demand much more detailed knowledge of concepts and ask you to apply them in new circumstances.

Keep up with the course material on a weekly basis. Read the appropriate chapter in the textbook before your instructor lectures on it. In this initial reading, don't worry about details or arguments you can't quite follow—just try to get a general understanding of the basic concepts and issues. You may be amazed at how your instructor's ability to teach improves when you come to class prepared. As soon as your instructor has finished covering a chapter, complete the corresponding *Study Guide* chapter. Avoid cramming the day before or even just the week before an exam. Because economics requires practice, cramming is an almost certain recipe for failure.

Keep a good set of lecture notes. Good lecture notes are vital for focusing your studying. Your instructor will only lecture on a subset of topics from the textbook. The topics your instructor covers in a lecture should usually be given priority when studying. Also give priority to studying the figures and graphs covered in the lecture. If you use the *Notetaker* (see description below) to insert key figures and graphs in your notes, you will have a clear and concise study aid.

Instructors do differ in their emphasis on lecture notes or the textbook, so ask early on in the course which is more important in reviewing for exams—lecture notes or the textbook. If your instructor answers that both are important, then ask the following, typically economic question: at the margin, which will be more beneficial—spending an extra hour re-reading your lecture notes or an extra hour re-reading the textbook? This question assumes that you have read each textbook chapter twice (once before lecture for a general understanding, and then later for a thorough understanding); that you have prepared a good set of lecture notes; and that you have worked through all of the problems in the appropriate *Study Guide* chapters. By applying this style of analysis to the problem of efficiently allocating your study time, you are already beginning to think like an economist!

Use your instructor and/or teaching assistants for help. When you have questions or problems with course material, come to the office to ask questions. Remember, you are paying for your education and instructors are there to help you learn. We are often amazed at how few students come to see us during office hours. Don't be shy. The personal contact that comes from one-on-one tutoring is professionally gratifying for us as well as (hopefully) beneficial for you.

Form a study group. A very useful way to motivate your studying and to learn economics is to discuss the course material and problems with other students. Explaining the answer to a question out loud is a very effective way of discovering how well you understand the question. When you answer a question only in your head, you often skip steps in the chain of reasoning without realizing it. When you are forced to explain your reasoning aloud, gaps and mistakes quickly appear, and you (with your fellow group members) can quickly correct your reasoning. The True/False/Uncertain questions in the *Study Guide* and the Review and Critical Thinking questions at the end of each textbook chapter are good study group material. You might also get together after having worked the *Study Guide* problems, but before looking at the answers, and help each other solve unsolved problems.

Work old exams. One of the most effective ways of studying is to work through exams your instructor has given in previous years. Old exams give you a feel for the style of question your instructor may ask, and give you the opportunity to get used to time pressure if you force yourself to do the exam in the allotted time. Studying from old exams is not cheating, as long as you have obtained a copy of the exam legally. Some institutions keep old exams in the library, others in the department or at the student union. Upper-year students who have previously taken the course are usually a good source as well. Remember, though, that old exams are a useful study aid only if you use them to understand the reasoning behind each question. If you simply memorize answers in the hopes that your instructor will repeat the identical question, you are likely to fail. From year to year, instructors routinely change the questions or change the numerical values for similar questions.

Use the other study aids. In addition to the *Study Guide*, there are two other study aids that we believe are worth purchasing for the help they will provide in mastering course material and doing well on examinations. However, don't just take our word for it— ask students who have used these aids for their opinions.

The *NoteTaker* (previously called *Graphpad*) contains all of the graphs from the textbook that your instructor is likely to use in class. This means that you do not have to spend time in class copying the graphs. Instead, just tear off the appropriate graph from the *NoteTaker* and insert it into your notebook. The graphs are printed on notebook-sized pages with three-ring binder holes already punched for convenience. In addition to the graphs, the pages are covered with grids for drawing additional graphs or taking notes. By eliminating tedious copying, the *NoteTaker* allows you to concentrate on understanding what your instructor is saying. And better understanding translates into better grades.

Economics in Action is a state-of-the-art interactive software for IBM-compatible computers. It is an integrated tutorial, graphing, demonstration, and testing program that covers all the main themes in the textbook using three modes. The tutorial mode places you in an economics-related job situation and leads you through assignments that reveal and explore

economic concepts and principles. The free mode allows you to interact with economic models by changing parameters and observing the effects on graphs. The quiz mode gives you graphical or data-related multiple-choice questions. When you select an answer, you are given a detailed explanation (and graphical illustration) of why your answer is right or wrong. All software modes are closely integrated with the textbook.

Using the Study Guide

You should only attempt to complete a chapter in the *Study Guide* after you have read the corresponding textbook chapter and listened to your instructor lecture on the material. Each *Study Guide* chapter contains the following sections.

Key Concepts This first section is a one- to two-page summary, in point form, of all key definitions, concepts, and material from the textbook chapter. The summary is organized using the same major section headings from the textbook chapter. Key terms from the textbook appear in bold. This section is designed to focus you quickly and precisely on the core material that you must master. It is an excellent study aid for the night before an exam. Think of it as crib notes that will serve as a final check of the key concepts you have studied.

Helpful Hints When you encounter difficulty in mastering concepts or techniques, you will not be alone. Many students find certain concepts difficult and often make the same kinds of mistakes. We have seen these common mistakes often enough to have learned how to help students avoid them. The hints point out these mistakes and offer tips to avoid them. The hints focus on the most important concepts, equations, and techniques for problem solving. They also review crucial graphs that appear on every instructor's exams. We hope that this section will be very useful, since instructors always ask exam questions designed to test these possible mistakes in your understanding.

This section sometimes includes extra material that your instructor may add to the course, but is not in textbook chapters. Examples of extra material include the mathematical solutions to demand and supply equations in the mathematical note to textbook Chapter 4 and the website appendix to textbook Chapter 19 on "Ideas About Fairness." This extra material is marked with the symbol ⓔ for extra, and may be skipped if your instructor does not cover it.

The symbol ⓔ is used in the *Study Guide* to identify questions and answers based on extra material.

Self-Test This will be one of the most useful sections of the *Study Guide*. The questions are designed to give you practice and to test skills and techniques you must master to do well on exams. There are plenty of the multiple-choice questions (25 for each chapter) that you are most likely to encounter on course tests and exams. There are other types of questions, described below, each with a specific pedagogical purpose. Questions (and answers) based on extra material covered in the Helpful Hints are marked with an ⓔ so that you can easily skip them if your instructor does not assign the extra material. Before we describe the three parts of the Self-Test section, here are some general tips that apply to all parts.

Use a pencil to write your answers in the *Study Guide*. This will allow you to erase your mistakes and have neat, completed pages from which to study. Draw graphs wherever they are applicable. Some questions will ask explicitly for graphs; many others will not but will require a chain of reasoning that involves shifts of curves on a graph. *Always draw the graph.* Don't try to work through the reasoning in your head—you are much more likely to make mistakes that way. Whenever you draw a graph, even in the margins of the *Study Guide*, label the axes. You may think that you can keep the labels in your head, but you will be confronting many different graphs with many different variables on the axes. Avoid confusion and label. As an added incentive, remember that on exams where graphs are required, instructors will deduct marks for unlabelled axes.

Do the Self-Test questions as if they were real exam questions, which means do them *without looking at the answers.* This is the single most important tip we can give you about effectively using the *Study Guide* to improve your test and exam performance. Struggling for the answers to questions that you find difficult is one of the most effective ways to learn. The athletic adage—no pain, no gain—applies equally well to studying. You will learn the most from right answers you had to struggle for and from your wrong answers and mistakes. Only after you have attempted all the questions should you look at the answers. When you finally do check the answers, be sure to understand where you went wrong and why the right answer is correct.

If you want to impose time pressure on yourself to simulate the conditions of a real exam, allow two minutes for each True/False/Uncertain and Multiple-Choice question. The Short Answer Problems vary considerably in their time requirements, so it is difficult to give time estimates for them. However, we believe that such time pressure is probably not a good idea for *Study Guide* questions. A state of mind of relaxed concentration is best for work in the *Study Guide*. Use old exams if you want practice with time pressure, or use the Part Overview Midterm Examinations (see description on page viii).

There are many questions in each chapter, and it will take you somewhere between two and five hours to answer all of them. If you get tired (or bored), don't burn yourself out by trying to work through all of the questions in one sitting. Consider breaking up your Self-Test over two (or more) study sessions.

The three parts of the Self-Test section are:

True/False/Uncertain and Explain   These questions test basic knowledge of chapter concepts and your ability to apply the concepts. Some of the questions challenge your understanding, to see if you can identify mistakes in statements using basic concepts. These questions will quickly identify gaps in your knowledge and are useful to answer out loud in a study group.

When answering, identify each statement as *true*, *false*, or whether you are *uncertain* because the statement may be true or false depending on circumstances or assumptions. Explain your answer in one sentence. The space underneath each question is sufficient for writing your answer.

Multiple-Choice   These more difficult questions test your analytical abilities by asking you to apply concepts to new situations, manipulate information, and solve numerical and graphical problems.

This is the most frequently used type of test and exam question, and the Self-Test contains 25 of them in a scrambled order to reflect a real exam situation. The *Test Bank* that your instructor will likely use to make up exams contains all of the *Study Guide* multiple-choice questions, numerous questions that closely "parallel" the *Study Guide* questions, plus many similar questions.

Read each question and all five choices carefully before you answer. Many of the choices will be plausible and will differ only slightly. You must choose the one best answer. A useful strategy in working these questions is first to eliminate any obviously wrong choices and then to focus on the remaining alternatives. Be aware that sometimes the correct answer will be "none of the above choices is correct." Don't get frustrated or think that you are dim if you can't immediately see the correct answer. These questions are designed to make you work to find the correct choice.

Short Answer Problems   The best way to learn to do economics is to do problems. Problems are also the second-most popular type of test and exam question— practice them as much as possible! Each Self-Test concludes with ten short answer, numerical or graphical problems, often based on economic policy issues. In many chapters, this is the most challenging part of the Self-Test. It is also likely to be the most helpful for deepening your understanding of the chapter material. We have, however, designed the questions to teach as much as to test. We have purposely arranged the parts of each multipart question to lead you through the problem-solving analysis in a gradual and sequential fashion, from easier to more difficult parts.

Difficult problems are marked with the symbol ⓓ for difficult, to alert you to the need for extra time and effort. These ⓓ symbols give you the same indication you would have on a test or exam from the number of marks or minutes allocated to a problem.

Answers   The Self-Test is followed by answers to all questions. But do not look at an answer until you have attempted a question. When you do finally look, use the answers to understand where you went wrong and why the right answer is correct.

Each True/False/Uncertain and Multiple-Choice answer includes a brief, point-form explanation to suggest where you might have gone wrong and the economic reasoning behind the answer. At the end of each answer are page numbers in the textbook where you can go to find a more complete explanation. Answers to difficult questions are marked with a ◑ to indicate why you might have struggled with that question! [We purposely did not mark which True/False/Uncertain and Multiple-Choice questions were difficult, to stay as close as possible to a real test or exam format. In an exam, all Multiple-Choice questions, for example, are worth the same number of marks, and you have no idea which questions are the difficult ones.]

The detailed answers to the Short Answer Problems should be especially useful in clarifying and illustrating typical chains of reasoning involved in economic analysis. Answers to difficult problems are marked with a ◑. If the answers alone do not clear up your confusion, go back to the appropriate sections of the textbook. If that still does not suffice, go to your instructor's or teaching assistants' office, or to your study group members, to get help and clarification.

Part Overview Problem and Midterm Examination   Every few chapters, at the end of each of the nine parts of the textbook, you will find a special problem (and answer). These multipart problems draw on material from all chapters in the part, and emphasize policy and real-world questions (for example, the impact of cigarette smuggling on tax revenues). These Overview Problems will help you integrate concepts from different chapters that may seem unconnected, but that are actually related. We often design exam questions similar to these problems.

Each Part Overview also contains a Midterm Examination, consisting of four multiple-choice questions from each chapter in the textbook part. The Midterm is set up like a real examination or test, with a time limit for working the questions. Like the other multiple-choice questions in the *Study Guide*, there are answers with point-form explanations as well as page numbers in the textbook where you can go to find more complete explanations.

If you effectively combine the use of the textbook, the *Study Guide*, the *NoteTaker*, *Economics in Action*, and all other course resources, you will be well prepared for exams. Equally importantly, you will also have developed analytical skills and powers of

reasoning that will benefit you throughout your life and in whatever career you choose.

Do You Have Any Friendly Advice For Us?

We have attempted to make this *Study Guide* as clear and as useful as possible, and to avoid errors. No doubt, we have not succeeded entirely, and you are the only judges who count in evaluating our attempt. If you discover errors, or if you have other suggestions for improving the *Study Guide*, please write to us. In future editions, we will try to acknowledge the names of all students whose suggestions help us improve the *Study Guide*. Send your correspondence or e-mail to either of us:

Professor Avi J. Cohen
Department of Economics
Vari Hall, York University
Toronto, Ontario M3J 1P3
avicohen@yorku.ca

Professor Harvey B. King
Department of Economics
University of Regina
Regina, Saskatchewan S4S 0A2
Harvey.King@uregina.ca

Acknowledgments

This third edition of the *Study Guide* has benefited from help and advice from many sources. We have adopted some ideas from the Australian *Study Guide* by Teresita Bentick, and from our co-author of the U.S. *Study Guide*, Mark Rush. Many colleagues have helped raise the quality of our questions with suggestions and corrections—we would especially like to thank Robin Bade, Gordon Church, Keith MacKinnon, Michael Parkin, Michael Rushton, and John Stewart. Various students have pointed out mistakes and ambiguities they found in using the *Study Guide*. Thanks to Rupert Baudais, Mark Burton, Henry Chan, Men Kim Chu, Aaron Dantowitz, Sachin Davé, Anna DeSantis, Lanna Fisher, Debra George (for explaining just what currency drain means), Stephen Kertzman, Filippo Lucchese, Shelly Sheets, and Edie Slugoski for helping us in this area. Thanks also to Joseph Gladstone, Pamela Erlichman, Dawn Lee, and Linda Scott for excellent editorial guidance. HK would like to thank Tracy, Harrison, and Morgan for being so patient and supportive while he hid away in his study all those nights and weekends, and Harrison for giving up his computer time. AJC would like to thank Susan for accommodation, encouragement, support, understanding, and for keeping him laughing.

Harvey King
Avi Cohen
January 1997

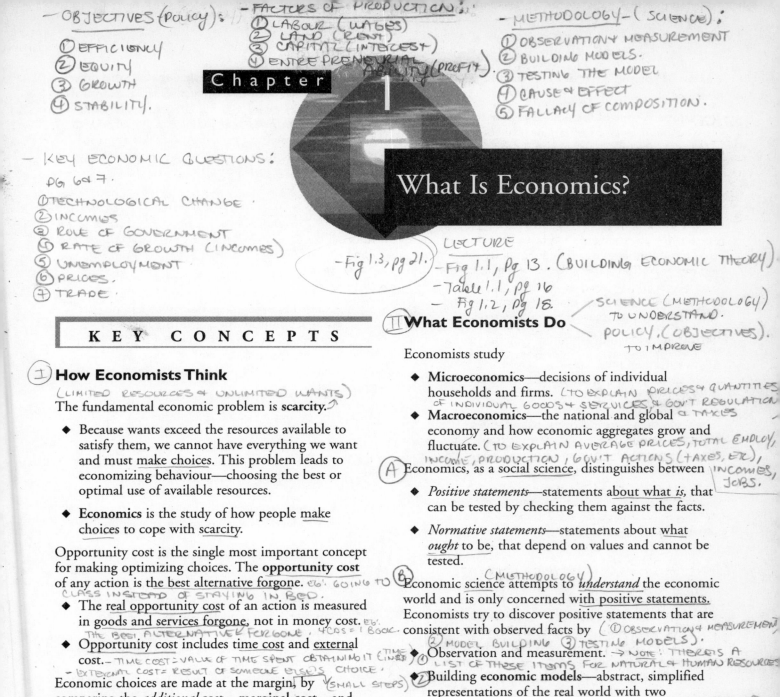

Handwritten annotations (top):

- OBJECTIVES (POLICY):
① EFFICIENCY
② EQUITY
③ GROWTH
④ STABILITY.

- FACTORS OF PRODUCTION:
① LABOUR (WAGES)
② LAND (RENT)
③ CAPITAL (INTEREST)
④ ENTREPRENEURIAL ABILITY (PROFIT).

- METHODOLOGY - (SCIENCE):
① OBSERVATION & MEASUREMENT
② BUILDING MODELS.
③ TESTING THE MODEL
④ CAUSE & EFFECT
⑤ FALLACY OF COMPOSITION.

- KEY ECONOMIC QUESTIONS:
PG 6 & 7.
① TECHNOLOGICAL CHANGE.
② INCOMES
③ ROLE OF GOVERNMENT
④ RATE OF GROWTH (INCOMES)
⑤ UNEMPLOYMENT
⑥ PRICES.
⑦ TRADE.

Chapter 1

What Is Economics?

- Fig 1.3, pg 21.

LECTURE
- Fig 1.1, Pg 13. (BUILDING ECONOMIC THEORY)
- Table 1.1, Pg 16
- Fig 1.2, Pg 18.

SCIENCE (METHODOLOGY)
TO UNDERSTAND.
POLICY. (OBJECTIVES).
TO IMPROVE

KEY CONCEPTS

I How Economists Think

(LIMITED RESOURCES & UNLIMITED WANTS)
The fundamental economic problem is **scarcity**.

- Because wants exceed the resources available to satisfy them, we cannot have everything we want and must make choices. This problem leads to economizing behaviour—choosing the best or optimal use of available resources.

- **Economics** is the study of how people make choices to cope with scarcity.

Opportunity cost is the single most important concept for making optimizing choices. The **opportunity cost** of any action is the best alternative forgone. EG: GOING TO CLASS INSTEAD OF STAYING IN BED.

- The real opportunity cost of an action is measured in goods and services forgone, not in money cost. EG: THE BEST ALTERNATIVE FORGONE, 4 CDS = 1 BOOK.
- Opportunity cost includes time cost and external cost. - TIME COST = VALUE OF TIME SPENT OBTAINING IT (TIME $). - EXTERNAL COST = RESULT OF SOMEONE ELSE'S CHOICE.

Economic choices are made at the margin, by (SMALL STEPS) comparing the *additional* cost—**marginal cost**—and *additional* benefit—**marginal benefit** of a small increase in an activity. If marginal benefit exceeds marginal cost, you choose to increase the activity.
EG: CHOOSE TO BUY THE EXTRA MEMORY FOR THE COMPUTER (B/C BENEFIT OUTWEIGHS THE COST.)

The **principle of substitution** states that when the opportunity cost of an activity increases, people substitute other activities in its place.
EG: SUBSTITUTE PEPSI FOR COKE (B/C COKE MORE EXPENSIVE)

- Changes in marginal costs (opportunity costs) and marginal benefits change the **incentives** people face and change their actions. ∴ OFFER DISCOUNTS / DEALS EG: DISCOUNT IN SUMMER FOR A WINTER SKI CHALET:
- Competition creates ripples along the chain of substitution—second round effects—that dominate first round effects.

∴? THINK: HOW WILL OPPORTUNITY COSTS CHANGE, & WHAT WILL BE THE SUBSTITUTION EFFECT. EG: FROST IN FLORIDA.... ∴↑ IN PRICE OF OJ, → ∴ SUB APPLE JUICE FOR OJ, ∴ ↑ IN PRICE OF APPLE JUICE →? ∴ SUB. EFFECT AGAIN (MAYBE CARROT JUICE) ↑ IN OPPORTUNITY COSTS

II What Economists Do

Economists study

- **Microeconomics**—decisions of individual households and firms. (TO EXPLAIN PRICES & QUANTITIES OF INDIVIDUAL GOODS & SERVICES & GOV'T REGULATION & TAXES)
- **Macroeconomics**—the national and global economy and how economic aggregates grow and fluctuate. (TO EXPLAIN AVERAGE PRICES, TOTAL EMPLOY, INCOME, PRODUCTION, GOV'T ACTIONS (TAXES, ETC), INCOMES, JOBS.

(A) Economics, as a social science, distinguishes between

- *Positive statements*—statements about what *is*, that can be tested by checking them against the facts.

- *Normative statements*—statements about what *ought* to be, that depend on values and cannot be tested.

(B) (METHODOLOGY) Economic science attempts to *understand* the economic world and is only concerned with positive statements. Economists try to discover positive statements that are consistent with observed facts by (① OBSERVATION & MEASUREMENT ② MODEL BUILDING ③ TESTING MODELS).

- ① Observation and measurement. → NOTE: THERE IS A LIST OF THESE ITEMS FOR NATURAL & HUMAN RESOURCES
- ② Building **economic models**—abstract, simplified representations of the real world with two components (INCLUDES ONLY THOSE FEATURES OF THE WORLD NEEDED FOR THE PURPOSE AT HAND.)
  - *Assumptions* about what is essential versus inessential detail. (WHAT IT INCLUDES & LEAVES OUT. RESULTS FROM ASSUMPTIONS)
  - *Implications* or *predictions* that can be tested by comparison with observed facts. (HOW A # OF VARIABLES ARE DETERMINED BY A # OF OTHER VARIABLES.)
- ③ Developing **economic theories**—generalizations for understanding economic choices developed by building and testing economic models (Text Fig. 1.1). (LECTURE) ∴ IMPLICATIONS ARE USED TO GENERATE PREDICTIONS, & THESE PREDICTIONS ARE TESTED. TO FORM THEORIES

Useful economic models and theories isolate important economic forces and disentangle cause and effect. This requires ① PAIRING OF EVENTS THAT ARE SIMILAR ② STATISTICAL TOOLS — ECONOMETRICS ③ EXPERIMENTS

- ④ *Ceteris paribus* assumptions to hold other things equal to isolate the effects of one force at a time. ∴ CHANGE ONE FACTOR AT A TIME, HOLDING OTHER THINGS CONSTANT, WE ∴ ISOLATE THE AREA OF INTEREST.

[handwritten top margin: EG: BIGGER NETS, CATCH MORE FISH (PART = FIRM) ∴ IF THE WHOLE DOES IT (ALL FIRMS), THE RESULT IS LESS FISH IN THE END (B/C OF RESOURCE DEPLETION)]

5 ◆ Avoiding errors of reasoning including the

[handwritten left margin: PARTS INTERACT TO PRODUCE AN OUTCOME FOR THE WHOLE THAT MIGHT DIFFER FROM THE INTENT OF THE PARTS.]

1 • Fallacy of composition—the false statement that what is true of the parts is true of the whole, or what is true of the whole is true of the parts.

2 • *Post hoc* fallacy—the false claim that event *a* caused event *b* just because event *a* occurred first. *[handwritten: EG: SEE A FLASH OF LIGHTNING FIRST, & LATER HEAR THUNDER ∴ LIGHTNING DID NOT CAUSE THUNDER]*

C Economic *policy* attempts to *improve* the economic world by achieving the objectives of

1 ◆ **Economic efficiency**—efficient production, *[handwritten: (LOW PRODUCTION + EXTERNAL COSTS)]* consumption, and exchange. *[handwritten: → PEOPLE SPECIALIZE TO MAKE A LIVING]*

[handwritten left margin: (PEOPLE BUY GOODS TO MAKE THEM WELL OFF)]

2 ◆ **Equity**—economic justice or fairness. *[handwritten: → ARE THINGS (INCOMES) DIVIDED EQUALLY.]*

3 ◆ **Economic growth**—increase in incomes and production per person. *[handwritten: B/C OF TECHNOLOGY, ↑ IN PRODUCTIVE EQUIPMENT, ↑ IN STANDARDS OF EDUCATION.]*

4 ◆ **Economic stability**—minimizing fluctuations in growth, employment, and average prices.

D *[handwritten: AGREEMENT & DISAGREEMENT (TABLE 1.1, PG 16). - POSITIVE & NORMATIVE MATTERS]*

III The Economy: An Overview

The economy is a mechanism that allocates scarce resources among competing uses. It determines *what, how, when,* and *where* to produce and *who* consumes what is produced. The economy consists of *[handwritten: Fig 1.2, Pg 18.]*

A

B ◆ Decision makers—households, firms, and governments. *[handwritten: → PRODUCERS OF GOODS & SERVICES]* *[handwritten: TRY TO INFLUENCE HOUSEHOLDS & FIRMS]* *[handwritten: ONLY GROUP THAT LIVES TOGETHER]*

C ◆ **Markets**—coordinate buying and selling plans of decision makers through prices. There are two kinds of markets. *[handwritten: ∴ (GET INFO & DO BUSINESS WITH EACH OTHER)]*

*[handwritten left margin: ** Fig 1.2, Pg 18]*

1 • *Goods markets*—for goods and services.

2 • *Factor markets*—for **factors of production** *[handwritten: ARE ....]* **(labour, land, capital, entrepreneurial ability)**

[handwritten: RETURNS: WAGES, RENT, INTEREST, PROFITS (ORGANIZES THE OTHER 3 FACTORS).]

D The Canadian economy is a(n) *[handwritten: Fig 1.3, Pg 21]*

[handwritten left margin: USES MARKET COORDINATING SYSTEM]

◆ *mixed economy* that operates mainly on the market mechanism, but also on command mechanisms. *[handwritten: → HIERARCHIAL ORGANIZATION GIVES INSTRUCTIONS TO BE FOLLOWED.]*

◆ *open economy* with economic links to other economies through exports and imports and through international borrowing and lending. A closed economy has no links with any other economy. *[handwritten: (THE ENTIRE WORLD IS EX. OF CLOSED)]*

[handwritten: - Fig 1.3, Pg 21. (GLOBAL ECONOMY)]

H E L P F U L   H I N T S

1 The definition of economics (how people use limited resources to try to satisfy unlimited wants) leads us directly to three important economic concepts—choice, opportunity cost, and competition. If wants exceed resources, we cannot have everything we want and therefore must make *choices* among alternatives. In making a choice, we forgo other alternatives, and the *opportunity cost* of any choice is the value of the best alternative forgone. Also, if wants exceed resources, then wants and individuals must *compete* against each other for the scarce resources.

2 Marginal analysis is a fundamental tool economists use to predict people's choices. The key to understanding marginal analysis is to focus on *additional*, rather than total, costs and benefits. For example, to predict whether or not Taejong will eat a fourth Big Mac, the economist compares Taejong's *additional* benefit or satisfaction from the fourth Big Mac with its *additional* cost. The total benefits and costs of all four Big Macs are not relevant. Only if the marginal benefit exceeds the marginal cost, will Taejong eat a fourth Big Mac.

3 In attempting to understand how and why something works (for example, an airplane, a falling object, an economy), we can try to use description or theory. A description is a list of facts about something. But it does not tell us which facts are essential for understanding how an airplane works (the shape of the wings) and which facts are less important (the colour of the paint).

Scientists use theory to abstract from the complex descriptive facts of the real world and focus only on those elements essential for understanding. Those essential elements are fashioned into models—highly simplified representations of the real world.

In physics and some other natural sciences, if we want to understand the essential force (gravity) that causes objects to fall, we use theory to construct a simple model, then test it by performing a controlled experiment. We create a vacuum to eliminate less important forces like air resistance.

Economic models are also attempts to focus on the essential forces (competition, self-interest) operating in the economy, while abstracting from less important forces (whims, advertising, altruism). Unlike physicists, economists cannot perform controlled experiments to test their models. As a result, it is difficult to conclusively prove or disprove a theory and its models.

4 Models are like maps, which are useful precisely because they abstract from real-world detail. A map that reproduced all of the details of the real world (streetlamps, fireplugs, electric wires)

would be useless. A useful map offers a simplified view, which is carefully selected according to the purpose of the map. Remember that economic models are not claims that the real world is as simple as the model. Models claim to capture the simplified effect of some real force operating in the economy. Before drawing conclusions about the real economy from a model, we must be careful to consider whether, when we reinsert all of the real-world complexities the model abstracted from, the conclusions will be the same as in the model.

5 The most important purpose of studying economics is not to learn what to think about economics but rather *how* to think about economics. The "what"—the facts and descriptions of the economy—can always be found in books. The value of an economics education is the ability to think critically about economic problems and *to understand how* an economy works. This understanding of the essential forces governing how an economy works comes through the mastery of economic theory and model-building.

SELF-TEST

True/False/Uncertain and Explain

1 Economics is the study of how to use unlimited resources to satisfy limited wants.

2 If Fred slept in instead of either going to lecture or jogging, the missed lecture is his opportunity cost of sleep.

3 When the opportunity cost of an activity increases, people substitute it for other activities.

4 In an economy in which economic activity is coordinated by a command mechanism, the decisions of *what, how, when,* and *who* are the result of price adjustment.

5 In economics, a closed economy is one in which there is very limited economic freedom.

6 Economics is not a science since it deals with the study of wilful human beings and not inanimate objects in nature.

7 A positive statement is about what *is,* while a normative statement is about what *will* be.

8 Macroeconomics includes the study of the causes of inflation.

9 Testing an economic model requires comparing its predictions against real-world events.

10 When the predictions of a model conflict with the relevant facts, a theory must be discarded or modified.

Multiple-Choice

1 The fact that human wants cannot be fully satisfied with available resources is called the problem of
a opportunity cost.
b scarcity.
c normative economics.
d what to produce.
e who will consume.

2 The problem of scarcity exists
a only in economies that rely on the market mechanism.
b only in economies that rely on the command mechanism.
c in all economies.
d only when people have not optimized.
e now but will be eliminated with economic growth.

3 When the government chooses to use resources to build a dam, those resources are no longer available to build a highway. This illustrates the concept of

a a market mechanism.
b macroeconomics.
c opportunity cost.
d a closed economy.
e cooperation.

4 A positive statement is

a about what ought to be.
b about what is.
c always true.
d capable of evaluation as true or false by observation and measurement.
e b and d.

5 A mixed economy has both

a internal and international trade.
b open and closed industries.
c positive and normative mechanisms.
d command and market mechanisms.
e wealth and poverty.

6 Renata has the chance either to attend an economics lecture or play tennis. If she chooses to attend the lecture, the value of playing tennis is

a greater than the value of the lecture.
b not comparable to the value of the lecture.
c equal to the value of the lecture.
d the opportunity cost of attending the lecture.
e zero.

7 The opportunity cost to a customer of getting a $10 haircut is the

a customer's best alternative use of the $10.
b customer's best alternative use of the time it takes to get a haircut.
c customer's best alternative use of both the $10 and the time it takes to get a haircut.
d value to the barber of $10.
e value to the barber of the time it takes to give a haircut.

8 All of the following are policy objectives *except*

a equity.
b efficiency.
c entrepreneurship.
d stability.
e growth.

9 Which of the following is an example of capital as a factor of production?

a money held by General Motors
b a General Motors bond
c an automobile factory owned by General Motors
d all of the above
e none of the above

10 An economic model is tested by

a examining the realism of its assumptions.
b comparing its predictions with the facts.
c comparing its descriptions with the facts.
d the Testing Committee of the Canadian Economic Association.
e all of the above.

11 All of the following are factors of production *except*

a natural resources.
b tools.
c entrepreneurship.
d government.
e land.

12 A closed economy is one that has

a more exports than imports.
b more imports than exports.
c strict government control of production.
d no economic links between households and government.
e no economic links with other economies.

13 The branch of economics that studies the decisions of individual households and firms is called

a macroeconomics.
b microeconomics.
c positive economics.
d normative economics.
e home economics.

14 Scarcity can be eliminated through

a cooperation.
b competition.
c market mechanisms.
d command mechanisms.
e none of the above.

15 The Canadian economy is best described as a

a closed economy.
b market economy.
c command economy.
d mixed economy.
e wealthy economy that avoids the problem of scarcity.

16 A normative statement is a statement regarding

a what is usually the case.

b the assumptions of an economic model.

c what ought to be.

d the predictions of an economic model.

e what is.

17 "The rich face higher income tax rates than the poor" is an example of

a a normative statement.

b a positive statement.

c a descriptive statement.

d a theoretical statement.

e b and c.

18 Other things being equal, which of the following statements is correct?

1 If unemployment increases, the opportunity cost of attending university decreases.

2 If men generally earn more than women in the labour market, the opportunity cost of attending university is higher for men than for women.

a 1 only

b 2 only

c 1 and 2

d neither 1 nor 2

e impossible to judge without additional information

19 Which of the following is *not* a capital resource?

a money

b a carpenter's hammer

c a shoe factory

d a bread-slicing machine

e the SkyDome

20 Which of the following is a positive statement?

a Low rents will restrict the supply of housing.

b High interest rates are bad for the economy.

c Housing costs too much.

d Owners of apartment buildings ought to be free to charge whatever rent they want.

e Government should control the rents that apartment owners charge.

21 All of the following are microeconomic questions *except*

a technological change.

b wages and earnings.

c national differences in wealth.

d production.

e consumption.

22 Which of the following is *not* part of the opportunity cost of attending university?

a cost of tuition

b cost of textbooks

c cost of meals

d income that could have been earned by working

e all of the above

23 Opportunity cost does *not* include

a external cost.

b the best alternative forgone.

c all alternatives forgone.

d time cost.

e real cost.

24 Which of the following statements is/are normative?

a Scientists should not make normative statements.

b Warts are caused by handling toads.

c As compact disc prices fall, people will buy more of them.

d If income increases, sales of luxury goods will fall.

e c and d.

25 Which of the following would *not* be considered a macroeconomic topic?

a the reasons for a decline in the price of orange juice

b the reasons for a decline in average prices

c the cause of recessions

d the effect of the government budget deficit on inflation

e the determination of aggregate income

Short Answer Problems

1 What is meant by scarcity, and why does the existence of scarcity mean that we must make choices?

2 If all people would only economize, the problem of scarcity would be solved. Agree or disagree and explain why.

3 Ashley, Doug, and Mei-Lin are planning to travel from Halifax to Sydney. The trip takes one hour by airplane and five hours by train. The air fare is $100 and train fare is $60. They all have to take time off from work while travelling. Ashley earns $5 per hour in her job, Doug $10 per hour, and Mei-Lin $12 per hour.

Calculate the opportunity cost of air and train travel for each person. Assuming they are all optimizers, how should each of them travel to Sydney?

4 Explain the interdependence that exists between households and firms in Text Fig. 1.2 on page 18 (ignore governments for this question).

5 Suppose the government builds and staffs a hospital in order to provide "free" medical care.
a What is the opportunity cost of the free medical care?
b Is it free from the perspective of society as a whole?

6 Indicate whether each of the following statements is positive or normative. If it is normative (positive), rewrite it so that it becomes positive (normative).
a The government ought to reduce the size of the deficit in order to lower interest rates.
b Government imposition of a tax on tobacco products will reduce their consumption.

7 Suppose we examine a model of plant growth that predicts that, given the amount of water and sunlight, the application of fertilizer stimulates plant growth.
a How might you test the model?
b How is the test different from what an economist could do to test an economic model?

8 When asked in a television interview what she felt she was missing out on because she spent most of her time training for the last Olympics, a rower answered, "A normal social life." She also revealed that she had given up a job that paid $20,000 per year in order to train full-time. She was fortunate to receive a grant from Sport Canada of $10,000 per year, but this was not enough to cover all of her expenses. Her food and rent were $5,000 per year and training expenses (coach's fee, equipment costs, etc.) were $16,000 per year.
a What is the annual opportunity cost of "going for Gold" for this rower?
b What is the annual opportunity cost to Canada of training this rower?
c In general, what is the annual opportunity cost to Canada of sending this rower and other athletes to the Olympics?

9 Why is the Canadian economy considered to be mixed?

10 Suppose your friend, who is a history major, claims that economic theories are useless because the models on which they are based are so unrealistic. He claims that since the models leave out so many descriptive details about the real world, they can't possibly be useful for understanding how the economy works. How would you defend your decision to study economic theory?

ANSWERS

True/False/Uncertain and Explain

1 F Limited resources and unlimited wants. (8–9)
2 U Opportunity cost is the *best* forgone alternative; don't know whether lecture or jogging more valuable to Fred. (8–9)
3 F People substitute other activities in place of the more expensive activity. (9–10)
4 F Price adjustments are the hallmarks of market mechanism. (19–20)
5 F Closed economy has no links with other economies. (20–21)
6 F Science not defined by subject, but by method of observation, measurement, and testing of theoretical models. (12–13)
7 F Normative statements are about what *ought* to be. (12–13)
8 T Inflation involves price level as a whole. (11–12)
9 T Test predictions, not assumptions. (12–13)
10 T A model's predictions must be consistent with the facts to become part of accepted theory. (12–13)

Multiple-Choice

1 b Definition. (1–2)
2 c With infinite wants and finite resources, scarcity will never be eliminated. (1–2)
3 c Highway is forgone alternative. (1–2)
4 e Definition. (12–13)
5 d Definition. (20–21)
6 d Choosing lecture means its value > tennis. Tennis = (best) forgone alternative to lecture. (8–9)
7 c Opportunity cost includes the real goods the $10 could buy and time costs. (8–9)
8 c Entrepreneurship is a factor of production. (15)
9 c Capital defined as manufactured goods used in production. (18–19)

10 **b** Assumptions not realistic descriptions; are simplified representations of world. (12–13)
11 **d** Government is decision maker. (18–19)
12 **e** Definition. (20–21)
13 **b** Definition. (11–12)
14 **e** Scarcity is inescapable fact of life. (8–9)
15 **d** Mixed economy relies on market and command mechanisms. (20–21)
16 **c** Key word for normative statements is *ought*. (12–13)
17 **e** Positive statements describe facts about what is. (12–13)
18 **c** Unemployment decreases expected average income from working. Higher opportunity cost for men may not be fair, but is a fact. (8–9)
19 **a** Money not a manufactured good used in production. (18–19)
20 **a** While **a** may be evaluated as true or false, other statements are matters of opinion. (12–13)
21 **c** **c** is a macroeconomic question. (11)
22 **c** Meals must be paid for whether or not one attends university, so are not forgone costs. (8–9)
23 **c** You do not forgo all alternatives. If you went to lecture, you could not have stayed in bed *and* gone jogging. (8–9)
24 **a** Key word is *should*. Even statement **b** is positive. (12–13)
25 **a** Price of individual good is a microeconomic topic. (11)

Short Answer Problems

1 Scarcity is the universal condition that human wants always exceed the resources available to satisfy them. The fact that goods and services are scarce means that individuals cannot have all of everything they want. It is therefore necessary to choose among alternatives.

2 Disagree. If everyone economized, then we would be making the best possible use of our resources and would be achieving the greatest benefits or satisfaction possible, given the limited quantity of resources. But this does not mean that we would be satisfying all of our limitless needs. The problem of scarcity can never be "solved" as long as people have infinite needs and finite resources for satisfying those needs.

3 The main point is that the total opportunity cost of travel includes the best alternative value of travel time as well as the train or air fare. The total costs of train and air travel for Ashley, Doug, and Mei-Lin are calculated in Table 1.1.

TABLE **1.1**

Traveller	Train	Plane
Ashley		
(a) Fare	$ 60	$100
(b) Opportunity cost of travel time at $5/hr	$ 25	$ 5
Total cost	**$ 85**	**$105**
Doug		
(a) Fare	$ 60	$100
(b) Opportunity cost of travel time at $10/hr	$ 50	$ 10
Total cost	**$110**	**$110**
Mei-Lin		
(a) Fare	$ 60	$100
(b) Opportunity cost of travel time at $12/hr	$ 60	$ 12
Total cost	**$120**	**$112**

Based on the cost calculation in Table 1.1, Ashley should take the train, Mei-Lin should take the plane, and Doug could take either.

4 Firms depend on households for the supply of factors of production. In exchange, households depend on firms for income. Households use that income to buy goods and services from firms, while firms depend on the money they get from household purchases to purchase more factors of production in the next period and renew the circular flow.

5 a Even though medical care may be offered without charge ("free"), there are still opportunity costs. The opportunity cost of providing such health care is the best alternative use of the resources used in the construction of the hospital, and the best alternative use of the resources (including human resources) used in the operation of the hospital.
b These resources are no longer available for other activities and therefore represent a cost to society.

6 a The given statement is normative. The following is positive: If the government reduces the size of the deficit, interest rates will fall.
b The given statement is positive. The following is normative: The government ought to impose a tax on tobacco products.

7 a The prediction of the model can be tested by conducting the following controlled experiment and carefully observing the outcome. Select a number of plots of ground of the same size that have similar characteristics and are subject to the same amount of water and sunlight. Plant equal quantities of seeds in all the plots. In some of the plots apply no fertilizer and in some of the plots apply (perhaps varying amounts of) fertilizer. When the plants have grown, measure the growth of the plants and compare the growth of the fertilized plots and the unfertilized plots. If plant growth is greater in fertilized plots, we provisionally accept the model and the theory on which it is based. If plant growth is not greater in fertilized plots, we discard the theory (model), or modify its assumptions. Perhaps the effective use of fertilizer requires more water.

Then construct a new model that predicts that given more water (and the same amount of sunlight), fertilized plants will grow larger than equivalently watered unfertilized plants. Test that model and continue modifying assumptions until predictions are consistent with the facts.

b Economists cannot perform such controlled experiments and instead must change one assumption at a time in alternative models and compare the results. Then differences in outcomes can only be tested against variations in data that occur naturally in the economy. This is a more difficult and less precise model-building and testing procedure than exists for the controlled fertilizer experiment.

8 a The point here is to realize which costs are specific to training for the Olympics. First, there is the value to the athlete of a forgone "normal social life." Second, because she is training for the Olympics, this rower forgoes her $20,000 salary. Third, her training expenses total $16,000, which are partially covered by her $10,000 government grant. She thus forgoes $6,000 worth of goods and services by training. Fourth, her ordinary living expenses are not part of the opportunity cost of training, since she incurs these whether or not she trains.

The total annual opportunity cost of training to this rower is $26,000 plus the value to her of a normal social life (a subjective cost that is difficult for others to measure).

b The annual opportunity cost to Canada of training this rower is $20,000 (opportunity cost of the rower's time) plus $16,000 training expenses (which are probably a good measure of the opportunity cost of the coach's services and equipment), plus the value to the rower of a forgone social life—a total cost of $36,000, plus

the value of the forgone social life. Had this rower not trained for the Olympics, the Canadian economy could have produced *alternative* goods and services worth $36,000.

c The annual opportunity cost to Canada of sending a team of athletes to the Olympics is the annual value of the goods and services that could have been produced with the resources devoted to training athletes.

9 The Canadian economy is a mixed economy because it relies on both the market and command mechanisms. Most coordination is carried out through the market mechanism, but governments and large firms also use command mechanisms.

10 A brief answer to your friend's challenge appears in Helpful Hint 3. Models are like maps, which are useful precisely because they abstract from real-world detail. A useful map offers a simplified view, which is carefully selected according to the purpose of the map. No map maker would claim that the world is as simple as her map, and economists do not claim that the real economy is as simple as their models. What economists claim is that their models isolate the simplified effect of some real forces (like optimizing behaviour) operating in the economy, and yield predictions that can be tested against real-world data.

Another way to answer your friend would be to challenge him to identify what a more realistic model or theory would look like. You would do well to quote Milton Friedman (a Nobel Prize winner in Economics) on this topic: "A theory or its 'assumptions' cannot possibly be thoroughly 'realistic' in the immediate descriptive sense. ... A completely 'realistic' theory of the wheat market would have to include not only the conditions directly underlying the supply and demand for wheat but also the kind of coins or credit instruments used to make exchanges; the personal characteristics of wheat-traders such as the color of each trader's hair and eyes, ... the number of members of his family, their characteristics, ... the kind of soil on which the wheat was grown, ... the weather prevailing during the growing season; ... and so on indefinitely. Any attempt to move very far in achieving this kind of 'realism' is certain to render a theory utterly useless."

From Milton Friedman, "The Methodology of Positive Economics," in *Essays in Positive Economics* (Chicago: University of Chicago Press, 1953), p. 32.

Chapter 2

Making and Using Graphs

Graphing Data

Graphs represent quantity as a distance. On a two-dimensional graph

- horizontal line is *x-axis*.

- vertical line is *y-axis*.

- intersection (0) is the *origin*.

Main types of economic graphs

- **Scatter diagram**—shows relationship between two variables, one measured on *x-axis*, the other measured on *y-axis*.

- **Time-series graph**—shows relationship between time (measured on *x-axis*) and other variable(s) (measured on *y-axis*). Reveals variable's level, direction of change, speed of change, and **trend** (general tendency to rise or fall).

- **Cross-section graph**—shows level of a variable across different groups at a point in time.

Misleading graphs often omit origin or stretch/squeeze measurement scale to exaggerate or understate variation. Always look closely at the values and labels on axes before interpreting a graph.

Graphs Used in Economic Models

Graphs showing relationships between variables fall into four categories

- **Positive (direct) relationship**—variables move together in same direction: upward sloping.

- **Negative (inverse) relationship**—variables move in opposite directions: downward sloping.

- Relationships with a maximum/minimum
  - Relationship slopes upward, reaches a maximum (zero slope), and then slopes downward.
  - Relationship slopes downward, reaches a minimum (zero slope), and then slopes upward.

- Unrelated (independent) variables—one variable changes while the other remains constant; graph is vertical or horizontal straight line.

The Slope of a Relationship

Slope of a relationship is change in value of variable on *y-axis* divided by change in value of variable on *x-axis*.

- Δ means "change in."

- Formula for slope is $\Delta y / \Delta x =$ rise/run.

- Straight line (**linear relationship**) has constant slope.
  - A positive, upward-sloping relationship has a positive slope.
  - A negative, downward-sloping relationship has a negative slope.

- Curved line has varying slope, which can be calculated
  - *at a point*—by drawing straight line tangent to the curve at that point and calculating slope of the line.
  - *across an arc*—by drawing straight line across two points on the curve and calculating slope of the line.

Graphing Relationships Among More Than Two Variables

Relationships among more than two variables can be graphed by holding constant the values of all variables except two. This is done by making a *ceteris paribus* assumption—"other things remaining the same."

H E L P F U L   H I N T S

1   Throughout the text, relationships among economic variables will almost invariably be represented and analysed graphically. An early, complete understanding of graphs will greatly facilitate your mastery of the economic analysis of later chapters. Avoid the common mistake of assuming that a superficial understanding of graphs will be sufficient.

2   If your experience with graphical analysis is limited, this chapter is crucial to your ability to readily understand later economic analysis. You will likely find significant rewards in occasionally returning to this chapter for review. If you are experienced in constructing and using graphs, this chapter may be "old hat." Even so, you should skim the chapter and work through the Self-Test in this *Study Guide*.

3   Slope is a *linear* concept since it is a property of a straight line. For this reason, the slope is constant along a straight line but is different at different points on a curved (nonlinear) line. For the slope of a curved line, we actually calculate the slope of a straight line. The text presents two alternatives for calculating the slope of a curved line: (1) slope at a point, and (2) slope across an arc. The first of these calculates the slope of the *straight line* that just touches (is tangent to) the curve at a point. The second calculates the slope of the *straight line* formed by the arc between two points on the curved line.

© 4   A straight line on a graph can also be described by a simple equation. The general form for the equation of a straight line is:

$$y = a + bx$$

If you are given such an equation, you can graph the line by finding the *y*-intercept (where the line intersects the vertical *y*-axis), finding the *x*-intercept (where the line intersects the horizontal *x*-axis), and then connecting those two points with a straight line:
To find the *y*-intercept, set $x = 0$.

$$y = a + b(0)$$
$$y = a$$

To find the *x*-intercept, set $y = 0$.

$$0 = a + bx$$
$$x = -a/b$$

Connecting these two points ($(x = 0, y = a)$ and $(x = -a/b, y = 0)$) or $(0, a)$ and $(-a/b, 0)$ yields the line in Fig. 2.1.

FIGURE **2.1**

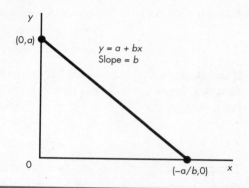

For any straight line with the equation of the form $y = a + bx$, the slope of the line is b. To see how to apply this general equation, consider this example:

$$y = 6 - 2x$$

To find the *y*-intercept, set $x = 0$.

$$y = 6 - 2(0)$$
$$y = 6$$

To find the *x*-intercept, set $y = 0$.

$$0 = 6 - 2x$$
$$x = 3$$

Connecting these two points, $(0, 6)$ and $(3, 0)$, yields the line in Fig. 2.2.

FIGURE **2.2**

The slope of this line is –2. Since the slope is negative, there is a negative relationship between the variables x and y.

SELF-TEST

True/False/Uncertain and Explain

1 A graph that omits the origin is misleading.

2 If the graph of the relationship between two variables slopes upward (to the right), the graph has a positive slope.

3 The graph of the relationship between two variables that are in fact unrelated is vertical.

4 The slope of a straight line is calculated by dividing the change in the value of the variable measured on the horizontal axis by the change in the value of the variable measured on the vertical axis.

5 In Fig. 2.3, the relationship between y and x is first negative, reaches a minimum, and then becomes positive as x increases.

FIGURE **2.3**

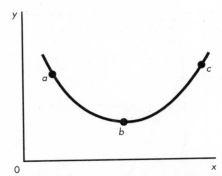

6 In Fig.2.3, the slope of the curve is increasing as we move from point b to point c.

7 In Fig. 2.3, the slope of the curve is approaching zero as we move from point a to point b.

8 In Fig. 2.3, the value of x is a minimum at point b.

9 For a straight line, if a small change in y is associated with a large change in x, the slope is large.

10 For a straight line, if a large change in y is associated with a small change in x, the line is steep.

Multiple-Choice

1 Figure 2.4 is
a a one-variable time-series graph.
b a two-variable time-series graph.
c a scatter diagram.
d b and c.
e none of the above.

FIGURE **2.4**

2 The dotted line in Fig. 2.4 represents variable *y*. Which of the following statements best describes the relationship between *x* and *y* in Fig. 2.4?

a *x* and *y* tend to move in opposite directions over time.

b *y* tends to move in the opposite direction from *x*, but one year later.

c *x* and *y* tend to move together over time.

d *x* tends to move in the same direction as *y*, but one year later.

e *y* tends to move in the same direction as *x*, but one year later.

3 From the data in Table 2.1, it appears that

a *x* and *y* have a negative relationship.

b *x* and *y* have a positive relationship.

c there is no relationship between *x* and *y*.

d there is first a negative and then a positive relationship between *x* and *y*.

e there is first a positive and then a negative relationship between *x* and *y*.

TABLE **2.1**

Year	x	y
1990	6.2	143
1991	5.7	156
1992	5.3	162

4 If variables *x* and *y* move up and down together, they are said to be

a positively related.

b negatively related.

c conversely related.

d unrelated.

e trendy.

5 The relationship between two variables that move in opposite directions is shown graphically by a line that is

a positively sloped.

b relatively steep.

c relatively flat.

d negatively sloped.

e curved.

6 To graph a relationship among more than two variables, what kind of assumption is necessary?

a normative

b positive

c linear

d independence of variables

e *ceteris paribus*

7 The tendency for a variable to rise or fall over time is called its

a slope.

b trend.

c *y*-coordinate.

d level.

e correlation.

8 In Fig. 2.5 the relationship between *x* and *y* as *x* increases is

a positive with slope decreasing.

b negative with slope decreasing.

c negative with slope increasing.

d positive with slope increasing.

e positive with slope first increasing then decreasing.

FIGURE **2.5**

9 What is the slope across the arc between *b* and *c* in Fig. 2.5?

a 1/2

b 2/3

c 1

d 2

e 3

10 In Fig. 2.5, consider the slopes of arc *ab* and arc *bc*. The slope at point *b* is difficult to determine exactly, but it must be

a greater than 5/2.

b about 5/2.

c between 5/2 and 1.

d about 1.

e less than 1.

11 Given the data in Table 2.2, holding income constant, the graph relating the price of strawberries (vertical axis) to the purchases of strawberries (horizontal axis)

a is a vertical line.
b is a horizontal line.
c is a positively sloped line.
d is a negatively sloped line.
e reaches a minimum.

TABLE **2.2**

Weekly Family Income ($)	Price per Box of Strawberries ($)	Number of Boxes Purchased per Week
300	$1.00	5
300	$1.25	3
300	$1.50	2
400	$1.00	7
400	$1.25	5
400	$1.50	4

12 Given the data in Table 2.2, suppose family income decreases from $400 to $300 per week. Then the graph relating the price of strawberries (vertical axis) to the purchases of strawberries (horizontal axis) will

a become negatively sloped.
b become positively sloped.
c shift to the right.
d shift to the left.
e no longer exist.

13 Given the data in Table 2.2, holding price constant, the graph relating family income (vertical axis) to the purchases of strawberries (horizontal axis) is a

a vertical line.
b horizontal line.
c positively sloped line.
d negatively sloped line.
e positively or negatively sloped line, depending on the price that is held constant.

14 In Fig. 2.6, x is

a positively related to y and negatively related to z.
b positively related to both y and z.
c negatively related to y and positively related to z.
d negatively related to both y and z.
e greater than z.

FIGURE **2.6**

15 In Fig. 2.6, a decrease in the value of z will cause, *ceteris paribus,*

a a decrease in the value of x.
b an increase in the value of x.
c an increase in the value of y.
d no change in the value of y.
e **a** and **d**.

16 In Table 2.3, suppose that w is the independent variable measured along the horizontal axis. The slope of the line relating w and u is

a positive with a decreasing slope.
b negative with a decreasing slope.
c positive with an increasing slope.
d negative with a constant slope.
e positive with a constant slope.

TABLE **2.3**

w	2	4	6	8	10
u	15	12	9	6	3

17 Refer to Table 2.3. Suppose that w is the independent variable measured along the horizontal axis. The slope of the line relating w and u is

a +3.
b −3.
c −2/3.
d +3/2.
e −3/2.

18 In Fig. 2.7, if household income increases by $1,000, household expenditure will

a increase by $1,333.
b decrease by $1,333.
c remain unchanged.
d increase by $1,000.
e increase by $750.

FIGURE **2.7**

FIGURE **2.8**

19 In Fig. 2.7, if household income is zero, household expenditure is

a 0.
b −$4,000.
c $4,000.
d $8,000.
e impossible to determine from the graph.

20 In Fig. 2.7, if household expenditure is $28,000, household income is

a $36,000.
b $32,000.
c $28,000.
d $25,000.
e none of the above.

21 At all points along a straight line, slope is

a positive.
b negative.
c constant.
d zero.
e none of the above.

22 What is the slope of the line in Fig. 2.8?

a 2
b 1/2
c 3
d 1/3
e −3

ⓔ 23 If the line in Fig. 2.8 were to continue down to the x-axis, what would the value of x be when y is zero?

a 0
b 2
c 2/3
d −2/3
e −3/2

ⓔ 24 If the equation of a straight line is $y = 6 + 3x$, then the slope is

a −3 and the y-intercept is 6.
b −3 and the y-intercept is −2.
c 3 and the y-intercept is 6.
d 3 and the y-intercept is −2.
e 3 and the y-intercept is −6.

ⓔ 25 If the equation of a straight line is $y = 8 − 2x$, then the slope is

a −2 and the x-intercept is −4.
b −2 and the x-intercept is 4.
c −2 and the x-intercept is 8.
d 2 and the x-intercept is −4.
e 2 and the x-intercept is 4.

Short Answer Problems

1 Draw a graph of variables x and y that illustrates each of the following relationships:
a x and y move up and down together.
b x and y move in opposite directions.
c as x increases y reaches a maximum.
d as x increases y reaches a minimum.
e x and y move in opposite directions, but as x increases y decreases by larger and larger increments for each unit increase in x.
f y is unrelated to the value of x.
g x is unrelated to the value of y.

2 What does it mean to say that the slope of a line is −2/3?

3 Explain two ways to measure the slope of a curved line.

4 How do we graph a relationship among more than two variables using a two-dimensional graph?

5 Consider the data in Table 2.4.
a Draw a time-series graph for the interest rate.
b Draw a two-variable time-series graph for both the inflation rate and the interest rate.
c Draw a scatter diagram for the inflation rate (horizontal axis) and the interest rate (vertical axis).
d Would you describe the general relationship between the inflation rate and the interest rate as positive, negative, or unrelated?

TABLE **2.4**

Year	Inflation Rate (%)	Interest Rate (%)
1970	5.4	6.4
1971	3.2	4.3
1972	3.4	4.1
1973	8.3	7.0
1974	11.8	7.9
1975	6.7	5.8
1976	4.9	5.0
1977	6.5	5.3
1978	8.6	7.2
1979	12.3	10.0

6 Compute the slopes of the lines in Fig. 2.9(a) and (b).

FIGURE **2.9**

(a)

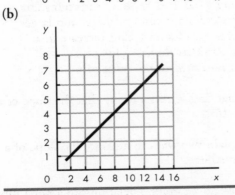

(b)

7 Draw each of the following:
a a straight line with slope −10 and passing through the point (2, 80).
b a straight line with slope 2 and passing through the point (6, 10).

8 The equation for a straight line is $y = 4 - 2x$.
a Calculate: the y-intercept; the x-intercept; the slope.
b Draw the graph of the line.

9 Use the graph in Fig. 2.10 to compute the slope
a across the arc between points a and b.
b at point b.
c at point c, and explain your answer.

FIGURE **2.10**

10 In Table 2.5, x represents the number of umbrellas sold per month, y represents the price of an umbrella, and z represents the average number of rainy days per month.
a On the same diagram, graph the relationship between x (horizontal axis) and y (vertical axis) when $z = 4$, when $z = 5$, and when $z = 6$. On average, it rains 6 days per month. This implies a certain average relationship between monthly umbrella sales and umbrella price. Suppose that the "greenhouse effect" reduces the average monthly rainfall to 4 days per month. What happens to the graph of the relationship between umbrella sales and umbrella prices?
b On a diagram, graph the relationship between x (horizontal axis) and z (vertical axis) when $y = \$10$ and when $y = \$12$. Is the relationship between x and z positive or negative?
c On a diagram, graph the relationship between y (horizontal axis) and z (vertical axis) when $x = 120$ and when $x = 140$. Is the relationship between y and z positive or negative?

TABLE **2.5**

Umbrellas Sold per Month (x)	Price per Umbrella (y)	Average Number of Rainy Days per Month (z)
120	$10	4
140	$10	5
160	$10	6
100	$12	4
120	$12	5
140	$12	6
80	$14	4
100	$14	5
120	$14	6

ANSWERS

True/False/Uncertain and Explain

1 U Sometimes it's misleading, sometimes omitting origin enables graph to reveal its information. (28–29, 32)

2 T Upward-sloping curves/lines have positive slopes. (32–33)

3 U Graph of unrelated variables may be vertical or horizontal. (34–35)

4 F Slope = (Δ variable on vertical (y) axis)/ (Δ variable on horizontal (x) axis). (36–37)

5 T Arc ab would have negative slope, arc bc positive slope. (33–35)

6 T Curve becomes steeper, meaning Δy increasing faster than Δx, so slope increasing. (32–33)

7 T At b, tangent has slope = 0, since $\Delta y = 0$ along horizontal line through b. (33–35)

8 F Value of y is minimum at point b. (34–35)

9 F Large slope means large Δy associated with small Δx. (36–37)

10 T Steep line has large slope, meaning large Δy associated with small Δx. (36–37)

Multiple-Choice

1 b Two variables are x and y. Scatter diagrams don't have time on an axis. (30–31)

2 e For example, x begins falling in 1991, y begins falling in 1992. (30–31)

3 a Higher values x (6.2) associated with lower values y (143). (32–34)

4 a Definition. (32–33)

5 d Graph may be steep, flat, or curved, but must have negative slope. (33–34)

6 e Must hold constant other variables to isolate relationship between two variables. (38–39)

7 b Definition. (30–31)

8 a Slope of arc ab = +2.5. Slope of arc bc = +1. (32–33)

9 c $\Delta y = 3$ (8 − 5); $\Delta x = 3$ (6 − 3). (37–38)

10 c 5/2 is slope of ab, while 1 is slope of bc. (37–38)

11 d Look *either* at data in top 3 rows (income = 300) *or* data in bottom 3 rows (income = 400). Higher price associated with lower purchases. (38–39)

⊘12 d At each price, fewer boxes will be purchased. (32–34)

⊘13 c For P = 1, two points on line are (5 boxes, $300) and (7 boxes, $400). Same relationship for other prices. (32–34)

14 c ↑y → ↓x holding z constant. ↑z → ↑x holding y constant. (38–39)

⊘15 a ↓z → ↓x holding y constant. ↓z → ↓y holding x constant. (38–39)

16 d As w↑, u↑. $\Delta u / \Delta w$ is constant. (36–37)

17 e Between any two points, $\Delta u = 3$, $\Delta w = -2$. (36–37)

18 e Slope ($\Delta y / \Delta x$) = 3/4. If Δx (Δ household income) = $1,000, then Δy (Δ household expenditure) = $750. (36–37)

19 c Where the line intersects the household expenditure (y)-axis. (27–28)

20 b From $28,000 on *vertical* (expenditure) axis, move across to line, then down to $32,000 on *horizontal* (income) axis. (27–28)

21 c Along straight line, slope may or may not be **a, b,** or **d.** (36–37)

22 c Between any two points, $\Delta y = 3$ and $\Delta x = 1$. (36–37)

⊘◎23 d Equation of line is y = 2 + 3x. Solve for x-intercept (set y = 0). (27–28)

◎24 c Use formula y = a + bx. Slope = b, y-intercept = a. (36–37)

◎25 b Use formula y = a + bx. Slope = b, x-intercept = −a/b. (36–37)

Short Answer Problems

1 Figure 2.11(a) through (g) illustrates the desired graphs.

2 The negative sign in the slope of −2/3 means that there is a negative relationship between the two variables. The value of 2/3 means that when the variable measured on the vertical axis decreases by 2 units (the *rise* or Δy), the variable measured on the horizontal axis increases by 3 units (the *run* or Δx).

2 The negative sign in the slope of −2/3 means that there is a negative relationship between the two variables. The value of 2/3 means that when the variable measured on the vertical axis decreases by 2 units (the *rise* or Δy), the variable measured on the horizontal axis increases by 3 units (the *run* or Δx).

3 The slope of a straight line can be measured at a point or across an arc. The slope at a point is measured by calculating the slope of the straight line that is tangent to (just touches) the curved line at the point. The slope across an arc is measured by calculating the slope of the straight line that forms the arc.

4 To graph a relationship among more than two variables, we hold all of the variables but two constant, and graph the relationship between the remaining two. Thus, we can graph the relationship between any pair of variables, given the constant values of the other variables.

5 a A time-series graph for the interest rate is given in Fig. 2.12(a).
  b Figure 2.12(b) is a two-variable time-series graph for both the inflation rate and the interest rate. The inflation rate is the dotted line; the interest rate is the solid line.
  c The scatter diagram for the inflation rate and the interest rate is given in Fig. 2.12(c).
  d From the graphs in Fig. 2.12(b) and (c), we see that the relationship between the inflation rate and the interest rate is generally positive.

6 To find the slope, pick any two points on a line and compute $\Delta y/\Delta x$. The slope of the line in Fig. 2.9(a) is −2/3, and the slope of the line in Fig. 2.9(b) is 1/2.

7 a The requested straight line is graphed in Fig. 2.13(a). First plot the point (2, 80). Then pick a second point whose *y*-coordinate decreases by 10 for every 1 unit increase in the *x*-coordinate, e.g., (5, 50). The slope between the two points is −30/3 = −10.
  b The requested straight line is graphed in Fig. 2.13(b). First plot the point (6, 10). Then pick a second point whose *y*-coordinate decreases by 2 for every 1 unit decrease in the *x*-coordinate, e.g., (5, 8). The slope between the two points is −2/−1 = 2.

FIGURE **2.11**

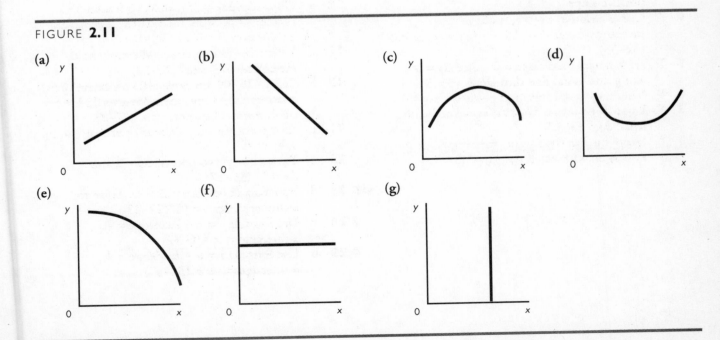

(a)   (b)   (c)   (d)

(e)   (f)   (g)

FIGURE **2.12**

(a)

(b)

(c)

FIGURE **2.13**

(a)

(b)

8 a To find the y-intercept, set $x = 0$.

$$y = 4 - 2(0)$$
$$y = 2$$

To find the x-intercept, set $y = 0$.

$$0 = 4 - 2x$$
$$x = 2$$

The slope of the line is -2, the value of the "b" coefficient on x.

b The graph of the line is shown in Fig. 2.14.

FIGURE **2.14**

9 a The slope across the arc between points *a* and *b* is –3/2.
  b The slope at point *b* is –3/4.
  c The slope at point *c* is zero because it is a minimum point. Nearby a minimum point the slope changes from negative to positive and must pass through zero, or no slope, to do so.

10 a The relationships between *x* and *y* for *z* = 4, 5, and 6 are graphed in Fig. 2.15(a). If the average monthly rainfall drops from 6 days to 4 days, the curve representing the relationship between umbrella sales and umbrella prices will shift from the curve labelled *z* = 6 to *z* = 4.
  b The relationships between *x* and *z* when *y* is $10 and when *y* is $12 are graphed in Fig. 2.15(b). The relationship between *x* and *z* is positive.
  c The relationships between *y* and *z* when *x* = 120 and when *x* = 140 are graphed in Fig. 2.15(c). The relationship between *y* and *z* is positive.

FIGURE **2.15**

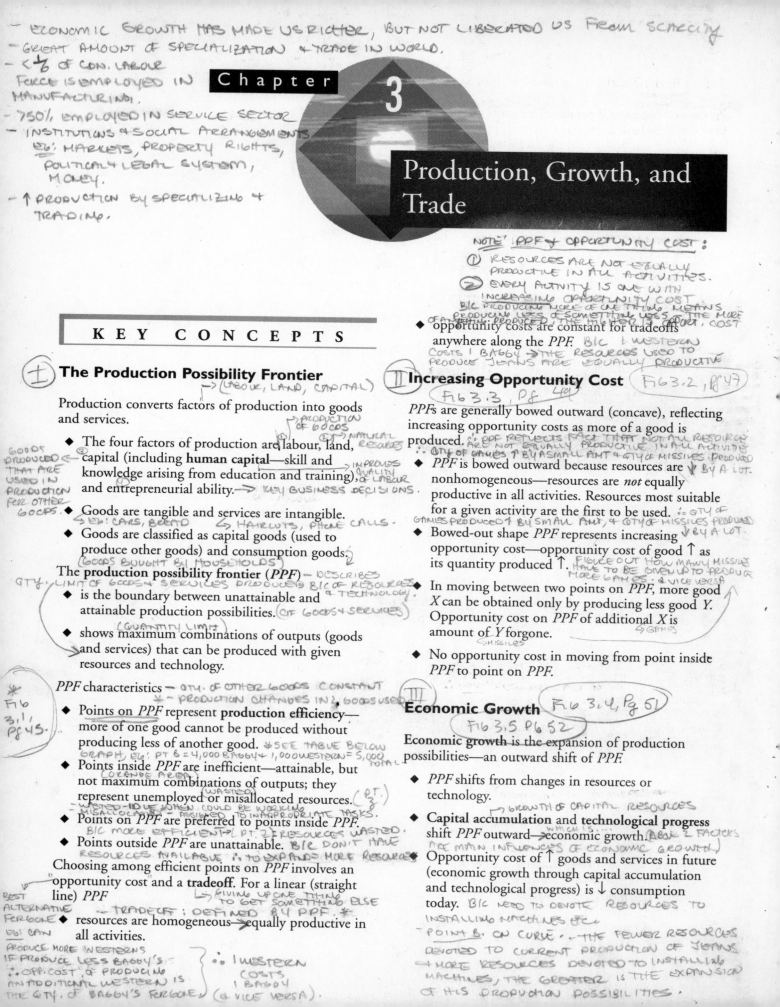

[Handwritten top margin:]
- ECONOMIC GROWTH HAS MADE US RICHER, BUT NOT LIBERATED US FROM SCARCITY
- GREAT AMOUNT OF SPECIALIZATION & TRADE IN WORLD.
- < 1/8 OF CDN. LABOUR FORCE IS EMPLOYED IN MANUFACTURING.
- 75% EMPLOYED IN SERVICE SECTOR
- INSTITUTIONS & SOCIAL ARRANGEMENTS EG: MARKETS, PROPERTY RIGHTS, POLITICALLY LEGAL SYSTEM, MONEY.
- ↑ PRODUCTION BY SPECIALIZING & TRADING.

Chapter 3

Production, Growth, and Trade

[Handwritten, right side:]
NOTE: PPF & OPPORTUNITY COST:
① RESOURCES ARE NOT EQUALLY PRODUCTIVE IN ALL ACTIVITIES.
② EVERY ACTIVITY IS ONE WITH INCREASING OPPORTUNITY COST B/C PRODUCING MORE OF ONE THING MEANS PRODUCING LESS OF SOMETHING ELSE. THE MORE OF A GOOD PRODUCED, THE HIGHER OPP. COST.

KEY CONCEPTS

(I) The Production Possibility Frontier

[Handwritten:] → (LABOUR, LAND, CAPITAL)

Production converts factors of production into goods and services. **[Handwritten:]** → PRODUCTION OF GOODS → NATURAL RESOURCES

[Handwritten left margin:] GOODS PRODUCED THAT ARE USED IN PRODUCTION FOR OTHER GOODS.

◆ The four factors of production are labour, land, capital (including **human capital**—skill and knowledge arising from education and training) and entrepreneurial ability. **[Handwritten:]** → IMPROVES QUALITY OF LABOUR → KEY BUSINESS DECISIONS

◆ Goods are tangible and services are intangible. **[Handwritten:]** → EG: CARS, BREAD → HAIRCUTS, PHONE CALLS.

◆ Goods are classified as capital goods (used to produce other goods) and consumption goods. **[Handwritten:]** (GOODS BOUGHT BY HOUSEHOLDS)

The **production possibility frontier** (*PPF*) — **[Handwritten:]** DESCRIBES QTY. LIMIT OF GOODS & SERVICES PRODUCED B/C OF RESOURCES & TECHNOLOGY.

◆ is the boundary between unattainable and attainable production possibilities. **[Handwritten:]** (OF GOODS & SERVICES)

◆ shows maximum combinations of outputs (goods **[Handwritten:]** (QUANTITY LIMIT) and services) that can be produced with given resources and technology.

PPF characteristics **[Handwritten:]** — QTY. OF OTHER GOODS CONSTANT — PRODUCTION CHANGES IN 2 GOODS USED

[Handwritten left margin:] ＃ FIG 3.1, Pg 45.

◆ Points on *PPF* represent **production efficiency**—more of one good cannot be produced without producing less of another good. **[Handwritten:]** ＃SEE TABLE BELOW GRAPH, EG: PT B = 4,000 BAGGY & 1,000 WESTERN = 5,000 TOTAL.

◆ Points inside *PPF* are inefficient—attainable, but not maximum combinations of outputs; they represent unemployed or misallocated resources. **[Handwritten:]** (WASTED) (PT. 3) (ORANGE AREA) — WASTED—IDLE WHEN COULD BE WORKING — MISALLOCATED — ASSIGNED TO INAPPROPRIATE TASKS.

◆ Points on *PPF* are preferred to points inside *PPF*. **[Handwritten:]** B/C MORE EFFICIENT — PT. 7 RESOURCES WASTED

◆ Points outside *PPF* are unattainable. **[Handwritten:]** B/C DON'T HAVE RESOURCES AVAILABLE ∴ TO EXPAND NEED MORE RESOURCES

Choosing among efficient points on *PPF* involves an opportunity cost and a **tradeoff**. For a linear (straight line) *PPF* **[Handwritten:]** → GIVING UP ONE THING TO GET SOMETHING ELSE → TRADEOFF: DEFINED BY PPF. ＃

[Handwritten left margin:] BEST ALTERNATIVE FORGONE

◆ resources are homogeneous → equally productive in all activities. **[Handwritten:]** EG: CAN PRODUCE MORE WESTERNS IF PRODUCE LESS BAGGY'S ∴ OPP.COST OF PRODUCING AN ADDITIONAL WESTERN IS THE QTY. OF BAGGY'S FORGONE. } ∴ 1 WESTERN COSTS 1 BAGGY (& VICE VERSA).

[Handwritten continuing right column:]
◆ opportunity costs are constant for tradeoffs anywhere along the *PPF*. **[Handwritten:]** B/C 1 WESTERN COSTS 1 BAGGY → THE RESOURCES USED TO PRODUCE JEANS ARE EQUALLY PRODUCTIVE

(II) Increasing Opportunity Cost **[Handwritten:]** FIG 3.2, Pg 47

[Handwritten:] FIG 3.3, Pg 49

*PPF*s are generally bowed outward (concave), reflecting increasing opportunity costs as more of a good is produced. **[Handwritten:]** ∵ PPF REFLECTS FACT THAT NOT ALL RESOURCES ARE EQUALLY PRODUCTIVE IN ALL ACTIVITIES ∴ QTY OF GAMES ↑ BY A SMALL AMT & QTY OF MISSILES PRODUCED ↓ BY A LOT.

◆ *PPF* is bowed outward because resources are nonhomogeneous—resources are *not* equally productive in all activities. Resources most suitable for a given activity are the first to be used. **[Handwritten:]** ∴ QTY OF GAMES PRODUCED ↑ BY SMALL AMT, & QTY OF MISSILES PRODUCED ↓ BY A LOT.

◆ Bowed-out shape *PPF* represents increasing opportunity cost—opportunity cost of good ↑ as its quantity produced ↑. **[Handwritten:]** ↓ BY A LOT FIGURE OUT HOW MANY MISSILES HAVE TO BE GIVEN UP TO PRODUCE MORE GAMES & VICE VERSA

◆ In moving between two points on *PPF*, more good *X* can be obtained only by producing less good *Y*. Opportunity cost on *PPF* of additional *X* is amount of *Y* forgone. **[Handwritten:]** X = GAMES Y = MISSILES

◆ No opportunity cost in moving from point inside *PPF* to point on *PPF*.

(III) Economic Growth **[Handwritten:]** FIG 3.4, Pg 51

[Handwritten:] FIG 3.5 Pg 52

Economic growth is the expansion of production possibilities—an outward shift of *PPF*.

◆ *PPF* shifts from changes in resources or technology. **[Handwritten:]** → GROWTH OF CAPITAL RESOURCES

◆ **Capital accumulation** and **technological progress** shift *PPF* outward → economic growth. **[Handwritten:]** WHICH IS.... (ABOVE 2 FACTORS ARE MAIN INFLUENCES OF ECONOMIC GROWTH.)

◆ Opportunity cost of ↑ goods and services in future (economic growth through capital accumulation and technological progress) is ↓ consumption today. **[Handwritten:]** B/C NEED TO DEVOTE RESOURCES TO INSTALLING MACHINES ETC.
[Handwritten:] - POINT B. ON CURVE ∴ THE FEWER RESOURCES DEVOTED TO CURRENT PRODUCTION OF JEANS & MORE RESOURCES DEVOTED TO INSTALLING MACHINES, THE GREATER IS THE EXPANSION OF ITS PRODUCTION POSSIBILITIES.

[handwritten top:] ∴ ECONOMIC GROWTH:
① RESULTS FROM TECHNOLOGICAL CHANGE & CAPITAL ACCUMULATION
② OPPORTUNITY COST OF FASTER ECONOMIC GROWTH IS A ↓ IN CURRENT CONSUMPTION.
③ BY ↓ CURRENT CONSUMPTION, WE CAN DEVOTE MORE RESOURCES TO DEVELOPING NEW TECHNOLOGIES & ACCUMULATING CAPITAL & SPEED UP THE R... ECONOMIC GROWTH & SEE FIG 3, 5.

IV Gains from Trade   *[handwritten:]* (Fig 3.6, P.55)

[handwritten:] ONLY THROUGH COMPARATIVE ADVANTAGE (NOT ABSOLUTE ADVANTAGE)

Production increases if people specialize in the activity in which they have a comparative advantage. *[hw:]* & TRADING
[hw:] DIFFERENCES IN OPPORT. COST ARE THE SOURCE OF GAINS IN SPECIALIZATION & TRADE.

◆ Person has **comparative advantage** in producing a good if she can produce at lower opportunity cost than anyone else. *[hw:]* EG: COSTS MARK LESS SKIRTS TO PRODUCE 1 JEAN)

◆ When each person specializes in producing a good at which she has comparative advantage and exchanges for other goods, there are gains from trade. *[hw:]* THEY PRODUCE THE GOOD WITH THE SMALLEST OPPORT. COST (EG: MARK PRODUCES JEANS) & THAN LATER TRADES WITH MARY, FOR SKIRTS — PRODS

◆ Specialization and exchange allow consumption *[hw:]* EFFICIENT! (not production) at points outside *PPF*. *[hw:]* B/C THEY CAN BUY (TRADE) AT LESS IF AN OPPORT. COST THAN PRODUCING GOODS THEMSELVES. (↑ HIGHER RETURN)

◆ Person has **absolute advantage** in producing all goods if, using the same quantity of inputs, she can produce more of all goods than anyone else. *[hw:]* (SOMETIMES DUE TO EFFICIENCY ADVANTAGES — CAN PRODUCE MORE OF BOTH GOODS @ SAME OPPORT. COSTS)

[hw left margin:] SAME OUTPUTS BUT MAKES A MORE EFFICIENT PRODUCTION PROCESS.

● Absolute advantage is *irrelevant* for specialization and gains from trade. *[hw:]* (NOT POSSIBLE TO HAVE AN ABSOLUTE & COMPARATIVE ADVANTAGE).

● Even a person with an absolute advantage gains by specializing in activity in which she has a comparative advantage and trading. *[hw:]* B/C OPPORTUNITY COSTS HAVEN'T CHANGED W/ ↑ EFFICIENCY.

◆ **Dynamic comparative advantage** results from specializing in an activity, **learning-by-doing**, and over time becoming the producer with the lowest opportunity cost. *[hw:]* EG: SINAPORE, SOUTH KOREA, TAIWAN HONG KONG HAVE PURSUED DYNAMIC COMPARATIVE ADVANTAGE VIGOROUSLY! (CALLED 4 TIGERS!)

V The Evolution of Trading Arrangements

Social arrangements that have evolved to help organize trade are *[hw:]* (TO GET GAINS FROM SPECIALIZATION & COMPARATIVE ADVANTAGE)

① ◆ Markets — *[hw:]* BUYERS/SELLERS GET INFO & DO BUSINESS - COMPARE MARKET PRICE W OPPORTUNITY COSTS & DECIDE WHETHER TO BE A BUYER OR SELLER.

② ◆ **Property rights**—governing ownership, use, and disposal of factors of production and goods and services. *[hw:]* PROTECT FROM STEALING B/C IF NOT THE INCENTIVE TO SPECIALIZE & PRODUCE GOODS WHERE PEOPLE HAVE A COMPARATIVE ADVANTAGE IS WEAKENED & GAINS FROM TRADE ARE LOST.

③ ◆ **Money**—monetary exchange overcomes **barter** problem of double coincidence of wants.
[hw:] - 2 WAYS TO TRADE: ① BARTER ② MONETARY EXCHANGE
- BARTER: DIRECT EXCHANGE OF ONE GOOD FOR ANOTHER (INEFFICIENT)
- MONETARY EXCHANGE: MONEY AS MEANS OF PAYMENT. (EFFICIENT B/C SAVE THE HASSLE OF BARTER).

H E L P F U L   H I N T S

I This chapter reviews the absolutely critical concept of *opportunity cost*—the best alternative forgone—that was introduced in Chapter 1. A very helpful formula for opportunity cost, which works well in solving problems, especially problems that involve moving up or down a production possibility frontier (*PPF*) is:

[hw left:] - USE FOR MOVING UP OR DOWN PPF

$$\text{Opportunity Cost} = \frac{\text{Give Up}}{\text{Get}}$$

[hw right:] MEASURED IN UNITS OF FORGONE GOOD.

[hw bottom:] NOTE: ∴ POSITIVE

Opportunity cost equals the quantity of goods you must give up divided by the quantity of goods you will get. This formula applies to all *PPF*s, whether they are linear as in Text Fig. 3.1 or bowed out as in Text Fig. 3.2. To illustrate, look again at the bowed-out *PPF*.

FIGURE **3.1**

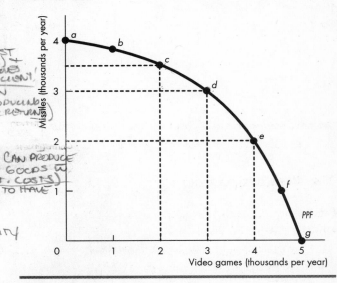

First, consider an example of moving down the *PPF*. In moving from *c* to *d*, what is the opportunity cost of an additional video game? This economy must *give up* 500 missiles (3,500 − 3,000) to *get* 1,000 video games (3,000 − 2,000). Substituting into the formula, the opportunity cost is:

$$\frac{500 \text{ missiles}}{1,000 \text{ video games}} = \frac{1}{2} \text{ missile per video game}$$

Next, consider an example of moving up the *PPF*. In moving from *d* to *c*, what is the opportunity cost of an additional missile? We must *give up* 1,000 video games (3,000 − 2,000) to *get* 500 missiles (3,500 − 3,000). Substituting into the formula, the opportunity cost is: *[hw:]* ALWAYS POSITIVE

$$\frac{1,000 \text{ video games}}{500 \text{ missiles}} = 2 \text{ video games per missile}$$

Opportunity cost is always measured in the units of the *forgone good*.

2 Opportunity cost can also be related to the slope of the *PPF*. As we move down between any two points on the *PPF*, the opportunity cost of an additional unit of the good on the *horizontal* axis is:

$$|\text{slope of } PPF|$$

[hw:] ∴ POSITIVE.

The slope of the *PPF* is negative, but economists like to describe opportunity cost in terms of a positive quantity of forgone goods. Therefore, we must use the *absolute value* of the slope to calculate the desired positive number.

As we move up between any two points on the *PPF*, the opportunity cost of an additional unit of the good on the *vertical* axis is:

$$\left| \frac{1}{\text{slope of } PPF} \right|$$

This is the reciprocal relation we saw between possibilities *c* and *d*. The opportunity cost of an additional video game (on the horizontal axis) between *c* and *d* is 1/2 missile. The opportunity cost of an additional missile (on the vertical axis) between *d* and *c* is 2 video games.

3 The missile/video games production possibility frontier assumes nonhomogeneous resources, that is, resources that are *not* equally useful in all activities. As a result of this assumption, opportunity cost increases as we increase the production of either good. In moving from possibility *c* to *d*, the opportunity cost per video game is 1/2 missile. But in increasing video game production from *d* to *e*, the opportunity cost per video game increases to 1 missile. In producing the first 1,000 video games, we use the resources best suited to video game production. As we increase video game production, however, we must use resources that are less well suited to video game production— hence increasing opportunity cost. A parallel argument accounts for the increasing opportunity cost of increasing missile production.

It is also possible to construct an even simpler model of a *PPF* that assumes homogeneous resources, resources that are *equally* useful in all activities. As a result of this assumption, opportunity cost is *constant* as we increase production of either good. Constant opportunity cost means that the *PPF* will be a straight line (rather than bowed out). As you will see in some of the following exercises, such a simple model is useful for illustrating the principle of comparative advantage, without having to deal with the complications of increasing opportunity cost.

⊚ **4** The text defines absolute advantage as a situation where one person has greater productivity than another in the production of all goods. We can also define *absolute advantage in the production of one good*. In comparing the productivity of two persons, this narrower concept of absolute advantage can be defined either in terms of greater output of the good per unit of inputs, or fewer inputs per unit of output. It is useful to understand these definitions of absolute advantage only to demonstrate that absolute advantage has *no role* in explaining specialization and trade. The gains from trade depend only on differing comparative advantages. People have a comparative advantage in producing a good if they can produce it at lower opportunity cost than others.

5 This chapter gives us our first chance to develop and use economic models. It is useful to think about the nature of these models in the context of the general discussion of models in Chapter 1. For example, one model in this chapter is a representation of the production possibilities in the two-person and two-good world of Mark and Marjorie. The model abstracts greatly from the complexity of the real world in which there are billions of people and numerous different kinds of goods and services. The model allows us to explain a number of phenomena that we observe in the world such as specialization and exchange. The model also has some implications or predictions. For example, countries that devote a larger proportion of their resources to capital accumulation will have more rapidly expanding production possibilities. The model can be subjected to "test" by comparing these predictions to the facts we observe in the real world.

SELF-TEST

True/False/Uncertain and Explain

Refer to the production possibility frontier (*PPF*) in Fig. 3.2 for Questions **1** to **4** .

FIGURE **3.2**

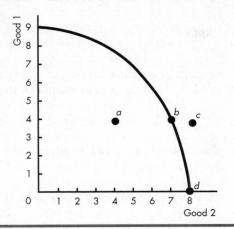

1 Point *a* is not attainable.

2 The opportunity cost of increasing the production of good 2 from 7 to 8 units is 4 units of good 1.

3 Point *c* is not attainable.

  4 In moving from point *b* to point *d*, the opportunity cost of increasing the production of good 2 equals the absolute value of the slope of the *PPF* between *b* and *d*.

5 Economic growth, by shifting out the *PPF*, eliminates the problem of scarcity.

6 In a model where capital resources can grow, points on the *PPF* that have more consumption goods yield faster growth.

7 The incentives for specialization and exchange do not depend on property rights but only on differing opportunity costs.

8 With specialization and trade, a country can produce at a point outside its *PPF*.

9 Canada has no incentive to trade with a cheap-labour country like Mexico.

10 A monetary exchange system requires a double coincidence of wants.

Multiple-Choice

1 If Harold can increase production of good *X* without decreasing the production of any other good, then Harold

a is producing on his *PPF*.
b is producing outside his *PPF*.
c is producing inside his *PPF*.
d must have a linear *PPF*.
e must prefer good *X* to any other good.

2 The bowed-out (concave) shape of a *PPF*

a is due to the equal usefulness of resources in all activities.
b is due to capital accumulation.
c is due to technological improvement.
d reflects the existence of increasing opportunity cost.
e reflects the existence of decreasing opportunity cost.

3 The economy is at point *b* on the *PPF* in Fig. 3.3. The opportunity cost of producing one more unit of *X* is

a 1 unit of *Y*.
b 20 units of *Y*.
c 1 unit of *X*.
d 8 units of *X*.
e 20 units of *X*.

FIGURE **3.3**

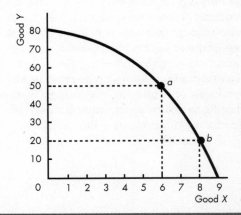

4 The economy is at point *b* on the *PPF* in Fig. 3.3. The opportunity cost of increasing the production of *Y* to 50 units is

a   2 units of *X*.
b   6 units of *X*.
c   8 units of *X*.
d   20 units of *Y*.
e   30 units of *Y*.

5 Refer to the *PPF* in Fig. 3.3. Which of the following statements is *false*?

a   Resources are nonhomogeneous.
b   Points inside the frontier represent unemployed resources.
c   Starting at point *a*, an increase in the production of good *Y* will shift the frontier out.
d   The opportunity cost of producing good *Y* increases as production of *Y* increases.
e   Shifts in preferences for good *X* or good *Y* will not shift the frontier.

6 Because productive resources are scarce, we must give up some of one good in order to acquire more of another. This is the essence of the concept of

a   specialization.
b   monetary exchange.
c   comparative advantage.
d   absolute advantage.
e   opportunity cost.

7 A movement *along* a given *PPF* will result from

a   technological change.
b   change in the stock of capital.
c   change in the labour force.
d   all of the above.
e   none of the above.

8 The opportunity cost of pushing the *PPF* outward is

a   capital accumulation.
b   technological change.
c   reduced current consumption.
d   the gain in future consumption.
e   all of the above.

In an eight-hour day, Andy can produce either 24 loaves of bread or 8 kilograms of butter. In an eight-hour day, Rolfe can produce either 8 loaves of bread or 8 kilograms of butter. Use this information to answer Questions **9** and **10**.

⊚ 9 Which of the following statements is *true*?

a   Andy has an absolute advantage in butter production.
b   Rolfe has an absolute advantage in butter production.
c   Andy has an absolute advantage in bread production.
d   Andy has a comparative advantage in butter production.
e   Rolfe has a comparative advantage in bread production.

10 Andy and Rolfe

a   can gain from exchange if Andy specializes in butter production and Rolfe specializes in bread production.
b   can gain from exchange if Andy specializes in bread production and Rolfe specializes in butter production.
c   cannot gain from exchange.
d   can exchange, but only Rolfe will gain.
e   can exchange, but only Andy will gain.

11 There are two goods—*X* and *Y*. If the opportunity cost of producing good *X* is lower for Pam than for Gino, then

a   Pam has an absolute advantage in the production of *X*.
b   Gino has an absolute advantage in the production of *Y*.
c   Pam has a comparative advantage in the production of *X*.
d   Gino has a comparative advantage in the production of *Y*.
e   c and d are true.

12 In general, the higher the proportion of resources devoted to technological research in an economy the

a   greater will be current consumption.
b   faster the *PPF* will shift outward.
c   faster the *PPF* will shift inward.
d   closer it will come to having a comparative advantage in the production of all goods.
e   more bowed out will be the shape of the *PPF*.

13 Anything that is generally acceptable in exchange for goods and services is

a   a commodity.
b   a medium of exchange.
c   private property.
d   a barter good.
e   called an exchange resource.

14 Mexico and Canada produce both oil and apples using labour only. A barrel of oil can be produced with 4 hours of labour in Mexico and 8 hours of labour in Canada. A bushel of apples can be produced with 8 hours of labour in Mexico and 12 hours of labour in Canada. Canada has

a   an absolute advantage in oil production.
b   an absolute advantage in apple production.
c   a comparative advantage in oil production.
d   a comparative advantage in apple production.
e   none of the above.

15 In Portugal, the opportunity cost of a bale of wool is 3 bottles of wine. In England, the opportunity cost of 1 bottle of wine is 3 bales of wool. Given this information,

a   England has an absolute advantage in wine production.
b   England has an absolute advantage in wool production.
c   Portugal has a comparative advantage in wine production.
d   Portugal has a comparative advantage in wool production.
e   no trade will occur.

16 The scarcity of resources implies that the *PPF* is

a   bowed inward (convex).
b   bowed outward (concave).
c   positively sloped.
d   negatively sloped.
e   linear.

17 If additional units of any good can be produced at a constant opportunity cost, the *PPF* is

a   bowed inward (convex).
b   bowed outward (concave).
c   positively sloped.
d   perfectly horizontal.
e   linear.

18 Refer to Fig. 3.4, which shows the *PPF* for an economy without discrimination operating at maximum efficiency. If discrimination against women workers is currently occurring in this economy, the elimination of discrimination would result in a(n)

a   movement from *a* to *b*.
b   movement from *b* to *c*.
c   movement from *a* to *c*.
d   outward shift of the *PPF*.
e   inward shift of the *PPF*.

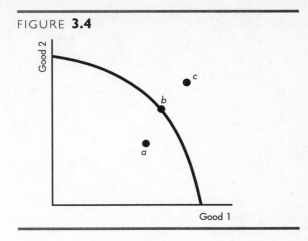

FIGURE **3.4**

Suppose a society produces only two goods—hockey sticks and maple leaves. Three alternative combinations on its *PPF* are given in Table 3.1. Use the information in Table 3.1 to answer Questions **19** and **20**.

TABLE **3.1**   PRODUCTION POSSIBILITIES

Possibility	Units of Hockey Sticks	Units of Maple Leaves
a	3	0
b	2	3
c	0	9

19 In moving from combination *c* to combination *b*, the opportunity cost of producing *one* additional hockey stick is

a   2 maple leaves.
b   1/2 maple leaves.
c   6 maple leaves.
d   1/6 maple leaves.
e   3 maple leaves.

20 According to this *PPF*

a   resources are homogeneous.
b   a combination of 3 hockey sticks and 9 maple leaves is attainable.
c   a combination of 3 hockey sticks and 9 maple leaves would not employ all resources.
d   the opportunity cost of producing hockey sticks increases as more hockey sticks are produced.
e   the opportunity cost of producing hockey sticks decreases as more hockey sticks are produced.

21 The *PPF* for wine and wool will shift if there is a change in

a   the price of resources.
b   the unemployment rate.
c   the quantity of resources.
d   preferences for wine and wool.
e   all of the above.

22 Refer to the *PPF* in Fig. 3.5. A politician who argues that "if our children are to be better off, we must invest now for the future" is recommending a current point like

a *a.*
b *b.*
c *c.*
d *d.*
e *e.*

FIGURE **3.5**

23 Refer to the *PPF* in Fig. 3.5. The statement that "unemployment is a terrible waste of human resources" refers to a point like

a *a.*
b *b.*
c *c.*
d *d.*
e *e.*

24 Which of the following is an advantage of a monetary exchange system over barter?

a A monetary exchange system eliminates the basis for comparative advantage.
b A monetary exchange system does not require a medium of exchange.
c Only in a monetary exchange system can gains from trade be realized.
d A monetary exchange system does not require a double coincidence of wants.
e All of the above are advantages of a monetary exchange system over barter.

25 Learning-by-doing is the basis of

a absolute comparative advantage.
b dynamic comparative advantage.
c intellectual property rights.
d monetary exchange.
e none of the above.

Short Answer Problems

I Why is a *PPF* negatively sloped? Why is it bowed out?

2 Consider two economies, one with no tool-making possibilities and one with tool-making.
 a With no tool-making possibilities (constant capital goods), what is the opportunity cost of moving from a point inside the economy's *PPF* to a point on the *PPF*? Explain.
 b In a tool-making economy, what is the opportunity cost of current consumption?

3 Lawyers earn $200 per hour while secretaries earn $15 per hour. Use the concepts of absolute and comparative advantage to explain why a lawyer who is a better typist than her secretary will still *specialize* in doing only legal work and will *trade* with the secretary for typing services.

4 Explain, using a specific example of exchange, why a monetary exchange system is more efficient than barter.

5 Suppose that an economy with unchanged capital goods has the *PPF* shown in Table 3.2.

TABLE **3.2** PRODUCTION POSSIBILITIES

Possibility	Maximum Units of Butter per Week	Maximum Units of Guns per Week
a	200	0
b	180	60
c	160	100
d	100	160
e	40	200
f	0	220

a On graph paper, plot these possibilities, label the points, and draw the *PPF*. (Put guns on the *x*-axis.)
b If the economy moves from possibility *c* to possibility *d*, the opportunity cost *per unit of guns* will be how many units of butter?
c If the economy moves from possibility *d* to possibility *e*, the opportunity cost *per unit of guns* will be how many units of butter?
d In general terms, what happens to the opportunity cost of guns as the output of guns increases?
e In general terms, what happens to the opportunity cost of butter as the output of butter increases? What do the results in parts **d** and **e** imply about resources?

f If (instead of the possibilities given) the *PPF* were a straight line joining points *a* and *f*, what would that imply about opportunity costs and resources?

g Given the original *PPF* you have plotted, is a combination of 140 units of butter and 130 units of guns per week attainable? Would you regard this combination as an efficient one? Explain.

h Given the original *PPF*, is a combination of 70 units of butter and 170 units of guns per week attainable? Is this an efficient combination? Explain.

6 If the following events occurred (each is a separate event, unaccompanied by any other event), what would happen to the *PPF* in Short Answer Problem 5?

a A new, easily exploited, energy source is discovered.

b A large number of skilled workers immigrate into the country.

c The output of butter increases.

d A new invention increases output per person in the butter industry but not in the guns industry.

e A new law is passed compelling workers, who could previously work as long as they wanted, to retire at age sixty.

7 France and Germany each produce both wine and beer, using a single homogeneous input— labour. Their production possibilities are:

France has 100 units of labour and can produce a maximum of 200 bottles of wine *or* 400 bottles of beer.

Germany has 50 units of labour and can produce a maximum of 250 bottles of wine *or* 200 bottles of beer.

a Complete Table 3.3.

TABLE **3.3**

	Bottles Produced by I Unit of Labour		Opportunity Cost of I Additional Bottle	
	Wine	Beer	Wine	Beer
France				
Germany				

Use the information in part **a** to answer the following questions.

b Which country has an absolute advantage in wine production?

c Which country has an absolute advantage in beer production?

d Which country has a comparative advantage in wine production?

e Which country has a comparative advantage in beer production?

f If trade is allowed, describe what specialization, if any, will occur.

8 Suppose the country of Quark has historically devoted 10 percent of its resources to the production of new capital goods. Use *PPF* diagrams like Text Fig. 3.5 on page 52 to compare the consequences (costs and benefits) of each of the following:

a Quark continues to devote 10 percent of its resources to the production of capital goods.

b Quark begins now to permanently devote 20 percent of its resources to the production of capital goods.

9 Tova and Ron are the only two remaining inhabitants of the planet Melmac. They spend their 30-hour days producing widgets and woggles, the only two goods needed for happiness on Melmac. It takes Tova 1 hour to produce a widget and 2 hours to produce a woggle, while Ron takes 3 hours to produce a widget and 3 hours to produce a woggle.

a For a 30-hour day, draw an individual *PPF* for Tova, for Ron.

b What does the shape of the *PPF*s tell us about opportunity costs? about resources?

c Assume initially that Tova and Ron are each self-sufficient. Define self-sufficiency. Explain what the individual consumption possibilities are for Tova, for Ron.

d Who has an absolute advantage in the production of widgets? of woggles?

e Who has a comparative advantage in the production of widgets? of woggles?

f Suppose Tova and Ron each specialize in producing only the good in which she/he has a comparative advantage (one spends 30 hours producing widgets, the other spends 30 hours producing woggles). What will be the total production of widgets and woggles?

g Suppose Tova and Ron exchange 7 widgets for 5 woggles. On your *PPF* diagrams, plot the new point of Tova's consumption, of Ron's consumption. Explain how these points illustrate the gains from trade.

10 The Netsilik and Oonark families live on the arctic coast, west of Hudson Bay. They often go fishing and hunting for caribou together. During an average working day, the Netsiliks can, at most, catch *either* 6 kilograms of fish or kill 6 caribou. The Oonarks can catch *either* 4 kilograms of fish or kill 4 caribou.

a Assuming linear *PPF*s, draw each family's *PPF* on the same diagram. Put fish on the horizontal axis and caribou on the vertical axis.

b Complete Table 3.4.

TABLE **3.4**

	Opportunity Cost of 1 Additional	
	Fish (kg)	Caribou
Netsiliks		
Oonarks		

c Which family has a comparative advantage in catching fish? in hunting caribou?

d Can specialization and trade increase the total output of fish and caribou produced by the two families? Explain.

A N S W E R S

True/False/Uncertain and Explain

1 F Attainable but not a maximum. (44–45)

2 T Moving from *b* to *d*, production good 1 ↓ by 4 units. (48–49)

3 T Outside *PPF*. (44–45)

4 T See Helpful Hint 2. (48–49)

5 F Cost of growth is forgone current consumption. (50–52)

6 F Points with capital goods yield faster growth. (51–53)

7 F Property rights prerequisite for specialization and exchange. (57–58)

8 F Can *consume* at point outside *PPF*. (53–55)

9 F Mutually beneficial trade depends on comparative advantage, not absolute advantage. (55–56)

10 F Monetary exchange eliminates problem of double coincidence wants. (58)

Multiple-Choice

1 c For 0 opportunity cost, must be unemployed resources. (44–45)

2 d a would be true if *un*equal resources; **b** and **c** shift *PPF*. (47–48)

3 b To ↑ quantity *X* to 9, must ↓ quantity *Y* from 20 to 0. (48–49)

4 a To move from *b* to *a*, quantity *X* ↓ from 8 to 6. (48–49)

5 c ↑ production *Y* moves up *along* *PPF*. (44–48)

6 e Definition. (45–46)

7 e **a, b**, and **c** all shift *PPF*. (50–52)

8 c **a** and **b** cause outward shift *PPF*, not opportunity cost; **d** effect of outward shift *PPF*. (50–52)

9 c Andy produces 3 loaves bread per hour; Rolfe produces 1 loaf per hour. (53–56)

10 b Andy has comparative advantage (lower opportunity cost) bread, Rolfe has comparative advantage butter production. (53–56)

11 e **c** by definition comparative advantage; **d** because opportunity cost *Y* reciprocal of opportunity cost *X*. (53–56)

12 b Technological progress shifts *PPF* outward at cost of current consumption. (51–53)

13 b Definition. (58)

14 d Opportunity cost oil in bushels of apples — Canada 2/3, Mexico 1/2. Opportunity cost apples in barrels of oil — Canada 3/2, Mexico 2. (53–54)

15 c Opportunity cost wine in bales of wool— Portugal 1/3, England 3. Opportunity cost wool in bottles of wine—Portugal 3, England 1/3. (53–54)

16 d Scarcity → opportunity cost → negative relationship—to get more of *X* you must give up *Y*. (45–46)

17 e Constant opportunity cost → constant slope *PPF*. (44–46)

18 a Discrimination causes underemployment of resources. Women not allowed to produce up to full abilities. (44–45)

19 e Give up 6 maple leaves to get 2 hockey sticks: 6/2 = 3 maple leaves per hockey stick. (44–46)

20 a Constant opportunity cost → resources equally useful for producing all goods. (44–47)

21 c Only changes in resources or technology shift *PPF*. (50–51)

22 a Producing more capital goods now, shifts *PPF* outward in future. (51–52)

23 d Points inside *PPF* represent unemployed resources, whether labour, capital, or land. (44–45)

24 d Money irrelevant to comparative advantage
(a) and gains from trade (c); monetary
exchange requires medium exchange (b). (58)

25 b Definition. (56)

Short Answer Problems

1 The negative slope of the *PPF* reflects
opportunity cost: in order to have more of one
good, some of the other must be forgone.

It is bowed out because the existence of
nonhomogeneous resources creates increasing
opportunity cost as we increase the production
of either good.

2 a In an economy with no tool-making
possibilities, a point inside the *PPF* represents
unemployed or underutilized resources. By
moving to a point on the frontier, more output
can be produced from the same resources,
simply by utilizing the resources more efficiently.
Since resources do not have to be withdrawn
from the production of any other good, the
opportunity cost of moving to a point on the
frontier is zero. This is the closest we get to a
"free lunch" in the discipline of economics.

b In a tool-making economy, we can forgo current
consumption to produce capital goods, which
subsequently increase future production and
consumption. By consuming all that is currently
produced, we forgo tool making and, ultimately,
increased future consumption.

3 The lawyer has an absolute advantage in
producing both legal and typing services relative
to the secretary. Nevertheless, she has a
comparative advantage in legal services, and the
secretary has a comparative advantage in typing.
To demonstrate these comparative advantages,
we can construct Table 3.5 of opportunity costs.

TABLE **3.5**

	Opportunity Cost of 1 Additional Hour ($)	
	Legal Services	**Typing**
Lawyer	200	200
Secretary	>200	15

Consider first the lawyer's opportunity costs.
The lawyer's best forgone alternative to providing
1 hour of legal services is the $200 she could earn
by providing another hour of legal services. If she
provides 1 hour of typing, she is also forgoing
$200 (1 hour) of legal services. What would the
secretary have to forgo to provide 1 hour of legal

services? He would have to spend 3 years in law
school, forgoing 3 years of income in addition to
the tuition he must pay. His opportunity cost is a
very large number, certainly greater than $200.
If he provides 1 hour of typing, his best forgone
alternative is the $15 he could have earned at
another secretarial job.

Thus Table 3.5 shows that the lawyer has a
lower opportunity cost (comparative advantage)
of providing legal services, and the secretary has
a lower opportunity cost (comparative
advantage) of providing typing services. It is on
the basis of comparative advantage (not absolute
advantage) that trade will take place from which
both parties gain.

4 The principal reason for the efficiency of a
monetary exchange system relative to barter is
that the monetary system does not require a
double coincidence of wants to complete a
successful exchange. For example, suppose you
specialize in the production of apples but like to
eat bananas. In a barter economy, you would
likely not be able to complete an exchange with
the first person you found who had bananas to
trade. It would be necessary for that person to
also want to trade the bananas for apples and not
for carrots or some other good. In a monetary
economy, you would always be able to make a
successful exchange with the first person you
found with bananas to trade since that person
would be willing to accept money in exchange.
Similarly, in a money exchange system, you
would be able to sell your apples for money to
the first person you found who wanted apples
(even if that person did not have bananas to sell).

5 a The graph of the *PPF* is given in Fig. 3.6.

FIGURE **3.6**

b In moving from *c* to *d*, in order to gain 60 units of guns, we must give up 160 − 100 = 60 units of butter. The opportunity cost per unit of guns is

$$\frac{60 \text{ units butter}}{60 \text{ units guns}} = 1 \text{ unit butter per unit of guns}$$

c In moving from *d* to *e*, in order to gain 40 units of guns, we must give up 100 − 40 = 60 units of butter. The opportunity cost per unit of guns is:

$$\frac{60 \text{ units butter}}{40 \text{ units guns}} = 1.5 \text{ unit butter per unit of guns}$$

d The opportunity cost of producing more guns increases as the output of guns increases.

e Likewise, the opportunity cost of producing more butter increases as the output of butter increases. Increasing opportunity costs imply that resources are nonhomogeneous; that is, they are not equally useful in gun and butter production.

f Opportunity costs would always be constant, regardless of the output of guns or butter. The opportunity cost per unit of guns would be

$$200/220 = 10/11 \text{ units of butter}$$

The opportunity cost per unit of butter would be

$$220/200 = 1.1 \text{ units of guns}$$

Constant opportunity costs imply that resources are homogeneous; that is, they are equally useful in gun and butter production.

g This combination is outside the *PPF* and therefore is not attainable. Since the economy cannot produce this combination, the question of efficiency is irrelevant.

h This combination is inside the *PPF* and is attainable. It is inefficient because the economy could produce more of either or both goods. Therefore some resources are not fully utilized.

6 a Assuming that both goods require energy for their production, the entire *PPF* shifts out to the northeast as in Fig. 3.7(a).

b Assuming that both goods use skilled labour in their production, the entire *PPF* shifts out to the northeast.

c The *PPF* does not shift. An increase in the output of butter implies a movement *along* the *PPF* to the left, not a shift of the *PPF* itself.

d The new invention implies that for every level of output of guns, the economy can now produce more butter. The *PPF* swings to the right, but remains anchored at point *f* as in Fig. 3.7(b).

e The entire *PPF* shifts in towards the origin.

FIGURE **3.7**

7 a The completed table is shown here as Table 3.3 Solution.

TABLE **3.3**   SOLUTION

	Bottles Produced by 1 Unit of Labour		Opportunity Cost of 1 Additional Bottle	
	Wine	**Beer**	**Wine**	**Beer**
France	2	4	2.0 beer	0.50 wine
Germany	5	4	0.8 beer	1.25 wine

b Germany, which can produce more wine (5 bottles) per unit of input, has an absolute advantage in wine production.

c Neither country has an absolute advantage in beer production, since beer output (4 bottles) per unit of input is the same for both countries.

d Germany, with the lower opportunity cost (0.8 beer), has a comparative advantage in wine production.

e France, with the lower opportunity cost (0.5 wine), has a comparative advantage in beer production.

f The incentive for trade depends only on differences in comparative advantage. Germany will specialize in wine production and France will specialize in beer production.

8 a The situation for Quark is depicted by Fig. 3.8. Suppose Quark starts on *PPF* 1. If it continues to devote only 10 percent of its resources to the production of new capital goods, then it is choosing to produce at a point like *a*. This will shift the *PPF* out in the next period, but only to the curve labelled 2 (where, presumably, Quark will choose to produce at point *b*).

FIGURE **3.8**

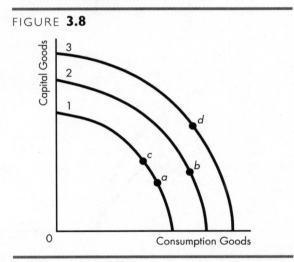

b Starting from the same initial *PPF*, if Quark now decides to increase the resources devoted to the production of new capital to 20 percent, it will be choosing to produce at a point like *c*. In this case, next period's *PPF* will shift further—to curve 3, and a point like *d*, for example.

Thus in comparing points *a* and *c*, we find the following costs and benefits: point *a* has the benefit of greater present consumption but at a cost of lower future consumption; point *c* has the cost of lower present consumption, but with the benefit of greater future consumption.

9 a The individual *PPF*s for Tova and Ron are given by Fig. 3.9(a) and (b), respectively.

FIGURE **3.9**

(a) Tova

(b) Ron

b The linear shape of the *PPF*s tells us that opportunity costs are constant along each frontier and that resources are homogeneous.

These linear *PPF*s with constant opportunity costs abstract from the complexity of the real world. The world generally has increasing opportunity costs, but that fact is not essential for understanding the gains from trade, which is the objective of this problem. Making the model more complex by including increasing opportunity costs would not change our results, but it would make it more difficult to see them.

c Individuals are self-sufficient if they consume only what they produce. This means there is no trade. Without trade, Tova's (maximum) consumption possibilities are exactly the same as her production possibilities—points along her *PPF*. Ron's (maximum) consumption possibilities are likewise the points along his *PPF*.

d Tova has an absolute advantage in the production of both widgets and woggles. Her absolute advantage can be defined either in terms of greater output per unit of inputs or fewer inputs per unit of output. A comparison of the *PPF*s in Fig. 3.9 shows that, for given inputs of 30 hours, Tova produces a greater output of widgets than Ron (30 versus 10) and a greater output of woggles than Ron (15 versus

10). The statement of the problem tells us equivalently that, per unit of output, Tova uses fewer inputs than Ron for both widgets (1 hour versus 3 hours) and woggles (2 hours versus 3 hours). Since Tova has greater productivity than Ron in the production of all goods (widgets and woggles), we say that overall she has an absolute advantage.

e Tova has a comparative advantage in the production of widgets, since she can produce them at lower opportunity cost than Ron (1/2 woggle versus 1 woggle). On the other hand, Ron has a comparative advantage in the production of woggles since he can produce them at a lower opportunity cost than Tova (1 widget versus 2 widgets).

f Tova will produce widgets and Ron will produce woggles, yielding a total production between them of 30 widgets and 10 woggles.

g After the exchange, Tova will have 23 widgets and 5 woggles (point *T*). Ron will have 7 widgets and 5 woggles (point *R*). These new post-trade consumption possibility points lie outside Tova's and Ron's respective pre-trade consumption (and production) possibilities. Hence trade has yielded gains that allow the traders to improve their consumption possibilities beyond those available with self-sufficiency.

10 a The *PPF*s of the Netsiliks and Oonarks are shown in Fig. 3.10.

FIGURE **3.10**

b The completed table is shown here as Table 3.4 Solution.

TABLE **3.4** SOLUTION

	Opportunity Cost of 1 Additional	
	Fish (kg)	**Caribou**
Netsiliks	1 caribou	1 kg fish
Oonarks	1 caribou	1 kg fish

c Neither family has a comparative advantage in catching fish since the opportunity cost of fish is the same (1 caribou) for each family. Similarly, neither family has a comparative advantage in hunting caribou since the opportunity cost of a caribou is the same (1 kg fish) for each family.

d Gains from specialization and trade are due to the existence of comparative advantage. In this case, no family has a comparative advantage in either fishing or hunting, so there are no gains from specialization and trade.

To illustrate the absence of gains, suppose that initially each family devoted half of its time to each activity. Then suppose that the Netsiliks specialized completely in catching fish and the Oonarks specialized completely in hunting caribou. Production before and after specialization is shown in Table 3.6.

TABLE **3.6**

	Before Specialization		After Specialization	
	Fish (kg)	**Caribou**	**Fish (kg)**	**Caribou**
Netsiliks	3	3	6	0
Oonarks	2	2	0	4
Total Production	5	5	6	4

Compare the total production of both commodities before and after specialization. Specialization has increased the total production of fish by 1 kilogram, but it has also led to a decrease in the total production of caribou by 1. There are no clear gains in consumption from specialization and trade.

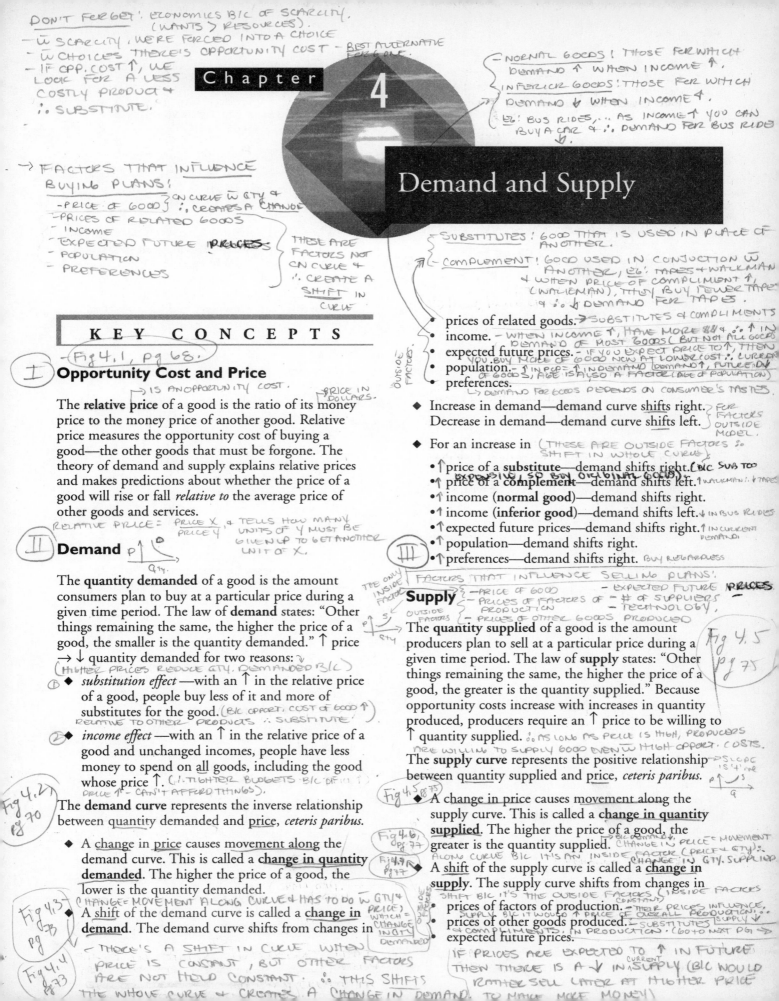

Handwritten notes (top left):

DON'T FORGET! ECONOMICS B/C OF SCARCITY.
(WANTS > RESOURCES).
— W SCARCITY, WE'RE FORCED INTO A CHOICE
— W CHOICES THERE'S OPPORTUNITY COST - BEST ALTERNATIVE FORGONE.
— IF OPP. COST ↑, WE LOOK FOR A LESS COSTLY PRODUCT ∴ SUBSTITUTE.

Handwritten notes (top right):

— NORMAL GOODS! THOSE FOR WHICH DEMAND ↑ WHEN INCOME ↑.
— INFERIOR GOODS! THOSE FOR WHICH DEMAND ↓ WHEN INCOME ↓.
EG: BUS RIDES, ∴ AS INCOME ↑ YOU CAN BUY A CAR ∴ DEMAND FOR BUS RIDE

Chapter 4

Demand and Supply

Handwritten notes (left of Key Concepts):

→ FACTORS THAT INFLUENCE BUYING PLANS!
— PRICE OF GOOD } ∴ CREATES A CHANGE ON CURVE W GTY ↓
— PRICES OF RELATED GOODS
— INCOME
— EXPECTED FUTURE PRICES
— POPULATION
— PREFERENCES

THESE ARE FACTORS NOT ON CURVE ∴ CREATE A SHIFT IN CURVE

KEY CONCEPTS

- Fig 4.1, pg 68.

Ⓘ **Opportunity Cost and Price**

→ IS AN OPPORTUNITY COST.   PRICE IN DOLLARS.

The **relative price** of a good is the ratio of its money price to the money price of another good. Relative price measures the opportunity cost of buying a good—the other goods that must be forgone. The theory of demand and supply explains relative prices and makes predictions about whether the price of a good will rise or fall *relative to* the average price of other goods and services.

RELATIVE PRICE = PRICE X / PRICE Y & TELLS HOW MANY UNITS OF Y MUST BE GIVEN UP TO GET ANOTHER UNIT OF X.

ⒾⒾ **Demand**

The **quantity demanded** of a good is the amount consumers plan to buy at a particular price during a given time period. The law of **demand** states: "Other things remaining the same, the higher the price of a good, the smaller is the quantity demanded." ↑ price → ↓ quantity demanded for two reasons:
(HIGHER PRICES REDUCE GTY. DEMANDED B/C)

① ◆ *substitution effect*—with an ↑ in the relative price of a good, people buy less of it and more of substitutes for the good. (B/C OPPORT. COST OF GOOD ↑ RELATIVE TO OTHER PRODUCTS ∴ SUBSTITUTE!)

② ◆ *income effect*—with an ↑ in the relative price of a good and unchanged incomes, people have less money to spend on all goods, including the good whose price ↑. (∴ TIGHTER BUDGETS B/C OF ↑↑ PRICE ↑ — CAN'T AFFORD THINGS).

The **demand curve** represents the inverse relationship between quantity demanded and price, *ceteris paribus*.

◆ A change in price causes movement along the demand curve. This is called a **change in quantity demanded**. The higher the price of a good, the lower is the quantity demanded.
(CHANGE = MOVEMENT ALONG CURVE & HAS TO DO W GTY ↓)

◆ A shift of the demand curve is called a **change in demand**. The demand curve shifts from changes in

— THERE'S A SHIFT IN CURVE WHEN PRICE IS CONSTANT, BUT OTHER FACTORS ARE NOT HELD CONSTANT. ∴ THIS SHIFTS THE WHOLE CURVE & CREATES A CHANGE IN DEMAND.

Handwritten (right column top):

— SUBSTITUTES! GOOD THAT IS USED IN PLACE OF ANOTHER.
— COMPLEMENT! GOOD USED IN CONJUNCTION W ANOTHER, EG! TAPES + WALKMAN ↑ WHEN PRICE OF COMPLIMENT ↑, (WALKMAN), THEY BUY FEWER TAPES ∴ ↓ DEMAND FOR TAPES.

- prices of related goods. → SUBSTITUTES & COMPLIMENTS
- income. — WHEN INCOME ↑, HAVE MORE $$ & ∴ ↑ IN DEMAND OF MOST GOODS (BUT NOT ALL GOODS)
- expected future prices. — IF YOU EXPECT PRICE TO ↑, THEN YOU BUY MORE OF GOOD NOW AT LOWER COST. CURRENT
- population. — ↑ IN POP = ↑ IN DEMAND (DEMAND), FUTURE ↑ OF GOODS, AGE IS ALSO A FACTOR (AGE OF POPULATION)
- preferences. → DEMAND FOR GOODS DEPENDS ON CONSUMER'S TASTES

◆ Increase in demand—demand curve shifts right. } FOR FACTORS OUTSIDE MODEL
Decrease in demand—demand curve shifts left.

◆ For an increase in (THESE ARE OUTSIDE FACTORS ∴ SHIFT IN WHOLE CURVE)
- ↑ price of a **substitute**—demand shifts right. (B/C SUB TOO EXPENSIVE, SO BUY ORIGINAL GOODS)
- ↑ price of a **complement**—demand shifts left. ↑ WALKMAN & TAPES
- ↑ income (**normal good**)—demand shifts right.
- ↑ income (**inferior good**)—demand shifts left. ↓ IN BUS RIDES
- ↑ expected future prices—demand shifts right. ↑ IN CURRENT DEMAND
- ↑ population—demand shifts right.
- ↑ preferences—demand shifts right. BUY REGARDLESS

ⒾⒾⒾ

Handwritten: THE ONLY INSIDE FACTOR

FACTORS THAT INFLUENCE SELLING PLANS!
— PRICE OF GOOD   — EXPECTED FUTURE PRICES
— PRICES OF FACTORS OF — # OF SUPPLIERS
  PRODUCTION   — TECHNOLOGY,
— PRICES OF OTHER GOODS PRODUCED

OUTSIDE FACTORS

Supply

The **quantity supplied** of a good is the amount producers plan to sell at a particular price during a given time period. The law of **supply** states: "Other things remaining the same, the higher the price of a good, the greater is the quantity supplied." Because opportunity costs increase with increases in quantity produced, producers require an ↑ price to be willing to ↑ quantity supplied. ∴ AS LONG AS PRICE IS HIGH, PRODUCERS ARE WILLING TO SUPPLY GOOD EVEN W HIGH OPPORT. COSTS.

The **supply curve** represents the positive relationship → SLOPE IS ↑VE between quantity supplied and price, *ceteris paribus*.

◆ A change in price causes movement along the supply curve. This is called a **change in quantity supplied**. The higher the price of a good, the greater is the quantity supplied. → B/C DEMAND & PRICE = MOVEMENT ALONG CURVE B/C IT'S AN INSIDE FACTOR (PRICE & GTY) ∴ CHANGE IN GTY. SUPPLIED

A **shift** of the supply curve is called a **change in supply**. The supply curve shifts from changes in SHIFT B/C IT'S THE OUTSIDE FACTORS (INSIDE FACTORS CONSTANT)

- prices of factors of production. — THEIR PRICES INFLUENCE SUPPLY B/C IT WOULD ↑ PRICE OF OVERALL PRODUCTION, SUPPLY ↓
- prices of other goods produced. — SUBSTITUTES SUPPLY & COMPLIMENTS IN PRODUCTION. (GO TO NEXT PG →)
- expected future prices.

IF PRICES ARE EXPECTED TO ↑ IN FUTURE THEN THERE IS A ↓ IN CURRENT SUPPLY (B/C WOULD RATHER SELL LATER AT HIGHER PRICE TO MAKE MORE MONEY!)

Handwritten margin figure labels: Fig 4.2 pg 70, Fig 4.3 pg 73, Fig 4.4 pg 73, Fig 4.5 pg 75, Fig 4.6 pg 77, Fig 4.7 pg 77

handwritten top margin left: FOR PRICES OF OTHER GOODS:
- SUBSTITUTE IN PRODUCTION: ↑ PRICE OF SUB. IN PRODUCTION

handwritten: ∴ ↓ SUPPLY OF GOOD.

handwritten: - COMPLEMENT IN PRODUCTION: WHEN 2 THINGS OF NECESSITY ARE PRODUCED TOGETHER (BY-PRODUCTS) ∴ ↑ IN PRICE OF BY-PRODUCT, ↑ SUPPLY OF OTHER BY-PRODUCTS

- • number of suppliers. *handwritten:* ↑ SUPPLIERS (FIRMS) ∴ ↑ IN SUPPLY OF GOOD (B/C MORE PRODUCERS)
handwritten left margin: MOST IMPORTANT *handwritten:* • technology. → ↑ IN TECH. MEANS WE USE LESS
handwritten: FACTORS OF PRODUCTION (SO CHEAPER TO PRODUCE) ∴ ↑ SUPPLY.

♦ Increase in supply—supply curve shifts right. *handwritten:* FOR OUTSIDE FACTORS.
Decrease in supply—supply curve shifts left.

♦ For an increase in *(handwritten:* THESE ARE OUTSIDE FACTORS ∴) *handwritten:* SHIFT IN WHOLE CURVE
  • ↑ price of factors of production—supply shifts left. *handwritten:* B/C IT COSTS MORE TO PRODUCE THE GOOD.
  • ↑ price of a substitute in production—supply shifts left.
  • ↑ price of a complement in production—supply shifts right.
  • ↑ expected future prices—supply shifts left. *handwritten:* B/C CAN SELL LATER
  • ↑ number of suppliers—supply shifts right. *handwritten:* B/C MORE IS BEING PRODUCED.
  • ↑ technology—supply shifts right. *handwritten:* - B/C IT USES LESS FACTORS OF PRODUCTION & ∴ COSTS LESS TO PRODUCE.

handwritten circle: IV
handwritten circle: Fig 4.8 Pg 78

Price Determination
handwritten: - WHEN PRICE ↑, DEMAND ↓ & ∴ SUPPLY ↑.

The **equilibrium price** is where the demand and supply curves intersect, where quantity demanded equals quantity supplied. *handwritten:* AT 3 [graph] P = $3.00 QTY = 4 MILLION

handwritten left: = SURPLUS S>D

♦ Above the equilibrium price, there is a surplus (quantity supplied > quantity demanded), and price will fall. *handwritten:* ↑ PRICE B/C THERE IS A SURPLUS & SO, BY ↓ PRICE, WE ↑ DEMAND & ∴ THAT ↓ SUPPLY.

handwritten left: = SHORTAGE S<D

♦ Below the equilibrium price, there is a shortage (quantity demanded > quantity supplied), and price will rise. *handwritten:* ↑ PRICE B/C THERE IS A SHORTAGE & WE NEED TO GET BACK TO EQUILIB. SO, BY ↑ PRICE YOU WILL ↓ DEMAND & ∴ ↑ SUPPLY AGAIN

handwritten left: AT EQUIL. BUYERS & SELLERS MATCH EACH OTHER

♦ Only in equilibrium is there no tendency for the price to change. The **equilibrium quantity** is the quantity bought and sold at the equilibrium price. *handwritten:* WHEN BUYERS SEEK LOWEST PRICE & SELLERS SEEK HIGHEST PRICE, THE PRICE AT WHICH TRADE TAKES PLACE IS AT EQUIL. (CAN'T DO BUSINESS AT A BETTER PRICE).

Predicting Changes in Price and Quantity
handwritten circle: V

When there is a single change *either* in demand *or* in supply, *ceteris paribus*, an

handwritten circle: Fig 4.9 Pg 80
♦ increase in demand → ↑ P and ↑ Q. *handwritten:* FOR A CHANGE IN DEMAND (ONLY DEMAND CURVE SHIFTS)
♦ decrease in demand → ↓ P and ↓ Q.
handwritten circle: Fig 4.10 Pg 81
♦ increase in supply → ↓ P and ↑ Q. *handwritten:* FOR A CHANGE IN SUPPLY (ONLY SUPPLY CURVE SHIFTS).
♦ decrease in supply → ↑ P and ↓ Q.

When there is a simultaneous change *both* in demand *and* supply, we can determine the effect on either price or quantity. But without information about the relative size of the shifts of the demand and supply curves, the effect on the other variable is ambiguous. *Ceteris paribus*, an

handwritten circle: Fig 4.11 Pg 82
♦ increase in both demand and supply → ↑, ↓, or constant P and ↑ Q. *handwritten:* SAME DIRECTION
♦ decrease in both demand and supply → ↑, ↓, or constant P and ↓ Q.

handwritten circle top right: Fig 4.12 Pg 83

♦ increase in demand and decrease in supply → ↑ P and ↑, ↓, or constant Q. *handwritten:* OPPOSITE DIRECTIONS
♦ decrease in demand and increase in supply → ↓ P and ↑, ↓, or constant Q.

handwritten circle: Fig 4.13 Pg 85
handwritten: ① SLIDE = ↑S > ↑D ∴ OVERTLY ↓ P
② ROCKET = ↓S > ↓D ∴ ROCKET ↑ P
③ POWER CONSTER = ↑↓S + D CONSTANT

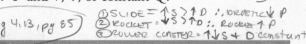

HELPFUL HINTS

1 When you are first learning about demand and supply it is useful to think in terms of concrete examples to help build an intuitive understanding. Have some favourite examples in the back of your mind. For example, in analysing complementary goods, think about hamburgers and french fries; in analysing substitute goods, think of hamburgers and hot dogs. This will help reduce the "abstractness" of the economic theory.

2 The statement that "price is determined by demand and supply" is a shorthand way of saying that price is determined by all of the factors affecting demand (prices of related goods, income, expected future prices, population, preferences) and all of the factors affecting supply (prices of other goods produced, prices of factors of production, expected future prices, number of suppliers, technology). The benefit of using demand and supply curves is that they allow us to sort out the influences on price of each of these separate factors systematically. Changes in the factors affecting demand shift the demand curve and move us up or down the given supply curve. Changes in the factors affecting supply shift the supply curve and move us up or down the given demand curve.

   Any demand and supply problem requires you to sort out these influences carefully. In so doing, *always draw a graph*, even if it is just a small graph in the margin of a true/false/uncertain or multiple-choice problem. Graphical representation is a very efficient way to "see" what happens. As you become comfortable with graphs, you will find that they are effective and powerful tools for systematically organizing your thinking.

   Do not make the common mistake of thinking that a problem is so easy that you can do it in your head, without drawing a graph. This mistake will cost you dearly on examinations. Also, when you do draw a graph, be sure to label the axes. As the course progresses, you will encounter many graphs with different variables on the axes. It is very easy to become confused if you do not develop the habit of labelling the axes.

3   Another very common mistake among students is failing to *distinguish* correctly *between a shift in a curve* and *a movement along a curve*. This distinction applies both to demand and supply curves. Many questions in the self-test are designed to test your understanding of this distinction, and you can be sure that your instructor will test you heavily on this. The distinction between "shifts in" versus "movements along" a curve is crucial for systematic thinking about the factors influencing demand and supply, and for understanding the determination of equilibrium price and quantity.

Consider the example of the demand curve. The quantity of a good demanded depends on its own price, the prices of related goods, income, expected future prices, population, and preferences. The term "demand" refers to the relationship between the price of a good and the quantity demanded, holding constant all of the other factors on which the quantity demanded depends. This demand relationship is represented graphically by the demand curve. Thus, the effect of a change in price on quantity demanded is already reflected in the slope of the demand curve; the effect of a change in the price of the good itself is given by a movement along the demand curve. This is referred to as a **change in quantity demanded**.

On the other hand, if one of the other factors affecting the quantity demanded changes, the demand curve itself will shift; the quantity demanded at each price will change. This shift of the demand curve is referred to as a **change in demand**. The critical thing to remember is that a change in the price of a good will not shift the demand curve, it will only cause a movement along the demand curve. Similarly, it is just as important to distinguish between shifts in the supply curve and movements along the supply curve.

To confirm your understanding, consider the effect (draw a graph!) of an increase in household income on the market for compact discs (CDs). First note that an increase in income affects the demand for CDs and not supply. Next we want to determine whether the increase in income causes a shift in the demand curve or a movement along the demand curve. Will the increase in income increase the quantity of CDs demanded even if the price of CDs does not change? Since the answer to this question is yes, we know that the demand curve will shift to the right. Note further that the increase in the

demand for CDs will cause the equilibrium price to rise. This price increase will be indicated by a movement along the supply curve (an increase in the quantity supplied) and will not shift the supply curve itself.

Remember: It is shifts in demand and supply curves that cause the market price to change, not changes in the price that cause demand and supply curves to shift.

4   When analysing the shifts of demand and supply curves in related markets (for substitute goods like beer and wine), it often seems as though the feedback effects from one market to the other can go on endlessly. To avoid confusion, stick to the rule that each curve (demand and supply) for a given market can shift a maximum of *once*. (See Short Answer Problems 4 and 6 on page 40 for further explanation and examples.)

ⓔ 5   The relationships between price and quantity demanded and supplied can be represented in three equivalent forms: demand and supply schedules, curves, and equations. Textbook Chapter 4 illustrates schedules and curves, but demand and supply equations are also powerful tools of economic analysis. The mathematical note to Chapter 4 provides the general form of these equations. The purpose of this helpful hint and the next is to further explain the equations and how they can be used to determine the equilibrium values of price and quantity.

Figure 4.1 presents a simple demand and supply example in three equivalent forms: (a) schedules, (b) curves, and (c) equations. The demand and supply schedules in (a) are in the same format as Text Fig. 4.8. The price—quantity combinations from the schedules are plotted on the graph in (b), yielding linear demand and supply curves. What is new about this example is the representation of those curves by the equations in (c).

If you recall (Chapter 2) the formula for the equation of a straight line ($y = a + bx$), you can see that the demand equation is the equation of a straight line. Instead of y, P is the dependent variable on the vertical axis, and, instead of x, Q_D is the independent variable on the horizontal axis. The intercept on the vertical axis a is +5, and the slope b is −1. The supply equation is also linear and graphed in the same way, but with Q_S as the independent variable. The supply curve intercept on the vertical axis is +1, and the slope is +1. The negative slope of the demand curve reflects the law of demand, and the positive slope of the supply curve reflects the law of supply.

You can demonstrate the equivalence of the demand schedule, curve, and equation by substituting various values of Q_D from the schedule into the demand equation, and calculating the associated prices. These combinations of quantity demanded and price are the coordinates (Q_D, P) of the points on the demand curve. You can similarly demonstrate the equivalence of the supply schedule, curve, and equation.

FIGURE **4.1**

(a) Demand and Supply Schedules

Price ($)	Q_D	Q_S	Shortage (–)/ Surplus (+)
1	4	0	–4
2	3	1	–2
3	2	2	0
4	1	3	+2
5	0	4	+4

(b) Demand and Supply Curves

(c) Demand and Supply Equations

Demand: $P = 5 - 1Q_D$
Supply: $P = 1 + 1Q_S$

The demand and supply equations are very useful for calculating the equilibrium values of price and quantity. As the schedules and curves both show, two things are true in equilibrium: (1) the price is the same for consumers (the highest price they are willing to pay for the last unit) and producers (the lowest price they are willing to accept for the last unit), and (2) the quantity demanded equals the quantity supplied, so that there are no surpluses or shortages. In terms of the demand and supply equations, this means that *in equilibrium*: (1) the price in both equations is the same. We will denote the equilibrium price as P^*. (2) $Q_D = Q_S =$ the equilibrium quantity bought and sold. We will denote the equilibrium quantity as Q^*. This means that, in equilibrium, the equations become

Demand: $P^* = 5 - 1Q^*$
Supply: $P^* = 1 + 1Q^*$

These equilibrium equations constitute a simple set of simultaneous equations. Since there are two equations (demand and supply) and two unknowns (P^* and Q^*), we can solve for the unknowns.

Begin the solution by setting demand equal to supply:

$$5 - 1Q^* = 1 + 1Q^*$$

Collecting like terms, we find

$$4 = 2Q^*$$
$$2 = Q^*$$

Once we have Q^* (equilibrium quantity), we can solve for the equilibrium price using *either* the demand or supply equations. Look first at demand:

$$P^* = 5 - 1Q^*$$
$$P^* = 5 - 1(2)$$
$$P^* = 5 - 2$$
$$P^* = 3$$

Alternatively, substituting Q^* into the supply equation yields the same result:

$$P^* = 1 + 1Q^*$$
$$P^* = 1 + 1(2)$$
$$P^* = 1 + 2$$
$$P^* = 3$$

Once you have solved for Q^*, the fact that substituting it into either the demand or supply equation yields the correct P^* provides a valuable check on your calculations. If you make a mistake in your calculations, when you substitute Q^* into the demand and supply equations, you will get two *different* prices. If that happens, you know to recheck your calculations. If you get the same price when you substitute Q^* into the demand and supply equations then you know your calculations are correct.

@ **6** Economists have developed the convention of graphing quantity as the independent variable and price as the dependent variable, and the forgoing equations reflect this. Despite this convention, economists actually consider real-world prices to be the independent variables and quantities as the dependent variables. In that case, the equations would take the form

Demand: $Q_D = 5 - 1P$
Supply: $Q_S = -1 + 1P$

You can solve these equations for yourself to see that they yield exactly the same values for P^* and Q^*. [*Hint*: First solve for P^* and then for Q^*.] Whichever form of the equations your instructor may use, the technique for solving the equations will be similar and the results identical.

SELF-TEST

True/False/Uncertain and Explain

1 The law of demand tells us that as the price of a good rises, demand decreases.

2 A decrease in income will shift the demand curve to the left.

3 A supply curve shows the maximum price at which the last unit will be supplied.

4 If A and B are substitutes, an increase in the price of A will shift the supply curve of B to the left.

5 When a cow is slaughtered for beef, its hide becomes available to make leather. Thus beef and leather are substitutes in production.

6 If the price of beef rises, there will be an increase in both the supply of leather and the quantity of beef supplied.

7 If the expected future price of a good increases, there will be an increase in equilibrium price and a decrease in equilibrium quantity.

8 Suppose new firms enter the steel market. The equilibrium price of steel will fall and the quantity will rise.

9 Suppose the demand for personal computers increases while the cost of producing them decreases. The equilibrium quantity of personal computers will rise and the price will fall.

10 When the actual price is above the equilibrium price, a shortage occurs.

Multiple-Choice

1 If an increase in the price of good A causes the demand curve for good B to shift to the left, then

a A and B are substitutes in consumption.
b A and B are complements in consumption.
c A and B are complements in production.
d B is an inferior good.
e B is a normal good.

2 Which of the following could *not* cause an increase in demand for a commodity?

a an increase in income
b a decrease in income
c a decrease in the price of a substitute
d a decrease in the price of a complement
e an increase in preferences for the commodity

3 The fact that a decline in the price of a good causes producers to reduce the quantity of the good supplied illustrates

a the law of supply.
b the law of demand.
c a change in supply.
d the nature of an inferior good.
e technological improvement.

4 A shift of the supply curve for rutabagas will be caused by

a a change in preferences for rutabagas.
b a change in the price of a related good that is a substitute in consumption for rutabagas.
c a change in income.
d a change in the price of rutabagas.
e none of the above.

5 If a resource can be used to produce either good *A* or good *B*, then *A* and *B* are

a substitutes in production.
b complements in production.
c substitutes in consumption.
d complements in consumption.
e normal goods.

6 If the market for twinkies is in equilibrium, then

a twinkies must be a normal good.
b producers would like to sell more at the current price.
c consumers would like to buy more at the current price.
d there will be a surplus.
e equilibrium quantity equals quantity demanded.

7 Some sales managers are talking shop. Which of the following quotations refers to a movement along the demand curve?

a "Since our competitors raised their prices our sales have doubled."
b "It has been an unusually mild winter; our sales of wool scarves are down from last year."
c "We decided to cut our prices, and the increase in our sales has been remarkable."
d "The Green movement has sparked an increase in our sales of biodegradable products."
e none of the above

8 Which of the following will definitely cause an increase in the equilibrium price?

a an increase in both demand and supply
b a decrease in both demand and supply
c an increase in demand combined with a decrease in supply
d a decrease in demand combined with an increase in supply
e none of the above

9 The price of a good will tend to fall if

a there is a surplus at the current price.
b the current price is above equilibrium.
c the quantity supplied exceeds the quantity demanded at the current price.
d all of the above are true.
e none of the above is true.

The market for coffee is initially in equilibrium with supply and demand curves of the usual shape. Pepsi is a substitute for coffee; cream is a complement for coffee. Questions **10** to **12** concern the market for *coffee*.

Assume that all *ceteris paribus* assumptions continue to hold *except* for the event(s) listed. Answer each question without considering the others.

10 Coffee is a normal good. A decrease in income will

a increase the price of coffee and increase the quantity demanded of coffee.
b increase the price of coffee and increase the quantity supplied of coffee.
c decrease the price of coffee and decrease the quantity demanded of coffee.
d decrease the price of coffee and decrease the quantity supplied of coffee.
e cause none of the above.

11 An increase in the price of Pepsi will

a increase the price of coffee and increase the quantity demanded of coffee.
b increase the price of coffee and increase the quantity supplied of coffee.
c decrease the price of coffee and decrease the quantity demanded of coffee.
d decrease the price of coffee and decrease the quantity supplied of coffee.
e cause none of the above.

12 A technological improvement lowers the cost of producing coffee. At the same time, preferences for coffee decrease. The *equilibrium quantity* of coffee will

a rise.
b fall.
c remain the same.
d rise or fall depending on whether the price of coffee falls or rises.
e rise or fall depending on the relative shifts of demand and supply curves.

13 Since 1960, there has been a dramatic increase in the number of working mothers. Based on this information alone, we can predict that the market for child-care services has experienced a(n)

a increase in demand.
b decrease in demand.
c increase in quantity demanded.
d decrease in quantity supplied.
e increase in supply.

14 If Hamburger Helper is an inferior good, then, *ceteris paribus*, a decrease in income will cause a

a leftward shift of the demand curve for Hamburger Helper.

b rightward shift of the demand curve for Hamburger Helper.

c movement up along the demand curve for Hamburger Helper.

d movement down along the demand curve for Hamburger Helper.

e none of the above.

15 A surplus can be eliminated by

a increasing supply.

b government raising the price.

c decreasing the quantity demanded.

d allowing the price to fall.

e allowing the quantity bought and sold to fall.

16 A decrease in quantity demanded is represented by a

a rightward shift of the supply curve.

b rightward shift of the demand curve.

c leftward shift of the demand curve.

d movement upward and to the left along the demand curve.

e movement downward and to the right along the demand curve.

17 If *A* and *B* are complementary goods (in consumption) and the cost of a resource used in the production of *A* decreases, then the price of

a both *A* and *B* will rise.

b both *A* and *B* will fall.

c *A* will fall and the price of *B* will rise.

d *A* will rise and the price of *B* will fall.

e *A* will fall and the price of *B* will remain unchanged.

18 All of the following "other things" are held constant along a demand curve *except*

a income.

b prices of related goods.

c the price of the good itself.

d preferences.

e all of the above.

19 Which of the following will shift the supply curve for good *X* leftward?

a a decrease in the wages of workers employed to produce *X*

b an increase in the cost of machinery used to produce *X*

c a technological improvement in the production of *X*

d a situation where quantity demanded exceeds quantity supplied

e all of the above

20 A shortage is the amount by which quantity

a demanded exceeds quantity supplied.

b supplied exceeds quantity demanded.

c demanded increases when the price rises.

d demanded exceeds the equilibrium quantity.

e supplied exceeds the equilibrium quantity.

21 Some producers are chatting over a beer. Which of the following quotations refers to a movement along the supply curve?

a "Wage increases have forced us to raise our prices."

b "Our new, sophisticated equipment will enable us to undercut our competitors."

c "Raw material prices have skyrocketed; we will have to pass this on to our customers."

d "We anticipate a big increase in demand. Our product price should rise, so we are planning for an increase in output."

e "New competitors in the industry are causing prices to fall."

22 If an increase in the price of good *A* causes the supply curve for good *B* to shift to the right, then

a *A* and *B* are substitutes in consumption.

b *A* and *B* are complements in consumption.

c *A* and *B* are substitutes in production.

d *A* and *B* are complements in production.

e *A* is a factor of production for making *B*.

23 "As domestic car prices have increased, consumers have found foreign cars to be a better bargain. Consequently, domestic car sales have fallen and foreign car sales have risen." Based on this information alone, there has been a

a shift in the demand curves for both domestic and foreign cars.

b shift in the supply curves for both domestic and foreign cars.

c movement along the demand curves for both domestic and foreign cars.

d movement along the demand curve for domestic cars and a shift of the demand curve for foreign cars.

e shift of the demand curve for domestic cars and a movement along the demand curve for foreign cars.

ⓔ **24** The demand curve for whatnots is $P = 75 - 6Q_D$ and the supply curve for whatnots is $P = 35 + 2Q_S$. What is the equilibrium price of a whatnot?

a $5

b $10

c $40

d $45

e none of the above

ⓔ **25** The demand curve for tribbles is $P = 300 - 6Q_D$. The supply curve for tribbles is $P = 20 + 8Q_S$. If the price of a tribble was set at $120, the tribble market would experience

a equilibrium.

b excess demand causing a rise in price.

c excess demand causing a fall in price.

d excess supply causing a rise in price.

e excess supply causing a fall in price.

Short Answer Problems

1 Explain the difference between wants and demands.

2 The price of personal computers has continued to fall even in the face of increasing demand. Explain.

3 A tax on crude oil would raise the cost of the primary resource used in the production of gasoline. A proponent of such a tax has claimed that it will not raise the price of gasoline using the following argument. While the price of gasoline may rise initially, that price increase will cause the demand for gasoline to decrease, which will push the price back down. What is wrong with this argument?

4 Brussel sprouts and carrots are substitutes in consumption and, since they can both be grown on the same type of land, substitutes in production too. Suppose there is an increase in the demand for brussel sprouts. Trace through the effects on price and quantity traded in both the brussel sprout and carrot markets. (Keep in mind Helpful Hint 4.)

5 The information given in Table 4.1 is about the behaviour of buyers and sellers of fish at the market on a particular Saturday.

TABLE **4.1** DEMAND AND SUPPLY SCHEDULES FOR FISH

Price (per fish)	Quantity Demanded	Quantity Supplied
$0.50	280	40
$1.00	260	135
$1.50	225	225
$2.00	170	265
$2.50	105	290
$3.00	60	310
$3.50	35	320

a On graph paper, draw the demand curve and the supply curve. Be sure to label the axes. What is the equilibrium price?

b We will make the usual *ceteris paribus* assumptions about the demand curve so that it does not shift. List five factors that we are assuming do not change.

c We will also hold the supply curve constant by assuming that five factors do not change. List them.

d Explain briefly what would happen if the price was initially set at $3.00.

e Explain briefly what would happen if the price was initially set at $1.00.

f Explain briefly what would happen if the price was initially set at $1.50.

6 The market for wine in Canada is initially in equilibrium with supply and demand curves of the usual shape. Beer is a close substitute for wine; cheese and wine are complements. Use demand and supply diagrams to analyse the effect of each of the following (separate) events on the equilibrium price and quantity in the Canadian wine market. Assume that all of the *ceteris paribus* assumptions continue to hold except for the event listed. For both equilibrium price and quantity you should indicate in each case whether the variable rises, falls, remains the same, or moves ambiguously (may rise or fall).

a The income of consumers falls (wine is a normal good).

b Early frost destroys a large part of the world grape crop.

c A new churning invention reduces the cost of producing cheese.

d A new fermentation technique is invented that reduces the cost of producing wine.

e A government study is published that links wine drinking and heart disease.

f Costs of producing both beer and wine increase dramatically.

7 A newspaper reported that "despite a bumper crop of cherries this year, the price drop for cherries won't be as much as expected because of short supplies of plums and peaches."

a Use a demand and supply graph for the cherry market to explain the effect of the bumper crop alone.

b On the same graph, explain the impact on the cherry market of the short supplies of plums and peaches.

8 Table 4.2 lists the demand and supply schedules for cases of grape jam.

TABLE **4.2** DEMAND AND SUPPLY SCHEDULES FOR GRAPE JAM PER WEEK

Price (per case)	Quantity Demanded (cases)	Quantity Supplied (cases)
$70	20	140
$60	60	120
$50	100	100
$40	140	80
$30	180	60

a On the graph in Fig. 4.2, draw the demand and supply curves for grape jam. Be sure to properly label the axes. Label the demand and supply curves D_0 and S_0, respectively.

FIGURE **4.2**

b What are the equilibrium price and quantity in the grape jam market? On your diagram, label the equilibrium point a.

c Is there a surplus or shortage at a price of $40? How much?

d The demand and supply schedules can also be represented by the following demand and supply equations:

Demand: $P = 75 - 0.25Q_D$
Supply: $P = 0.5Q_S$

Use these equations to solve for the equilibrium quantity (Q^*); equilibrium price (P^*). [*Hint*: Your answers should be the same as those in **8b**.]

e Suppose the population grows sufficiently that the demand for grape jam increases by 60 cases per week at every price.

i Construct a table (price, quantity demanded) of the new demand schedule.

ii Draw the new demand curve on your original graph and label it D_1.

iii Label the new equilibrium point b. What are the new equilibrium price and quantity?

iv What is the new demand equation? [*Hints*: What is the new slope? What is the new price-axis intercept?]

9 The demand equation for dweedles is

$$P = 8 - 1Q_D.$$

The supply equation for dweedles is

$$P = 2 + 1Q_S,$$

where P is the price of a dweedle in dollars, Q_D is the quantity of dweedles demanded, and Q_S is the quantity of dweedles supplied. The dweedle market is initially in equilibrium and income is $300.

a What is the equilibrium quantity (Q^*) of dweedles?

b What is the equilibrium price (P^*) of a dweedle?

c As a result of an increase in income to $500, the demand curve for dweedles shifts (the supply curve remains the same). The new demand equation is

$$P = 4 - 1Q_D$$

Use this information to calculate the new equilibrium quantity of dweedles; calculate the new equilibrium price of a dweedle.

d On the graph in Fig. 4.3, draw and label: (1) the supply curve, (2) the initial demand curve, (3) the new demand curve.

e Are dweedles a normal or inferior good? How do you know?

FIGURE **4.3**

10 The demand equation for flubits is

$$P = 80 - 2Q_D.$$

The supply equation for flubits is

$$P = 50 + 1Q_S,$$

where P is the price of a flubit in dollars, Q_D is the quantity of flubits demanded, and Q_S is the quantity of flubits supplied. Assume that there are no changes in *ceteris paribus* assumptions.

a If the price of flubits was set at $56, calculate the exact surplus or shortage of flubits.

b Explain the adjustment process that will bring the situation above to equilibrium.

c What is the equilibrium quantity (Q^*) of flubits?

d What is the equilibrium price (P^*) of a flubit?

e Now assume that as a result of technological advance, the supply curve for flubits shifts (the demand curve remains the same). The new supply equation is

$$P = 20 + 1Q_S$$

Use this information to calculate the new equilibrium quantity of flubits; calculate the new equilibrium price of a flubit.

A N S W E R S

True/False/Uncertain and Explain

1 F As price rises, quantity demanded decreases. (69–70)

2 U Leftward shift for normal good, rightward shift for inferior good. (71–72)

3 F Supply curve shows minimum price at which last unit supplied. (74–75)

4 U True if A and B substitutes in production, but false if substitutes in consumption. (74–76)

5 F Beef and leather complements in production because produced together of necessity. (74–76)

6 T For complements in production, ↑ price for one good → ↑ quantity supplied and ↑ supply other good. (74–76)

7 U ↑ expected future prices → rightward shift demand and leftward shift supply. Price ↑ but Δ quantity depends on relative magnitude shifts. (71–72, 75–76)

8 T ↑ number firms → rightward shift supply → ↓ price and ↑ quantity. (75–77)

9 U Quantity will ↑ but Δ price depends on relative magnitude shifts in demand and supply. (82–83)

10 F At $P >$ equilibrium P, there is surplus (quantity supplied > quantity demanded). (78–79)

Multiple-Choice

1 b For example, ↑ price french fries → ↓ demand hamburgers. (71–72)

2 c Both income answers could be correct if commodity were normal (**a**) or inferior (**b**). (71–72)

3 a Question describes movement down along supply curve. (74–75)

4 e Answers **a**, **b**, and **c** shift demand, while **d** causes movement along supply curve. (74–75)

5 a Definition of substitute in production. (75)

6 e At equilibrium price, plans producers and consumers match; quantity demanded = quantity supplied. (78–79)

7 c Other answers describe shifts of demand curve. (71–73)

8 c Answers **a** and **b** have indeterminate effect on price, while **d** → ↓ price. (82–84)

9 d All answers describe price above equilibrium price. (78–79)

10 d Demand shifts left. (80–81)

11 b Demand shifts right. (80–81)

12 e Supply shifts right, and demand shifts left. (82–84)

13 a ↑ working mothers → ↑ preferences for child care → ↑ demand child-care services. (71–73)

14 b Changes in income shift demand curve rather than causing movement along demand curve. (71–72)

15 d Other answers make surplus (excess quantity supplied) larger. (78–79)

16 d ↓ Quantity demanded is movement up along demand curve. Could also be caused by leftward shift supply. (72–73)

17 c Supply *A* shifts right → ↓ price *A* This → ↑ demand for *B* → ↑ price *B*. (71–73)

18 c "Other things" shift demand curve. Only price can change along fixed demand curve. (71–73)

19 b ↑ price factor of production shifts supply left. (75–77)

20 a Shortage is horizontal distance between demand and supply curves at price below equilibrium price. (78–79)

21 d Other answers describe shifts of supply curve. (76–77)

22 d Definition complements in production. Price changes related goods in consumption shift demand. (75–76)

23 d ↑ price domestic cars due to leftward shift supply. Domestic and foreign cars substitutes → rightward shift demand foreign cars. (71–72, 75–76)

24 d Set demand equal to supply, solve for $Q^* = 5$. Substitute $Q^* = 5$ into either demand or supply equation to solve for P^*. (96)

25 b At $P = \$120$, $Q_D = 30$, and $Q_S = 12.5$. Excess demand so price will ↑. (78–79, 96)

Short Answer Problems

1 Wants reflect our unlimited desires for goods and services without regard to our ability or willingness to make the sacrifices necessary to obtain them. The existence of scarcity means that many of those wants will not be satisfied. On the other hand, demands refer to plans to buy and, therefore, reflect decisions about which wants to satisfy.

2 Due to the tremendous pace of technological advance, not only has the demand for personal computers been increasing, but the supply has been increasing as well. Indeed, supply has been increasing much more rapidly than demand, which has resulted in falling prices. Thus *much* (but not all) of the increase in sales of personal computers reflects a movement down along a demand curve rather than a shift in demand.

3 This argument confuses a movement along an unchanging demand curve with a shift in the demand curve. The proper analysis is as follows. The increase in the price of oil (the primary resource in the production of gasoline) will shift the supply curve of gasoline leftward. This will cause the equilibrium price of gasoline to increase and thus the quantity demanded of gasoline will decrease. Demand itself will not decrease, that is, the demand curve will not shift. The decrease in supply causes a movement along an unchanged demand curve.

4 The answer to this question requires us to trace through the effects on the two graphs in Fig. 4.4—(a) for the brussel sprout market and (b) for the carrot market. The sequence of effects occurs in order of the numbers on the graphs.

Look first at the market for brussel sprouts. The increase in demand shifts the demand curve rightward from D_0 to D_1 (1), and the price of brussel sprouts rises. This price rise has two effects (2) on the carrot market. Since brussel sprouts and carrots are substitutes in consumption, the demand curve for carrots shifts rightward from D_0 to D_1. And, since brussel sprouts and carrots are substitutes in production, the supply curve of carrots shifts leftward from S_0 to S_1. Both of these shifts in the carrot market raise the price of carrots, causing feedback effects on the brussel sprout market. But remember the rule (Helpful Hint 4) that each curve (demand and supply) for a given market can shift a maximum of *once*. Since the demand curve for brussel sprouts has already shifted, we can only shift the supply curve from S_0 to S_1 (3) because of the substitutes in production relationship. Each curve in each market has now shifted once and the analysis must stop. We can predict that the net effects are increases in the equilibrium prices of both brussel sprouts and carrots, and indeterminate changes in the equilibrium quantities in both markets.

FIGURE **4.4**

(a) Brussel Sprout Market

(b) Carrot Market

5 a The demand and supply curves are shown in Fig. 4.5. The equilibrium price is $1.50 per fish.

FIGURE **4.5**

b Prices of related goods; income; expected future prices; population; preferences.

c Prices of factors of production; prices of other goods produced; expected future prices; number of suppliers; technology.

d At a price of $3.00, quantity supplied (310) exceeds quantity demanded (60). Fish sellers find themselves with surplus fish. Rather than be stuck with unsold fish (which yields no revenue), some sellers cut their price in an attempt to increase the quantity of fish demanded. Competition forces other sellers to follow suit, and the price falls until it reaches the equilibrium price of $1.50, while quantity demanded increases until it reaches the equilibrium quantity of 225 units.

e At a price of $1.00, the quantity demanded (260) exceeds the quantity supplied (135)— there is a shortage. Unrequited fish buyers bid up the price in an attempt to get the "scarce" fish. As prices continue to be bid up as long as there is excess demand, quantity supplied increases in response to higher prices. Price and quantity supplied both rise until they reach the equilibrium price ($1.50) and quantity (225 units).

f At a price of $1.50, the quantity supplied exactly equals the quantity demanded (225). There is no excess demand (shortage) or excess supply (surplus), and therefore no tendency for the price or quantity to change.

6 The demand and supply diagrams for parts **a** to **e** are shown in Fig. 4.6.

FIGURE **4.6**

(a)

(b)

(c)

(d)

(e)

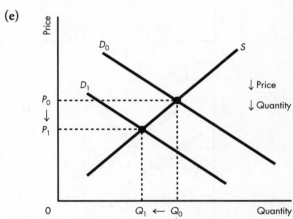

f Questions like this require the examination of two separate but related markets—the beer and wine markets. Since this kind of question often causes confusion for students, Fig. 4.7 gives a more detailed explanation of the answer.

Look first at the beer market. The increase in the cost of beer production shifts the supply curve of beer leftward from S_0 to S_1. The resulting rise in the price of beer affects the wine market since beer and wine are substitutes (in consumption).

Turning to the wine market, there are two shifts to examine. The increase in beer prices causes the demand for wine to shift rightward from D_0 to D_1. The increase in the cost of wine production shifts the supply curve of wine leftward from S_0 to S_1. This is the end of the analysis, since the question only asks about the wine market. The final result is a rise in the equilibrium price of wine and an ambiguous change in the quantity of wine. Although the diagram shows $Q_1 = Q_0$, Q_1 may be $\geq$ or $\leq Q_0$.

FIGURE **4.7**

(a) Beer Market

(b) Wine Market

Many students rightfully ask, "But doesn't the rise in wine prices then shift the demand curve for beer rightward, causing a rise in beer prices and an additional increase in the demand for wine?" This question, which is correct in principle, is about the dynamics of adjustment, and these graphs are only capable of analysing once-over shifts of demand or supply. We could shift the demand for beer rightward, but the resulting rise in beer prices would lead us to shift the demand for wine a *second time*. In practice, stick to the rule that each curve (demand and supply) for a given market can shift a maximum of *once*.

7 a The demand and supply curves for the cherry market are shown in Fig. 4.8.

FIGURE **4.8**

Suppose D_0 and S_0 represent the demand and supply curves for cherries last year. This year's bumper crop increases supply to S_1. Other things being equal, the price of cherries would fall from P_0 to P_1.

b But other things are not equal. Short supplies of plums and peaches (their supply curves have shifted left) drive up their prices. The increase in the prices of plums and peaches, which are substitutes in consumption for cherries, increases the demand for cherries to D_1. The net result is that the price of cherries only falls to P_2 instead of all the way to P_1.

8 a The demand and supply curves for grape jam are shown in Fig. 4.2 Solution.

FIGURE **4.2** SOLUTION

b The equilibrium is given at the intersection of the demand and supply curves (labelled point *a*). The equilibrium price is $50 per case and the equilibrium quantity is 100 cases per week.

c At a price of $40 there is a shortage of 60 cases per week.

@ **d** In equilibrium, the equations become:

Demand: $P^* = 75 - 0.25Q^*$
Supply: $P^* = 0.5Q^*$

To solve for Q^*, set demand equal to supply:

$$75 - 0.25Q^* = 0.5Q^*$$
$$75 = 0.75Q^*$$
$$100 = Q^*.$$

To solve for P^*, we can substitute Q^* into either the demand or supply equations. Look at demand first:

$$P^* = 75 - 0.25Q^*$$
$$P^* = 75 - 0.25(100)$$
$$P^* = 75 - 25$$
$$P^* = 50$$

Alternatively, substituting Q^* into the supply equation yields the same result:

$$P^* = 0.5Q^*$$
$$P^* = 0.5(100)$$
$$P^* = 50$$

e i   Table 4.3 also contains the (unchanged) quantity supplied, for reference purposes.

TABLE **4.3** DEMAND AND SUPPLY SCHEDULES FOR GRAPE JAM PER WEEK

Price (per case)	Quantity Demanded (cases)	Quantity Supplied (cases)
$70	80	140
$60	120	120
$50	160	100
$40	200	80
$30	240	60

ii   The graph of the new demand curve, D_1, is shown in Fig. 4.2 Solution.
iii   The new equilibrium price is $60 per case and the quantity is 120 cases of grape jam per week.
@ **iv**   The new demand equation is $P = 90 - 0.25Q_D$. Notice that the slope of the new demand equation is the same as the slope of the original demand equation. An increase in demand of 60 cases at every price results in a rightward *parallel* shift of the demand curve. Since the two curves are parallel, they have the same slope. The figure of 90 is the price-axis intercept of the new demand curve, which you can see on your graph. *Remember* that the

demand equation is the equation of a straight line ($y = a + bx$); in this case, $a = 90$.

If you want additional practice in the use of demand and supply equations for calculating equilibrium values of price and quantity, you can use the new demand curve equation together with the supply curve equation to calculate the answers you found in **e iii**.

@ **9**   In equilibrium, the equations become

Demand: $P^* = 8 - 1Q^*$
Supply: $P^* = 2 + 1Q^*$

a   To solve for Q^*, set demand equal to supply:

$$8 - 1Q^* = 2 + 1Q^*$$
$$6 = 2Q^*$$
$$3 = Q^*$$

b   To solve for P^*, we can substitute Q^* into either the demand or supply equations. Look first at demand:

$$P^* = 8 - 1Q^*$$
$$P^* = 8 - 1(3)$$
$$P^* = 8 - 3$$
$$P^* = 5$$

Alternatively, substituting Q^* into the supply equation yields the same result:

$$P^* = 2 + 1Q^*$$
$$P^* = 2 + 1(3)$$
$$P^* = 2 + 3$$
$$P^* = 5$$

c   In equilibrium, the equations are

Demand: $P^* = 4 - 1Q^*$
Supply: $P^* = 2 + 1Q^*$

To solve for Q^*, set demand equal to supply:

$$4 - 1Q^* = 2 + 1Q^*$$
$$2 = 2Q^*$$
$$1 = Q^*$$

To solve for P^*, we can substitute Q^* into either the demand or supply equations. Look first at demand:

$$P^* = 4 - 1Q^*$$
$$P^* = 4 - 1(1)$$
$$P^* = 4 - 1$$
$$P^* = 3$$

Alternatively, substituting Q^* into the supply equation yields the same result:

$$P^* = 2 + 1Q^*$$
$$P^* = 2 + 1(1)$$
$$P^* = 2 + 1$$
$$P^* = 3$$

d The supply curve, initial demand curve, and new demand curve for dweedles are shown in Fig. 4.3 Solution.

FIGURE **4.3** SOLUTION

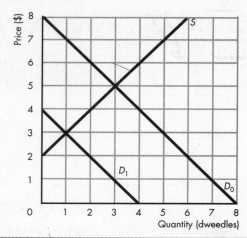

e Dweedles are an inferior good. An increase in income (from \$300 to \$500) caused a decrease in demand—the demand curve for dweedles shifted leftward.

10 a Substitute the price of \$56 into the demand and supply equations to calculate the quantities demanded and supplied at that price. This is the mathematical equivalent of what you do on a graph when you identify a price on the vertical axis, move your eye across to the demand (or supply) curve, and then move your eye down to read the quantity on the horizontal axis.

Substituting into the demand equation we find

$$P = 80 - 2Q_D$$
$$56 = 80 - 2Q_D$$
$$2Q_D = 24$$
$$Q_D = 12.$$

Substituting into the supply equation

$$P = 50 + 1Q_S$$
$$56 = 50 + 1Q_S$$
$$6 = Q_S$$

Quantity demanded exceeds quantity supplied by 6 (12 – 6), so there is a shortage of 6 flubits.

b A shortage means the price was set below the equilibrium price. Competition between consumers for the limited number of flubits will bid up the price and increase the quantity supplied until we reach the equilibrium price and quantity.

c In equilibrium, the equations are

Demand: $P^* = 80 - 2Q^*$
Supply: $P^* = 50 + 1Q^*$

To solve for Q^*, set demand equal to supply:

$$80 - 2Q^* = 50 + 1Q^*$$
$$30 = 3Q^*$$
$$10 = Q^*$$

d To solve for P^*, substitute Q^* into the demand equation:

$$P^* = 80 - 2Q^*$$
$$P^* = 80 - 2(10)$$
$$P^* = 80 - 20$$
$$P^* = 60$$

You can check this answer yourself by substituting Q^* into the supply equation.

e The new equilibrium equations are

Demand: $P^* = 80 - 2Q^*$
Supply: $P^* = 20 + 1Q^*$

To solve for Q^*, set demand equal to supply:

$$80 - 2Q^* = 20 + 1Q^*$$
$$60 = 3Q^*$$
$$20 = Q^*$$

To solve for P^*, substitute Q^* into the supply equations:

$$P^* = 20 + 1Q^*$$
$$P^* = 20 + 1(20)$$
$$P^* = 20 + 20$$
$$P^* = 40$$

You can check this answer yourself by substituting Q^* into the demand equation.

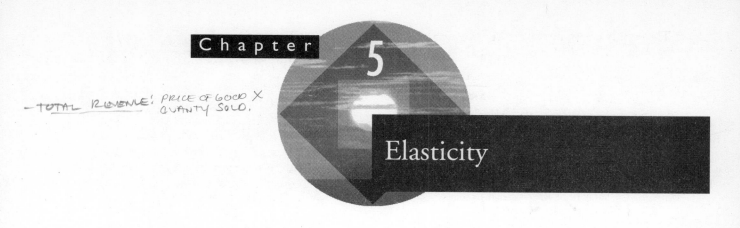

Chapter 5

Elasticity

— TOTAL REVENUE: PRICE OF GOOD × QUANTITY SOLD.

KEY CONCEPTS

① Elasticity of Demand

Price elasticity of demand (η) measures *responsiveness* of quantity demanded to change in price.

◆ η is units-free measure of responsiveness.

Fig 5.2 Pg 101

◆ $\eta = \left|\dfrac{\% \Delta \text{ quantity demanded}}{\% \Delta \text{ in price}}\right| = \left|\dfrac{(\Delta Q / Q_{ave})}{(\Delta P / P_{ave})}\right| = \dfrac{\%\Delta q}{\%\Delta p}$

PERCENTAGE CHANGE   *(x-y) / ((x+y)/2)*

#150 - #30 / #120   *#50 + #30 = #40 ∴ 20/40*

◆ Elasticity is *not* equal to slope. Moving down along a linear demand curve, slope ($\Delta P / \Delta Q$) is constant but elasticity ↓ as P_{ave} ↓ and Q_{ave} ↑

∴ LOWER THE AV. PRICE THE LESS ELASTIC DEMAND.   *LOWER THE AVERAGE PRICE, THE GREATER THE AVERAGE QTY DEMANDED.*

◆ **When**   **Demand is**

When	Demand is
η = ∞	**perfectly elastic (horizontal)** *(INFINITELY RESPONSIVE TO % Δ PRICE)*
1 < η < ∞	**elastic** *(% Δ QTY > % Δ PRICE)*
η = 1	**unit elastic** *(% Δ QTY = % Δ PRICE)*
0 < η < 1	**inelastic** *(% Δ QTY < % Δ PRICE)*
η = 0	**perfectly inelastic (vertical)** *(QTY DEMANDED IS CONSTANT, REGARDLESS OF PRICE)*

Fig 5.3 Pg 102   *Fig 5.4 Pg 103*

Elasticity of demand depends on

① ◆ *closeness of substitutes*—closer substitutes for a good → ↑ elasticity. *WHEN YOU HAVE A DECENT SUBSTITUTE FOR A GOOD IT ↑ ELASTICITY B/C YOU DON'T HAVE TO BUY ORIGINAL GOOD (USE SUB).*

• Necessities generally have poor substitutes and inelastic demands.

• Luxuries generally have many substitutes and elastic demands.

② ◆ *proportion of income spent on good*—higher proportion of income spent on a good → ↑ elasticity. *THE MORE EXPENSIVE THE PRODUCT, THE MORE THE PROPORTION OF YOUR INCOME IT REQUIRES, SO IF TEXTBOOK PRICE ↑ = ↑ ELASTICITY, B/C YOU WOULD RATHER SUB.*

③ ◆ *time elapsed since price change*—longer time elapsed → ↑ elasticity. *B/C WILL EVENTUALLY BUY THE CHEAPER SUBSTITUTE (WHICH WILL ∴ ↓ QTY PURCHASED).*

— 2 TIME FRAMES!

① SHORT - RUN DEMAND

② LONG - RUN DEMAND.

• Short-run demand describes responsiveness to a change in price *before* sufficient time for all substitutions to be made.

• Long-run demand describes responsiveness to a change in price *after* sufficient time for all substitutions to be made.

• Short-run demand is usually less elastic than long-run demand. *B/C IN LONG RUN YOU CAN FIND MORE SUBSTITUTES WHICH ∴ ↑ ELASTICITY.*

Elasticity and **total revenue** ($P \times Q$)—the **total revenue test**

◆

Fig 5.6, Pg 106

When demand is	*↑ Price causes*
inelastic (η < 1)	↑ total revenue *(B/C YOU NEED IT & CAN'T SUB).*
unit elastic (η = 1)	no change total revenue
elastic (η > 1)	↓ total revenue *(B/C YOU CAN SUB).*

② More Elasticities of Demand

① **Cross elasticity of demand (η_x)** measures the *responsiveness* of quantity demanded of good *A* to a change in price of good *B*. *(PRICE OF GOOD COMPARED TO IT'S SUBSTITUTES & COMPLEMENTS).*

◆ $\eta_x = \dfrac{\% \Delta \text{ quantity demanded good } A}{\% \Delta \text{ price good } B}$

NOTE: NO ABSOLUTE VALUE SIGNS ∴ (+ or -)

Fig 5.7, pg 107

◆ $\eta_x > 1 \,(+)$ Goods are substitutes *B/C ↑ P. OF ORIGINAL GOOD ∴ ↑ D. OF SUBSTITUTE (SHIFTS R & POSITIVE)*

◆ $\eta_x < 0 \,(-)$ Goods are complements *B/C ↑ P. OF COMPLEMENT ∴ ↓ D. OF ORIGINAL (SHIFTS L & NEGATIVE)*

② **Income elasticity of demand (η_y)** measures *responsiveness* of demand to change in income.

NOTE: NO! ABSOLUTE VALUE SIGNS ∴ CAN BE (+) OR (-)

◆ $\eta_y = \dfrac{\% \Delta \text{ quantity demanded}}{\% \Delta \text{ income}}$ *← PRICE ASSUMED CONSTANT*

Fig 5.8 pg 108

◆ **When**   **Demand is**

When	Demand is
$\eta_y > 1$	income elastic (normal good) – *↑ Y & ↑ Q (FASTER)*
$0 < \eta_y < 1$	income inelastic (normal good) *↑ Q & ↑ Y (FASTER)*
$\eta_y < 0$	negative income elasticity (inferior good)

INTIALLY: ↑ Q & ↑ Y = POSITIVE
HITS MAX
THEN: ↓ Q & ↑ Y = NEGATIVE

3 RANGES

+   - / M (max)

Elasticity of Supply

(III)

Elasticity of supply (η_s) measures *responsiveness of* quantity supplied to change in price.

② PRICE TO SELL ANY QTY. DEMANDED, THEN SUPPLY CURVE IS HORIZONTAL & Ns = ∞ (PERFECTLY ELASTIC)

NOTE: 2 IMPORTANT CASES FOR Ns!

*NOTE! NO! ABSOLUTE VALUE SIGNS, CAN BE (+) OR (−)

◆ $\eta_s = \dfrac{\% \, \Delta \text{ quantity supplied}}{\% \, \Delta \text{ price}}$

PRICE ASSUMED CONSTANT

① QTY. SUPPLIED IS FIXED REGARDLESS OF PRICE, THEN SUPPLY CURVE IS VERTICAL & Ns = 0 (PERFECTLY INELASTIC) (GO TO TOP).

Elasticity of supply depends on

① ◆ factor substitution possibilities—the more common the factors of production used → ↑ η_s.
∴ SUPPLY CURVE HORIZONTAL & ↑ Ns TO ∞.

② ◆ time frame for supply decision—η_s ↑ with ↑ time from momentary, to short-run, to long-run supply.

Fig 5.10 pg 111

- Momentary supply describes responsiveness of quantity supplied immediately following a price change. *VERTICAL SUPPLY CURVE ∴ PERFECTLY INELASTIC.*

- Short-run supply describes responsiveness of quantity supplied to a price change when *some* technologically possible adjustments to production have been made. *CAN MAKE ADJUSTMENTS TO SUPPLY QUICKLY B/C OF*

- Long-run supply describes responsiveness of quantity supplied to a price change when *all* technologically possible adjustments to production have been made. *(MOST ELASTIC).* *PRICE CHANGES.*

H E L P F U L   H I N T S

1 There are many elasticity formulae in this chapter, but they are all based on the same simple, intuitive principle—*responsiveness*. All of the demand and supply elasticity formulae measure the *responsiveness* (sensitivity) *of quantity* (demanded or supplied) to changes in something else. Thus percentage change in quantity is always in the numerator of the relevant formula. As you come to understand how quantity responds to changes in price, income, and prices of related goods, you will be able to work out each elasticity formula, even if you have temporarily forgotten it.

2 The complete formula (see Text Fig. 5.2, page 101) for calculating the price elasticity of demand between two points on the demand curve is

$$\eta = \dfrac{\% \, \Delta \text{ quantity demanded}}{\% \, \Delta \text{ in price}}$$

$$= \left| \left(\dfrac{\Delta Q}{Q_{ave}} \right) \Big/ \left(\dfrac{\Delta P}{P_{ave}} \right) \right|$$

The law of demand assures us that price and quantity demanded always move in opposite

directions along any demand curve. Thus without the absolute value sign, the formula for the price elasticity of demand would yield a negative number. Because our main interest is in the *magnitude* of the response in quantity demanded to a change in price, for simplicity, we take the absolute value to guarantee a positive number. Whenever you see the often-used shorthand term, *elasticity* of demand, remember that it means the absolute value of the *price* elasticity of demand.

3 Elasticity is *not* the same as slope (although they are related). Along a straight-line demand curve the slope is constant, but the elasticity varies from infinity to zero as we move down the demand curve. To see why, look at the formula below, which is just a rearrangement of the elasticity formula in Helpful Hint 2.

$$\eta = \left| \left(\dfrac{\Delta Q}{\Delta P} \right) \times \left(\dfrac{P_{ave}}{Q_{ave}} \right) \right|$$

The term in the first parentheses is simply the inverse of the slope. Since the slope is constant everywhere along a straight-line demand curve, so is the inverse of the slope. Consider, however, what happens to the term in the second parentheses as we move down the demand curve. At the "top" of the demand curve, P_{ave} is very large, Q_{ave} is very small, so the term in the second parentheses is large. As we move down the demand curve, P_{ave} becomes smaller and Q_{ave} becomes larger, so the term in the second parentheses falls in value. The net result is that the absolute value of the price elasticity of demand falls as we move down the demand curve.

4 One of the most practical and important uses of the concept of elasticity of demand is that it allows us to predict the effect on total revenue of a change in price. A fall in price will increase total revenue if demand is elastic, leave total revenue unchanged if demand is unit elastic, and decrease total revenue if demand is inelastic. Because price and quantity demanded always move in opposite directions along a demand curve, a fall in price will cause an increase in quantity demanded. Since total revenue equals price times quantity, the fall in price will tend to decrease total revenue, while the increase in quantity demanded will increase total revenue. The net effect depends on which of these individual effects is larger.

The concept of elasticity of demand conveniently summarizes the net effect. For example, if demand is elastic, the percentage change in quantity demanded is greater than the percentage change in price. Hence, with a fall in price, the quantity effect dominates and total revenue will increase. If, however, demand is inelastic, the percentage change in quantity demanded is less than the percentage change in price. Hence, with a fall in price, the price effect dominates and total revenue will decrease.

5 Two other important elasticity concepts are the income elasticity of demand and the cross elasticity of demand

Income elasticity of demand

$$\eta_y = \frac{\% \, \Delta \text{ quantity demanded}}{\% \, \Delta \text{ income}}$$

$$= \left(\frac{\Delta Q}{Q_{ave}}\right) \bigg/ \left(\frac{\Delta Y}{Y_{ave}}\right)$$

Cross elasticity of demand

$$\eta_x = \frac{\% \, \Delta \text{ quantity demanded of good } A}{\% \, \Delta \text{ in price of good } B}$$

$$= \left(\frac{\Delta Q^A}{Q^A_{ave}}\right) \bigg/ \left(\frac{\Delta P^B}{P^B_{ave}}\right)$$

Notice that these two elasticity formulae do *not* have absolute value signs and can take on either positive or negative values. While these formulae measure responsiveness, both the magnitude *and the direction* of the response are important. In the case of income elasticity of demand, the response of quantity demanded to an increase in income will be positive for a normal good and negative for an inferior good. In the case of cross elasticity of demand, the response of the quantity demanded of good *A* to an increase in the price of good *B* will be positive if the goods are substitutes and negative if the goods are complements.

In calculating an income elasticity or a cross elasticity, be alert to the fact that the *price of the good in the numerator* of the formula *is assumed constant*. Income elasticity measures the quantity response to a change in income, *ceteris paribus*. Cross elasticity measures the quantity response of good *A* to a change in the price of good *B*, *ceteris paribus*. This means that we cannot simply read numerical values for calculating these elasticities from the equilibrium positions of a set of demand and supply curves. For example, when income increases, demand shifts right (for a normal good), and the new equilibrium quantity will also have a higher equilibrium

price. To calculate income elasticity correctly, we compare the income and quantity demanded of the initial equilibrium with the new income and quantity demanded. To obtain the correct new quantity demanded, we must use the new demand curve, but must calculate the quantity demanded that would have prevailed at the *initial*, unchanged price. (See Short Answer Problems **9** and **10** for examples.)

SELF-TEST

True/False/Uncertain and Explain

1 The price elasticity of demand measures how responsive prices are to changes in demand.

2 The demand for gasoline is likely to become more inelastic with the passage of time after a price increase.

3 Price elasticity of demand is constant along a linear demand curve.

4 If you like Pepsi Cola and Coca-Cola about the same, your demand for Pepsi is likely to be elastic.

5 If your expenditures on toothpaste are a small proportion of your total income, your demand for toothpaste is likely to be inelastic.

6 The more narrowly we define a good, the more elastic is its demand.

7 An inferior good will have a negative cross elasticity of demand.

8 If a 10 percent increase in the price of widgets causes a 6 percent increase in the quantity of woozles demanded, then widgets and woozles must be complements.

9 If a decrease in supply causes revenue to increase, then demand must be inelastic.

10 If a 9 percent increase in price leads to a 5 percent decrease in quantity demanded, total revenue has decreased.

Multiple-Choice

1 If price elasticity of demand is zero, then as the price falls

a total revenue does not change.
b quantity demanded does not change.
c quantity demanded falls to zero.
d total revenue increases from zero.
e none of the above occurs.

2 There are two points on the demand curve for volleyballs, as shown in Table 5.1.

TABLE **5.1**

Price per Volleyball	Quantity Demanded
$19	55
$21	45

What is the elasticity of demand between these two points?

a 2.5
b 2.0
c 0.5
d 0.4
e none of the above

3 The fact that butter has margarine as a close substitute in consumption

a makes the supply of butter more elastic.
b makes the supply of butter less elastic.
c makes the demand for butter more elastic.
d makes the demand for butter less elastic.
e does not affect butter's elasticity of supply or demand.

4 A sudden end-of-summer heat wave increases the demand for air conditioners and catches suppliers with no reserve inventories. The momentary supply curve for air conditioners is

a perfectly elastic.
b perfectly inelastic.
c elastic.
d upward sloping.
e horizontal.

5 A technological breakthrough lowers the cost of photocopiers. If the demand for photocopiers is price inelastic, we predict that photocopier sales will

a fall and total revenue will rise.
b fall and total revenue will fall.
c rise and total revenue will rise.
d rise and total revenue will fall.
e rise but changes in total revenue will depend on elasticity of supply.

6 A perfectly vertical demand curve has a price elasticity of

a zero.
b greater than zero but less than one.
c one.
d greater than one.
e infinity.

7 If a 10 percent increase in income causes a 5 percent increase in quantity demanded (at a constant price), what is the income elasticity of demand?

a 0.5
b −0.5
c 2.0
d −2.0
e none of the above

8 If the price elasticity of demand is 2, then a 1 percent decrease in price will

a double the quantity demanded.
b reduce the quantity demanded by half.
c increase the quantity demanded by 2 percent.
d reduce the quantity demanded by 2 percent.
e increase the quantity demanded by 0.5 percent.

9 A given percentage increase in the price of a good is likely to cause a larger percentage decline in quantity demanded

a the shorter the passage of time.
b the larger the proportion of income spent on it.
c the harder it is to obtain good substitutes.
d all of the above.
e none of the above.

10 A negative value for

a price elasticity of supply implies an upward-sloping supply curve.

b cross elasticity of demand implies complementary goods.

c price elasticity of demand implies an inferior good.

d income elasticity of demand implies a normal good.

e income elasticity of demand implies an error in your calculation.

11 A decrease in tuition fees will decrease the university's total revenue if the price elasticity of demand for university education is

a negative.

b greater than zero but less than one.

c equal to one.

d greater than one.

e less than the price elasticity of supply.

12 When price goes from $1.50 to $2.50, quantity supplied increases from 9,000 to 11,000 units. What is the price elasticity of supply?

a 0.4

b 0.8

c 2.5

d 4.0

e none of the above

13 If the demand for frozen orange juice is price elastic, then a severe frost that destroys large quantities of oranges will likely

a reduce the equilibrium price of juice, but increase total consumer spending on it.

b reduce the equilibrium quantity of juice as well as total consumer spending on it.

c reduce both the equilibrium quantity and the price of juice.

d increase the equilibrium price of juice as well as total consumer spending on it.

e increase the equilibrium price of juice, but leave total consumer spending on it constant.

14 If a 4 percent rise in the price of peanut butter causes total revenue to fall by 8 percent, then demand for peanut butter

a is elastic.

b is inelastic.

c is unit elastic.

d has an elasticity of 1/2.

e has an elasticity of 2.

15 Tina and Brian work for the same recording company. Tina claims that they would be better off by increasing the price of their CDs while Brian claims that they would be better off by decreasing the price. We can conclude that

a Tina thinks the demand for CDs has price elasticity of zero, and Brian thinks price elasticity equals one.

b Tina thinks the demand for CDs has price elasticity equal to one, and Brian thinks price elasticity equals zero.

c Tina thinks the demand for CDs is price elastic, and Brian thinks it is price inelastic.

d Tina thinks the demand for CDs is price inelastic and Brian thinks it is price elastic.

e Tina and Brian should stick to singing and forget about economics.

16 The cross elasticity of the demand for white tennis balls with respect to the price of yellow tennis balls is probably

a negative and high.

b negative and low.

c positive and high.

d positive and low.

e zero.

17 Preferences for brussel sprouts increase. The price of brussel sprouts will not change if the price elasticity of

a demand is 0.

b demand is 1.

c supply is 0.

d supply is 1.

e supply is infinity.

18 A union leader who claims that "higher wages increase living standards without causing unemployment" believes that the demand for labour is

a income elastic.

b income inelastic.

c perfectly elastic.

d perfectly inelastic.

e unit elastic.

19 Luxury goods tend to have income elasticities of demand that are

a greater than one.

b greater than zero but less than one.

c positive.

d negative.

e first positive and then negative as income increases.

20 Given the relationship shown in Fig. 5.1 between total revenue from the sale of a good and the quantity of the good sold, then

a this is an inferior good.
b this is a normal good.
c the elasticity of demand is zero.
d the elasticity of demand is infinity.
e the elasticity of demand is one.

FIGURE **5.1**

21 If a 4 percent decrease in income (at a constant price) causes a 2 percent decrease in the consumption of dweedles, then

a the income elasticity of demand for dweedles is negative.
b dweedles are a necessity and a normal good.
c dweedles are a luxury and a normal good.
d dweedles are an inferior good.
e a and d are true.

22 The long-run supply curve is likely to be

a more elastic than momentary supply, but less elastic than short-run supply.
b less elastic than momentary supply, but more elastic than short-run supply.
c less elastic than both momentary and short-run supply curves.
d more elastic than both momentary and short-run supply curves.
e vertical.

23 Business people speak about price elasticity of demand without using the actual term. Which of the following statements reflect elastic demand for a product?

a "A price cut won't help me. It won't increase sales, and I'll just get less money for each unit that I was selling before."
b "I don't think a price cut will make any difference to my bottom line. What I may gain from selling more I would lose on the lower price."
c "My customers are real bargain hunters. Since I set my prices just a few cents below my competitors, customers have flocked to the store and sales are booming."
d "With the recent economic recovery, people have more income to spend and sales are booming, even at the same prices as before."
e None of the above.

24 If the Jets decrease ticket prices and find that total revenue does not change, then the price elasticity of demand for tickets is

a zero.
b greater than zero, but less than one.
c equal to one.
d greater than one.
e inferior.

25 Long-run elasticity of supply of a good is greater than short-run elasticity of supply because

a more substitutes in consumption for the good can be found.
b more complements in consumption for the good can be found.
c more technological ways of adjusting supply can be exploited.
d income rises with more elapsed time.
e the long-run supply curve is steeper.

Short Answer Problems

1 Why is elasticity superior to slope as a measure of the responsiveness of quantity demanded to changes in price?

2   In each of the following, compare the price elasticity of demand for each pair of goods and explain why the demand for one of the goods is more elastic than demand for the other.

a   IBM personal computers before the development of other "clone" personal computers versus IBM personal computers after the production of such clones

b   television sets versus matches

c   electricity just after an increase in its price versus electricity two years after the price increase

d   acetaminophen versus Tylenol-brand acetaminophen

3   Why does supply tend to be more elastic in the long run?

4   In Fig. 5.2, which demand curve (D_A or D_B) is more elastic in the price range P_1 to P_2? Explain why. [*Hint*: Use the formula for price elasticity of demand.]

FIGURE **5.2**

5   Consider the demand curve in Fig. 5.3(a). A portion of the demand curve is also described by the demand schedule in Table 5.2.

FIGURE **5.3**

(a)

(b)

TABLE **5.2**

Price ($)	Quantity Demanded	Total Revenue
22	0	
20	1	
18	2	
16	3	
14	4	
12	5	
10	6	
8	7	
6	8	

Fill in the numbers for total revenue in the last column of Table 5.2, and graph your results on Fig. 5.3(b). Describe the shape of the total revenue curve as quantity increases (price decreases).

6 Using the same information for the demand curve in Short Answer Problem 5:

a Complete the second and third columns of Table 5.3: η (the price elasticity of demand) and ΔTR (the change in total revenue) as the price falls from the higher price to the lower price. Describe the relationship between elasticity and change in total revenue as price falls (moving down the demand curve).

TABLE **5.3**

ΔP ($)	η	ΔTR($)	η′	$\Delta TR′$ ($)
16 — 14				
14 — 12				
12 — 10				
10 — 8				
8 — 6				

b Suppose income increases from $10,000 to $14,000, causing an increase in demand: at every price, quantity demanded increases by 2 units. Draw the new demand curve on Fig. 5.3(a) and label it $D′$. Use this new demand curve to complete the last two columns of Table 5.3 for η′ (the new price elasticity of demand) and $\Delta TR′$ (the new change in total revenue).

c Using the price range between $16 and $14, explain why $D′$ is more inelastic than D.

d Calculate the income elasticity of demand, assuming the price remains constant at $12. Is this a normal or inferior good? Explain why you could have answered the question even without calculating the income elasticity of demand.

⊚ⓓ 7 The demand equation for woozles is $P = 60 - 2Q_D$. The supply equation for woozles is $P = 32 + 5Q_S$, where P is the price of a woozle in dollars, Q_D is the quantity of woozles demanded, and Q_S is the quantity of woozles supplied.

a Calculate the price elasticity of demand for woozles between $Q_D = 4$ and $Q_D = 6$.

b Initially, the woozle market is in equilibrium with $P^* = 52$ and $Q^* = 4$. Then, the supply curve shifts (the demand curve remains

constant) yielding a new equilibrium price of $P^* = 48$.

Using all of the relevant information above, show *two separate methods* for determining whether total revenue increases, decreases, or remains constant in moving from the initial equilibrium to the new equilibrium.

8 Suppose Jean loses his present job and his monthly income falls from $10,000 to $6,000, while his monthly purchases of grits increase from 200 to 400.

a Calculate his income elasticity of demand for grits.

b Are grits a normal or inferior good? Explain why.

⊚ 9 The demand equation for tribbles is $P = 50 - 1Q_D$. The supply equation for tribbles is $P = 20 + 0.5Q_S$ where P is the price of a tribble in dollars, Q_D is the quantity of tribbles demanded, and Q_S is the quantity of tribbles supplied. The tribble market is initially in equilibrium, and income is $180.

a What is the equilibrium quantity (Q^*) of tribbles?

b What is the equilibrium price (P^*) of a tribble?

c As a result of a decrease in income to $120, the demand curve for tribbles shifts (the supply curve remains the same). The new demand equation is:

$$P = 110 - 1Q_D$$

Use this information to calculate the new equilibrium quantity of tribbles; calculate the new equilibrium price of a tribble.

d Calculate the income elasticity of demand for tribbles. Are tribbles a normal or inferior good? [*Hint*: In your calculation be sure to: (1) use the information about the *initial* equilibrium conditions (price, quantity, and income), and (2) keep in mind that price is assumed *constant* in calculating income elasticity. Only income and quantity change.]

10 Table 5.4 gives the demand schedules for good A when the price of good B (P_B) is $8 and $12. Complete the last column of the table by computing the cross elasticity of demand between goods A and B for each of the three prices of A. Are A and B complements or substitutes?

TABLE **5.4** DEMAND SCHEDULES FOR GOOD A

	$P_B = \$8$	$P_B = \$12$	
P_A	Q_A	Q'_A	η_x
$8	2,000	4,000	
$7	4,000	6,000	
$6	6,000	8,000	

A N S W E R S

True/False/Uncertain and Explain

1 F Responsiveness quantity demanded to ΔP. (99–100)

2 F Elasticity $\uparrow$ with elapsed time. (104–105)

3 F Slope constant; $\eta \downarrow$ as move down demand curve. (102–103)

4 T Colas are substitutes for you. (103)

5 T $\downarrow$ proportion income spent on good, more inelastic demand. (104)

6 T Narrower definition $\rightarrow$ more substitutes. (103)

⊙ 7 U Inferior good has negative income elasticity; cross elasticity sign depends on whether substitute or complement. (107–108)

⊙ 8 F η_x positive so goods are substitutes. (107)

9 T $\downarrow S \rightarrow \uparrow P \rightarrow \uparrow$ total revenue, so demand inelastic. (105–106)

10 F (% $\uparrow P$) > (% $\downarrow Q$), so total revenue ($P \times Q$) $\uparrow$. (105–106)

Multiple-Choice

1 b Demand curve vertical so $\downarrow P \rightarrow$ no Δ quantity demanded. (101–102)

2 b $|(-10/50)/(2/20)| = 2$. (100–101)

3 c Closer substitutes $\rightarrow \uparrow$ elasticity demand. (103–104)

4 b Definition. (110–111)

⊙ 5 d Rightward shift supply $\rightarrow \uparrow$ quantity sold and $\downarrow P$, with inelastic demand $\rightarrow \downarrow$ total revenue. (105–106)

6 a Definition. (101–102)

7 a $\eta_y = (\% \Delta Q_D)/(\% \Delta \text{income}) = 5/10 = 0.5$. (107–108)

8 c $\eta = |(\% \Delta Q_D)/(\% \Delta P)|$. $2 = |2/-1|$. Q_D and P always inversely related on demand curve. (100–101)

9 b $\eta \uparrow$ with $\uparrow$ proportion income spent on good. $\eta \uparrow$ when longer time passage and easier to obtain substitutes. (103–105)

10 b η_s and η never negative. η_y negative for inferior good. (107–108)

11 b $\downarrow P \rightarrow \downarrow$ total revenue when $\eta < 1$. η never negative. (105–106)

12 a $\eta_s = (\% \Delta Q_S)/(\% \Delta P) = (2,000/10,000)/(1/2) = 0.4$. (110–111)

13 b $\downarrow S \rightarrow \downarrow Q_D$ and $\uparrow P$. Since $\eta > 1$, $\uparrow P \rightarrow \downarrow$ expenditure. (105–106)

⊙ 14 a If $\uparrow P \rightarrow \downarrow$ total revenue, then η must be > 1. Must know (% ΔQ_D) to precisely calculate η. (105–106)

15 d Better off means $\uparrow$ total revenue. By definition relation $\uparrow P$, η, and total revenue. (105–106)

16 c Close substitutes so η_x positive and very elastic (high). (107)

17 e $\uparrow D \rightarrow$ no ΔP if supply curve horizontal (η_s = infinity). (110–111)

18 d Labour demand curve would be vertical. (101–102)

19 a See answer to **25** below. **c** correct, but **a** best answer. (107–109)

⊙ 20 e Note total revenue (*TR*) on *y*-axis. Since *TR* constant as $\uparrow Q$ (and presumably $\downarrow P$), $\eta = 1$. **a**, **b** depend on η_y. (105–106)

⊙ 21 b $\eta_y > 0$ so normal good. Necessities tend to have $\eta_y < 1$, while luxuries tend to have $\eta_y > 1$. (107–109)

22 d Definition. Momentary supply curve most vertical. (110–111)

23 c Small $\downarrow P \rightarrow$ large $\uparrow$ quantity demanded. **a** inelastic, **b** unit elastic, **d** on income elasticity. (101–102)

24 c Total revenue test. (105–106)

25 c Definition. **a**, **b**, **d** affect demand, not supply. Long-run supply curve flatter than short-run. (110–111)

Short Answer Problems

1 The slope of a demand curve tells us how much quantity demanded changes when price changes. However, the numerical value of the slope depends on the units we use to measure price and quantity and will change if the unit of measure is changed even though demand is unchanged. For example, if we change the unit of measure for quantity from tonnes to kilograms, the new slope of the (same) demand curve will be 1,000 times the old slope. On the other hand, elasticity gives a unit-free measure of the responsiveness of quantity demanded to price changes.

2 a The demand for IBM personal computers will be more elastic after the production of clone personal computers since there would then be more readily available substitutes.

b The demand for television sets will be more elastic since they will generally take a larger proportion of consumer income.

c The demand for electricity after the passage of two years will be more elastic since consumers will have more time to find substitutes for electricity, for example, a gas stove.

d The demand for Tylenol is more elastic. There are far more substitutes for Tylenol (other brands of acetaminophen) than for acetaminophen in general.

3 Supply is more elastic in the long run because the passage of time allows producers to find better (more efficient) ways of producing that are not available in the short run. The responsiveness of production to an increase in price will increase as firms have time to discover and implement new technologies or to increase the scale of operation.

4 D_A is more elastic than D_B. To see why, look at the formula for price elasticity of demand:

$$\eta = \left| \frac{\% \, \Delta \text{ quantity demanded}}{\% \, \Delta \text{ price}} \right|$$

The percentage change in price is the same for the two demand curves. But the percentage change in quantity is greater for D_A. At P_1, the initial quantity demanded is the same for both demand curves (Q_1). With the fall in price to P_2, the increase in quantity demanded is greater for D_A (to Q_{2A}) than for D_B (to Q_{2B}). Therefore D_A is more elastic than D_B

FIGURE **5.2** SOLUTION

5 The numbers for total revenue are shown in Table 5.2 Solution. The total revenue curve is shown in Fig. 5.3(b) Solution. The total revenue curve first increases (at a diminishing rate—its slope is decreasing as we move up the curve), then reaches a maximum between $Q = 5$ and $Q = 6$, and then decreases. We will encounter this pattern of changing total revenue again in studying monopoly in Chapter 12.

TABLE **5.2** SOLUTION

Price ($)	Quantity Demanded	Total Revenue
22	0	0
20	1	20
18	2	36
16	3	48
14	4	56
12	5	60
10	6	60
8	7	56
6	8	48

FIGURE **5.3**(b) SOLUTION

6 a The completed columns of Table 5.3 are shown here. The second and third columns of the table show that as price falls, total revenue increases when demand is elastic; total revenue remains constant when demand is unit elastic; total revenue falls when demand is inelastic.

TABLE **5.3**   SOLUTION

ΔP ($)	η	ΔTR($)	η′	ΔTR′ ($)
16 — 14	2.14	+8	1.36	+4
14 — 12	1.44	+4	1.00	0
12 — 10	1.00	0	0.73	−4
10 — 8	0.69	−4	0.53	−8
8 — 6	0.47	−8	0.37	−12

b The new demand curve is labelled D' in Fig 5.3(a) Solution. The last two columns of the table have been completed on the basis of the new demand curve.

FIGURE **5.3** (a)   SOLUTION

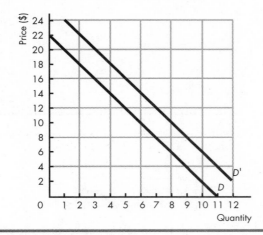

c Since they are parallel, D' and D have exactly the same slope. Thus we know that for a given change in price, the change in quantity demanded will be the same for the two curves. However, elasticity is determined by *percentage* changes, and the percentage change in quantity demanded is different for the two curves, although the percentage change in price will be the same. For a given percentage change in price, the percentage change in quantity demanded will always be less for D'. For example, as the price falls from $16 to $14 (a 13 percent change), the quantity demanded increases from 5 to 6 units along D', but from 3 to 4 along D. The percentage change in quantity demanded is only 18 percent along D' and 29 percent along D. Since the percentage change in price is the same for both curves, D' is more inelastic than D.

d Income increases from $10,000 to $14,000. At a constant price of $12, the increase in income, which shifts out the demand curve to D', increases the quantity consumers will demand from 5 units to 7 units. Substituting these numbers into the formula for the income elasticity of demand yields

$$\eta_y = \left(\frac{\Delta Q}{Q_{ave}}\right)\bigg/\left(\frac{\Delta Y}{Y_{ave}}\right)$$

$$= \left(\frac{2}{6}\right)\bigg/\left(\frac{4,000}{12,000}\right) = +1$$

The income elasticity of demand is a positive number, since both ΔQ and ΔY are positive. Therefore, this is a normal good. We already knew that from the information in part **b**, which stated that the demand curve shifted rightward with an increase in income. If this were an inferior good, the increase in income would have shifted the demand curve leftward and the income elasticity of demand would have been negative.

7 a In order to calculate price elasticity of demand, we need to know two points (each point a combination of price and quantity demanded) on the demand curve. We only are given the quantity demanded coordinate of each point. By substituting $Q_D = 4$ and $Q_D = 6$ into the demand equation, we can solve for the two price coordinates:

At $Q_D = 4$; $P = 60 - 2(4) = 52$
At $Q_D = 6$; $P = 60 - 2(6) = 48$

These price and quantity demanded coordinates can now be substituted into the formula for the price elasticity of demand:

$$\eta = \left|\left(\frac{\Delta Q}{Q_{ave}}\right)\bigg/\left(\frac{\Delta P}{P_{ave}}\right)\right|$$

$$= \left|\left(\frac{-2}{5}\right)\bigg/\left(\frac{4}{50}\right)\right| = 5$$

b One method is simply to compare total revenue ($P \times Q$) at each equilibrium.

Initial equilibrium:
Total revenue = $(P \times Q) = (52 \times 4) = 208$.

New equilibrium:
If $P^* = 48$, Q^* can be calculated by substituting P^* into the demand equation:

$$48 = 60 - 2\,Q^*$$
$$2\,Q^* = 12$$
$$Q^* = 6$$

So total revenue = $(P \times Q) = (48 \times 6) = 288$.

In moving from the initial to the new equilibrium, total revenue has increased.

A second method is to use the information from part **a** on the price elasticity of demand. We know that between $Q_D = 4$ and $Q_D = 6$

on the demand curve, demand is elastic. These two points correspond to the initial equilibrium and, after the shift of the supply curve, the new equilibrium. Since demand here is elastic, we know that the fall in price from $P = 52$ to $P = 48$ will increase total revenue.

8 a Using the formula for income elasticity of demand

$$\eta_y = \left(\frac{\Delta Q}{Q_{ave}} \right) \Big/ \left(\frac{\Delta Y}{Y_{ave}} \right)$$

$$= \left(\frac{200 - 400}{\tfrac{1}{2}(200 + 400)} \right) \Big/ \left(\frac{10,000 - 6,000}{\tfrac{1}{2}(10,000 + 6,000)} \right)$$

$$= \left(\frac{-200}{300} \right) \Big/ \left(\frac{4,000}{8,000} \right) = -\frac{4}{3}$$

b Grits are an inferior good because the income elasticity of demand is negative.

9 a The initial equilibrium quantity (Q^*) of tribbles is 20. [Refer to *Study Guide* Chapter 4 if you need help in solving demand and supply equations.]

b The initial equilibrium price (P^*) of a tribble is $30. [Refer to *Study Guide* Chapter 4 if you need help in solving demand and supply equations.]

c The new equilibrium quantity of tribbles is 60. The new equilibrium price of a tribble is $50.

d At the initial income of $180 and price of $30, the quantity of tribbles demanded is 20. In order to find the new quantity demanded at income of $120, we have to use the new demand equation. But since *price* is assumed constant in calculating income elasticity, we have to substitute $P = 30$ into the new demand equation to get the appropriate new quantity. It would be *incorrect* to use the new equilibrium quantity, because that quantity corresponds to a *different price* ($50).

$$P = 110 - 1Q_D$$
$$30 = 110 - 1Q_D$$
$$Q_D = 80$$

We now have appropriate information about the initial quantity demanded (20) and income ($180), and about the new quantity demanded (80) and income ($120). Substituting this information into the formula for income elasticity of demand yields

$$\eta_y = \left(\frac{\Delta Q}{Q_{ave}} \right) \Big/ \left(\frac{\Delta Y}{Y_{ave}} \right)$$

$$= \left(\frac{-60}{50} \right) \Big/ \left(\frac{60}{150} \right) = -3$$

Since the income elasticity of demand for tribbles is negative, tribbles are an inferior good.

10 The cross elasticities of demand between *A* and *B* are listed in Table 5.4 Solution. Since the cross elasticities are positive, we know that *A* and *B* are substitutes.

TABLE **5.4** SOLUTION DEMAND SCHEDULES FOR GOOD A

P_A	$P_B = \$8$	$P_B = \$12$	
	Q_A	Q'_A	η_x
$8	2,000	4,000	1.67
$7	4,000	6,000	1.00
$6	6,000	8,000	0.71

Fig 6.1, pg 121

- SHORT-RUN SUPPLY: SHOWS HOW QTY. OF HOUSING SUPPLIED VARIES AS PRICE VARIES, (WHILE # OF HOUSES REMAINS CONSTANT)
- SUPPLY RESPONSE VARIATION IS DUE TO EXTENT TO WHICH HOUSING IS USED (ROOM RENT PREVIOUSLY OR NOT)
- LONG-RUN SUPPLY: SHOWS HOW QTY VARIES FROM TIME PASSING (TO BUILD/DESTROY BUILDINGS).
- SHOWN PERFECTLY ELASTIC — SAYING COST OF BUILDING AN APT. IS ≈ THE SAME, REGARDLESS OF # OF EXISTING APT. BUILDINGS).

THESE PEOPLE PAY ABOVE MARKET PRICE B/C OF SHORTAGE
RENT CEILING
$10,000 $100,000
SHORTAGE OF 56,000
THESE PEOPLE HAVE RENT [CONTROL]

KEY CONCEPTS

Ⅰ Housing Markets and Rent Ceilings
Fig 6.1, pg 121

A In an unregulated housing market (EARTHQUAKE)

- Shortage → ↑ rents (B/C OF SUPPLY SHORTAGE) → economizing on space, (RENT OUT ROOMS) ∴ ↑ quantity supplied (short run), and building activity shifts supply rightward (long run).

- Rents ↓ and the housing stock ↑.

B In a regulated housing market

- A **rent ceiling** (a **price ceiling** applied to rents) makes it illegal to ↑ rents. ONLY WORKS WHEN BELOW EQUILIB PRICE, B/C FORCES OF LAW & MARKET IN CONFLICT.
  RENT CEILING (BELOW EQUILIB).

Fig 6.2, pg 122

- Housing stocks are lower than in an unregulated market both in short and long run. No incentive to economize on space or build new housing. — NOT AT A FIXED RENT W/ A SHORTAGE IN HOUSING (IF UNREGULATED THEY COULD ↑ RENT ∴ INCENTIVE IS THERE TO BUILD MORE

- Shortage → excess demand → B/C D>S. = SHORTAGE

  {2 THINGS THAT OCCUR B/C OF RENT CEILINGS THAT TRY & BLOCK MARKET MECHANISM}
  - **search activity** (time spent looking for someone with whom to do business) and (B/C NOTHING TO BUY & NOTHING TO SELL — W/ REGULATED, SEARCH ACTIVITY ↑ - COSTLY
  - **black markets** (illegal trading arrangements at prices in excess of ceilings). EG: TICKET SCALPING.

- Total housing cost in regulated market, including cost of search activity, may be > cost in unregulated market. *greater* ∴ RENT CEILINGS ONLY CONTROL RENT PORTION, & NOT TOTAL COST, SO TOTAL COST WILL BE HIGHER THAN UNREGULATED MARKET PRICE.
  = RENT (REGULATED) + TIME & RESOURCES SPENT SEARCHING (UNREDUCED)

The Labour Market and Minimum Wages
Fig 6.3, pg 124   Fig 6.4, pg 125

Minimum wage laws make it illegal to hire labour below a specified wage. MIN. WAGE SET ABOVE EQUILIB PRICE (OTHERWISE HAS NO EFFECT)

- Minimum wages create excess supply of labour and lower the quantity of labour demanded and hired.
  B/C D<S = EXCESS OF WORKERS WHO WILL WORK FOR LESS THAN MIN. WAGE.

- Unemployed workers willing to work at a lower wage spend more time searching for work. B/C D>S = EXCESS WILLING TO WORK FOR LESS THAN MIN WAGE (SEE SUPPLY SIDE IN FIG 6.7).

RENT CEILINGS ARE SUPPOSED TO HELP THE POOR, BUT DON'T B/C D>S = SHORTAGE, 44,000 HOUSES AVAILABLE AT RENT CONTROLLED PRICE, WHEN ABOUT THE 56,000 SHORTAGE, THESE PEOPLE PAY IN THE BLACK MARKET W/ UNREGULATED PRICE.

- THE HIGHER THE WAGE RATE, ↑S & ↓D.
- B/C AT ↓, S↓ & ↑D. B/C CHEAPER LABOUR.
- THE LOWER THE WAGE RATE ↑D & ↓S (WHO WANTS TO WORK FOR $ LOW)

- Minimum wage laws contribute to high unemployment among unskilled and younger workers. B/C S>D

- IN SHORT RUN SUPPLY: ↓ WAGES = ↓ S (LABOUR) & ↑ D, B/C COMPANIES WANT TO HIRE CHEAP LABOUR.
- IN LONG RUN: ↓ WAGES ENCOURAGES WORKERS TO LEAVE MARKET & GET SKILLS ∴ S↓ & ↑ WAGES (B/C ↑D).

Taxes
Fig 6.7, pg 129   DEMAND CURVE DOES NOT CHANGE W/ TAX

Sales tax shifts up supply curve by vertical distance equal to amount of tax. Who pays tax depends on elasticities of supply and demand. B/C ↑P = ↓QTY SUPPLIED — SUPPLY ↓ (SHIFTS LEFT) & DISTANCE BETWEEN S AND S+TAX IS THE ACTUAL TAX

- *Supply elasticity and tax division* *Fig 6.7, pg 129*
  - Perfectly inelastic supply—sellers pay all. (THE TAX) *Fig 6.7A, pg 129* EG: WATER SPRING THAT CAN'T BE CONTROLLED, KEEP SUPPLYING REGARDLESS OF PRICE
  - More inelastic supply—more sellers pay. NOTE: THE MORE ELASTIC THE SUPPLY, THE LARGER IS THE PROPORTION OF TAX PAID BY CONSUMER
  - More elastic supply—more buyers pay.
  - Perfectly elastic supply—buyers pay all. (THE TAX) *Fig 6.7B, pg 129* EG: SAND, TAX SHIFTS SUPPLY CURVE UPWARDS

- *Demand elasticity and tax division* *Fig 6.6, pg 128* Ⓐ
  - Perfectly inelastic demand—buyers pay all. (THE TAX) EG: INSULIN, PRICE INELASTIC B/C BUY REGARDLESS OF PRICE
  - More inelastic demand—more buyers pay. & NOTE: THE MORE INELASTIC DEMAND, THE LARGER THE PORTION OF TAX PAID BY THE CONSUMER
  - More elastic demand—more sellers pay.
  - Perfectly elastic demand—sellers pay all. (THE TAX) *Fig 6.6B, pg 128.* EG: PINK MARKERS, PRICE ELASTIC B/C CAN SUBSTITUTE FOR LOWER COST MARKERS.

Markets for Prohibited Goods — EG: DRUGS.
Fig 6.8, pg 131

Penalizing dealers for selling illegal goods → ↑ cost selling goods and ↓ supply. Penalizing buyers for consuming illegal goods → ↓ willingness to pay and ↓ demand. — THE MORE SEVERE THE PENALTY ON THE SUPPLIER/SELLER — ↑P.

- (Sellers' penalties > buyers' penalties) → ↓ Q, ↑ P. = SUPPLY
- (Sellers' penalties < buyers' penalties) → ↓ Q, ↓ P. = DEMAND
  — WHEN BOTH PENALIZED IT ↓D & ↓S.
- Taxing (decriminalized) goods can achieve the same consumption levels as prohibition. ∴ ↑P to ↓S (HIGH RATE) (LOW CONSUMP)

Fig 6.9, pg 132. — ∴ CONSUMERS PAY A HIGH PRICE & SUPPLIERS RECEIVE A SMALL AMT. OF THAT PRICE ∴ LARGE AMT IS TAX REVENUE (GOVT).

NOTE: MOST ITEMS THAT ARE TAXED ARE INELASTIC (B/C ELASTIC MEANS SUBSTITUTION FOR UN-TAXED GOODS). ∴ BUYER PAYS THE TAX.

Fig 6.10, pg 133

Stabilizing Farm Revenue

CONSUMERS BUY OF ↑ REGARDLESS OF PRICE ∴ ↑P = ↑TR.

Demand for most farm products is inelastic → large variations farm revenue.

↑ IN REV > ↓ IN REV.

◆ Poor harvest (↓ S) → ↑ P, ↑ total revenue. *Fig 6.10, pg 133*
  B/C INELASTIC ↑ TR FROM ↑P (∴ MAKING PROFIT OFF OTHER
◆ Bumper harvest (↑ S) → ↓ P, ↓ total revenue. *OPPORTUNITY (COSTS).*
  B/C INELASTIC ∴ ↓TR FROM ↓P ↓ IN REV > ↑ IN REV

Fig 6.10 pg 133

Farm revenue is stabilized through speculation by *↑ BY PUTTING INVENTORIES TO SELL LATER* inventory holders, who buy at low prices and sell at *Fig 6.11 pg 133* high prices, reducing price fluctuations. *REDUCE PRICE FLUCTUATIONS BY ADDING/SELLING INVENTORIES, KEEPS CONSUMER BUYING SAME AMT. AT SAME PRICE*

Farm stabilization agencies (**farm marketing boards**) also limit price fluctuations by setting *↓STABILIZE PRICES OF CERTAIN GOODS.*

Fig 6.12 pg 136 ① price floors → ↑ market price and surpluses.
  FIG 6.12, PG 136. B/C THEY ARE MORE EXPENSIVE THAN COMPETITIVE PRICE ∴ ↑P = ↓ DS, ↑S ∴ SURPLUS.

Fig 6.13 ② **quotas** (quantity restrictions on production) → *SUPPLY IS PERFECTLY INELASTIC* ↑ P and ↓ Q grown. *& YOU PRODUCE SAME AMT W/↑ IN P. FARMERS WANT TO PRODUCE MORE OUTPUT AT LOWER PRICE BUT THAT WILL RESTORE COMPETITIVE PRICE "NO!*

Fig 6.14 ③ **subsidies** (payments to producers by governments) *↓ LOWERS THE PRICE PAID BY CONSUMER* → ↑ supply and ↓ market price (but farmers receive market price + subsidy). *FARMERS GAIN B/C PRODUCING AT LOWER COST & TAX PAYERS PAY SUBSIDY. ∴ SUBSIDY LOWERS COST TO CONSUMER BUT AT HIGH COSTS TO TAXPAYER*

NOTE: INVENTORIES DON'T STABILIZE FARM REVENUE FARM REVENUE FLUCTUATES AS PRODUCTION FLUCTUATES

H E L P F U L   H I N T S

1 In the real world we frequently observe market regulation by governments in the form of price constraints of one form or another. It is thus important to study the effects of such regulation. Another benefit of studying government regulation is to obtain an understanding of how markets work when, by contrast, the government does *not* affect the normal operation of markets.

   Whenever something disturbs an equilibrium in an unregulated (free) market, the desires of buyers and sellers are brought back into balance by price movements. If prices are controlled by government regulation, however, the price mechanism can no longer serve this purpose. Thus, *balance* must be restored in some other way. In the case of price ceilings, black markets are likely to arise. If black markets cannot develop because of strict enforcement of price ceilings, then demanders will be forced to bear the costs of increased search activity, waiting in line, or something else.

2 This chapter discusses government price constraints in three specific markets: rental housing, labour, and farm products. The principles raised in those discussions, however, can be generalized to other markets.

   In any market with a legal price ceiling set below the market-clearing price, we will observe excess quantity demanded, because the price cannot increase to eliminate it. As a

consequence, the value of the last unit of the good available will exceed the controlled price. Demanders are willing to engage in costly activities up to the value of that last unit (search activity, waiting lines, and black market activity) in order to obtain the good.

   Furthermore, if price is allowed to increase in response to a decrease in supply or an increase in demand, there are incentive effects for suppliers to produce more and demanders to purchase less (movements along the supply and demand curves). Indeed, it is the response to these incentives that restores equilibrium in markets with freely adjusting prices. If, however, the price cannot adjust, these price-induced incentive effects do not have a chance to operate. Specifically, in the case of rent ceilings, the inability of rents (price) to rise means that: (1) there is no inducement to use the current stock of housing more intensively in the short run and (2) there is no incentive to construct new housing in the long run. Similarly, the effects on any market in which a minimum price (price floor) is set above the market-clearing (equilibrium) price will be similar to those discussed in the text for the labour market under a minimum wage or price floors in agricultural markets.

3 The division of the burden of a tax is also called tax incidence. Who pays a sales tax imposed on producers depends on the elasticities of demand and supply. The general principles of tax incidence are

- The more inelastic the demand, the more consumers pay.
- The more elastic the demand, the more producers pay.
- The more inelastic the supply, the more producers pay.
- The more elastic the supply, the more consumers pay.

S E L F - T E S T

True/False/Uncertain and Explain

1 When rents in an unregulated housing market rise due to a decrease in supply, people who are unable to pay the higher rents will not get housing.

2 The more elastic demand is for a product, the larger is the fraction of a sales tax paid by consumers.

3 If a rent ceiling exceeds people's willingness to pay, search activity and black markets will increase.

4 The statement "if we legalize and tax drugs, tax revenues could be used to finance more drug education programs" is normative.

5 An increase in the minimum wage will reduce the number of workers employed.

6 The impact of minimum wage laws on unemployment among young workers tends to be about the same as it is for older workers.

7 Suppose the supply curve for corn fluctuates widely but the demand curve is stable. The price of corn will fluctuate more if demand is elastic rather than inelastic.

8 If the price is higher than an inventory holder's expected future price, she sells goods from inventory.

9 If penalties are imposed on both sellers and buyers in a market for prohibited goods, the price remains constant and the quantity bought decreases.

10 A subsidy shifts the demand curve for a good rightward.

Multiple-Choice

1 The short-run supply curve for rental housing is positively sloped because

a the supply of housing is fixed in the short run.
b the current stock of buildings will be used more intensively as rents rise.
c the cost of constructing new buildings increases as the number of buildings increases.
d the cost of constructing new buildings is about the same regardless of the number of buildings in existence.
e new buildings will be constructed as rents rise.

2 Rent ceilings imposed by governments

a keep rental prices below the unregulated market price.
b keep rental prices above the unregulated market price.
c keep rental prices equal to the unregulated market price.
d increase the stock of rental housing.
e increase the intensity of use of the current stock of rental housing.

3 Figure 6.1 shows the market for frisbees before and after a sales tax is imposed. The sales tax on each frisbee is

a $0.40.
b $0.60.
c $1.00.
d $5.60.
e $6.60.

FIGURE **6.1**

4 Refer to Fig. 6.1. For each frisbee, the sellers' share of the tax burden is

a $0.40.

b $0.60.

c $1.00.

d $5.60.

e $6.60.

5 Refer to Fig. 6.1. For each frisbee, the buyers' share of the tax burden is

a $0.40.

b $0.60.

c $1.00.

d $5.60.

e $6.60.

6 Refer to Fig. 6.1. Government revenue from the tax is

a $4,000.

b $5,000.

c $22,400.

d $26,400.

e $30,000.

7 From Fig. 6.1 we can deduce that between 4,000 and 5,000 units, the demand for frisbees is

a inelastic.

b unit elastic.

c elastic.

d more elastic than the supply (S) of frisbees.

e soaring.

8 European Union (EU) countries have been accumulating butter and cheese mountains and wine lakes. These surpluses are consistent with

a floor prices for agricultural products that are below market prices.

b floor prices for agricultural products that are above market prices.

c ceiling prices for agricultural products that are below market prices.

d ceiling prices for agricultural products that are above market prices.

e quotas for agricultural products.

9 A momentary supply curve is

a elastic since price is fixed.

b relatively more elastic than a short-run supply curve.

c relatively inelastic since yields are known, but sales are not.

d inelastic since output is fixed.

e as ephemeral as gossamer wings.

10 A price ceiling set below the equilibrium price will result in

a excess supply.

b excess demand.

c the equilibrium price.

d an increase in supply.

e a decrease in demand.

11 If the minimum wage is set at $2 per hour in Fig. 6.2, what is the level of unemployment in millions of hours?

a 50

b 40

c 20

d 10

e 0

FIGURE **6.2**

12 With inventory speculation, a bumper crop of barley will

a decrease farm revenue, while a poor harvest will increase farm revenue.

b increase farm revenue, while a poor harvest will decrease farm revenue.

c decrease farm revenue as will a poor harvest.

d increase farm revenue as will a poor harvest.

e do none of the above.

13 If enforcement is aimed at sellers of a prohibited good,

a price and quantity bought will decrease.

b price and quantity bought will increase.

c price will increase and quantity bought will decrease.

d price will decrease and quantity bought will increase.

e price change will be uncertain and quantity bought will decrease.

14 If the price of a good is not affected by a sales tax, then

a supply is perfectly elastic.
b demand is perfectly elastic.
c elasticity of supply is greater than elasticity of demand.
d elasticity of demand is greater than elasticity of supply.
e none of the above.

15 Which of the following statements is *false*?

a Buying goods to put into inventory is equivalent to decreasing quantity supplied.
b Selling goods from inventory is equivalent to increasing quantity supplied.
c In a market with inventories, producers' supply differs from market supply.
d Producers' supply is the sum of market supply and inventory supply.
e Inventory holders must forecast future prices.

16 Which of the following is *not* a likely outcome of rent ceilings?

a a black market for rent-controlled housing
b long waiting lists of potential renters of rent-controlled housing
c a short-run shortage of housing
d black market prices below the rent ceiling prices
e increased search activity for rent-controlled housing

17 Figure 6.3 illustrates the short-run demand and supply curves in the wheat bran market. If the Wheat Marketing Board sets a quota of 50 million bushels, then the market-clearing price of a bushel of wheat bran is

a $1.00.
b $3.00.
c $5.00.
d two scoops of raisins.
e none of the above.

FIGURE **6.3**

18 Refer to Fig. 6.3. With the quota of 50 million bushels, farmers have an incentive to

a decrease output because the market-clearing price is below cost of production.
b decrease output because there is a surplus at the market-clearing price.
c increase output because the market-clearing price is above cost of production.
d increase output because there is a shortage at the market-clearing price.
e stick to the quota.

19 Refer to Fig. 6.3. Suppose the marketing board develops a new kind of subsidy called a direct payment plan. Farmers are told, "We will guarantee you $5.00 per bushel, but everything you produce at this price must be sold on the market for whatever buyers will pay; then we will give you (at taxpayers' expense) the difference between the market price and $5.00 per bushel." How many bushels of wheat bran will be sold?

a 20 million
b 50 million
c 60 million
d 70 million
e none of the above

20 Refer to Fig. 6.3. The amount of taxpayers' money that the marketing board pays to farmers in Question **19** is

a zero.
b $70 million.
c $250 million.
d $280 million.
e $350 million.

21 Which of the following statements about prohibited goods is *true*?

a Taxes are more effective in changing preferences than prohibition.

b Prohibition is more effective in generating revenue than an equivalent tax.

c Taxes and penalties cannot be set so as to yield equivalent outcomes.

d Taxes generate revenues, while prohibition generates more enforcement expenses.

e None of the above is true.

22 Which of the following types of labour would be most significantly affected by an increase in the legal minimum wage?

a professional athletes

b young, unskilled labour

c skilled union workers

d university professors

e self-employed labour

23 Which of the following combinations would generally yield the greatest price fluctuation?

a large supply shifts and inelastic demand

b large supply shifts and elastic demand

c large supply shifts and perfectly elastic demand

d small supply shifts and inelastic demand

e small supply shifts and elastic demand

24 With inventory speculation

a prices stabilize but farm revenue does not.

b prices do not stabilize but farm revenue does.

c bumper crops bring decreased total revenue.

d poor harvests bring increased total revenue.

e c and d.

25 An agricultural subsidy

a shifts the supply curve rightward.

b benefits consumers by lowering product prices.

c benefits farmers by raising the price they receive.

d imposes major costs on taxpayers.

e does all of the above.

Short Answer Problems

1 Suppose there is a significant reduction in the supply of gasoline. Explain how an unregulated market adjusts. What is it that induces consumers to reduce their consumption of gasoline willingly?

2 Governments tend to place high sales taxes (often called "sin" taxes) on liquor and cigarettes. Aside from moral and health reasons, why are these goods chosen as a source of tax revenue?

3 The supply of fruit is subject to unpredictable fluctuations. Why does the price of fresh fruit fluctuate much more than the price of canned fruit?

4 Suppose the Nudist Party wins the next federal election because all the clothed citizens forgot to vote. The Nudists pass a law making clothes illegal. Unfortunately for the Nudists, the police don't take the law seriously (where would officers pin their badges?) and put almost no effort into enforcement. Use a diagram to explain why the black market price of now illegal clothes will be close to the unregulated market equilibrium price.

5 Suppose that the market for rental housing is initially in long-run equilibrium. Use graphs to answer the following:

a Explain how an unregulated market for rental housing would adjust, if there is a sudden significant increase in demand. What will happen to rent and the quantity of units rented in the short run and in the long run? Be sure to discuss the effect on incentives (in both the short run and the long run) as the market-determined price (rent) changes.

b Now explain how the market would adjust to the increase in demand, if rent ceilings are established at the level of the initial equilibrium rent. What has happened to supplier incentives in this case?

6 The demand for and supply of gasoline are given in Table 6.1.

a What are the equilibrium price and quantity of gasoline?

TABLE **6.1**

Price ($ per litre)	Quantity Demanded	Quantity Supplied
	(millions of litres per day)	
1.40	8	24
1.30	10	22
1.20	12	20
1.10	14	18
1.00	16	16
0.90	18	14

b Suppose that the quantity of gasoline supplied suddenly declines by 8 million litres per day at every price. Construct a new table of price, quantity demanded, and quantity supplied, and draw a graph of the demand curve and the initial and new supply curves. Assuming that the market for gasoline is unregulated, use either your table or graph to find the new equilibrium price and quantity of gasoline.

c How has the change in price affected the behaviour of demanders? the behaviour of suppliers?

7 Suppose that the government imposes a price ceiling of $1 per litre of gasoline at the same time as the decrease in supply reported in Short Answer Problem **6b**.

a What is the quantity of gasoline demanded? quantity supplied?

b What is the quantity of gasoline actually sold?

c What is the excess quantity of gasoline demanded?

d What is the highest price demanders are willing to pay for the last litre of gasoline available?

e Geordi values gasoline as in **d**. How long would Geordi be willing to sit in line to buy 10 litres of gasoline if the best alternative was to work at a wage rate of $8 per hour?

8 The Ministry of Treasury has been authorized to levy a 15¢ per unit excise (sales) tax on one of two goods—comic books or dog biscuits. As a summer student at the Ministry, you are given an assignment by the Director of Taxes, Dr. More. You must choose the good that meets two objectives: (1) it will yield the greatest tax revenue, and (2) the major burden of the tax will fall on consumers. Ministry researchers have estimated the supply and demand curves (without the tax) for each market. The comic book market is shown in Fig. 6.4 and the dog biscuit market in Fig. 6.5. The following questions will help you complete your assignment.

FIGURE **6.4**

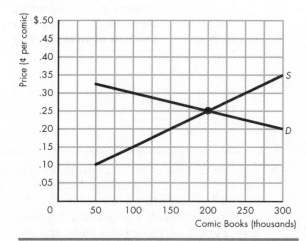

Comic Books (thousands)

a For the comic book market, shift the appropriate curve to reflect the tax and draw it on Fig. 6.4. Label the curve either *S + tax* or *D + tax*. Identify the new equilibrium price and quantity. Compare the total expenditure in the original and new equilibria.

b Calculate the total tax revenue collected, and indicate it as an area on Fig. 6.4.

c How much of the tax is paid by consumers? by producers?

FIGURE **6.5**

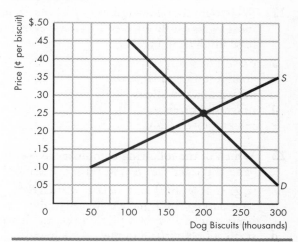

Dog Biscuits (thousands)

d Now perform the same analysis on the dog biscuit market. Shift the appropriate curve to reflect the tax and draw it on Fig. 6.5. Label the curve either *S + tax* or *D + tax*. Identify the new equilibrium price and quantity. Compare the total expenditure in the original and new equilibria.

e Calculate the total tax revenue collected, and indicate it as an area on Fig. 6.5.

f How much of the tax is paid by consumers? by producers?

g What is your recommendation to Dr. More? Explain.

9 Dr. More was pleased with your excise tax recommendation in Short Answer Problem **8**, but you can't stop wondering about his comment, "Hmm, I thought you would do it the other way." If you haven't already figured out to what he was referring, the following questions will help.

a For the comic book market, calculate the elasticity of demand between the original and new equilibrium points. Is demand elastic or inelastic?

b Perform the same calculation for the dog biscuit market. Is demand elastic or inelastic?

c What do you know about demand elasticities that would have allowed you to complete your assignment "the other way" and predict which market would yield maximum tax revenue, and which market would place most of the tax burden on consumers?

⌖ **10** Figure 6.6 shows the demand curve in the market for grinola seeds. Grinola is difficult to grow—simply a frown from a farmer in the field causes the seeds to develop split ends which makes them worthless. As a result, grinola harvests fluctuate widely.

FIGURE **6.6**

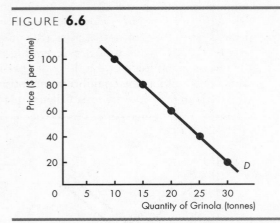

a If there are no inventory speculators in the grinola market, what will the market price be when momentary supply is 25 tonnes? 20 tonnes? 15 tonnes?

b Suppose inventory speculators discover that grinola can be stored easily and enter the market looking for a profit. They forecast an expected price of $60 per tonne. Explain what happens when the momentary supply is 25 tonnes. Identify the amount the inventory speculators buy or sell, the quantity bought by consumers, and the market price.

c Repeat the analysis in part **b** for a momentary supply of 20 tonnes.

d Repeat the analysis in part **b** for a momentary supply of 15 tonnes.

e What has happened to price fluctuations in the grinola market?

f Inventory speculators don't operate out of the goodness of their hearts. Have they made a profit in grinola? Explain your calculation.

ANSWERS

True/False/Uncertain and Explain

1 T At equilibrium rent, all who can afford housing get it, but not necessarily those who need housing. (120–121)

2 F More elastic demand → more substitutes → better able to escape tax by not buying. (127–128)

3 F Ceiling is above market price so search activity won't ↑ and black markets won't arise. (122–123)

⌖ **4** F Positive statement; can be verified by observation. (130–132)

5 T ↑ minimum wage → ↓ quantity labour demanded. (125–126)

6 F Greater impact on young workers since they have lower wages. (125–126)

7 F Fluctuate more if demand inelastic. (133–134)

8 T Buy low, sell high. (134–135)

⌖ **9** U Effect on P depends on relative magnitude of penalties. (130–132)

10 F Shifts supply rightward. (137)

Multiple-Choice

1 b **c**, **d**, and **e** refer to long run. (120–121)

2 a Definition. **d** and **e** result of ↑ rent in unregulated market. (122–123)

3 c Equals the vertical distance between the two supply curves. (126–127)

4 a Original $P = \$6$, new $P = \$6.60$. Sellers pay $1 tax and get $0.60 more from buyers, so sellers pay $0.40. (126–127)

5 b See previous answer. (126–127)

6 a $1 per frisbee × 1,000 units sold. (126–127)

⌖ **7** c ↑ P ($6 to $6.60) → ↓ total revenue ($30,000 to $26,400). **d** wrong—$\eta = 2.3$ and $\eta_s = 3.2$. (126–130)

8 b Floor above market P → excess supply. (135–137)

9 d Definition. (133–134)

10 b Draw graph. No Δ *ceteris paribus* assumptions → no shift supply or demand. (122–123)

⌖ **11** e Floor below equilibrium P doesn't prevent market from reaching equilibrium. (124–126)

12 b Price remains constant so total revenue is positively correlated with output. (134–135)

13 c Supply shifts leftward as penalties are added to other costs. (130–132)

14 b **a** would ↑ P by full amount tax. **c** and **d** affect P but amounts uncertain. (127–128)

15 d Market supply = producers' supply + inventory supply. (134–135)

16 d Black market prices will be above ceiling. (122–123)

17 c Where momentary supply curve at 50 million bushels intersects demand. (135–137)

◉ 18 c Farmers receiving $5 but willing to supply this quantity at (their cost of) $1. (135–137)

◉ 19 d Quantity supplied at $P = \$5$. (135–137)

◉ 20 d 70 million bushels sell for $1 per bushel. Taxpayers make up difference of $4 per bushel × 70 million. (135–137)

21 d Reverse taxes and prohibition to make **a** and **b** true. (130–132)

22 b Lowest wage labour. (124–126)

23 a Draw graphs to see. (133–134)

24 a Quantities (and revenues) still fluctuate. **c** and **d** true if reverse decrease and increase. (134–135)

25 e Definition. (137)

Short Answer Problems

1 If the market for gasoline is initially in equilibrium and there is a significant reduction in supply, there will be excess quantity demanded at the existing price. As a result, the price of gasoline will rise, which will cause movements along the new supply curve and the demand curve. As the price rises there will be a price-induced increase in quantity supplied and a price-induced decrease in quantity demanded. The price continues to rise until the excess quantity demanded is eliminated. The price increase causes consumers to reduce their desired consumption of gasoline.

2 Because alcohol and nicotine are addictive, the demands for liquor and cigarettes are relatively inelastic. When liquor and cigarette prices are increased by "sin" taxes, the percentage fall in quantity demanded is less than the percentage increase in price. Thus total revenue increases as does tax revenue. To raise a fixed amount of revenue, it takes a much smaller per unit tax on goods with inelastic demand than on goods with elastic demand. Inelastic demand also means, *ceteris paribus*, that a greater portion of the tax is borne by consumers rather than producers.

3 The key difference between the two goods is that most fresh fruit cannot be stored effectively while canned fruit is stored easily. Without storage, inventory speculation is difficult, and fresh fruit prices fluctuate widely with variations in the momentary supply curve. Since canned fruit can be stored, inventory holders operate to make the supply of canned fruit perfectly elastic at the inventory holders' expected price. Thus supply-induced price fluctuations for canned fruit are eliminated. Canned fruit prices can still fluctuate if the inventory holders' expected price changes.

4 The clothing market is illustrated in Fig. 6.7. The demand curve is D and the supply curve is S. The equilibrium price is P_c and the quantity is Q_c. Since police enforcement is lax, the cost of breaking the law (CBL) is very small for both buyers and sellers. Thus the curves that incorporate CBL are very close to the original demand and supply curves. The intersection of $D - CBL$ and $S + CBL$ yields a new equilibrium price identical to the original price (the price may be slightly higher or lower depending on the relative magnitude of the shifts of demand and supply) and a new equilibrium quantity (Q_p) only slightly less than the original quantity.

FIGURE **6.7**

5 a Figure 6.8 corresponds to an unregulated market for rental housing. The initial demand, short-run supply, and long-run supply curves are D_0, SS_0, and LS respectively. The market is initially in long-run equilibrium at point a corresponding to rent R_0 and quantity of rental units Q_0. Demand then increases to D_1, creating excess quantity demanded of $Q_2 - Q_0$ at the initial rent. In the short run, in an unregulated market, rent will rise to R_1 to clear the markets and the equilibrium quantity of housing rented is Q_1 (point b). Note that as the rent rises, the quantity of rental housing supplied increases (a movement from point a to point b along supply curve SS_0) as the existing stock of housing is used more intensively. Also the quantity of housing demanded decreases (a movement from point c to point b along demand curve D_1). Together, these movements eliminate the excess quantity demanded. The higher rent also provides an incentive to construct new housing in the long run. This is illustrated by the shift in the supply curve from SS_0 to SS_1. Finally, a new long-run equilibrium is achieved at point c, with rent restored to its original level and the number of units rented equal to Q_2.

FIGURE **6.8**

Quantity of Rental Units

b We can also use Fig. 6.8 to discuss the behaviour of a market with a rent ceiling set at R_0. Start in the same long-run equilibrium at point a. Once again we observe an increase in demand from D_0 to D_1. In this case, however, the rent cannot rise to restore equilibrium. There will be no incentive to use the existing stock of housing more intensively in the short run or to construct new housing in the long run. The quantity of rental housing supplied will remain at Q_0. Since the last unit of rental housing is valued at R_2, but rent is fixed at R_0, demanders of rental housing will be willing to bear additional costs up to $R_2 - R_0$ (in the form of additional search activity or illegal payments) in order to obtain rental housing.

6 a The equilibrium price of gasoline is $1.00 per litre since, at that price, the quantity of gasoline demanded is equal to the quantity supplied (16 million litres per day). The equilibrium quantity of gasoline is 16 million litres per day.

b The new table and graph are shown in Table 6.2 and Fig. 6.9.

TABLE **6.2**

Price	Quantity Demanded (millions of litres per day)	Quantity Supplied (millions of litres per day)
1.40	8	16
1.30	10	14
1.20	12	12
1.10	14	10
1.00	16	8
0.90	18	6

FIGURE **6.9**

Quantity of Gasoline (millions of litres per day)

The new equilibrium price is $1.20 per litre since, at that price, the quantity of gasoline demanded equals the new quantity supplied (12 million litres per day). The new equilibrium quantity is 12 million litres of gasoline per day.

c The increase in price has caused the quantity of gasoline demanded to decrease by 4 million litres per day (from 16 to 12 million). Given the new supply curve S_1, the increase in price from $1.00 to $1.20 per litre increases the quantity of gasoline supplied by 4 million litres per day (from 8 to 12 million).

7 a At the ceiling price of $1.00, quantity demanded is 16 million litres per day, quantity supplied is 8 million litres per day.

b The quantity of gasoline actually sold is 8 million litres per day. When, at a given price, quantity demanded and quantity supplied differ, whichever quantity is *less* determines the quantity actually sold.

c The excess quantity of gasoline demanded is 8 million litres per day.

d The highest price consumers are willing to pay for the last unit of gasoline supplied (the 8-millionth litre per day) is $1.40. You can obtain this answer from your graph by imagining a vertical line from the quantity 8 million litres up to where it intersects the demand curve at $1.40. The demand curve shows the highest price consumers are willing to pay for that last litre supplied.

e The regulated price of gasoline is $1.00 per litre but the value to Geordi of the last litre is $1.40, so he would be willing to bear costs of $4.00 above the regulated price of gasoline to obtain 10 litres ($0.40 × 10 litres). If the best alternative is to earn $8.00 per hour, Geordi would be willing to spend up to half an hour sitting in line to buy 10 litres.

8 a See Fig. 6.4 Solution. In the comic book market, the supply curve shifts up vertically by an amount equal to the tax (15¢). The original equilibrium price is 25¢ and quantity is 200,000. The new equilibrium price is 30¢ and quantity is 100,000. Total expenditure has decreased, from $50,000 (25¢ × 200,000) to $30,000 (30¢ × 100,000).

FIGURE **6.4** SOLUTION

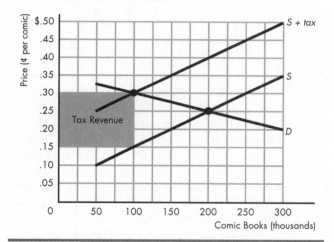

b Total tax revenue is 15¢ per comic book × 100,000 units sold = $15,000 and is indicated by the shaded area on Fig. 6.4 Solution.

c As a result of the tax, the price to consumers has gone up by 5¢ (from 25¢ to 30¢). Consumers' share of the tax burden is $5,000 (5¢ × 100,000). Producers pay the 15¢ tax to government, but only get back 5¢ of it from consumers. Therefore producers' share of the tax burden is $10,000 (10¢ × 100,000).

d See Fig. 6.5 Solution. In the dog biscuit market, the supply curve shifts up vertically by an amount equal to the tax (15¢). The original equilibrium price is 25¢ and quantity is

200,000. The new equilibrium price is 35¢ and quantity is 150,000. Total expenditure has increased, from $50,000 (25¢ × 200,000) to $52,500 (35¢ × 150,000).

FIGURE **6.5** SOLUTION

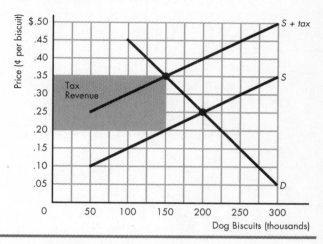

e Total tax revenue is 15¢ per dog biscuit × 150,000 units sold = $22,500 and is indicated by the shaded area on Fig. 6.5 Solution.

f As a result of the tax, the price to consumers has gone up by 10¢ (from 25¢ to 35¢). Consumers' share of the tax burden is $15,000 (10¢ × 150,000). Producers pay the 15¢ tax to government, and get back 10¢ of it from consumers. Therefore producers' share of the tax burden is $7,500 (5¢ × 150,000).

g You confidently recommend to Dr. More that the Ministry tax dog biscuits. An excise tax on dog biscuits meets both objectives: (1) it will raise more tax revenue than a tax on comic books ($22,500 versus $15,000), and (2) it will place more of the tax burden on consumers. In the dog biscuit market, consumers will pay $15,000, which is 67 percent of the tax burden. In the comic book market, consumers will pay only $5,000, which is 33 percent of the tax burden.

9 You are kicking yourself because you forgot that there is a relationship between elasticity of demand and both (1) a change in total revenue for a (tax-induced) increase in price, and (2) whether consumers or producers bear more of the burden of a tax.

a For the comic book market, the elasticity of demand calculation is

$$\eta = \left|\left(\frac{\Delta Q}{Q_{ave}}\right)\middle/\left(\frac{\Delta P}{P_{ave}}\right)\right|$$

$$= \left|\left(\frac{100-200}{150}\right)\middle/\left(\frac{.30-.25}{.275}\right)\right|$$

$$= \left|\left(\frac{-.667}{-.182}\right)\right| = 3.67$$

Demand is elastic.

b For the dog biscuit market, the elasticity of demand calculation is

$$\eta = \left|\left(\frac{\Delta Q}{Q_{ave}}\right)\middle/\left(\frac{\Delta P}{P_{ave}}\right)\right|$$

$$= \left|\left(\frac{150-200}{175}\right)\middle/\left(\frac{.35-.25}{.30}\right)\right|$$

$$= \left|\left(\frac{-.286}{.333}\right)\right| = 0.86$$

Demand is inelastic.

c You forgot that an increase in price increases total expenditure when demand is inelastic, and decreases total expenditure when demand is elastic. Thus you could have used elasticity data to predict that expenditure would increase in the dog biscuit market. An increase in expenditure is not the same as an increase in tax revenue, but if more money is being spent, there is more to be spent on taxes. You also forgot that the more inelastic demand is, the more of a tax consumers pay.

If you had thought of the elasticity approach without prompting, good for you! Dr. More will be calling on you again for advice. If you didn't think of it, time to return to Drs. Parkin and Bade for a refresher.

◑ 10 Refer to Fig. 6.6 Solution.

FIGURE **6.6** SOLUTION

a When momentary supply is 25 tonnes, $P = \$40$. When momentary supply is 20 tonnes, $P = \$60$. When momentary supply is 15 tonnes, $P = \$80$.

b The expected future price is $60. When momentary supply is 25 tonnes, the market price of $40 would be below the expected future price so speculators buy grinola to store. They start buying at $40, but their added demand pushes up the price until it quickly reaches $60. The speculators buy 5 tonnes, paying somewhere between $40 and $60 per tonne. Consumers buy the remaining 20 tonnes, and the final market price is $60.

c In this case, the expected future price and the market price are identical ($60), so speculators take no action. The market price is $60.

d The expected future price is $60. When momentary supply is 15 tonnes, the market price of $80 would be above the expected future price so speculators sell grinola from their inventories. They start selling at $80, but their added supply pushes down the price until it quickly reaches $60. The speculators sell 5 tonnes, receiving somewhere between $80 and $60 per tonne. Consumers buy 20 tonnes (15 from producers and 5 from speculators), and the final market price is $60.

e Price fluctuations for consumers have been largely eliminated since, regardless of the momentary supply, the market price moves quickly to $60.

f It is likely that the inventory speculators have made a profit. In part **b**, they bought 5 tonnes at a price somewhere between $40 and $60 per tonne. Therefore they spent between $200 and $300. They made no transactions in part **c**. In part **d**, they sold 5 tonnes at a price somewhere between $80 and $60 per tonne. Therefore they earned between $400 and $300. Their net profit is somewhere between a maximum of $200 ($400 – $200) and a minimum of zero ($300 – $300).

PROBLEM

The finance minister has asked your boss at the finance department, Dr. Ina Lastic, to estimate the effects of levying a $24-per-carton tax on cigarettes. Dr. Lastic predicts that the tax will raise significant tax revenues (at least $30 million) because cigarette demand is inelastic.

Unfortunately, Dr. Lastic is unaware of a recent study you read in the *Globe and Mail* about past tax increases that found "that Ottawa has not received the entire tax windfall it expected from increased cigarette levies because of growing tobacco smuggling."

She has asked you to perform the following detailed analysis for her predictions. The demand and supply curves (without taxes) for cigarettes are given in Fig. P1.1. The before-tax price is $28 per carton, and the before-tax quantity is 2.25 million cartons per year.

a Draw the new *S + tax* curve on Fig. P1.1.

b According to Dr. Lastic's predictions, what is the after-tax equilibrium price? equilibrium quantity?

c Calculate her predicted tax revenues.

d Check to see if Dr. Lastic's claim that the demand for cigarettes is inelastic is correct by calculating η between the before-tax equilibrium and the after-tax equilibrium. Was she right?

FIGURE **P1.1** CANADIAN CIGARETTE MARKET

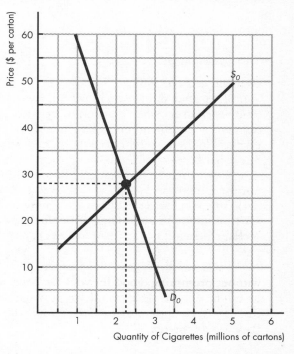

d e Dr. Lastic gets high marks for economics so far. Nonetheless, you respectfully point out that her revenue prediction is wrong because she hasn't taken into account the effects of smuggling. Showing an uncharacteristic willingness to stretch herself, she replies, "I'm listening. What's *your* prediction of tax revenue?"

Here's your chance to impress the boss. You know that the supply curve of cigarettes in the United States is the same as the before-tax supply curve in Canada. You have estimated the cost of breaking the law (*CBL*) to suppliers at $16 per carton and risk to consumers of buying smuggled cigarettes is so small that their *CBL* is effectively zero. Use this information to answer the following questions.

i   Draw and label any appropriate new curve(s) on Fig. P1.1.

ii   What is *your* prediction of the after-tax price of a carton of cigarettes? the quantity of cigarettes sold legally? the quantity of smuggled cigarettes sold illegally? [*Hint*: the price of legal and illegal cigarettes will be equal because they are perfect substitutes.]

iii What is *your* prediction of tax revenue?

MIDTERM EXAMINATION

You should allocate 48 minutes for this examination (24 questions, 2 minutes per question). For each question, choose the one *best* answer.

1   The Canadian economy relies

a   exclusively on the market mechanism.

b   extensively on the market mechanism in a mixed economy.

c   exclusively on the command mechanism.

d   extensively on the command mechanism in a mixed economy.

e   equally on market and command mechanisms in a mixed economy.

2   Francesca makes $25 an hour as a welder. She must take 2 hours off work (without pay) to go to the dentist for a filling. The dentist charges $100. The opportunity cost of Francesca's trip to the dentist is

a $125.

b $100.

c $50.

d $150.

e   none of the above.

3   A conventional *PPF* shows that

a   there is a limit to the production of any one good.

b   to produce more of one good, we must produce less of another good.

c   there are limits to total production with given resources and technology.

d   all of the above are true.

e   none of the above is true.

4   If individuals *a* and *b* can both produce only goods *X* and *Y* and *a* does *not* have a comparative advantage in the production of either *X* or *Y*, then we know that

a   *b* has an absolute advantage in the production of *X* and *Y*.

b   *a* and *b* have the same opportunity cost for *X* and for *Y*.

c   *b* has a comparative advantage in the production of both *X* and *Y*.

d   there will be gains from trade.

e   **b** and **d**.

5   The magnitude of *both* the elasticity of demand and the elasticity of supply depends on

a   the factor substitution possibilities.

b   the proportion of income spent on a good.

c   the time elapsed since the price change.

d   the technological conditions of production.

e   none of the above factors.

6   If an increase in price causes a decrease in total revenue then price elasticity of demand is

a   negative.

b   zero.

c   greater than zero but less than one.

d   equal to one.

e   greater than one.

7   The data in Table P1.1 could *not* be represented by

a   two one-variable time-series graphs.

b   one two-variable time-series graph.

c   a three-variable time-series graph.

d   a scatter diagram.

e   any of the above.

TABLE **P1.1**

Year	x	y
1990	6.2	143
1991	5.7	156
1992	5.3	162

8 If the price of an umbrella is low and the number of rainy days is large, more umbrellas will be sold. If the price of an umbrella is high and there are few rainy days, fewer umbrellas will be sold. On the basis of this information, the number of

a umbrellas sold and the price of an umbrella are positively related, holding the number of rainy days constant.

b umbrellas sold and the price of an umbrella are negatively related, holding the number of rainy days constant.

c rainy days and the number of umbrellas sold are negatively related, holding the price of an umbrella constant.

d rainy days and the price of an umbrella are negatively related, holding the number of umbrellas sold constant.

e times you scratch your head over this question is 44.

9 Inventory holders

a sell goods from inventory when price is less than the expected future price.

b buy goods to put into inventory when price is greater than the expected future price.

c make the market supply curve perfectly elastic at the inventory holders' expected future price.

d do all of the above.

e do none of the above.

10 The tax burden on consumers will be greater the more

1 elastic is demand.
2 inelastic is demand.
3 elastic is supply.
4 inelastic is supply.

a 2 only
b 1 and 3
c 1 and 4
d 2 and 3
e 2 and 4

Suppose a society produces only two goods—guns and butter. Three alternative combinations on its *PPF* are given in Table P1.2. Use the information in Table P1.2 to answer Questions **11** and **12**.

TABLE **P1.2** PRODUCTION POSSIBILITIES

Possibility	Units of Butter	Units of Guns
a	8	0
b	6	1
c	0	3

11 In moving from combination *b* to combination *c*, the opportunity cost of producing *one* additional unit of guns is

a 2 units of butter.
b 1/2 unit of butter.
c 6 units of butter.
d 1/6 unit of butter.
e 3 units of butter.

12 According to this *PPF*

a a combination of 6 butter and 1 gun would not employ all resources.

b a combination of 0 butter and 4 guns is attainable.

c resources are homogeneous.

d the opportunity cost of producing guns increases as more guns are produced.

e the opportunity cost of producing guns decreases as more guns are produced.

13 Which of the following is a normative statement?

a Pollution is an example of an external cost.
b Pollution makes people worse off.
c Firms that pollute should be forced to shut down.
d Pollution imposes opportunity costs on others.
e None of the above.

14 Economic decisions in markets are *coordinated* by

a firms.
b households.
c governments.
d price adjustments.
e all of the above.

15 If both demand and supply increase, then equilibrium price

a will rise and quantity will increase.
b will fall and quantity will increase.
c could rise or fall and quantity will increase.
d will rise and quantity could either increase or decrease.
e will fall and quantity could either increase or decrease.

16 If turnips are an inferior good, then, *ceteris paribus,* an increase in the price of turnips will cause

a a decrease in the demand for turnips.
b an increase in the demand for turnips.
c a decrease in the supply of turnips.
d an increase in the supply of turnips.
e none of the above.

17 In Fig. P1.2, if the minimum wage is set at $6 per hour, what is the level of unemployment in millions of hours?

a 50
b 40
c 0
d 10
e 20

FIGURE **P1.2**

18 A price floor set below the equilibrium price results in
a excess supply.
b excess demand.
c the equilibrium price.
d an increase in supply.
e a decrease in demand.

19 If a 10 percent increase in income causes a 10 percent decrease in the consumption of widgets (at a constant price), then
a the price elasticity of demand for widgets equals 1.
b the income elasticity of demand for widgets is negative.
c the income elasticity of demand for widgets equals 1.
d widgets are a normal good.
e none of the above is true.

20 A decrease in the price of X from $6 to $4 causes an increase in the quantity of Y demanded (at the current price of Y) from 900 to 1,100 units. What is the cross elasticity of demand between X and Y?

a 0.5
b −0.5
c 2
d −2
e **a** or **b**, depending on whether X and Y are substitutes or complements

21 The graph of the relationship between two variables that are negatively related
a is horizontal.
b slopes upward to the right.
c is vertical.
d slopes downward to the right.
e is linear.

22 In Fig. P1.3, the slope of the line is
a 1.00.
b 1.25.
c 1.50.
d 0.75.
e 0.50.

FIGURE **P1.3**

23 A decrease in quantity supplied is represented by a
a movement down the supply curve.
b movement up the supply curve.
c leftward shift of the supply curve.
d rightward shift of the supply curve.
e rightward shift of the demand curve.

24 Farmland can be used to produce either cattle or corn. If the demand for cattle increases then

a demand for corn will increase.
b supply of corn will increase.
c demand for corn will decrease.
d supply of corn will decrease.
e b and c.

A N S W E R S

Problem

a See Fig. P1.1 Solution. Ignore the curve S + CBL for now.

FIGURE **P1.1** SOLUTION
CANADIAN CIGARETTE MARKET

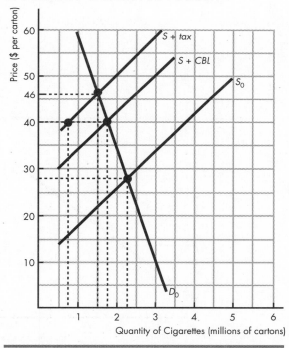

b The after-tax equilibrium price is $46 per carton. The after-tax equilibrium quantity is 1.5 million cartons per year.

c Tax revenue is 1.5 million cartons × $24 per carton = $36 million per year.

d $$\eta = \left| \frac{\dfrac{\Delta Q}{Q_{ave}}}{\dfrac{\Delta P}{P_{ave}}} \right|$$

$$\eta = \left| \frac{\dfrac{-0.75}{1.875}}{\dfrac{18}{37}} \right| = \frac{.4}{.486} = .82$$

The demand curve is inelastic ($\eta < 1$) between the two equilibrium points. Dr. Lastic's predictions about tax revenue (without smuggling) and elasticity were correct.

e **i** See Fig. P1.1 Solution. Since the *CBL* to consumers is zero, the demand curve does not shift. The smugglers' supply curve is *S + CBL*.
ii Since consumers can buy cigarettes from smugglers at a price of $40 per carton, no one is willing to buy at the higher legal price of $46. The legal price is bid down to $40. At that price, legal suppliers will supply 0.75 million cartons, and total market demand is 1.75 million cartons. Smugglers supply the difference, 1 million cartons.
iii Tax revenue is 0.75 million cartons × $24 per carton = only $18 million per year.

Dr. Lastic is impressed. She says, "When I studied economics, we were taught that illegal activities were the business of law enforcement officials, not economists. What you have shown is that almost any activity can be analysed from an economic perspective. Well done. Let's draft our reply to the minister."

Midterm Examination

1 b Definition. (19–20)
2 d $100 which could have been spent on other goods plus time cost ($25 × 2 hours). (8–9)
3 d a and b show scarcity, c shows opportunity cost. (44–46)
4 b No comparative advantage means equal opportunity cost. No information on absolute advantage. (53–56)
5 c a, d affect η_s only. b affects η only. (103–105, 110–111)
6 e Total revenue test. (105–106)
7 c There are two variables plus time, which could be represented by a, b, or d.(27–31)
8 b c would be true if change "negatively" to "positively." Can't judge d without additional information. (38–39)
9 c a and b would be true if reversed "less" and "greater." (134–135)
10 d Definition. (127–130)
11 e Give up 6 butter to get 2 guns: 6/2 = 3 butter per gun. (47–48)

12 **d** Opportunity cost gun between a and $b = 2$ butter; between b and $c = 3$ butter. **a** on *PPF*, **b** outside *PPF*. (47–48)

13 **c** **a** and **b** are true statements; **d** is a positive statement that can be tested. (12–13)

14 **d** Price adjustments coordinate choices made by firms, households, and governments. (19–20)

15 **c** Rightward shifts demand and supply must $\rightarrow \uparrow$ equilibrium quantity, but effect on price indeterminate. (82–83)

16 **e** $\uparrow P \rightarrow$ movement along demand curve. (72–73)

17 **b** Quantity supplied (50) > quantity demanded (10). (125–126)

18 **c** Draw graph. Floor doesn't prevent $\uparrow P$ from excess demand. (124–126)

19 **b** $\eta_y = (\% \, \Delta \, Q_D)/(\% \, \Delta \text{ income}) = -10/10 = -1$; widgets inferior good. (107–108)

20 **b** $\eta_x = (\% \, \Delta \, Q^Y_D)/(\% \, \Delta \, P^X) = (200/1{,}000)/(-2/5) = -0.5.$ (107)

21 **d** As $x \uparrow$, $y \downarrow$. (33–34)

22 **d** For example, using points (0, 4) and (16, 16): $\Delta y = 12$ (16 − 4), $\Delta x = 16$ (16 − 0). (36–37)

23 **a** Illustration of law of supply. (74–77)

24 **d** Cattle and corn substitutes in production. $\uparrow$ demand for cattle $\rightarrow \uparrow$ price cattle $\rightarrow \downarrow$ supply corn. (75–76)

Chapter 7

Utility and Demand

KEY CONCEPTS

I — Household Consumption Choices

Household consumption choices are determined by: ① *BUDGET CONSTRAINTS* & ② *PREFERENCES*.

①◆ Budget constraint

- Income and prices (*P*) of goods and services are given. *GIVEN AMT. OF INCOME & CANNOT INFLUENCE PRICES OF GOODS IT BUYS.* Budget line marks boundary between <u>affordable</u> (points on line or inside) and unaffordable (outside line) choices. *BUDGET LINE = LIMITS TO CONSUMPTION. — BUDGET IS A CONSTRAINT OF CHOICES (UNAFFORDABLE)*

Fig 7.1 pg 149

②◆ Preferences—likes and dislikes based on utility. *SATISFACTION YOU GET FROM CONSUMPTION OF GOOD.*

Utility is benefit or satisfaction from consumption. *(ABSTRACT CONCEPT W ARBITRARY UNITS).*

◆ <u>Total utility</u> (*TU*) is <u>total</u> benefit or satisfaction from consumption of goods and services. ↑ consumption → ↑ total utility. *B/C TU DEPENDS ON PERSON'S LEVEL OF CONSUMPTION. ∴ ↑C = ↑TU.*

Table 7.1 pg 150

◆ Marginal utility (*MU*) is Δ total utility from one-unit *CHANGE* increase in quantity good consumed. *MU* positive, but due to **diminishing marginal utility**, ↓ as consumption good ↑. *∴ NOTE THAT MU HAS DIMINISHING*

Fig 7.2 pg 151

THESE 2 FEATURES: ① POSITIVE ② ↑C = ↓MU. EG: IDEA OF TOO MUCH OF ONE THING — GET SICK OF IT SO YOU ↓ SATISFACTION.

II — Maximizing Utility

→ 2 WAYS... ① CONSUMER EQUILIB. ② MU PER DOLLAR SPENT

Consumers strive for utility maximization. *MAKE CHOICES BASED ON WHAT WILL SATISFY THEM THE MOST & MAX THIS BENEFIT.*

◆ Given income and the prices of goods and services, ①**consumer equilibrium** occurs when consumer allocates income in way that maximizes total utility. *∴ GET INDIV. TU FOR POP & MOVIES THEN TU FOR BOTH POP & MOVIES → THE HIGHEST TU IS THE EQUILIB (BEST MAX).*

Table 7.2 pg 152

◆ Total utility is maximized when all income is spent ②and **marginal utility per dollar spent** is equal for all goods. For substitute goods movies (*m*) and pop (*p*), this occurs when

Table 7.3 pg 153

∴ MU PER DOLLAR SPENT
$$\frac{MU_m}{P_m} = \frac{MU_p}{P_p}$$
PRICE MOVIES. PRICE PP

EG: $\frac{38}{32} = \frac{19}{16}$

6.33 = 6.33.

∴TU IS MAXIMIZED.

Fig 7.3 pg 153

NOTE: MU ↓ AS C↑.

The <u>power of marginal analysis</u> for predicting economic choices stems from a simple rule—if the marginal gain from an action exceeds the marginal loss, take the action. *IF BENEFIT > COST.*

Fig 7.3 pg 153

- The rule applied to the utility maximization example is—if the marginal utility per dollar spent on movies exceeds the marginal utility per dollar spent on pop, buy more movies and less pop. *& VICE VERSA.*
- The marginal gain from more movies exceeds the marginal loss from less pop.

III — Predictions of Marginal Utility Theory

Fig 7.4, Pg 154

↓ P OF MOVIES = MOVEMENT ALONG MOVIE DEMAND CURVE (BY MORE & SHIFT OF POP DEMAND CURVE (LEFT))

- *Ceteris paribus*, ↓ P_m → ↑ Q_m consumed (movement down along demand curve for movies) and → leftward shift demand curve for pop. *SUBSTITUTE*

↑ P OF POP = MOVEMENT ALONG MOVIE DEMAND CURVE (BUY ↓ POP) & SHIFT OF MOVIE DEMAND CURVE (RIGHT)

- *Ceteris paribus*, ↑ P_p → ↓ Q_p consumed (movement up along demand curve for pop) and → rightward shift demand curve for movies. *B/C SHE SUBSTITUTES MOVIES FOR POP WHEN P↑ FOR POP.*

Fig 7.5 pg 156

Movies and pop normal goods. *Ceteris paribus*, ↑ income → ↑ consumption movies and pop (rightward shifts both demand curves). *B/C ↑ INCOME = ↑ CONSUMPTION (BUYING) OF BOTH GOODS. NOTE: WHEN INCOME ↑, YOU CONSUME MORE OF A 'NORMAL' GOOD & LESS OF AN 'INFERIOR' GOOD.*

Marginal utility theory allows us to derive and predict the above results which, in Chapter 4, were just *assumptions* about consumer demand.

Table 7.7 pg 157

Individual and market demand:

- Individual demand—relationship between quantity demanded and price for single individual.

- Market demand—sum of individual demands; relationship between total quantity demanded and price.

Fig 7.6 pg 156

- Market demand curve—horizontal sum of individual demand curves. *(IS FORMED BY ADDING THE QUANTITIES DEMANDED BY EACH INDIV. AT EACH PRICE).*

& MARKET DEMAND SLOPES DOWNWARD

→ ASSUMED THAT: - PEOPLE GET UTILITY FROM CONSUMPTION.
- THAT CONSUMPTION YIELDS MORE UTILITY
- THAT M.U. DIMINISHES
- & PEOPLE TRY TO MAXIMIZE UTILITY.

ⓘⱽ Criticisms of Marginal Utility Theory

① Utility can't be observed. But utility does not need to be observed to be used. We do observe incomes and quantities and prices of goods and services. Utility theory allows us to understand consumption choices and predict effects of changes in prices and incomes on these choices. *CONSUMERS MAXIMIZE T.U. BY MAKING M.U. PER DOLLAR SPENT ON EACH GOOD EQUAL.*

② Consumers aren't as smart as the theory implies. But the theory makes no predictions about real consumers' thought processes. It simply predicts real consumers' *actions.* — *CONFUSES PEOPLE'S ACTIONS (REAL WORLD) ū THOSE OF PEOPLE IN A MODEL ECONOMY.... .: NOT REAL!*

ⓥ Implications of Marginal Utility Theory

- GAIN BY SPECIALIZATION (COMPARATIVE ADVANTAGE) & THEN TRADING.

Consumer surplus:

Fig 7.7 pg 161

◆ **Value** of a good is maximum amount person would be willing to pay for it.
- PRICE: IS AMT. ACTUALLY PAID FOR GOOD.

◆ **Consumer surplus** is the value of a good minus its price. *AF → (BASE × HEIGHT) ÷ 2*

CONSUMER SURPLUS.

◆ Consumer surplus is the area under the demand curve, but above market price (see Text Fig. 7.7, page 161). *- SHOWS THE DIFFERENCE BETWEEN VALUE SHE PLACES ON 1ST, 2ND, 3RD ETC. MOVIE & THE PRICE SHE ACTUALLY PAYS .: THERE IS A GAIN → CONSUMER SURPLUS.*

Distinction between total utility and marginal utility resolves diamond–water paradox.

◆ Diamonds, though less useful (low *TU*) than water, have higher price (high *MU*).

◆ Water more useful (high *TU*), but has lower price (low *MU*).

.: B/C OF THEORY OF M.U. → AS TU↑ = ↑C = ↓MU.
SO B/C WATER ⟹ TU↑ = ↓MU.
.°. MU PER DOLLAR SPENT IS EQUAL FOR DIAMONDS & WATER
B/C MU(DIAMONDS)/P(DIAMONDS) = MU(WATER)/P(WATER)

H E L P F U L   H I N T S

I Utility is an extremely useful abstract concept that allows us to think more clearly about consumer choice. Do not be confused by the fact that arbitrary units are used to measure utility. The only important basis for marginal utility theory is that you are able to judge whether the additional satisfaction per dollar spent on good *X* is greater or less than the additional satisfaction per dollar spent on *Y*. If it is greater, then you decide to consume an additional unit of *X*. How much greater is irrelevant for the decision.

2 The marginal utility per dollar spent on good *X* can be written as MU_X/P_X where MU_X is the marginal utility of the last unit of *X* consumed and P_X is the price of a unit of good *X*. The consumer equilibrium (utility-maximizing)

condition for goods *X* and *Y* can thus be written

$$\frac{MU_X}{P_X} = \frac{MU_Y}{P_Y}$$

This implies that, in consumer equilibrium, the ratio of marginal utilities will equal the ratio of prices of the two goods:

$$\frac{MU_X}{MU_Y} = \frac{P_X}{P_Y}$$

This result is often useful.

3 If an individual is not in consumer equilibrium, then the preceding equation is not satisfied. For example, consider spending all of one's income on a consumption plan where

$$\frac{MU_X}{P_X} > \frac{MU_Y}{P_Y}$$

or, equivalently,

$$\frac{MU_X}{MU_Y} > \frac{P_X}{P_Y}$$

Since P_X and P_Y are given, this means that MU_X is "too large" and MU_Y is "too small." Utility can be increased by increasing consumption of *X* (and thereby decreasing MU_X due to the principle of diminishing marginal utility) and decreasing consumption of *Y* (and thereby increasing MU_Y due to diminishing marginal utility).

4 Text Table 7.7 on page 157 is a good review device.

S E L F - T E S T

True/False/Uncertain and Explain

I The market demand curve is the horizontal sum of all individual demand curves.

2 The principle of diminishing marginal utility means that as consumption of a good increases, total utility increases but at a decreasing rate.

3 When the price of good X rises, the marginal utility from the consumption of X decreases.

4 If the marginal utilities from consuming two goods are not equal, then the consumer cannot be in equilibrium.

5 If the marginal utility per dollar spent on good X exceeds the marginal utility per dollar spent on good Y, total utility will increase by increasing consumption of X and decreasing consumption of Y.

6 When income decreases, the marginal utility derived from a good will increase.

7 Because utility cannot be observed or measured, marginal utility theory is essentially useless.

8 The value of a good is equal to the price of the good.

9 Consumer surplus for relatively cheap goods like water will be relatively low.

10 If a shift in supply decreases the price of a good, consumer surplus increases.

Multiple-Choice

1 If Ms. Petersen is maximizing her utility in the consumption of goods A and B, which of the following statements must be *true*?

a $MU_A = MU_B$

b $\dfrac{MU_A}{P_A} = \dfrac{MU_B}{P_B}$

c $\dfrac{MU_A}{P_B} = \dfrac{MU_B}{P_A}$

d $TU_A = TU_B$

e $\dfrac{TU_A}{P_A} = \dfrac{TU_B}{P_B}$

2 Samir consumes apples and bananas and is in consumer equilibrium. The marginal utility of the last apple is 10 and the marginal utility of the last banana is 5. If the price of an apple is $0.50, then what is the price of a banana?

a $0.05
b $0.10
c $0.25
d $0.50
e $1.00

3 Market demand is the

a sum of the prices that each individual is willing to pay for each quantity demanded.
b sum of the quantities demanded by each individual at each price.
c sum of the consumer surplus of each individual.
d difference between the maximum amount each individual is willing to pay for a good and the market price.
e difference between the market price and the maximum amount each individual is willing to pay for a good.

4 If Soula is maximizing her utility and two goods have the same marginal utility then she will

a buy only one.
b buy equal quantities of both.
c be willing to pay the same price for each.
d get the same total utility from each.
e do none of the above.

5 Bikes and roller blades are substitutes. Marginal utility theory predicts that when the price of bikes increases, the quantity demanded of bikes

a decreases and the demand curve for roller blades shifts rightward.

b decreases and the demand curve for roller blades shifts leftward.

c decreases and the demand curve for roller blades will not shift.

d increases and the demand curve for roller blades shifts rightward.

e increases and the demand curve for roller blades shifts leftward.

6 Total utility is always

a greater than marginal utility.

b less than marginal utility.

c decreasing when marginal utility is decreasing.

d decreasing when marginal utility is increasing.

e increasing when marginal utility is positive.

7 Bill and Ted consume 15 chocolate bars each at the current price. If Bill's demand curve is more elastic than Ted's demand curve, then

a Bill's willingness to pay for the last chocolate bar is greater than Ted's.

b Ted's willingness to pay for the last chocolate bar is greater than Bill's.

c Bill's consumer surplus is greater than Ted's.

d Ted's consumer surplus is greater than Bill's.

e Bill's consumer surplus equals Ted's.

8 If a consumer is in equilibrium, then

a total utility is maximized given the consumer's income and the prices of goods.

b marginal utility is maximized given the consumer's income and the prices of goods.

c marginal utility per dollar spent is maximized given the consumer's income and the prices of goods.

d the marginal utility of each good will be equal.

e none of the above is true.

9 Squid costs $2 per kilogram and octopus costs $1 per kilogram. Jacques buys only octopus and gets 10 units of utility from the last kilogram he buys. Assuming that Jacques has maximized his utility, his marginal utility, in units, from the first kilogram of squid must be

a more than 10.

b less than 10.

c more than 20.

d less than 20.

e zero.

10 Suppose that Arnie spends his entire income of $10 on law books and silk ties. Law books cost $2 and silk ties cost $4 (see Table 7.1). The marginal utility of each good is independent of the amount consumed of the other good.

TABLE **7.1**

| | Marginal Utility | |
Quantity	Law Books	Silk Ties
1	12	16
2	10	12
3	8	8
4	6	4

If Arnie is maximizing his utility, how many silk ties does he buy?

a 0

b 1

c 2

d 3

e 4

11 Total utility equals

a the sum of the marginal utilities of each unit consumed.

b the area below the demand curve but above the market price.

c the slope of the marginal utility curve.

d the marginal utility of the last unit divided by price.

e the marginal utility of the last unit consumed multiplied by the total number of units consumed.

12 A household's consumption choices are determined by

a prices of goods and services.

b income.

c preferences.

d all of the above.

e a and b only.

13 The high price of diamonds relative to the price of water reflects the fact that at typical levels of consumption

a the total utility of water is relatively low.

b the total utility of diamonds is relatively high.

c the marginal utility of water is relatively high.

d the marginal utility of diamonds is relatively low.

e none of the above is true.

14 The demand schedule for marbles is shown in Table 7.2.

TABLE **7.2** DEMAND SCHEDULE FOR MARBLES

Price ($ per marble)	Quantity Demanded
10	1
9	2
8	3
7	4
6	5

If the actual price is $7, what is total consumer surplus?

a $3
b $4
c $6
d $12
e $27

15 Sergio is maximizing his utility in his consumption of beer and bubblegum. If the price of beer is greater than the price of bubblegum, then we know with *certainty* that

a Sergio buys more beer than bubblegum.
b Sergio buys more bubblegum than beer.
c the marginal utility of the last purchased beer is greater than the marginal utility of the last purchased bubblegum.
d the marginal utility of the last purchased bubblegum is greater than the marginal utility of the last purchased beer.
e the marginal utilities of the last purchased beer and bubblegum are equal.

16 Chuck and Barry have identical preferences but Chuck has a much higher income. If each is maximizing his utility, then

a they will have equal total utilities.
b Chuck will have lower total utility than Barry.
c Chuck will have lower marginal utility than Barry for most goods.
d Chuck will have higher marginal utility than Barry for most goods.
e they will have equal marginal utilities for most goods.

17 Which of the following is *not* a prediction of marginal utility theory?

a other things remaining the same, the higher the price of a good, the lower is the quantity demanded
b other things remaining the same, the higher the price of a good, the higher is the consumption of substitutes for that good
c other things remaining the same, the lower the price of a good, the lower is the consumption of substitutes for that good
d the law of demand
e diminishing marginal utility

18 According to the principle of diminishing marginal utility, as consumption of a good increases, total utility

a decreases and then eventually increases.
b decreases at an increasing rate.
c decreases at a decreasing rate.
d increases at an increasing rate.
e increases at a decreasing rate.

19 Suppose that Madonna spends her entire income of $6 on purple nail polish and leather outfits. Nail polish costs $1 per unit and outfits cost $2 per unit (see Table 7.3). The marginal utility of each good is independent of the amount consumed of the other good.

TABLE **7.3**

	Marginal Utility	
Quantity	Nail Polish	Outfits
1	8	16
2	6	12
3	4	10
4	3	6

If Madonna is maximizing her utility, what is her *total* utility?

a 19
b 28
c 38
d 42
e none of the above

20 In consumer equilibrium, a consumer equates the

a total utility from each good.
b marginal utility from each good.
c total utility per dollar spent on each good.
d marginal utility per dollar spent on each good.
e total income spent on each good with total utility from each good.

21 The relative prices of beer to back bacon are 2:1. If Bob's current consumption is at a level where $MU_{beer}/MU_{back\ bacon}$ is 1:2, then to achieve maximum utility Bob must

a consume more beer and less back bacon.
b not change his current consumption of beer and back bacon.
c consume less beer and more back bacon.
d increase the price of beer.
e consume twice as much beer and one-half as much back bacon.

22 The value of a good is defined as the

a market price.
b average price paid by individuals in a market.
c cost of producing the good.
d highest price an individual is willing to pay.
e total utility to an individual of all units of the good.

23 If potato chips were free, individuals would consume

a an infinite quantity of chips.
b the quantity of chips at which total utility from chips falls to zero.
c the quantity of chips at which marginal utility from chips falls to zero.
d zero chips since this equates marginal utility and price.
e none of the above.

24 Broomhilda is initially maximizing her utility in her consumption of goods X and Y. The price of good X doubles, *ceteris paribus*. For Broomhilda to once again maximize her utility, her *quantity of X* consumed must

a rise until the marginal utility of X has doubled.
b fall to one-half its previous level.
c fall until the marginal utility of X has doubled.
d fall until the marginal utility of X falls to one-half its previous level.
e yield infinite bliss.

25 Beverly is currently in consumer equilibrium. An increase in her income will

a increase her total utility.
b decrease her total utility.
c increase her marginal utility of all goods.
d decrease her marginal utility of all goods.
e increase her consumption of all goods.

Short Answer Problems

1 A consumer is initially maximizing his utility in the consumption of goods A and B so that

$$\frac{MU_A}{P_A} = \frac{MU_B}{P_B}$$

The price of A then rises as a result of the shift in supply shown in Fig. 7.1.

FIGURE **7.1**

Use the above condition for utility maximization to explain how the consumer will move to a new utility-maximizing equilibrium. Show the connection between your explanation and the change on the diagram.

2 Consider the following information relevant to a consumer who is trying to allocate her income between goods X and Y so as to maximize utility. The price of X is \$2 and the price of Y is \$1 per unit. When all income is spent, the marginal utility of the last unit of X is 20 and the marginal utility of the last unit of Y is 16.

a Why is the consumer not in equilibrium?
b To increase utility, which good should this consumer consume more of and which less of?

3 Explain why the consumer equilibrium condition and the principle of diminishing marginal utility imply the law of demand.

4 An apparent paradox that bothers many people is that although childcare workers are usually paid low salaries, it is often said that "they have the most important job in the world." Use economic reasoning to resolve this paradox.

5 Table 7.4 gives the demand schedules for broccoli for three individuals: Tom, Jana, and Ted.

TABLE **7.4** INDIVIDUAL DEMAND FOR BROCCOLI

Price	Quantity Demanded (kilograms per week)		
($ per kilogram)	Tom	Jana	Ted
0.50	10	4	10
0.75	9	2	7
1.00	8	0	4
1.25	7	0	1

a Calculate the market demand schedule.
b On a single diagram, draw the individual demand curves for Tom, Jana, and Ted, as well as the market demand curve.

6 Tables 7.5 and 7.6 give Amy's utility from the consumption of popcorn and candy bars during a week.

TABLE **7.5** AMY'S UTILITY FROM POPCORN

Bags of Popcorn	Total Utility	Marginal Utility
1	20	
2	36	
3	50	
4		12
5	72	
6	80	

TABLE **7.6** AMY'S UTILITY FROM CANDY BARS

Number of Candy Bars	Total Utility	Marginal Utility
1	14	
2	26	
3		10
4	44	
5	51	
6	57	

a Complete the tables.
b Suppose the price of a bag of popcorn is $1.00 and the price of a candy bar is $0.50. Given the information in Tables 7.5 and 7.6, complete Table 7.7 where *MU/P* means marginal utility divided by price, which is equivalent to marginal utility per dollar spent.

TABLE **7.7**

Bags of Popcorn	MU/P	Number of Candy Bars	MU/P
1		1	
2		2	
3		3	
4		4	
5		5	
6		6	

c Amy's weekly allowance is $4.00. Answer the following if she spends her entire allowance on popcorn and candy.
  i How much popcorn and how many candy bars will Amy consume each week if she maximizes her utility?
  ii Show that the utility maximum condition is satisfied.
  iii What is total utility?
  iv If, instead, Amy consumed 3 bags of popcorn and 2 candy bars, explain why she would not be maximizing her utility using figures for both total utility and for the terms *MU/P*.

7 Suppose that Amy's preferences remain as they were in Short Answer Problem **6**, but the price of a candy bar doubles to $1.00.
a Construct a new table (similar to Table 7.7) of *MU/P* for popcorn and candy bars.
b Amy's allowance continues to be $4.00. After the price change, how much popcorn and how many candy bars will she consume each week?
c Are popcorn and candy bars substitutes or complements for Amy? Why?
d Based on the information you have obtained, draw Amy's demand curve for candy bars.

e Suppose that both bags of popcorn and candy bars continue to sell for $1.00 each, but now Amy's allowance increases to $6.00 per week.
i How many candy bars and bags of popcorn will Amy choose to consume per week under the new situation?
ii Are popcorn and candy bars normal goods? Why or why not?

8 Suppose that Andre Agassi spends his entire income of $8 on hairbands and toy tennis rackets (see Table 7.8). The price of a hairband is $2 and the price of a tennis racket is $4. The marginal utility of each good is independent of the amount consumed of the other good.

TABLE **7.8**

Quantity	Marginal Utility	
	Hairbands	**Rackets**
1	20	36
2	18	32
3	16	20
4	8	16

a If Andre is maximizing his utility, how many units of each good should he purchase?
b If Andre's income rises to $24, how many units of each good should he purchase?
c Using the information above, calculate Andre's income elasticity of demand for hairbands.

9 Suppose that Igor maximizes his utility by spending his entire income on bats and lizards (see Table 7.9). The marginal utility of each good is independent of the amount consumed of the other good.

TABLE **7.9**

Quantity	Marginal Utility	
	Bats	**Lizards**
1	20	45
2	18	40
3	16	25
4	8	20

Igor's income is $16. The price of a bat is $2, and he buys 3 bats. If the marginal utility of the last lizard he buys is 40, calculate the price of a lizard using *two* separate methods.

10 Andy's weekly demand schedule for pizza is shown in Table 7.10.

TABLE **7.10** DEMAND SCHEDULE FOR PIZZA

Price ($ per pizza)	Quantity Demanded
15	1
12	2
10	3
9	4
8	5

If the price of a pizza is $9, what is Andy's consumer surplus for the following number of pizzas that he buys at that price?
a first pizza
b second pizza
c total number of pizzas

ANSWERS

True/False/Uncertain and Explain

1 T Definition. (158)
2 T Because *MU* positive but diminishing. (150–151)
3 F $\uparrow P \rightarrow \downarrow Q \rightarrow \uparrow MU$. (154–156)
4 F If prices unequal, then marginal utilities unequal in consumer equilibrium. (152–153)
5 T $\uparrow$ consumption $X \rightarrow \downarrow MU_X$.
$\downarrow$ consumption $Y \rightarrow \uparrow MU_Y$. Moves ratios *MU/P* toward equality. (152–154)
6 U True for normal good; may be false for inferior good. (157)
7 F Theory makes predictions that can be tested against observed data. (159–160)
8 U True if last unit consumed, false (value > price) otherwise. (160–161)
9 F Since many units consumed, many earlier units have willingness to pay > price. (160–161)
10 T Rightward shift supply ($\rightarrow \downarrow P$) $\rightarrow$ $\uparrow$ quantity consumed, so more units with willingness to pay > price. (160–161)

Multiple-Choice

1 b Definition. (152–153)
2 c Solve $10/.5 = 5/P_b$ for P_b. (152–153)
3 b See text discussion. (158)

4 c From maximum condition of equal MU/P. No necessary relation between MU and quantity or TU. (152–154)

5 a See text discussion. (155–156)

6 e $TU \uparrow$ when MU positive, whether $MU \downarrow$ or $\uparrow$. TU may be $\lessgtr MU$. (150–151)

7 d Ted's steeper demand curve $\rightarrow \uparrow$ willingness to pay for previous units. Willingness to pay for last unit equal. (160–161)

8 a Consumers maximize TU. **c** and **d** wrong because MU/P equal for TU maximization. (152–154)

☉ 9 d For octopus, $MU_o/P_o = 10$. For squid, $MU_s/2$ would need to be $= 10$, so MU_s must be < 20. (152–153)

10 b Buys 1 tie ($MU/P = 16/4$) and 3 books ($MU/P = 8/2$). (152–154)

11 a **b** is consumer surplus. For **c**, $MU =$ slope TU curve. **d** and **e** nonsense. (150–151)

12 d Preferences and constraints. (149–150)

13 e For diamonds: TU relatively low, MU relatively high. For water: TU relatively high, MU relatively low. (160–161)

14 c For 4 marbles consumed, consumer surplus (in \$) $= (10 - 7) + (9 - 7) + (8 - 7) + (7 - 7)$. (160–161)

☉ 15 c From maximum condition of equal MU/P. No necessary relation between MU and quantity. (152–154)

16 c Chuck consumes greater quantities of each good, so MU lower. (157)

17 e $\downarrow MU$ is *assumption* of theory. (154–157)

☉ 18 e Because marginal utility is positive but diminishing with $\uparrow$ consumption. (150–151)

19 d Buys 2 polish and 2 outfits. $TU = 8 + 6 + 16 + 12$. (150–153)

20 d Definition. MU/P key to utility maximization. (152–153)

21 c To equalize MU/P must $\uparrow MU_{beer}$ and $\downarrow MU_{back\ bacon}$. **d** wrong because no control over prices. (152–154)

22 d Definition. (160)

☉ 23 c Maximizes TU. With fewer chips, MU still positive, so TU could $\uparrow$. With more, MU turns negative so TU would $\downarrow$. (152–154)

24 c From maximum condition of equal MU/P. No necessary relation between MU and quantity consumed. (152–154)

☉ 25 a For inferior goods, consumption may $\downarrow$ and $MU \uparrow$. (157)

Short Answer Problems

1 When the price of A rises, *ceteris paribus*:

$$\frac{MU_A}{P_A} < \frac{MU_B}{P_B}$$

The consumer is no longer in equilibrium. In order to restore the equality in the equilibrium condition, the consumer must change his consumption to make MU_A rise and MU_B fall. (The consumer cannot change the prices of A and B.) Since marginal utility diminishes with increases in quantity consumed, the consumer must decrease consumption of A and increase consumption of B. Decreased consumption of A moves the consumer up to the left on the demand curve, from the initial intersection of D and S_0 to the new intersection of D and S_1. In the new consumer equilibrium, equality will be restored in the equilibrium condition.

2 a This consumer is not in equilibrium because the marginal utility per dollar spent is not the same for goods X and Y. The marginal utility per dollar spent on X is $MU_X/P_X = 20/2 = 10$, which is less than the marginal utility per dollar spent on Y: $MU_Y/P_Y = 16$.

b To equate the marginal utilities per dollar spent (and thus increase utility), this consumer should increase consumption of Y and decrease consumption of X. The principle of diminishing marginal utility implies that this will decrease the marginal utility of Y and increase the marginal utility of X.

3 Suppose we observe an individual in consumer equilibrium consuming X_0 units of good X and Y_0 units of good Y with the prices of X and Y given by P_X and P_Y respectively. This means that at consumption levels X_0 and Y_0, the marginal utility per dollar spent on X equals the marginal utility per dollar spent on Y. Now let the price of X increase to P^1_X. The marginal utility per dollar spent on X declines and thus is now less than the marginal utility per dollar spent on Y. To restore equilibrium, our consumer must increase the marginal utility of X and decrease the marginal utility of Y. From the principle of diminishing marginal utility we know that the only way to do this is to decrease the consumption of X and increase the consumption of Y. This demonstrates the law of demand since an increase in the price of X has been shown to require a decrease in the consumption of X to restore consumer equilibrium.

4 While most parents place a high value on childcare services, there are many childcare workers willing to provide those services. While the total utility provided by the services of childcare workers is high, the marginal utility of those (abundantly supplied) services is low.

5 a The market demand schedule is obtained by adding the quantities demanded by Tom, Jana, and Ted at each price (see Table 7.11).

TABLE **7.11** MARKET DEMAND SCHEDULE FOR BROCCOLI

Price ($ per kilogram)	Quantity Demanded (kilograms per week)
0.50	24
0.75	18
1.00	12
1.25	8

b Figure 7.2 illustrates the individual demand curves for Tom, Jana, and Ted as well as the market demand curve.

FIGURE **7.2**

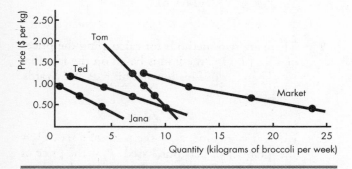

6 a The tables are completed in Table 7.5 Solution and Table 7.6 Solution.

TABLE **7.5** SOLUTION
AMY'S UTILITY FROM POPCORN

Bags of Popcorn	Total Utility	Marginal Utility
1	20	20
2	36	16
3	50	14
4	62	12
5	72	10
6	80	8

TABLE **7.6** SOLUTION
AMY'S UTILITY FROM CANDY BARS

Number of Candy Bars	Total Utility	Marginal Utility
1	14	14
2	26	12
3	36	10
4	44	8
5	51	7
6	57	6

b The table is completed in Table 7.7 Solution.

TABLE **7.7** SOLUTION

Bags of Popcorn	MU/P	Number of Candy Bars	MU/P
1	20	1	28
2	16	2	24
3	14	3	20
4	12	4	16
5	10	5	14
6	8	6	12

c i 2 bags of popcorn and 4 candy bars.
ii The utility maximum condition is satisfied since Amy spends all of her income ($4.00), and the marginal utility per dollar spent is the same for popcorn and candy bars (16).
iii Total utility is the utility from the consumption of 2 bags of popcorn (36) plus the utility from the consumption of 4 candy bars (44) = 80.
iv If Amy consumed 3 bags of popcorn and 2 candy bars, total utility would be 76, which is less than 80, the total utility from the consumption of 2 bags of popcorn and 4 candy bars. For the combination of 3 bags of popcorn and 2 candy bars, *MU/P* for popcorn is 14 while *MU/P* for candy bars is 24. Since *MU/P* is not the same for both goods, this combination does not meet the condition for utility maximization.

7 a See Table 7.12.

TABLE **7.12**

Bags of Popcorn	MU/P	Number of Candy Bars	MU/P
1	20	1	14
2	16	2	12
3	14	3	10
4	12	4	8
5	10	5	7
6	8	6	6

b 3 bags of popcorn and 1 candy bar. Amy spends all of her income ($4.00) and the marginal utility per dollar spent is the same for popcorn and candy bars (14).

c Popcorn and candy bars are substitutes for Amy, since an increase in the price of a candy bar causes an increase in the demand for popcorn.

d Amy's demand curve for candy bars is given in Fig. 7.3. Two points on the demand curve have been identified: when the price of a candy bar is $1.00, 1 candy bar will be demanded, and when the price is $0.50, 4 candy bars will be demanded. The demand curve is a line through these two points.

FIGURE **7.3**

e i Now, Amy will choose to consume 4 bags of popcorn and 2 candy bars (instead of 3 bags of popcorn and 1 candy bar). Amy spends all of her income ($6.00) and the marginal utility per dollar spent is the same for popcorn and candy bars (12).

ii Popcorn and candy bars are both normal goods for Amy since the increase in income (allowance) leads to increases in the demand for both goods.

8 a The utility-maximizing combination of goods is shown in Table 7.13.

TABLE **7.13**

Quantity	MU/P Hairbands	Rackets
1	10	9
2	9	8
3	8	5
4	4	4

Andre should purchase 2 hairbands and 1 racket. Andre spends all of his income ($8), and the marginal utility per dollar spent is the same for hairbands and rackets (9).

b Andre should purchase 4 hairbands and 4 rackets. He spends all of his income ($24), and the marginal utility per dollar spent is the same for hairbands and rackets (4).

c The income elasticity of demand for hairbands is

$$\eta_y = \frac{\frac{\Delta Q}{Q_{ave}}}{\frac{\Delta Y}{Y_{ave}}} = \frac{\frac{4-2}{\frac{1}{2}(4+2)}}{\frac{24-8}{\frac{1}{2}(24+8)}} = \frac{\frac{2}{3}}{\frac{16}{16}} = \frac{2}{3}$$

9 There are two methods for calculating the price of a lizard. One method is based on the fact that Igor spends all of his income on bats and lizards. This means that

$$Y = P_B Q_B + P_L Q_L$$

where Y = income, P_B = the price of a bat, Q_B = the quantity of bats purchased, P_L = the price of a lizard, and Q_L = the quantity of lizards purchased. We know $Y = 16$, $P_B = 2$, $Q_B = 3$, and if the marginal utility of the last lizard is 40, then $Q_L = 2$. Substituting in these values, we can solve for P_L.

$$16 = 2(3) + P_L(2)$$
$$10 = P_L(2)$$
$$5 = P_L$$

The second method uses the condition for utility maximization:

$$\frac{MU_B}{P_B} = \frac{MU_L}{P_L}$$

We know that $MU_L = 40$, $P_B = 2$, and if Igor buys 3 bats, $MU_B = 16$. Substituting in these values, we can solve for P_L.

$$\frac{16}{2} = \frac{40}{P_L}$$
$$80 = 16P_L$$
$$5 = P_L$$

10 a The most Andy would be willing to pay for the first pizza is $15, but the price is only $9. His consumer surplus is $6 ($15 – $9).

  b Andy's consumer surplus on the second pizza is the difference between the most he would be willing to pay ($12) and the price ($9). His consumer surplus is $3.

  c At a price of $9, Andy will buy 4 pizzas. He will receive consumer surplus on the first three pizzas in the amount of $6, $3, and $1, respectively. Thus, his total consumer surplus is $10.

8

Possibilities, Preferences, and Choices

KEY CONCEPTS

Consumption Possibilities

Budget line shows limits to household consumption, given income, and prices of goods and services. Consider example of movies (horizontal axis) and pop (vertical axis).

◆ Budget equation is

$$Q_p = \frac{y}{P_p} - \frac{P_m}{P_p} Q_m$$

◆ Magnitude of slope of budget equation (P_m/P_p) equals **relative price** of movies in terms of pop.

◆ Intercepts measure household's **real income** in movies (*x*-intercept) and pop (*y*-intercept).

◆ $\uparrow P_m \rightarrow$ steeper budget line, fixed pop-intercept.

◆ $\uparrow P_p \rightarrow$ flatter budget line, fixed movie-intercept.

◆ $\uparrow y \rightarrow$ rightward parallel shift budget line.

Preferences and Indifference Curves

Indifference curve maps household preferences, joining combinations goods giving equal satisfaction.

◆ Indifference curves generally slope downward and bow towards the origin (convex).

◆ Indifference curves farther from the origin represent higher levels of satisfaction.

◆ Indifference curves never intersect.

◆ **Marginal rate of substitution** (MRS) is magnitude of slope of indifference curve—rate at which household gives up good *y* (pop) for additional unit good *x* (movies) and still remains indifferent.

◆ **Diminishing marginal rate of substitution** is tendency for MRS to $\downarrow$ as move down along an indifference curve. Accounts for bowed-towards-the-origin shape of indifference curves.

◆ $\uparrow$ substitutability between goods $\rightarrow$ straighter indifference curves.
$\downarrow$ substitutability between goods $\rightarrow$ more tightly curved indifference curves.

The Household's Consumption Choice

Given income and prices of goods, household allocates income to maximize satisfaction. Household chooses best affordable point, which is on budget line and on highest possible indifference curve. At the best affordable point

◆ household spends all its income and achieves maximum satisfaction.

◆ budget line and indifference curve are tangent and have same slope—MRS equals the relative price.

Predicting Consumer Behaviour

Price effect is Δ consumption resulting from Δ price of a good. Price effect = substitution effect + income effect.

◆ **Substitution effect**—Δ consumption resulting from Δ price accompanied by (hypothetical) Δ income leaving household indifferent between initial and new situations. For normal and inferior goods, substitution effect of $\downarrow$ price $\rightarrow$ $\uparrow$ consumption.

◆ **Income effect**—Δ consumption resulting from (hypothetically) restoring original income but keeping prices constant at new level. For normal goods, income effect of (hypothetical) $\uparrow$ income $\rightarrow \uparrow$ consumption. For inferior goods, (hypothetical) $\uparrow$ income $\rightarrow \downarrow$ consumption.

◆ The downward-sloping demand curve is a consequence of the consumer choosing his best affordable combination of goods. The demand curve can be derived from the price effect—by tracing the best affordable quantity of a good as its price changes.

For normal goods, substitution and income effects work in same direction, so $\downarrow$ price $\rightarrow \uparrow$ consumption.

For inferior goods, substitution and income effects work in opposite directions, but net effect of $\downarrow$ price usually $\rightarrow$ (smaller) $\uparrow$ consumption.

HELPFUL HINTS

1 Although the analysis in this chapter may seem restrictive, it is helpful to maintain a broad perspective. From a general economic perspective, the consumer's problem is to do the best given the constraints faced. These constraints, which limit the range of possible choices, depend on income and the prices of goods and are represented graphically by the budget line. Doing the best means finding the most preferred outcome consistent with those constraints. In this chapter, preferences are represented graphically by indifference curves.

Graphically, the consumer problem is to find the highest indifference curve attainable given the budget line. To make graphical analysis feasible, we restrict ourselves to choices between only two goods, but the same principles apply in the real world to a broader array of choices.

2 The budget equation for pop and movies on text page 170 is

$$Q_p = \frac{y}{P_p} - \frac{P_m}{P_p} Q_m$$

This is the type of straight line equation ($y = a + bx$) that we discussed in Chapter 2. The differences are that Q_p is the dependent variable (instead of y) and Q_m is the independent variable (instead of x). We can use the budget equation to graph the budget line by finding the Q_p-intercept (where the line intersects the

vertical Q_p axis), finding the Q_m-intercept (where the line intersects the horizontal Q_m axis), and then connecting those two points with a straight line.

To find the Q_p-intercept, set $Q_m = 0$.

$$Q_p = \frac{y}{P_p} - \frac{P_m}{P_p}(0)$$

$$Q_p = \frac{y}{P_p}$$

To find the Q_m-intercept, set $Q_p = 0$.

$$0 = \frac{y}{P_p} - \frac{P_m}{P_p} Q_m$$

$$\frac{P_m}{P_p} Q_m = \frac{y}{P_p}$$

$$Q_m = \frac{y}{P_m}$$

The Q_p-intercept, $Q_p = y/P_p$, is the consumer's real income in terms of pop. It tells us how much pop could be purchased if all income was spent on pop. The Q_m-intercept, $Q_m = y/P_m$, is the consumer's real income in terms of movies. It tells us how many movies could be purchased if all income was spent on movies. These intercepts provide an easy method for drawing a budget line. Each of the two endpoints (the intercepts) is just income divided by the price of the good on that axis. Connecting those endpoints with a straight line yields the budget line.

The slope of the budget line provides additional information for the consumer's choice. The magnitude (absolute value) of the slope equals the relative price (or opportunity cost) of movies in terms of pop. In other words, the magnitude of the slope equals the number of units of pop it takes to buy one movie. More generally, the magnitude of the slope of the budget line (P_x/P_y) equals the relative price (or opportunity cost) of the good on the horizontal x-axis in terms of the good on the vertical y-axis; or the number of units of vertical-axis goods it takes to buy one unit of the horizontal-axis good.

© 3 The marginal rate of substitution (MRS) is the rate at which a consumer gives up good Y for an additional unit of good X and still remains indifferent. The MRS equals the magnitude of the slope of the indifference curve, $\Delta Q_Y/\Delta Q_X$.

Because indifference curves are bowed towards the origin (convex), the magnitude of the slope and hence the MRS diminish as we move down an indifference curve. The diminishing MRS means that the consumer is willing to give up less of good Y for each additional unit of good X. As the consumer moves down an indifference curve, she is coming to value good Y more and value good X less. This is easily explained by the principle of diminishing marginal utility, which underlies the following equation (which also appear in the website appendix to the chapter).

$$\text{Marginal rate of substitution} = \frac{MU_X}{MU_Y}$$

At the top of the indifference curve, the consumer is consuming little X and much Y, so the marginal utility of X (MU_X) is high and the marginal utility of Y (MU_Y) is low. Moving down the curve, as the quantity of X consumed increases, MU_X decreases; and as the quantity of Y consumed decreases, MU_Y increases. Thus the principle of diminishing marginal utility provides an intuitive understanding of why the MRS diminishes as we move down an indifference curve.

ⓔ **4** At the consumer's best affordable point, the budget line is just tangent to the highest affordable indifference curve, so the magnitude of the slope of the budget line equals the magnitude of the slope of the indifference curve. Combining the information from Helpful Hint **2** (the magnitude of the slope of the budget line equals P_X/P_Y) and Helpful Hint **3** (the magnitude of the slope of the indifference curve equals MU_X/MU_Y) yields

$$\frac{P_X}{P_Y} = \frac{MU_X}{MU_Y}$$

Rearranging terms yields

$$\frac{MU_X}{P_X} = \frac{MU_Y}{P_Y}$$

This is the equation for utility maximization from Chapter 7. You can now see why the budget equation/indifference curve analysis of consumer choice developed here complements the marginal utility analysis of Chapter 7.

5 Understanding the distinction between the income and substitution effects of a change in the price of a good is often challenging for students. Consider a decrease in the price of

good A. This has two effects that will influence the consumption of A. First, the decrease in the price of A will reduce the relative price of A and, second, it will increase real income. The substitution effect is the answer to the question: How much would the consumption of A change as a result of the relative price decline if we also (hypothetically) reduce income by enough to leave the consumer indifferent between the new and original situations? The income effect is the answer to the question: How much more would the consumption of A change if we (hypothetically) restore the consumer's real income but leave relative prices at the new level?

SELF-TEST

True/False/Uncertain and Explain

1 The graph of a budget line will be bowed towards the origin.

2 *Ceteris paribus*, an increase in the price of goods means that real income falls.

3 We assume that more of any good is preferred to less of the good.

4 Higher indifference curves represent higher levels of income.

5 The principle of the diminishing marginal rate of substitution explains why indifference curves are bowed towards the origin.

6 Perfect substitutes will have L-shaped indifference curves.

7   At the best affordable consumption point of movies and pop, the marginal rate of substitution equals the ratio of the price of movies to the price of pop.

8   When the relative price of a good decreases, the income effect leads to increased consumption of the good.

9   The law of demand can be derived from an indifference curve model by tracing the impact on quantity demanded of an increase in price.

10   The theory of consumer choice claims that people actually compute marginal rates of substitution and set them equal to relative prices in order to make spending decisions.

Multiple-Choice

1   Which of the following statements best describes a consumer's budget line?
a   the amount of each good a consumer can purchase
b   the limits to a consumer's set of affordable consumption choices
c   the desired level of consumption for the consumer
d   the consumption choices made by a consumer
e   the set of all affordable consumption choices

2   Real income is measured in
a   monetary units.
b   price units.
c   units of satisfaction.
d   units of indifference.
e   units of goods.

3   For an increase in price, the substitution effect
a   always increases consumption.
b   increases consumption for normal goods only.
c   decreases consumption for normal goods only.
d   decreases consumption for inferior goods only.
e   does none of the above.

4   If two goods are perfect substitutes, then their
a   indifference curves are positively sloped straight lines.
b   indifference curves are negatively sloped straight lines.
c   indifference curves are L-shaped.
d   marginal rate of substitution is zero.
e   marginal rate of substitution is infinity.

5   Consider the budget line and indifference curve in Fig. 8.1. If the price of good X is $2, what is the price of good Y?
a $0.37
b $0.67
c $1.50
d $2.67
e   impossible to calculate without additional information

FIGURE **8.1**

6   The initial budget equation for pop and movies is $Q_p = 20 - 4Q_m$, and the price of pop (P_p) is $5. If the price of pop falls to $4, which of the following is the new budget equation?
a $Q_p = 25 - 2Q_m$
b $Q_p = 25 - 4Q_m$
c $Q_p = 25 - 5Q_m$
d $Q_p = 20 - 5Q_m$
e   none of the above

7   Which of the following statements is *false*?
a   indifference curves are negatively sloped
b   a preference map consists of a series of nonintersecting indifference curves
c   indifference curves are bowed out from the origin
d   the marginal rate of substitution is the magnitude of the slope of an indifference curve
e   the marginal rate of substitution increases with movement up an indifference curve

8 The initial budget line labelled *RS* in Fig. 8.2 would shift to *RT* as a result of a(n)

a increase in the price of good *X*.
b decrease in the price of good *X*.
c decrease in preferences for good *X*.
d increase in the price of good *Y*.
e increase in real income.

FIGURE **8.2**

9 When the initial budget line labelled *RS* in Fig. 8.2 shifts to *RT*, the substitution effect is illustrated by the move from point

a *a* to *b*.
b *a* to *c*.
c *a* to *d*.
d *b* to *d*.
e *d* to *c*.

10 When the initial budget line labelled *RS* in Fig. 8.2 shifts to *RT*, the income effect is illustrated by the move from point

a *a* to *b*.
b *a* to *c*.
c *a* to *d*.
d *b* to *c*.
e *b* to *d*.

11 Zarina's income allows her to afford 3 tomatoes and no toothbrushes, or 2 toothbrushes and no tomatoes. The relative price of toothbrushes (price toothbrush/price tomato) is

a 2/3.
b 3/2.
c 6/1.
d 1/6.
e impossible to calculate without additional information.

12 In general, as a consumer moves down an indifference curve, increasing consumption of good *X* (measured on the horizontal axis),

a more of *Y* must be given up for each additional unit of *X*.
b a constant amount of *Y* must be given up for each additional unit of *X*.
c less of *Y* must be given up for each additional unit of *X*.
d the relative price of *Y* increases.
e the relative price of *Y* decreases.

13 If the price of the good measured on the vertical axis increases, the budget line will

a become steeper.
b become flatter.
c shift leftward but parallel to the original budget line.
d shift rightward but parallel to the original budget line.
e shift leftward and become steeper.

14 Which of the following statement(s) about Fig. 8.3 is/are *true*?

a Point *s* is preferred to point *q*, but *s* is not affordable.
b Points *q* and *r* yield the same utility, but *q* is more affordable.
c Point *t* is preferred to point *q*, but *t* is not affordable.
d Points *q* and *s* cost the same, but *q* is preferred to *s*.
e All of the above statements are true.

FIGURE **8.3**

15 If income increases, the budget line will

a become steeper.

b become flatter.

c shift leftward but parallel to the original budget line.

d shift rightward but parallel to the original budget line.

e shift parallel but leftward or rightward depending on whether a good is normal or inferior.

16 If the price of good X (measured on the horizontal axis) falls, the substitution effect is represented by a movement to a

a higher indifference curve.

b lower indifference curve.

c steeper part of the same indifference curve.

d flatter part of the same indifference curve.

e flatter part of a higher indifference curve.

17 A change in the price of the good measured on the horizontal (x) axis changes which aspect(s) of the budget equation?

a slope and y-intercept

b slope and x-intercept

c x- and y-intercepts but not slope

d slope only

e none of the above

18 Bill consumes apples and bananas. Suppose Bill's income doubles and the prices of apples and bananas also double. Bill's budget line will

a shift left but not change slope.

b remain unchanged.

c shift right but not change slope.

d shift right and become steeper.

e shift right and become flatter.

19 When the price of an inferior good falls, the

1 income and substitution effects both move quantity demanded in the same direction.

2 income and substitution effects move quantity demanded in opposite directions.

3 income effect is usually larger than the substitution effect.

4 substitution effect is usually larger than the income effect.

a 1 and 2

b 1 and 4

c 2 and 3

d 2 and 4

e none of the above

20 Which of the following statements about the budget line is *false*? The budget line

a divides affordable from unaffordable consumption points.

b is based on fixed prices.

c is based on fixed income.

d is based on fixed quantities.

e constrains consumer choices.

21 When Clark Gable took off his shirt in *It Happened One Night*, he was not wearing an undershirt. As a result, men's undershirt sales plummeted. *Ceteris paribus*, we can conclude that men's undershirt

a preferences changed when prices changed.

b preferences changed when income changed.

c choices changed when preferences changed.

d choices changed when prices changed.

e choices changed when income changed.

22 In moving down along an indifference curve, the marginal rate of substitution (MRS) for complements will

a increase faster than the MRS for substitutes.

b increase more slowly than the MRS for substitutes.

c be relatively constant.

d decrease faster than the MRS for substitutes.

e decrease more slowly than the MRS for substitutes.

23 The income effect

a usually dominates the substitution effect.

b usually dominates the price effect.

c plus the price effect equals the substitution effect.

d minus the price effect equals the substitution effect.

e plus the substitution effect equals the price effect.

24 The budget line depends on

a income.

b prices.

c income and prices.

d preferences.

e preferences and prices.

25 The shape of an indifference curve depends on

a the prices of goods.

b household income.

c the substitutability between goods for the household.

d the level of satisfaction for the household.

e all of the above.

Short Answer Problems

1 Why is an indifference curve negatively sloped?

2 Explain why it is logically impossible for indifference curves to intersect each other, by comparing points *a*, *b*, and *c* in Fig. 8.4.

FIGURE **8.4**

⊚ 3 In Helpful Hint 3 (as well as in the website Appendix to Chapter 8), it is established that the

$$\text{Marginal rate of substitution} = \frac{\text{marginal utility of movies}}{\text{marginal utility of pop}}$$

As we move down an indifference curve, use the principle of diminishing marginal utility to explain why the marginal rate of substitution diminishes.

4 For normal goods,

- an increase in income causes an *increase in demand* (demand curve shifts to the right).
- the income effect (due to a decrease in price) causes *an increase in quantity demanded.*

Explain why these two statements are or are not contradictory. Be sure to define clearly any important concepts.

5 Jan and Dan both like bread and peanut butter and have the same income. Since they face the same prices, they have identical budget lines. Currently, Jan and Dan consume exactly the same quantities of bread and peanut butter; they have the same best affordable consumption point. Jan, however, views bread and peanut butter as close (though not perfect) substitutes, while Dan considers bread and peanut butter to be quite (but not perfectly) complementary.

a On the same diagram, draw a budget line and representative indifference curves for Jan and Dan. (Measure the quantity of bread on the horizontal axis.)

b Now, suppose the price of bread declines. Graphically represent the substitution effects for Jan and Dan. For whom is the substitution effect greater?

◉ 6 Figure 8.5 illustrates a consumer's indifference map for food and clothing.

FIGURE **8.5**

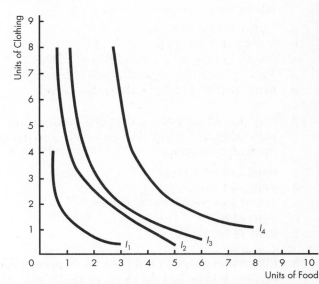

a i Initially, the price of a unit of clothing is $P_c = \$1.00$ and the price of a unit of food is $P_f = \$1.50$. If income is $y = \$9.00$, draw the consumer's budget line on Fig. 8.5 and label the best affordable point as point *a*. What is the quantity of food consumed?

ii What is the equation of the budget line in terms of P_c, P_f, and y? What is the equation of the budget line in numerical terms? Express the magnitude (absolute value) of the slope of the budget line as a ratio of P_c and P_f.

iii At point *a*, what is the value of the marginal rate of substitution (or equivalently, MU_f/MU_c)?

iv Use your answers in parts **ii** and **iii** to derive the formula for utility maximization. Explain.

b If P_f increases to $\$3.00$ per unit while income and P_c remain unchanged, draw the new budget line and label the new best affordable point as point *b*. What is the new quantity of food consumed?

c If P_f increases again to $\$4.50$ per unit while income and P_c remain unchanged, draw the corresponding budget line and label the best affordable point as point *c*. What is the quantity of food consumed?

d On a separate graph, plot and draw the demand curve for food that corresponds to points *a*, *b*, and *c*. Be sure to clearly label the axes.

e Suppose prices remain at their initial values ($P_c = \$1.00$, $P_f = \$1.50$) but income falls to $3.00. Draw the new budget line and label the best affordable point as point *z*. What is the quantity of food consumed? Is food a normal or inferior good? Explain. On your demand curve graph from part **d**, plot point *z* and roughly sketch a demand curve corresponding to the new income level.

7 Sharon, a fitness fanatic, plays squash and takes aerobics classes at her health club. Squash courts rent for $2 per hour and aerobics classes are $1 per hour. Sharon has decided to spend $12 per week for fitness activities. Figure 8.6 illustrates several indifference curves for squash and aerobics on Sharon's preference map.

FIGURE **8.6**

a How many hours of squash and aerobics will Sharon consume at her best affordable point?

b Suppose that squash rentals fall to $1 per hour.
  i How many hours of squash and aerobics will Sharon now consume? What is the increase in her hours of squash?
  ii Of the total increase in hours of squash, how many hours are due to the substitution effect of the price fall?
  iii Of the total increase in hours of squash, how many hours are due to the income effect of the price fall?

c On a separate graph, plot two points on Sharon's demand curve for squash and draw her straight line demand curve.

d The price of squash continues to be $1 but Sharon's fitness budget increases to $14. How many hours of squash and aerobics will Sharon now consume?

8 Ms. Muffet consumes both curds and whey. The initial price of curds is $1.00 per unit, and the price of whey is $1.50 per unit. Ms. Muffet's initial income is $12.00.

a What is the relative price of curds?

b Derive Ms. Muffet's budget equation and draw her budget line on a graph. (Measure curds on the horizontal axis.)

c On your graph, draw an indifference curve so that the best affordable point corresponds to 6 units of curds and 4 units of whey.

d What is the marginal rate of substitution of curds for whey at this point?

e Show that any other point on the budget line is inferior.

9 Given the initial situation described in Short Answer Problem **8**, suppose Ms. Muffet's income now increases.

a Illustrate graphically how the consumption of curds and whey are affected if both goods are normal. (Numerical answers are not necessary. Just show whether consumption increases or decreases.)

b Draw a new graph showing the effect of an increase in Ms. Muffet's income if whey is an inferior good.

10 Return to the initial circumstances described in Short Answer Problem **8**. Now, suppose the price of curds doubles to $2.00 a unit, while the price of whey remains at $1.50 per unit and income remains at $12.00.

a Draw the new budget line.

b Why is the initial best affordable point (label it point *r*) no longer the best affordable point?

c Using your graph, show the new best affordable point and label it *t*. What has happened to the consumption of curds?

d Decompose the effect on the consumption of *X* into the substitution effect and the income effect. On your graph, indicate the substitution effect as movement from point *r* to point *s* (which you must locate) and indicate the income effect as movement from point *s* to point *t*.

A N S W E R S

True/False/Uncertain and Explain

1 F Budget lines straight. Indifference curves bowed towards origin. (169–170)
2 T Real income = income/price goods. (170–171)
3 T See text discussion. (172–173)
4 F Represent higher levels satisfaction. (172–173)
5 T See text discussion. (173–174)
6 F True for perfect complements. (175–176)
⊙ 7 T Budget line tangent to indifference curve. (176–177)
⊙ 8 U True for normal, false for inferior goods. (177–181)
9 T See text discussion. (177–178)
10 F Claims only choices made by real people resemble choices predicted by model. (159–160)

Multiple-Choice

1 b **a** should be combinations of goods; **c** about indifference curves; **d** about best affordable point; **e** includes area inside budget line. (169–170)
2 e See text discussion. (170)
3 e For ↑ price, substitution effect always → ↓ consumption for both normal and inferior goods. (179–181)
4 b With constant slope = 1. (175–176)
5 c Income = \$12 (\$2 × 6 units X), so price Y = \$12/8 units Y. (169–171)
⊙ 6 c From $Q_p = (y/P_p) - (P_m/P_p)Q_m$. If P_p = \$5, then y = \$100 and P_m = \$20. Then recalculate Q_p equation for P_p = \$4. (170–171)
7 c Indifference curves bow in towards the origin. (172–174)
8 a With same income, ↓ X can be purchased. **c** relates to indifference curves. ↑ real income is move from point b to c. (170–171)
9 a Budget line with new prices tangent to original indifference curve. (179–181)
10 d Hypothetically restore original income (reverse ↑ real income) but keep prices constant at new level. (179–181)
⊙ 11 b (3 × price tomato) = (2 × price toothbrush). Divide both sides equation by price tomato and by 2. (169–171)
12 c Due to diminishing MRS. **d** and **e** wrong since relative price relates to budget line, not indifference curve. (172–174)
13 b y-intercept shifts down, x-intercept unchanged. (170–171)

14 c t on higher indifference curve, but outside budget line. s and q yield same utility so **a**, **d** wrong. q preferred to r so **b** wrong. (176–177)
15 d ↑ income does not change slope but ↑ x- and y-intercepts. (170–171)
16 d New budget line flatter and drawn tangent to same indifference curve. (179–181)
⊙ 17 b See Helpful Hint 2 and analyse ΔP_m (movies on horizontal axis). (170–171)
18 b Numerators and denominators of both intercepts double, so intercepts do not change. (170–171)
19 d See text discussion. (181)
20 d Quantities vary along budget line. (169–170)
21 c Gable's influence → ↓ preference undershirts. Combined with unchanged prices and incomes → ↓ consumption. (172–173)
⊙ 22 d MRS always ↓ moving down indifference curve. Complements have more tightly curved indifference curves. (175–176)
23 e See text discussion. Reverse of **a**, **b** true. (179–181)
24 c See text discussion. (169–170)
25 c Budget line depends on **a** and **b**. At any level satisfaction, indifference curve could be any shape. (175–176)

Short Answer Problems

1 An indifference curve tells us how much the consumption of one good must increase as the consumption of another good decreases in order to leave the consumer indifferent (no better or worse off). It is negatively sloped because the goods are both desirable. As we *decrease* the consumption of one good, in order to not be made worse off, consumption of the other good must *increase*. This implies a negative slope.

2 The explanation takes the form of a proof by contradiction. Since points a and b are on the same indifference curve (I_1), the consumer is indifferent between them. Since points a and c are on the same indifference curve (I_2), the consumer is also indifferent between them. If the consumer is indifferent between a and b and between a and c, this implies an indifference between b and c. But indifference between points b and c is logically impossible, because we assume that more of any good is preferred to less of that good. Since point c has more of both good X and good Y than point b, the consumer cannot be indifferent between b and c. Indifference between b and c contradicts the assumption that more is preferred to less. Hence indifference curves cannot intersect.

⊛ 3 As we move down an indifference curve for pop and movies, such as in Text Fig. 8.5 on page 174, we increase the quantity of movies consumed and decrease the quantity of pop consumed. As movie consumption increases, each additional movie yields lower marginal utility because of the principle of diminishing marginal utility. Thus the value of the numerator on the right-hand side of the equation below decreases.

$$\text{Marginal rate of substitution} = \frac{\text{marginal utility of movies}}{\text{marginal utility of pop}}$$

As pop consumption decreases, each previous pop consumed yields higher marginal utility. Thus, the value of the denominator on the right-hand side of the equation increases. The combined effect of a decrease in the numerator and an increase in the denominator is that the ratio MU_{movies}/MU_{pop} falls as we move down an indifference curve, corresponding to a diminishing marginal rate of substitution on the left-hand side of the equation.

4 These statements appear to be contradictory because an increase in income leads, in the first statement, to a shift of the demand curve but, in the second statement, to a movement along the demand curve. The reason the statements are *not* contradictory has to do with a crucial distinction between *nominal* income and *real* income.

The first statement (an increase in income causes an increase in *demand* [demand curve shifts rightward]) describes how an increase in *nominal* income shifts the demand curve. *Nominal* income is measured in dollars.

The second statement (the income effect [due to a decrease in price] causes an increase in *quantity demanded*) describes how an increase in *real* income causes a movement along the stationary demand curve.

Real income is measured in purchasing power, or the quantities of goods that nominal income can buy. When the price of a good decreases, your *real* income goes up because you can now purchase more of that good with the same, unchanged, *nominal* income. Because *nominal* income is unchanged in the second statement, the demand curve does not shift. But because *real* income has increased, the decrease in price leads to an increase in *quantity demanded*.

5 a Initially, Jan and Dan are at point *c* on the budget line labelled *AB* in Fig. 8.7. Jan's indifference curve is illustrated by I_J. Note that her indifference curve is close to a straight line reflecting the fact that bread and peanut butter are close substitutes. On the other hand, since Dan considers bread and peanut butter to be complementary, his indifference curve, I_D, is more tightly curved.

FIGURE **8.7**

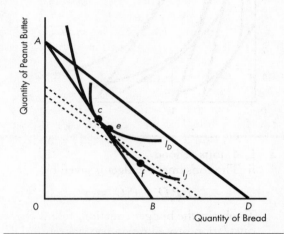

b If the price of bread declines, the budget line will become flatter, such as the line labelled *AD* in Fig. 8.7. In order to measure the substitution effect, find the point on the original indifference curve that has the same slope as the new budget line. Since Dan's indifference curve is more sharply curved, it becomes flatter quite rapidly as we move away from point *c*. Thus the substitution effect is quite small, from *c* to point *e*. Since Jan's indifference curve is almost a straight line, the substitution effect must be much larger, from *c* to point *f.*

◑ 6 The consumer's budget line is shown in Fig. 8.5 Solution.

FIGURE **8.5** SOLUTION

a i 4 units of food
ii The consumer's budget is given by

$$P_c Q_c + P_f Q_f = y$$

To obtain the budget equation, follow the calculation procedure on text page 170. Divide by P_c to obtain

$$Q_c + \frac{P_f}{P_c} Q_f = \frac{y}{P_c}$$

Subtract $(P_f/P_c)Q_f$ from both sides to obtain

$$Q_c = \frac{y}{P_c} - \frac{P_f}{P_c} Q_f$$

To obtain the budget equation in numerical terms, substitute in the values $P_c = \$1.00$, $P_f = \$1.50$, and $y = \$9.00$.

$$Q_c = \frac{9}{1} - \frac{1.50}{1} Q_f$$

$$Q_c = 9 - 3/2 Q_f$$

The magnitude (absolute value) of the slope of the budget line is 3/2, which is the ratio of P_f/P_c. Note that this price ratio cannot be read directly off the graph since the axes measure quantities, not prices.
iii The marginal rate of substitution at point a is defined as the magnitude of the slope of the indifference curve at point a. Since the slope of the indifference curve at point a is equal to the slope of the tangent at a, and since the budget line is tangent at a, the magnitude of the slope of the indifference curve is 3/2. This magnitude is equivalent to MU_f/MU_c.
iv The magnitude of the slope of the budget line is P_f/P_c and the magnitude of the slope of

the indifference curve at a is MU_f/MU_c. Since the two magnitudes are equal, $P_f/P_c = MU_f/MU_c$ or $MU_f/P_f = MU_c/P_c$.
b See Fig. 8.5 Solution: 2 units of food.
c See Fig. 8.5 Solution: 1 unit of food.
d The demand curve for food is shown in Fig. 8.8.

FIGURE **8.8**

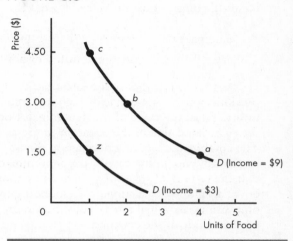

e See Fig. 8.5 Solution. 1 unit of food. Food is a normal good because a *decrease* in income (with prices constant) causes a decrease in food consumption (from 4 units to 1 unit). See Fig. 8.8 for the new demand curve (income = $3).

7 a In order to find Sharon's best affordable point, draw the budget line in Fig. 8.6 Solution. The initial budget line is labelled AB and Sharon's best affordable point is point c on indifference curve I_2. Thus Sharon consumes 3 hours of squash and 6 hours of aerobics per week.

FIGURE **8.6** SOLUTION

b If the price of squash falls to $1, the budget line becomes *AD*.

i Now Sharon's best affordable point is point *e* on indifference curve I_3. This corresponds to consumption of 6 hours of squash and 6 hours of aerobics per week. Her squash consumption has increased by 3 hours.

ii To measure the substitution effect, shift the new budget line leftward in parallel fashion until it is tangent to the indifference curve I_2, where Sharon was before the fall in the price of squash. In effect, budget line *A′B′* removes the increase in real income due to the price fall in order to isolate the substitution effect of the price fall on Sharon's consumption of squash. Point *f* is what Sharon would have consumed at the new prices if her income fell just enough to return her to her original indifference curve. The substitution effect of the fall in the price of squash is the movement from initial point *c* to point *f*, which is an increase in squash hours consumed of 2 (from 3 to 5 hours).

iii To measure the income effect, shift the budget line *A′B′* rightward in parallel fashion until it is tangent to the indifference curve I_3, where Sharon was before we hypothetically reduced her real income. In effect, this shift isolates the income effect by restoring the increase in real income due to the price fall while keeping prices constant at their new values. The income effect of the fall in the price of squash is the movement from point *f* to point *e*, which is an increase in squash hours consumed of 1 (from 5 to 6 hours).

The results are summarized in Table 8.1.

TABLE **8.1**   PRICE EFFECT FROM FIGURE 8.6 SOLUTION

Effect	Move from Point	↑ Hours Squash
Substitution effect	c to f	2
+ Income effect	f to e	1
= Price effect	c to e	3

c In parts **a** and **b**, income spent on fitness was constant at $12 and the price of aerobics was constant at $1 per hour. When the price of squash was $2 per hour, Sharon wanted to consume 3 hours of squash and when the price of squash was $1, Sharon wanted to consume 6 hours of squash. This gives us two points on Sharon's demand curve for squash, which are labelled *a* and *b* in Fig. 8.9. Drawing a line passing through these points allows us to obtain her straight line demand curve, labelled *D*.

FIGURE **8.9**

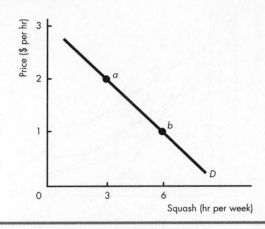

d When Sharon's fitness budget increases to $14, the budget line shifts right to the line labelled *GH* in Fig. 8.6 Solution. Sharon's best affordable point is now at *j*, which corresponds to 7 hours of squash and 7 hours of aerobics consumed per week.

⊘ 8 a The relative price of curds is the price of curds divided by the price of whey:

$$\frac{\$1.00}{\$1.50} = \frac{2}{3}$$

b Let P_c = the price of curds, P_w = the price of whey, Q_c = quantity of curds, Q_w = quantity of whey, and y = income. The budget equation, in general form, is

$$Q_w = \frac{y}{P_w} - \frac{P_c}{P_w}Q_c$$

Since P_c = $1.00, P_w = $1.50, and y = $12.00, Ms. Muffet's budget equation is specifically given by

$$Q_w = 8 - 2/3 \ Q_c$$

The graph of this budget equation, the budget line, is given by the line labelled *AB* in Fig. 8.10.

FIGURE **8.10**

FIGURE **8.11**

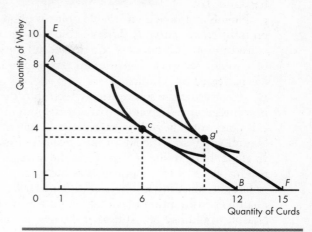

c   If the best affordable point corresponds to 6 units of curds and 4 units of whey, then the relevant indifference curve must be tangent to (just touch) the budget line *AB* at *c*, which is indifference curve I_1.

d   The marginal rate of substitution is given by the magnitude of the slope of the indifference curve at point *c*. We do not know the slope of the indifference curve directly, but we can easily compute the slope of the budget line. Since, at point *c*, the indifference curve and the budget line have the same slope, we can obtain the marginal rate of substitution of curds for whey. Since the slope of the budget line is −2/3, the marginal rate of substitution is 2/3. For example, Ms. Muffet is willing to give up 2 units of whey in order to receive 3 additional units of curds and still remain indifferent.

e   Since indifference curves cannot intersect each other and since indifference curve I_1 lies everywhere above the budget line (except at point *c*), we know that every other point on the budget line is on a lower indifference curve. For example, point *d* lies on indifference curve I_0. Thus every other point on the budget line is inferior to point *c*.

9 a   An increase in income will cause a parallel rightward shift of the budget line, for example, to *EF* in Fig. 8.10. If both curds and whey are normal goods, Ms. Muffet will move to a point like *g* at which the consumption of both goods has increased.

b   If whey is an inferior good, then its consumption will fall as income rises. This is illustrated in Fig. 8.11. Once again the budget line shifts from *AB* to *EF*, but Ms. Muffet's preferences are such that her new consumption point is given by a point like *g'* where the consumption of whey has actually declined.

10 a   Ms. Muffet's initial budget line is *AB* and the initial best affordable point is *r* in Fig. 8.12. Note that point *r* in Fig. 8.12 is the same as point *c* in Fig. 8.10. The new budget line following an increase in the price of curds to $2.00 (income remains at $12.00) is *AH*.

FIGURE **8.12**

b   After the price increase, point *r* is no longer the best affordable point since it is no longer even affordable.

c   The new best affordable point (labelled *t* in Fig. 8.12) indicates a decrease in the consumption of curds.

d   The substitution effect of the increase in the price of curds is indicated by the movement from *r* to *s* in Fig. 8.12. This gives the effect of the change in relative prices while keeping Ms. Muffet on the same indifference curve. The income effect is indicated by movement from *s* to *t*.

Chapter 9

Organizing Production

KEY CONCEPTS

The Firm and Its Economic Problem

[handwritten: EXISTS B/C OF SCARCITY]

A **firm** is an institution that hires and organizes factors of production to produce and sell goods and services. Firms strive for maximum profit and efficient, lowest-cost production. Firms organize production by using

[handwritten: ORGANIZATION IS A FUNDAMENTAL PROBLEM]

[handwritten: 2 SYSTEMS ① COMMAND ② INCENTIVE FOR ORGANIZING PRODUCTION]

◆ Command systems based on a managerial hierarchy. *[handwritten: COMMUNICATION IS DOWNWARD & ∴ NO KNOWLEDGE BY TOP EXECUTIVES]*

◆ Incentive systems to overcome problems of uncertainty and incomplete information. *[handwritten: & B/C OF INCOMPLETE INFO THERE'S COMPENSATION PACKAGES OFFERED TO STRENGTHEN INCENTIVES & PRODUCTIVITY TO SOLVE]*

With incomplete information, the **principal–agent problem** arises when agents (those employed by others) do not act in the best interests of the principals (employers of the agents). *[handwritten: TO DEVISE COMPENSATION RULES TO INDUCE AN AGENT TO ACT IN BEST INTEREST OF A PRINCIPAL]*

[handwritten: SOLN: CREATE INCENTIVES THAT INDUCE AGENT TO WORK IN INTERESTS OF PRINCIPAL]

[handwritten: 3 WAYS: ① OWNERSHIP ② INCENTIVE PAY ③ LONG-TERM CONTRACTS TO ↑ PROFITS, EFFICIENCY PRODUCTION.]

◆ Strategies for coping with the principal–agent problem and inducing agents to act in the best interests of the principals include ownership, incentive pay, and long-term contracts. *[handwritten: ② RELATED TO PERFORMANCE ③ TIE THEM IN FOR LONG-TERM SUCCESS & FORTUNE]*

◆ To cope with uncertainty and incomplete information, firms have devised different forms of business organization: *[handwritten: CAN MAKE A BUSINESS FAIL ∴ THESE THINGS LEAD TO DIFFERENT FORMS OF ORGANIZATION.]*

[handwritten: 3 FORMS OF BUSINESS ORGANIZATION - EACH ONE INFLUENCES MANAGEMENT STRUCTURE, AMT COMPENSATION FOR FACTORS OF PRODUCTION, AMT OF TAX OWNERS PAY, WHO GETS PROFITS, & LIABLE FOR DEBTS.]

◆ ① *Sole proprietorship*—single owner with unlimited liability. *[handwritten: LEGAL RESPONSIBILITY FOR ALL DEBTS OF THE FIRM UP TO THE AMOUNT EQUAL TO THE ENTIRE WORTH OF THE OWNER.]*

◆ ② *Partnership*—two or more owners with unlimited liability.

◆ ③ *Corporation*—owned by limited liability stockholders. *[handwritten: OWNERS HAVE LEGAL LIABILITY ONLY FOR THE VALUE OF THEIR INITIAL INVESTMENT. AREN'T FORCED TO USE PERSONAL ASSETS TO PAY DEBT.]*

Business Finance

[handwritten: (RAISE FUNDS)]

Firms finance expenses by *[handwritten: ① SELLING STOCK ② SELLING BONDS]* *[handwritten: OWNER'S STAKE IN BUSINESS.]*

◆ Selling stock. Corporations raise **equity** by selling shares of stock. The shareholders are owners of a corporation, and an owner's stake in a business is called equity.

◆ ② Selling bonds. A **bond** is a legally enforceable obligation to pay specified money at future dates. *[handwritten: & INTEREST]*

• **Capital gain** is income received by selling a stock or bond for a higher price than the original price paid for it.

Present value of future amount of money is amount which, if invested today, will grow as large as the future amount, taking account of earned interest. **Discounting** is the conversion of a future amount of money to its present value.

[handwritten: FUTURE AMT = PRESENT VALUE × (1 + r)]

◆ Present value = $\dfrac{\text{amount money available } n \text{ years}}{(1 + r)^n}$ *[handwritten: INTEREST RATE]*

◆ Firms decide whether or not to borrow by evaluating net benefit of borrowing = (marginal benefit – marginal cost). Present value of net benefit is net present value. If net present value is positive, firm ↑ profit by borrowing. *[handwritten: ↑ WEIGHING BENEFITS AGAINST COST = NET BENEFIT OF BORROWING]*

Opportunity Cost and Economic Profit

[handwritten: ↳ BEST ALTERNATIVE FORGONE.] *[handwritten: ① EXPLICIT COSTS ② IMPLICIT COSTS.]*

A firm's opportunity costs of production consist of explicit costs (paid directly in money) and *implicit costs* (opportunities forgone but not paid for directly in money). Major implicit costs include *[handwritten: THESE FACTORS OF PRODUCTION: ① CAPITAL ② INVENTORIES ③ OWNER'S RESOURCES]*

◆ Cost of capital—the **economic depreciation** of capital is the change in market price of a capital asset. (Accountants apply conventional depreciation rates to the purchase price to calculate depreciation.) Other cost of capital is forgone interest. *[handwritten: ∴ OPPORTUNITY COST OF USING CAPITAL ASSET IS ① DEPRECIATION & ② INTEREST.]*

• **Implicit rental rate** (= economic depreciation + forgone interest). *[handwritten: WHEN A FIRM RENTS CAPITAL TO ITSELF]*

• **Sunk cost** (= past economic depreciation) is *not* an opportunity cost of capital. *[handwritten: B/C THAT PAST OPPORTUNITY CANNOT BE RETRIEVED.]*

◆ Cost of inventories—must be replaced when used. *[handwritten: OPPORTUNITY COSTS OF USING THEM FROM INVENTORY IS ITS MARKET PRICE (CURRENT)]*

[Handwritten top margin: OPPORTUNITY COST IS WAGE INCOME FORGONE OF ALTERNATIVE JOB. TIME & ORGANIZATION OF FACTORS OF PRODUCTION TO RUN BUSINESS]

③ ◆ <u>Cost of owner's resources</u>—owners supply entrepreneurial ability. **Normal profit** is the expected return to entrepreneurial ability and is part of a firm's opportunity costs of production. B/C *[IT IS THE COST OF THE ALTERNATIVE FORGONE)]*

Economists' costs and profits: 2 *[(RUNNING ANOTHER FIRM) CALCULATES TIME, INVESTMENT, RISK & DEPRECIATION]*

◆ *Opportunity costs* = explicit costs + implicit costs

◆ **Economic profits** = revenues − (explicit costs + implicit costs) *[OPPORTUNITY COSTS]*

◆ Because normal profits are part of implicit costs, economic profits (when positive) are over and above normal profits.

Accountants' costs and profits: *[ONLY USES CONVENTIONAL LIFE PRESUMPTIONS FOR CALCULATION.]*

◆ Accounting costs = explicit costs + conventional depreciation

◆ Accounting profits = revenues − (explicit costs + conventional depreciation) *[MONEY COSTS]*

◆ Accounting profits do *not* subtract normal profits or other implicit costs. *[LIKE: ↓ IN MARKET VALUE OF ASSETS, ROCKY'S WAGES (IF WORKED ELSEWHERE), INTEREST ON $ INVESTED (IF PUT $ IN BANK), & NORMAL PROFIT.]*

Economic Efficiency
[2 COMPONENTS OF EFFICIENCY.]

Technological efficiency—not possible to ↑ output without ↑ inputs. *[— MAY NOT BE ECONOMICALLY EFFICIENT]*

Economic efficiency—lowest possible cost of producing given output. *[— DEPENDS ON THE PRICES OF THE FACTORS OF PRODUCTION. — IS ALWAYS TECHNOLOGICALLY EFFICIENT.]*

Firms and Markets

Firms coordinate economic activity when *[THEY]* perform task more efficiently than markets. Firms often have advantages of *[(REASONS WHY FIRMS ARE MORE EFFICIENT AS COORDINATORS OF ECONOMIC ACTIVITY): ③]*

① • lower **transactions costs**—costs arising from finding someone with whom to do business. *[— CONTRACTS & NEGOTIATIONS.]*

② • **economies of scale**—↓ unit cost of producing good as output rate ↑. *[B/C OF SPECIALIZATION]*

③ • economies of <u>team production</u>—individuals in production process specializing in mutually supportive tasks. *[EG: TEAM ACTIVITY— SPECIALIZE IN PITCHING, SOME IN BATTING.]*

HELPFUL HINTS

1 The concept of *present value* is fundamental in thinking about the value today of an investment or of future amounts of money. It gives us a method of comparing investments that have payments that occur at different points in time. The intuition behind present value is that a dollar today is worth more than a dollar in the future because today's dollar can be invested to earn interest. To calculate the value *today* of an amount of money that will be paid in the future, we must discount that future amount to compensate for the forgone interest. The *present value* of a future amount of money is the amount that, if invested today, will grow as large as that future amount, taking into account the interest that it will earn.

2 In this chapter, we again meet our old friend opportunity cost. Here we look at the costs firms face with a special emphasis on the differences between *opportunity cost* measures used by economists and *accounting cost* measures. Opportunity cost, which is the concept of cost relevant for economic decisions, includes *explicit* and *implicit* costs. Important examples of implicit costs include the owner's/investor's forgone interest, implicit rent, economic depreciation, and normal profits. Accounting cost includes only explicit, out-of-pocket costs and conventional depreciation. These differences in cost measures between accountants and economists lead to differences in profit measures as well, as outlined here.

Economists

Opportunity costs = explicit costs + implicit costs

Economic profits = revenues − (explicit costs + implicit costs) *[= OPPORTUNITY COST]*

Accountants

Accounting costs = explicit costs + conventional depreciation

Accounting profits = revenues − (explicit costs + conventional depreciation)

Implicit costs, which economists include but accountants exclude, are the key to difference between economists' and accountants' measures of cost and profit. Accounting profits do *not* subtract normal profits or other implicit costs, so accounting profits are generally greater than economic profits.

Because normal profits are part of implicit costs, economic profits are profits over and above normal profits. If we think of normal profits as average profits, economic profits are *above-average* profits. Economic profits are a signal to firms that they are earning a greater return on investment than could be earned on average elsewhere in the economy.

Economic profits can also be negative if revenues are less than opportunity costs. As we will see in Chapter 11, such *economic losses* are a signal to firms that they are earning a *lower* return on investment than could be earned on average elsewhere.

3 It is important to distinguish between *technological efficiency* and *economic efficiency*. The difference is critical since economic decisions will be made only on the basis of economic efficiency. Technological efficiency is an engineering concept and occurs when it is not possible to increase output without increasing inputs. There is no consideration of input costs. Economic efficiency occurs when the *cost* of producing a given output is at a minimum. All technologically efficient production methods are not economically efficient. But all economically efficient methods are also technologically efficient. Competition favours firms that choose economically efficient production methods, and penalizes firms that do not.

S E L F - T E S T

True/False/Uncertain and Explain

1 Giving corporate managers stock in their companies is a strategy for coping with a principal–agent problem.

2 Normal profit is the expected return for supplying entrepreneurial ability.

3 If the interest rate is 10 percent a year, then the present value of $100 received in one year is $110.

4 In a principal–agent relationship between the stockholders and managers of Scotiabank, the stockholders are agents and the managers are principals.

5 Opportunity cost is greater than accounting cost.

6 When a firm produces using its own machine, its opportunity cost is lower than if it had rented the machine.

7 The opportunity cost of using inventories is the current market price.

8 An economically efficient production process becomes economically inefficient if the relative prices of inputs change.

9 For a capital asset, economic depreciation is less than conventional depreciation.

10 Markets will coordinate economic activity in situations where there are economies of scale.

Multiple-Choice

1 Which of the following statements is *not* true of firms?
a Firms and markets are institutions for coordinating economic activity.
b Firms organize factors of production in order to produce goods and services.
c Firms sell goods and services.
d Technologically efficient firms can eliminate scarcity.
e Firms use command systems to organize production.

2 A firm that has two or more owners with joint unlimited liability is
a a proprietorship.
b a partnership.
c a conglomerate.
d a corporation.
e none of the above.

3 Which of the following may vary over the term of a bond?

a present value
b redemption value
c redemption date
d annual coupon value
e none of the above

4 Bart buys a bow tie business for $100,000. To pay for the business, he borrows $60,000 from the bank at 12 percent interest and sells $40,000 worth of bonds. The bonds pay 10 percent interest per year. The opportunity cost of running the business in its first year includes

a only the $7,200 interest paid to the bank.
b only the $4,000 interest paid to bondholders.
c both the $7,200 bank interest and the $4,000 bondholders' interest.
d neither the $7,200 bank interest nor the $4,000 bondholders' interest.
e none of the above.

5 In general,
1 opportunity cost is greater than accounting cost.
2 opportunity cost is less than accounting cost.
3 economic profit is greater than accounting profit.
4 economic profit is less than accounting profit.

a 1 only
b 1 and 3
c 1 and 4
d 2 and 3
e 2 and 4

6 The rate of interest is 10 percent per year. You invest $50,000 of your own money in a business and earn *accounting* profits of $20,000 after one year. *Ceteris paribus*, what are your *economic* profits?

a $20,000
b $15,000
c $5,000
d $2,000
e – $15,000

7 The owner's stake in a business is called

a present value.
b redemption value.
c sunk cost.
d equity.
e inventories.

8 Which of the following is *not* an implicit cost?

a economic depreciation
b forgone interest
c implicit rent
d sunk cost
e normal profit

9 In Table 9.1, which method(s) of making a photon torpedo is/are technologically efficient?

a 1
b 2
c 3
d all of the above
e 1 and 3 only

TABLE **9.1** THREE METHODS OF MAKING ONE PHOTON TORPEDO

| | Quantities of Inputs | |
Method	Labour	Capital
1	5	10
2	10	7
3	15	5

10 Refer to Table 9.1. If the price of labour is $10 per unit and the price of capital is $20 per unit, which method(s) is/are economically efficient?

a 1
b 2
c 3
d all of the above
e 1 and 3 only

11 What is a *disadvantage* of a corporation relative to a proprietorship or partnership?

a owners have unlimited liability
b profits are taxed as corporate profits and as dividend income to stockholders
c there is difficulty in raising money
d perpetual life
e none of the above

12 Which of the following statements is *true*?

a All technologically efficient methods are also economically efficient.
b All economically efficient methods are also technologically efficient.
c Technological efficiency changes with changes in relative input prices.
d Technologically efficient firms will be more likely to survive than economically efficient firms.
e None of the above.

13 Firms will be more efficient than the market as a coordinator of economic activity when firms have

a lower transactions costs.
b lower monitoring costs.
c economies of scale.
d economies of team production.
e all of the above.

14 If the annual rate of interest is 10 percent, what is the present value of $100 received one year from now?

a $90.00
b $90.91
c $95.45
d $100.00
e $110.00

15 The possibility that an employee may not work hard is an example of the

a limited liability problem.
b principal–agent problem.
c transactions cost problem.
d technological efficiency problem.
e partnership problem.

16 Which of the following types of firms issue(s) shares of stock?

a proprietorship
b partnership
c corporation
d all of the above
e b and c only

17 Which of the following groups is the residual claimant of a corporation?

a stockholders
b bondholders
c banks and other creditors
d government taxing agencies
e managers

18 The construction cost of a building is $100,000. The conventional depreciation allowance is 5 percent per year. At the end of the first year the market value of the building is $80,000. For the first year, the depreciation cost is

a $20,000 to an accountant or an economist.
b $5,000 to an accountant or an economist.
c $5,000 to an accountant but $20,000 to an economist.
d $20,000 to an accountant but $5,000 to an economist.
e none of the above.

19 Abdul operates his own business and pays himself a salary of $20,000 per year. He refused a job that pays $30,000 per year. What is the opportunity cost of Abdul's time in the business?

a $10,000
b $20,000
c $30,000
d $50,000
e zero

20 Economic profit is revenues minus

a explicit costs.
b implicit costs.
c opportunity costs.
d accounting costs.
e (explicit costs + conventional depreciation).

21 Economies of scale exist when

a transactions costs are high.
b transactions costs are low.
c hiring additional inputs does not increase the price of inputs.
d the cost of producing a unit of output falls as the output rate increases.
e the firm is too large and too diversified.

22 Suppose that the trademark "Vice–President's Choice" currently has a market value of $10,000. After one year, the market value increases to $15,000. The opportunity cost of using the trademark during the year is

a zero
b –$5,000
c $5,000
d $10,000
e $15,000

23 The present value of a future payment of money will be higher the

a higher the interest rate or the further in the future the payment.
b lower the interest rate or the further in the future the payment.
c higher the interest rate or the nearer the date of the future payment.
d lower the interest rate or the nearer the date of the future payment.
e lower the interest rate and independent of the date of the future payment.

24 If the present value of $500 received one year from now is $463, what is the annual interest rate?

a 5 percent
b 8 percent
c 10 percent
d 20.8 percent
e 37 percent

25 If the annual interest rate is 10 percent, what is the present value of $100 *two* years from now?

a $80.00
b $82.64
c $90.91
d $120.00
e $121.00

Short Answer Problems

1 Give the meaning of present value by explaining (in words) why $110 received one year from now has a present value of $100 if the interest rate is 10 percent per year.

2 The standard tip in a restaurant is 15 percent. Restaurants could raise their prices 15 percent, set a no-tipping policy, and pay servers the extra 15 percent. Use principal–agent analysis to explain why most restaurants prefer tipping.

3 Compare the accounting cost and opportunity cost approaches in each of the following cases:
a depreciation cost.
b the firm borrows money to finance its operation.
c the firm uses its own funds rather than borrowing.
d the value of the firm's owner's resources.

4 Distinguish between technological efficiency and economic efficiency.

5 Markets and firms are alternative ways of coordinating economic activity that arise because of scarcity. Why do both firms and markets exist?

6 Complete Table 9.2 by computing the present value of each of three future payment sequences, first assuming the annual interest rate is 10 percent ($r = 0.1$), then assuming it is 5 percent ($r = 0.05$). The three future payment sequences are
A: $100 paid after one year.
B: $100 paid after two years.

C: A 2-year, $1,000 bond with a coupon payment of $100 per year. For example, the bondholder will receive a $100 coupon payment at the end of one year and again at the end of two years. At the end of two years, the bondholder will also receive $1,000 (the face value of the bond).

TABLE **9.2**

Future Payment Sequence	Present Value ($)	
	$r = 0.1$	$r = 0.05$
A		
B		
C		

7 Bonds *A* and *B* are described as follows.
   A: Pays $220 after two years.
   B: Pays $110 after one year and $110 after two years.
   For which of these bonds would you be willing to pay more? Why? [*Hint*: You do not need to know the interest rate to answer this question.]

8 A year ago, Frank, the bricklayer, decided to start a business manufacturing doll furniture. Frank has two sisters; Angela is an accountant and Edith is an economist. (Both sisters are good with numbers, but Edith doesn't have enough personality to be an accountant.) Each of the sisters computes Frank's cost and profit for the first year using the following information.

1. Frank took no income from the firm. He has a standing offer to return to work as a bricklayer for $30,000 per year.
2. Frank rents his machinery for $9,000 a year.
3. Frank owns the garage in which he produces, but could rent it out at $3,000 per year.
4. To start the business, Frank used $10,000 of his own money and borrowed $30,000 at the market rate of interest of 10 percent per year.
5. Frank hires one employee at an annual salary of $20,000.
6. The cost of materials during the first year is $40,000.
7. End of year inventory is zero.
8. Frank's entrepreneurial abilities are worth $14,000.
9. Frank's revenue for his first year is $100,000.

a Set up a table indicating how Angela and Edith would compute Frank's cost. Ignore any depreciation. What is Frank's cost as computed by Angela? by Edith?

b What is Frank's profit (or loss) as computed by Angela? by Edith?

9 According to your roommate, it is always more economically efficient to produce wheat using some machinery than using only labour. Suppose that there are two technologically efficient methods of producing one tonne of wheat.

Method 1 requires 20 machine hours plus 20 hours of labour.

Method 2 requires 100 hours of labour.

Country A has a highly developed industrial economy, while country B is less developed. In country A the price of an hour of labour (the wage rate) is $8, while the wage rate in country B is $4. The price of a machine hour is $20 in both countries. Which method is economically efficient in country A? in country B? Explain.

10 Consider countries A and B described in Short Answer Problem 9.

a What wage rate in country B would make the two methods equally efficient in country B?

b What price of a machine hour would make the two methods equally efficient in country A?

A N S W E R S

True/False/Uncertain and Explain

1 T Makes managers' (agents) incentives same as shareholders' (principal). (189–190)

2 T Definition. (198)

3 F PV of $110 received in one year is $100. (194–196)

4 F Stockholders' (principals) profits depend on job done by managers (agents). (190–192)

5 U Usually true, but depends on existence of implicit costs and differences between economic and conventional depreciation. (196–199)

6 F Opportunity cost equal for ownership or rental. (196–197)

7 T See text discussion. (198)

8 U Depends on magnitude price change. (200–201)

9 U Depends on whether ↓ market value is ≶ conventional depreciation calculation. (196–197)

10 F Firms more efficient if economies of scale. (202–203)

Multiple-Choice

1 d Scarcity can never be eliminated. (189–190)

2 b Definition. (191–192)

3 a PV changes with changes in r. All other parameters fixed. (194–195)

4 c Both explicit costs, part of opportunity cost. (196–197)

5 c See formulae in Helpful Hint 2. (196–199)

☉ 6 b Economic profits = accounting profits – implicit costs = $20,000 – (0.10 × $50,000). (196–199)

7 d Definition. (193)

8 d Sunk cost is past economic depreciation; past forgone opportunity cannot be retrieved. (196–198)

9 d No method has more of one input and same amount of other input, compared with alternative method. (200–201)

10 b 2 costs $240 while 1 and 3 cost $250. (200–201)

11 b d advantage. a, c disadvantages proprietorship and partnership. (191–192)

12 b c true for economic efficiency. Reverse of d true. (200–201)

13 e See text discussion. (202–203)

14 b $PV = \$100/(1 + 0.1)$. (194–195)

15 b See text discussion. (190–191)

16 c See text discussion. (191–192)

17 a Others have fixed claims. (191–192)

18 c Accountant's depreciation = (5 %) × $100,000. Economist's depreciation = Δ market value. (197–198)

19 c Forgone income. (198)

20 c Definition. (198)

21 d See text discussion. (203)

22 b ↑ value = negative opportunity cost. (196–198)

23 d Since $(1 + r)^n$ in denominator of PV formula, lower r and n make PV higher. (194–196)

☉ 24 b $463 = $500/(1 + r)$. Solve for r. (194–196)

☉ 25 b $PV = \$100/(1 + 0.1)^2$. (194–196)

Short Answer Problems

1 The present value of $110 received one year from now is the amount that, if invested today at the market rate of interest, would grow to be $110 in one year. Since the interest rate is 10 percent, $100 invested today at 10 percent would grow to be $110 in one year. Thus $100 is the present value of $110 in one year.

2 Restaurants face a classic principal–agent problem because servers may provide poor service to customers and drive away future business. Instead of having managers try to closely monitor each server, it is more efficient to delegate monitoring to customers. Customers tip based on quality of service, creating an incentive for the server—the agent—to provide good service. This is exactly what the restaurant owner—the principal—wants.

3 a From the accounting cost approach, depreciation cost is computed as a prespecified percentage of the original purchase price of the capital good, with no reference to current market value. The opportunity cost approach measures economic depreciation cost as the change in the market value of the capital good over the period in question.

b If a firm borrows money, the accounting and opportunity cost approaches will be the same; both will include the explicit interest payments.

c If a firm uses its own funds rather than borrowing, the accounting and opportunity cost approaches will differ. The accounting cost will be zero since there are no explicit interest payments. The opportunity cost approach recognizes that those funds could have been loaned and thus the (implicit) interest income forgone is the opportunity cost.

d If the owner could have worked elsewhere, the forgone wages are an opportunity cost but not an accounting cost. If the owner pays herself a salary, that will be counted as both an opportunity and accounting cost. In addition to supplying labour, the owner supplies entrepreneurial ability that also could be applied elsewhere. The cost of entrepreneurial ability is normal profit, which is an opportunity cost but not an accounting cost.

4 A method is technologically efficient if it is not possible to increase output without increasing inputs. A method is economically efficient if the cost of producing a given level of output is as low as possible. Technological efficiency is independent of prices while economic efficiency depends on the prices of inputs. An economically efficient method of production is always technologically efficient, but a technologically efficient method is not necessarily economically efficient.

5 As we saw in the example on text page 203, car repair can be coordinated by the market or by a firm. The institution (market or firm) that actually coordinates in any given case will be the one that is more efficient. In cases where there are significant transactions costs, economies of scale, or economies of team production, firms are likely to be more efficient, and firms will dominate the coordination of economic activity. But the efficiency of firms is limited, and there are many circumstances where market coordination of economic activity dominates because it is more efficient.

6 The completed table is shown here as Table 9.2 Solution. While each answer is a straightforward application of the present value formula, here are details for computing the present value of future payment sequence C when $r = 0.05$. Payment sequence C is best thought of as a two-part promise: (1) $100 after one year and (2) $1,100 after two years (the sum of value of the bond and the second coupon payment). The present value is then the sum of the present values of the two parts. The present value of (1) is $100/1.05 = $95.24, and the present value of (2) is $1,100/(1.05)^2 = $997.73. Therefore, the present value of the two-year bond is the sum $95.24 + $997.73 = $1,092.97.

TABLE **9.2** SOLUTION

Future Payment Sequence	Present Value ($)	
	$r = 0.1$	$r = 0.05$
A	90.91	95.24
B	82.64	90.70
C	1,000.00	1,092.97

7 A bondholder would be willing to pay more for bond B than bond A because bond B has a higher present value. While both bonds pay the same total dollar amount over two years, bond B pays half of that amount after only one year. A holder of bond A, however, must wait two years for the full amount.

    If we think of the $220 payment of bond A as two $110 payments, each paid after two years, each payment is discounted by (divided by) $(1 + r)^2$. The second $110 payment of bond B is also paid after two years and is also discounted by $(1 + r)^2$. So one $110 payment from bond A and one $110 payment from bond B have equal present values. But the first $110 payment of bond B is paid after one year and is therefore only discounted by $(1 + r)$, which is a smaller number than the discount of $(1 + r)^2$ which applies to the other \$110 payment of bond A. Since this discount factor is in the denominator of the present value formula, the smaller denominator for the bond B calculation means a higher present value than for the bond A calculation. This result is shown in the following expression comparing the present values of bond A (PV_A) and bond B (PV_B).

$$PV_B = \frac{110}{1 + r} + \frac{110}{(1 + r)^2} \quad \text{is greater than}$$

$$PV_A = \frac{110}{(1 + r)^2} + \frac{110}{(1 + r)^2} = \frac{220}{(1 + r)^2}$$

8 a Table 9.3 gives the cost as computed by Angela and Edith. The item numbers correspond to the item numbers in the problem.

TABLE **9.3**

Item Number	Angela's Accounting Computation (accounting cost)	Edith's Economic Computation (opportunity cost)
1.	\$0	\$30,000
2.	9,000	9,000
3.	0	3,000
4.	3,000	4,000
5.	20,000	20,000
6.	40,000	40,000
7.	0	0
8.	0	\$14,000
Total Cost	\$72,000	\$120,000

b Revenue is \$100,000. Angela's accounting computation of profit uses this formula:

Accounting profits = revenues − explicit costs
= \$100,000 − \$72,000
= \$28,000

Edith's economic computation of profit uses this formula:

Economic profits = revenues − opportunity costs
= \$100,000 − \$120,000
= − \$20,000 (an economic loss)

9 Both production methods are technologically efficient. The economically efficient production method has the lower cost of producing a tonne of wheat. In country A, the price of an hour of labour is \$8 and the price of a machine hour is \$20. The cost of producing a tonne of wheat is \$560 using method 1 and \$800 using method 2.

Therefore method 1 is economically efficient for country A.

The price of an hour of labour is \$4 in country B, and thus it will face different costs of producing a tonne of wheat. Under method 1, the cost will be \$480 but under method 2, which uses only labour, the cost will be \$400. So method 2 is economically efficient for country B.

The reason for this difference is that economic efficiency means producing at lowest cost. If the relative prices of inputs are different in two countries, there will be differences in the relative costs of production using alternative methods. Therefore your roommate is wrong.

⚙10 a If the wage rate in country B were to increase to \$5 an hour, then production of a tonne of wheat would be \$500 under either method. How did we obtain this answer? Express the cost under method 1 (C_1) and the cost under method 2 (C_2) as follows:

$$C_1 = 20P_m + 20P_h$$
$$C_2 = 100P_h$$

where P_m is the price of a machine hour and P_h is the price of an hour of labour (the wage rate). We are given that $P_m = \$20$ and asked to find the value of P_h that makes the two methods equally efficient; the value of P_h that makes $C_1 = C_2$. Thus we solve the following equation for P_h:

$$20P_m + 20P_h = 100P_h$$
$$20(\$20) + 20P_h = 100P_h$$
$$\$400 = 80P_h$$
$$\$5 = P_h$$

b If the price of a machine hour is \$32, production of a tonne of wheat would be \$800 under either method in country A. This question asks: Given the wage rate of \$8 (P_h) in country A, what value of P_m makes $C_1 = C_2$? Thus we solve the following equation for P_m:

$$20P_m + 20P_h = 100P_h$$
$$20P_m + 20(\$8) = 100(\$8)$$
$$20P_m = \$640$$
$$P_m = \$32$$

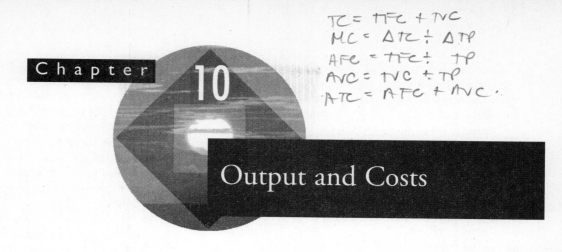

[handwritten top right]
TC = TFC + TVC
MC = ΔTC ÷ ΔTP
AFC = TFC ÷ TP
AVC = TVC ÷ TP
ATC = AFC + AVC.

Chapter 10

Output and Costs

KEY CONCEPTS

The Firm's Objective and Constraints

[handwritten: FIRM TRIES TO USE SCARCE RESOURCES EFFICIENTLY]

Firm's objective is profit maximization. Limits to profit maximization are *[handwritten: ① MARKET CONSTRAINTS ② TECHNOLOGY CONSTRAINTS.]*

① ◆ Market constraints

   [handwritten: (CONSUMERS WILL ONLY BUY IF PRICES LOWER)]

   • Limited demand for firm's output and limited supply factor inputs. *[handwritten: → B/C THEY HAVE LIMITS TO WHAT THEY GIVE & WILL ONLY SUPPLY IT FOR HIGHER PRICES.]*
   • For small firms, market constraints take form of given prices for outputs and inputs. *[handwritten: (MEANS THIS FIRM CAN'T INFLUENCE PRICES FOR OUT/INPUTS SELLING/BUYING)]*

② ◆ Technology constraints *[handwritten: LIMITS TO QTY OF OUTPUT THAT CAN BE PRODUCED BY USING GIVEN QTY OF INPUTS (FACTORS OF PRODUCTION)]*

Firm has two planning horizons.

   ◆ **Short run**—at least one fixed input. Other inputs are variable inputs. *[handwritten: EG: SEWING MACHINE]*

   ◆ **Long run**—all inputs are variable. *[handwritten: EG: LABOUR.]*

Short-Run Technology Constraint

[handwritten: CHANGE IN VARIABLE INPUT CAN BE DESCRIBED BY THESE ③ CONCEPTS]

Short-run production described by

[handwritten: Fig 10.1 pg 212] ① ◆ **Total product** curve (*TP*)—maximum attainable output with fixed quantity capital as quantity labour varies/changes. *[handwritten: (INPUT) UNATTAIN TP ATTAIN TECH INEFFICIENT ONLY PTS ON CURVE ARE TECH EFFICIENT]*

[handwritten: Fig 10.2 pg 213.] ② ◆ **Marginal product** curve (*MP*)—Δ*TP* resulting from one-unit ↑ variable input. *[handwritten: ↑ STEEPER THE SLOPE OF TP, THE LARGER MP. = ↑ IN ΔTP / ↑ INPUT EMPLOYED.]* *[handwritten: MP]*

[handwritten: Fig 10.3 pg 214] ③ ◆ **Average product** curve (*AP*)—*TP* per unit variable input. *[handwritten: = TP / INPUT EMPLOYED. & AP IS LARGEST WHEN AP = MP (AT A MAX). AP]*

◆ As ↑ variable input, *MP* ↑ (**increasing marginal return**), reaches maximum, and then ↓ (**decreasing marginal return**). When *MP* > *AP*, *AP* ↑. When *MP* < *AP*, *AP* ↓. When *MP* = *AP*, maximum *AP*.

[handwritten: EG: 6PA, IF MP = 3 & AP = 2 THEN IT ↑ AP OVERALL (6PA)]

[handwritten bottom left: = INCREASING MARGINAL RETURNS: WHEN MP OF AN ADDITIONAL WORKER > MP OF PREVIOUS WORKER. EG: 2 PEOPLE ARE MORE EFFICIENT THAN ONE]

[handwritten top: ↑ ONE MORE WORKER'S MP < MP OF PREVIOUS WORKERS ∴ ↑ OUTPUT, BUT NOT AS MUCH ↑ IN OUTPUT WHEN YOU HIRED 2ND WORKER ∴ HIRING MORE WORKERS EVENTUALLY ↑ OUTPUT BY SMALLER & SMALLER AMTS ∴ MP↓]

◆ **Law of diminishing returns**—with quantity fixed inputs constant, as firm uses more variable input, its *MP* eventually diminishes. *[handwritten: B/C MP↓ SO DOES AP↓.]*

Short-Run Cost

Short-run cost curves determined by technology and product curves.

◆ **Total cost** (*TC*) = *TFC* + *TVC*. *[handwritten: FIXED COST / VARIABLE COST]*

   • **Total fixed cost** (*TFC*)—cost of fixed inputs.
   • **Total variable cost** (*TVC*)—cost of variable inputs. *[handwritten: → ↑ MC AS YOU ↑ LABOUR FOR ADDITIONAL UNIT]*
   • **Marginal cost** (*MC*)—Δ*TC* resulting from one-unit ↑ output. *[handwritten: = ↑ IN TC / ↑ IN OUTPUT. EG: 70-013 = 3 ∴ 25/3 = 8.33 75-2100 = 25]*

◆ **Average total cost** (*ATC*) = *AFC* + *AVC*. *[handwritten: ⇒ TC = TFC + TVC / Q Q Q]*

   • **Average fixed cost** (*AFC*)—total fixed cost per unit output. *[handwritten: AFC↓ AS OUTPUT↑ B/C ITS SPREAD OVER LARGER OUTPUT]*
   • **Average variable cost** (*AVC*)—total variable cost per unit output.
   • *AFC* curve ↓ constantly as output ↑. *[handwritten: Fig 10.5 pg 218]*
   • *AVC*, *ATC*, and *MC* curves are U-shaped. *[handwritten: AVERAGES OUT USES OF A COST B/C OUTPUT↑ B/C (AVC)]*
   • As ↑ output, *MC* ↓, reaches minimum, and then ↑. *[handwritten: ① SPREADING FIXED COST OVER LARGER OUTPUT ② EVENTUALLY DIMINISHING RETURNS]*
   • When *MC* < *ATC*, *ATC* ↓. When *MC* > *ATC*, *ATC* ↑. When *MC* = *ATC*, minimum *ATC*. Same relation *MC* and *AVC*. *[handwritten: MC ATC AVC AFC. TVC TFC TC MC < AC. Fig 10.6 pg 219.]*

Plant Size and Cost

Long-run cost—cost of production when all inputs, including plant size, adjusted to economically efficient levels. *[handwritten: + DEPENDS ON PRODUCTION FN.]* *[handwritten: Fig 10.7 pg 221]*

Production function—relationship between maximum attainable output and quantities of inputs when *all* inputs variable. *[handwritten: = MAX OUTPUT ATTAINABLE & QTYS OF ALL OUTPUTS USED.]*

◆ **Returns to scale**—↑ output resulting from ↑ all inputs by same percentage. Three possibilities: *[handwritten: = EQUAL %AGE CHANGE IN USE OF ALL THE FIRM'S OUTPUTS.]*

1. **Constant returns to scale**—percentage ↑ firm's output = percentage ↑ inputs.
2. **Increasing returns to scale (economies of scale)**—percentage ↑ firm's output > percentage ↑ inputs. *[handwritten: MEANS IF DOUBLE INPUT, IT'S OUTPUT MORE THAN DOUBLE.]*
3. **Decreasing returns to scale (diseconomies of scale)**—percentage ↑ firm's output < percentage ↑ inputs. *[handwritten: MEANS IF DOUBLE INPUT, OUTPUT LESS THAN DOUBLE.]*

[handwritten margin: Fig 10.9 pg 224]

◆ **Long-run average cost curve (*LRAC*)**—traces U-shaped relation between lowest attainable *ATC* and output when all inputs variable. When *LRAC* ↓, increasing returns to scale. When *LRAC* horizontal, constant returns to scale. When *LRAC* ↑, decreasing returns to scale.

[handwritten diagrams and notes: economies of scale, under utilizing plant, start, scale b, over utilizing plant]

HELPFUL HINTS

1 This chapter introduces many new concepts and graphs and may at first appear overwhelming. Don't get lost among the trees and lose sight of the forest. There is a simple and fundamental relationship between production functions and cost functions.

The chapter begins with the short-run production function and concepts of total product, marginal product, and average product. This is followed by the short-run cost function and concepts of total cost, marginal cost, average variable cost, and average total cost.

But all of these seemingly disparate concepts are related to the law of diminishing returns. The law states that as a firm uses additional units of a variable input, while holding constant the quantity of fixed inputs, the marginal product of the variable input will eventually diminish. This law explains why the marginal product and average product curves eventually fall, and why the total product curve becomes flatter. When productivity falls, costs increase, and the law explains the eventual upward slope of the marginal cost curve. When marginal product falls, marginal cost increases.

The marginal cost curve, in turn, explains the U-shape of the average variable cost and average total cost curves. When the marginal cost curve is below the average variable (or total) cost curve, the average variable (or total) cost curve is falling. When marginal cost is above the average variable (or total) cost curve, the average variable (or total) cost curve is rising. The marginal cost curve intersects the average variable (or total) cost curve at the minimum point on the average variable (or total) cost curve.

Use the law of diminishing returns as the key to understanding the relationships between the many short-run concepts and graphs in the chapter. But all concepts and graphs are not equally important. Pay most attention to the unit cost concepts and graphs—especially marginal cost, average variable cost, and average total cost—because these will be used the most in later chapters to analyse the behaviour of firms.

2 Be sure to thoroughly understand Fig. 10.1 (Text Fig. 10.5b on page 218). It is the most important graph in the chapter and one of the most important graphs in all of microeconomics.

FIGURE **10.1**

The curves for average total cost (*ATC*), average fixed cost (*AFC*), and average variable cost (*AVC*) are derived by taking the values for *TC*, *TFC*, and *TVC* and dividing by quantity of output. Since these are average values for a fixed quantity of output, they are plotted directly above the corresponding units of output. On the other hand, marginal cost (*MC*) is the *change* in total cost (or equivalently, in total variable cost) resulting from a one-unit increase in output. It is plotted *midway* between the corresponding units of output. The *ATC*, *AVC*, and *MC* curves are crucially important. The *ATC* and *AVC* curves are both U-shaped. The *MC* curve is also U-shaped and intersects the *ATC* and *AVC* curves at their minimum points. The *MC* curve is below the *ATC* and *AVC* curves when *ATC* and *AVC* are falling, and above the *ATC* and *AVC* curves when they are rising. The less important *AFC* curve falls continuously as output increases.

3 You will probably draw a graph like the one in Fig. 10.1 at least one hundred times in this course. Here are some hints on drawing the graph quickly and easily.

Be sure to label the axes; quantity of output (Q) on the horizontal axis and average cost on the vertical axis.

Draw an upward-sloping marginal cost curve, as shown here in Fig. 10.2. The marginal cost curve can have a small downward-sloping section at first, but this is not important for subsequent analysis. Next, draw a shallow U-shaped curve that falls until it intersects the marginal cost curve, and then rises. Then pick a point further up the marginal cost curve. Draw another shallow U-shaped curve whose minimum point passes through your second point. Finally, label the curves.

Any time a test question (including those in the Self-Test) asks about these curves, *draw a graph* before you answer.

FIGURE **10.2**

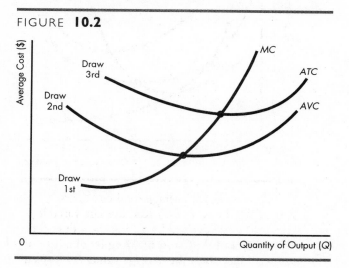

4 Be sure to understand how economists use the terms *short run* and *long run*. These terms do *not* refer to any notion of calendar time. They are better thought of as planning horizons. The short run is a planning horizon short enough that while some inputs are variable, at least one input cannot be varied but is fixed. The long run refers to a planning horizon that is long enough that all inputs can be varied.

5 The later sections of the chapter explain the long-run production function and cost function when plant size is variable. While diminishing returns was the key for understanding short-run costs, the concept of returns to scale is the key for understanding long-run costs. Returns to scale are the increase in output relative to the

increase in inputs when *all inputs* are increased by the same percentage. Returns to scale can be increasing, constant, or decreasing, and correspond to the downward-sloping, horizontal, and upward-sloping sections of the long-run average cost curve.

SELF-TEST

True/False/Uncertain and Explain

1 Limitations on the feasible ways in which inputs can be converted into outputs is an example of a market constraint on firm profitability.

2 Given a fixed quantity of capital, if 2 additional labourers produce 15 additional units of output, the marginal product of labour is 15 units of output.

3 The average product curve cuts the marginal product curve from above at the maximum point on the marginal product curve.

4 The law of diminishing returns implies that eventually the marginal product curve will be negatively sloped as the variable input increases.

5 The law of diminishing returns implies that we will not observe a range of increasing marginal returns.

6 Average variable cost reaches its minimum at the same level of output at which average product is a maximum.

7 If average variable cost is decreasing then marginal cost is decreasing.

8 No part of any short-run average total cost curve can lie below the long-run average cost curve.

9 Increasing returns to scale means that the long-run average cost curve is negatively sloped.

10 In the long run, the total cost and total variable cost curves are the same.

Multiple-Choice

1 In economics, the short run is a time period in which
a one year or less elapses.
b all inputs are variable.
c all inputs are fixed.
d there is at least one fixed input and at least one variable input.
e all inputs are variable but the technology is fixed.

2 The marginal cost (*MC*) curve intersects the
a *ATC, AVC,* and *AFC* curves at their minimum points.
b *ATC* and *AFC* curves at their minimum points.
c *AVC* and *AFC* curves at their minimum points.
d *ATC* and *AVC* curves at their minimum points.
e *TC* and *TVC* curves at their minimum points.

3 Marginal cost is the amount that
a total cost increases when one more labourer is hired.
b fixed cost increases when one more labourer is hired.
c variable cost increases when one more labourer is hired.
d total cost increases when one more unit of output is produced.
e fixed cost increases when one more unit of output is produced.

4 A rise in the price of a fixed input will cause a firm's
a average variable cost curve to shift up.
b average total cost curve to shift up.
c average total cost curve to shift down.
d marginal cost curve to shift up.
e marginal cost curve to shift down.

5 A field of ripe corn is waiting to be harvested. Labour is the only variable input, and the total product (in bushels) of various numbers of labourers is given in Table 10.1.

TABLE **10.1**

Number of Labourers	Total Product
0	0
1	3
2	7
3	10
4	12

Diminishing returns *begin* when you add which labourer?
a 1st labourer
b 2nd labourer
c 3rd labourer
d 4th labourer
e there are no diminishing returns since total product always rises

6 When the marginal product of labour is less than the average product of labour,
a the average product of labour is increasing.
b the marginal product of labour is increasing.
c the total product curve is negatively sloped.
d the firm is experiencing diminishing returns.
e none of the above is true.

7 If all inputs are increased by 10 percent and output increases by less than 10 percent, it must be the case that
a average total cost is decreasing.
b average total cost is increasing.
c the *LRAC* curve is negatively sloped.
d there are increasing returns to scale.
e there are decreasing returns to scale.

8 A technological advance will shift
1 *TP, AP,* and *MP* curves up.
2 *TP, AP,* and *MP* curves down.
3 *TC, ATC,* and *MC* curves up.
4 *TC, ATC,* and *MC* curves down.

a 1 and 3
b 1 and 4
c 2 and 3
d 2 and 4
e none of the above

9 The vertical distance between the *TC* and *TVC* curves is

a decreasing as output increases.
b increasing as output increases.
c equal to *AFC*.
d equal to *TFC*.
e equal to *MC*.

10 Total cost is $20 at 4 units of output and $36 at 6 units of output. Between 4 and 6 units of output, marginal cost

a is less than average total cost.
b is equal to average total cost.
c is equal to average variable cost.
d is greater than average total cost.
e cannot be compared with any average cost without additional information.

11 The long-run average cost curve

a shifts up when fixed costs increase.
b shifts down when fixed costs increase.
c is the short-run average total cost curve with the lowest cost.
d traces the minimum points on all the short-run average total cost curves for each scale of plant.
e traces the minimum short-run average total cost for each output.

12 The average variable cost curve will shift up if

a there is an increase in fixed costs.
b there is a technological advance.
c the price of variable input decreases.
d the price of output increases.
e none of the above occurs.

13 A firm's fixed costs are $100. If total costs are $200 for one unit of output and $310 for two units, what is the marginal cost of the second unit?

a $100
b $110
c $200
d $210
e $310

14 A firm will want to increase its scale of plant if

a it persistently produces on the upward-sloping part of its short-run average total cost curve.
b it persistently produces on the downward-sloping part of its short-run average total cost curve.
c it is producing below capacity.
d marginal cost is below average total cost.
e marginal cost is below average variable cost.

15 If *ATC* is falling then *MC* must be

a rising.
b falling.
c equal to *ATC*.
d above *ATC*.
e below *ATC*.

16 In the long run,

a only the scale of plant is fixed.
b all inputs are variable.
c all inputs are fixed.
d a firm must experience decreasing returns to scale.
e none of the above is true.

17 Constant returns to scale means that as all inputs are increased,

a total output remains constant.
b average total cost remains constant.
c average total cost increases at the same rate as inputs.
d long-run average cost remains constant.
e long-run average cost rises at the same rate as inputs.

18 According to the law of diminishing returns,

1 marginal productivity eventually rises.
2 marginal productivity eventually falls.
3 marginal cost eventually rises.
4 marginal cost eventually falls.

a 1 and 3
b 1 and 4
c 2 and 3
d 2 and 4
e 4 only

19 The average product of labour is

a the slope of the total product curve.
b the slope of the marginal product curve.
c the increase in total product divided by the increase in labour employed.
d the total product divided by the quantity of labour employed.
e none of the above.

20 In the short run, a profit-maximizing firm is constrained by

a limited demand for its product.
b limited input supplies.
c limited number of technologically efficient production methods.
d limited planning horizon.
e all of the above.

21 Which of the following does *not* cause decreasing *ATC*?

a decreasing marginal cost
b decreasing average variable cost
c decreasing average fixed cost
d increasing marginal product
e increasing returns to scale

22 Refer to Fig. 10.3 illustrating Swanky's short-run total product curve. Which of the following statements is *true*?

a Points above the curve are attainable and are inefficient.
b Points below the curve are attainable and are inefficient.
c Points below the curve are unattainable and are inefficient.
d Points on the curve are unattainable and are efficient.
e Points on the curve all have equal marginal products.

FIGURE **10.3**

23 Refer to Fig. 10.3 illustrating Swanky's short-run total product curve. Marginal product reaches a maximum when you add which labourer?

a 1st labourer
b 2nd labourer
c 3rd labourer
d 4th labourer
e 5th labourer

24 Average variable cost is at a minimum at the same output where

a average product is at a maximum.
b average product is at a minimum.
c marginal product is at a maximum.
d marginal product is at a minimum.
e marginal cost is at a minimum.

25 Which of the following statements by a restaurant owner refers to the law of diminishing returns?

a "The higher the quality of the ingredients we use, the higher the cost of producing each meal."
b "If we double the size of our premises and double everything else—kitchen staff, serving staff, equipment—we can increase the number of meals we serve, but not to double current levels."
c "We can increase the number of meals we serve by just adding more kitchen staff, but each additional worker adds fewer meals than the previous worker because traffic in the kitchen will get worse."
d "We can serve the same number of meals with fewer kitchen staff, but we would have to buy more labour-saving kitchen equipment."
e "We can serve the same number of meals with less kitchen equipment, but we would have to hire more kitchen staff."

Short Answer Problems

1 Why must the marginal product curve intersect the average product curve at the maximum point of the average product curve?

2 Why must the marginal cost curve intersect the average total cost curve at the minimum point of the average total cost curve?

3 Explain the connection, if any, between the U-shape of the average total cost curve and (a) fixed costs, and (b) the law of eventually diminishing returns.

4 Use the concepts of marginal and average to answer the following question. Suppose the worst student at Hubertville High School transfers to Histrionic High School. Is it possible that the average grade-point of the students at each school rises? Explain.

5 What is the difference, if any, between diminishing returns and decreasing returns to scale?

6 How is the long-run average cost curve obtained and how does it differ from Jacob Viner's mistaken conception of it?

7 For a given scale of plant, Table 10.2 gives the total monthly output of golf carts attainable using varying quantities of labour.

TABLE **10.2** MONTHLY GOLF CART PRODUCTION

Labourers (per month)	Output (units per month)	Marginal Product	Average Product
0	0		
1	1		
2	3		
3	6		
4	12		
5	17		
6	20		
7	22		
8	23		

a Complete the table for the marginal product and average product of labour. (Note that marginal product should be entered *midway* between rows to emphasize that it is the result of *changing* inputs—moving from one row to the next. Average product corresponds to a *fixed* quantity of labour and should be entered on the appropriate row.)

b Label the axes and draw a graph of the total product curve (*TP*).

c On a separate piece of paper, label the axes and draw a graph of both marginal product (*MP*) and average product (*AP*). (Marginal product should be plotted *midway* between the corresponding units of labour, as in Text Fig. 10.2(b) on page 213, while average product should be plotted directly above the corresponding units of labour, as in Text Fig. 10.3 on page 214.)

8 Now let's examine the short-run costs of golf cart production. The first two columns of Table 10.2 are reproduced in the first two columns of Table 10.3. The cost of 1 labourer (the only variable input) is $2,000 per month. Total fixed cost is $2,000 per month.

TABLE **10.3** SHORT-RUN COSTS (MONTHLY)

L	Q	TFC ($)	TVC ($)	TC ($)	MC ($)	AFC ($)	AVC ($)	ATC ($)
0	0	2,000						
1	1							
2	3							
3	6							
4	12							
5	17							
6	20							
7	22							
8	23							

a Given this information, complete Table 10.3 by computing total fixed cost (*TFC*), total variable cost (*TVC*), total cost (*TC*), marginal cost (*MC*), average fixed cost (*AFC*), average variable cost (*AVC*), and average total cost (*ATC*). Your completed table should look like Text Table 10.2 on page 217, with marginal cost entered *midway* between the rows.

b Label the axes and draw the *TC*, *TVC*, and *TFC* curves on a single graph.

c Label the axes and draw the *MC*, *ATC*, *AVC*, and *AFC* curves on a single graph. Be sure to plot *MC midway* between the corresponding units of output.

d Now suppose that the price of a labourer increases to $2,500 per month. Construct a table for the new *MC* and *ATC* curves (output, *MC*, *ATC*). Label the axes and draw a graph of the new *MC* and *ATC* curves. What is the effect of the increase in the price of the variable input on these curves?

9 Return to the original price of labour of $2,000 per month. Now suppose that we double the quantity of fixed inputs so that total fixed costs also double to $4,000 per month. This increases the monthly output of golf carts for each quantity of labour as indicated in Table 10.4.

TABLE **10.4** NEW MONTHLY PRODUCTION OF GOLF CARTS

Labourers (per month)	Output (units per month)
0	0
1	1
2	4
3	10
4	19
5	26
6	31
7	34
8	36

a Construct a table for the new *MC* and *ATC* curves (output, *MC*, *ATC*). Label the axes and draw a graph of the new *MC* and *ATC* curves.

b What is the effect on these curves (compared with the original *MC* and *ATC* curves in Short Answer Problem **8c**) of an increase in "plant size"? Are there economies of scale?

c Draw the long-run average cost (*LRAC*) curve if these are the only two plant sizes available.

10 Figure 10.4 gives a sequence of short-run *ATC* curves numbered 1 through 7 corresponding to seven different plant sizes.

FIGURE **10.4**

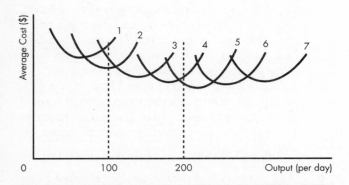

a Draw the long-run average cost curve on Fig. 10.4.

b If the desired level of output is 100 units per day, what is the best plant size? (Give the number of the associated short-run *ATC* curve.) What if the desired level of output is 200 units per day?

ANSWERS

True/False/Uncertain and Explain

1 F Example of technology constraint. (211)

2 F $\Delta TP/\Delta L = 15/2 = 7.5$. (212–214)

⊙3 F True if switch terms "average product" and "marginal product." (214)

4 T *MP* must eventually ↓ with ↑ *L*. (215)

5 F *Eventually* diminishing returns. *MP* can initially ↑. (215)

⊙6 T $AVC = TVC/Q = WL/Q = W/(Q/L) = W/AP$. (219)

⊙7 U *MC* must be below *AVC*, but *MC* may be ↑ or ↓. (218–219)

8 T Definition *LRAC*. (224)

9 T See text discussion. (222–225)

10 T All costs variable in long run. (211)

Multiple-Choice

1 d Definition. (211)

2 d *AFC* always ↓, *TC* and *TVC* always ↑. (217–219)

3 d Definition. (216–217)

4 b Won't affect *AVC* or *MC*. (220)

5 c *MP* 1st = 3, *MP* 2nd = 4, *MP* 3rd = 3. (215)

6 d When *MP* < *AP*, *MP* ↓ (diminishing returns), *AP* ↓, and *TP* positively sloped. (213–214)

7 e Definition. Since all inputs variable, **a** and **b** irrelevant. (222–225)

8 b Productivity ↑, costs ↓. (219–220)

9 d *TC* = *TFC* + *TVC*. Distance constant. (217–218)

⊙10 d $MC = 16/2 = 8$. *ATC* is \$5 at 4 units and \$6 at 6 units. (216–218)

11 e Definition. **d** is Jacob Viner's mistake. **a** and **b** short run since fixed costs. (224)

12 e **a** and **d** don't affect *AVC*. **b** and **c** shift *AVC* down. (220)

13 b Fixed costs irrelevant. $\Delta TC/\Delta Q = (\$310 - \$200)/(2 - 1)$. (216–217)

14 a **b** and **c** plant too big. **d** and **e** relate to short run. (224–225)

⊙15 e *MC* could be ↑ or ↓ below *ATC* when *ATC* ↓. (218–219)

16 b Definition. All returns to scale possible in long run. (211, 222)

17 d *LRAC* horizontal. (225)

18 c ↓ *MP* → ↑ *MC*. (218–219)

19 d Definition. (212–214)

20 e Market constraints and technology constraints. (211)

21 **e** ↑ returns to scale is long-run concept; *ATC* is short-run concept. (218–219)

22 **b** Attainable but not maximum *TP*. (212–213)

23 **b** *MP* = slope *TP* curve = 6 for 2nd labourer. (212–214)

24 **a** *AVC* ↓ as long as *AP* ↑ . See Text Fig. 10.6. (219)

25 **c** *MP* ↓ as restaurant uses more variable input (labour). (215)

Short Answer Problems

1 Since the average product curve first rises and then falls, when average product is rising, marginal product must be greater than average product, and when average product is falling, marginal product must be lower than average product. Therefore the marginal product curve must intersect the average product curve at its maximum point. In order for average product to increase, it must have been *pulled up* by a larger increase in product from the last unit of input. Therefore marginal product is higher than average product. Similarly, when average product is falling, it must be that it has been *pulled down* by a lower marginal product. When average product is at its maximum, it is neither rising nor falling, so marginal product cannot be higher or lower than average product. Therefore marginal product must be equal to average product.

2 The answer to this problem is just the mirror image of the answer to Short Answer Problem 1. The average total cost curve is U-shaped, first falling and then rising as output increases. When average total cost is falling, marginal cost must be less than average total cost, and when average total cost is rising, marginal cost must be greater than average total cost. Therefore the marginal cost curve must intersect the average total cost curve at its minimum point. In order for average total cost to fall, it must have been *pulled down* by a smaller increase in cost from the last unit of output. Therefore marginal cost is lower than average total cost. Similarly, when average total cost is rising, it must be that it has been *pulled up* by a higher marginal cost. When average total cost is at its minimum, it is neither falling nor rising, so marginal cost cannot be lower or higher than average total cost. Therefore, marginal cost must be equal to average total cost.

3 The U-shape of the average total cost (*ATC*) curve arises from the opposing forces of (a) spreading fixed costs over a larger output and (b) the law of eventually diminishing returns.

As output increases, fixed costs are spread over a larger output so average fixed cost (*AFC*) falls. Initially, as output increases, the marginal productivity of the variable factor rises, causing average variable cost (*AVC*) to fall. Falling *AVC*, together with falling *AFC*, cause average total cost (*ATC*) to fall, contributing to the downward-sloping portion of *ATC*. Eventually, as output increases, diminishing returns set in, marginal productivity falls, and *AVC* rises. Eventually, *AVC* rises more quickly than *AFC* falls, contributing to the upward sloping portion of *ATC*.

4 Yes, it is possible that the average grade-point of the students at each school rises. Think of the transferring student as the *marginal* student. If his grade-point average, although the lowest at Hubertville High, is higher than the *average* grade-point at Histrionic High, then the results are: the *average* grade-point at Hubertville High rises with the elimination of the lowest grade-point; and the *average* grade-point at Histrionic High rises because the transferring (*marginal*) student's grade-point pulls up the *average* grade-point.

5 The law of diminishing returns states that as a firm uses additional units of a variable input, *while holding constant the quantity of fixed inputs*, the marginal product of the variable input will eventually diminish. Decreasing returns to scale occur when a firm increases *all of its inputs by an equal percentage*, and this results in a lower percentage increase in output. Diminishing (marginal) returns is a short-run concept since there must be a fixed input. Decreasing returns to scale is a long-run concept since all inputs must be variable.

6 Any given level of output can be produced using alternative scales of plant, but for each level of output, one scale of plant results in the lowest short-run average total cost. The scale of plant can be varied in the long run, and the long-run average cost curve traces out the lowest short-run average total cost at each level of output. Jacob Viner's mistaken conception of the long-run average cost curve was that (a) it must pass through the minimum point of each short-run average cost curve (which is incorrect) and, (b) it must not be above any short-run cost curve at any point (which is correct). The mistake is that these two properties cannot be satisfied simultaneously. Indeed, the long-run average cost curve does *not* pass through the minimum point of each of the short-run average cost curves.

7 a The completed Table 10.2 is shown here as Table 10.2 Solution.

TABLE **10.2** SOLUTION
MONTHLY GOLF CART PRODUCTION

Labourers (per month)	Output (units per month)	Marginal Product	Average Product
0	0		0
		 1	
1	1		1.00
		 2	
2	3	·	1.50
		 3	
3	6		2.00
		 6	
4	12		3.00
		 5	
5	17		3.40
		 3	
6	20		3.33
		 2	
7	22		3.14
		 1	
8	23		2.88

b Figure 10.5 gives the graph of the total product curve.

FIGURE **10.5**

c Figure 10.6 gives the graphs of marginal product and average product.

FIGURE **10.6**

8 a Completed Table 10.3 is given here as Table 10.3 Solution.

TABLE **10.3** SOLUTION
SHORT-RUN COSTS (MONTHLY)

L	Q	TFC ($)	TVC ($)	TC ($)	MC ($)	AFC ($)	AVC ($)	ATC ($)
0	0	2,000	0	2,000		—	—	—
					2,000			
1	1	2,000	2,000	4,000		2,000	2,000	4,000
					1,000			
2	3	2,000	4,000	6,000		667	1,333	2,000
					667			
3	6	2,000	6,000	8,000		333	1,000	1,333
					333			
4	12	2,000	8,000	10,000		167	667	833
					400			
5	17	2,000	10,000	12,000		118	588	706
					667			
6	20	2,000	12,000	14,000		100	600	700
					1,000			
7	22	2,000	14,000	16,000		91	636	727
					2,000			
8	23	2,000	16,000	18,000		87	696	783

b The *TC, TVC,* and *TFC* curves are graphed in Fig. 10.7.

FIGURE **10.7**

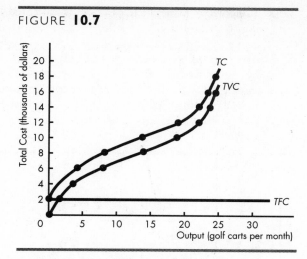

c The *MC, ATC, AVC,* and *AFC* curves are
graphed in Fig. 10.8.

FIGURE **10.8**

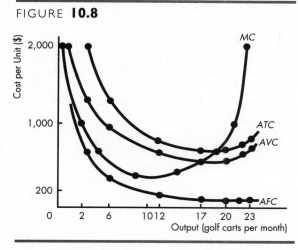

d The new *MC* and *ATC* curves (and the
associated table) are given in Fig. 10.9. The
original curves, MC_1 and ATC_1, are indicated for
reference. The new curves are labelled MC_2 and
ATC_2. Both curves have shifted up as a result of
an increase in the price of labour.

FIGURE **10.9**

Output	MC ($)	ATC ($)
0		0
	2,500	
1		4,500
	1,250	
3		2,333
	833	
6		1,583
	417	
12		1,000
	500	
17		853
	833	
20		850
	1,250	
22		886
	2,500	
23		957

9 a The new *MC* and *ATC* curves (and the
associated table) are given in Fig. 10.10. The
new curves are labelled MC_3 and ATC_3. The
original curves, MC_1 and ATC_1, are indicated for
reference.

FIGURE **10.10**

Output	MC ($)	ATC ($)
0		0
	2,000	
1		6,000
	667	
4		2,000
	333	
10		1,000
	222	
19		632
	286	
26		538
	400	
31		516
	667	
34		529

b The curves have shifted (generally) down and to the right as a result of increasing the plant size. There are economies of scale (increasing returns to scale) up to the level of output at which MC_3 intersects ATC_3 (approximately 32 units).

c The long-run average cost curve is indicated in Fig. 10.10 by the heavy line tracing out the lowest short-run average total cost of producing each level of output. In this example, that happens to correspond entirely to ATC_3.

10 a The long-run average cost curve is indicated in Fig. 10.4 Solution by the heavy scalloped-shaped curve tracing out the lowest short-run average cost of producing each level of output.

b For output of 100 units, the best plant size is associated with short-run average total cost curve 2. For output of 200 units, the best plant size is associated with short-run average total cost curve 5.

FIGURE **10.4** SOLUTION

KEY CONCEPTS

Perfect Competition

Perfect competition is a model that assumes many firms; identical products; many buyers; free entry; complete information.

◆ Each firm is a **price taker.** → *CAN'T INFLUENCE PRICE OF A GOOD OR SERVICE*

◆ Each firm faces a perfectly elastic demand curve at the market price. *(CAN SUBSTITUTE FOR CHEAPER ALTERNATIVE)*.

Firm maximizes profit (**normal profit + economic profit**).

◆ Normal profit = expected return to entrepreneurial ability.

◆ Economic profit = total revenue – total cost (total cost includes normal profit).

◆ **Total revenue** (TR)—price (P) × quantity (Q).

- **Average revenue** (AR)—TR/Q.
- **Marginal revenue** (MR)—$\Delta TR/\Delta Q$.
- In perfect competition, $AR = MR = P$.

In short run, firm decides what quantity to produce or to shut down. *① ② @ WHAT QTY TO PRODUCE - LONGRUN: ① to ↑ or ↓ PLANT SIZE ② STAY IN INDUSTRY OR LEAVE*

◆ Profit maximized at quantity where $MR = MC$:

- If $MR > MC$, firm $\uparrow Q$ to $\uparrow$ profit.
- If $MR < MC$, firm $\downarrow Q$ to $\uparrow$ profit.

◆ Three possible short-run profit-maximizing outcomes:

- $P (= AR = MR) > ATC \rightarrow$ economic profits.
- $P (= AR = MR) = ATC \rightarrow$ zero economic profits (*break-even point* at minimum ATC; firm just earning normal profits).
- $P (= AR = MR) < ATC \rightarrow$ economic losses (firm earning less than normal profits).

◆ For firm suffering economic losses:

- If $P > AVC$, firm will continue to produce.
- If $P < AVC$, firm will temporarily shut down. →
- **Shutdown point** at minimum AVC.

Perfectly competitive firm's supply curve is its MC curve above minimum AVC.

Output, Price, and Profit in the Short Run

Short-run industry supply curve is horizontal sum of individual firm supply curves.

Equilibrium market price and quantity determined by industry demand and supply curves.

◆ In the short run, perfectly competitive firms can make an economic profit, normal profit (zero economic profit), or suffer an economic loss. *BREAKEVEN = NORMAL PROFIT*

◆ In the short run, the number of firms and their plant size are fixed.

Output, Price, and Profit in the Long Run

In the long run, the number of firms in the industry and the plant size of each firm can adjust. Economic profits/losses are signals for firms to enter/exit the industry and cause reallocation of resources. *BASED ON ENTRY & EXIT*

◆ Economic profits → *MEANS* new entry *@ A* → rightward shift industry $S \rightarrow \downarrow P \rightarrow$ elimination profits. *+ MORE NORMAL PROFIT*

◆ Economic losses → existing firms exit → leftward shift industry $S \rightarrow \uparrow P \rightarrow$ elimination losses. *↑ PROFIT TO NORMAL PROFIT*

In long-run competitive equilibrium *= NORMAL PROFIT. (ECO. PROFIT IS ZERO).*

◆ $MR = P = MC$. Firms maximize short-run profits.

◆ $P =$ minimum ATC. Economic profits are zero. No incentive for firms to enter or exit industry.

◆ P = minimum *LRAC*. Optimum plant size. No incentive for firm to change plant size.

Changing Tastes and Advancing Technology

For a permanent shift in demand

◆ ↓ Demand → ↓ P, economic loss and exit → ↓ industry supply → ↑ P. In long run, enough firms exit so remaining firms earn normal profit.

◆ ↑ Demand → ↑ P, economic profit and entry → ↑ industry supply → ↓ P. In long run, enough firms enter so economic profit eliminated and firms earn normal profit.

The change in long-run equilibrium price from a permanent shift in demand depends on

◆ **external economies**—factors beyond control of firm that lower costs as *industry* output ↑.

◆ **external diseconomies**—factors beyond control of firm that raise costs as *industry* output ↑.

The shape of the **long-run industry supply curve** depends on existence of external economies or diseconomies. The long-run industry supply curve shows how industry quantity supplied varies as market price varies after all possible adjustments, including changes in plant size and number of firms. Shape may be

◆ horizontal for constant cost industry.

◆ upward sloping for increasing cost industry with external diseconomies.

◆ downward sloping for decreasing cost industry with external economies.

New technology → ↓ costs, ↑ industry supply → ↓ P. New technology firms make economic profit and enter. Old technology firms suffer economic loss and exit or switch to new technology. In long run, all firms use new technology and earn normal profit

Competition and Efficiency

Allocative efficiency—no one can be made better off without making someone else worse off; no wasted resources. Requires

◆ **Consumer efficiency**—maximum utility. All points on market demand curve achieve consumer efficiency if there are no **external benefits**—benefits accruing to people other than buyer of good.

◆ **Producer efficiency**—technological efficiency and economic efficiency. All points on market supply curve achieve producer efficiency if there are no **external costs**—cost borne by people other than producer of good.

◆ **Exchange efficiency**—all gains from trade realized. Total gains from trade are sum of

• **Consumer surplus**—value of goods to consumers – price paid = area below demand curve and above market price.

• **Producer surplus**—total revenue – opportunity cost = area below market price and above supply curve.

Perfect competition achieves allocative efficiency at the market equilibrium price and quantity if there are no external benefits and costs.

HELPFUL HINTS

1   Although perfectly competitive markets are rare in the real world, there are three important reasons to develop a thorough understanding of their behaviour.

First, many markets closely approximate perfectly competitive markets. The analysis in this chapter gives direct and useful insights into the behaviour of these markets.

Second, the theory of perfect competition allows us to isolate the effects of competitive forces that are at work in *all* markets, even in those that do not match the assumptions of perfect competition.

Third, the perfectly competitive model serves as a useful benchmark for evaluating relative allocative efficiency.

2   In the short run, a perfectly competitive firm cannot change the size of its plant—it has fixed inputs. The firm also is a price taker; it always sells at the market price, which it cannot influence. The only variable that the firm controls is its level of output. The short-run condition for profit maximization is to choose the level of output at which marginal revenue equals marginal cost. This is a general condition which, as we will see in subsequent chapters, applies to other market structures such as monopoly and monopolistic competition. Since for the perfectly competitive firm, marginal revenue is equal to price, this profit-maximizing condition takes a particular form; choose the level of output at which price is equal to marginal cost ($P = MC$).

3 Many students have trouble understanding why a firm continues to operate at the break-even point, where economic profits are zero. The key to understanding lies in the definition of which costs are included in the average total cost curve. Recall from Chapter 9 that the economist defines a firm's total costs as *opportunity costs*, which include both explicit costs and *implicit costs*.

Implicit costs include forgone interest, forgone rent, and forgone cost of the owner's resources. Owners supply their time, which could have been used to earn income elsewhere. Owners also supply entrepreneurial ability. Normal profit is the expected return to entrepreneurial ability and is part of a firm's implicit costs.

At the break-even point where total revenue equals total cost (or, equivalently, average revenue equals average total cost), the owners of the firm are still earning a return on their investment, time, and entrepreneurial ability, which is equal to the best return that they could earn elsewhere. That is the definition of opportunity cost—the best alternative forgone. As the phrase "normal profits" implies, these are profits that could normally be earned as a return to entrepreneurial ability, on average, in any other industry. At the break-even point, the firm is earning normal profits even though its economic profits (sometimes called "extra-normal," or "above-average," profits) are zero. In earning normal profits, the firm is earning just as much profit as it could anywhere else, and is therefore totally content to continue producing in this industry.

4 When the price of output falls below the break-even point, but is above the shutdown point, the firm will continue to produce even though it is suffering economic losses. In this price range, the firm is no longer earning normal profit and theoretically could earn more by switching to another industry. Nonetheless, the firm will continue to operate in the short run because switching has costs. In order to switch industries, the firm must shut down, which entails still paying its total fixed costs.

As long as price is above the shutdown point (minimum average variable cost), a firm will decide to produce since it will be covering total variable cost and part of total fixed cost. Its loss will be less if it continues to produce at the output where $P = MC$ than if it shuts down.

If price falls below the shutdown point, a firm that produces output will not only lose its total fixed costs, it will lose additional money on every unit of output produced, since average revenue is less than average variable cost. Thus when price is less than average variable cost, the firm will choose to minimize its loss by shutting down.

5 In the long run, fixed costs disappear, and the firm can switch between industries and change plant size without cost. Economic profits serve as the signal for the movement or reallocation of firm resources until long-run equilibrium is achieved. Firms will move out of industries with negative economic profits and into industries with positive economic profits. Only when economic profits are zero will there be no tendency for firms to exit or enter industries.

The fact that there are no restrictions on entry into the industry is what assures that economic profits will be zero and that firms will be producing at the minimum of their long-run average cost curves in long-run equilibrium.

6 In long-run equilibrium, three conditions are satisfied for each firm in an industry:
  i $MR = P = MC$. This implies that profits are maximized for each firm.
  ii $P = ATC$. This implies that economic profits are zero and each firm is just earning normal profit.
  iii $P = $ minimum $LRAC$. This implies that production takes place at the point of minimum long-run average cost.

SELF-TEST

True/False/Uncertain and Explain

1 The industry demand curve in a perfectly competitive industry is horizontal.

2 The objective of firms in a competitive industry is to maximize revenue.

3 Firms can make losses in the long run but not the short run.

4 A perfectly competitive industry will achieve allocative efficiency if there are no external costs or external benefits.

5 At prices below minimum average total cost, a firm will shut down.

6 The supply curve of a perfectly competitive firm gives the quantities of output supplied at alternative prices as long as the firm earns economic profits.

7 In long-run equilibrium, each firm in a perfectly competitive industry will choose the plant size associated with minimum long-run average cost.

8 If, in a competitive industry, there are external economies, the long-run industry supply curve is positively sloped.

9 Suppose a competitive industry is in long-run equilibrium when there is a substantial increase in total fixed costs. All firms will now be making economic losses and some firms will go out of business.

10 When the quantity of a good bought by a consumer at a given price is a point on the demand curve, consumer efficiency has occurred.

Multiple-Choice

1 Which of the following is *not* a characteristic of a perfectly competitive industry?
a downward-sloping industry demand curve
b perfectly elastic demand curve for each individual firm
c each firm decides its quantity of output
d slightly differentiated products
e many firms each supplying a small fraction of industry supply

2 If a firm faces a perfectly elastic demand for its product, then
a it is not a price taker.
b it will want to lower its price to increase sales.
c it will want to raise its price to increase total revenue.
d its marginal revenue curve is equal to the price of the product.
e it will always earn zero economic profits.

3 In a perfectly competitive industry, the market price is $10. An individual firm is producing the output at which $MC = ATC = \$15$. AVC at that output is $10. What should the firm do to maximize its short-run profits?
a shut down
b expand output
c contract output
d leave output unchanged
e insufficient information to answer

4 Refer to Fact 11.1. If the price of fiddleheads last month was $15 per bag, Franklin
a should have shut down because total revenue did not cover total variable cost.
b made an economic loss of $135.
c made zero economic profits.
d made an economic profit of $50.
e made an economic profit of $100.

FACT **11.1**

Franklin is a fiddlehead farmer. He sold 10 bags of fiddleheads last month, with total fixed cost of $100 and total variable cost of $50.

---

5 Refer to Fact 11.1. If fiddlehead prices fell to $10 per bag while production and cost figures remained the same, Franklin would
a shut down immediately.
b break even because total revenues just cover total fixed costs.
c be indifferent between producing and shutting down because his loss of $50 just covers total variable costs.
d continue producing despite his loss of $50.
e continue producing despite his loss of $100.

6 Refer to Fact 11.1. Suppose the price of fiddleheads is expected to stay at $10 per bag, and Franklin's production and cost figures are expected to stay the same. His total fixed cost consists entirely of rent on land, and his five-year lease on the land runs out at the end of the month. Should Franklin renew the lease?

a Yes, because total revenue will still cover total fixed cost.

b Yes, because total revenue will still cover total variable cost and a portion of total fixed cost.

c No, because total revenue must cover all costs for resources to remain in fiddlehead farming in the long run.

d No, because in the long run, zero economic profits are a signal to move resources out of fiddlehead farming.

e Insufficient information to answer.

7 In which of the following situations will a perfectly competitive firm earn economic profits?

a $MR > AVC$

b $MR > ATC$

c $ATC > MC$

d $ATC > AR$

e $AR > AVC$

8 In the price range below minimum average variable cost, a perfectly competitive firm's supply curve is

a horizontal at the market price.

b vertical at zero output.

c the same as its marginal cost curve.

d the same as its average variable cost curve.

e none of the above.

9 The short-run industry supply curve is

a the horizontal sum of the individual firms' supply curves.

b the vertical sum of the individual firms' supply curves.

c vertical at the total level of output being produced by all firms.

d horizontal at the current market price.

e none of the above.

10 Mugs can be produced from labour alone. Table 11.1 shows two output/input combinations.

TABLE **11.1**

Mugs	Labour-Hours
25	4
27	5

If the price of a mug is $100 and labour costs $50 per hour, what is the marginal cost of production in this range of output?

a $25

b $40

c $50

d $100

e none of the above

11 A firm in a perfectly competitive industry is maximizing its short-run profits by producing 500 units of output. At 500 units of output, which of the following *must be false*?

a $MC < AVC$

b $MC < ATC$

c $MC > ATC$

d $AR < ATC$

e $AR > AVC$

12 If a profit-maximizing firm in perfect competition is earning economic profits, then it must be producing a level of output where

a price is greater than marginal cost.

b price is greater than marginal revenue.

c marginal cost is greater than marginal revenue.

d marginal cost is greater than average total cost.

e average total cost is greater than marginal cost.

13 If an industry experiences external economies as the industry expands in the long run, the long-run industry supply curve will

a be perfectly inelastic.

b be perfectly elastic.

c have a positive slope.

d have a negative slope.

e have allocative inefficiency.

14 Under which of the following circumstances would a long-run equilibrium in a perfectly competitive industry *not* be allocatively efficient?

a firms are price takers

b new technologies are developed

c external economies or external diseconomies are present

d external costs or external benefits are present

e free entry to the industry

15 Figure 11.1 illustrates the cost curves for a perfectly competitive firm. The current market price is $11 and the firm has the plant size shown by $SRAC_1$. The firm's short-run equilibrium output is
a 7 units.
b 9 units.
c 10 units.
d 17 units.
e 18 units.

FIGURE **11.1**

16 Refer to Fig. 11.1. The current market price is $11 and the firm has the plant size shown by $SRAC_1$. In the long run, the firm will
a exit from the industry.
b keep its current plant size, and other firms will enter the industry.
c keep its current plant size, and other firms will exit from the industry.
d increase its plant size, and other firms will enter the industry.
e increase its plant size, and other firms will exit from the industry.

17 Refer to Fig. 11.1. The long-run equilibrium price and quantity combination is
a $6 and 7 units.
b $6 and 17 units.
c $8 and 9 units.
d $8 and 18 units.
e $9 and 7 units.

18 A perfectly competitive industry is in short-run equilibrium with price below average total cost. Which of the following is *not* a prediction of the long-run consequences of such a situation?
a price will increase
b the output of the industry will increase
c firms will leave the industry
d the output of each remaining firm will increase
e economic profits will be zero

19 The supply curve for an individual firm in a perfectly competitive industry is $P = 1 + 2Q_S$. If the industry consists of 100 identical firms, then what is industry supply when $P = 7$?
a 300
b 400
c 600
d 800
e none of the above

20 If a perfectly competitive firm in the short run is able to pay its variable costs and part, but not all, of its fixed costs, then it is operating in the range on its marginal cost curve that is
a above the break-even point.
b below the break-even point.
c above the shutdown point.
d below the shutdown point.
e between the shutdown and break-even points.

21 A perfectly competitive firm is maximizing profit if
a marginal cost equals price and price is above minimum average variable cost.
b marginal cost equals price and price is above minimum average fixed cost.
c total revenue is at a maximum.
d average variable cost is at a minimum.
e average total cost is at a minimum.

22 The maximum loss a firm will experience in long-run equilibrium is
a zero.
b its total cost.
c its total variable cost.
d its average total cost.
e none of the above.

23 For a perfectly competitive firm in long-run equilibrium, which of the following is *not* equal to price?

a short-run average total cost
b short-run average variable cost
c short-run marginal cost
d long-run average cost
e average revenue

24 When economic profits are zero

a the product will not be produced in the short run.
b the product will not be produced in the long run.
c firms will leave the industry.
d revenues are not covering implicit costs.
e none of the above will occur.

25 Which of the following is *not* true of a new long-run equilibrium resulting from a new technology in a perfectly competitive industry?

a price will be lower
b industry output will be greater
c firm profits will be greater
d all firms in the industry will be using the new technology
e average total cost will be lower

Short Answer Problems

1 Why will a firm in a perfectly competitive industry choose *not* to charge a price either above or below the market price?

2 Why will economic profits tend to zero in long-run equilibrium in a perfectly competitive industry?

3 Suppose we observe a perfectly competitive industry in a long-run equilibrium when there is a permanent decrease in demand for the industry's product. There are no external economies or diseconomies. How does the industry adjust to a new long-run equilibrium? What happens to price, quantity, firm profits, and the number of firms during the adjustment process?

4 In a perfectly competitive industry with no external benefits or costs, suppose output is restricted to a quantity less than the equilibrium quantity. Explain why this level of output is allocatively inefficient.

5 Table 11.2 gives the total cost structure for one of many identical firms in a perfectly competitive industry.

a Complete the table by computing total variable cost, average total cost, average variable cost, and marginal cost at each level of output. [*Remember*: As in the problems in Chapter 10, marginal cost should be entered *midway* between rows.]

TABLE **11.2**

Quantity (units per day)	Total Cost ($)	Total Variable Cost ($)	Average Total Cost ($)	Average Variable Cost ($)	Marginal Cost ($)
0	12				
					...
1	24				
					...
2	32				
					...
3	42				
					...
4	54				
					...
5	68				
					...
6	84				

b Complete Table 11.3 by computing the profit (per day) for the firm at each level of output if the price of output is $9; $11; $15.

TABLE **11.3**

Quantity (units per day)	Profit P = $9	Profit P = $11	Profit P = $15
0			
1			
2			
3			
4			
5			
6			

c Consider the profit-maximizing output decision of the firm at alternative prices. How much will the firm produce if the price of output is $9? $11? $15? Explain each of your answers.

6 A firm will maximize profit if it produces every unit of output for which marginal revenue exceeds marginal cost. This is called the marginal approach to profit maximization. Using the marginal approach, determine the profit-maximizing level of output for the firm in Short Answer Problem 5 when the price of output is $15. How does your answer here compare with your answer in 5c?

7 This problem concerns a hypothetical pottery manufacturing firm that produces ceramic mugs for sale in a purely competitive market. With a plant of given size, the firm can turn out the quantities of ceramic mugs shown in Table 11.4, by varying the amount it uses of a single variable input, labour.

TABLE **11.4**

Number of Mugs	Labour-Hours (per day)
20	6.50
40	11.00
60	14.50
80	17.50
100	20.50
120	23.75
140	27.50
160	32.00
180	37.50
200	44.50
220	53.50
240	65.00
260	79.50
280	97.50

Suppose the firm can hire all the labour it would ever want at the going wage of $8 per labour-hour. The firm's total fixed costs are $64 per day.

a Draw a table showing output, total variable cost (*TVC*), total cost (*TC*), average variable cost (*AVC*), average total cost (*ATC*), and marginal cost (*MC*). [*Remember:* Marginal cost should be entered *midway* between rows of output.]

b On a graph with *Mugs (per day)* on the horizontal axis, draw the three "per-unit" cost curves, *AVC*, *ATC*, and *MC*. [Note that the marginal cost values from your table should be plotted on the graph *midway* between the corresponding units of output.]

c Consider (separately) the following alternative market prices that the firm might face: *P* = $3.20, *P* = $2, *P* = $1.65, *P* = $1.40. Assuming that the firm wants to maximize its profit, for *each* of the above prices, answer the following questions: Approximately how many mugs per day would the firm produce? How do you know? Is the firm making a profit at that price? And if so, approximately how much?

8 Suppose that the ceramic pottery mug industry consists of 60 firms, each identical to the single firm discussed in Short Answer Problem 7. Table 11.5 represents some points on the industry demand schedule for ceramic pottery mugs.

TABLE **11.5**

Price ($)	Quantity Demanded
1.00	15,900
1.60	14,400
2.20	12,900
2.80	11,400
3.40	9,900
4.00	8,400
4.60	6,900
5.20	5,400
5.80	3,900
6.40	2,400
7.00	900

a On a new graph, draw the industry short-run supply curve. Draw the industry demand curve on the same graph.
b What is the short-run equilibrium price of ceramic pottery mugs?
c Is the ceramic pottery mug industry in long-run equilibrium? Explain your answer.

9 A perfectly competitive industry has 100 identical firms in the short run, each of which has the short-run cost curves listed in Table 11.6.

TABLE **11.6**

Output (units)	Average Total Cost ($)	Average Variable Cost ($)	Marginal Cost ($)
11	20.5	13.1	
			·········· 12
12	19.8	13.0	
			·········· 14
13	19.3	13.1	
			·········· 16
14	19.1	13.3	
			·········· 18
15	19.0	13.6	
			·········· 20
16	19.1	14.0	
			·········· 22
17	19.2	14.5	
			·········· 24
18	19.5	15.0	
			·········· 26
19	19.8	15.6	
			·········· 28
20	20.3	16.2	
			·········· 30
21	20.7	16.9	

This short-run average total cost curve touches the long-run average cost curve at the minimum point on the long-run average cost curve as point *m* in Text Fig. 11.9 on page 245. The industry demand schedule is the same in the long and the short run. Table 11.7 represents some points on the demand schedule.

TABLE **11.7**

Price ($)	Quantity Demanded
11	3,200
13	3,000
15	2,800
17	2,600
19	2,400
21	2,200
23	2,000
25	1,800
27	1,600
29	1,400
31	1,200

a What is the quantity of output corresponding to the firm's break-even point? the shutdown point? Explain your answers.

b What is the short-run equilibrium price in this market? Show how you found your answer.

c What amount of profit or loss is being made by each firm at the short-run equilibrium price? Is this industry in long-run equilibrium at its present size? Why or why not?

d Exactly how many firms will exist in this industry in the long run? Explain your answer. How much economic profit will each firm earn in the long run?

10 Consider a perfectly competitive industry in long-run equilibrium. All the firms in the industry are identical.

a Draw a two-part graph illustrating the long-run equilibrium for the industry—part (a) on the left—and for the typical firm—part (b) on the right. The graph of the firm should include the *MC*, *ATC*, *MR*, and *LRAC* curves. Assume that the *LRAC* curve is U-shaped as it is in Text Fig. 11.9 on page 245. Label the equilibrium price P_0, the equilibrium industry quantity Q_0, and the output of the firm q_0.

b Now, suppose there is a decline in industry demand. Using your graphs from part **a**, show what happens to market price, firm output, firm profits, and industry equilibrium quantity in the short run (assume that the shutdown point is not reached).

Then show what happens to market price, firm output, firm profits, and industry equilibrium quantity in the long run (assume that there are no external economies or diseconomies). What has happened to the number of firms?

A N S W E R S

True/False/Uncertain and Explain

1 F Individual firm demand curve horizontal. Industry demand curve downward sloping. (234–235)

2 F Maximize total profit. (236–237)

3 F Losses in short run but not long run. (243–244)

4 T "Invisible hand" → economic efficiency and consumer efficiency. (249–251)

5 U True if $P <$ minimum *AVC*. False if $P >$ minimum *AVC* but $<$ minimum *ATC*. (240–241)

6 F   As long as P > minimum AVC. (240–241)

7 T   Otherwise firm driven out of business by lower-cost firms. (245)

8 F   Negatively sloped. (247–248)

◑9 T ATC shifts ↑ with no ΔMC. Economic losses → exit. (243–244)

10 T   Definition. (249–250)

Multiple-Choice

1 d   Identical products. (234–235)

2 d   Firm can ↑ Q without ΔP, so MR from additional $Q = P$. (234–235)

◑3 c   Draw graph. Firm should choose lower Q where $P = MC$. If AVC at current Q = $10, minimum AVC must be < $10, so new Q > minimum AVC. (238–240)

4 c   Profits = TR ($15 × 100) – TC ($100 + $50) = 0. (238–240)

◑5 d TR ($10 × 10) – TC ($100 + $50) = –$50. Shutting down would bring bigger loss of $100 (fixed costs). (238–240)

◑6 c   He is making long-run decision. **a, b** refer to short run. **d** false because *losses* signal to move resources. (243–244)

7 b   Since $MR = AR$, AR > ATC. Multiply by Q → TR > TC, so economic profits. (238–240)

8 b   Firm stays shut down ($Q = 0$) until P reaches minimum AVC. (240–241)

9 a   Definition. **c** is momentary supply curve. **d** is demand curve facing individual firm. (240–241)

10 a $MC = \Delta TC/\Delta Q$ = $50/2. Mug price irrelevant. (216–217)

◑11 a   **a** implies shutdown. Other answers possible with losses (**b, d**) or profits (**c, e**). (238–240)

12 d   ($MC = P =$) AR > ATC. **a, b, c** not consistent with profit maximization. **e** implies losses. (238–240)

13 d   Because ↓ costs as industry Q ↑. (247–248)

14 d   **a, e** conditions perfect competition. **b, c** affect shape long-run supply curve but not allocative efficiency. (249–250)

15 c   Choose Q where $P = MC$. (238–240)

16 d   Profits → new entry → ↓ P and incentive to build larger, lower cost plant. (243–245)

17 b   Long-run equilibrium at intersection $SRAC$, $SRMC$, and $LRAC$ curves. (243–245)

18 b   As firms exit, supply shifts left → ↓ industry Q and ↑ P → ↑ Q remaining firms. (243–244)

◉19 a   For one firm: $7 = 1 + 2Q_S$; $2Q_S = 6$; $Q_S = 3$. For 100 firms, $3 × 100 = 300$. (241)

20 e   If couldn't pay variable costs → below shutdown. If paying all variable and fixed costs → break even. (238–240)

21 a AFC irrelevant. Maximizing profit ≠ maximizing revenue. **d, e** might be true depending on P. (238–240)

22 a   Definition long-run equilibrium → zero economic profits. (243–244)

23 b   Long-run equilibrium at intersection ATC, MC, and $LRAC$ curves. (244–245)

◑24 e   Product produced in short and long run, revenues exactly cover all costs (including implicit). (243–245)

25 c   In long-run equilibrium, economic profits always zero. (248–249)

Short Answer Problems

1   If a firm in a perfectly competitive industry charged a price even slightly higher than the market price, it would lose all of its sales. Thus it will not charge a price above the market price. Since it can sell all it wants at the market price, it would not be able to increase sales by lowering its price. Thus it would not charge a price below the market price since this would decrease total revenue and profits.

2   In a perfectly competitive industry, the existence of positive economic profits will attract the entry of new firms, which will shift the industry supply curve rightward, causing the market price to fall and firm profits to decline. This tendency will exist as long as there are positive economic profits. Similarly, the existence of economic losses will cause firms to exit from the industry, which will shift the industry supply curve leftward, causing the market price to rise and firm profits to rise (losses to decline). This tendency will exist as long as losses are being made. Thus, the only point of rest in the long run (the only equilibrium) occurs when economic profits are zero.

3   The decrease in market demand causes the market price to fall. Since, in the initial long-run equilibrium, each firm was earning zero economic profit, the fall in price means that profits will fall and firms will now be making losses. Since the decrease in demand is permanent, these losses will induce some firms to leave the industry. This will shift the industry supply curve leftward, causing an increase in market price. The increasing price causes profits to increase for the remaining firms, so their losses will decline. The exit of firms continues until losses are eliminated. Costs have not been affected by the decrease in demand, so if there are no external economies or diseconomies, the price must continue rising until it reaches its original level in the new long-run equilibrium. The output of each firm will also equal its original level, but the equilibrium quantity at the industry level will be less because the number of firms has declined.

4 Refer to Text Fig. 11.12 on page 250. If output is restricted to quantity Q_0, the value to consumers of an additional unit of the good is V_0, while producers would be willing to supply additional goods for any price at or above C_0. If more goods are produced and sold at any price in between V_0 and C_0, consumers will be better off because they value the goods more than the price paid, and producers will be better off because they receive a higher price than the minimum necessary to induce production. Consumers and producers could be made better off without making someone else worse off. Therefore at quantity Q_0, there are unrealized gains from trade (more consumer and producer surplus is possible), and this level of output is allocatively inefficient.

5 a Completed Table 11.2 is shown here as Table 11.2 Solution.

TABLE **11.2** SOLUTION

Quantity (units per day)	Total Cost ($)	Total Variable Cost ($)	Average Total Cost ($)	Average Variable Cost ($)	Marginal Cost ($)
0	12	0	—	—	
					… 12
1	24	12	24.00	12.00	
					… 8
2	32	20	16.00	10.00	
					… 10
3	42	30	14.00	10.00	
					… 12
4	54	42	13.50	10.50	
					… 14
5	68	56	13.60	11.20	
					… 16
6	84	72	14.00	12.00	

b Completed Table 11.3 is given here as Table 11.3 Solution. The values for profit are computed as total revenue minus total cost, where total revenue is price times quantity and total cost is given in Table 11.2.

TABLE **11.3** SOLUTION

Quantity (units per day)	Profit P = $9	Profit P = $11	Profit P = $15
0	**-12**	-12	-12
1	-15	-13	-9
2	-14	-10	-2
3	-15	**-9**	3
4	-18	-10	6
5	-23	-13	**7**
6	-30	-18	6

c If the price is $9, profit is maximized (actually loss is minimized) when the firm shuts down and produces zero units. If the firm chooses to produce, its loss will be at least $14, which is greater than the fixed cost loss of $12. If the price is $11, the firm is still unable to make a positive economic profit. The loss is minimized (at $9) if the firm produces 3 units. At this price, all of variable cost and part of fixed cost can be recovered. At a price of $15, the firm will maximize profit (at $7) at an output of 5 units per day.

6 The marginal approach to profit maximization states that the firm should produce all units of output for which marginal revenue exceeds marginal cost. For a perfectly competitive firm, marginal revenue equals price, so (equivalently) the firm should produce every unit for which price exceeds marginal cost. If the price of output is $15, we can see from Table 11.2 Solution that the firm should produce 5 units. Since the marginal cost of moving from the 4th to the 5th unit ($14) is less than price ($15), the 5th unit should be produced. The marginal cost of moving to the 6th unit ($16), however, is greater than price. It should not be produced. The answer here is the same as the answer in 5c.

7 a With only one variable input (labour), *TVC* (for any level of output) = (labour hours × wage rate). The requested table is Table 11.8.

TABLE **11.8**

Output (per day)	TVC ($)	TC ($)	AVC ($)	ATC ($)	MC ($)
0	0	64	—	—	
					⋯ 2.60
20	52	116	2.60	5.80	
					⋯ 1.80
40	88	152	2.20	3.80	
					⋯ 1.40
60	116	180	1.93	3.00	
					⋯ 1.20
80	140	204	1.75	2.55	
					⋯ 1.20
100	164	228	1.64	2.28	
					⋯ 1.30
120	190	254	1.58	2.12	
					⋯ 1.50
140	220	284	1.57	2.03	
					⋯ 1.80
160	256	320	1.60	2.00	
					⋯ 2.20
180	300	364	1.67	2.02	
					⋯ 2.80
200	356	420	1.78	2.10	
					⋯ 3.60
220	428	492	1.95	2.24	
					⋯ 4.60
240	520	584	2.17	2.43	
					⋯ 5.80
260	636	700	2.45	2.69	
					⋯ 7.20
280	780	844	2.79	3.01	

b The graph appears in Fig. 11.2. It also illustrates the answers to part **c**.

FIGURE **11.2**

c In every case, at the profit-maximizing output, marginal revenue (which, for a price-taking firm in a perfectly competitive market, is the same as market price) is equal to marginal cost, provided that price is greater than average variable cost.

Profit "per unit of output" is the difference between average revenue (price) and average total cost at the level of output. Total profit is "per unit profit" × number of units of output. Economic profit might be zero or negative (a loss) and still be the best the firm can attain in the short run. The calculations of total profit at each price appear in Table 11.9.

TABLE **11.9**

Price ($)	Output Chosen	Per Unit Profit ($)	Total Profit ($)
3.20	200	1.10	220.00
2.00	160	0	0
1.65	140	-0.38	-53.20
1.40	0	0	-64.00

Note the following:

1. Marginal cost is $3.20 at approximately 200 units.
2. The per unit profit is $P - ATC$.
3. 160 units is the "break-even" level of output, where MC = minimum ATC and the firm is just covering all its opportunity costs.
4. At an output of 140 units, the firm continues to produce in the short run because it can more than cover its variable costs. If it produced zero units, its loss would be greater, $64, which is the amount of its fixed costs.
5. Any positive output increases losses when the price is below the shutdown price, which here is approximately $1.57. When price is less than minimum AVC, the firm would not only lose its fixed costs, it would also lose additional money on every unit it produced.

8 There are 60 identical price-taking firms. For every possible price (above minimum AVC of approximately $1.57), each firm will supply the quantity at which $P = MC$. We can derive (in Table 11.10) the industry supply schedule from the MC curve of an individual firm.

TABLE **11.10**

Price ($)	Quantity Supplied by 1 Firm	Quantity Supplied by 60 Firms
1.57	134	8,040
1.80	150	9,000
2.20	170	10,200
2.80	190	11,400
3.60	210	12,600
4.60	230	13,800
5.80	250	15,000
7.20	270	16,200

a The graph of the industry supply curve appears in Fig. 11.3, together with the industry demand curve.

FIGURE **11.3**

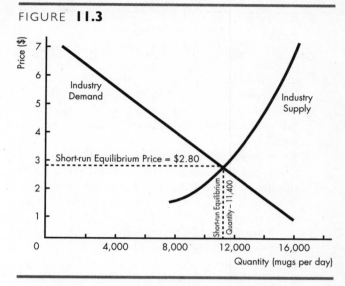

b The short-run equilibrium price is $2.80 (where a total of 11,400 mugs per day are supplied and sold; or 190 mugs per day supplied by each firm at MC of $2.80).

c At a price of $2.80 and output of 190, for each firm, $P > ATC$ where $ATC = 2.06. So all existing firms are making economic profits after covering *all* opportunity costs including a normal profit. (See Helpful Hint 3.) The industry will attract new entrants because it offers more than normal profits. Even though the industry is in short-run equilibrium, it is *not* in long-run equilibrium because the number of firms has not "stabilized." New firms will enter the industry, the industry supply curve will shift rightward, and price will fall until no firm is making economic profits.

9 a The break-even point occurs at 15 units of output. At this level of output, ATC is at its minimum ($19) and is equal to MC. Since the MC of moving from the 14th to the 15th unit is $18, and the MC of moving from the 15th to the 16th units is $20, we can interpolate the MC exactly at 15 units as midway between $18 and $20, or as $19. The shutdown point occurs at 12 units of output. At this level of output, AVC is at its minimum ($13) and is equal to MC. The interpolated value of MC at exactly 12 units of output is midway between $12 and $14, or is $13.

b The short-run equilibrium price is $25. This is the price at which industry quantity supplied equals quantity demanded as shown in Table 11.11.

c At a price of $25, each firm produces 18 units of output. At 18 units, ATC is $19.50, so economic profits are being earned. The amount of profit is ($25 − $19.50 per unit =) $5.50 per unit. Total economic profit per *firm* is $5.50/unit × 18 units = $99. This means that new entrants will be attracted to the industry. We conclude that the industry is *not* in long-run equilibrium.

d Entry continues until economic profits are competed away, and all firms are operating at the minimum point of the *LRAC* curve (which, in this problem, is also the minimum point of the given short-run average total cost curve).

    Minimum *ATC* for each firm occurs at 15 units of output, when $ATC = MC = \$19$, so price in the long run *must* be $19. At a price of $19, consumers demand 2,400 units (from Table 11.11). It follows that when the industry is in long-run equilibrium, there must be 2,400 units/15 units per firm = 160 firms in the industry, each producing 15 units of output, at *zero economic profit.*

TABLE **11.11**

$P = MC$ ($)	Quantity Supplied by 1 Firm	Quantity Supplied by 100 Firms	Quantity Demanded
13	12	1,200	3,000
15	13	1,300	2,800
17	14	1,400	2,600
19	15	1,500	2,400
21	16	1,600	2,200
23	17	1,700	2,000
25	**18**	**1,800**	**1,800**
27	19	1,900	1,600
29	20	2,000	1,400

10 a A long-run equilibrium in a perfectly competitive industry is illustrated in Fig. 11.4.

    Part (a) illustrates industry equilibrium at the intersection of industry demand (D_0) and industry supply (S_0): point *a*. The equilibrium industry quantity is labelled Q_0 and the equilibrium market price is labelled P_0.

    Part (b) illustrates the situation for a single firm in long-run equilibrium. The firm is at point *a′*, the minimum point of both the short-run average total cost curve (*ATC*) and the long-run average cost curve (*LRAC*). The firm is producing the output labelled q_0 and earning zero economic profit.

FIGURE **11.4**

(a) Industry

(b) Firm

b The new short-run equilibrium is also illustrated in Fig. 11.4. The decrease in demand shifts the market demand curve leftward, from D_0 to D_1. The new market equilibrium is at point b. The price has fallen from P_0 to P_1 and the industry equilibrium quantity has fallen from Q_0 to Q_1. The fall in price induces firms to reduce output as shown by the move from point a' to point b' on the MC curve in part (b). Since P_1 is less than minimum ATC, firms are making losses in the new short-run equilibrium.

The new long-run equilibrium is also illustrated in Fig. 11.4. With short-run losses, firms will exit from the industry in the long run. This causes the industry supply curve to shift leftward, causing the price to rise and thus reducing losses. Firms continue to leave until the industry supply curve has shifted enough to eliminate losses, from S_0 to S_1. This gives a new long-run industry equilibrium at point c and the price has returned to its initial level, P_0, but industry quantity has fallen to Q_2.

As firms exit and the market price rises, remaining firms will increase their output (moving up the MC curve from point b' to point a') and their losses will be reduced. When sufficient firms have left the industry, the price will have risen (returned) to P_0 and firms will have returned to point a' in part (b). At this point, each firm is again earning zero economic profit and firm output has returned to q_0. But, since there are now fewer firms, industry equilibrium quantity is less.

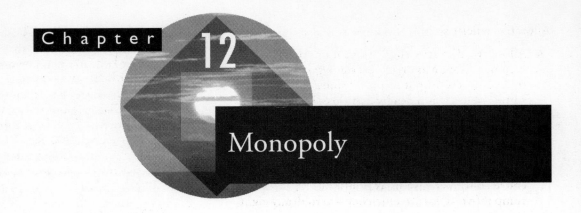

Chapter

12

Monopoly

How Monopoly Arises

Monopoly—industry with one supplier of product with no close substitutes. Arises from

- **Barriers to entry**—impediments protecting firm from competition from potential new entrants.

  - Legal barriers to entry—for a **legal monopoly**, competition and entry restricted by public franchise, *government licence, patent,* or *copyright.*
  - Natural barriers to entry—a **natural monopoly** occurs when, due to economies of scale, one firm can supply the market at lower *ATC* than multiple firms can.

Single-Price Monopoly

Single-price monopoly charges same price for every unit output.

- Monopoly's demand curve is industry demand curve.

- Marginal revenue (*MR*) < price (*P*). To sell additional output, must lower *P* on *all* output.

- In moving down the monopoly's demand curve

  - when total revenue (*TR*) ↑, *MR* positive, η > 1.
  - when *TR* maximum, *MR* zero, η = 1.
  - when *TR* ↓, *MR* negative, η < 1.

- Monopoly's technology and costs like firm in perfect competition.

- Profit-maximizing monopoly chooses output at which *MR* = *MC*, charges maximum price consumers willing to pay (on demand curve).

- Monopoly never operates in inelastic range demand curve. Monopoly has no supply curve.

- Monopoly can make economic profits even in long run because barriers prevent entry of new firms.

Price Discrimination

Price discrimination—charging some customers lower price than others for *identical* good; or charging an individual customer a lower price on a large purchase than a small, even though selling costs are identical.

Price discrimination can increase profits by enabling firm to capture more of the consumer surplus.

- *Perfect price discrimination*—different price for each unit sold; obtains maximum price each consumer willing to pay.

  - *MR* curve same as demand curve. Same output as perfectly competitive industry.
  - But all consumer surplus captured as profit.

- Price discrimination requires

  - Good cannot be resold.
  - Charge lower *P* to higher elasticity group. Charge higher *P* to lower elasticity group.

- Price discriminating monopoly produces greater output than single-price monopoly.

Comparing Monopoly and Competition

Price and output

- Single-price monopoly *P* > competitive *P*.

- Single-price monopoly *Q* < competitive *Q*.

  - The more perfectly the monopoly can price discriminate, the closer its *Q* gets to competitive *Q*.

Allocative efficiency

◆ Allocative efficiency single-price monopoly
< competition. Monopoly prevents gains from
trade: restricts output, captures some consumer
surplus, but creates **deadweight loss**—total loss of
consumer surplus and **producer surplus** (revenue
– opportunity cost production) below efficient
levels.

◆ Perfect price discriminating monopoly captures
entire consumer surplus as profit, but achieves
competitive allocative efficiency—zero deadweight
loss.

Costs of monopoly

◆ Deadweight loss.

◆ Cost of resources used **rent seeking**—searching out
profitable monopoly opportunities.

◆ If no barriers to entry, cost of resources used rent
seeking = value monopoly profit (if there is rent
seeking).

◆ Social cost of monopoly = deadweight loss +
monopoly's economic profit (if there is rent
seeking).

Gains from monopoly

◆ *Economies of scale* (↓ *LRAC* through ↑ *Q*).

◆ **Economies of scope** (↓ *ATC* through ↑ range of
goods produced).

◆ ↑ innovation and technological change (in some
cases).

HELPFUL HINTS

1 The opposite extreme of perfect competition is
monopoly. While in perfect competition there
are many firms that can decide only on quantity
produced but not on price, a monopoly is a
single firm with the ability to set both quantity
and price. These differences create differences in
the revenue situation facing the monopoly. The
cost curves for the two market structures are
assumed to be the same.

Because there is only one firm, the industry
demand curve is also the firm demand curve.
Facing a negatively sloped demand curve, if a
single-price monopoly wants to sell one more
unit of output, it must lower its price. This has
two effects on revenue. First, the sale of an
additional unit will increase revenue by the
amount of the price. However, since the firm
must also *drop the price on previous units*, revenue

on these will decrease. The net change in
revenue, the marginal revenue, will be less than
price and the marginal revenue curve will lie
below the demand curve.

Combining this new revenue situation with
our familiar cost curves from Chapter 10 yields
the important Text Fig. 12.4(b), which is
reproduced below as Fig. 12.1. Notice the
following points about this graph.

FIGURE **12.1**

The profit maximization rule for a single-
price monopoly is to find the quantity of output
where *MR* = *MC*. This is the same rule that
applies to a perfectly competitive firm.

For a perfectly competitive firm *MR* is also
equal to price, so the intersection of *MR* and
MC yields the profit-maximizing output and
price. That is not true for the monopolist. *MR* is
not equal to price, and once the profit-
maximizing output is identified, the monopolist
still has to set the price.

To find the profit-maximizing price, draw
an imaginary vertical line up to the demand
curve from the intersection of *MR* and *MC*.
Then draw an imaginary horizontal line to the
price axis to read the price.

Understanding what the vertical and
horizontal distances of the economic profit area
represent will make you less likely to make
mistakes in drawing that area. The vertical
distance is between the demand (or average
revenue) curve and the average total cost curve.
That distance measures average revenue minus
average total cost, which equals average
economic profit, or economic profit per unit.
The horizontal distance is just the number of
units produced. So the area of the rectangle
(vertical distance × horizontal distance)
= economic profit per unit × number of units

= total economic profit. Do *not* make the mistake of drawing the vertical distance down to the intersection of *MC* and *MR*. That intersection has no economic meaning for the calculation of total economic profit.

2   There is an easy trick for drawing the marginal revenue curve corresponding to any linear demand curve. The price intercept (where $Q = 0$) is the same as for the demand curve, and the quantity intercept (where $P = 0$) is exactly *half* of the output of the demand curve. The marginal revenue curve is, therefore, a downward-sloping straight line whose slope is twice as steep as the slope of the demand curve.

3   Price discrimination can be profitable for a monopoly only if different consumer groups have different elasticities of demand for the good. If such differences exist, the price-discriminating monopolist treats the groups as different markets. The profit maximization rule for a price-discriminating monopoly is to find the quantity of output where *MR in each market* = *MC*. Then, in each market, charge the maximum price the consumer group is willing to pay for that output (on demand curve). With different elasticities of demand between groups, this rule will yield different prices in the two markets.

   If, however, the elasticities of demand in the two markets are equal, then marginal revenues are equal and the prices corresponding to the marginal revenues are also equal. There is no point in charging different prices, and the profit-maximizing rule for price discrimination collapses back into the rule for single-price monopoly.

4   The absence of entry barriers into a perfectly competitive industry is the basis for the prediction that any short-run economic profits in perfect competition will be competed away in the long run. Conversely, the presence of entry barriers in monopoly is the basis for the prediction that monopoly profits can persist in the long run. However, when rent-seeking activity is taken into account, there may be no long-run economic profits, even in monopoly. Rent seeking is any activity aimed at obtaining existing monopoly rights or creating new monopoly rights. Competition among rent seekers bids up the cost of rent seeking until it just equals the value of the potential monopoly profits, leaving the rent-seeker-turned-monopolist with little or no economic profit.

S E L F - T E S T

True/False/Uncertain and Explain

1   Over the output range where total revenue is decreasing, marginal revenue is positive.

2   The supply curve of a monopoly firm is its marginal cost curve.

3   A monopoly will make economic profits.

4   For a perfect price-discriminating monopolist, the demand curve is also the marginal revenue curve.

5   Price discrimination only works for goods that can be readily resold.

6   In moving from perfect competition to single-price monopoly, part of the deadweight loss is due to a reduction in producer surplus.

7   No deadweight loss results from monopoly because the monopoly gains everything the consumer loses.

8   Because of the existence of rent seeking, the social cost of monopoly is smaller than the deadweight loss.

9   When rent seeking is taken into account, economic profits from monopoly are guaranteed in the long run.

10 A monopoly industry with large economies of scale and scope may produce more output and charge a lower price than does a perfectly competitive industry.

Multiple-Choice

1 Which of the following is a *natural* barrier to the entry of new firms in an industry?

a licensing of professions
b economies of scale
c issuing a patent
d a public franchise
e all of the above

2 In order to increase sales from 7 units to 8 units, a single-price monopolist must drop the price from $7 per unit to $6 per unit. What is marginal revenue in this range?

a $48
b $6
c $1
d −$1
e none of the above

3 If marginal revenue is negative at a particular output, then

a price must be negative.
b the monopolist should increase output.
c the elasticity of demand is less than 1 at that output.
d demand must be elastic at that output.
e the monopolist should shut down.

4 *Disadvantages* of monopoly include

a economies of scope.
b economies of scale.
c diffusion of technological advances.
d rent-seeking behaviour.
e all of the above.

5 Taking rent-seeking activity into account, the social cost of monopoly is equal to the

a deadweight loss from monopoly.
b monopoly profit.
c deadweight loss plus monopoly profit.
d deadweight loss minus monopoly profit.
e consumer surplus lost plus producer surplus lost.

6 If a single-price monopoly has shut down, then at the level of output where marginal cost and marginal revenue intersect, it *must be true* that

a marginal revenue is less than average variable cost.
b marginal cost is less than average variable cost.
c price is less than average variable cost.
d total revenue is less than total cost.
e all of the above are correct.

7 For the single-price monopoly depicted in Fig. 12.2, when profit is maximized, quantity is

a 3 and price is $3.
b 3 and price is $6.
c 4 and price is $4.
d 4 and price is $5.
e 5 and price is $4.

FIGURE **12.2**

8 If the single-price monopoly depicted in Fig. 12.2 is maximizing profit, what is total economic profit?

a $3
b $4
c $6
d $9
e none of the above

9 The output of a (not perfect) price-discriminating monopoly will be

a less than a single-price monopoly.
b more than a single-price monopoly, but less than a perfectly competitive industry.
c the same amount as a perfectly competitive industry.
d more than a perfectly competitive industry.
e none of the above.

10 Consider the industry demand curve in Fig. 12.3. If the industry operates under perfect competition, which area in the diagram indicates consumer surplus?

a *aek*
b *dhk*
c *dik*
d *dih*
e none of the above

FIGURE **12.3**

11 Consider the industry demand curve in Fig. 12.3. If the industry operates under perfect competition, which area in the diagram indicates producer surplus?

a *aek*
b *dhk*
c *dik*
d *dih*
e none of the above

12 Consider the industry demand curve in Fig. 12.3. Which area in the diagram indicates the deadweight loss from a single-price monopoly?

a *eacf*
b *acd*
c *abd*
d *bcd*
e none of the above

13 Which area in Fig. 12.3 indicates the deadweight loss from a perfect price-discriminating monopoly?

a *eacf*
b *acd*
c *abd*
d *bcd*
e none of the above

14 Four monopolists were overheard talking at an expensive restaurant. Which of their statements below contains a correct strategy for maximizing profits?

a "In my company, we don't increase output unless we know that the larger output will raise total revenue."
b "I think cost minimization is the key to maximizing profits."
c "We try to make the most of our equipment by producing at maximum capacity."
d "I don't really keep close tabs on total profits, but I don't approve any business deal unless it increases my revenue more than it increases my costs."
e None of the above.

15 A monopoly has economies of scope if

a average total cost declines as the firm's scale increases.
b average total cost declines as output increases.
c total profit declines as output increases.
d average total cost declines as the number of different goods produced increases.
e total profit declines as the number of different goods produced increases.

16 If a profit-maximizing monopoly is producing at an output at which marginal cost exceeds marginal revenue, it

a should raise price and lower output.
b should lower price and raise output.
c should lower price and lower output.
d is making losses.
e is maximizing profit.

17 A profit-maximizing monopoly will never produce at an output level

a at which it would make economic losses.
b where marginal revenue is less than price.
c at which average cost is greater than marginal cost.
d in the inelastic range of its demand curve.
e in the inelastic range of its marginal revenue curve.

18 A perfect price-discriminating monopoly

a has a demand curve which is also its average revenue curve.
b will maximize revenue.
c is assured of making a profit.
d will produce the quantity at which the marginal cost curve intersects the demand curve.
e will be allocatively inefficient.

19 A monopoly will go out of business in the short run if

a it is making an economic loss.
b MR is less than AVC.
c the price is less than AVC.
d the profit-maximizing level of output is in the elastic range of the demand curve.
e MR is less than AR.

20 Table 12.1 lists marginal costs for the XYZ firm. If XYZ sells 3 units at a price of $6 each, what is its producer surplus?

a $2
b $6
c $7
d $9
e $12

TABLE **12.1**

Quantity	Marginal Cost
1	2
2	3
3	4
4	5

21 A single-price monopolist will maximize profits if it produces the output where

a price equals marginal cost.
b price equals marginal revenue.
c marginal revenue equals marginal cost.
d average revenue equals marginal cost.
e average revenue equals marginal revenue.

22 Many video stores charge a lower rental for Wednesday nights compared with weekends. This price discrimination is profitable only if the elasticity of demand for videos on Wednesdays is

a greater than the elasticity of demand for videos on weekends.
b less than the elasticity of demand for videos on weekends.
c positive and the elasticity of demand for videos on weekends is negative.
d negative and the elasticity of demand for videos on weekends is positive.
e equal to one.

23 Activity for the purpose of creating monopoly is

a called rent seeking.
b illegal in Canada.
c called price discrimination.
d called legal monopoly.
e costless.

24 Which of the following is true for a producing single-price monopolist but not for a producing perfect competitor?

a The firm maximizes profit by setting marginal cost equal to marginal revenue.
b The firm is a price-taker.
c The firm can sell any level of output at any price it sets.
d The firm's marginal cost is less than average revenue.
e None of the above statements is true.

25 When perfect price discrimination occurs, which of the following statements is *false*?

a Buyers cannot resell the product.
b The firm can distinguish between buyers.
c The firm sets prices.
d The firm captures consumer surplus.
e Allocative efficiency is worse than with single-price monopoly.

Short Answer Problems

1 Why is marginal revenue less than price for a single-price monopoly?

2 Explain why the output of a competitive industry will always be greater than the output of the *same* industry under single-price monopoly.

3 The price of the last unit sold and the quantity sold are exactly the same in an industry under perfect competition and under a perfect price-discriminating monopoly. Are consumers therefore indifferent between the two? Explain.

4 Under what circumstances would a monopoly be more efficient than a large number of competitive firms? Illustrate graphically such a situation where a monopoly produces more and charges a lower price than would be the case if the industry consisted of a large number of perfectly competitive firms.

5 A single-price monopoly is the only seller of skyhooks in the Canadian market. The firm's total fixed cost is $112 per day. Its total variable costs and total costs (both in dollars per day) are shown in Table 12.2.
  a Complete the table by computing marginal cost, average variable cost, and average total cost. [*Remember*: Marginal cost should be entered *midway* between rows of output.]

TABLE **12.2**

Quantity	Total Variable Cost (TVC)	Total Cost (TC)	Marginal Cost (MC)	Average Variable Cost (AVC)	Average Total Cost (ATC)
9	135	247			
10	144	256			
11	155	267			
12	168	280			
13	183	295			
14	200	312			
15	219	331			
16	240	352			
17	263	375			
18	288	400			
19	315	427			
20	344	456			

b Table 12.3 lists some points on the demand curve facing the firm, as well as the total cost information from part **a**. Complete the table by copying your values for marginal cost from Table 12.2 and by computing total revenue, marginal revenue, and economic profit. [*Remember:* Marginal revenue, like marginal cost, should be entered *midway* between rows of output.]

What is the firm's profit-maximizing quantity of output? At what price will it sell skyhooks? What will be its total economic profit? Explain your answers.

TABLE **12.3**

Price (P)	Quantity Demanded (Q_D)	Total Revenue (TR)	Marginal Revenue (MR)	Total Cost (TC)	Marginal Cost (MC)	Economic Profit (TR–TC)
57	9			247		
56	10			256		
55	11			267		
54	12			280		
53	13			295		
52	14			312		
51	15			331		
50	16			352		
49	17			375		
48	18			400		
47	19			427		
46	20			456		

c On the graph in Fig. 12.4, plot the demand curve and the *MR, AVC, ATC,* and *MC* curves corresponding to the data in parts **a** and **b**. Show the equilibrium output and the area of economic profit on your diagram.

FIGURE **12.4**

d The firm's cost curves are unchanged, but now consumer demand shifts. Table 12.4 lists some points on the new demand curve, as well as the total cost information from part **a**. Complete the table by copying your values for marginal cost from Table 12.2, and by computing the new values for total revenue, marginal revenue, and economic profit.

TABLE **12.4**

Price (P)	Quantity Demanded (Q_D)	Total Revenue (TR)	Marginal Revenue (MR)	Total Cost (TC)	Marginal Cost (MC)	Economic Profit (TR–TC)
24.50	9			247		
24.00	10			256		
23.50	11			267		
23.00	12			280		
22.50	13			295		
22.00	14			312		
21.50	15			331		
21.00	16			352		
20.50	17			375		
20.00	18			400		
19.50	19			427		
19.00	20			456		
18.50	21			487		

What is the firm's new profit-maximizing quantity of output? At what price will it now sell skyhooks? What will be its total economic profit? Explain your answers.

e On the graph in Fig. 12.5, plot the new demand curve and *MR* curve. Copy the *AVC*, *ATC*, and *MC* curves from Fig. 12.4. Show the new equilibrium output and the area of economic profit on your diagram.

FIGURE **12.5**

f Suppose demand falls even further so that the new demand curve equation is $P = 19 - 1/2Q_D$. On the graph in Fig. 12.6, plot this demand curve and copy the *AVC* curve from Fig. 12.4. Explain why the monopolist will shut down in the short run.

FIGURE **12.6**

⊚ⓓ6 You are given the following information about an industry consisting of 100 identical firms. The demand curve facing the industry is

$$P = 36 - 0.01Q$$

The marginal revenue curve facing the industry is

$$MR = 36 - 0.02Q$$

The marginal cost curve of an individual firm is

$$MC = -12 + 2Q$$

The horizontal sum of the marginal cost curves of all of the firms in the industry is

$$MC = -12 + 0.02Q$$

Use this information to answer the following questions.

a Suppose all 100 firms are controlled by a single-price monopolist. Calculate the profit-maximizing quantity of output for the monopolist. Calculate the price per unit of output that the monopolist will charge.

b Suppose instead that the 100 firms operate independently as a perfectly competitive industry. Calculate the short-run equilibrium quantity of output for the industry as a whole. Calculate the short-run equilibrium price for the industry.

c *Without* using your answer about industry output to part **b**, calculate the short-run equilibrium output per firm.

d Compare the monopoly price and quantity outcomes with the perfect competition price and quantity outcomes.

7 Barney's Bistro has two kinds of customers for lunch: stockbrokers and retired senior citizens. The demand schedules for lunches for the two groups are given in Table 12.5.

Barney has decided to price discriminate between the two groups by treating each

demand separately and charging the price that maximizes profit in each of the two submarkets. Marginal cost and average total cost are equal and constant at $2 per lunch.

a Complete Table 12.5 by computing the total and marginal revenue associated with stockbroker demand (TR_{SB} and MR_{SB}) as well as the total and marginal revenue associated with senior citizen demand (TR_{SC} and MR_{SC}). [*Remember*: Marginal revenue should be entered *midway* between rows.]

b What are the profit-maximizing output and price for stockbrokers?

c What are the profit-maximizing output and price for senior citizens?

d What is total economic profit?

e Show that the total economic profit in part **d** is the maximum by comparing it with total economic profit if instead Barney served: 1 additional lunch *each* to stockbrokers and senior citizens; 1 less lunch *each* to stockbrokers and senior citizens.

f What is the consumer surplus for stockbrokers? for senior citizens? for all customers?

8 The stockbrokers complain bitterly about Barney's discriminatory pricing policy, and threaten to bring bag lunches unless Barney charges a uniform price to all customers. Barney buckles under the pressure, and sits down with

TABLE 12.5

	Stockbrokers				Senior Citizens		
Price (P)	Quantity Demanded (Q_D)	Total Revenue (TR_{SB})	Marginal Revenue (MR_{SB})		Quantity Demanded (Q_D)	Total Revenue (TR_{SC})	Marginal Revenue (MR_{SC})
8	0				0		
7	1				0		
6	2				0		
5	3				1		
4	4				2		
3	5				3		
2	6				4		
1	7				5		
0	8				6		

his calculator to figure out his profit-maximizing output and price as a single-price monopolist. Using the previous information in Short Answer Problem 7, can you figure it out for him *without* looking at the hints below? If not, answer these questions.

a Calculate Barney's demand schedule by adding up the quantity demanded by stockbrokers and senior citizens at each price. Construct a table similar to Table 12.3, with columns for price, quantity demanded, total revenue, and marginal revenue. [*Remember*: Marginal revenue should be entered *midway* between rows.]

b Marginal cost and average total cost remain unchanged at $2 per lunch. What are Barney's profit-maximizing output and price?

c What is Barney's total economic profit as a single-price monopolist? How does this compare with his total economic profit as a price-discriminating monopolist?

d What is the consumer surplus for all customers? How does this compare with the consumer surplus for all customers when Barney price discriminated?

9 Figure 12.7 gives the demand, marginal revenue, and marginal cost curves for a certain industry. Your task is to illustrate how consumer and producer surplus are distributed under each of four ways of organizing the industry. In each case redraw any relevant part of Fig. 12.7 and then (1) indicate the region of the graph corresponding to consumer surplus by drawing horizontal lines through it; (2) indicate the region corresponding to producer surplus by drawing vertical lines through it; and (3) indicate the region (if any) corresponding to deadweight loss by putting dots in the area.

a The industry consists of many perfectly competitive firms.

b The industry is a single-price monopoly.

c The industry is a price-discriminating monopoly charging two prices: P_1 and P_3.

d The industry is a perfect price-discriminating monopoly.

FIGURE **12.7**

10 Before every Olympic Games, the International Olympic Committee (IOC) auctions off the rights to televise the Games to the highest bidder. NBC won the bid for the Summer 1996 Olympics, paying US$456 million. The television rights gave NBC a monopoly. Yet analysts (correctly) predicted that NBC would not make a profit. Their prediction was reasonable, since NBC failed to make a profit on similar telecasts of the 1988 and 1992 Olympics. The questions below will help to understand this apparent paradox.

a What kind of monopoly does NBC have?

b NBC earns revenue by selling airtime to commercial sponsors. Assume that NBC faces a normal, downward-sloping demand curve in selling 30-second commercial spots. Let's ignore for the moment the payment to the IOC and assume that marginal cost and average total cost of delivering the airtime are equal and constant. Draw a diagram representing NBC's profit-maximizing decision. Although you do not have enough information to calculate precise numbers, indicate generally the quantity of commercial spots sold and the price per commercial spot.

c On your diagram, indicate the area representing economic profit. If the analysts' predictions were correct, what is the value of this area?

d Why did NBC fail to realize this economic profit?

A N S W E R S

True/False/Uncertain and Explain

1   F   *MR* is negative. (263–264)
2   F   Monopolist has no supply curve. (265–266)
3   U   Monopoly no guarantee of profits if rent seeking is costly enough. (275–276)
⊙ 4   T   Demand curve gives revenue for each successive unit. (269–271)
5   F   Can*not* be readily resold. (271)
6   T   Area below competitive price and above *MC*. (273–274)
⊙ 7   U   True for perfect price-discriminating monopoly, false for all other monopoly. (273–275)
⊙ 8   F   Greater. Resources used in rent-seeking cost to society. (275–276)
9   F   In equilibrium, economic profits may be totally eliminated by rent-seeking costs. (275–276)
10   T   Advantages of monopoly. (276–277)

Multiple-Choice

1   b   Others are legal barriers. (260–261)
2   d   *TR* (*P* = $7) = $7 × 7 = $49. *TR* (*P* = $6) = $6 × 8 = $48. *MR* = Δ*TR* = $48 − $49. (261–263)
3   c   See text discussion. Should ↓ output. Shutdown decision premature since monopolist can change price. (261–264)
4   d   Others are advantages. Rent seeking diverts resources that could be used productively. (275–277)
5   c   Monopoly profit = resources used rent seeking. (275–276)
6   c   a, b irrelevant comparisons marginal and average quantities. d true *if TR* < *TVC*. (265–266)
7   b   *Q* where *MR* = *MC*. Highest *P* consumers will pay for 3 units. (265–266)
⊙ 8   c   (*AR* − *ATC*) × *Q* = ($6 − $4) × 3. (265–266)
9   b   c true for perfect price discrimination. (272–273)
10   b   Area above price but below demand (willingness to pay). (273–274)
11   d   Area below price but above *MC*. (273–274)
12   b   Sum of lost producer (*bcd*) and consumer (*abd*) surplus compared to competitive outcome. (273–274)
13   e   Deadweight loss is zero. (273–274)

14   d   *MR* − *MC* comparisons are key. Revenue **a** and cost **b** are important, but must be *compared* for profitability. (265–266)
15   d   Definition. (276–277)
16   a   Draw graph. $Q_{current}$ > *Q* corresponding to *MR* = *MC*. (265–266)
17   d   *TR* would be ↓ needlessly. Monopolist could ↓ *Q* and ↑ *P* to ↑ *TR*. (263–264)
⊙ 18   d   Same outcome as perfectly competitive industry, so e wrong. *D* = *MR* so a wrong. Profit maximizing so b wrong. (269–271)
19   c   Shutdown rule same as perfect competition. (265–266)
⊙ 20   d   Sum of (*P* − *MC*) for each unit output. (273–274)
21   c   Rule for choosing output. (265–266)
22   a   Charge lower price with higher η and higher price with lower η. (268–271)
23   a   Definition. Activity has costs. (275–276)
⊙ 24   d   a true for both. b true competitor only. c false for both. (265–266)
25   e   Allocative efficiency same as perfect competition. (273–274)

Short Answer Problems

1   In order to sell an additional unit of output, a monopoly must drop the price. This has two effects on revenue: one positive and equal to price, and the other negative. Marginal revenue is the net effect, which must be less than price. First, the additional unit sold at the new lower price adds an amount to revenue equal to the price. But, a single-price monopoly must also lower the price to previous customers who would have paid more. The net effect on marginal revenue is equal to the price minus the loss of revenue from lowering the price to previous customers. This difference must necessarily be less than price.

2   A competitive industry will produce the level of output at which the industry marginal cost curve intersects the demand curve facing the industry. A single-price monopoly will produce at the level of output at which the industry marginal cost curve intersects the monopoly marginal revenue curve. Since the marginal revenue curve lies below the demand curve, this implies a lower level of output in the monopoly industry.

3   While the quantity sold and the price charged to the last customer are the same in the cases of perfect competition and a perfect price discriminator, the distribution of consumer surplus is not the same. Since a perfect price

discriminator charges each customer the most she is willing to pay, there is no consumer surplus. Any consumer surplus that would have occurred under perfect competition now accrues to the monopoly. Consumers would like to obtain more consumer surplus, and therefore pay less for the same amount. Consequently, consumers prefer perfect competition.

4   A monopoly would be more efficient than perfect competition if the monopoly has sufficient economies of scale and/or scope. Those economies must be large enough that the monopoly produces more than the competitive industry and sells it at a lower price. Figure 12.8 illustrates such a situation. The important feature is that the marginal cost curve for the monopoly must not only be lower than the supply curve of the competitive industry, but it must also be sufficiently lower so that it intersects the *MR* curve at an output greater than *C* (the competitive output). Such a situation could arise if there are extensive economies of scale and/or scope.

FIGURE **12.8**

5 a   Completed Table 12.2 is given here as Table 12.2 Solution.

TABLE **12.2**   SOLUTION

Quantity	Total Variable Cost (TVC)	Total Cost (TC)	Marginal Cost (MC)	Average Variable Cost (AVC)	Average Total Cost (ATC)
9	135	247		15.00	27.44
			... 9		
10	144	256		14.40	25.60
			... 11		
11	155	267		14.09	24.27
			... 13		
12	168	280		14.00	23.33
			... 15		
13	183	295		14.08	22.69
			... 17		
14	200	312		14.29	22.29
			... 19		
15	219	331		14.60	22.07
			... 21		
16	240	352		15.00	22.00
			... 23		
17	263	375		15.47	22.06
			... 25		
18	288	400		16.00	22.22
			... 27		
19	315	427		16.58	22.47
			... 29		
20	344	456		17.20	22.80

b Completed Table 12.3 is shown here as Table 12.3 Solution.

TABLE **12.3** SOLUTION

Price (P)	Quantity Demanded (Q_D)	Total Revenue (TR)	Marginal Revenue (MR)	Total Cost (TC)	Marginal Cost (MC)	Economic Profit (TR–TC)
57	9	513		247		266
			... 47		... 9	
56	10	560		256		304
			... 45		... 11	
55	11	605		267		338
			... 43		... 13	
54	12	648		280		368
			... 41		... 15	
53	13	689		295		394
			... 39		... 17	
52	14	728		312		416
			... 37		... 19	
51	15	765		331		434
			... 35		... 21	
50	16	800		352		448
			... 33		... 23	
49	17	833		375		458
			... 31		... 25	
48	18	864		400		464
			... 29		... 27	
47	19	893		427		466
			... 27		... 29	
46	20	920		456		464

Equilibrium output occurs where $MC = MR = 28$, $Q = 19$, $P = \$47$, economic profit = $466 per day.

The profit-maximizing quantity of output occurs where marginal cost equals marginal revenue, at 19 units. The maximum price the firm can charge and still sell 19 units is $47. This combination of quantity and price yields a total economic profit of $466, which, as can be seen from the table, is the maximum possible profit.

c The requested diagram appears in Fig. 12.4 Solution.

FIGURE **12.4** SOLUTION

d Completed Table 12.4 is given here as Table 12.4 Solution.

TABLE **12.4** SOLUTION

Price (P)	Quantity Demanded (Q_D)	Total Revenue (TR)	Marginal Revenue (MR)	Total Cost (TC)	Marginal Cost (MC)	Economic Profit (TR–TC)
24.50	9	220.50		247		−26.50
			... 19.50		... 9	
24.00	10	240.00		256		−16.00
			... 18.50		... 11	
23.50	11	258.50		267		−8.50
			... 17.50		... 13	
23.00	12	276.00		280		−4.00
			... 16.50		... 15	
22.50	13	292.50		295		−2.50
			... 15.50		... 17	
22.00	14	308.00		312		−4.00
			... 14.50		... 19	
21.50	15	322.50		331		−8.50
			... 13.50		... 21	
21.00	16	336.00		352		−16.00
			... 12.50		... 23	
20.50	17	348.50		375		−26.50
			... 11.50		... 25	
20.00	18	360.00		400		−40.00
			... 10.50		... 27	
19.50	19	370.50		427		−56.50
			... 9.50		... 29	
19.00	20	380.00		456		−76.00

Equilibrium output occurs where $MC = MR = 16$, $Q = 13$, $P = \$22.50$, economic profit = −$2.50.

The profit-maximizing quantity of output occurs where marginal cost equals marginal revenue, now at 13 units. The maximum price the firm can charge and still sell 13 units is $22.50. This combination of quantity and price yields a total economic profit of –$2.50 (an economic loss). As can be seen from the table, this is the minimum possible loss. The firm will continue to produce in the short run because this loss is less than its shutdown loss which would be $112, the amount of its fixed cost.

e   The requested diagram appears in Fig. 12.5 Solution.

FIGURE **12.5**   SOLUTION

f   The requested diagram appears in Fig. 12.6 Solution. Since the demand curve is everywhere below the *AVC* curve, no matter what quantity of output the firm might produce, price will be less than *AVC*. This means that the firm will lose money on every unit produced in addition to losing its total fixed cost. The monopolist will minimize loss in this case by shutting down and losing just its fixed cost ($112).

FIGURE **12.6**   SOLUTION

⊚**⏀ 6 a**   The monopolist will choose the quantity of output where marginal revenue equals marginal cost. To calculate this quantity, set the equation for marginal revenue equal to the equation for *industry* marginal cost (since the monopolist controls all of the firms).

$$36 - 0.02Q = -12 + 0.02Q$$
$$48 = .04Q$$
$$1,200 = Q$$

To calculate the price that the monopolist will charge, substitute the quantity 1,200 into the demand equation. This is the mathematical equivalent of graphically, after finding the quantity corresponding to the intersection of *MC* and *MR*, moving your eye up to the demand curve to read the price.

$$P = 36 - 0.01Q$$
$$P = 36 - 0.01(1,200)$$
$$P = 36 - 12$$
$$P = 24$$

b   The perfectly competitive industry's short-run equilibrium quantity of output occurs where industry demand intersects industry supply. Set the industry demand equation equal to the industry supply equation, which is the horizontal sum of the marginal cost curves of all the firms in the industry.

$$36 - 0.01Q = -12 + 0.02Q$$
$$48 = 0.03Q$$
$$1,600 = Q$$

To calculate the short-run equilibrium price for the industry, we can substitute the quantity 1,600 into either the industry demand equation or the industry supply equation.

Using the industry demand equation yields

$$P = 36 - 0.01Q$$
$$P = 36 - 0.01(1,600)$$
$$P = 36 - 16$$
$$P = 20$$

Using the industry supply equation yields the same result

$$P = -12 + 0.02Q$$
$$P = -12 + 0.02(1,600)$$
$$P = -12 + 32$$
$$P = 20$$

c If industry output is 1,600 units and there are 100 identical firms, then obviously the output per firm is 1,600 units/100 firms equals 16 units/firm. But the question specifically asks you not to use the information about industry output.

　　The other way to calculate the short-run equilibrium output per firm is to substitute the equilibrium price of 20 into the individual firm's marginal cost curve, which is also its short-run supply curve.

$$P = -12 + 2Q$$
$$20 = -12 + 2Q$$
$$32 = 2Q$$
$$16 = Q$$

d The monopoly price ($24) is higher than the perfect competition price ($20) and the monopoly quantity of output (1,200) is lower than the perfect competition quantity of output (1,600).

7 a The completed table is given in Table 12.5 Solution.

b The profit-maximizing output for stockbrokers occurs when $MC = \$2 = MR_{SB}$. This is at 3 lunches and the price is $5 per lunch to stockbrokers.

c The profit-maximizing output for senior citizens occurs when $MC = \$2 = MR_{SC}$. This occurs at 2 lunches and the price to senior citizens is $4 per lunch.

d Total revenue is $15 from stockbrokers and $8 from senior citizens, or $23. Since average total cost is $2 per lunch, total cost is $2 × 5 lunches = $10. Thus total economic profit is $13.

e If Barney served 1 additional lunch each to stockbrokers and senior citizens, that would make 4 lunches for stockbrokers (at $4 per lunch) and 3 lunches for senior citizens (at $3 per lunch). Since average total cost is $2 per lunch, the total cost is $2 × 7 lunches = $14. Total revenue is $16 from stockbrokers and $9 from senior citizens, or $25. Thus total economic profit is $11, less than the $13 in part **d**.

TABLE **12.5** SOLUTION

	Stockbrokers				Senior Citizens		
Price (P)	Quantity Demanded (Q_D)	Total Revenue (TR_{SB})	Marginal Revenue (MR_{SB})		Quantity Demanded (Q_D)	Total Revenue (TR_{SC})	Marginal Revenue (MR_{SC})
8	0	0			0	0	
			 7				 0
7	1	7			0	0	
			 5				 0
6	2	12			0	0	
			 3				 5
5	3	15			1	5	
			 1				 3
4	4	16			2	8	
			.... −1				 1
3	5	15			3	9	
			.... −3				.... −1
2	6	12			4	8	
			.... −5				.... −3
1	7	7			5	5	
			.... −7				.... −5
0	8	0			6	0	

If Barney served 1 less lunch each to stockbrokers and senior citizens, that would make 2 lunches for stockbrokers (at $6 per lunch) and 1 lunch for senior citizens (at $5 per lunch). Since average total cost is $2 per lunch, the total cost is $2 × 3 lunches = $6. Total revenue is $12 from stockbrokers and $5 from senior citizens, or $17. Thus total economic profit is $11, less than the $13 in part **d**.

f The consumer surplus of stockbrokers is

$$($7 - $5) + ($6 - $5) + ($5 - $5) = $3.$$

The consumer surplus of senior citizens is

$$($5 - $4) + ($4 - $4) = $1.$$

The consumer surplus of all customers is

$$$3 + $1 = $4.$$

⏱ 8 a The requested table is given as Table 12.6 Solution.

TABLE **12.6** SOLUTION

Price (P)	Quantity Demanded (Q_D)	Total Revenue (TR)	Marginal Revenue (MR)
8	0	0	
			········ 7
7	1	7	
			········ 5
6	2	12	
			········ 4
5	4	20	
			········ 2
4	6	24	
			········ 0
3	8	24	
			········ −2
2	10	20	
			········ −4
1	12	12	
			········ −6
0	14	0	

b The profit-maximizing output occurs when MC = $2 = MR. This occurs halfway between a combination of 4 lunches at $5 per lunch, and 6 lunches at $4 per lunch. Either combination yields the same economic profit. Let's look at the combination of 6 lunches at $4 per lunch.

c Total revenue is $4 per lunch × 6 lunches = $24. Average total cost is $2 per lunch. Total cost is $2 × 6 lunches = $12. Thus total economic profit is $12.

Barney's economic profits as a single-price monopolist ($12) are less than his economic profits as a price-discriminating monopolist ($13).

d From the demand curves we can tell that there is 1 customer (stockbroker) who values lunch at $7, 1 customer (stockbroker) who values lunch at $6, 2 customers (stockbroker and senior) who value lunch at $5, and 2 customers (stockbroker and senior) who value lunch at $4. The consumer surplus for all customers is

$$1($7 - $4) + 1($6 - $4) + 2($5 - $4) + 2($4 - $4) = $7.$$

This consumer surplus without price discrimination ($7) is greater than consumer surplus with price discrimination ($4).

9 a Under perfect competition, price equals marginal cost. The amount of consumer surplus is given by the area under the demand curve but above the price (P_0) while the amount of producer surplus is given by the area above the MC curve but below the price; see Fig. 12.7 Solution (a).

b If the industry is a single-price monopoly, price will be greater than MC and output will be less than under competition. Consumer surplus is still given by the area under the demand curve but above the price (P_2), while producer surplus is given by the area above the MC curve but below the price up to the monopoly level of output. The remaining part of the large triangle is a deadweight loss since it is the amount of surplus under competition that is lost under a single-price monopoly; see Fig. 12.7 Solution (b).

c Similar reasoning allows us to establish regions in Fig. 12.7 Solution (c) corresponding to consumer surplus, producer surplus, and deadweight loss.

d Under perfect price discrimination, all of the potential surplus is captured by the producer and there is no deadweight loss (or consumer surplus). See Fig. 12.7 Solution (d).

FIGURE **12.7** SOLUTION

(a)

(b)

(c)

(d)

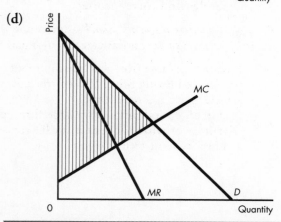

10 a NBC had a legal monopoly, based on a public franchise—an exclusive right granted to a firm to supply a good or service.

   b The requested diagram is shown in Fig. 12.9 Solution. The quantity of commercial spots sold is Q_{CS} and the price is P_{CS}.

FIGURE **12.9** SOLUTION

   c The shaded rectangle above ATC and below P_{CS} in Fig. 12.9 Solution represents economic profit. That profit, which is based on costs that exclude the US$456 payment to the IOC, will be US$456 if the analysts are correct.

   d NBC fails to make an economic profit because of the costs of rent seeking. NBC had to compete for the monopoly rights to televise the Olympics. It makes sense for bidders to continue to offer a higher price for those rights up to the point where the price of the rights equals the value of the economic profit to be earned from owning them.

Monopolistic Competition and Oligopoly

KEY CONCEPTS

Varieties of Market Structure

Market structure of most industries lies between extremes of perfect competition and monopoly.

◆ To evaluate competitiveness of a market, economists use two measures of industrial concentration:

- **Four-firm concentration ratio**—percentage of industry sales made by largest four firms.
- **Herfindahl–Hirschman Index (HHI)**—sum of squared market shares of 50 largest firms in industry.

◆ High concentration ratios usually → low degree competition.

◆ Problems with concentration ratios:
- national, but many industries local/international.
- no indication entry barriers.
- firms operate in other industries.

Monopolistic Competition

Monopolistic competition is market structure where many firms compete through **product differentiation**—making similar but slightly different products. This gives firms an element of monopoly power. There is free entry and exit.

◆ Implications
- Firm faces downward-sloping demand curve.
- Marginal revenue curve ≠ demand curve.
- Firm can choose price and output.

◆ Outcomes
- Profit maximization: choose Q where $MC = MR$, charge highest price (on demand curve).

- Short-run economic profits possible, attract entry → leftward shift demand curve facing each firm.
- Long-run economic profits = 0, $P = ATC$, ATC not minimum (*excess capacity*).
- Losses of ↓ allocative efficiency and high advertising expenditure must be weighed against gains of ↑ product variety, ↑ product innovation, and ↑ information to consumers.

Oligopoly

Oligopoly is market structure where few firms compete and *strategically interact*. Firm considers effects of its actions on behaviour of others and actions of others on its own profit.

◆ *Kinked demand curve model* assumes if firm ↑ price, no firms follow, and if firm ↓ price, all firms follow. Result is each firm faces kinked demand curve, with kink at current P, Q.

- Predictions: sticky prices—kink causes break in MR curve so MC curve can vary within break without affecting price or quantity.
- Problems: no indication how current P determined or how firms react if discover beliefs about demand curve incorrect.

◆ *Dominant firm oligopoly model* assumes one large firm with major cost advantage, many small firms.

- Predictions: large firm acts like monopoly, sets profit-maximizing price. Small firms take price, act like perfect competitors.
- Problems: no indication why large firm has cost advantage or what happens if small firms acquire low-cost technology.

Game Theory

Game theory analyses strategic behaviour. Games have

- **Rules**—specify permissible actions by players.

- **Strategies**—actions such as raising or lowering price, output, advertising, or product quality.

- Payoffs—profits and losses of players. **Payoff matrix** relates payoffs and strategies.

A "prisoners' dilemma" is a one-time, two-person game. Each player has a dominant strategy of cheating, that is, confessing. Concepts include

- *Dominant strategy*—unique best strategy independent of other player's action.

- **Dominant strategy equilibrium**—occurs when there is a dominant strategy for each player.

- **Nash equilibrium**—*A* takes best possible action given action *B*, and *B* takes best possible action given action *A*.

Oligopoly Game

Duopoly is a market structure with two firms.

- In a duopoly game, each firm can *comply* with a **collusive agreement** to restrict output and ↑ price, or it can *cheat*.

- A **cartel** is a group of firms in a collusive agreement.

- In a one-time game, a "prisoners' dilemma" solution occurs—each firm has the dominant strategy of cheating, even though both firms would be better off if they could trust each other and comply.

- In a repeated game, other strategies can create a **cooperative equilibrium** where each firm complies with the collusive agreement.
  - A *tit-for-tat strategy* is taking the same action the other player took last period.
  - A *trigger strategy* is cooperating until the other player cheats, and then cheating forever.

Game theory can be used to analyse other choices facing firms—how much to spend on research and development or on advertising, whether to enter or exit an industry, etc.

In a **contestable market** there are few firms but free entry and exit so existing firms face perfect competition from *potential* entrants. Existing firms may use strategies of

- An entry-deterrence game—set a competitive price and earn normal profit to keep out a potential competitor.

- **Limit pricing**—compared to monopoly outcome, ↓ price and ↑ quantity in order to deter entry.

HELPFUL HINTS

1 Most industries are neither perfectly competitive nor pure monopolies; they lie somewhere between these two extremes. This does not mean that the last two chapters have been wasted. By examining firms under these extreme market structures, we are now able to discuss the wide range of industries between them in just a single chapter.

The intermediate forms of market structure share many of the characteristics of perfect competition and/or monopoly. Consider the profit-maximizing rule of choosing the output where $MC = MR$. The rule applies not only in perfect competition and monopoly, but also in monopolistic competition, kinked demand curve, and dominant firm oligopoly models. Free entry leads to zero long-run economic profits both in perfect competition and monopolistic competition. The downward-sloping demand and marginal revenue curves of monopoly also apply to monopolistic competition, kinked demand curve, and dominant firm oligopoly models.

The extreme and unrealistic assumptions of models of perfect competition and monopoly allow us to isolate the impact of important forces like profit maximization and important constraints like competition and market demand. These forces and constraints also operate in more realistic market structures. But it was necessary to isolate these forces and constraints beforehand rather than attempt to immediately analyse "realistic" market structures like monopolistic competition and oligopoly, which would have been a confusing jumble of details and possible outcomes. It would have been like driving in a strange, large city without a road map.

2 In graphing a monopolistically competitive firm in long-run equilibrium, be sure that the *ATC* curve is tangent to the demand curve at the same level of output at which the *MC* and *MR* curves intersect. Also be sure that the *MC* curve intersects the *ATC* curve at the minimum point on the *ATC* curve.

3 This chapter uses elementary game theory to explain oligopoly. The prisoners' dilemma game illustrates the most important game theory concepts (rules, strategies, payoffs), which are then used in more complex game theory models like those of repeated games.

It is important to learn how to find the equilibrium of a prisoners' dilemma-type game. Take the example of players A and B, where each player has to choose between two strategies—confess or deny. First set up the payoff matrix. Then look at the payoff matrix from A's point of view. A does not know if B is going to confess or deny, so A asks two questions: (1) Assuming that B confesses, do I get a better payoff if I confess or deny? (2) Assuming that B denies, do I get a better payoff if I confess or deny?

If A's best strategy is to confess, regardless of whether B confesses or denies, confessing is A's dominant strategy. Next, look at the payoff matrix from B's point of view. Let B ask the equivalent two questions, and find B's dominant strategy. The combination of A's dominant strategy and B's dominant strategy comprises the equilibrium outcome of the game.

4 The key insight of the prisoners' dilemma game is the *tension* between the equilibrium outcome (where both players' best strategy is to confess because they can't trust each other) and the fact that both players could make themselves better off if only they would cooperate. All of the equilibrium situations we have examined up until now have been stable outcomes where all agents' self-interests (utility and profit) have been maximized. Remember, equilibrium is defined as a situation where there is no tendency to change. The equilibrium of the prisoner's dilemma is different. Even though both players confess, their individual self-interests are *not* maximized. It is the additional possibility of *strategic interaction* (to trust or not trust the other player) that creates the instability of outcomes.

The instability of outcomes in this simple game helps us to understand more complex market phenomena such as gasoline price-wars. When gasoline station owners trust each other, prices remain relatively high and profits are maximized. But there is always an incentive to cheat on a collusive agreement. Once cheating begins, trust breaks down and the owners are driven to the equilibrium outcome where all owners cheat, prices fall, and profits are reduced. Eventually, the reduced profits lead the owners to take a chance on trusting each other again, since they figure it couldn't be worse than the existing low prices and profits. All stations raise their prices, and the cycle begins again. This instability of price and profit outcomes stems from the cycle of trust and not-trust. In other words, the instability arises from strategic interaction between station owners.

SELF-TEST

True/False/Uncertain and Explain

1 A high concentration ratio indicates a low degree of competition.

2 Product differentiation gives a monopolistically competitive firm some monopoly power.

3 Free entry is the key characteristic of monopolistic competition that produces excess capacity.

4 The kinked demand curve model predicts that price and quantity will be sensitive to small cost changes.

5 When a monopolistically competitive industry is in long-run equilibrium, economic profits are zero and price equals minimum average total cost.

6 Advertising by monopolistic competitors is allocatively inefficient.

7 An oligopolist will consider the reaction of other firms before it decides to cut its price.

8 A Nash equilibrium occurs when *A* takes the best possible action given the action of *B*, and *B* takes the best possible action given the action of *A*.

9 If duopolists agree to collude, they can (jointly) make as much profit as a single monopoly.

10 In the case of colluding duopolists, the dominant strategy equilibrium is for both firms to cheat.

Multiple-Choice

1 The four-firm concentration ratio measures the share of the largest four firms in total industry

a profits.
b sales.
c cost.
d capital.
e none of the above.

2 For a monopolistically competitive firm in long-run equilibrium,

a $P = MC$.
b $MC = ATC$.
c $AR = ATC$, but $P > MC$.
d $MC = AR$, but $ATC > AR$.
e none of the above is true.

3 Figure 13.1 represents a monopolistically competitive firm in short-run equilibrium. What is the firm's level of output?

a Q_1
b Q_2
c Q_3
d Q_4
e zero

FIGURE **13.1**

4 Figure 13.1 represents a monopolistically competitive firm in short-run equilibrium. What is the firm's economic profit *per unit*?

a $P_4 - P_2$
b $P_4 - P_1$
c P_4
d P_3
e none of the above

5 Figure 13.1 represents a monopolistically competitive firm in short-run equilibrium. In the long run,

a new firms will enter, and each existing firm's demand shifts leftward.
b new firms will enter, and each existing firm's demand shifts rightward.
c existing firms will leave, and each remaining firm's demand shifts leftward.
d existing firms will leave, and each remaining firm's demand shifts rightward.
e there will be no change from the short run.

6 In the dominant firm model of oligopoly, the smaller firms act like

a oligopolists.
b monopolists.
c monopolistic competitors.
d perfect competitors.
e a cartel.

7 Which of the following is *not* an aspect common to all games?

a rules
b collusion
c strategies
d payoffs
e the analysis of strategic interaction

8 In the prisoners' dilemma with players Art and Bob, each prisoner would be best off if

a both prisoners confess.

b both prisoners deny.

c Art denies and Bob confesses.

d Bob denies and Art confesses.

e none of the above is done.

9 Limit pricing refers to

a the highest price a monopolist can set.

b a firm lowering its monopoly price to deter entry.

c a strategy used by entering firms in contestable markets.

d the price determined in a kinked demand curve model.

e none of the above.

10 Which of the following is *not* a problem with concentration ratios as a measure of industry competitiveness?

a Concentration ratios are national measures, but firms in some industries operate in regional markets.

b Concentration ratios are national measures, but firms in some industries operate in international markets.

c Concentration ratios tell us nothing about the severity of barriers to entry in the industry.

d Concentration ratios tell us nothing about how cost varies among firms in the industry.

e Concentration ratios have difficulty classifying multiproduct firms by industry.

11 Under monopolistic competition, long-run economic profits tend towards zero *because of*

a product differentiation.

b the lack of barriers to entry.

c excess capacity.

d inefficiency.

e the downward-sloping demand curve each firm faces.

12 Each of the following is a characteristic of monopolistic competition. Which is *not* a characteristic of oligopoly?

a Each firm faces a downward-sloping demand curve.

b Firms are profit-maximizers.

c The sales of one firm will not have a significant effect on other firms.

d There is more than one firm in the industry.

e Firms set prices.

13 If a duopoly with collusion maximizes profit,

a each firm must produce the same amount.

b each firm must produce its maximum output possible.

c industry marginal revenue must equal industry marginal cost at the level of total output.

d industry demand must equal industry marginal cost at the level of total output.

e total output will be greater than without collusion.

14 In the long run, a monopolistically competitive firm will earn the same economic profits as

a a monopolistically competitive firm in the short run.

b a member of a cartel.

c a pure price-discriminating monopolist.

d a perfectly competitive firm.

e none of the above.

15 The firms Trick and Gear form a cartel to collude to maximize profit. If this game is nonrepeated, the dominant strategy equilibrium is

a both firms cheat on the agreement.

b both firms comply with the agreement.

c Trick cheats, while Gear complies with the agreement.

d Gear cheats, while Trick complies with the agreement.

e indeterminate.

16 Consider the same cartel consisting of Trick and Gear. Now, however, the game is repeated indefinitely and each firm employs a tit-for-tat strategy. The equilibrium is

a both firms cheat on the agreement.

b both firms comply with the agreement.

c Trick cheats, while Gear complies with the agreement.

d Gear cheats, while Trick complies with the agreement.

e indeterminate.

17 The equilibrium in Question 16 is called a

a credible strategy equilibrium.

b dominant player equilibrium.

c duopoly equilibrium.

d trigger strategy equilibrium.

e cooperative equilibrium.

18 Which of the following is true for perfect competition, monopolistic competition, and single-price monopoly?

a homogeneous product
b zero long-run economic profits
c short-run profit-maximizing quantity where *MC* = *MR*
d easy entry and exit
e none of the above

19 Which of the following statements about the sections of kinked demand curve in Fig. 13.2 is *correct*?

a *AB* assumes new firms will enter the industry, while *BC* assumes no new firms will enter.
b *AB* assumes no new firms will enter the industry, while *BC* assumes new firms will enter.
c The kink between sections reflects market imperfections.
d *AB* assumes other firms will match a price increase, while *BC* assumes other firms will not match a price decrease.
e *AB* assumes other firms will not match a price increase, while *BC* assumes other firms will match a price decrease.

FIGURE **13.2**

20 In the long run, the firm in monopolistic competition will

a face a perfectly elastic demand curve.
b produce more than the quantity that minimizes *ATC*.
c produce less than the quantity that minimizes *ATC*.
d produce the quantity that minimizes *ATC*.
e earn economic profits.

21 Table 13.1 gives the payoff matrix in terms of profit for firms *A* and *B*, when there are two strategies facing each firm: (1) charge a low price or (2) charge a high price. The equilibrium in this game (played once) is a dominant strategy equilibrium since

a firm *B* will reduce profit by more than *A* if both charge a lower price.
b firm *B* is the dominant firm.
c the best strategy for each firm does not depend on the strategy chosen by the other.
d there is no credible threat by either firm to punish the other if it breaks the agreement.
e all of the above are true.

TABLE **13.1**

		Firm B	
		Low Price	High Price
Firm A	Low Price	A: $2 B: $5	A: $20 B: −$15
	High Price	A: −$10 B: $25	A: $10 B: $20

22 Refer to the nonrepeated game in Table 13.1. In equilibrium, what are firm *A*'s profits?

a −$10
b $2
c $10
d $20
e indeterminate.

23 Refer to the nonrepeated game in Table 13.1. If both firms could agree to collude, what would be firm *A*'s profits?

a −$10
b $2
c $10
d $20
e indeterminate.

24 In the long run, a monopolistically competitive firm will produce the output at which price equals

a marginal cost.
b marginal revenue.
c average variable cost.
d average total cost.
e **b** and **d**.

25 Which of the following characteristics is *not* shared by single-price monopoly and monopolistic competition?
a firms face a downward-sloping demand curve
b profit-maximizing quantity where $MC = MR$
c equilibrium ATC above minimum ATC
d positive long-run economic profits
e positive long-run normal profits

Short Answer Problems

1 Considering the geographical scope of markets, how might a concentration ratio *understate* the degree of competitiveness in an industry? How might it *overstate* the degree of competitiveness?

2 Compare the advantages and disadvantages of perfect competition and monopolistic competition in terms of allocative efficiency.

3 Consider the case of two colluding duopolists in a nonrepeated game. In equilibrium, will the firms comply or cheat on the agreement? Explain why.

4 How can a price war that eliminates profits be explained using game theory?

5 Consider a single firm in a monopolistically competitive industry in the short run. Using axes like those shown in Fig. 13.3, draw a new graph for each of the following situations.

FIGURE **13.3**

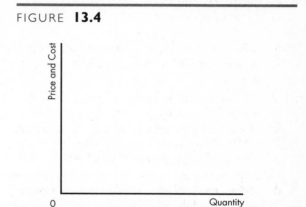

a The firm is making an economic profit.
b The firm is making a loss that will cause shutdown.
c The firm is making a loss, but is still producing.
d Starting from the situation in part **c**, explain what will happen in this industry and how your graph in part **c** will be affected? (No new graph required.)
e The firm is in long-run equilibrium.

6 Consider a monopolistically competitive industry in long-run equilibrium. Firm A in this industry attempts to increase profits by advertising.
a On the graph in Fig. 13.4, show what will happen in the short run as a result of the decision to advertise. Briefly explain your graph.

FIGURE **13.4**

b If the firm is successful in raising profits in the short run, what will happen in the long run?

7 A small prairie town has two bakeries—Always Fresh and Never Stale. Transportation costs are high relative to the price of bread, so the bakeries do not get any out-of-town competition; the local bread industry is a duopoly. Always Fresh and Never Stale have the same cost curves, and each currently makes an annual profit of $2,000.

Suppose that a new advertising service, Philomena's Flyers, starts up. If one bakery advertises in Philomena's Flyers, its annual profits will increase to $5,000, while the other bakery will lose $2,000. If both advertise, each will make a zero profit. If neither advertises, each bakery will continue to make an annual profit of $2,000.
a Represent this duopoly as a game by identifying the players, strategies, and possible outcomes.
b Construct the payoff matrix.
c What is the equilibrium outcome? Explain.

8 Figure 13.5(a) gives the identical average total cost (ATC) curve for Always Fresh and Never Stale. Figure 13.5(b) gives the town's market demand curve for bread and the firms' joint marginal cost curve. Suppose that the two bakeries collude to maximize profit and agree to divide output equally for a single year.
a How much will each bakery produce and what price per loaf will they charge?
b What is each bakery's average total cost and profit?

FIGURE **13.5**

(a) *ATC* Curve for Each Bakery

(b) **Market Demand for Bread and Firm's Joint *MC* Curve**

⌀ 9 Now suppose that Never Stale convinces Always Fresh that demand has decreased and they must reduce their price by 10 cents per loaf in order to sell their agreed upon quantity. Of course, demand has *not* decreased, but Always Fresh produces its agreed amount and charges 10 cents less per loaf. Never Stale, the cheater, also charges 10 cents less than before, but increases output sufficiently to satisfy the rest of demand at this price.

a How many loaves of bread does Never Stale produce?

b What is Always Fresh's average total cost and profit?

c What is Never Stale's average total cost and profit?

10 Return to the initial situation. The firms are preparing to enter into a *long-term* collusive agreement. Always Fresh credibly assures Never Stale that if Never Stale cheats, Always Fresh will undercut Never Stale's price as soon as the cheating is discovered. Would Never Stale want to cheat on the agreement now? Why or why not?

ANSWERS

True/False/Uncertain and Explain

1 U Often true, but depends on geographical scope market, barriers to entry, and multimarket firms. (286–289)

2 T Creates downward-sloping demand curve. (290–291)

3 F Product differentiation → downward-sloping demand. (291–292)

4 F Insensitive to small cost changes. (293–294)

5 F Zero profits, but P > minimum *ATC*. (290–292)

⌀ 6 U Depends on information content advertising and gains from ↑ product variety. (292–293)

7 T Oligopoly involves strategic behaviour. (293, 296)

8 T Definition. (297–298)

9 T With collusion, they act exactly like monopoly. (300–301)

⌀ 10 U True for nonrepeated game but may be false for repeated game. (303–305)

Multiple-Choice

1 b Definition. (286–287)

⌀ 2 c Demand curve ($AR = P$) tangent to *ATC* and above *MC*. (290–291)

3 b Where $MC = MR$. (290–291)

⌀ 4 a At Q_2, $AR - ATC$. (290–291)

5 a With new entrants, industry demand divided among more firms so each firm's demand curve shifts left. (290–291)

6 d Dominant firm sets price, smaller firms take that price as given. (294–295)

7 b No collusion in prisoners' dilemma. (296–298)

8 b But doesn't happen because players cannot trust each other enough to collude. (296–298)

9 b Definition. **c** would be true for *existing* firms. (308–309)

10 d Concentration ratios do not attempt to measure cost. (286–289)

11 b a and e → possibility profits, c and d are outcomes, not forces → zero profits. (290–292)

◑ 12 c Oligopoly involves interdependence between firms. (290–293)

13 c See Text Fig.13.6(b). (298–301)

14 d Zero economic profits. (290–292)

15 a Similar to prisoners' dilemma outcome. (302–304)

◑ 16 b Cooperative equilibrium; each player responds rationally to credible threat of other. (304–305)

17 e Definition. (304–305)

18 c b and d false for monopoly. a false for monopolistic competition. (290–293)

19 e *AB* more elastic than *BC* because price changes unmatched. (293–294)

20 c Excess capacity at *Q* where demand tangent to downward slope *ATC*. (290–292)

21 c Definition of dominant strategy equilibrium. (302–304)

22 b Both firms charge low price. (302–304)

23 c Both firms charge high price. (302–304)

24 d Where demand curve tangent to *ATC*. (290–291)

◑ 25 d Zero long-run economic profits for monopolistic competition. (290–293)

Short Answer Problems

1 Concentration ratios are calculated from a national geographical perspective. If the actual scope of the market is not national, the concentration ratio will likely misstate the degree of competitiveness in an industry. If the actual market is global, the concentration ratio will understate the degree of competitiveness. A firm may have a concentration ratio of 100 as the only producer in the nation, but may face a great deal of international competition. When the scope of the market is regional, the concentration ratio will overstate the degree of competitiveness. The concentration ratio includes firms elsewhere in the nation that are not real competitors in the region.

2 The advantage of perfect competition is that it leads to production at minimum average total cost, while monopolistic competition leads to a higher average total cost due to reduced output and high advertising expenditures.

The advantage of monopolistic competition is that it leads to greater product variety, which consumers value, while in a perfectly competitive industry there is a single, identical product produced by all firms. Monopolistic competition also leads to greater product innovation and, as a positive by-product of greater advertising, valuable information to consumers. Thus the loss in allocative efficiency and greater advertising costs (higher *ATC*) that occur in monopolistic competition have to be weighed against the gains of greater product variety, greater product innovation, and more valuable information provided to consumers.

3 Each firm's best strategy is to cheat regardless of the strategy of the other firm. Call the firms *A* and *B*. Firm *A* knows that if firm *B* follows the collusive agreement, *A* can increase its profit by cheating. If firm *B* cheats, then firm *A* knows that it must also cheat to minimize its loss of profit. Thus cheating is the dominant strategy for firm *A*. Accordingly, it is also the dominant strategy for firm *B*.

4 Game theory explains price wars as the consequence of firms in a colluding industry responding to the cheating of a firm. If one firm cheats by cutting its price, then all other firms will cut their prices, and a price war will ensue. Once the price has fallen sufficiently (perhaps to the zero profit level), the firms will again have a strong incentive to rebuild their collusion.

5 a Figure 13.3 Solution (a) illustrates a monopolistically competitive firm making an economic profit in the short run. The important feature of the graph is that at the profit-maximizing output, price is greater than average total cost. The economic profit is indicated by the shaded area.

FIGURE **13.3** SOLUTION
(a)

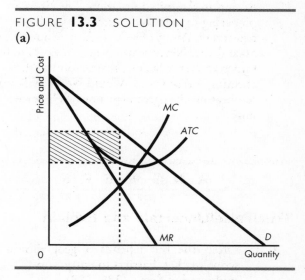

b Figure 13.3 Solution (b) illustrates a firm that will shut down in the short run since price is less than average variable cost at the profit-maximizing (loss-minimizing) level of output.

FIGURE **13.3** SOLUTION
(b)

c Figure 13.3 Solution (c) illustrates a firm making a loss but continuing to produce. The loss is indicated by the shaded area. Note that, at the profit-maximizing output, price is less than *ATC* but greater than *AVC*.

FIGURE **13.3** SOLUTION
(c)

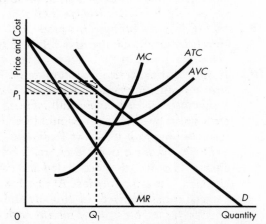

d Since firms are typically experiencing a loss, firms will leave the industry. This means that the demand curves facing each of the remaining firms will begin to shift rightward as they each attract some of the customers of the departing firms. As the firms' demand curves shift rightward, losses are reduced. Firms will continue to have an incentive to leave until losses have been eliminated. Thus firms' demand curves will continue to shift until they are tangent to the *ATC* curve.

e Figure 13.3 Solution (d) illustrates a typical monopolistically competitive firm in long-run equilibrium. The key feature is that the demand curve facing the firm is tangent to the ATC curve at the profit-maximizing output. Thus the firm is making a zero economic profit.

FIGURE **13.3** SOLUTION
(d)

6 a Advertising will increase firm A's cost, but also increase demand (it hopes). If the increase in demand (revenue) is greater than the increase in cost, then firm A will have increased its profit. Figure 13.4 Solution illustrates this situation. The initial curves are given by D_0, ATC_0, and MR_0.

Initially the firm is producing Q_0 and selling at price P_0 and making zero economic profit. Advertising, which is a fixed cost, raises the ATC curve to ATC_1 (MC does not shift), but also increases the demand and marginal revenue curves to D_1 and MR_1, respectively. The shift in the demand curve is sufficiently great that there is now a positive economic profit at the new profit-maximizing level of output (Q_1). The economic profit is indicated by the shaded area.

FIGURE **13.4** SOLUTION

b No doubt other firms will also begin to advertise in an attempt to increase their profit (or recover lost profit). As all other firms advertise, the demand curve for our firm will shift back to the left as it loses some of the customers it has gained. In the long run, once again, all firms will be making zero profit even after advertising.

7 a The players are Always Fresh and Never Stale. Each firm has two strategies: to advertise or not to advertise. There are four possible outcomes: (1) both firms advertise, (2) Always Fresh advertises but Never Stale does not, (3) Never Stale advertises but Always Fresh does not, and (4) neither firm advertises.

b The payoff matrix is given in Table 13.2. The entries give the profit earned by Always Fresh (*AF*) and Never Stale (*NS*) under each of the four possible outcomes.

TABLE **13.2**

		Never Stale	
		Advertise	Not Advertise
Always Fresh	Advertise	AF: 0 NS: 0	AF: $5,000 NS: –$2,000
	Not Advertise	AF: –$2,000 NS: $5,000	AF: $2,000 NS: –$2,000

c First, consider how Always Fresh decides which strategy to pursue. If Never Stale advertises, Always Fresh can advertise and make zero profit or not advertise and make a $2,000 loss. Thus Always Fresh will want to advertise if Never Stale does.

If Never Stale does not advertise, Always Fresh can advertise and make a $5,000 profit or not advertise and make a $2,000 profit.

Therefore Always Fresh will want to advertise whether Never Stale advertises or not. Never Stale will come to the same conclusion. The dominant strategy equilibrium is that both firms advertise.

8 a The firms will agree to produce 30,000 loaves each and sell at a price of 50 cents per loaf. We determine this by noticing (Fig. 13.5b) that the profit-maximizing (monopoly) output is 60,000 loaves for the industry ($MR = MC$ at 60,000) and the industry price is 50 cents per loaf. Since the firms have agreed to divide output equally, each will produce 30,000 loaves.

b From Fig. 13.5(a) we determine that, at 30,000 loaves, each firm's average total cost is 40 cents per loaf. Since price is 50 cents per loaf, profit will be $3,000 for each firm.

9 a At the new price of 40 cents per loaf, the total quantity demanded is 80,000 loaves. Since Always Fresh continues to produce 30,000 loaves, this means that Never Stale will produce the remaining 50,000 loaves demanded.

b Since Always Fresh continues to produce 30,000 loaves, its average total cost continues to be 40 cents per loaf. With the new price also at 40 cents, Always Fresh will make a zero economic profit.

c Never Stale has increased output to 50,000 loaves, which implies average total cost of 30 cents per loaf. Thus, given a price of 40 cents, Never Stale's economic profit will be $5,000.

10 Given that the agreement is long term, Never Stale would almost surely not cheat. The reason is that, while Never Stale could increase short-term profit by cheating, it would lose much more future profit if Always Fresh retaliates.

The key point is that Never Stale's behaviour changes, not because cost or demand have changed, but rather because Always Fresh's behaviour has changed. In duopoly and oligopoly, the best strategy for any firm depends on the behaviour of other firms.

PROBLEM

FIGURE **P2.1**

(a) Industry

(b) Firm

Despite significant differences between perfect competition, monopoly, and monopolistic competition, all of these market structures can be analysed using the diagrams in Fig. P2.1.

Figure P2.1(a) shows an industry in short-run equilibrium at the intersection of the demand (D_0) and supply (S_0) curves. Ignore for the moment the other supply curve (S_1) and the marginal revenue curve (MR). Long-run market demand is the same as short-run market demand. There are no external economies or diseconomies. Figure P2.1(b) shows the cost curves of one of the many identical firms in the industry.

Let's first suppose this is a perfectly competitive (pc) industry.

a Describe the demand curve facing an individual firm; describe the marginal revenue curve.

b On Fig. P2.1, identify and label the industry short-run equilibrium price (P_{pc}) [this is a giveaway!], output (Q_{pc}), and individual firm output (q_{pc}). Is each individual firm making a profit or loss? Explain.

c What happens in the long run? On Fig. P2.1, identify and label the industry long-run equilibrium price (P^{LR}_{pc}), output (Q^{LR}_{pc}), and individual firm ouput (q^{LR}_{pc}).

Now suppose that the market in Fig. P2.1(a) is supplied by a single-price monopolist (m) with a legal monopoly. S_1 is the monopolist's marginal cost curve. Ignore S_0 and part (b) of the figure.

d   Describe the demand curve facing the monopolist; describe the supply curve of the monopolist.

e   On Fig. P2.1(a), identify and label the industry short-run equilibrium price (P_m) and output (Q_m).

f   At Q_m, if the monopolist's average total cost is less than P_m, explain what happens in the long run. On Fig. P2.1(a), identify and label the industry long-run equilibrium price (P^{LR}_m) and output (Q^{LR}_m).

g   Compare the long-run allocative efficiency of this industry under monopoly versus under perfect competition. Identify any deadweight loss on the appropriate figure.

Finally, suppose that the industry in Fig. P2.1(a) is supplied by many monopolistically competitive (mc) firms. The industry supply curve is S_0, and at price P_{pc}, each firm is in long-run equilibrium. Ignore S_1 and MR. Each firm has the cost curves in Fig. P2.1(b), but produces a slightly differentiated product.

h   Describe the demand curve facing an individual firm and draw it on Fig. P2.1(b).

i   On Fig. P2.1(b), identify and label the long-run output (q_{mc}) for an individual monopolistically competitive firm. Describe one point that you can identify precisely on the marginal revenue curve facing an individual firm. Explain why this is a long-run equilibrium.

j   Compare the long-run allocative efficiency of this industry under monopolistic competition versus under perfect competition. What consideration must be taken into account that is not taken into account for a monopoly?

MIDTERM EXAMINATION

You should allocate 56 minutes for this examination (28 questions, 2 minutes per question). For each question, choose the one *best* answer.

1   Marginal utility equals
a   total utility divided by price.
b   total utility divided by the total number of units consumed.
c   the slope of the total utility curve.
d   the inverse of total utility.
e   the area below the demand curve but above market price.

2   A consumer maximizes his utility by purchasing 2 units of good X at \$5/unit and 3 units of good Y at \$7/unit. What is the ratio of the marginal utility of X to the marginal utility of Y?
a   5/7
b   7/5
c   2/3
d   3/2
e   10/21

3   The supply curve for a single-price monopoly is
a   its marginal cost curve.
b   its marginal cost curve above minimum average variable cost.
c   its average variable cost curve.
d   its marginal revenue curve.
e   none of the above.

4   A successful price-discriminating firm must be able to
a   prevent consumer resale.
b   differentiate consumers with high price elasticity of demand and charge them low prices.
c   differentiate consumers with low price elasticity of demand and charge them high prices.
d   do all of the above.
e   do none of the above.

5   The marginal cost curve slopes upward because of
a   diminishing marginal utility.
b   diminishing marginal returns.
c   technological inefficiency.
d   economic inefficiency.
e   none of the above.

6   In economics, the long run is a time period in which
a   one year or more elapses.
b   all inputs are variable.
c   all inputs are fixed.
d   there is at least one fixed input and at least one variable input.
e   all inputs are variable but plant size is fixed.

7 Suppose good X is measured on the horizontal axis and good Y on the vertical axis. The marginal rate of substitution is best defined as the

a relative price of good X in terms of good Y.
b relative price of good Y in terms of good X.
c rate at which a consumer will give up good Y in order to obtain more of good X and remain indifferent.
d rate at which a consumer will give up good X in order to obtain more of good Y and remain indifferent.
e slope of the budget line.

8 When the price of a good changes, the change in consumption that leaves the consumer indifferent is called the

a utility effect.
b substitution effect.
c income effect.
d price effect.
e inferior effect.

9 Figure P2.2 represents a monopolistically competitive firm in short-run equilibrium. What is the firm's price?

a P_1
b P_2
c P_3
d P_4
e P_5

FIGURE **P2.2**

10 Figure P2.2 represents a monopolistically competitive firm in short-run equilibrium. In the long run, what is the firm's economic profit *per unit*?

a $P_4 - P_2$
b $P_4 - P_1$
c P_3
d P_2
e none of the above

11 For a single-price monopolist, which of the following statements is *false*?

a There is no unique one-to-one relationship between price and quantity supplied.
b For any output greater than zero, $MR < AR$.
c The industry demand curve is the monopolist's demand curve.
d The intersection of MR and MC provides all information necessary for identifying the profit-maximizing quantity and price.
e Total revenue is at a maximum where $MR = 0$.

12 A single-price monopoly never operates

a on an elastic portion of the demand curve.
b on a portion of the demand curve that is unit elastic.
c on an inelastic portion of the demand curve.
d at a quantity where marginal revenue is positive since total revenue is not at a maximum.
e under any of the above conditions.

13 Shelley is maximizing her utility in her consumption of mink coats and Porsches. If the marginal utility of her last purchased mink coat is twice the marginal utility of her last purchased Porsche, then we know with certainty that

a Shelley buys twice as many mink coats as Porsches.
b Shelley buys twice as many Porsches as mink coats.
c Shelley buys more Porsches than mink coats, but we do not know how many more.
d the price of a mink coat is twice the price of a Porsche.
e the price of a Porsche is twice the price of a mink coat.

14 The difference between the value of a good and its price is known as

a excess demand.
b excess supply.
c consumer surplus.
d consumer excess.
e marginal utility.

15 If the present value of 100 received one year from now is $80, what is the annual interest rate?

a 50 percent
b 10 percent
c 20 percent
d 25 percent
e 8 percent

16 A firm has $200 in explicit costs and sells the resulting output for $250. The normal rate of profit is 10 percent. Which of the following statements is *true*?

a Implicit costs are $25.
b Economic profits are $20.
c Economic profits are $50.
d Economic profits exceed accounting profits.
e Explicit costs exceed implicit costs.

17 In a perfectly competitive industry of 100 firms, the demand curve facing the individual firm

a has unitary elasticity.
b is identical to the industry demand curve.
c is 1/100 of the industry demand curve.
d is one where $AR = MR$.
e is none of the above.

18 If economic profits are being made by firms in a competitive industry, new firms will enter. This will shift

a the industry demand curve to the left, causing market price to fall.
b the industry demand curve to the right, causing market price to rise.
c the industry supply curve to the left, causing market price to rise.
d the industry supply curve to the right, causing market price to fall.
e none of the above curves.

19 A change in income changes which aspect(s) of the budget equation?

a slope and *y*-intercept
b slope and *x*-intercept
c *x*- and *y*-intercepts but not slope
d slope only
e none of the above

20 When the price of a normal good rises, the income effect

a increases consumption of the good and the substitution effect decreases consumption.
b decreases consumption of the good and the substitution effect increases consumption.
c and the substitution effect both increase consumption of the good.
d and the substitution effect both decrease consumption of the good.
e is always larger than the substitution effect.

21 If *AFC* is falling then *MC* must be

a rising.
b falling.
c above *AFC*.
d below *AFC*.
e none of the above.

22 If all inputs are increased by 10 percent and output increases by more than 10 percent, it must be the case that

a average total cost is decreasing.
b average total cost is increasing.
c the *LRAC* curve is positively sloped.
d there are increasing returns to scale.
e there are decreasing returns to scale.

23 In Table P2.1, which method(s) of making a medical hologram is/are technologically efficient?

a 1
b 2
c 3
d all of the above
e 1 and 3 only

TABLE **P2.1** THREE METHODS OF MAKING ONE MEDICAL HOLOGRAM

| | Quantities of Inputs | |
Method	Labour	Capital
1	5	10
2	10	15
3	15	5

24 Refer to Table P2.1. If the price of labour is $20 per unit and the price of capital is $10 per unit, which method(s) is/are economically efficient?

a 1
b 2
c 3
d 2 and 3 only
e 1 and 3 only

25 The kinked demand curve model

a suggests that price will remain constant even with fluctuations in demand.

b suggests how the current price is determined.

c assumes that marginal revenue sometimes increases with output.

d assumes that competitors will match price cuts and ignore price increases.

e suggests none of the above.

26 In the prisoners' dilemma with players Art and Bob, the dominant strategy equilibrium is

a both prisoners confess.

b both prisoners deny.

c Art denies and Bob confesses.

d Bob denies and Art confesses.

e indeterminate.

27 In a perfectly competitive industry, the market price is $5. An individual firm is producing the level of output at which marginal cost is $5 and is increasing, and average total cost is $25. What should the firm do to maximize its short-run profits?

a shut down

b expand output

c contract output

d leave output unchanged

e insufficient information to answer

28 The long-run competitive industry supply curve will be positively sloped if there are

a external economies.

b external diseconomies.

c no external economies or diseconomies.

d external costs.

e external benefits.

ANSWERS

Problem

a The individual firm's demand curve and marginal revenue curve is a horizontal line at P_{pc}.

b See Fig. P2.1(b) Solution. Each firm is making economic profits because at output q_{pc}, price (P_{pc} = average revenue) is greater than average total cost.

c See Fig. P2.1 Solution. In response to economic profits, new firms enter the industry, causing the industry supply curve to shift rightward until it reaches S_1. When the price has fallen to P^{LR}_{pc}, economic profits have been eliminated and each firm is earning normal profits only.

d The monopolist's demand curve is the industry demand curve D_0. The monopolist does not have a supply curve since she can choose a combination of price and quantity.

e See Fig. P2.1(a) Solution.

FIGURE **P2.1** SOLUTION

(a) Industry

(b) Firm

f Even though the monopolist is earning economic profits, nothing happens in the long run because legal barriers prevent new entry. Long-run equilibrium price and output are the same as short-run price (P_m) and output (Q_m).

g Monopoly is less efficient than perfect competition, by the shaded area of deadweight loss indicated on Fig. P2.1(a) Solution.

h See Fig. P2.1(b) Solution. Since the firm is in long-run equilibrium, the downward-sloping demand curve must be tangent to the ATC curve at the equilibrium price P_{pc}.

i See Fig. P2.1 Solution. A profit-maximizing firm chooses the output (q_{mc}) where MC intersects MR. Hence the MR curve must intersect MC at q_{mc}. This is a long-run equilibrium because the firm is earning zero economic profits, so there is no incentive for entry or exit.

j Under monopolistic competition, ATC is higher (P_{pc}) than under perfect competition (P^{LR}_{pc}), implying less efficiency. However, the loss in allocative efficiency of monopolistic competition must be weighed against the gain in increased product variety.

Midterm Examination

1 c $MU = \Delta$ total utility/Δ quantity. (150–151)

2 a Quantities irrelevant. Ratios MUs must be = ratio prices. (152–154)

3 e Monopoly has no supply curve. (265–266)

4 d See text discussion. (271)

5 b $\downarrow$ marginal returns = $\downarrow MP \rightarrow \uparrow MC$. (216–219)

6 b Definition. All inputs and plant size variable. (211)

7 c Definition. **a** and **b** relate to slope budget line. MRS = **e** only at best affordable point. (173–179)

8 b Definition. (179–181)

9 d Highest possible price to sell Q_2. (290–292)

10 e Long-run economic profit per unit = zero. (290–292)

⊘11 d Need demand curve to identify price. (265–266)

12 c If demand is inelastic $\rightarrow MR < 0$. But MR must always be > 0 to intersect (positive) MC. (263–264)

13 d From maximum condition of equal MU/P. No necessary relation between MU and quantity. (152–154)

14 c Definition. (160–161)

15 d $\$80 = \$100/(1 + r)$. Solve for r. (194–196)

16 e Implicit costs = .10 ($\$200$) = $\$20$; economic profits = $\$25$; accounting profits = $\$50$. (196–198)

17 d Horizontal at market price. Infinite elasticity. (234–235)

18 d Economic profits/losses signal for supply shifts. Profits $\rightarrow$ entry new firms. (243–244)

⊘19 c See Chapter 8 Helpful Hint **2**. Δ income (y) does not change slope (P_m/P_p) but does Δ intercepts (y/P_m) and (y/P_p). (170–171)

20 d Both work in same direction. $\uparrow P \rightarrow \downarrow$ consumption. (179–181)

21 e AFC always $\downarrow$; no necessary relation to MC. See Text Fig. 10.5(b). (216–219)

22 d Definition. Since all inputs variable, **a** and **b** irrelevant. (222–225)

23 e 2 uses more labour and more capital than 1. (200–201)

24 a 1 costs $\$200$ while 2 and 3 cost $\$350$. (200–201)

25 d **a** true if fluctuation in MC. MR always $\downarrow$ with $\uparrow Q$ so **c** false. (293–294)

26 a Outcome of game. (296–298)

⊘27 e Firm at Q where $P = MC$, but losing \$ since $AR < ATC$. Need AVC information to determine if **a** or **d** correct. (238–239)

28 b $\uparrow$ costs as industry $Q \uparrow$ (247–248).

Chapter 14

Pricing and Allocating Factors of Production

KEY CONCEPTS

Factor Prices and Incomes

Firms hire the *services* of factors of production (labour, capital, land, entrepreneurship) to produce output.

◆ Demand and supply in factor markets for labour, capital, and land determine those factor prices (PF) (wages, interest, rent) and quantities (QF).

- Factor income = $(PF \times QF)$.
- The factor price for entrepreneurship is normal profit. Economic profit/loss is a residual income going to a firm's owners.

◆ ↑ demand for factor → ↑ PF, ↑ QF, and ↑ income.
↓ demand for factor → ↓ PF, ↓ QF, and ↓ income.

◆ ↑ supply of factor → ↓ PF, ↑ QF, and ↑ income if $\eta_D > 1$; ↓ income if $\eta_D < 1$.

◆ ↓ supply of factor → ↑ PF, ↓ QF, and ↓ income if $\eta_D > 1$; ↑ income if $\eta_D < 1$.

Demand for Factors

Demand for factors is a **derived demand**, stemming from firms' profit-maximizing objective and technology and market constraints.

◆ **Marginal revenue product** (MRP) is extra revenue from employing one more unit of factor.

- $MRP = MP \times MR$
- For a perfectly competitive firm, $MR = P$ output. So $MRP = MP$ (additional output produced by employing additional unit of a factor) $\times P$ output.

◆ Profit-maximizing firm hires additional units of factor up to point where $MRP = PF$. For labour (L), this is where MRP_L = wage rate.

◆ Firm's demand curve for factor is identical to the marginal revenue product curve of the factor.

◆ Firm's demand curve for labour shifts right if

- ↑ P output.
- ↑ price other inputs.
- technological change ↑ MP labour.

◆ Market demand curve for labour—sum of quantities of labour demanded by all firms at each wage rate.

$$\text{Elasticity of demand for labour} = \left| \frac{\% \Delta \text{ quantity labour demanded}}{\% \Delta \text{ wage rate}} \right|$$

Demand for labour will be *more elastic*

◆ when production is more labour-intensive (wages a greater percentage of total cost)

◆ the slower the MP labour diminishes

◆ the greater the elasticity of demand for the final product

◆ the greater the substitutability of capital for labour in the long run

Supply of Factors

Supply of labour determined by households' decisions of allocating time between **market activity** (work) and **nonmarket activity** (leisure, nonmarket production).

◆ At wage rates above household's **reservation wage**, household supplies labour.

◆ *Substitution effect* from ↑ wage → ↑ quantity labour supplied.

◆ *Income effect* from ↑ wage → ↓ quantity labour supplied.

◆ When wage ↑, quantity labour supplied ↑ when substitution effect > income effect.

◆ Individual household labour supply curve bends backward when income effect > substitution effect.

◆ Market supply of labour curve is horizontal sum of all household supply curves. Upward sloping on normal range of wage rates.

Supply of capital determined by households' saving decisions. Households supply *financial capital* that firms use to buy physical capital goods.

◆ Quantity of financial capital supplied ↑ when

  • current income > expected future income.
  • interest rates ↑.

◆ Market supply of capital curve is horizontal sum of all household supply curves. Short-run supply is inelastic. Long-run supply is more elastic.

◆ To an individual firm, short-run supply of capital is fixed. Long-run supply is perfectly elastic.

Supply of land is fixed and perfectly inelastic. But to an individual firm, supply of land is elastic.

Incomes, Economic Rent, and Transfer Earnings

Economic rent is income received by factor owner *above* amount required to induce supply. Income required to induce supply is **transfer earnings**. Transfer earnings are the opportunity cost of using a factor.

◆ Income consists of transfer earnings (area under supply curve) and economic rent (area above supply curve but below factor price).

◆ The more inelastic the supply of a factor, the greater the proportion of its income that is economic rent.

◆ Distinction between *rent* (price paid to factor of production, land) and *economic rent* (component of income of almost every factor production).

H E L P F U L   H I N T S

I This chapter gives a broad overview of the characteristics that are common to all markets for factors of production. For example, the assumption that firms are profit-maximizers implies that they will hire each factor of production up to the point where marginal revenue product is equal to the marginal cost of the factor, regardless of whether the factor of production is labour, land, or capital.

2 Distinguish carefully between the marginal revenue product of a factor of production and the marginal revenue of a unit of output. As noted in the text, the marginal revenue product of a factor of production can be calculated by multiplying marginal revenue and marginal product ($MRP = MR \times MP$). We can think of this intuitively as follows: marginal product tells us how much more output we receive from using more of a factor, and marginal revenue tells us how much more revenue we receive from selling each unit of that additional output. Therefore MP times MR tells us how much more revenue we receive from using more of the factor (the MRP).

3 The most important graph in this chapter appears in Text Fig. 14.4, reproduced here as Fig. 14.1. Using the example of Max's Wash 'n' Wax, the figure demonstrates that a firm's demand for labour curve is the same as its marginal revenue product curve of labour.

FIGURE **14.1**

(a)

(b)

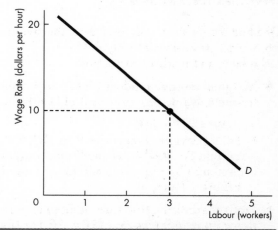

Part (a) of the figure shows the marginal revenue product curve (*MRP*) that is based on the numbers in Text Table 14.1 on page 324. Notice that the values for *MRP* are plotted midway between the labour inputs used in their calculation. For example, the *MRP* of moving from 0 to 1 labourer is 20, so the value of 20 on the *MRP* curve is plotted midway between 0 and 1 labourers.

Part (b) constructs Max's demand for labour by asking how much labour Max would be willing to hire at alternative wage rates. Since Max is a profit-maximizer, he will want to hire labour up to the point where the marginal revenue product of labour is equal to the wage rate. For example, if the wage rate is $10 per hour, Max will hire 3 workers since marginal revenue product is $10 when 3 workers are hired. Other points on the labour demand curve can be obtained in similar fashion. The result is that the labour demand curve is the same as the *MRP* curve.

S E L F - T E S T

True/False/Uncertain and Explain

1 Economic profit is the factor price of entrepreneurship.

2 If the production of good *A* is labour-intensive, the demand for labour used in the production of good *A* tends to be inelastic.

3 An increase in the supply of labour increases labour income.

4 A household supplies no labour at wage rates below its reservation wage.

5 A backward-bending supply curve for labour will arise if the substitution effect dominates the income effect.

6 If a household's current income is low compared with its expected future income, it will save very little.

7 The supply curve of capital is highly elastic.

8 The market supply of a particular piece of land is perfectly elastic.

9 If the supply of a factor of production is perfectly inelastic, its entire income is transfer earnings.

10 If Lloyd Robertson would be willing to read the news for $100,000 per year, and he is paid $2,100,000 per year to do so, he is earning economic rent of $2,000,000.

Multiple-Choice

1 Factor prices are wages for labour, rent for land,
a normal profit for capital, and interest for money.
b dividends for capital, and interest for money.
c interest for capital, and normal profit for entrepreneurship.
d interest for capital, and economic profit for entrepreneurship.
e economic profit for capital, and normal profit for entrepreneurship.

2 Suppose that the supply of a factor of production is very elastic. An increase in the demand for that factor results in a
a large increase in the quantity supplied of the factor and a small increase in its price.
b small increase in the quantity supplied of the factor and a large increase in its price.
c large increase in the supply of the factor and a small increase in its price.
d small increase in the supply of the factor and a large increase in its price.
e small increase in the supply of the factor and a small increase in its price.

3 An increase in the supply of a factor of production will

a increase the factor's income if the elasticity of factor demand is less than 1.

b decrease the factor's income if the elasticity of factor demand is less than 1.

c increase the factor's income if the elasticity of factor supply is less than 1.

d decrease the factor's income if the elasticity of factor supply is less than 1.

e always decrease the factor's income.

4 When a firm is a price-taker in the labour market, its marginal revenue product of labour curve is also its

a marginal cost curve for labour.

b demand curve for labour.

c supply curve of labour.

d supply curve of output.

e average revenue curve.

5 A profit-maximizing firm will continue to hire units of a variable factor of production until the

a marginal cost of the factor equals its marginal product.

b marginal cost of the factor equals its average revenue product.

c average cost of the factor equals its marginal revenue product.

d marginal cost of the factor equals its marginal revenue product.

e factor's marginal revenue product equals zero.

6 If the wage rate increases, the *substitution* effect will give a household an incentive to

a raise its reservation wage.

b increase its nonmarket activity and decrease its market activity.

c increase its market activity and decrease its nonmarket activity.

d increase both market and nonmarket activity.

e decrease both market and nonmarket activity.

7 If the wage rate increases, the *income* effect will give a household an incentive to

a raise its reservation wage.

b increase its nonmarket activity and decrease its market activity.

c increase its market activity and decrease its nonmarket activity.

d increase both market and nonmarket activity.

e decrease both market and nonmarket activity.

8 If the price of its output falls, a perfectly competitive firm will hire

a less labour, causing the wage to fall.

b less labour, causing the marginal product of labour to rise.

c less labour, causing the marginal product of labour to fall.

d more labour, causing the marginal product of labour to rise.

e more labour, causing the marginal product of labour to fall.

9 A technological change that causes an increase in the marginal product of labour will shift

a the labour demand curve leftward.

b the labour demand curve rightward.

c the labour supply curve leftward.

d the labour supply curve rightward.

e **b** and **d**.

10 In the short run, a firm faces a supply of capital that is

a perfectly elastic.

b perfectly inelastic.

c positively sloped.

d negatively sloped.

e backward bending.

11 If the desire for leisure increased, the wage rate would

a rise and the quantity of labour hired would fall.

b rise and the quantity of labour hired would rise.

c fall and the quantity of labour hired would fall.

d fall and the quantity of labour hired would rise.

e fall and the quantity of labour demanded would rise.

12 As the wage rate rises, a household will have a backward-bending supply of labour curve if

a the income effect is in the same direction as the substitution effect.

b the wage rate rises above the reservation wage.

c the substitution effect dominates the income effect.

d the income effect dominates the substitution effect.

e leisure is an inferior good.

13 An example of derived demand is the demand for

a sweaters derived by an economics student.

b sweaters produced by labour and capital.

c labour used in the production of sweaters.

d sweater brushes.

e none of the above.

14 The change in total revenue resulting from employing an additional unit of capital is the

a marginal product of capital.
b marginal revenue of capital.
c marginal revenue cost of capital.
d marginal revenue product of capital.
e average revenue product of capital.

15 Other things remaining the same, the larger the proportion of total cost coming from labour, the

a more elastic is the demand for labour.
b less elastic is the demand for labour.
c more elastic is the supply of labour.
d less elastic is the supply of labour.
e lower is the demand for labour.

16 Which of the following statements about the short-run demand for labour, *ceteris paribus*, is *true*?

a The larger the elasticity of demand is for the product, the less elastic is the demand for labour.
b The higher the labour intensity of the production process is, the less elastic is the demand for labour.
c The more rapidly the marginal product of labour curve diminishes, the less elastic is the demand for labour.
d All of the above are true.
e None of the above is true.

17 Consider the supply schedule of a factor of production given in Table 14.1. If 4 units of the factor are supplied at a price of $8 per unit, what are the transfer earnings?

a $8
b $12
c $20
d $32
e none of the above

TABLE **14.1**

Price of Factor ($)	Quantity of Factor Supplied
2	1
4	2
6	3
8	4
10	5

18 Consider the supply schedule of a factor of production given in Table 14.1. If 4 units of the factor are supplied at a price of $8 per unit, what is the economic rent?

a $8
b $12
c $20
d $32
e none of the above

19 Whether a household's current income is high or low *compared with expected future income* is influenced by

a the stage of the life cycle the household is in.
b whether the household is rich or poor.
c whether interest rates are high or low.
d whether saving is high or low.
e all of the above.

20 Economic rent is the

a price paid for the use of a hectare of land.
b price paid for the use of a unit of capital.
c income required to induce a given quantity of a factor of production to be supplied.
d income received above the amount required to induce a given quantity of a factor of production to be supplied.
e transfer earnings of a factor of production.

21 The supply curve of labour facing the individual firm in a perfectly competitive labour market is

a upward sloping.
b backward bending.
c first upward sloping and then backward bending as the wage increases.
d vertical.
e horizontal.

22 The income effect of a higher wage is

a the increased income workers must be paid to be willing to work more.
b the increased prices of consumer goods that result from increased worker incomes.
c the increased demand for leisure that results from increased worker incomes.
d the increased workers' purchasing power that results from increased worker incomes.
e all of the above.

23 Which of the following will *not* be true in a profit-maximizing equilibrium?

a marginal revenue equals marginal product
b marginal revenue equals marginal cost
c marginal revenue times marginal product of a factor equals marginal factor cost
d marginal revenue product of a factor equals marginal factor cost
e marginal revenue product of a factor divided by marginal factor cost equals marginal product of a factor

24 The income of a factor in relatively inelastic supply will consist of

a transfer earnings only.
b economic rent only.
c more transfer earnings than economic rent.
d more economic rent than transfer earnings.
e equal amounts of transfer earnings and economic rent.

25 A factor that affects *only* the long-run elasticity of demand for labour is

a the labour intensity of the production process.
b the substitutability of capital for labour.
c the elasticity of demand for the product.
d how rapidly the marginal product of labour curve diminishes.
e none of the above.

Short Answer Problems

1 Why isn't the factor price for capital the price of the specific pieces of capital equipment that the firm buys?

2 Discuss the substitution and income effects on the quantity of labour supplied if the wage rate *decreases*.

3 Why do younger households tend to save less than older households?

4 Are prices of retail goods in Toronto's trendy Yorkville district high because rents are high, or are rents high because prices are high? Explain.

5 Table 14.2 gives the total and marginal product schedules for a firm that sells its output and buys labour in competitive markets. Initially the price at which the firm can sell any level of output is $5 per unit and the wage rate at which it can purchase any quantity of labour is $15 per unit.

TABLE **14.2**

Quantity Labour (L)	Output (Q)	Marginal Product (MP_L)	P = $5 Total Revenue (TR)	P = $5 Marginal Revenue Product (MRP_L)	P = $3 Total Revenue (TR)	P = $3 Marginal Revenue Product (MRP_L)
0	0					
		... 12				
1	12					
		... 10				
2	22					
		... 8				
3	30					
		... 6				
4	36					
		... 4				
5	40					
		... 2				
6	42					

a Complete the first two blank columns in Table 14.2 by computing the *TR* and MRP_L corresponding to a price of output = $5.

b The marginal revenue product of labour (MRP_L) can be computed by either of the following formulas:

$$MRP_L = \Delta TR / \Delta L$$
$$MRP_L = MR \times MP_L$$

where ΔTR = the change in total revenue, ΔL = the change in labour, MR = marginal revenue, and MP_L = marginal product of labour. Show that these two formulas are equivalent for the case when the quantity of labour changes from 1 to 2 units.

c If the firm maximizes profit, what quantity of labour will it hire? How much output will it produce?

d If total fixed cost is $125, what is the amount of profit?

e What is its profit if the firm hires one more unit of labour than the profit-maximizing quantity? one less unit of labour than the profit-maximizing quantity?

f Draw a graph of the demand for labour and the supply of labour and illustrate labour market equilibrium.

6 Now, suppose that the market demand for the output of the firm in Short Answer Problem 5 decreases, causing the price of output to decrease to $3 per unit. The total and marginal product schedules remain unchanged.

  a Complete the last two blank columns in Table 14.2 by computing the TR and MRP_L corresponding to price of output = $3.

  b If the wage remains at $15 per unit of labour, what is the profit-maximizing quantity of labour that the firm will hire? How much output will it produce?

  c Total fixed cost continues to be $125. What is the amount of profit?

  d Will the firm shut down in the short run? Explain.

  e Draw a new graph of the new labour market equilibrium.

7 The price of output for the firm in Short Answer Problem **6** remains at $3, but the wage now rises to $21 per unit of labour. The total and marginal product schedules remain unchanged.

  a What happens to the demand curve for labour (the MRP of labour curve)?

  b Under these circumstances, what is the profit-maximizing quantity of labour that the firm will hire? How much output will it produce?

  c Total fixed cost continues to be $125. What is the amount of profit?

  d Draw a graph of the labour market equilibrium.

©⦾ **8** A perfectly competitive firm in long-run equilibrium produces flubits using only two factors of production—labour and capital. Each factor is sold in a perfectly competitive factor market. Labour costs $30 per unit and capital costs $50 per unit.

  a Assuming the firm has hired the profit-maximizing quantity of capital in part **b** of this question, the marginal revenue product of labour curve is

$$MRP_L = 110 - 8/5 \ Q_L$$

where MRP_L is the marginal revenue product of labour and Q_L is the quantity (in units) of labour hired. How many units of labour does the firm hire?

  b Assuming the firm has hired the profit-maximizing quantity of labour in part **a** of this question, the marginal revenue product of capital curve is

$$MRP_K = 125 - 75/40 \ Q_K$$

where MRP_K is the marginal revenue product of capital and Q_K is the quantity (in units) of capital hired. How many units of capital does the firm hire?

  c The price of a flubit is $10.

  i How many flubits is the firm producing? [*Hint*: Remember that the firm is in long-run equilibrium.]

  ii What is the marginal (physical) product of the 25th unit of labour hired?

9 Table 14.3 gives the market labour demand and supply schedules.

TABLE **14.3**

Wage Rate (dollars per hour)	Quantity of Labour Supplied (hours)	Quantity of Labour Demanded (hours)
0	0	240
1	20	200
2	40	160
3	60	120
4	80	80
5	100	40
6	120	0

  a What is the equilibrium wage rate and the quantity of labour hired?

  b What is the total amount of income received by labour in this market?

  c Represent the market graphically. Identify the equilibrium wage and quantity of labour.

  d Based on your graph from part **c**, how much of labour income is transfer earnings? How much is economic rent?

  e Now suppose that the demand for labour increases by 60 hours at each wage rate.

  i What are the new equilibrium wage rate and quantity of labour?

  ii What is the new total amount of labour income?

  iii How much of this income is transfer earnings? How much is economic rent?

⦾ **10** A constant cost perfectly competitive industry is initially in long-run equilibrium at P_0 and Q_0 in Fig. 14.2. Each firm in the industry faces the marginal revenue product (MRP^0_L) and wage curves in Fig. 14.3, and initially hires QL_0 units of labour.

FIGURE **14.2** INDUSTRY

FIGURE **14.3** FIRM

a A decrease in preferences causes industry demand to shift to D_1. As a result of decrease in demand, draw the appropriate new curves (if any) on Fig. 14.3 and explain any shifts. What happens to the short-run quantity of labour hired by the individual firm?

b There are no further shifts in demand. Explain what will happen in the long run and why. Draw any necessary additional curve(s) on Figs. 14.2 and 14.3 showing the final long-run equilibrium.

A N S W E R S

True/False/Uncertain and Explain

1 **F** Normal profit. Economic profit is residual income to firm's owners, who may include the entrepreneur. (320)

2 **F** Tends to be elastic. (328)

3 **U** True if elasticity demand for labour > 1; false if < 1. (321–322)

4 **T** Reservation wage minimum for labour supply. (329–330)

5 **F** Income effect dominates substitution effect. (329–330)

6 **T** Saving for greater future consumption not sensible if expect to be better off in future anyway. (331–332)

ⓓ 7 **U** True for long run, false for short run. (331–332)

8 **F** Perfectly inelastic. (332–333)

9 **F** Entire income is economic rent. (334–335)

10 **T** Excess of income over transfer earnings. (334–335)

Multiple-Choice

1 **c** Definition. (320)

2 **a** Movement up along flat supply curve. (321–322)

3 **b** $\uparrow PF$ with inelastic demand $\rightarrow \uparrow (PF \times QF)$. (321–322)

4 **b** Shows quantity labour hired at each wage rate. (325)

5 **d** Where supply curve of factor to firm (MC) intersects demand curve for factor (MRP). (325–326)

6 **c** Substitute work for leisure. (329–330)

7 **b** Consume more normal goods, including leisure, which entails working less. (329–330)

ⓓ 8 **b** Labour demand curve shifts left. Supply horizontal. Because of diminishing MP, $\downarrow L \rightarrow \uparrow MP$. (326–327)

9 **b** See text discussion. (326–327)

10 **b** Fixed in specific capital equipment. (331–332)

11 **a** Labour supply would shift left. (329–330)

12 **d** Income and substitution effects opposite for labour. (329–330)

13 **c** Factor of production used as input. (323–324)

14 **d** Revenue from selling marginal product of capital. (323–324)

15 **a** $\uparrow$ wage $\rightarrow$ greater $\uparrow$ total costs and $\uparrow$ product $P \rightarrow$ greater $\downarrow$ sales and $\downarrow$ labour hired. (328)

ⓓ 16 **c** Reverse of **a**, **b** true. (328)

17 **c** $2 + $4 + $6 + $8. (334–335)

ⓓ 18 **b** Total income ($32 = 4 \times $8) minus transfer earnings ($20). (334–335)

ⓓ 19 **a** Younger households have relatively low current income, older households relatively high current income. (331–332)

20 **d** Definition. Price paid for land use is rent. (334–335)

21 **e** Because firm small part of labour market, can buy as much labour as desired at market wage. (329–330)

22 c ↑ wage → ↑ income → ↑ demand for normal goods, including leisure. (329–330)

◔ 23 a *MR* measured in $, *MP* measured in physical units. Other answers definitions or profit-maximizing conditions. (325–326)

24 d Draw graph with steep supply and compare areas above and below supply curve at equilibrium *PF* and *QF.* (334–335)

25 b a, c, d affect both short and long run. (327–328)

Short Answer Problems

1 In general, factor prices represent the *opportunity cost* to the firm of *using* that factor of production. Wages are the cost of using labour and rent is the cost of using land. The cost of using a piece of capital equipment bought by the firm is the interest that must be paid (explicitly or implicitly) on the funds tied up in the purchase of the equipment. Capital equipment lasts for a long period of time. The cost of capital during any one period is not the purchase price of the equipment, it is the cost of the funds tied up in the equipment over the period.

2 If the wage rate decreases, the opportunity cost of leisure decreases and households will have a tendency to shift from work to leisure (the substitution effect), thereby reducing the quantity of labour supplied. The lower wage also decreases the household's income and, thus causes the household to reduce its demand for leisure and other normal goods (the income effect) thereby increasing the quantity of labour supplied.

3 Households will tend to save less when current income is low relative to expected future income and save more when current income is high relative to expected future income. Younger households are largely in this first situation, while older households are largely in the second.

4 Rents are high because prices are high. Land in Yorkville has a perfectly inelastic supply, so the price of land (its rent) is determined entirely by demand for the land.

Demand is high because merchants know that the prime retail location will allow them to charge higher prices and potentially earn higher profits than in other locations.

5 a The completed columns for *TR* and MRP_L corresponding to a price of output = $5 are shown in Table 14.2 Solution. The values for *TR* are obtained by multiplying the quantity of

output by the price of output ($5). The values for MRP_L between any two quantities of labour are obtained by dividing the change in *TR* by the change in quantity of labour, or by multiplying *MR* ($5) by MP_L.

TABLE **14.2** SOLUTION

Quantity Labour (L)	Output (Q)	Marginal Product (MP_L)	P = $5 Total Revenue (TR)	P = $5 Marginal Revenue Product (MRP_L)	P = $3 Total Revenue (TR)	P = $3 Marginal Revenue Product (MRP_L)
0	0		0		0	
		⋯ 12		⋯ 60		⋯ 36
1	12		60		36	
		⋯ 10		⋯ 50		⋯ 30
2	22		110		66	
		⋯ 8		⋯ 40		⋯ 24
3	30		150		90	
		⋯ 6		⋯ 30		⋯ 18
4	36		180		108	
		⋯ 4		⋯ 20		⋯ 12
5	40		200		120	
		⋯ 2		⋯ 10		⋯ 6
6	42		210		126	

b From part **a**, the formula $MRP_L = \Delta TR/\Delta L$, yields a marginal revenue product of labour of 50 when the quantity of labour changes from 1 to 2 units. To confirm that the second formula ($MRP_L = MR \times MP_L$) gives the same answer when the quantity of labour changes from 1 to 2 units, substitute in the values for *MR* ($5, the price of an additional unit of output) and MP_L (10 units of output). This yields the same marginal revenue product of labour as above; $5 × 10 units = $50.

c The firm maximizes profit by hiring labour up to the point where the *MRP* of labour is equal to the marginal cost of labour (the wage rate). That point occurs at 5 units of labour. The *MRP* of moving from 4 to 5 units of labour is 20, and the *MRP* of moving from 5 to 6 units of labour is 10. Thus by interpolation, the *MRP* at exactly 5 units of labour is 15 (midway between 20 and 10). So when 5 units of labour are hired, the *MRP* of labour is equal to the wage rate ($15). Given that 5 units of labour are hired, the profit-maximizing output will be 40 units (from Table 14.2 Solution).

d To calculate profit, we must first calculate total revenue and then subtract total cost. Total revenue is $200 (40 units of output × $5 per unit) and total cost is also $200—the sum of total variable (labour) cost of $75 (5 units of labour × $15 per unit) and total fixed cost of $125. Thus profit is zero.

e If the firm hires one more unit of labour (6 units), total revenue will be $210 (42 units of output × the $5 price). Total cost will be the $125 fixed cost plus $90 in total variable cost (6 units of labour × the $15 wage rate) or $215. Thus profit will be a negative $5 (a $5 loss).

If the firm hires one less unit of labour (4 units), total revenue will be $180 (36 units of output × the $5 price). Total cost will be the $125 fixed cost plus $60 in total variable cost (4 units of labour × the $15 wage rate) or $185. Thus profit will be a negative $5 (a $5 loss).

f The graph of labour market equilibrium appears in Fig. 14.4. The demand for labour is given by the firm's MRP_L curve which is labelled D_0 (D_1 will be discussed in Short Answer Problem 6).

Notice that the values for MRP are plotted midway between the corresponding quantities of labour. For example, MRP of 60 is plotted midway between 0 and 1 units of labour.

Since the firm purchases labour in a perfectly competitive labour market, the supply of labour to the firm is perfectly elastic at the market wage rate. The labour supply curve is labelled $W = 15. The equilibrium is at the intersection of these curves, and corresponds to a wage rate of $15 and a quantity of labour hired of 5 units.

FIGURE **14.4**

6 a The completed columns for TR and MRP_L corresponding to price of output = $3 are shown in Table 14.2 Solution. The values for TR are obtained by multiplying the quantity of output by the price of output ($3). The values for MRP_L between any two quantities of labour are obtained by dividing the change in TR by the change in quantity of labour, or by multiplying MR ($3) by MP_L.

b If the wage rate remains at $15, the profit-maximizing quantity of labour will fall to 4 units since MRP_L equals the wage rate at 4 units of labour. The MRP of moving from 3 to 4 units of labour is 18, and the MRP of moving from 4 to 5 units of labour is 12. Thus, by interpolation, the MRP at exactly 4 units of labour is 15 (midway between 18 and 12). Given that 4 units of labour are employed, the profit-maximizing output will be 36 units (from Table 14.2 Solution).

c Profit equals total revenue minus total cost. Total revenue is $108 (36 units of output × $3 per unit) and total cost is $185—the sum of total variable (labour) cost of $60 (4 units of labour × $15 per unit) and total fixed cost of $125. Thus profit is –$77, or a loss of $77.

d The firm will not shut down since total revenue ($108) is enough to cover total variable cost ($60) and part of fixed cost. If the firm decided to shut down, it would lose the $125 of fixed cost rather than just $77.

e The graph of labour market equilibrium appears in Fig. 14.4. The new demand for labour is given by the firm's new MRP_L curve, which is labelled D_1. The supply of labour has not changed; it continues to be horizontal at $15, the competitive market wage. The new equilibrium is at the intersection of these curves and corresponds to a wage rate of $15 and a quantity of labour hired of 4 units.

7 a Since marginal revenue and the marginal product of labour are unaffected by a change in the wage rate, the demand curve for labour (the MRP of labour) will remain at D_1.

b If the wage rate rises to $21, the profit-maximizing quantity of labour will fall to 3 units since MRP_L equals the wage rate at 3 units of labour. Given that 3 units of labour are employed, the profit-maximizing output will be 30 units (from Table 14.2 Solution).

c Profit equals total revenue minus total cost. Total revenue is $90 (30 units of output × $3 per unit) and total cost is $188—the sum of total variable (labour) cost of $63 (3 units of labour × $21 per unit) and total fixed cost of $125. Thus profit is –$98, or a loss of $98.

d See Fig. 14.4. The relevant demand for labour curve continues to be D_1, but the labour supply curve reflects the rise in the competitive wage rate; it is now horizontal at a wage rate of $21 (labelled $W = 21). The equilibrium is at the intersection of these curves and corresponds to a wage rate of $21 and a quantity of labour hired of 3 units.

⊚ⓞ 8 a By assuming that the firm has already hired its capital, we know (in principle) fixed costs and can calculate the profit-maximizing quantity of the variable factor (labour) by setting the MRP_L equal to the wage rate ($30).

$$30 = 110 - 8/5 \ Q_L$$
$$8/5 \ Q_L = 80$$
$$Q_L = 50$$

b By assuming that the firm has already hired its labour, we can treat labour as the fixed cost and treat capital as the variable factor of production. Calculate the profit-maximizing quantity of the capital hired by setting the MRP_K equal to the cost of a unit of capital ($50).

$$50 = 125 - 75/40 \ Q_K$$
$$75/40 \ Q_K = 75$$
$$Q_K = 40$$

c i The fact that the firm is in long-run equilibrium provides the key to calculating the quantity of flubits produced. In long-run equilibrium, the firm earns zero economic profit, so total revenue is exactly equal to total cost.

We can calculate total cost by adding the costs of the (only) two factors of production. Labour cost is 50 units of labour × $30 per unit or $1,500. Capital cost is 40 units of capital × $50 per unit or $2,000. Total cost is, therefore, $3,500.

Total revenue must also be equal to $3,500. Since total revenue (TR) is just the price of output (P) times quantity sold (Q), we can calculate Q by substituting in the values we have for TR ($3,500) and P ($10).

$$TR = P \times Q$$
$$\$3,500 = \$10 \times Q$$
$$Q = 350$$

ii To calculate the marginal product of the 25th unit of labour, we begin by calculating the marginal *revenue* product of the 25th unit of labour. Substituting $Q_L = 25$ into the equation for MRP_L yields

$$MRP_L = 110 - 8/5 \ (25)$$
$$= 110 - 40$$
$$= 70$$

One definition of the marginal revenue product of labour is the marginal product of labour (MP_L) times marginal revenue (MR) or $MRP_L = MP_L \times MR$. Rearranging to solve for MP_L yields

$$MP_L = MRP_L/MR$$

Substituting in the values for the marginal revenue product of the 25th unit of labour (70) and for MR (the price of output $10) yields

$$MP_L = 70/10$$
$$MP_L = 7$$

9 a The equilibrium wage rate is $4 per hour and the quantity of labour hired is 80 hours.

b Total income is $320 ($4 per hour × 80 hours).

c The supply and demand curves for labour are given in Fig. 14.5. The supply of labour is given by S_0 and the initial demand for labour is represented by D_0. The equilibrium occurs at the intersection of these two curves. You can see that the equilibrium wage is $4 per hour and the quantity of labour is 80 hours.

FIGURE **14.5**

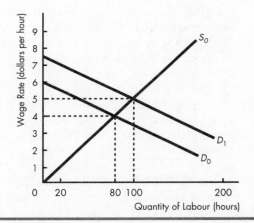

d Given that the supply of labour curve is a 45-degree line starting at the origin, half of income is transfer earnings (the area below the supply curve) and the other half is economic rent (the area above the supply curve). Since income is $320, each of these is $160.

e i Each entry in the last column of Table 14.3 will increase by 60 units. The new equilibrium wage rate is $5 per hour and the new equilibrium quantity of labour is 100 hours. The new labour demand curve appears in Fig. 14.5 as D_1.

ii Total income is now $500 ($5 per hour × 100 hours).

iii Once again the slope of the labour supply curve (which has not changed) implies that income is split evenly between transfer earnings and economic rent. Each will be equal to $250.

☉ 10 a See Fig.14.2 Solution and Fig.14.3 Solution. The decrease in demand causes the industry price of output to fall to P_1, which causes each firm's marginal revenue product of labour curve to shift leftward. There is no change in the wage, so the quantity of labour hired by the individual firm decreases to QL_1.

b The key to understanding what will happen in the long run is the fact that this is a constant cost industry initially in long-run equilibrium. At P_0 and Q_0, firms earn zero economic profits. When price falls to P_1, firms make economic losses. This leads some firms to exit the industry, causing the industry supply curve to shift leftward. Because this is a constant cost industry, we know that the new long-run equilibrium, even at reduced levels of output, must occur at the same price as the initial equilibrium. Thus the industry supply curve shifts to S_1. The final long-run equilibrium for the industry is back at the original price P_0 and new quantity Q_2.

As the price of output returns to P_0, the marginal revenue product of labour curve for each remaining firm shifts back to the right, ending up at its original position. The quantity of labour hired by each remaining firm increases from QL_1 to QL_0.

When firms exit, industry supply decreases, price increases, and the quantity supplied by each remaining firm increases. In Chapter 10, we saw that this means each remaining firm moves up its marginal cost curve. Here, we can see why. Each remaining firm increases its hiring of the variable factor of production, labour. Because of diminishing returns, the marginal (physical) product of labour falls. With a fixed wage, marginal cost ($MC = W/MP_L$) increases.

FIGURE **14.2** SOLUTION INDUSTRY

FIGURE **14.3** SOLUTION FIRM

KEY CONCEPTS

Skill Differentials

Skill differentials arise because of difference in

◆ Demand—skilled labour has higher marginal revenue product (*MRP*) than unskilled labour. Higher *MRP* → higher demand.

◆ Supply—skills costly to acquire. **Human capital** is accumulated skill and knowledge human beings. Costs of acquiring skill → supply curve skilled labour above supply curve unskilled labour.

Union-Nonunion Wage Differentials

Labour unions are organized groups of workers.

◆ **Craft union**—group of workers with similar range of skills working for different firms/industries.

◆ **Industrial union**—group of workers with variety of skills and job types working for same firm/industry.

◆ **Rand formula** requires all workers in a *closed shop* to contribute to the union whether or not they belong.

◆ **Collective bargaining**—process of negotiation between unions and employers.

Labour unions' objectives are increasing compensation, improving working conditions, and expanding job opportunities. Methods of achieving objectives include

◆ Restricting supply of labour.

◆ ↑ demand for union labour or making demand more inelastic by encouraging import restrictions, supporting minimum wage laws and immigration restrictions, ↑ product demand, ↑ marginal product union members.

Monopsony—market structure in which there is a single buyer. Firm that is only employer in town is monopsonist in the labour market.

◆ To hire more labour, monopsonist must pay a higher wage. Marginal cost of labour curve (*MCL*) for monopsonist is upward sloping and above and steeper than the market supply curve of labour.

◆ Profit-maximizing rule for monopsonist is to hire quantity of labour where *MCL* curve intersects *MRP* curve, then offer lowest wage for which labour will work (on supply curve).

◆ For monopsonist, employment and wage are lower than for competitive labour market. More elastic supply of labour → ↓ *opportunity* for monopsony to ↓ wages, to ↓ employment or to ↑ economic profit.

◆ Adding union to a monopsony labour market can → **bilateral monopoly**, where wage determined by relative bargaining strength firm and union. Highest possible wage where *MCL* intersects *MRP*. Lowest possible wage is pure monopsony wage.

◆ Adding a minimum wage law to a monopsony labour market can → ↑ wage and ↑ employment.

Wage Differentials Between the Sexes

Wage differentials between men and women because of

◆ Job types—men and women doing different jobs; men's jobs often better paid than women's jobs.

◆ Discrimination—results in lower wages and employment for those discriminated against.

◆ Differences in human capital—differences in schooling (mostly eliminated), work experience, and job interruptions (lessened recently).

◆ Differences in degree of specialization—because of social conventions men have specialized in market activities, while women have divided their time between market activities and nonmarket activities.

- *Household production* creates goods and services consumed within household rather than supplied to market.
- Market specialization → ↑ productivity and ↑ wages.

Pay Equity Laws

Pay equity laws determine wages by assessing value of jobs on objective characteristics rather than on what the market will pay.

◆ *Pay equity*—paying same wage for different jobs judged objectively to be comparable.

◆ Pay equity laws can → ↑ equity where discrimination exists.

◆ Pay equity laws can → unintended consequences of ↑ unemployment for women where existing market wage differentials are productivity-based.

H E L P F U L   H I N T S

1 This chapter introduces the concept of a monopsonist, a firm that is the only buyer in a market, such as labour. The monopsonist faces an upward-sloping supply curve of labour. As a result, its marginal cost of labour curve (*MCL*) is different from the labour supply curve.

There is a close parallel between (a) the relationship between the labour supply curve and the *MCL* curve for the monopsonist and (b) the already familiar relationship (Chapter 12) between the demand curve and the marginal revenue curve (*MR*) for the monopolist. Both sets of relationships stem from the assumption of a single price for labour or output in the relevant market.

The monopolist, as the only seller in an output market, faces a downward-sloping demand curve. The marginal revenue from the sale of an additional unit of output is *less* than the selling price because the monopolist must *lower* the price on all previous units as well. Thus the *MR* curve lies *below* the demand curve for the single-price monopolist.

For the monopsonist in a labour market, the marginal cost of hiring an additional unit of labour is *higher* than the wage because the

monopsonist must *raise* the wage on all previous units of labour as well. Thus the *MCL* curve lies *above* the supply of labour curve for the monopsonist.

S E L F - T E S T

True/False/Uncertain and Explain

1 The marginal revenue product of unskilled workers is lower than that of skilled workers.

2 The vertical distance between the labour supply curves for skilled and unskilled workers is the marginal revenue product of the skill.

3 The larger the marginal revenue product of the skill and the more costly it is to acquire, the smaller is the wage differential between skilled and unskilled workers.

4 Unions support minimum wage laws in part because they increase the cost of unskilled labour, a substitute for skilled union labour.

5 For a firm that is a monopsonist in the labour market, the supply curve of labour is the marginal cost of labour curve.

6 The more elastic is labour supply, the less opportunity a monopsonist has to make an economic profit.

7 The introduction of a minimum wage that is above the current wage will raise the wage but reduce employment.

8 In the case of bilateral monopoly in a labour market, the wage depends on the bargaining strength of the two traders.

9 Economic theory tells us that discrimination in employment will result in wage differentials.

10 If males on average earn more than females, there is discrimination.

Multiple-Choice

1 Which of the following is *not* a reason why the wage of skilled workers exceeds the wage of unskilled workers?

a The market for skilled workers is more competitive than the market for unskilled workers.

b The marginal revenue product of skilled workers is greater than that of unskilled workers.

c The cost of training skilled workers is greater than the cost of training unskilled workers.

d Skilled workers have acquired more human capital than unskilled workers.

e The demand curve for skilled workers lies to the right of the demand curve for unskilled workers.

2 Other things remaining the same, if education costs rise substantially, we would expect to see a(n)

a decrease in the marginal revenue product of skilled workers.

b decrease in the demand for skilled workers.

c increase in the supply of skilled workers.

d increase in the wage of skilled workers.

e increase in the number of skilled workers employed.

3 A union that organizes workers with a similar skill regardless of the firm or industry that employs them is a(n)

a industrial union.

b craft union.

c local union.

d national union.

e public sector union.

4 Figure 15.1 illustrates a monopsonist in the labour market (*MCL* = marginal cost of labour). The profit-maximizing wage rate and quantity of labour hired will be

a $4 per hour and 800 hours of labour.

b $4 per hour and 400 hours of labour.

c $7 per hour and 600 hours of labour.

d $9 per hour and 400 hours of labour.

e none of the above.

FIGURE **15.1**

5 If the labour market illustrated in Fig. 15.1 became competitive, the equilibrium wage rate and quantity of labour hired would be

a $4 per hour and 800 hours of labour.

b $4 per hour and 400 hours of labour.

c $7 per hour and 600 hours of labour.

d $9 per hour and 400 hours of labour.

e none of the above.

6 If a union forms to face the monopsonist in Fig. 15.1, the situation is one of

a binding arbitration.

b derived demand.

c duopoly.

d collusive oligopoly.

e bilateral monopoly.

7 If a union and the monopsonist in Fig. 15.1 agree to collective bargaining, the outcome will be an hourly wage

a of $7.

b between $4 and $7.

c between $4 and $9.

d between $7 and $9.

e that is indeterminate without additional information.

8 Wage differentials between males and females can be explained by

a occupational differences.
b human capital differences.
c degree of specialization differences.
d discrimination.
e all of the above.

9 If discrimination takes the form of restricting a group's access to education and training, the effect on this group of workers will be to shift the

a *MRP* curve rightward and increase the wage.
b *MRP* curve leftward and decrease the wage.
c *MRP* curve rightward and decrease the wage.
d supply of labour curve up and decrease the wage.
e supply of labour curve down and decrease the wage.

10 The Rand formula made

a collective bargaining compulsory.
b it compulsory for all workers in a partially unionized plant to contribute to the union.
c binding arbitration legal.
d strikes and lockouts illegal under some circumstances.
e none of the above.

11 Pay equity is an attempt to pay women and men the same wage

a for doing the same job.
b for household production as for market activity.
c for different jobs that are judged to be comparable.
d regardless of their jobs.
e regardless of gender.

12 Refer to Fig. 15.2. For any given quantity of labour employed,

a the elasticity of demand for skilled workers is less than the elasticity of demand for unskilled workers.
b skilled workers will receive a lower wage than unskilled workers.
c skilled workers will receive a higher wage than unskilled workers.
d the vertical distance between the curves is the compensation for the cost of acquiring skill.
e the vertical distance between the curves is the present value of human capital.

FIGURE **15.2**

13 The vertical distance between the two supply curves in Fig. 15.3

a is the compensation for the cost of acquiring skill.
b is the *MRP* of skill.
c is the result of discrimination against unskilled workers.
d will disappear if there is free entry in the skill market.
e will disappear with equal pay for work of equal value.

FIGURE **15.3**

14 Refer only to the information in Fig. 15.3. For any given wage rate, more hours of

a unskilled labour will be demanded than skilled labour.
b skilled labour will be demanded than unskilled labour.
c unskilled labour will be supplied than skilled labour.
d skilled labour will be supplied than unskilled labour.
e unskilled labour will be supplied if the *MRP* of skill increases.

15 If a strike or lockout occurs in a bilateral monopoly situation, it is usually because the

a demand for labour is relatively inelastic.
b demand for labour is relatively elastic.
c supply of labour is relatively inelastic.
d supply of labour is relatively elastic.
e union or firm has misjudged the bargaining situation.

16 Which of the following would unions be *least* likely to support?

a increasing the legal minimum wage
b restricting immigration
c encouraging imports
d increasing demand for the goods their workers produce
e increasing the marginal product of union labour

17 Productivity differences in competitive labour markets cause the wage paid to secretaries to be substantially higher than the wage paid to cleaners. A new pay equity law judges secretaries and cleaners to be comparable. To equalize wages, the wage rate for cleaners is forced up and the wage rate for secretaries is forced down. Employment of secretaries

a will rise, while employment of cleaners will fall.
b will fall, while employment of cleaners will rise.
c and cleaners will rise.
d and cleaners will fall.
e and cleaners will remain unchanged.

18 Refer again to the situation in Question 17. As a result of the pay equity law, *unemployment* of

a secretaries will rise.
b cleaners will rise.
c secretaries and cleaners will rise.
d secretaries and cleaners will fall.
e secretaries and cleaners will remain unchanged.

19 Which of the following statements is *false*? Human capital

a is the accumulated skill and knowledge of human beings.
b is costly to acquire.
c increases from on-the-job training.
d increases from higher wages.
e increases from education.

20 When compared with a competitive labour market with the same marginal revenue product and labour supply curves, a monopsonist labour market has a(n)

a lower wage and lower employment.
b lower wage and higher employment.
c higher wage and lower employment.
d higher wage and higher employment.
e indeterminate outcome.

21 A union is formed to restrict labour supply in a previously perfectly competitive labour market. If the union succeeds in raising the wage,

a employment will fall.
b employment will rise.
c employment will not change.
d the total wage bill will rise.
e the total wage bill will fall.

22 Pay equity laws

a cannot achieve their objective if wage differentials are discrimination-based.
b can achieve their objective if wage differentials are productivity-based.
c can achieve their objective if wage differentials are discrimination-based.
d analyse job characteristics and determine their worth on market grounds.
e compare the market value of objective job characteristics.

23 For the monopsonist employer illustrated in Fig. 15.4, the profit-maximizing wage rate and quantity of labour hired will be

a $9 per hour and 300 hours of labour.
b $8 per hour and 350 hours of labour.
c $8 per hour and 500 hours of labour.
d $7 per hour and 400 hours of labour.
e $6 per hour and 300 hours of labour.

FIGURE **15.4**

24 Suppose the government passes a minimum wage law that prohibits anyone from hiring labour at less than $8 per hour. In Fig. 15.4, the marginal cost of labour (*MCL*) for the monopsonist

a is not affected.
b equals $8 only from 0 to 250 hours of labour.
c equals $8 only from 0 to 350 hours of labour.
d equals $8 only from 0 to 500 hours of labour.
e shifts up by a vertical distance of $8.

25 A working arrangement in which all workers must be members of the union before they can be hired by the firm is called a(n)

a open shop.
b closed shop.
c union shop.
d craft shop.
e professional association.

Short Answer Problems

1 Members of labour unions earn wages well above the minimum wage. Even so, why is it in the interest of a union to support increases in the legal minimum wage?

2 Bob and Sue form a household. They have decided that Sue will fully specialize in market activity and Bob will pursue activities both in the job market and in the household. If most households are like Bob and Sue, why would the result be a difference between the earnings of men and women, even if there is no discrimination?

3 Suppose the labour market for investment advisors is exactly as shown in Text Fig. 15.8 on page 356, where there is discrimination against female advisors and discrimination for male advisors. Explain the effects of introducing a scheme of pay equity that equalizes wage rates at $40,000 per year.

4 In what situations can laws enforcing pay equity achieve their objective of greater equity? In what situations can such laws not achieve their objectives?

5 Figure 15.5 shows the demand and supply of unskilled and skilled labour. S_U and S_S are the supply curves for unskilled and skilled workers, respectively, and D_U and D_S are the demand curves for unskilled and skilled workers, respectively.

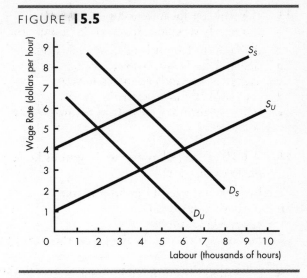

FIGURE **15.5**

a What is the *MRP* of skill if 5,000 hours of each kind of labour are hired?
b What amount of extra compensation per hour is required to induce the acquisition of skill at the same level of hiring?
c What are the equilibrium wage and quantity of labour in the market for skilled labour?
d What are the equilibrium wage and quantity of labour in the market for unskilled labour?

6 Yuri has an opportunity to increase his human capital by taking a training course that will raise his income by $100 every year for the rest of his life. Assume that there are no other benefits of the course. The cost of the course is $1,200 and Yuri's best alternative investment pays an interest rate of 10 percent per year for the rest of his life. Should Yuri pay the $1,200 and take the course? Explain.

7 Initially we observe an industry facing a competitive labour market in which the supply of labour comes from two sources: domestic workers and foreign workers. All workers have similar skills. Also assume that the output of the industry competes with imported goods.

a In Fig. 15.6, graphically represent the initial competitive labour market. Draw the labour demand and supply curves and identify the equilibrium wage rate and level of employment.

FIGURE **15.6**

b Now suppose a union consisting of domestic workers is formed. Through its support a law is passed that prohibits firms from hiring foreign workers. What effect will this have on employment and the wage rate? Illustrate graphically using the graph in part **a**.

c Finally, the industry and union support the passage of a law that legally restricts imports that compete with industry output. Using the same graph, show the consequences for the wage rate and employment.

8 Pollutionless Paper is a pulp and paper mill that employs almost all of the labour in a small town in New Brunswick. The town's labour market, which approximates a monopsony, is illustrated in Fig. 15.7, where *S* is the supply curve of labour, and *MRP* and *MCL* are Pollutionless Paper's marginal revenue product of labour and marginal cost of labour curves, respectively.

FIGURE **15.7**

a If Pollutionless Paper is a profit-maximizing monopsonist, what wage rate will it pay and how much labour will it employ? What is the value of labour's *MRP* at this level of employment?

b If the town had a competitive labour market with the same *MRP* curve, what would the equilibrium wage rate and the level of employment be? Compare these outcomes with the monopsony outcomes in part **a**.

9 Consider the following alternatives for the labour market in Fig. 15.7.

a Suppose the government imposes a minimum wage of $4 per hour. What wage rate will Pollutionless Paper pay and how much labour will it employ? Compare these outcomes with the monopsony outcomes in Short Answer Problem **8a**.

b Suppose there is no legal minimum wage, but the workers form a union. If the union tries to negotiate a higher wage rate while maintaining employment at the monopsony level, what is the maximum wage rate that Pollutionless Paper will be willing to pay? What is the minimum wage rate that the union will accept?

10 Consider the negotiations between Pollutionless Paper and the union in Short Answer Problem **9b**.

a What determines the wage rate that will actually be paid?

b If Pollutionless Paper and the union are equally strong and realize it, what will the wage rate likely be?

c If Pollutionless Paper and the union are equally strong, but the union mistakenly believes it is stronger, what is the likely outcome of negotiations?

d If Pollutionless Paper and the union are equally strong, but Pollutionless Paper mistakenly believes it is stronger, what is the likely outcome of negotiations?

ANSWERS

True/False/Uncertain and Explain

1 T Consequences → demand unskilled workers to left of demand skilled workers. (346–347)
2 F Vertical distance compensation for cost of acquiring skill. (346–347)
3 F The larger the wage differential. (346–347)

4 T ↑ price substitute → ↑ demand union labour. (351–352)

5 F *MCL* curve above supply curve of labour. (352–353)

◑ **6 T** ↑ η labour supply → ↓ differences between *MCL* and wage. (352–353)

◑ **7 U** True for competitive labour market, false for monopsonistic labour market (where ↑ wage and ↑ employment). (354)

8 T See text discussion. (352–353)

9 T ↓ wages for discriminated against and ↑ wages for discriminated for. (355–357)

10 U Differences may be due to job type differences, discrimination, human capital differences, and/or specialization differences. (356–358)

Multiple-Choice

1 a Wage differences not due to competitive differences. In any case, ↑ competitiveness would → ↓ skilled wages. (346–347)

2 d ↑ cost acquiring skill → upward shift supply curve skilled workers. (346–347)

3 b Definition. (348–349)

4 b *QL* where *MCL* intersects *MRP*. Then lowest wage required for labour to supply that *QL* (on supply curve). (352–353)

5 c Where *S* intersects *MRP*. (352–353)

6 e See text discussion. (352–353)

7 c Between minimum firm can achieve ($4) and maximum union can achieve ($9). (352–353)

8 e All can contribute to differentials. (355–358)

9 e Education and training would ↑ human capital and shift supply curve labour up. (356–357)

10 b See text discussion. (348–349)

11 c See text discussion. (358–359)

◑ **12 c** Reverse **a** true. **d** applies to supply. **e** nonsense. (346–347)

13 a See Text Fig. 15.1. (346–347)

14 c No demand curves on figure. ↑ *MRP* skill shifts demand, not supply. (346–347)

15 e **a** – **d** may affect relative bargaining strength but do not cause strikes or lockouts. (352–353)

16 c ↑ imports → ↓ domestically produced goods → ↓ demand for domestic, union labour. (351–352)

17 d But ↓ employment secretaries due to shortages and ↓ employment cleaners due to unemployment. (358–359)

18 b Labour market for secretaries experiences shortage, not unemployment. (358–359)

19 d ↑ wages are often an effect, but not a cause, of ↑ human capital. (346–347)

20 a See Text Fig. 15.5. (352–353)

21 a Leftward shift supply → ↓ employment. Impact on wage bill depends on elasticity of demand for labour. (350–351)

22 c Reverse **a**, **b** true. Assess job characteristics on objective grounds, not market value. (358–359)

23 e *QL* where *MCL* intersects *MRP*. Then lowest wage required for labour to supply that *QL* (on supply curve). (352–353)

◑ **24 d** *MCL* horizontal at minimum wage until intersects *S*. Firm must then ↑ wage to get ↑ quantity supplied labour. (354)

25 b Definition. (348–349)

Short Answer Problems

1 An increase in the minimum wage will increase the cost of hiring unskilled labour, which will tend to increase the demand for skilled labour which is a substitute.

2 If Sue specializes in market activity while Bob is diversified, it is likely that Sue's earning ability will exceed Bob's because of the gains from her specialization. If most households followed this pattern of specialization, the income of women would exceed that of men even without discrimination.

3 The wages of female investment advisors will increase from $20,000 to $40,000 per year and employment will increase from 1,000 to 2,000. The wages of male investment advisors will decrease from $60,000 to $40,000 per year and employment will decrease from 3,000 to 2,000. The effects of the scheme will be to produce the competitive outcome that would have prevailed without discrimination. There is no excess demand or supply of either female or male advisors.

4 Laws enforcing pay equity can achieve their objective of greater equity in situations where discrimination is the source of wage differentials. The wages of the lower paid group that is discriminated against can be raised to reflect their true productivity without increasing their unemployment.

Such laws cannot achieve their objectives in situations where wage differentials arise from differences in productivity. If productivity differences exist, pay equity laws can have the unintended consequence of increasing unemployment among the lower paid group of workers.

5 a The *MRP* of skill is the difference between the *MRP* of skilled versus unskilled labour; the vertical distance between the demand curves for skilled and unskilled labour. In Fig. 15.5, the *MRP* of skill is $3 per hour when 5,000 hours of each kind of labour are employed.

b Since labour supply curves give the minimum compensation workers are willing to accept in return for supplying a given quantity of labour, the extra compensation for skill is the vertical distance between the supply curves of skilled and unskilled labour. At 5,000 hours of employment for both kinds of labour, this is $3 per hour.

c In equilibrium in the market for skilled labour, the wage rate will be $6 per hour and employment will be 4,000 hours of labour. This occurs at the intersection of the D_S and S_S curves.

d In equilibrium in the market for unskilled labour, the wage rate will be $3 per hour and employment will be 4,000 hours of labour. This occurs at the intersection of the D_U and S_U curves.

6 Yuri should take the course only if the value of the course exceeds the cost of the course. The cost of the course is $1,200 while the value of the course is the present value of the extra $100 in income Yuri can expect to receive each year for the rest of his life. The present value of this income stream is the amount of money which, if invested today at 10 percent (Yuri's best alternative return), would yield an equivalent stream of income. Thus the present value of the extra income is $1,000. Since this is less than the cost of the training course, Yuri should *not* take it.

7 a The initial competitive demand for labour and supply of labour curves are given by D_C and S_C respectively, in Fig. 15.6 Solution (ignore the other curves for now). The equilibrium wage rate is W_C and the competitive equilibrium level of employment is QL_C

FIGURE **15.6** SOLUTION

b If a law is passed prohibiting firms from hiring foreign workers, the labour supply curve (now under a union) will shift leftward (to S_U in Fig. 15.6 Solution). This will have the effect of raising the wage rate to W_1 and decreasing the quantity of labour employed to QL_1.

c Restrictions on imports will increase the demand for the product produced in the industry and thus increase the derived demand (*MRP*) of labour in the industry. In Fig. 15.6 Solution this is illustrated by a shift from D_C to D_U. The result will be a further increase in the wage rate to W_2 and an increase in employment to QL_2. Whether the quantity of labour hired now exceeds the initial competitive quantity depends on the magnitude of the shift in the labour demand curve.

8 a A profit-maximizing monopsonist will hire additional labour up to the point where *MCL* equals *MRP*. Referring to Fig. 15.7, this means that Pollutionless Paper will hire 6,000 hours of labour. To hire that quantity of labour, the labour supply curve *S* tells us that the wage rate must be $3 per hour. This is less than the $6 per hour marginal revenue product of labour.

b In a competitive labour market, the wage rate would be $4 per hour and 8,000 hours of labour would be employed. The competitive labour market results in a higher wage rate and a higher level of employment than the monopsony outcomes.

9 a If the government establishes a minimum wage at $4 per hour, the marginal cost of labour to Pollutionless Paper becomes constant at $4 per hour (up to 8,000 hours of labour). Thus equating the marginal cost of labour and the marginal revenue product of labour leads to a wage rate of $4 and 8,000 hours of labour employed. The addition of a minimum wage to the monopsony labour market results in a higher wage rate and a higher level of employment.

b The maximum wage rate Pollutionless Paper is willing to pay for 6,000 hours of labour is $6 per hour (the *MRP* of that amount of labour). The minimum wage rate that the union will accept for 6,000 hours of labour is $3 per hour (the supply price of that amount of labour).

10 a The wage rate that will actually be paid as the outcome of bargaining depends on the relative bargaining strengths of the firm and the union. Bargaining strength depends on the costs (from lockouts and strikes) that each side can inflict on the other if there is a failure to agree.

b Pollutionless Paper and the union will split the difference between $6 and $3 and agree on a wage rate of $4.50.

c If the union holds out for more than a $4.50 wage rate, Pollutionless Paper will likely lockout the workers.

d If Pollutionless Paper holds out for less than a $4.50 wage rate, the union will likely strike. When lockouts or strikes occur, it is usually because one side has misjudged the situation.

Chapter 16

Capital and Natural Resource Markets

KEY CONCEPTS

The Structure of Capital Markets

Capital markets link saving decisions households (supply of financial capital) and investment decisions firms (demand for financial capital to buy capital goods).

- The price of capital is the interest rate.

- **Financial intermediaries** facilitate transactions in the three capital markets.

  - **Stock market**—stocks of corporations traded.
  - **Bond market**—bonds of corporations and governments traded.
  - **Loan market**—households and firm borrow and lend.

The Demand for Capital

Capital is a *stock*.

Net investment = Δ capital stock.
   = *Gross investment* (*flow* purchase of new capital) − *Depreciation* (*flow* amount of capital stock that wears out)

Demand for capital determined by firms' profit-maximizing choices.

- Profit-maximizing rule for *renting* capital—use additional capital until marginal revenue product equals price of using capital. Price of using capital is the interest rate.

- Profit-maximizing rule for *buying* capital—buy additional capital until present value of future flow of marginal revenue products equals purchase price. Or, buy additional capital when **net present value** (*NPV*) is positive.

- *NPV* = present value of future flow of marginal revenue products − purchase price.

Market demand curve for capital is horizontal sum of individual firm demand curves.

- $\uparrow r \rightarrow \downarrow NPV \rightarrow \downarrow$ quantity capital demanded.

- Rightward shift demand curve for capital because of

  - technological change
  - population growth

The Supply of Capital

Supply of capital determined by households' saving decisions.

- Saving (income − consumption) is a *flow* addition to household **wealth** (stock of accumulated past saving).

- Household's decision how to allocate its wealth across various assets is called *portfolio choice*.

- Saving determined by

  - income—$\uparrow$ income $\rightarrow \uparrow$ saving.
  - expected future income—when current income > expected future income $\rightarrow \uparrow$ saving.
  - interest rate—substitution effect from $\uparrow r \rightarrow \uparrow$ saving. Income effect from $\uparrow r \rightarrow \uparrow$ saving for net lender and $\downarrow$ saving for net borrower.

Market supply curve of capital curve is horizontal sum of all household supply curves. Short-run supply is inelastic. Long-run supply is more elastic.

- $\uparrow r \rightarrow \uparrow$ quantity capital supplied.

- Rightward shift supply curve for capital because of

  - $\uparrow$ income or $\uparrow$ population.
  - more unequal distribution income or more middle-aged distribution of population.

Interest Rates and Stock Prices

Interest rates and asset prices adjust to achieve equality between quantity capital demanded and supplied. Interest rate on a stock is the *stock yield* (stock dividend/stock price). Interest rate on a bond is the *bond yield* (coupon payment/bond price).

◆ Price of stock ↑ if

- expected future dividend ↑.
- interest rate ↓ .

◆ *Price-earnings ratio*—ratio of current price of stock share to current profit per share.

- If expected future profit > current profit → ↑ price-earnings ratio.
- Volume trading ↑ with divergent expectations future profits.

◆ **Takeover** when stock market value firm < present value expected future profits from operating firm.

◆ **Merger** when two firms believe that combining assets → ↑ combined stock market values.

Natural Resource Markets

Natural resources are nonproduced factors of production. **Exhaustible natural resource** can only be used once and cannot be replaced. **Nonexhaustible natural resource** can be used repeatedly (with careful management) and not be depleted.

◆ For a natural resource; the stock is the total amount that exists; the flow is the rate of use.

◆ Demand for stock of a natural resource determined by expected interest rate from holding the stock. Expected interest rate on stock of a natural resource = rate of economic profit from using the resource + expected rate of price appreciation.

Stock equilibrium for a natural resource occurs when expected interest rate on owning natural resource stock equals the interest rate on assets of comparable risk.

◆ **Hotelling Principle**—price natural resource will grow at rate = interest rate on other assets.

◆ **Choke price**—price at which use of the natural resource (the flow demand) is zero.

◆ The price of a natural resource is such that its future price is expected to rise at a rate equal to the interest rate, and to reach the choke price at the moment the resource is exhausted. Price and rate of use depend on

- Interest rate—↑ r → ↓ current price and ↑ current use.

- Demand for flow—↑ demand → ↑ current price and ↑ current use.
- Stock resource remaining—↑ current stock → ↓ current price and ↑ current use.

HELPFUL HINTS

1 A profit-maximizing firm will hire an additional factor as long as the factor's use adds more to revenue than to cost; in other words, as long as its marginal revenue product (*MRP*) is greater than its marginal cost (*MC*). The profit-maximizing quantity will be the quantity at which the marginal revenue product of a factor is just equal to its marginal cost. Since, in a competitive market, the marginal cost is the price of the factor (*PF*), this profit-maximizing condition becomes *MRP* = *PF* in a competitive factor market. This implies that the demand curve for a factor is given by its *MRP* curve.

2 The profit-maximizing condition given in Helpful Hint **1** generally applies to all competitive factor markets. However, in the case of capital markets, the condition must be adapted depending on whether the firm rents or buys capital.

The profit-maximizing firm will **rent** *capital equipment up to the point at which the marginal revenue product per rental period is equal to the rent per period.* This is the "flow version" of the profit-maximizing condition for the firm's capital input.

If, however, a firm considers buying capital rather than renting it, we must adapt the profit-maximizing condition. The reason is that capital is generally operated over more than one period and will generate marginal revenue products that are distributed over time. The purchase price, however, must be paid now. In order to compare the purchase price (*PF*) with the stream of marginal revenue products, we must compute the present value of that stream.

In the case of capital equipment that will be used over more than one period, the profit-maximizing condition becomes: buy an additional unit of capital until the present value of the stream of marginal revenue products is equal to the price of the unit of capital. Since the net present value (*NPV*) of an investment is defined as the present value of the stream of marginal revenue products minus the price of the unit of capital, an equivalent condition is: **buy** *capital equipment until the net present value* *of investment is zero.* This is the "stock version" of the profit-maximizing condition for the firm's capital input. (If you need to review the concept of present value, return to Chapter 9.)

3 You may have wondered why financial analysts equate a *rise* in bond prices with a *fall* in interest rates. This chapter explains why interest rates and all asset prices (including bond prices) are inversely related.

   The interest rate or yield on an asset is equal to the income from the asset divided by the price of the asset.

$$\text{interest rate} = \frac{\text{fixed income}}{\text{price of asset}}$$

   Given a *fixed* annual income from the asset, the higher the price of the asset, the lower is the interest rate or yield. For example, if a Northern Telecom bonds pays a fixed annual income of $10, and the price of a Northern Telecom bond is $100, the interest rate or yield on the bond is $10/$100 = 0.1 or 10 percent. A fall in the price of the bond to $91 will cause the yield on the bond to rise to $10/91 = 0.11 or 11 percent. Thus a fall in bond prices is equivalent to a rise in the interest rate on bonds, and vice versa.

4 The inverse relationship between the interest rate and assets prices also applies to prices of shares of stock. The relationship is slightly more complicated because the annual income from a stock—its dividend—is *variable* instead of *fixed*. Nonetheless, *ceteris paribus*, a rise in interest rates will cause a fall in stock prices, and vice versa.

SELF-TEST

True/False/Uncertain and Explain

1 Natural resources can be used only once and cannot be replaced.

2 If the price of a unit of capital exceeds the present value of its marginal revenue product, a profit-maximizing firm should buy it.

3 A new machine that is expected to last one year and, at the end of the year, to increase firm revenue by $1,050, sells at a price of $1,000. The firm should buy the machine if the interest rate is 6 percent.

4 If a household has negative net financial assets, a decrease in the interest rate will increase its saving.

5 The Hotelling Principle states that equilibrium occurs in the market for hotel stocks when the stock price is expected to rise at the rate of interest.

6 To say that the price of a bond has risen is the same as saying that the yield on the bond has declined.

7 A takeover of firm *A* by firm *B* would occur if firm *B* believes that the stock market value of firm *A* is greater than the present value of expected future profits from operating firm *A*.

8 While markets may efficiently allocate goods that can be replaced or reproduced, they cannot allocate exhaustible natural resources efficiently.

9 If a cheap substitute for oil is developed, we would expect to see the choke price for oil decline.

10 The economic model of exhaustible natural resources implies that the market will provide an automatic incentive to conserve as the resource gets closer to being depleted.

Multiple-Choice

1 Which of the following is physical capital?

a a shovel
b IBM stock
c money
d a General Motors bond
e all of the above

2 Which of the following is an example of a stock?

a investment
b depreciation
c capital
d income
e none of the above

3 The decline in the value of capital resulting from its use over time is given by

a the level of saving.
b investment.
c net investment.
d gross investment minus net investment.
e net present value.

4 A firm is expected to pay an $8 dividend per share of stock each year indefinitely. If the market rate of interest is 8 percent, what will be the price of a share of stock in this firm?

a $8
b $8.64
c $64
d $80
e $100

5 The yield on a stock will rise when

a either the dividend increases or the share price of the stock increases.
b either the dividend increases or the share price of the stock decreases.
c either the dividend decreases or the share price of the stock increases.
d either the dividend decreases or the share price of the stock decreases.
e none of the above occurs.

6 Bond *A* is more risky than bond *B*. Then, in equilibrium,

a the interest rate on *A* must be higher than that on *B*.
b the interest rate on *A* must be lower than that on *B*.
c the interest rate on *A* must be equal to the interest rate on *B*.
d no one will want to buy bond *A*.
e only those who prefer risk will buy bond *A*.

7 Which of the following is an exhaustible natural resource?

a coal
b land
c water
d trees
e none of the above

8 The yield on a stock of a natural resource is the

a rate of interest on the loan used to buy the resource.
b marginal revenue product of the resource.
c marginal revenue product of the resource divided by its price.
d marginal revenue product of the resource multiplied by the market interest rate.
e rate of change in the price of the resource.

9 In Table 16.1, which company has the highest price-earnings ratio?

a Company A
b Company B
c Company C
d All have the same ratio.
e Insufficient information to calculate.

TABLE **16.1**

Data	Company A	Company B	Company C
Last year's profits per share	$8	$10	$5
Dividend per share	$4	$2	$5
Value of stock per share	$80	$20	$25
Outstanding shares	1,000	10,000	3,000
Present value of expected profit	$200,000	$200,000	$50,000

10 In Table 16.1, which company has the highest yield?

a Company A
b Company B
c Company C
d All have the same yield.
e Insufficient information to calculate.

11 In Table 16.1, which company is the most likely target of a takeover?

a Company A
b Company B
c Company C
d All are equally likely targets.
e Insufficient information to calculate.

12 The higher the rate of interest, the

a higher the net present value of an investment.
b lower the present value of the flow of marginal revenue products of an investment.
c greater the quantity of capital demanded.
d greater the marginal revenue product of capital.
e lower the marginal revenue product of capital.

13 If the interest rate increases, the

a substitution effect encourages more saving only if the household is a net borrower.
b substitution effect encourages more saving only if the household is a net lender.
c income effect encourages more saving only if the household is a net borrower.
d income effect encourages more saving only if the household is a net lender.
e statements in **b** and **d** are true.

14 Household determination of how much to hold in various assets and how much to owe in various liabilities is called

a investment.
b balance sheet decision making.
c portfolio choice.
d the price-earnings problem.
e the net present value problem.

15 If the market for a stock of a natural resource is in equilibrium, then the price of the resource is

a expected to rise at a rate equal to the rate of interest.
b expected to fall at a rate equal to the rate of interest.
c equal to the choke price of the resource.
d equal to the marginal revenue product of the resource.
e equal to the Hotelling price of the resource.

16 The current price of a natural resource is higher when

a its marginal revenue product is lower.
b the stock of the resource remaining is larger.
c the interest rate is lower.
d the choke price is lower.
e none of the above is true.

17 A bond has a redemption value of $100 and pays $10 interest each year. If you paid $100 for the bond and its price today is $98, what is its current yield?

a 2 percent
b 8.2 percent
c 10 percent
d 10.2 percent
e 12.2 percent

18 The price of a share of XYZ Corporation's stock is $80, and the current dividend payment is $4. What is the stock yield?

a 3.2 percent
b 4 percent
c 5 percent
d 8 percent
e 20 percent

19 An event occurs which almost everyone agrees will cause a decline in the future profit of the XYZ Corporation. Immediately after the event becomes known, the price of XYZ stock will

a fluctuate up and down with a high volume of trading.
b fluctuate up and down with a low volume of trading.
c fall gradually with a high volume of trading.
d fall quickly with a low volume of trading.
e fall quickly with a high volume of trading.

20 A *takeover* of a firm is likely to occur when

a the stock market value of the firm is higher than the present value of expected future profit from operating the firm.
b the stock market value of the firm is lower than the present value of expected future profit from operating the firm.
c current firm profit is higher than the present value of expected future profit from operating the firm.
d current firm profit is lower than the present value of expected future profit from operating the firm.
e interest rates are high.

21 Institutions that are primarily engaged in taking deposits, making loans, and buying securities are called

a brokers.
b financial intermediaries.
c insurance companies.
d monopsonists.
e pension funds.

22 A profit-maximizing firm will choose to buy an extra unit of capital whenever

a the present value of the flow of marginal revenue product is greater than zero.
b the cost of capital exceeds the present value of the flow of marginal revenue product.
c the cost of capital equals the present value of the flow of marginal revenue product.
d net present value is greater than zero.
e none of the above occurs.

23 Firms will invest as long as net present value

a exceeds the rate of interest.
b equals the rate of interest.
c is less than the rate of interest.
d is positive.
e is zero.

24 Which of the following would cause the supply of capital curve to shift rightward?

a an increase in the proportion of young households in the population
b an increase in the interest rate
c a decrease in the interest rate
d an increase in average household income
e an increase in the marginal revenue product of capital

25 A machine that costs $2,000 will generate marginal revenue product of $1,100 at the end of one year and the same amount at the end of two years. What is the net present value of the machine if the rate of interest is 10 percent?

a −$90.91
b −$49.90
c $0
d $90.91
e $1,909.09

Short Answer Problems

1 Why does the quantity of capital demanded increase when the interest rate falls?

2 Suppose firms A and B earned the same amount of profit per share in the most recent year but that the price of a share of stock in firm A is higher than for firm B. What does this imply about the two firms' price-earnings ratios? What does this reflect about expected future profits of the two firms?

3 Exxoff Oil Co. experiences a large and potentially very costly oil spill Sunday night. What can we infer about the degree of consensus among stock market participants' beliefs if on Monday: the price of Exxoff stock declines significantly at the opening of the stock market and remains there? the price of Exxoff stock fluctuates narrowly all day with a large volume of trade?

4 Why does a higher interest rate imply a lower current price of an exhaustible resource?

5 Larry's Lawn Care began the year with a stock of capital equal to $100,000. The capital stock depreciated by 12 percent during the year. Larry also bought $10,000 worth of new lawn care equipment during the year. What was Larry's gross investment during the year? net investment?

6 Larry's Lawn Care is considering the purchase of additional lawn mowers. These lawn mowers have a life of two years and cost $120 each. Marginal revenue products for each year are given in Table 16.2.

TABLE **16.2**

Number of Lawn Mowers	MRP in First Year	MRP in Second Year	NPV ($r = 0.05$)	NPV ($r = 0.10$)	NPV ($r = 0.15$)
1st	100	80			
2nd	80	64			
3rd	72	62			

a Complete Table 16.2 by computing net present values (*NPV*) if the interest rate is 5 percent ($r = 0.05$), 10 percent ($r = 0.10$), or 15 percent ($r = 0.15$).
b How many lawn mowers will Larry's Lawn Care purchase if the interest rate is 15 percent? 10 percent? 5 percent?
c Construct an approximate lawn mower demand curve for Larry's Lawn Care by graphically representing the three points identified in part **b** and drawing a curve through them.

7 The present value of expected future profits for Larry's Lawn Care is $400,000. There are 8,000 outstanding shares of stock in Larry's Lawn Care. The dividend paid in the current year was $7.50 a share.

  a What is the market price of a share of Larry's Lawn Care stock?

  b What is the stock yield?

8 The city of Metropolis (in which Larry's Lawn Care operates) initiates a "Yard Beautiful" award with a cash prize. As a result, the present value of expected future profits for Larry's Lawn Care increases to $600,000.

  a If the market price of a share of Larry's Lawn Care stock does not change, will there be a takeover? If so, what is the highest price someone would pay for a share of stock?

  b If the share price now changes to the market price and the dividend remains at $7.50 a share, what is the stock yield?

9 Gunk is an exhaustible natural resource which is running out. Only 1,215 barrels of gunk remain. Table 16.3 gives the marginal revenue product schedule for gunk.

TABLE **16.3**

Barrels of Gunk per Year	Marginal Revenue Product ($)
0	14.64
133	13.31
254	12.10
364	11.00
464	10.00
555	9.09

  a Draw a graph of the demand curve for gunk (as a flow).

  b What is the choke price of gunk?

☉10 You remain mired in the gunk problem. Suppose that the interest rate is 10 percent.

  a What is the current equilibrium price of a barrel of gunk? How did you determine this?

  b If the current year is year 1, complete Table 16.4 for each year until the stock of gunk is exhausted.

TABLE **16.4**

Year	Price	Initial Stock of Gunk	Final Stock of Gunk
1		1,215	
2			
3			
4			
5			

A N S W E R S

True/False/Uncertain and Explain

1 **U** True for exhaustible, false for nonexhaustible natural resources. (377–378)

2 **F** Reverse is true. (369–370)

☉3 **F** $PV = \$1,050/(1 + .06) = \$990.56$. $NPV = \$990.56 - \$1,000 = -\$9.44$. Since NPV negative, don't buy. (369–370)

☉4 **U** Depends on relative strength income effect ($\uparrow$ savings) and substitution effect ($\downarrow$ savings). (372–373)

5 **F** True for market for natural resources. (378)

6 **T** Bond yield = (fixed earnings)/(price of bond). (374–375)

7 **F** Reverse true—if value firm *A less than ...* (376–377)

8 **F** Markets can be efficient if no externalities. As resource used up, price $\uparrow \rightarrow \downarrow$ quantity demanded and $\uparrow$ use substitutes. (381)

9 **T** Less demand for oil so people would stop using it at a lower price. (378–379)

10 **T** Because price will $\uparrow$. (380–381)

Multiple-Choice

1 **a** Others are financial capital. (368–369)

2 **c** Others are flows. (368–369)

3 **d** Equals depreciation. (368–369)

4 **e** r = dividend/share price. .08 = $8/share price. Share price = $8/.08. (375–376)

5 **b** Yield = dividend/share price. (374–376)

6 **a** Higher return necessary to compensate for higher risk if investor willing to hold bond. (374–375)

7 a Others are nonexhaustible natural resources. (377)

8 e See text discussion. (378–379)

9 a Current share price/most recent profit per share = $80/$8. (375–376)

10 c Dividend/share price = $5/$25. (375–376)

◑ 11 a Stock market value company ($80/share × 1,000 shares = $80,000) < present value expected profit ($200,000). (376–377)

12 b Reverse **a, c** true. *r* does not affect *MRP* capital. (369–370)

13 d Because ↑ household income from lending. Substitution effect always → ↑ savings. (372–373)

14 c Definition. (372–373)

15 a This is the Hotelling Principle. (378–379)

◑ 16 c Reverse **a, b** true. No direct relation current and choke prices. (378–380)

17 d Yield = yearly earnings/price bond. (374–375)

18 c Yield = dividend/share price. (375–376)

19 d ↓ expected future profit → ↓ price. Agreement → low volume. (376–377)

20 b Cost of buying < value of firm. (376–377)

21 b Definition. **c** is example of financial intermediary. (367–368)

22 d When present value flow marginal product > cost of capital. (369–370)

23 d **a, b,** and **c** are nonsense comparisons. (369–370)

24 d **a** → leftward shift. **b** and **c** → movement along supply curve. **e** shifts demand curve. (373–374)

◑ 25 a $NPV = [\$1,100/(1.1) + \$1,100/(1.1)^2] - \$2,000.$ (369–370)

Short Answer Problems

1 Profit-maximizing firms will demand capital as long as the present value of the stream of future marginal revenue product from the new capital exceeds the price of the new capital; in other words, as long as its net present value is positive. Since a lower interest rate implies that the present value of any given future stream of marginal revenue product will be larger, the net present value will be positive for a *larger* number of additional capital goods and thus more capital will be purchased. Therefore, the quantity of capital demanded increases as the interest rate falls.

2 The price-earnings ratio is the current price of a share of stock divided by the most recent profits per share. Thus, the price-earnings ratio of firm *A*'s stock is greater than the price-earnings ratio of firm *B*'s stock. This implies that, although the

recent profits (per share) of the two firms may be the same, future profits (per share) for firm *A* are expected to be higher than for firm *B*.

The price of a share of stock represents the present value of *expected* future profits, so a higher price implies higher expected future profits.

3 A significant decline in the price of Exxoff stock with little volume of trade implies that there is wide consensus that the oil spill means a significant reduction in the present value of future Exxoff profits.

If, on the other hand, there is a large volume of trade in Exxoff stock with little net price movement, it implies that there is little consensus about the implications of the oil spill for the future profitability of Exxoff.

4 In equilibrium, the current price of the resource will be the price which, if the price continues to increase at a rate equal to the interest rate, the choke price will be reached at the same time that the resource is depleted. A higher interest rate means that the price is expected to rise at a faster rate. Therefore if it is to reach the choke price at the right time, it must start from a lower current price.

Another answer from a portfolio choice perspective is: the higher interest rate raises the relative attractiveness of financial assets, lowering the demand for resource assets and therefore lowering the price of a resource.

5 Gross investment is $10,000, the amount of the purchase of new capital. Net investment is –$2,000, the amount of gross investment minus depreciation of $12,000.

◑ 6 a Completed Table 16.2 appears here as Table 16.2 Solution. *NPV* is calculated as the present value of the stream of marginal revenue products resulting from an investment minus the cost of the investment. For lawn mowers with a two-year life, the *NPV* is calculated using the following equation:

$$NPV = \frac{MRP_1}{1+r} + \frac{MRP_2}{(1+r)^2} - P_L$$

In this equation, MRP_1 and MRP_2 are the marginal revenue products in the first and second years, respectively, and P_L is the price of a lawn mower. The values of MRP_1 and MRP_2 are given in Table 16.2 for the first, second, and third lawn mowers and P_L is given as $120. The values for *NPV* given in Table 16.2 Solution are obtained by substituting these values into the above equation and evaluating the expression for the alternative values of *r*, the interest rate.

TABLE **16.2** SOLUTION

Number of Lawn Mowers	MRP in First Year	MRP in Second Year	NPV (r = 0.05)	NPV (r = 0.10)	NPV (r = 0.15)
1st	100	80	47.80	37.02	27.45
2nd	80	64	14.24	5.62	−2.04
3rd	72	62	4.81	−3.31	−10.51

  b If the interest rate is 15 percent, only one additional lawn mower will be purchased since the second lawn mower has negative net present value. If the interest rate is 10 percent, two lawn mowers will be purchased, and if the interest rate is 5 percent, three lawn mowers will be purchased.

  c The approximate lawn mower demand curve is illustrated in Fig. 16.1. The curve indicates that, at an interest rate of 15 percent, one lawn mower will be demanded. At an interest rate of 10 percent, two lawn mowers will be demanded and, at an interest rate of 5 percent, three lawn mowers will be demanded.

FIGURE **16.1**

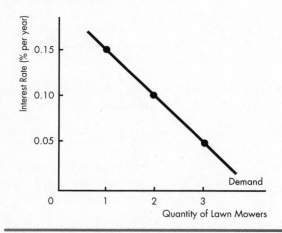

7 a The market price of a share of Larry's Lawn Care stock will be the present value of expected future profits for the firm divided by the number of shares outstanding: $50.

  b The stock yield is 15 percent. This is the dividend ($7.50) as a percentage of the price of a share of stock ($50).

8 a Yes, there will be a takeover because the stock market value ($400,000) is less than the present value of expected future profits ($600,000). The highest price someone would pay for a share of stock is $75, the present value of expected future profits divided by the number of shares ($600,000/8,000).

  b The stock yield will now be 10 percent. This is the dividend ($7.50) as a percentage of the new market price of a share of stock ($75).

9 a The demand curve for gunk is given by the marginal revenue product curve. It is illustrated in Fig. 16.2.

FIGURE **16.2**

  b The choke price for gunk is $14.64. This is the price that is high enough that the resource will not be used at all.

10 a If the interest rate is 10 percent, the current price of a barrel of gunk is $10. We know that the current (equilibrium) price must be such that if the price of gunk is increasing at a rate of 10 percent per year (equal to the rate of interest), the stock will be depleted just as the choke price is achieved. We can find the current price by noting that (1) the choke price is $14.64 and (2) the remaining stock is 1,215 barrels, and then working backward.

  Since the price of gunk is growing at the rate of 10 percent per year, the price in the year before the choke price is reached must be $14.64 (the choke price) divided by 1.10 (1 + the 10% growth rate of price) or $13.31. From Table 16.3 (and recognizing that gunk is just depleted as the $14.64 price is reached) we can infer that 133 barrels of gunk would be purchased in that year. Proceeding in a similar manner, working backward until all 1,215 barrels of gunk have been purchased, we discover that the current equilibrium price must be $10.

b Using the procedure outlined in part **a**, Table 16.4 can be completed as shown in Table 16.4 Solution.

TABLE **16.4** SOLUTION

Year	Price	Initial Stock of Gunk	Final Stock of Gunk
1	10.00	1,215	751
2	11.00	751	387
3	12.10	387	133
4	13.31	133	0
5	14.64	0	

Chapter 17

Uncertainty and Information

Uncertainty and Risk

Uncertainty—more than one event may occur, but we don't know which one. Related concepts are

◆ *Probability*—number between 0 and 1 measuring the chance of an event occurring.

◆ **Risk**—can estimate the probability of uncertain events.

Facing uncertainty, individuals maximize **expected utility**—average utility from all possible events. Expected utility may differ from *actual* utility (utility the individual actually gets when an event actually occurs).

◆ **Utility of wealth**—utility an individual gets from wealth. ↑ wealth → ↑ utility, but *marginal utility of wealth* ↓. Utility of wealth curve measures cost of risk.

◆ Cost of risk = amount expected wealth must ↑ to → same expected utility as no-risk situation.

◆ The more *risk averse* (prefer less risk), the more rapidly marginal utility wealth ↓ (the more curved is utility of wealth curve) and the greater the cost of risk.

◆ For a *risk-neutral* individual, risk is costless and her utility of wealth curve is linear.

Insurance

People buy insurance to reduce risk.

◆ Insurance works by pooling a large number of risks so that the total number of adverse outcomes is relatively certain. Insurance companies collect premiums from everyone to cover total cost of accidents, but payout benefits only to those suffering losses.

◆ Insurance is profitable because people are risk averse and will pay to ↓ risk. People pay a small premium to insure that they will not suffer a large loss.

Information

Economic information reduces uncertainty, but gathering information has an opportunity cost—**information cost**. Because information is costly, people economize on its use.

◆ Buyers searching for lowest price use *optimal-search rule*:

• search until expected marginal benefit search = marginal cost search, then buy; or
• search until a price ≤ **reservation price** (highest price buyer willing to pay) is found, then buy.

Sellers advertise to persuade and inform.

◆ Quality of *experience goods* can only be assessed after they are bought → advertising for *experience goods* usually persuades.

◆ Quality of *search goods* can be assessed before they are bought → advertising for *search goods* usually informs.

Advertising → ↑ costs, ↑ competition, and possibly → ↓ costs if allow economies of scale.

Private Information

Private information is available to one person but too costly for others to obtain → two problems.

◆ **Moral hazard**—post-agreement incentive to ↑ personal benefits at expense of uniformed party.

◆ **Adverse selection**—tendency for people to accept contracts with private information that can be used to their own advantage and to disadvantage of uninformed.

Information problems can be overcome through **signals**—actions conveying information that can be used by market. Examples are warranties on used cars; credit information and loan limits in the loan market; driving record and deductibles in car insurance.

Asymmetric Information in Labour Markets

Asymmetric information in labour markets → difficulty for employer to monitor efforts employee.

◆ Employers use compensation schemes (sales commissions, **rank-tournament compensation schemes**, profit shares) to spur employees to unmonitored actions that maximize profit.

Managing Risk in Financial Markets

Risk in financial markets can be lowered through diversifying asset holdings (don't put all eggs in same basket).

In an **efficient market**, if something can be anticipated, it will be, and the anticipation will affect the current price.

◆ Actual price = expected future price and embodies all available information.

◆ No forecastable profit opportunities available.

The stock market is an efficient market. Stock prices fluctuate when new information becomes available.

HELPFUL HINTS

1 Uncertainty plays a part in almost every economic decision. Yet in previous chapters we have ignored uncertainty in analysing consumers' and firms' choices. Why? To keep the analysis simple and because uncertainty usually does not negate important economic rules. For example, the key rule for understanding profit maximization is for the firm to choose the level of output where $MC = MR$. The firm may be uncertain about both its MC and MR, but it still tries to find the level of output where they are equal. If we had incorporated uncertainty into the analysis from the start, the profit-maximizing rule would have been more complicated, and it

would have been harder to see the $MC = MR$ rule.

A correct model-building strategy initially leaves out the complication of uncertainty. Remember from Chapter 1 that models are highly simplified representations of the real world that attempt to focus on essential forces (like profit maximization) while abstracting from some less important real-world detail (like uncertainty). Before drawing final conclusions about the real world from simple models, it is important to consider whether, when we reinsert real-world complexities like uncertainty, the outcomes will be the same. This chapter on uncertainty provides some basic tools that can be used, in more advanced courses, to "complicate" or enrich the simple models of consumers' and firms' choices.

2 The existence of risk and uncertainty is an objective feature of reality. How decision makers cope with uncertainty, however, depends on their *attitudes* towards risk. Some people are more risk averse than others.

A person's *utility of wealth* schedule reflects her degree of risk aversion. Economists believe that most people's utility of wealth schedules exhibit diminishing marginal utility as wealth increases. However, for two people, for example, Alexis and Madeleine, Alexis's marginal utility of wealth may decrease at a faster rate than Madeleine's. Alexis would be more risk averse than Madeleine and less likely to undertake risky ventures that offer the possibility of a high return at the cost of a greater probability of loss. *Ceteris paribus*, Alexis would be less likely to undertake risky ventures because she will attach a relatively greater utility weight to the probable decrease of wealth from a loss than to the probable increase in wealth from a success. Because of these relative weights, a risk averse person is also more likely to take out insurance against loss.

There are many markets besides that for insurance (e.g., the stock market) that exist, in part, to allow risk averse people to offload risk to those who are less risk averse.

3 Two important concepts for analysing choice under uncertainty are *expected wealth* and *expected utility*. Expected wealth (sometimes called expected value) is the average wealth arising from all possible outcomes. It is computed as the weighted average of the wealth associated with each possible outcome, where the weights are the probabilities of each outcome.

For example, if there are three possible outcomes yielding wealth of W_1, W_2, and W_3, and the probabilities associated with these outcomes are p_1, p_2, and p_3, respectively, then expected wealth equals

$$(W_1 \times p_1) + (W_2 \times p_2) + (W_3 \times p_3).$$

Expected utility is the average utility arising from all possible outcomes. It is calculated in the same way. If the utilities associated with each possible wealth outcome are U_1, U_2, and U_3, respectively, then expected utility equals

$$(U_1 \times p_1) + (U_2 \times p_2) + (U_3 \times p_3).$$

In analysing choice under uncertainty, we must first calculate expected wealth. But a decision is ultimately based on the expected utility associated with that expected wealth.

S E L F - T E S T

True/False/Uncertain and Explain

1 Risk is a state in which more than one event may occur, but we don't know which one.

2 The more rapidly your marginal utility of wealth diminishes, the less risk averse you are.

3 A risk-neutral person has a constant marginal utility of wealth.

4 If Petro-Canada drills in an uncharted region of the Northwest Territories without any idea of the likelihood of striking oil, Petro-Canada faces uncertainty rather than risk.

5 Advertising for search goods is designed mainly to inform rather than persuade.

6 If you are careless with matches because you know you have fire insurance, an adverse selection problem exists.

7 An efficient compensation scheme maximizes both profits for the firm and compensation for the employee.

8 Diversified investment portfolios are preferable to undiversified portfolios.

9 In an efficient market, the actual price is rarely equal to the expected future price.

10 If prices in an efficient market are volatile, expectations about future prices must be volatile.

Multiple-Choice

1 The more rapidly a person's marginal utility of wealth diminishes, the
a more risk inclined the person is.
b more risk-neutral the person is.
c more risk averse the person is.
d more likely it is that the person has a moral hazard problem.
e less likely the person is to take out insurance.

2 The expected value of a game that gives a 50 percent chance of winning $60 and a 50 percent chance of winning nothing is
a $10.
b $20.
c $30.
d $60.
e none of the above.

3 On a normal utility of wealth curve diagram with wealth on the horizontal axis and utility on the vertical axis, the marginal utility of wealth is
a a point on the horizontal axis.
b a point on the vertical axis.
c an area under the utility of wealth curve.
d the slope of a ray from the origin to a point on the utility of wealth curve.
e the slope of the utility of wealth curve.

4 Goods whose quality can be assessed only after they are bought are called

a private information goods.
b search goods.
c experience goods.
d inferior goods.
e lemons.

5 The buyer's reservation price is

a the lowest price that the buyer is willing to pay.
b the highest price that the buyer is willing to pay.
c the price equating the expected marginal benefit and marginal cost of searching.
d a and c.
e b and c.

6 Warranties will distinguish good cars from lemons only if

a warranties cost the dealer nothing.
b car prices are not affected by whether or not the dealer gives a warranty.
c providing warranties is worthwhile for dealers of good cars and too costly for dealers of lemons.
d providing warranties is worthwhile for both dealers of good cars and lemons.
e a and b.

7 According to the utility of wealth schedules in Table 17.1,

a Chloe is more risk averse than Esther.
b Esther is more risk averse than Chloe.
c Chloe is risk-neutral, while Esther is risk averse.
d Esther is risk-neutral, while Chloe is risk averse.
e it is impossible to calculate risk aversion and risk neutrality.

TABLE **17.1** UTILITY OF WEALTH

Wealth ($)	Utility (units)	
	Chloe	Esther
0	0	0
20	45	60
40	80	90
60	110	100
80	130	105

8 Chloe's expected *wealth* from an investment opportunity that will pay either $40 or $80 with equal probability is

a $60.
b $105.
c $120.
d $210.
e none of the above.

9 Refer to Table 17.1 and Fact 17.1. If Esther has no sickness insurance, her expected *wealth* is

a $30.
b $48.
c $60.
d $80.
e $100.

FACT **17.1**

Esther earns $60 if she stays healthy and works, but earns zero if she gets sick and cannot work. Esther has an 80 percent chance of staying healthy and a 20 percent chance of getting sick.

10 Refer to Table 17.1 and Fact 17.1. If Esther has no sickness insurance, her expected *utility* is

a 0.
b 50.
c 80.
d 100.
e none of the above.

11 Refer to Table 17.1 and Fact 17.1. Esther pays $20 for sickness insurance that pays out $60 if she is sick and nothing if she is healthy. Esther's expected *wealth* is now

a $36.
b $40.
c $56.
d $100.
e none of the above.

12 Refer to Table 17.1 and Fact 17.1. Esther pays $20 for sickness insurance that pays out $60 if she is sick and nothing if she is healthy. Esther's expected *utility* is now

a 40.
b 90.
c 92.
d 100.
e none of the above.

13 Which compensation scheme is most likely to be efficient in the case of a chief executive officer of a corporation?

a commission on sales
b share of total firm profits
c salary based on years of employment
d tournament-like prize
e b and d

14 Which compensation scheme is most likely to be efficient in the case of a salesperson?

a hourly wage rate
b commission on sales
c share of total firm profits
d salary based on years of employment
e none of the above

15 Mira must choose Option *A* or Option *B*. Option *A* guarantees her $10,000. Option *B* gives her $5,000 with probability 0.5 and $15,000 with probability 0.5. Having a normal utility of wealth curve, Mira will

a prefer and choose *A*.
b prefer and choose *B*.
c prefer *A* but choose *B*.
d prefer *B* but choose *A*.
e be indifferent between *A* and *B*.

16 If there are three possible events and each has a probability of occurrence of one-third, then

a neither uncertainty nor risk exists.
b uncertainty exists, but not risk.
c risk exists, but not uncertainty.
d both uncertainty and risk exist.
e there is not enough information to distinguish between uncertainty and risk.

17 In an efficient market, which of the following statements is *false*?

a The current price is equal to the expected future price.
b The current price embodies all available information.
c No forecastable profit opportunities exist.
d Prices are stable.
e Expectations are subject to fluctuations.

18 An efficient compensation scheme

a cannot incorporate the effects of luck.
b will not be accepted by the employee.
c splits revenues equally between the employee and employer.
d maximizes the employee's expected income.
e maximizes the employer's expected profit.

19 Optimizing buyers will devote additional resources searching for information when

a expected marginal benefit is positive.
b expected marginal benefit is less than the marginal cost of searching.
c expected marginal benefit equals the marginal cost of searching.
d marginal cost of searching is positive.
e none of the above.

20 If buyers cannot assess the quality of used cars and there are no warranties,

a only bad used cars will be sold.
b only good used cars will be sold.
c good cars will be sold at a higher price than bad cars.
d there is a moral hazard problem.
e there is no adverse selection problem.

21 An increase in Robin's wealth from $3,000 to $6,000 raises her utility from 80 units to 100. If she has a normal utility of wealth curve, with wealth of $9,000 her utility might be

a 100 units.
b 115 units.
c 120 units.
d 125 units.
e 180 units.

22 The cost of risk is the amount by which expected wealth must increase to give the same

a marginal utility as a no-risk situation.
b expected utility as a no-risk situation.
c expected wealth as a no-risk situation.
d probability as a no-risk situation.
e insurance as a no-risk situation.

23 After purchasing theft insurance, you decide to spend less on home security devices. Your behaviour is an example of

a adverse selection.
b free riding.
c insurance market signalling.
d asymmetric information.
e moral hazard.

24 Advertising

a for search goods is designed to persuade.
b for experience goods is designed to inform.
c that is persuasive increases competition.
d is costly.
e is all of the above.

25 Stock market prices are volatile because

a expectations are irrational.
b expectations change frequently due to new information.
c stock markets are inefficient markets.
d stockholders do not behave like inventory holders.
e all of the above statements are true.

Short Answer Problems

1 If you agree to pay the first $200 worth of damage ($200 deductible), your car insurance premium might be $1,000 per year. But if you agree to a $500 deductible, your insurance premium might be $800 per year. Why do insurance companies charge premiums that are related inversely to the total loss that the customer agrees to bear?

2 Why do banks often lend more readily to people who have credit cards and have previously borrowed from the bank than to people who have always paid in cash and never borrowed?

3 Many large firms are owned by a group of stockholders who hire managers to run the firm. Why is profit sharing a good compensation scheme for top management in such a firm?

4 What is meant by an efficient market? Explain why the current market price will always be equal to the expected future price in an efficient market.

5 Figure 17.1 presents Katherine's utility of wealth curve. She is considering an investment that will pay either W_1 with a 50 percent probability or W_2 with a 50 percent probability.
 a Label as U_1 Katherine's utility if she receives W_1. Label as U_2 Katherine's utility if she receives W_2. Label Katherine's expected wealth EW and her expected utility U. What does her expected wealth equal?
 b What is Katherine's cost of risk? Explain.

FIGURE **17.1**

6 Table 17.2 presents the utility of wealth schedules for Ren and Stimpy. Who is more risk averse, Ren or Stimpy? Explain.

TABLE **17.2** UTILITY OF WEALTH

Wealth ($)	Utility (units)	
	Ren	Stimpy
0	0	0
20	100	60
40	150	110
60	175	150
80	187	180
100	193	200

7 Suppose that Ren and Stimpy initially have $40 each. They are offered a chance to play a game that costs $20 to play. There is a 50 percent chance of winning $60 and a 50 percent chance of winning nothing.
 a What is the expected value (*expected wealth*) of the game?
 b What is the *expected utility* of the game for Ren? for Stimpy?
 c If Ren and Stimpy are optimizers, who will be willing to play the game and who will prefer not to play and hold on to the initial $40? Explain.

◑ 8 Table 17.3 presents Leonard's utility of wealth schedule. Leonard is considering an investment project that will pay either zero or $20,000 with equal probability.

TABLE **17.3** LEONARD'S UTILITY OF WEALTH

Wealth (000 $)	Utility (units)
0	0
4	52
5	60
8	79
10	87
15	98
20	104

a What is Leonard's expected wealth from the project?
b What is Leonard's expected utility?
c What is Leonard's cost of risk?
d Is Leonard willing to undertake the project if it costs him $5,000?

◑ 9 Suppose that there are many investment projects identical to the one in Short Answer Problem **8**, and many individuals with the same utility of wealth schedule as Leonard. Leonard wants to buy insurance against the failure of the project (the zero payment outcome).

a What is the most that Leonard would be willing to pay for an insurance policy that pays him $20,000 if the project fails? [*Hint*: You do not need to consider the cost of the project.]
b What is the least an insurance company would charge if its operating cost (above money paid out in claims) is $1,000 per policy?
c Is there a market opportunity for insurance?

◑ 10 Dylan owns some land on which he usually grows vegetables. This year he has accepted a job as a bartender and will not be able to tend the vegetable patch. Dylan is thinking of hiring Thomas, who has some gardening experience, to grow vegetables for him.

Thomas has been milking cows for a dairy farmer, and working very hard for $30 per day. From conversations with Thomas, Dylan gathers that Thomas places a value of $10 on relaxation —Thomas prefers to relax rather than to work, but a day of working for $10 or a day of relaxing are equally acceptable.

Dylan knows that income from growing vegetables depends on how hard the cultivator works and on weather conditions. Table 17.4 gives the alternative total incomes from the possible combinations of work effort and weather conditions. There is a 50 – 50 chance of good or bad weather.

TABLE **17.4** INCOME FROM VEGETABLE GROWING ($ PER DAY)

Weather	Worker's Effort	
	Works Hard	Relaxes
Good	$160	$80
Bad	$80	$80

Dylan is considering two alternative compensation schemes.

Scheme 1 Dylan pays Thomas $31 per day.
Scheme 2 Dylan pays Thomas $10 per day plus 26 percent of the income from vegetable growing.

Using this information, work out which compensation scheme Dylan should adopt. [*Remember*: An efficient compensation scheme has two features. It must maximize profit for the principal and be acceptable to the agent (make the agent at least as well off as in the best alternative job).]

A N S W E R S

True/False/Uncertain and Explain

1	F	Definition uncertainty. (389)
2	F	More risk averse. (389–391)
3	T	See text discussion. Linear marginal utility of wealth curve. (391)
4	T	Risk means probabilities could be estimated. (389)
5	T	Quality can be assessed before buying. (394)
6	F	Moral hazard problem. (395, 397–398)
7	F	Maximize profit and be acceptable to employee. (398)
◑ 8	U	True if investor risk averse, but may be false otherwise. (402–403)
9	F	Actual price = expected future price. (403)
10	T	See text discussion. (403)

Multiple-Choice

1 c Moral hazard irrelevant. More likely to insure. (389–391)

2 c ($60 × 0.5) + ($0 × 0.5). (389–391)

3 e Δ utility/Δ wealth. (389–390)

4 c Definition. (394)

◑ **5** e See text discussion. (393–394)

6 c Buyers believe warranty signal because cost of false signal high. (395–396)

7 b Marginal utility of wealth diminishes more rapidly. (389–391)

8 a ($40 × 0.5) + ($80 × 0.5). (389–391)

9 b ($60 × 0.8) + ($0 × 0.2). (390–392)

◑ **10** c (100 × 0.8) + (0 × 0.2). (389–392)

11 b (($60 – $20) × 0.8) + (($60 – $20) × 0.2). (389–392)

◑ **12** b Wealth in either case = $40 ($60 – $20). Expected utility = (90 × 0.8) + (90 × 0.2). (389–392)

13 e Strong connection effort/competition and profit. (398–401)

14 b Directly links unmonitored effort to outcome. (398–400)

◑ **15** a Expected value *A* and *B* equal, but *A* less risky, so preferable. (389–391)

16 d Definitions. Risk is subset of uncertainty. (389)

17 d Prices fluctuate with changes in expectations. (403)

18 e Designed by principal and must be acceptable to agent. (398)

19 e When expected marginal benefit > marginal cost. (393–394)

20 a Opposite **d**, **e** true. (395–396)

◑ **21** b With diminishing marginal utility of wealth, must be < 120. (389–391)

22 b See text discussion. (391)

23 e See text discussion. (395)

24 d **a**, **b**, **c** true if reverse persuade and inform. (394)

25 b Only source of change in efficient market. (403)

Short Answer Problems

1 By allowing customers to pay lower premiums if they agree to bear a higher share of total damages, insurance companies alleviate the adverse selection problem. High-risk drivers know that they are accident prone and are willing to pay higher premiums for nearly full coverage, while low-risk drivers know that they seldom have accidents and will choose lower premiums with lower coverage. With deductibles, the adverse-selection problem of high-risk people driving low-risk people out of the market is less likely to occur. The insurance company can charge differential premiums that reflect the different risks that it is insuring.

2 Banks have more information about the ability and willingness to pay of people who have previously borrowed from them or from other financial institutions. A good loan repayment record is evidence (a signal) that the customer is a low-risk borrower. If a customer has never borrowed before, the bank must find other ways to assess whether the customer is a high-risk or a low-risk borrower.

3 Neither the effort nor the output of the managers can be monitored easily by the stockholders. But since the decisions of managers have a direct and significant bearing on the profit of the firm, their incentive is to make decisions that maximize stockholder profit if they share in any increase in profit through a profit-sharing compensation scheme.

4 An efficient market is one in which the actual price embodies all available relevant information. The price will thus be equal to the expected future price and there will be no forecastable profit opportunities. The current market price will always be equal to the expected future price in an efficient market because any deviation would be eliminated immediately since it provides an expected profit opportunity.

5 a Figure 17.1 Solution illustrates Katherine's utilities if she receives W_1 and W_2. Her expected wealth (*EW*) equals the probability of receiving W_1 multiplied by W_1, plus the probability of receiving W_2 multiplied by W_2. Because each probability equals 0.5, *EW* is simply the average of (halfway between) W_1 and W_2. In a similar calculation, expected utility (*U*) is the weighted average of (halfway between) U_1 and U_2.

b The cost of risk is the amount expected wealth must increase to give the same expected utility as a no-risk situation. If Katherine receives wealth *W* with no-risk, that gives the same level of utility as does *EW*. Katherine's expected wealth (*EW*) needs to be greater than the no-risk wealth (*W*) by the amount (*EW* – *W*) in order for her to be indifferent between the two outcomes. Therefore, (*EW* – *W*) is the cost of risk.

FIGURE **17.1** SOLUTION

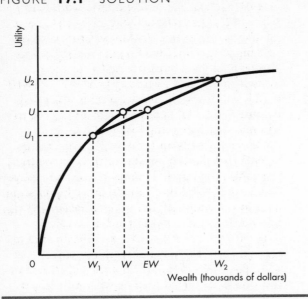

6 To find out who is more risk averse, we must determine whose marginal utility of wealth decreases faster as wealth increases. Table 17.6 presents the total and marginal utility of wealth for Ren and Stimpy. Since Ren's marginal utility of wealth decreases faster than Stimpy's, Ren is the more risk averse.

TABLE **17.6** TOTAL/MARGINAL UTILITY OF WEALTH

	Ren		Stimpy	
Wealth ($)	Total Utility (units)	Marginal Utility (units)	Total Utility (units)	Marginal Utility (units)
0	0		0	
		 100		 60
20	100		60	
		 50		 50
40	150		110	
		 25		 40
60	175		150	
		 12		 30
80	187		180	
		 6		 20
100	193		200	

7 a The expected value of the game, or the *expected wealth* from playing the game, can be calculated using the method in Helpful Hint **3**. Multiply each possible wealth outcome by its probability of occurrence and sum the results. Winning the game yields a wealth of $80 ($40 to start − $20 to play + $60 prize). Losing yields a wealth of $20 ($40 to start − $20 to play). The expected value or expected wealth of the game is ($80 × 0.5) + ($20 × 0.5) = $50.

b The *expected utility* of the game can also be calculated using the method in Helpful Hint **3**. Multiply the utility of each possible wealth outcome by its probability of occurrence and sum the results.

For Ren, expected utility is (187 × 0.5) + (100 × 0.5) = 143.5 units. For Stimpy, expected utility is (180 × 0.5) + (60 × 0.5) = 120 units.

c To decide whether or not to play the game, each player compares the expected utility of the outcome of the game with the expected utility of not playing the game and keeping $40.

For Ren, the expected utility of the game is 143.5 units, which is less than the 150 units of utility of keeping the $40 wealth. Ren will not play the game. For Stimpy, the expected utility of the game is 120 units, which is more than the 110 units of utility of keeping the $40 wealth. Stimpy will play the game. These results are not surprising, since Ren is more risk averse than Stimpy and, *ceteris paribus*, is less likely to play a game of chance and more likely to hold on to a sure $40.

8 a Leonard's expected wealth is ($0 × 0.5) + ($20,000 × 0.5) = $10,000.

b Leonard's expected utility is (0 × 0.5) + (104 × 0.5) = 52 units.

c Uncertain wealth of $0 or $20,000 yields expected wealth of $10,000 and expected utility of 52 units. From Table 17.3, we can see that certain (no-risk) wealth of $4,000 also yields utility of 52 units. The cost of risk is $6,000, the amount by which expected wealth must be increased beyond no-risk wealth to give the same utility as the no-risk situation ($10,000 − $4,000).

d For Leonard, the forgone utility of the $5,000 cost of investing in the project (60 units) is greater than the expected utility of the risky project (52 units). Leonard is not willing to undertake the project.

9 a Leonard is willing to buy insurance as long as the utility from the certain outcome after buying insurance yields at least as much expected utility as the risky project. Since the expected utility of the project (52 units) is the same as the expected utility of a certain outcome of $4,000, Leonard would be willing to pay up to $16,000 for an insurance policy that pays him $20,000 if the project fails. With insurance, Leonard will receive $20,000 whether the project succeeds or fails. Subtracting an insurance premium of $16,000 leaves him with a certain net income of $4,000. Leonard would be indifferent between purchasing insurance and taking the risk on the project. At any premium less than $16,000, Leonard would be better off with insurance. He would have a certain net income greater than $4,000 and a utility of greater than 52 units.

b A profit-maximizing insurance company would charge at least enough to cover its expected costs per project—the expected payout plus operating costs. Since half of the projects fail, the expected payout is $10,000 per project ($20,000 × 0.5). With operating costs of $1,000 per project, the least an insurance company would charge is $11,000 ($10,000 + $1,000).

c Since individuals are willing to pay $16,000, which is more than the minimum price insurance companies must charge to make a profit ($11,000), there is a market for insurance. Compared with a situation with no insurance, individuals and insurers will both be better off at any premium between $11,000 and $16,000.

10 Income depends on whether Thomas works hard or relaxes and whether there is good or bad weather. The probability of good or bad weather is 0.5.

If Thomas works hard, expected total income is ($160 × 0.5) + ($80 × 0.5) = $120.

If Thomas relaxes, expected total income is ($80 × 0.5) + ($80 × 0.5) = $80.

To see which compensation scheme is efficient, calculate the outcome of each scheme for the principal and the agent.

Scheme 1: Dylan (principal) pays Thomas (agent) $31 per day. Will Thomas work hard or relax? If Thomas relaxes, he receives $31. Since he does not have to exert himself, the value of relaxing is also $31. If Thomas works hard, he also receives $31, but since he has to exert himself, the value of working hard is $31 − $10 = $21. Thomas will choose to relax. Expected income will be $80 per day, with $31 going to Thomas and $49 going to Dylan.

Scheme 2: Dylan (principal) pays Thomas (agent) $10 plus 26 percent of the income from vegetable growing. If Thomas relaxes, he receives $10 + (0.26 × $80) = $30.80. Since he does not have to exert himself, the value of relaxing is also $30.80. If Thomas works hard, he receives $10 + (0.26 × $120) = $41.20. Since he has to exert himself, the value of working hard is $41.20 − $10 = $31.20. Thomas will choose to work hard. Expected income will be $120 per day, with $41.20 going to Thomas and $78.80 going to Dylan.

Both Dylan and Thomas are better off under compensation scheme 2.

But is Thomas better off growing vegetables under compensation scheme 2 than he would be milking cows? If Thomas milks cows, he earns $30, but since he has to work hard, the value to him is $30 − $10 = $20. This is lower than the value he receives working hard growing vegetables under scheme 2. Therefore, compensation scheme 2 is more efficient.

PROBLEM

FIGURE **P3.1** LABOUR MARKETS FOR PROGRAMMERS

(a) Left-Handed

(b) Right-Handed

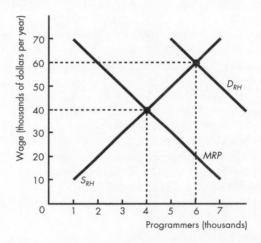

Suppose the computer software industry uses only two inputs—programmers (labour) and computers (capital). All programmers, whether left-handed or right-handed, have computer science degrees, are equally skilled and productive, and have the marginal revenue product (*MRP*) curve in Fig. P3.1(a) and (b).

Software firms (run mostly by right-handers) discriminate against left-handed programmers, believing (wrongly) that left-handers are less productive than right-handers. Figure P3.1(a) shows the supply curve of left-handed programmers and firms' demand curve for left-handed programmers.

Software firms also discriminate in favour of right-handed programmers, believing (wrongly) that right-handers are more productive than left-handers. Figure P3.1(b) shows the supply curve

of right-handed programmers and firms' demand curve for right-handed programmers.

a What is the relationship between the wage and the marginal revenue product for left-handed programmers? for right-handed programmers?

b Explain the competitive forces that would tend to eliminate this form of discrimination, even without government legislation.

c If owners of firms are so strongly prejudiced against left-handers that they are willing to accept lower profits rather than employ left-handers, will competitive forces eliminate this discrimination?

d The government introduces pay equity legislation, designed to equalize wages between left-handers and right-handers. The legislation includes an educational program to inform firms of the true and equal productivity of all programmers, regardless of their "handedness." If the program is successful, what will be the wage of programmers? the employment of left-handed programmers? the employment of right-handed programmers?

e With equalized programmer wages, what is now the relationship between the wage and the marginal revenue product for left-handed programmers? for right-handed programmers? What other meaning does *pay equity* have besides paying different groups equal wages?

f As a result of the pay equity legislation, what has happened to the *average* wage of programmers? Assuming programmers and capital are substitute inputs, use a diagram to explain the impact on each firm's demand for capital. What will happen to the price and employment of capital in the software industry in the short run? in the long run?

g As a result of the pay equity legislation, what has happened to the average wage of *left-handed* programmers? Explain the impact on the decisions of left-handers to invest in human capital.

MIDTERM EXAMINATION

You should allocate 32 minutes for this examination (16 questions, 2 minutes per question). For each question, choose the one *best* answer.

1 Refer to Fig. P3.2. If demand for a factor of production increases from D_0 to D_1, the *change* in transfer earnings is

a area *ihfc*.
b area *jcfk*.
c area *0fk*.
d area *0fh*.
e none of the above

FIGURE **P3.2**

2 Household savings are larger when either current income is

a low compared with expected future income or interest rates are high.
b low compared with expected future income or interest rates are low.
c high compared with expected future income or interest rates are high.
d high compared with expected future income or interest rates are low.
e above or below the reservation wage.

3 An increase in Katherine's wealth from $3,000 to $6,000 raises her utility from 80 units to 100. If she is risk-neutral, with wealth of $9,000, her utility might be

a 100 units.
b 115 units.
c 120 units.
d 125 units.
e 180 units.

4 A department store that pays clerks a fixed wage that does not depend on sales is likely to have problems of

a moral hazard.
b adverse selection.
c private information.
d creating work incentives.
e all of the above.

5   XYZ Corporation is expected to pay a dividend of $5 a share every year. If the annual interest rate is 5 percent, what is the market price of a share of XYZ stock?

a $50.00
b $5.00
c $5.25
d $4.76
e $100.00

6   The choke price of a natural resource is the price at which

a   the resource will begin to be used.
b   no one uses the resource.
c   the resource will be used as a substitute for other scarce resources.
d   the resource will begin to be conserved.
e   economists check into the Heartbreak Hotelling.

7   The demand curve for a factor of production will shift rightward as a result of a(n)

a   decrease in the price of the factor.
b   increase in the price of the factor.
c   decrease in the price of a substitute factor.
d   increase in the price of a substitute factor.
e   decrease in the price of output.

8   Suppose a profit-maximizing firm hires labour in a competitive labour market. If the marginal revenue product of labour is greater than the wage, the firm should

a   increase the wage rate.
b   decrease the wage rate.
c   increase the quantity of labour it hires.
d   decrease the quantity of labour it hires.
e   shift to a more labour-intensive production process.

9   A group of union workers with a variety of skills who work for the same firm or industry is a(n)

a   industrial union.
b   craft union.
c   local union.
d   national union.
e   public sector union.

10   Refer to Fig. P3.3. For any given wage,

a   the elasticity of demand for skilled workers is greater than the elasticity of demand for unskilled workers.
b   more skilled workers will be hired than unskilled workers.
c   more unskilled workers will be hired than skilled workers.
d   the horizontal distance between the curves is the compensation for the cost of acquiring skill.
e   the horizontal distance between the curves is the *MRP* of skill.

FIGURE **P3.3**

11   A high price-earnings ratio means

a   current share price is higher than the expected future share price.
b   investors will want to sell the stock to realize profits.
c   future profits are expected to be high relative to current profits.
d   future profits are expected to be low relative to current profits.
e   none of the above.

12   If the net present value of a new machine is positive then

a   the firm should not buy the machine.
b   the present value of the machine's stream of marginal revenue products is greater than the purchase price.
c   the present value of the machine's stream of marginal revenue products is less than the purchase price.
d   a and b.
e   a and c.

13 Which of the following statements is/are *true*?

1 Quality of search goods can only be assessed after they are bought.

2 Quality of search goods can be assessed before they are bought.

3 Advertising for experience goods usually persuades.

4 Advertising for experience goods usually informs.

a 1 and 3

b 1 and 4

c 2 and 3

d 2 and 4

e none of the above

14 Insurance is most likely to be purchased by someone whose

a total utility of wealth diminishes rapidly.

b total utility of wealth diminishes slowly.

c marginal utility of wealth diminishes rapidly.

d marginal utility of wealth diminishes slowly.

e marginal utility of wealth is constant.

15 For a monopsonist facing an upward-sloping supply curve of labour (*S*), the marginal cost of labour (*MCL*) curve

a intersects the *MRP* curve of labour at the equilibrium wage.

b is below and parallel to *S*.

c is identical to *S*.

d is above and parallel to *S*.

e is none of the above.

16 Suppose the government passes a minimum wage law that prohibits anyone from hiring labour at less than $8 per hour. In Fig. P3.4, the monopsonist will hire

a 250 hours of labour.

b 300 hours of labour.

c 350 hours of labour.

d 400 hours of labour.

e 500 hours of labour.

FIGURE **P3.4**

ANSWERS

Problem

a For the 2,000 left-handed programmers employed, the wage ($20,000 per year) is much less than the marginal revenue product of $60,000 per year. For the 6,000 right-handed programmers employed, the wage ($60,000 per year) is much more than the marginal revenue product of $20,000 per year.

b A nondiscriminating firm could earn higher profits by employing more left-handed programmers as long as their marginal revenue product exceeds the wage. Similarly, profits will increase by employing fewer right-handed programmers as long as their wage exceeds their marginal revenue product. The competitive outcome would be a wage of $40,000 per year for every programmer, and employment of 4,000 left-handed and 4,000 right-handed programmers.

c No. Firms can continue to discriminate if they "pay" for the discrimination in the form of lower profits.

d A successful education program alter's firms' beliefs about left-handed and right-handed programmers and moves the demand curves to the true *MRP* curves. The outcome will be the same as the competitive outcome—a wage of $40,000 per year for every programmer, and employment of 4,000 left-handed and 4,000 right-handed programmers.

e The wage is equal to the marginal revenue product for every programmer. Pay equity also means each labourer being paid an amount *equal* to the value of his or her marginal revenue product.

f Before legislation, the average yearly wage of programmers was a weighted (by employment) average of the wages of left-handers and right-handers.

$$\frac{(\$20,000 \times 2,000) + (\$60,000 \times 6,000)}{8,000} = \$50,000$$

After legislation, the average yearly wage has fallen to $40,000. The decrease in wages causes a decrease in the demand for capital, as firms try to economize on the now relatively more expensive capital input (see Fig. P3.5).

FIGURE **P3.5** CAPITAL MARKET FOR COMPUTERS

In the short run, the supply of capital (SS_0) is perfectly inelastic. The decrease in demand from D_0 to D_1 causes the price of capital to fall to R_1, while the quantity employed remains constant. In the long run, the supply curve of capital to the industry (LS) is perfectly elastic at the economy-wide interest rate R. The fall in price eventually shifts capital resources out of this industry into other industries where the rate of interest is higher. The short-run supply curve shifts to SS_1, the price of capital returns to R, and the quantity of capital employed decreases.

g The average yearly wage of left-handed programmers has increased from $20,000 to $40,000. This creates an incentive for more left-handers to invest in the necessary human capital (computer science degrees) to become a programmer, increasing the quantity supplied of left-handed programmers.

Midterm Examination

1 b ↑ in area under supply curve. (334–335)

2 c See text discussion. (331–332)

3 c Risk-neutral → constant marginal utility wealth. Marginal utility of extra $3,000 is 20 units utility. (389–391)

4 e All are problems created by private information. (395, 398–400)

5 e For indefinite future, PV = yearly amount paid/r = $5/0.05. (375–376)

6 b Definition. (378–379)

7 d Firm demands more of this now relatively cheaper factor at every price for factor. **a** and **b** move along curve, **e** shifts curve left. (327)

8 c Hiring ↑ labour → ↑ profit since $MRP > MC$. Firm can't change wage. (325–326)

9 a Definition. (348–349)

⊘10 b Reverse **a** true. **d** true for vertical distance between supply. **e** true for vertical distance. (346–347)

⊘11 c Reverse of **a**, **b** true. (375–376)

12 b Definition. Firm should buy machine. (369–370)

13 c Definition for search goods. Experience goods cannot be judged in advance so advertising for information purposes is useless. (394)

14 c More rapidly marginal utility wealth ↓, the more risk averse the person. Total utility wealth always ↑. (391–392)

⊘15 e MCL is above, but not parallel to S. MCL intersects S at equilibrium QL, not wage. (352–354)

⊘16 c New MCL flat at $8 until it hits S curve → QL where new MCL intersects MRP. (352–354)

Chapter 18

Market Failure and Public Choice

KEY CONCEPTS

The Government Sector

Total spending by all levels of government (federal, provincial, local) in Canada is 46 percent of total income. Eleven percent of the Canadian labour force is employed by government. Government expenditure peaked in 1992 at 50 percent of total income and has since declined.

The Economic Theory of Government

Government economic activity stems from attempts to correct

◆ **Market failure**—inability of unregulated market to achieve allocative efficiency. There are three cases:

- **Public goods**—goods and services that can be consumed simultaneously by everyone and from which no one can be excluded.
- *Monopoly*—output restriction by monopolies and cartels and rent seeking prevent efficient allocation resources.
- **Externalities**—production of goods and services creates *external costs* or *external benefits* that fall on people not involved in the transaction.

◆ Economic inequality—an unregulated market economy produces what most people regard as an inequitable distribution of income.

Public Choice and the Political Marketplace

Public choice theory analyses government as a political marketplace analogous to the economic marketplace. Actors are

◆ Voters—consumers of the outcomes of the political process. They express their demand by voting, lobbying, and making campaign contributions.

◆ Politicians—officials elected by voters. Objective is to get and stay elected.

◆ Bureaucrats—officials hired by politicians who work in government. Objective is to maximize budget of their agency.

Political equilibrium is situation where choices of voters, politicians, and bureaucrats are compatible, and no group will be better off with a different choice.

Public Goods

Pure public goods can be consumed by everyone, no one can be excluded. They have two features:

◆ **Nonrivalry**—one person's consumption does not ↓ amount available for another.

- Opposite is **rival good**—one person's consumption ↓ amount available for another (e.g., a hot dog).

◆ **Nonexcludability**—no one can be excluded from consuming.

- Opposite is **excludable good**—can exclude others from consuming (e.g., cable television).

Public goods → **free rider** (someone who consumes without paying) and *free-rider problem*—tendency for too little of public good to be provided if produced and sold privately.

◆ Efficient scale of provision of public good occurs where net benefit is maximized or where marginal benefit equals marginal cost of public good.

- *Total benefit* is total $ value placed on public good.

- *Net benefit* is total benefit − total cost.
- **Marginal benefit** is ↑ total benefit from a unit ↑ public good.

◆ Private provision of a public good creates a free-rider problem and provides less than the efficient quantity of the good.

◆ Government provision can provide an efficient quantity of a public good, where politicians compete for votes of well-informed voters.

The quantity of government provision of a public good generally depends on the political marketplace and the actions of voters, politicians, and bureaucrats.

◆ Politicians tend to follow **principle of minimum differentiation**—tendency for competitors to make themselves identical to appeal to maximum number voters/clients.

◆ Voters may be **rationally ignorant**—deciding not to acquire information because cost of acquisition > expected benefit. Then politicians, influenced by bureaucrats and special-interest lobbyists, may allow inefficient overprovision of a public good.

Taxes

Income taxes generate large percentage of government revenues.

◆ High-income voters prefer lower tax rates and fewer government benefits.

◆ Low-income voters prefer higher tax rates and greater benefits.

◆ Tax policy is outcome of **median voter theorem**—political parties pursue policies maximizing net benefit of median voter.

Excise tax is tax on sale of particular good.

◆ Tax on good → supply curve shifts upward, ↑ equilibrium *P*, ↓ equilibrium *Q*, and ↑ *deadweight loss*.

◆ Size of deadweight loss depends on elasticity of demand. To minimize deadweight loss, governments place highest tax rates on goods with lowest elasticities of demand.

H E L P F U L   H I N T S

1 The criterion economists use to judge the success of the market (or any other institution for that matter) is allocative efficiency. Allocative efficiency means that the economy is producing

all goods and services up to the point at which the marginal cost is equal to the marginal benefit. In such a state, no one can be made better off without making someone else worse off.

When the market fails to achieve this "ideal" state of efficiency, we call it *market failure.* The market can fail by producing too little if the marginal benefit of the last unit exceeds the marginal cost. On the other hand, the market can fail by producing too much if the marginal cost of the last unit exceeds the marginal benefit.

In this chapter (and in Chapter 20), we learn that governments can correct market failures, but can also fail to achieve allocative efficiency. Since both markets and governments can fail, the relevant economic question in each case is: Which fails less?

2 Public choice theory provides a theory of the political marketplace that parallels the economic theory of markets for goods and services. It is useful to draw analogies between the operation of political markets and ordinary markets.

In political markets, the demanders are voters, whereas in ordinary markets, the demanders are consumers. In both cases, demanders are concerned about their costs and benefits.

The suppliers in political markets are politicians and bureaucrats, whereas in ordinary markets, the suppliers of goods and services are firms.

In political markets, voters express their demands by means of votes, political contributions, and lobbying. This occurs because the suppliers (politicians) in this market are motivated by a desire to retain political office. In ordinary markets, consumers express their demands by means of dollars, since suppliers are motivated by a desire to maximize profit.

In both markets, equilibrium is a state of rest. In equilibrium there is no tendency to change because participants cannot become better off by making a different choice or by engaging in an additional transaction.

3 Understand the logic behind the median voter theorem. Politicians want to be elected and then remain in office. To do so they must receive a majority of votes; they must win at least one more than 50 percent of the votes. Since all politicians realize this, the median voter, the "middle" voter, becomes the key voter. A politician who offers a platform that deviates from the preferences of the median voter will lose to a politician who offers a platform closer to those preferences.

4 Well-informed special interest groups are able to induce the government to conduct programs that do not maximize net benefits because most voters are *rationally* ignorant. For most voters, it does not pay to be well informed about any particular issue. As a result, a small, well-informed interest group will be able to have an influence on government programs that greatly exceeds its size relative to all voters.

5 All goods provided by the government are not necessarily public goods. A public good is defined by the characteristics of nonrivalry and nonexcludability, not by whether or not it is publicly provided. For example, many cities and communities provide swimming pools and residential garbage pickup. Neither of these is a pure public good in spite of the fact that each may be provided by the government. Indeed, in many other communities, the same services are provided by the private market.

6 It is important to understand why the properties of nonrivalry and nonexcludability associated with pure public goods imply that we obtain the marginal benefit curve for the economy as a whole differently than for private goods.

A private good is a rival in consumption. Therefore to obtain the demand curve for the whole economy, we sum the individual marginal benefit (demand) curves *horizontally*. However, the economy's marginal benefit curve for a public good is obtained by summing the individual marginal benefit curves *vertically*. This is the relevant marginal benefit curve for evaluating the efficient provision level of the public good.

S E L F - T E S T

True/False/Uncertain and Explain

1 Restriction of output by monopolies is an example of market failure.

2 According to public choice theory, not only is there possibility of market failure, but there is also the possibility of "government failure."

3 The existence of public goods gives rise to the free-rider problem.

4 The economy's marginal benefit curve for a public good is obtained by adding the marginal benefits of each individual at each quantity of provision.

5 The private market will produce much less than the efficient quantity of pure public goods.

6 Net benefit is zero when the allocatively efficient level of output is obtained.

7 The public choice theory of government behaviour assumes that politicians and bureaucrats are motivated primarily by concern for the public interest.

8 Political parties will tend to propose fundamentally different policies in order to give voters a clearer choice.

9 If politicians respond to voters, government policies will maximize net benefit.

10 It is irrational for voters to be uninformed about an issue as important as national defence.

Multiple-Choice

1 The market demand curve for a *private* good is obtained by

a summing the individual marginal cost curves horizontally.

b summing the individual marginal cost curves vertically.

c summing the individual marginal benefit curves horizontally.

d summing the individual marginal benefit curves vertically.

e none of the above methods.

2 The economy's total demand curve for a *public* good is obtained by

a summing the individual marginal cost curves horizontally.

b summing the individual marginal cost curves vertically.

c summing the individual marginal benefit curves horizontally.

d summing the individual marginal benefit curves vertically.

e none of the above methods.

3 The efficient scale of provision of a public good occurs where

a net benefit is at a maximum.

b marginal benefit is at a maximum.

c marginal benefit minus marginal cost equals zero.

d marginal cost is at a minimum.

e a and c are true.

4 When a city street is not congested, it is like a(n)

a external good.

b internal good.

c rival good.

d private good.

e public good.

5 Governments provide pure public goods like national defence because

a governments are more efficient than private firms at producing such goods.

b of the free-rider problems that result in underproduction by private markets.

c people do not value national defence very highly.

d of the potential that private firms will make excess profits.

e of external costs.

6 Which of the following goods has the nonexcludability feature?

a city bus

b toll bridge

c lighthouse

d art museum

e all of the above

7 The quantity of public goods produced by an unregulated market tends to be

a less than the allocatively efficient quantity.

b equal to the allocatively efficient quantity.

c greater than the allocatively efficient quantity.

d that which maximizes total public benefit.

e that which maximizes net public benefit.

8 Public choice theory

a argues that government has a tendency to conduct policies that help the economy towards allocative efficiency.

b argues that politicians and bureaucrats tend to be more concerned about the public interest than individuals in the private sector.

c argues that the public choices of government maximize net benefits.

d applies economic tools used to analyse markets to the analysis of government behaviour.

e applies the tools of political analysis to the analysis of economic markets.

9 According to public choice theory, a voter will favour a candidate whose political program is

a perceived to offer the greatest personal benefit to the voter.

b best for the majority of the people.

c closest to allocative efficiency.

d favoured by the median voter.

e all of the above.

10 In general, a tax of $3 per unit of good *A* will shift the supply curve of *A* up by

a $3 and increase the price of *A* by $3.

b $3 and increase the price of *A* by less than $3.

c $3 and increase the price of *A* by more than $3.

d more than $3 and increase the price of *A* by $3.

e less than $3 and increase the price of *A* by $3.

11 The deadweight loss due to a price increase resulting from a tax is the loss of

a consumer surplus.

b producer surplus.

c consumer surplus plus the loss of producer surplus.

d consumer surplus minus the loss of producer surplus.

e tax revenue from the decreased equilibrium quantity.

12 Figure18.1 gives the demand and supply for imported cheese. If the government imposes a $3 tax per kilogram of imported cheese, price will increase by

a $3 to $7.

b $3 to $6.

c $2 to $6.

d $2 to $5.

e none of the above.

FIGURE **18.1**

13 Competitors who make themselves identical to appeal to the maximum number of voters illustrate the

a principle of maximum differentiation.

b principle of minimum differentiation.

c principle of rational ignorance.

d principle of nonrivalry.

e Niskanen theory of bureaucratic behaviour.

14 Refer to Fig. 18.2 which shows the total cost and total benefit of proposals for building four different-sized high schools. The proposal with the largest net benefit is

a A.

b B.

c C.

d D.

e impossible to identify without additional information.

FIGURE **18.2**

15 Refer to Fig. 18.2 which shows the total cost and total benefit of proposals for building four different-sized high schools. The proposal most likely to appeal to voters in an election is

a A.

b B.

c C.

d D.

e impossible to identify without additional information.

16 Refer to Fig. 18.2 which shows the total cost and total benefit of proposals for building four different-sized high schools. The proposal that best meets the goals of the school district's bureaucrats is

a A.

b B.

c C.

d D.

e impossible to identify without additional information.

17 If voters have similar views and are well informed, the quantity of national defence provided by the government will tend to be

a greater than the allocatively efficient quantity.
b less than the allocatively efficient quantity.
c the least costly quantity.
d the quantity that maximizes net benefit.
e the quantity that maximizes the Ministry of Defence budget.

18 Competition between two political parties will cause those parties to propose policies

a that are quite different.
b that are quite similar.
c of rational ignorance.
d that reduce the well-being of middle-income families and increase the well-being of the rich and the poor.
e that equate total costs and total benefits.

19 Rational ignorance

a results when the cost of information exceeds the benefits of having the information.
b allows special interest groups to exert political influence.
c combined with special interest groups can yield allocative inefficiency in the provision of public goods.
d results in all of the above.
e results in none of the above.

20 Refer to Fig. 18.3. Pre-tax consumer surplus is equal to triangle

a *gmc.*
b *gkc.*
c *mkc.*
d *dac.*
e *dbc.*

FIGURE **18.3**

21 Refer to Fig. 18.3. Pre-tax producer surplus is equal to triangle

a *gmc.*
b *gkc.*
c *mkc.*
d *dac.*
e *abc.*

22 Refer to Fig. 18.3. Deadweight loss from the tax is equal to triangle

a *abc.*
b *dbc.*
c *dac.*
d *edc.*
e *gdj.*

23 According to public choice theory, a voter will tend to be well informed if the issue in question

a is complicated and difficult to understand.
b affects everyone a little.
c is of special interest to a small group to which the voter does not belong.
d has a large direct effect on the voter.
e is important even if it does not directly affect the voter.

24 The budget of a government bureau is likely to increase beyond the quantity that maximizes net benefit of the economy if

a voters are well informed.
b there is rational voter ignorance combined with special interest lobbying.
c it is allocatively efficient to do so.
d bureaucrats are rationally ignorant.
e there are negative externalities.

25 On any given spending issue subject to a vote, the median voter is the one who favours

a the least spending.
b the most spending.
c the efficient level of spending.
d the average level of spending.
e spending more than the level favoured by half the voters and less than the level favoured by half the voters.

Short Answer Problems

1 Explain the *nonrivalry* and *nonexcludability* features of a pure public good.

2 What is the free-rider problem?

3 Briefly compare an equilibrium in a political market with an equilibrium in a market for goods and services.

4 Explain why it may be rational for voters to be ignorant.

5 Why does the imposition of an excise tax cause the supply curve of the taxed good to shift upward?

6 Heritage Apartments has 100 residents who are concerned about security. Table 18.1 gives the total cost of hiring a 24-hour security guard service as well as the marginal benefit to each of the residents.

TABLE **18.1**

Number of Guards	Total Cost per Day ($)	Marginal Benefit per Resident ($)	Marginal Benefit to All Residents ($)
1	300	10	
2	600	4	
3	900	2	
4	1,200	1	

a Why is a security guard a public good for the residents of Heritage Apartments?
b Why will zero guards be hired if each of the residents must act individually?
c Complete the last column of Table 18.1 by computing the marginal benefit of security guards to all of the residents together.

⊘ 7 Now suppose that the residents form an Apartment Council that acts as a governing body to address the security issue.
a What is the optimal (allocatively efficient) number of guards? What is the net benefit at the optimal number of guards?
b Show that net benefit is less for either one less guard or for one more guard than the net benefit for the optimal number of guards.
c How might the Apartment Council pay for the optimal number of guards?

8 Two candidates are competing in an election for president of the Economics Club. The only issue dividing them is how much will be spent on the annual Economics Club party. It is well known that the seven voting members of the club (*A* through *G*) have preferences as shown in Table 18.2. These are strongly held preferences regarding exactly how much should be spent on the party.

TABLE **18.2**

Voting Member	Proposed Amount ($)
A	10
B	20
C	30
D	40
E	50
F	60
G	70

a How much will each candidate propose to spend?
b To demonstrate that your answer to part **a** is correct, consider the outcome of the following two contests.
   i Candidate 1 proposes the amount you gave in part **a** and candidate 2 proposes $1 less. Which candidate will win? Why?
   ii Candidate 1 proposes the amount you gave in part **a** and candidate 2 proposes $1 more. Which candidate will win? Why?
c Suppose that the Sociology Club is also electing a president and that the same single issue prevails. It is well known that the seven voting members of the Sociology Club have the following strongly held preferences regarding exactly how much should be spent on their party (see Table 18.3).

TABLE **18.3**

Voting Member	Proposed Amount ($)
T	0
U	0
V	0
W	40
X	41
Y	42
Z	43

How much will each of the two candidates propose in this case?

9 Table 18.4 gives three alternative income distributions for five individuals, *A* through *E*. Currently income is distributed according to distribution 1 (given in the first column of the table). Consider alternative proposed distributions 2 and 3 one at a time.

TABLE **18.4**

Individual	Distribution 1 ($)	Distribution 2 ($)	Distribution 3 ($)
A	0	200	150
B	200	300	250
C	400	350	450
D	700	600	600
E	1,000	850	850

a If distribution 2 is proposed as an alternative to distribution 1, will it have majority support? Why or why not?

b If distribution 3 is proposed as an alternative to distribution 1, will it have majority support? Why or why not?

10 Figure 18.4 gives the supply and demand for movie tickets in Ourtown. The market is initially in equilibrium (point *a*) with a price of $5 per ticket and 5,000 tickets sold per week. Suppose that the town government establishes a new tax of $2 per movie ticket.

FIGURE **18.4**

a Illustrate the effect of the new tax graphically. What will the new equilibrium price and quantity be?

b How much of the $2 tax is paid by consumers in the form of a higher price and how much is paid by movie ticket sellers in the form of reduced revenue per ticket?

c How much tax revenue will be collected each week?

d How much consumer surplus will be lost due to the tax? How much producer surplus will be lost? What is the deadweight loss of the tax?

A N S W E R S

True/False/Uncertain and Explain

1 T Allocatively inefficient output. (416–417)
2 T Believe government agents act in own interest, not necessarily public interest. (418–419)
3 T Nonexcludability → no incentive to pay. (416–417)
4 T See text discussion. (420–422)
5 T Because no accounting for external benefits. (420–422)
6 F Net benefit is maximized. (420–422)
7 F Concern for own self-interest. (418–419)
8 F Propose similar policies as vote-maximizing strategy appealing to median voter. (422–424)
9 U True if voters well informed, false if voters rationally ignorant. (424–425)
10 F May pay to be rationally ignorant. (424–425)

Multiple-Choice

1 c See text discussion. (420–422)
2 d See Text Fig. 18.4. (420–422)
3 e Equivalent conditions. (420–422)
4 e Features nonrivalry and nonexcludability. Congestion → rivalry. (416–417)
5 b Would not be profitable for private firms. (419–423)
6 c Can't prevent ships from seeing the light. (416–417)
7 a Private production unprofitable because of free-rider problem. (422–423)
8 d Political marketplace. (418–419)
9 a Voter assumed concerned only with own self-interest. (418–419)
10 b Draw graph. **a** true only for perfectly elastic supply. Other answers always false. (427–429)
11 c See text discussion. (427–428)

12 c Draw graph. Shift supply upward by $3. (427–429)

13 b Definition. (423–424)

14 b Largest $TB - TC$. (420–423)

15 b Maximizes net benefit. (420–423)

16 d Public choice theory assumes bureaucrats maximize budget (TC). (424–425)

17 d Government will respond to demands of voters. (424–425)

18 b Vote maximizing by principle minimum differentiation. (422–424)

◑ 19 d a definition, **b, c** outcomes of rational ignorance. (424–425)

20 b Area below demand, above market price. (249–250)

21 c Area above supply, below market price. (249–250)

22 c Lost consumer + producer surplus. (427–429)

23 d Information acquired only if value > cost acquisition. (424–425)

24 b Bureaucratic overprovision. (424–425)

25 e Median = exactly halfway between. (426–427)

Short Answer Problems

1 A good has the nonrivalry feature if its consumption by one person does not reduce the amount available for others. The nonexcludability feature means that if the good is produced and consumed by one person, others cannot be excluded from consuming it as well.

2 The free-rider problem is the problem of unregulated markets producing too little of a pure public good because there is little incentive for individuals to pay for the good. The reason is that the person's payment will likely have no perceptible effect on the amount the person will be able to consume.

3 In both cases, the equilibrium is a state of rest in the sense that no group has an incentive to change their choices. In the case of equilibrium in an ordinary market for goods and services, neither demanders nor suppliers are able to make an exchange that will make them better off. Similarly, when a political market is in equilibrium, neither demanders (voters) nor suppliers (politicians and bureaucrats) are able to make an alternative choice that will make them better off.

4 Most issues have only a small and indirect effect on most voters. In such cases it would be irrational for a voter to spend much time and effort to become well informed because the additional cost would quickly exceed any additional benefit. Only if the voter is significantly and directly affected by an issue will it pay to become well informed. As a result, most voters will be rationally ignorant regarding any given issue.

5 When an excise tax is imposed on a supplier, it raises the minimum price the supplier must receive in order to be willing to offer any given quantity for sale. This is nothing more than an upward shift in the supply curve. It is useful to think of a new excise tax as an increase in the cost of production.

6 a A security guard is a public good because, in this case, it has the features of nonrivalry and nonexcludability. It has nonrivalry because one resident's *consumption* of the security provided by a guard does not reduce the security of anyone else. The nonexcludability property is evidenced by the fact that once a security guard is in place, all residents enjoy the increased security; none can be excluded.

b If each resident must act individually in hiring a security guard none will be hired because each resident receives only $10 in benefit from the first guard, which costs $300 per day.

c The entries in the last column of Table 18.1 Solution are obtained by multiplying the marginal benefit per resident by the number of residents, 100. This multiplication is the numerical equivalent of summing the individual marginal benefit curves vertically for each quantity of guards.

TABLE **18.1** SOLUTION

Number of Guards	Total Cost per Day ($)	Marginal Benefit per Resident ($)	Marginal Benefit to All Residents ($)
1	300	10	1,000
2	600	4	400
3	900	2	200
4	1,200	1	100

◑ 7 a If the Apartment Council hires each guard for whom the marginal benefit exceeds the marginal cost, they will hire the optimal number of guards. The marginal cost of each additional guard is $300. The marginal benefit of the first guard is $1,000, so he will be hired. Similarly, the marginal benefit of the second guard is $400, and she will be hired.

The marginal benefit of the third guard, however, is only $200, which is less than marginal cost. Therefore we conclude that the allocatively efficient (optimal) number of guards is two. For two guards, the net benefit is $800: total benefit ($1,400) minus total cost ($600).

b For one guard, the net benefit is $700: total benefit ($1,000) minus total cost ($300). For three guards, the net benefit is also $700: total benefit ($1,600) minus total cost ($900). Thus the net benefit of $800 is greatest for two guards.

c The Apartment Council might pay for the optimal number of guards by collecting a security fee of $6 per day from each of the 100 residents in order to hire two security guards.

8 a Each candidate will propose spending $40 since that is the preference of the median voter (voter *D*).

b **i** Candidate 1 will win because *D*, *E*, *F*, and *G* will vote for that candidate because $40 comes closer to matching their preferences than the $39 proposed by candidate 2. Only *A*, *B*, and *C* will vote for candidate 2.

ii Candidate 1 will win because *A*, *B*, *C*, and *D* will vote for that candidate while only *E*, *F*, and *G* will vote for candidate 2.

c Once again, the candidates will both propose spending $40 on the party since that is the preference of the median voter. Note that in this case, the median voter's view is not "average."

9 a Only *A* and *B* are better off under distribution 2. Distribution 2 will receive the support of only *A* and *B* with *C*, *D*, and *E* opposed. Note particularly that the median voter (*C*) is worse off under distribution 2.

b Distribution 3 will receive majority support since it makes the median voter better off. It will be supported by *A*, *B*, and *C* and opposed by *D* and *E*.

10 a The new tax shifts the supply curve for movie tickets up by $2, the amount of the tax. In Fig. 18.4 Solution, the new curve is labelled S_1. The new equilibrium (point *b*) price and quantity are $6 per ticket and 4,000 tickets per week, respectively.

FIGURE **18.4** SOLUTION

b Of the $2 tax, $1 is paid by consumers since the price of a ticket rises from $5 to $6, and $1 is paid by sellers, since the revenue per ticket they receive falls from $5 to $4.

c Total tax revenue will be $8,000 per week: $2 per ticket times 4,000 tickets sold.

d The loss of consumer surplus is given by the area of triangle *abc* in Fig. 18.4 Solution and is equal to $500 (from the formula for the area of a right-angled triangle—area = 1/2 × base (*ac*) × height (*bc*) = 1/2 × 1,000 × $1). Similarly, the loss of producer surplus is given by the area of triangle *adc*, and is equal to $500. Thus the deadweight loss is $1,000, the sum of consumer and producer surplus.

Chapter 19

Inequality and Redistribution

KEY CONCEPTS

Economic Inequality in Canada

There is a great deal of inequality of income and wealth. The degree of inequality is measured by the Lorenz curve.

◆ The **Lorenz curve** for income (wealth) graphs the cumulative percentage of income (wealth) against the cumulative percentage of families.

◆ The 45° "line of equality" represents a hypothetically equal distribution of income (wealth).

◆ The farther the Lorenz curve is from the line of equality, the more unequal the distribution.

◆ The distribution of wealth in Canada is even more unequal than the distribution of income.

Poverty exists when families cannot buy adequate food, shelter, and clothing.

◆ **Low-income cutoff** (families spending 54.7 percent or more of their income on food, shelter, and clothing) is used to measure poverty. In Canada, 13.5 percent of families have incomes below the low-income cutoff.

◆ Most important factors influencing poverty are source of income, family type, and age of household head.

Comparing Like with Like

Wealth is the *stock* of assets owned by an individual. Wealth includes *human capital* as well as *tangible assets*. *Income* is the *flow* of earning received by an individual from his or her stock of wealth.

◆ Data used to construct wealth distributions do not include human capital and therefore overstate wealth inequalities.

◆ Distributions of annual income and wealth are more unequal than distributions of lifetime income and wealth.

◆ Even correcting for these factors, there are significant inequalities in distributions of income and wealth in Canada.

Factor Prices, Endowments, and Choices

The unequal distribution of income arises from unequal wage rates, unequal distribution of endowments, and personal choices.

◆ Inequalities can be bequeathed to the next generation through *bequests* (gifts to next generation) and *assortative mating* (marrying within one's own socioeconomic class).

Income Redistribution

Income is redistributed by governments through income taxes, income maintenance programs, and provision of goods and services below cost.

◆ **Income taxes** can be

- **Progressive**—marginal tax rate ↑ with ↑ level income.
- **Regressive**—marginal tax rate ↓ with ↑ level income.
- **Proportional** (*flat-rate tax*)—marginal tax rate constant at all levels income.

◆ Income maintenance programs include social security, unemployment compensation, and welfare.

◆ Provision of education and health-care services below cost (often for free) reduces inequality.

Income redistribution creates a **big tradeoff** between inequality and efficiency. Redistribution uses scarce resources and weakens incentives, so a more equally shared pie results in a smaller pie. The "big tradeoff" problem can be approached with

◆ Piecemeal reforms → limited response to most pressing current problems.

◆ Radical reforms including a **negative income tax**— give every family *guaranteed annual income* and decrease family benefits at specified *benefit-loss rate* as market income ↑. Negative income tax avoids most problems of existing programs, but is costly.

Ideas About Fairness (see website)

A theory of distributive justice is a set of principles for testing the fairness of the distribution of economic well-being. Two classes of such theories are the

◆ End-state theory of distributive justice—focus on fairness of *outcomes* or *ends* (equality of outcome).

• *Utilitarian* theory—outcome must maximize the sum of the utilities of all individuals. Redistribute income until marginal utility of last dollar spent by each individual is equal. Complete equality of income → maximum total utility.

• *Maximin* theory—outcome must yield maximum possible utility (income) for the person with the minimum utility (income). Fairest distribution is not complete equality but redistribution only until least well-off person can gain no more.

◆ Process theory of distributive justice—focus on fairness of *process* or *means* by which outcomes achieved (equality of opportunity). Classical liberalism emphasizes equality of opportunity and voluntary exchange, and any outcome resulting from this process is fair.

H E L P F U L   H I N T S

1 Statistics used to construct Lorenz curves do not always give an accurate picture of inequality. It is important to understand why inaccurate pictures might arise. For example, you should understand why a distribution of wealth that excludes the value of human capital will give a distorted picture relative to the distribution of income.

You should also understand why the distribution of annual (static) income will give a distorted picture relative to the distribution of lifetime (dynamic) income. Finally, you should understand why the distribution of before-tax, before-transfer income will give a distorted picture relative to the distribution of after-tax, after-transfer income.

2 The issue of fairness discussed in this chapter is a normative issue. Note, however, that the tradeoff between equity and economic efficiency (the so-called big tradeoff) is a positive issue.

S E L F - T E S T

True/False/Uncertain and Explain

1 In Canada, income is more unequally distributed than wealth.

2 The farther the Lorenz curve is from the 45° line, the more equal the distribution of income.

3 Under a proportional income tax, total taxes rise as income rises.

4 The marginal tax rate does not change as income rises.

5 A regressive income tax redistributes income from the rich to the poor.

6 Compared with the market distribution of income, government benefits and taxes reduce the inequality of income distribution.

7 The financial wealth distribution ignores the distribution of human capital and thus *overstates* inequality among individuals.

8 If debts could be bequeathed, the distribution of wealth would become more equal over time.

9 A negative income tax creates a welfare trap by discouraging employment.

10 In general, reducing income inequality by redistributing income from the rich to the poor will lead to greater production of goods and services.

Multiple-Choice

I Differences in the wage rates received by different individuals reflect differences in

a marginal product of labour.
b natural ability.
c human capital.
d all of the above.
e none of the above.

2 A bequest is a(n)

a mistake.
b tax on inherited wealth.
c gift from one generation to another.
d incentive for one generation to work harder.
e conditional inheritance.

3 Assortative mating means that

a poor women tend to marry rich men.
b rich women tend to marry rich men.
c rich women tend to marry poor men.
d same sex marriages occur because "like attracts like."
e same sex marriages are prohibited.

4 Consider the Lorenz curves in Fig. 19.1. Which Lorenz curve corresponds to the greatest income *inequality*?

a *A*
b *B*
c *C*
d *D*
e impossible to tell without additional information

FIGURE **19.1**

5 In Fig. 19.1, what is curve *A* (a straight line) called?

a market distribution line
b line of equality
c fairness line
d Okun tradeoff curve
e none of the above

6 Which point in Fig. 19.1 indicates that the richest 20 percent of families earn 40 percent of the income?

a *a*
b *b*
c *c*
d *d*
e none of the above

7 Even if the distribution of wages is symmetric, the distribution of income will be skewed because

a abilities are distributed symmetrically.
b abilities are distributed asymmetrically.
c individuals tend to supply more labour at higher wages.
d individuals tend to supply less labour at higher wages.
e **b** and **d** are true.

8 Which of the following *reduces* the inequality of income or wealth relative to the market distribution?

a government payments to the poor
b a regressive income tax
c large bequests
d assortative mating
e all of the above

9 A theory of distributive justice that emphasizes the mechanism by which distribution takes place is a(n)

a   utilitarian theory.
b   end-state theory.
c   maximin theory.
d   process theory.
e   outcomes theory.

10 Wealth differs from income in that

a   income is a stock, wealth is a flow.
b   wealth is derived from income.
c   income is what you earn, wealth is what you own.
d   income is what you own, wealth is what you earn.
e   wealth is preferable to income.

11 In Table 19.1, which tax plan is proportional?

a   Plan *A*
b   Plan *B*
c   Plan *C*
d   Plan *D*
e   impossible to calculate without additional information

TABLE **19.1**

Current Gross Income	Tax Payment Plan A	Tax Payment Plan B	Tax Payment Plan C	Tax Payment Plan D
0	0	0	0	200
1,000	100	100	200	200
2,000	200	400	200	200
4,000	400	1,600	200	200

12 In Table 19.1, which tax plan is progressive?

a   Plan *A*
b   Plan *B*
c   Plan *C*
d   Plan *D*
e   c and d

13 The distribution of *annual income*

a   understates the degree of inequality because it does not take into account the family's stage in its life cycle.
b   understates the degree of inequality because it does not take into account the distribution of human capital.
c   overstates the degree of inequality because it does not take into account the family's stage in its life cycle.
d   overstates the degree of inequality because it does not take into account the distribution of human capital.
e   is an accurate measure of the degree of inequality.

14 The distribution of *wealth*

a   understates the degree of inequality because it does not take into account the family's stage in its life cycle.
b   understates the degree of inequality because it does not take into account the distribution of human capital.
c   overstates the degree of inequality because it does not take into account the family's stage in its life cycle.
d   overstates the degree of inequality because it does not take into account the distribution of human capital.
e   is an accurate measure of the degree of inequality.

15 According to the maximin theory, income should be redistributed if the

a   average person can be made better off.
b   poorest person can be made better off.
c   richest person can be made worse off.
d   wage rate is greater than the marginal product of labour.
e   wage rate is less than the marginal product of labour.

16 Which of the following is an example of an end-state theory of distributive justice?

a   marginal product theory
b   classical liberalism theory
c   utilitarian theory
d   process theory
e   none of the above

17 In Fig. 19.2, the richest 20 percent of all families receive what share of all income?

a 10 percent
b 20 percent
c 30 percent
d 40 percent
e none of the above

FIGURE **19.2**

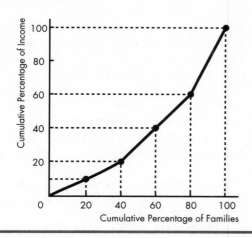

18 In Fig. 19.2, the poorest 20 percent of all families receive what share of income?

a 10 percent
b 20 percent
c 30 percent
d 40 percent
e none of the above

19 In Fig. 19.2, the middle 20 percent of all families receive what share of income?

a 10 percent
b 20 percent
c 30 percent
d 40 percent
e none of the above

20 The curve in Fig. 19.2 represents the

a line of market income distribution.
b line of perfect equality.
c Okun tradeoff curve.
d Nozick curve.
e Lorenz curve.

21 Suppose that if a family earns zero income, it receives a monthly transfer payment of $1,000 from the government. If the family earns $400 in a month, the government payment drops to $700. What is the marginal tax rate in this case?

a 0 percent
b 10 percent
c 40 percent
d 50 percent
e 75 percent

22 The most important factor influencing the incidence of low income is

a source of income.
b sex of household head.
c age of household head.
d family type.
e geographical region.

23 If the marginal tax rate increases as income increases, the income tax is defined as

a progressive.
b proportional.
c negative.
d regressive.
e excessive.

24 Redistribution of income from the rich to the poor will lead to a reduction in total output. This is known as the

a market distribution.
b process theory of distributive justice.
c end-state theory of distributive justice.
d big tradeoff.
e capitalist dilemma.

25 Which diagram is used by economists to illustrate the distribution of income or wealth?

a Lorenz curve
b normal distribution
c Rawls curve
d Okun tradeoff curve
e none of the above

Short Answer Problems

1 Explain the differences and connections between the concepts of wealth and income.

2 What are the two factors that determine a person's income? To what extent are these factors the result of forces beyond the control of the individual and to what extent are they the result of individual choice?

3 The two classes of theories of distributive justice are process theories and end-state theories. What is the principal characteristic of a process theory of distributive justice? Why is the utilitarian theory an end-state theory of distributive justice?

4 Why is there a "big tradeoff" between fairness and efficiency?

5 Table 19.2 gives information regarding the distribution of income in an economy which generates $100 billion in total annual income.

TABLE **19.2** TOTAL FAMILY INCOME

Percentage of Families	Total Income (billions of $)	Income Share (%)	Cumulative Percentage of Families	Cumulative Percentage of Income
Poorest 20%	5			
Second 20%	10			
Third 20%	15			
Fourth 20%	20			
Richest 20%	50			

a Complete Table 19.2 by computing the entries in the last three columns.
b Draw the Lorenz curve for income in this economy and label it *A*.

6 Now suppose that a progressive income tax is levied on the economy. The distribution of after-tax income is given in Table 19.3. We have assumed that none of the revenue is redistributed to families in the economy. Note that total after-tax income is $71 billion.

TABLE **19.3** AFTER-TAX FAMILY INCOME

Percentage of Families	After-Tax Income (billions of $)	After-Tax Income Share (%)	Cumulative Percentage of Families	Cumulative Percentage of After-Tax Income
Poorest 20%	5			
Second 20%	9			
Third 20%	12			
Fourth 20%	15			
Richest 20%	30			

a Complete Table 19.3.
b Draw the Lorenz curve for after-tax income on the same graph you used for Short Answer Problem **5b** and label it *B*.
c What effect has the progressive income tax had on inequality?

7 Finally, suppose that, in addition, the government redistributes all of the tax revenue so that the after-transfer (after-tax) income distribution is that given in Table 19.4. For example, those in the poorest group receive transfer income in the amount of $10 billion so that their after-transfer income becomes $15 billion.

TABLE **19.4** AFTER-TRANSFER FAMILY INCOME

Percentage of Families	After-Transfer Income Share (billions of $)	After-Transfer Income Share (%)	Cumulative Percentage of Families	Cumulative Percentage of After-Transfer Income
Poorest 20%	15			
Second 20%	16			
Third 20%	18			
Fourth 20%	20			
Richest 20%	31			

a Complete Table 19.4.
b Draw the Lorenz curve for after-transfer income on the same graph you used for Short Answer Problems **5b** and **6b** and label it *C*.
c What effect has income redistribution through transfer payments had on inequality?

8 Consider an economy consisting of 100 individuals who are identical in every way. Each lives to be 80 years of age and no older. Between birth and the age of 20 years they earn zero income; between the ages of 21 and 35 each earns an annual income of $30,000; between the ages of 36 and 50 each earns an annual income of $40,000; between the ages of 51 and 65 each receives an annual income of $60,000; and between the ages of 66 and 80 each receives an annual income of $20,000. At any given time there are 20 individuals in each of the 5 age groups. For simplicity we assume that there are no bequests. This information is summarized in Table 19.5.

TABLE **19.5** LIFETIME INCOME PATTERNS

Age Group (years)	Number in Age Group	Individual Annual Income ($)
0–20	20	0
21–35	20	30,000
36–50	20	40,000
51–65	20	60,000
66–80	20	20,000

a Draw the Lorenz curve for lifetime income in this economy and label it *A*.

b Draw the Lorenz curve for annual income in this economy and label it *B*.

c Which of these is a better measure of the inequality among individuals in this economy? Why?

9 Consider the worlds of Vulcan and Klingon. The Vulcan Lorenz curve is given in Fig. 19.3, and the Klingon income distribution data are given in Table 19.6.

FIGURE **19.3**

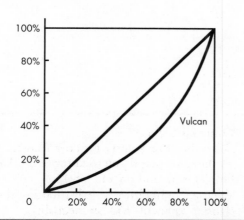

TABLE **19.6** KLINGON INCOME DISTRIBUTION

Family Income Rank	Percentage Share Total Income
Lowest 20%	10%
Second 20%	10%
Middle 20%	20%
Fourth 20%	30%
Highest 20%	30%

a Label the axes of Fig. 19.3 and explain what the diagonal line represents.

b Using the data from Table 19.6, draw the Klingon Lorenz curve on Fig. 19.3.

10 There are two major theories of distributive justice.
a State and define one theory.
b State and define the other theory.
c Using *only* the information in Short Answer Problem 9, which theory(s) of distributive justice can be used to judge Vulcan and Klingon? Which world is more just according to the theory(s)?

ANSWERS

True/False/Uncertain and Explain

1 F See Text Fig. 19.1. (437–438)
2 F More unequal. (437–438)
3 T Marginal tax rate constant, but total taxes ↑. (443–444)
4 U Depends if tax regressive (**F**), proportional (**T**), or progressive (**F**). (443–444)
5 F From poor to rich. (443–444)
6 T See Text Fig. 19.5. (444–445)
7 T Human capital wealth more equally distributed than financial wealth. (440)
8 T Only assets can be bequeathed. (442–443)
9 F Removes welfare trap and encourages employment. (446–447)
10 F Lower production due to the big tradeoff. (445–446)

Multiple-Choice

1 d All affect marginal revenue product of labour. (441–443)
2 c Definition. (442–443)
3 b Marriage within socioeconomic class. (443)
4 d Curve farthest from 45° line. (437–438)
5 b Definition. (437–438)
6 c Moving from 80 percent to 100 percent of families (richest 20 percent) moves income from 60 percent to 100 percent of total (40 percent). (437–438)
7 c Higher wages associated with even higher incomes (wage × quantity labour). (441–442)
8 a Others increase inequality. (443–445)
9 d Definition. (See website.)
10 c Wealth is a stock, income a flow derived from wealth. (437–438)
11 a Taxes always 10 percent of income. (443–444)
12 b With ↑ income, tax rate ↑ from 0 percent, to 10 percent, to 20 percent, to 40 percent. (443–444)

☉ 13   c   Human capital affects distribution of wealth, not income. (440)

☉ 14   d   Life cycle biases distribution income, not wealth. (440)

☺ 15   b   Definition. (See website.)

☺ 16   c   Maximize sum of utilities (end-states) of individuals. (See website.)

17   d   100 percent – 60 percent of cumulative income. (437–438)

18   a   10 percent – 0 percent of cumulative income. (437–438)

19   b   40 percent – 20 percent of cumulative income. (437–438)

20   e   Definition. (437–438)

☉ 21   e $\Delta T/\Delta Y = \$300/\$400$. (446–447)

22   a   See Text Fig. 19.3 notes. (438–439)

23   a   Definition. (443–444)

24   d   See text discussion. (445–446)

25   a   Definition. (437–438)

Short Answer Problems

1   Wealth is the *stock* of assets owned by an individual, while income is the *flow* of earnings received by an individual. The concepts are connected in that an individual's income is the earnings that flow from her stock of wealth.

2   A person's income is determined by the market prices for productive resource services and the quantity of resource services the person is able and willing to sell at those prices. These two factors depend on a number of things, some of which are (at least partially) under the control of the individual and some of which are not.

   The price of labour services, the wage rate, is determined in the market for labour. But, as we learned in Chapters 14 and 15, the wage rate will depend on the marginal product of labour, which is affected by individual choices about training and education as well as personal inherent ability.

   The quantity of labour services supplied will also depend on personal choices about how to spend one's time. The quantity of other resource services supplied will also depend on personal choices as well as the individual's endowment of the factor.

☺ 3   A process theory of distributive justice focuses on the fairness of the process or mechanisms by which results are achieved instead of focusing on the results themselves. The utilitarian theory suggests that the fairest system is one in which the sum of the utilities in the society is a maximum. Since the theory focuses on the outcome or the ends, it is an end-state theory of distributive justice.

4   If greater fairness means increasing the equality of income, it can only be achieved by income redistribution; the income of some must be taxed in order to make transfer payments to others. However, there are incentive effects that reduce the total amount of income available to be distributed.

   If productive activities such as work are taxed, there will be a tendency to reduce time spent in those activities. Furthermore, any redistribution program would require the use of resources to administer it and thus leave fewer resources for other productive activities. Thus we arrive at the insight: A more equally shared pie results in a smaller pie.

5 a   Table 19.2 is completed as Table 19.2 Solution. The income share for each group of families is the total income of that group as a percent of total income in the economy ($100 billion). The cumulative percentage of income (last column) is obtained by adding the percentage income share of the group (from the third column) to the total percentage income share of all poorer groups of families.

TABLE **19.2**   SOLUTION
TOTAL FAMILY INCOME

Percentage of Families	Total Income (billions of $)	Income Share (%)	Cumulative Percentage of Families	Cumulative Percentage of Income
Poorest 20%	5	5	20	5
Second 20%	10	10	40	15
Third 20%	15	15	60	30
Fourth 20%	20	20	80	50
Richest 20%	50	50	100	100

b   The curve labelled *A* in Fig. 19.4 is the Lorenz curve for total family income. This simply plots the values in the last two columns of Table 19.2 Solution.

FIGURE **19.4**

6 a Table 19.3 is completed as Table 19.3 Solution.

TABLE **19.3** SOLUTION
AFTER-TAX FAMILY INCOME

Percentage of Families	After-Tax Income (billions of $)	After-Tax Income Share (%)	Cumulative Percentage of Families	Cumulative Percentage of After-Tax Income
Poorest 20%	5	7	20	7
Second 20%	9	13	40	20
Third 20%	12	17	60	37
Fourth 20%	15	21	80	58
Richest 20%	30	42	100	100

b The curve labelled *B* in Fig. 19.4 is the Lorenz curve for after-tax family income.

c The progressive income tax has reduced inequality by taking a larger percentage of income from higher income groups.

7 a Table 19.4 is completed as Table 19.4 Solution.

TABLE **19.4** SOLUTION
AFTER-TRANSFER FAMILY INCOME

Percentage of Families	After-Transfer Income Share (billions of $)	After-Transfer Income Share (%)	Cumulative Percentage of Families	Cumulative Percentage of After-Transfer Income
Poorest 20%	15	15	20	15
Second 20%	16	16	40	31
Third 20%	18	18	60	49
Fourth 20%	20	20	80	69
Richest 20%	31	31	100	100

b The curve labelled *C* in Fig. 19.4 is the Lorenz curve for after-tax, after-transfer family income.

c Income redistribution through transfer payments has reduced inequality.

⊘ 8 a Since each individual in the economy earns exactly the same lifetime income, the Lorenz curve for lifetime income coincides with the line of equality and is labelled *A* in Fig. 19.5.

FIGURE **19.5**

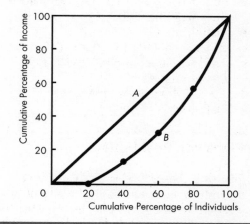

b The Lorenz curve for annual income is labelled *B* in Fig. 19.5. It reflects the fact that the poorest 20 percent of the individuals (0–20 years) receive 0 percent of the annual income; the second poorest 20 percent, those 60–80 years, receive 13 percent of the annual income; the third poorest 20 percent, those 21–35 years, receive 20 percent of the annual income; the fourth poorest 20 percent, those 36–50 years, receive 27 percent of the annual income; and the richest 20 percent, those 51–65 years, receive 40 percent of the annual income.

c The distribution of lifetime income is a better measure of the degree of inequality. In this imaginary economy all individuals are identical (equal), a fact that is reflected by equal lifetime incomes. The only reason annual income distribution in this economy is not equal is because the individuals are at different stages of identical life cycles.

9 a See Fig. 19.3 Solution. The diagonal line represents hypothetical income equality.

b See Fig. 19.3 Solution.

FIGURE **19.3** SOLUTION

10 a An end-state theory of distributive justice focuses on the fairness of *outcomes* (equality of outcomes).

b A process theory of distributive justice focuses on the fairness of the *process* by which outcomes are achieved (equality of opportunity).

c Since we have information only on income outcomes and not on the process by which they are achieved, only the end-state theory of distributive justice can be used to judge Vulcan and Klingon. Since the Klingon Lorenz curve is closer to the line of equality, the Klingon world is more just according to the end-state theory.

Competition Policy

Market Intervention

Forms of government intervention in monopolistic and oligopolistic markets:

- Regulation—rules determining prices, product standards, and entry conditions. *Deregulation*—removing rules.

- Public ownership—publicly owned firms are **Crown corporations. Privatization**—selling publicly owned corporation to private shareholders.

- **Anti-combine law**—makes some market behaviour (monopolistic practices) illegal.

Government intervention designed to influence surpluses. **Total surplus** represents the combined gains from trade to consumers and producers; sum of *consumer surplus* and *producer surplus*.

- *Consumer surplus*—value of goods to consumers – price paid = area below demand curve and above market price.

- *Producer surplus*—total revenue – opportunity cost = area below market price and above supply curve.

Total surplus maximized under competition when *deadweight loss* = 0.

- Under monopoly, ↑ producer surplus, ↓ consumer surplus and creation *deadweight loss*.

- Monopolistic practices create a tension between consumer interests and producer interests. This tension is the key to the economic theory of regulation.

Economic Theory of Regulation

Economic theory of regulation part of broader theory of public choice (Chapter 18), but emphasizing government regulation.

- Demand for regulation ↑ with ↑

  - consumer surplus per buyer.
  - number buyers.
  - producer surplus per firm.
  - number firms.

- Supply of regulation ↑ with ↑

  - consumer surplus per buyer.
  - producer surplus per firm.
  - number people affected.

In political equilibrium, no interest group presses for changes in existing regulation, and no politicians plan to offer different regulations. There are two theories of political equilibrium.

- **Public interest theory**—predicts regulations supplied to maximize total surplus and eliminate deadweight loss. Government will act in the public interest to eliminate waste and achieve allocative efficiency.

- **Capture theory**—predicts regulations supplied to maximize producer surplus and economic profit. Government "captured" by interests of producers.

Regulation and Deregulation

Government regulatory agencies set rules for prices, quantities, and market access.

Natural monopoly (because of economies of scale, one firm can supply the market at lower *ATC* than multiple firms can) can be regulated with the following rules.

◆ **Marginal cost pricing rule**—set price equal to marginal cost. Maximizes total surplus, but not viable because firm makes economic loss.

◆ **Average cost pricing rule**—set price equal to average total cost. May be most efficient even though deadweight loss.

◆ **Rate of return regulation**—set price to achieve specified target rate of return on capital.

- Ideally, yields normal profit only; same outcome as average-cost pricing rule.
- But there is a problem of incentive for firm to inflate cost (of capital) to yield economic profits.

◆ Evidence mixed, but regulated natural monopolies seem to earn profits equal to or greater than average, supporting more of predictions of capture theory than public interest theory.

Cartel (collusive agreement among firms in an oligopoly to restrict output and ↑ price) can be regulated with the following rules.

◆ Set price and quantity at competitive levels (intersection of industry demand and *MC* curves). Public interest theory outcome.

◆ Set price and quantity to maximize profit (highest price associated with quantity at intersection of industry *MC* and *MR* curves). Capture theory outcome.

◆ Evidence mixed, but regulated cartels seem to earn profits equal to or greater than average, supporting more of predictions of capture theory than public interest theory.

Public Ownership

Publicly owned corporations can be operated with the following objectives:

◆ Allocative efficiency—set price equal to marginal cost and subsidize the economic loss. Maximizes consumer surplus.

◆ Budget maximization with marginal cost pricing—set price equal to marginal cost but pad production costs to maximum. Allocatively efficient, but maximizes producer benefits.

◆ Budget maximization at zero price—↑ output until price falls to zero. Inefficient (deadweight loss), results in overproduction and maximizes producer benefits.

◆ Evidence suggests publicly owned firms will overproduce and be less efficient than a private firm. Recent tendency to privatize publicly owned firms.

Anti-Combine Law

Competition Act of 1986 distinguishes between

◆ Criminal actions (conspiracy to fix prices, bid-rigging, false advertising) dealt with by courts.

◆ Noncriminal actions (mergers, abuse of market position, exclusive dealing) dealt with by Competition Tribunal.

Evidence suggests anti-combine laws have served the public interest.

HELPFUL HINTS

I Figure 20.1 depicts revenue and marginal cost curves for an industry. Use this figure to think of regulation as determining the division of the potential total surplus (the area of triangle *abc*) among consumer surplus, producer surplus, and deadweight loss.

FIGURE **20.1**

If the industry is perfectly competitive, then output will be Q_c and the market price will be P_c. Total surplus is maximized and is given by the area of triangle *abc*. Total surplus is equal to the sum of consumer surplus (triangle *dbc*) and producer surplus (triangle *adc*). There is no deadweight loss.

If the industry is a profit-maximizing monopoly, output will be Q_m and the price will be P_m. In this case, total surplus is represented by the area of trapezoid *abfg*. Because of monopoly restriction of output, total surplus under monopoly is less than under competition. The difference is the deadweight loss from monopoly, the amount of total surplus that is lost when we go from competition to monopoly. The deadweight loss is given by the area of triangle *gfc*. Total surplus can be divided into consumer surplus (triangle *ebf*) and producer surplus (trapezoid *aefg*). Consumer surplus is quite small, but producer surplus is at a maximum.

Actual output is likely to be between these bounds. As output moves from Q_c to Q_m, consumer surplus decreases, while producer surplus and the deadweight loss both increase. If this industry is regulated, the public interest theory of intervention predicts that the result will be a level of output close to Q_c, while the capture theory of intervention predicts a level of output closer to Q_m.

SELF-TEST

True/False/Uncertain and Explain

1 In a monopoly industry, producer surplus is maximized at the profit-maximizing level of output.

2 In a monopoly industry, total surplus is maximized at the profit-maximizing level of output.

3 Evidence of higher-than-normal rates of return for regulated natural monopolies matches the predictions of the capture theory.

4 The evidence that producers are strongly supporting deregulation matches the predictions of the capture theory.

5 Government intervention will move the economy closer to allocative efficiency.

6 According to the capture theory, government regulatory agencies eventually capture the profits of the industries they regulate.

7 In practice, rate of return regulation is equivalent to marginal cost pricing.

8 Under rate of return regulation, firms can get closer to maximizing producer surplus if they inflate their costs.

9 If industry prices and profits fall after *deregulation*, the regulation was likely serving the interest of consumers.

10 Anti-combine laws have generally been directed towards achieving allocative efficiency and serving the public interest.

Multiple-Choice

1 Which of the following is *not* a federal regulatory agency?
a Atomic Energy Control Board
b Canadian Radio-television and Telecommunications Commission
c Petro-Canada
d Canadian Transport Commission
e National Farm Products

2 The difference between the maximum amount consumers are willing to pay and the amount they actually do pay for a given quantity of a good is called
a government surplus.
b consumer surplus.
c producer surplus.
d total surplus.
e deadweight surplus.

3 Which of the following is *least* likely to be a *natural monopoly*?
a subway service
b electric utilities
c water and sewer service
d taxi cab service
e cable TV service

4 The supply of economic regulation originates with

a monopolists.
b labour unions.
c fair trade associations.
d voters.
e politicians and bureaucrats.

5 Total surplus is maximized when

a marginal cost equals marginal revenue.
b marginal cost equals average total cost.
c price equals marginal cost.
d price equals average total cost.
e price equals average variable cost.

6 In a monopoly industry, producer surplus is maximized when

a marginal cost equals marginal revenue.
b marginal cost equals average total cost.
c price equals marginal cost.
d price equals average total cost.
e price equals average variable cost.

7 A large demand for intervention by *producers* will result when there is a

a small consumer surplus per buyer.
b large consumer surplus per buyer.
c large number of buyers.
d small producer surplus per firm.
e large producer surplus per firm.

8 The supply of intervention increases with

a smaller consumer surplus per buyer.
b larger producer surplus per firm.
c smaller number of people affected.
d all of the above.
e none of the above.

9 The total number of Crown corporations in Canada is about

a 25.
b 35.
c 90.
d 125.
e 1,000.

10 Figure 20.2 gives the revenue and cost curves for an industry. This industry will become a natural monopoly because

a one firm can supply the entire market at a lower price than can two or more firms.
b there are decreasing returns to scale over the entire range of demand.
c there are diseconomies of scale over the entire range of demand.
d even a single firm will be unable to earn a positive profit in this industry.
e all of the above are true.

FIGURE **20.2**

11 Consider the natural monopoly in Fig. 20.2. If the firm is unregulated and operates as a private profit-maximizer, what output will it produce?

a 0, because the firm suffers economic losses when $P = MC$
b Q_0
c Q_1
d Q_2
e Q_3

12 Consider the natural monopoly in Fig. 20.2. If a regulatory agency sets a price just sufficient for the firm to earn normal profits, what output will it produce?

a 0, because the firm suffers economic losses when $P = MC$
b Q_0
c Q_1
d Q_2
e Q_3

13 Consider the natural monopoly in Fig. 20.2. Total surplus is a maximum when quantity is

a Q_0 and price is P_3.
b Q_1 and price is P_1.
c Q_1 and price is P_4.
d Q_2 and price is P_2.
e Q_3 and price is P_0.

14 Consider the natural monopoly in Fig. 20.2. If a regulator uses a marginal cost pricing rule, what line segment gives the amount of subsidy (per unit of output) required to assure that the monopolist remains in business?

a *ba*
b *ea*
c *fc*
d *gd*
e *eb*

15 Consider the natural monopoly in Fig. 20.2. What region in the graph represents the deadweight loss arising from an average cost pricing rule?

a *abc*
b *cdg*
c *cfg*
d *aeg*
e none of the above

16 A monopolist under rate of return regulation has an incentive to

a pad costs.
b produce more than the efficient quantity of output.
c charge a price equal to marginal cost.
d maximize consumer surplus.
e do **a** and **b**.

17 Which of the following is consistent with the public interest theory of intervention?

a regulation of a natural monopoly by setting price equal to marginal cost
b regulation of a competitive industry in order to increase output
c regulation of the airline industry by establishing minimum airfares
d regulation of agriculture by establishing barriers to exit from the industry
e none of the above

18 Which of the following is consistent with the capture theory of intervention?

a regulation of a natural monopoly by setting price equal to marginal cost
b regulation of a competitive industry in order to increase output
c regulation of the airline industry by establishing minimum airfares
d regulation of agriculture by establishing barriers to exit from the industry
e none of the above

19 In a political equilibrium,

a allocative efficiency must be achieved.
b no one wants to change his or her proposal.
c firms will be making zero economic profit.
d all parties will agree that the appropriate level of regulation has been achieved.
e all of the above are true.

20 Anti-combine laws attempt to

a support prices.
b establish Crown corporations.
c prevent monopoly practices.
d establish fair trade laws.
e regulate monopolies.

21 A Crown corporation that maximizes its budget together with marginal cost pricing will

a produce the efficient level of output.
b produce more than the efficient level of output.
c maximize consumer surplus.
d maximize producer surplus.
e do **a** and **d**.

22 The public interest theory of intervention predicts that government regulation will

a promote the interests of public officials.
b attempt to maximize total surplus.
c attempt to maximize producer surplus.
d attempt to minimize producer surplus.
e attempt to maximize consumer surplus.

23 Allocative efficiency is achieved when

a consumer surplus is maximized.
b producer surplus is minimized.
c total surplus is maximized.
d total surplus is minimized.
e none of the above.

24 Regulation refers to

a the discipline of the marketplace.

b rules administered by a government agency.

c selling a publicly owned corporation to private shareholders.

d cartelization of a competitive industry.

e the formation of monopolies.

25 A natural monopoly is likely to have

a low fixed cost and low marginal cost.

b low fixed cost and high marginal cost.

c high fixed cost and low marginal cost.

d high fixed cost and high marginal cost.

e high fixed cost and increasing marginal cost.

Short Answer Problems

1 Regulation of monopoly is necessary because of the tension between the public interest and the producer's interest. Explain.

2 In the regulation of a natural monopoly, when would an average cost pricing rule be better than a marginal cost pricing rule?

3 Why is rate of return regulation equivalent to average cost pricing?

4 Explain the problem that the recent deregulation process poses for the capture theory of intervention.

5 Suppose the government tried to eliminate monopoly profit by taxing each unit of monopoly output.

a What effect would such a policy have on the quantity a monopolist produces and the price it charges?

b What is the effect on economic efficiency?

ⓔⓓ**6** The demand for Aerodisks, a disk made from a unique material that flies a considerable distance when thrown, is given by the equation

$$P = 10 - 0.01 Q_D.$$

The corresponding marginal revenue (MR) equation is

$$MR = 10 - 0.02 Q.$$

The Aerodisk Company is a natural monopoly. The firm's total fixed cost is $700 and the marginal cost is constant at $2 per disk. [*Note*: This implies that average variable cost is also constant at $2 per disk.] Suppose that the Aerodisk Company is *not* regulated.

a What will be the quantity sold and the price of an Aerodisk?

b How much is economic profit or loss?

c How much is producer surplus?

d How much is consumer surplus?

e How much is total surplus?

ⓔⓓ**7** Now suppose that the Aerodisk Company becomes regulated and that the regulator uses a marginal cost pricing rule.

a What will be the quantity sold and the price of an Aerodisk?

b How much is economic profit or loss?

c How much is producer surplus?

d How much is consumer surplus?

e How much is total surplus?

8 Suppose that the regulator of the Aerodisk Company uses an average cost pricing rule.

a What will be the price of an Aerodisk and how many will be sold?

b How much is economic profit or loss?

c How much is producer surplus?

d How much is consumer surplus?

e How much is total surplus?

9 Since the Aerodisk Company will make a loss under marginal cost pricing, the government must subsidize the production of Aerodisks in order for the firm to be willing to produce.

a What is the total subsidy necessary under a marginal cost pricing rule to leave the firm with a zero economic profit?

b What is the amount of the deadweight loss associated with an average cost pricing rule?

c In order to pay the necessary subsidy under the marginal cost rule, the government must raise tax revenue in the amount of the subsidy. If the deadweight loss associated with the tax is $100, which pricing rule is superior?

10 Figure 20.3 illustrates the industry demand, marginal revenue (MR) and marginal cost (MC) curves in an oligopoly industry. The industry is regulated.

a What price and quantity will be predicted by the public interest theory of regulation? Why?

b What price and quantity will be predicted by the capture theory of regulation? Why?

c Can you explain why the firms in this industry might be demanders of regulation?

FIGURE **20.3**

A N S W E R S

True/False/Uncertain and Explain

1	T	See text discussion. (455–456)
2	F	True for competition. (455–456)
3	T	Regulators act in interest of monopoly. (462–463)
4	F	Matches public interest theory. (462–465)
5	U	True according to public interest theory, false according to capture theory. (457–458)
6	F	Industry captures more of total surplus. (457–458)
7	F	More like average cost pricing. (460–462)
8	T	↑ costs → ↑profits. (462–463)
9	F	Serving producers. (463–465)
10	T	See text discussion. (468–469)

Multiple-Choice

1	c	Crown corporation. (458–459)
2	b	Definition. (455–456)
3	d	No major economies of scale. (459–460)
4	e	Create legislation. (456–457)
5	c	Pricing rule for allocative efficiency. (455–456)
6	a	Pricing rule of monopoly profit maximization. (455–456)
7	e	b, c → ↑ demand by buyers. (456–457)
8	b	Reverse a, c true. (456–457)
9	d	See Text Table 20.2. (465–466)
10	a	Definition natural monopoly. (459–460)
11	c	Where $MC = MR$. (459–461)
12	d	Where $P = ATC$. (459–461)
13	e	Where $P = MC$. (459–461)
14	d	To cover loss per unit of output. (460–461)
15	c	See Text Fig. 20.3. (459–461)
16	a	To increase profits. (461–462)
17	a	Only option → ↑ efficiency. (457–458)
18	c	Helps airline firms, not consumers. (457–458)
19	b	See text discussion. (457–458)
20	c	See text discussion. (455)
21	e	See Text Fig. 20.7(b). (465–467)
22	b	Attempt to achieve allocative efficiency. (457–458)
23	c	See text discussion. (455–456)
24	b	See text discussion. (455)
25	c	Yielding always downward sloping ATC. (459–460)

Short Answer Problems

1 It is in the public interest to achieve allocative efficiency; that is, to expand output to the level that maximizes total surplus. On the other hand, it is in the interest of the monopoly producer to restrict output in order to maximize producer surplus and thus monopoly profit.

Since these interests are not the same, monopoly must be regulated in order to achieve allocative efficiency. The public interest theory of regulation suggests that this is the principle that guides regulation of monopoly industries.

2 An average cost pricing rule will create a deadweight loss but so will a marginal cost pricing rule, through the need to impose a tax.

Since, for a natural monopoly, marginal cost is less than average total cost, regulation by use of a marginal cost pricing rule requires the government to pay a subsidy in order for the firm to be willing to produce at all.

In order to pay that subsidy the government must levy a tax that will impose a deadweight loss on the economy. If the deadweight loss associated with the tax (for example, the deadweight loss of the marginal cost pricing rule with its attendant subsidy) is greater than the deadweight loss of an average cost pricing rule, the average cost pricing rule is superior.

3 The key here is to recall that economic cost includes a normal rate of return. Thus because rate of return regulation sets a price that allows the firm to achieve a normal rate of return, it is setting the price equal to average total cost.

4 The capture theory predicts that producers will capture the regulatory process and use it to maximize producer surplus. But if the producer lobby was strong enough to achieve regulation, why have producers been unable to stop deregulation? A further question is why do many producers *favour* deregulation? The capture theory has no good answers to these questions.

5 a Imposing a tax on each unit sold by a monopolist will increase marginal cost. As a consequence the profit-maximizing monopolist will raise the price and reduce the quantity produced.

b The tax will certainly reduce the profit of the monopolist and may even eliminate it, but the consequence will be to make the inefficiency due to monopoly even worse. This is illustrated in Fig. 20.4. The curve *MC* is the marginal cost curve before the tax. An unregulated monopolist will produce amount Q_2, while the economically efficient output is Q_3. The tax, however, causes the monopolist to reduce output from Q_2 to Q_1, which moves the market outcome farther away from efficiency.

FIGURE **20.4**

©Ø 6 Figure 20.5 will be helpful in answering questions about the Aerodisk market. It gives the relevant revenue and cost curves for the Aerodisk Company.

FIGURE **20.5**

a In an unregulated market, the Aerodisk Company will choose output so as to maximize profit, where $MR = MC$. To calculate this output, set $MR = MC = 2$ and solve for Q:

$$10 - 0.02Q = 2$$
$$8 = 0.02Q$$
$$400 = Q$$

To calculate price, substitute $Q = 400$ into the demand equation:

$$P = 10 - 0.01Q_D$$
$$= 10 - 0.01(400)$$
$$= 10 - 4$$
$$= 6$$

400 Aerodisks will be produced and sold at a price of $6 each.

b To determine economic profit we first determine average total cost (*ATC*) when output (*Q*) is 400 units.

$$ATC = AFC + AVC$$
$$= (TFC/Q) + AVC$$
$$= (700/400) + 2$$
$$= 3.75$$

Therefore economic profit is the difference between price (average revenue) and *ATC* times the quantity sold. This is equal to $900 and is represented in Fig. 20.5 by region *fbdg*.

c Producer surplus is the difference between the producer's revenue and the opportunity cost of production. Total revenue is $2,400 ($6 × 400 units) and total opportunity cost is $800 ($2 × 400 units). Thus producer surplus is $1,600. Graphically, producer surplus is the area of rectangle *abde* in Fig. 20.5.

d Consumer surplus is readily obtained graphically as the area in triangle *bcd* in Fig. 20.5. The area of that triangle is $800.

e Total surplus is $2,400, the sum of producer and consumer surplus.

7 a Under a marginal cost pricing rule, the price of an Aerodisk will be equal to marginal cost or $2. To calculate the quantity sold, substitute the price into the demand equation:

$$P = 10 - 0.01Q_D$$
$$2 = 10 - 0.01Q_D$$
$$0.01Q_D = 8$$
$$Q_D = 800.$$

b To determine the amount of economic profit or loss, we must first determine ATC when output is 800. Using the procedure in the previous problem we find that at $Q = 800$, ATC is $2.875, which is greater than price by $0.875 (87.5¢). Therefore the Aerodisk Company will make a loss in the amount of $700 ($0.875 × 800). Alternatively, since MC is constant, if the price is set equal to MC which is equal to AVC, the total loss will be just TFC or $700.

c Producer surplus is zero.

d Consumer surplus is given by the area of triangle *ach* in Fig. 20.5, which is $3,200.

e Total surplus is $3,200 (a maximum).

8 a Computation of ATC at various levels of output allows us to determine that the ATC curve crosses the demand curve when $Q = 700$ and $ATC = \$3$. Thus under an average cost pricing rule, the price of an Aerodisk will be $3 and 700 units will be sold.

b Since price is equal to average total cost, economic profit is zero.

c Producer surplus is $700, area *aijh* in Fig. 20.5.

d Consumer surplus is $2,450, the area of triangle *ijc* in Fig. 20.5.

e Total surplus is $3,150.

9 a The total subsidy is equal to the loss under marginal cost pricing. In Short Answer Problem **7b** we computed this to be $700.

b The deadweight loss associated with the average cost pricing rule is the loss of total surplus relative to the marginal cost pricing rule. We have computed the total surplus under marginal cost pricing ($3,200) in Short Answer Problem **7e** and the total surplus under average cost pricing ($3,150) in Short Answer Problem **8e**. The deadweight loss is the difference: $50.

c The average cost pricing rule is superior because it has the smaller deadweight loss.

10 a The public interest theory predicts that regulators will set price and quantity so as to maximize total surplus. This means that they will choose quantity (and price) where MC is equal to demand. This corresponds to a quantity of 500 units and a price of $4 per unit.

b The capture theory predicts that the regulator will choose quantity and price so as to maximize the profit of the industry. This is the quantity that would be chosen by a profit-maximizing monopolist, 300 units, where $MC = MR$. The highest price that could be charged and still sell that quantity can be read from the demand curve: $6 per unit.

c Firms in the industry would be demanders of regulation if the regulation had the effect of increasing profit to the industry. As we discovered in Chapter 13, cartels are unstable because there is always an incentive to cheat on output restriction agreements and it is very difficult to enforce the agreements. If, however, the firms in an industry can get the government, through regulation, to enforce a cartel agreement, they will want to do it.

Externalities, the Environment, and Knowledge

Externalities

Externality is cost or benefit from production or consumption activities that affects people who are not part of the original activity. Externalities may be negative (from pollution) or positive (from education).

◆ *External cost* (negative externality)—cost of producing a good/service not borne by consumers but by others.

◆ *External benefit* (positive externality)—benefit from consuming a good/service going not to consumers but to others.

Externalities create market failure (allocative *in*efficiency). Markets overproduce goods/services with external costs and underproduce goods/services with external benefits.

Economics of the Environment

Many people assume that all environmental damage must be stopped. Economic analysis of the environment, however, evaluates the costs and benefits of actions in order to identify efficient amounts of pollution or environmental damage.

◆ Demand ↑ over time for a cleaner environment due to ↑ incomes (high-quality environment is a normal good) and ↑ knowledge about environmental problems. Environmental problems include air pollution, water pollution, and land pollution.

Externalities arise because of an *absence* of property rights.

◆ **Property rights** are social arrangements governing ownership, use, and disposal of factors of production and goods and services. In Canada, property rights are legally established titles enforceable in court.

◆ Without property rights, for example in a river, the marginal cost (*MC*) of polluting the river is zero. Firms will pollute as long as a marginal benefit (*MB*) of polluting is greater than zero. Negative externalities like pollution can often be corrected by establishing property rights.

◆ **Coase theorem**—if property rights are established and transactions costs are low, there will be no externalities and private transactions will be efficient. How property rights are assigned will *not* affect the efficiency of the outcome, but will affect the distribution of costs and benefits.

Where property rights cannot be established or transactions costs are high, other policies can be used by government regulators to achieve efficiency even with externalities.

◆ To achieve efficiency, policies must yield a quantity of output where marginal social cost = marginal social benefit.

• **Marginal social cost** (*MSC*) equals marginal private cost directly incurred by producer *plus* marginal cost imposed as externality on others.
• **Marginal social benefit** (*MSB*) equals marginal private benefit directly received by consumer *plus* marginal benefit received as externality by others.

◆ Emission charges—policy of setting a price per unit of pollution so that *MSC* = *MSB*. In practice,

• difficult to determine marginal benefit of pollution
• polluters have incentive to mislead regulators about benefit.

◆ Marketable permits—quantitative limits on emissions that overcome the need for the regulator to know firms' marginal benefits of pollution. Each firm given a pollution limit (permit) that can be bought and sold.

- Firms reducing their pollution below their limit can sell the "excess" reduction to other firms who then can pollute more.
- In a competitive market for permits, price of permits will yield efficient outcome where $MSC = MSB$.

◆ Taxes—to control a negative externality, regulator can impose a tax equal to external marginal cost.

- This makes the MSC curve the relevant MC curve for the polluting producer's decision → output where $MSC = MSB$.

A carbon-fuel tax would limit carbon emissions and potentially limit global warming of the atmosphere.

◆ There is no such tax because there is scientific uncertainty about carbon dioxide's contribution to global warming and uncertainty about the costs of global warming; costs would be borne now while uncertain benefits would accrue only in the future; and there are problems of international cooperation.

◆ Industrial and developing countries are in a prisoners' dilemma game where no one cuts back carbon dioxide emissions because it is in every country's interest to let others carry the costs of environmental policies.

The Economics of Knowledge

Knowledge creates significant external benefits, so that the marginal social benefit (MSB) exceeds the marginal private benefit (MPB). Market outcomes that result from choosing quantities where $MPB = MSC$ yield less than the efficient quantity of knowledge; there is *market failure*.

To achieve efficiency, policies must yield a quantity of knowledge output where $MSB = MSC$.

◆ Subsidies—payment by government to producers of knowledge-based goods/services.

- To encourage production of goods/services with a positive externality, pay subsidy to producers equal to external marginal benefit.
- This makes the MSB curve the relevant MB curve for the knowledge producer's decision → output where $MSB = MSC$.

◆ Below-cost provisions—government provides the good/service (public education) and charges a price (often zero) below cost.

◆ **Patents** and **copyrights**—provide creators of knowledge with **intellectual property rights** in their discoveries, and help insure that the creator will profit.

- Because knowledge does not seem to have *diminishing marginal productivity*, incentives must be created to encourage an efficient level of development of new ideas.
- Patents and copyrights encourage development of new knowledge, but create a temporary monopoly, so gains from ↑ knowledge must be balanced against loss from monopoly.

H E L P F U L   H I N T S

1 A competitive market will result in the quantity of output at which the marginal private cost is equal to the marginal private benefit. The efficient quantity is the quantity at which marginal social cost is equal to marginal social benefit.

The difference between *marginal social cost* and *marginal private cost* is external cost, and the difference between *marginal social benefit* and *marginal private benefit* is external benefit.

In most economic activities, people who are not part of the original activity are not affected, so there are no external costs or benefits. This means that private and social costs and benefits coincide and competitive markets will be efficient. However, when third parties are affected, there are external costs or benefits and competitive markets will *not* be efficient. Markets overproduce goods/services with external costs and underproduce goods/services with external benefits.

2 Competitive markets with externalities are not efficient because some of the costs or benefits are *external*. If those costs or benefits could be *internalized* somehow, then the market would be efficient. There are two main approaches to internalizing externalities that are discussed in this chapter.

The first is to clearly define and strictly enforce property rights. Then costs imposed on people who are not part of the original activity can be recovered through the legal process and will thus be paid by those involved in the activity: the costs will become internal (private).

The second approach to internalizing externalities is to tax activities that generate external costs and subsidize activities that generate external benefits. By charging a tax equal to the external cost, the entire cost becomes internal. Similarly, by paying a subsidy in the amount of external benefits, the entire benefit becomes internal.

3 If the production of a good or service produces external costs, a competitive market will result in a quantity that exceeds the allocatively efficient level. Text Fig. 21.7, reproduced as Fig. 21.1, illustrates that taxing the production of that good or service can induce the allocatively efficient quantity. The example is of transportation services, which produce external costs of pollution and congestion.

FIGURE **21.1**

The demand curve for transportation services is the same as the marginal benefit curve. The marginal private cost (MPC) and marginal social cost (MSC) curves are *not* the same, however. The MPC curve reflects the costs that directly accrue to the producer of transportation services. There are, however, other costs in the form of pollution and congestion that are imposed on others. The MSC curve reflects both the marginal cost incurred by the producer and these external costs.

The allocatively efficient quantity of transportation services occurs at Q_1, the intersection of the $D = MB$ curve and the MSC curve. A competitive market, however, will result in the quantity at which the D and MPC curves intersect since producers only take private costs into account; market price will be P_0 and

quantity will be Q_0, which is greater than the allocatively efficient quantity.

If, however, a tax is levied on producers in the amount of the external costs, the MSC curve becomes the new relevant marginal cost curve for producers. As a result, the market price will rise to P_1 and the quantity will fall to Q_1, and allocative efficiency is achieved. Note that the efficient quantity of output is not zero, which means that there will be some pollution and congestion. The efficient (optimal) level of pollution/congestion is not zero.

Generally, the costs saved by reducing pollution to zero are less than the benefits lost (benefits from consuming goods whose production created pollution as a by-product).

SELF-TEST

True/False/Uncertain and Explain

1 If negative externalities exist, marginal social cost and external cost are equivalent.

2 If the production of a good involves no external cost, then marginal social cost is equal to marginal private cost.

3 Externalities often arise from the absence of private property rights.

4 The existence of external benefits means that marginal social cost is less than marginal private cost.

5 When external costs are present, the private market will tend to produce more than the allocatively efficient level of output.

6 Assigning property rights solves the problem of a negative externality.

7 The allocatively efficient quantity of pollution is always zero.

8 Patents encourage invention and innovation.

9 Marketable pollution permits require regulators to know firms' marginal benefit schedules.

10 The outcome of a global warming dilemma game is that industrial countries control pollution and developing countries pollute.

Multiple-Choice

1 An externality is a cost or benefit arising from an economic activity that falls on
a consumers but not producers.
b producers but not consumers.
c free riders.
d rivals.
e none of the above.

2 Figure 21.2 depicts the demand for good *A* as well as the marginal private cost (*MPC*) and marginal social cost (*MSC*) associated with the production of good *A*. Production of the sixth unit of output generates an *external*
a cost of $1.50.
b cost of $3.
c cost of $6.
d benefit of $3.
e benefit of $6.

FIGURE **21.2**

3 In Fig. 21.2, how many units of good *A* will be produced in an unregulated market?
a 0 units
b 5 units
c 6 units
d 8 units
e impossible to calculate without additional information

4 In Fig. 21.2, what is the allocatively efficient quantity of good *A*?
a 0 units
b 5 units
c 6 units
d 8 units
e impossible to calculate without additional information

5 At the current level of production of buckyballs, marginal social benefit is less than marginal social cost. To achieve allocative efficiency,
a buckyballs should be taxed.
b buckyballs should not be produced.
c output of buckyballs should increase.
d output of buckyballs should decrease.
e property rights in buckyballs should be established.

6 Which of the following illustrates the concept of external cost?
a Bad weather reduces the size of the wheat crop.
b A reduction in the size of the wheat crop causes the income of wheat farmers to fall.
c Smoking harms the health of the smoker.
d Smoking harms the health of nearby nonsmokers.
e Public health services reduce the transmission of disease.

7 The production of too many goods with negative externalities is an example of
a redistribution.
b consumer sovereignty.
c producer sovereignty.
d public failure.
e market failure.

8 Figure 21.3 depicts the demand curve for good *B*, the marginal social benefit (*MSB*) curve, and marginal private and social cost (*MPC = MSC*) curve. How many units of good *B* will be produced and consumed in an unregulated market?

a 0 units
b 3 units
c 5 units
d 6 units
e 9 units

FIGURE **21.3**

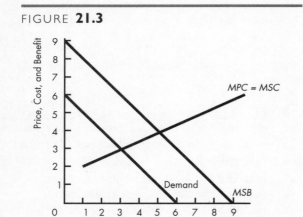

9 In Fig. 21.3, what is the allocatively efficient quantity of good *B*?

a 0 units
b 3 units
c 5 units
d 6 units
e 9 units

10 In Fig. 21.3, which of the following government policies would induce the market to achieve allocative efficiency?

a Tax the production of *B* at $3 per unit.
b Tax the production of *B* at $4 per unit.
c Subsidize the consumption of *B* at $1 per unit.
d Subsidize the consumption of *B* at $3 per unit.
e Subsidize the consumption of *B* at $4 per unit.

11 When market failure occurs, the government will act to reduce the level of inefficiency. This is a prediction of a(n)

a end-state theory of government behaviour.
b process theory of government behaviour.
c public interest theory of government behaviour.
d public choice theory of government behaviour.
e rent-seeking theory of government behaviour.

12 An externality is

a the amount by which price exceeds marginal private cost.
b the amount by which price exceeds marginal social cost.
c the effect of government regulation on market price and output.
d someone who consumes a good without paying for it.
e a cost or benefit that arises from a decision but is not borne by the decision maker.

13 The marginal private cost curve (*MPC*) is a positively sloped straight line starting at the origin. If external costs per unit of output are constant, then the marginal *social* cost curve is a positively sloped straight line

a parallel to and above *MPC*.
b parallel to and below *MPC*.
c starting at the origin and above *MPC*.
d starting at the origin and below *MPC*.
e identical to *MPC*.

14 A market economy tends to _____ goods with negative externalities and _____ goods with positive externalities.

a overproduce; overproduce
b overproduce; underproduce
c underproduce; overproduce
d underproduce; underproduce
e produce; consume

15 Policies for correcting problems of negative externalities include all of the following *except*

a emission charges.
b patents.
c quantitative limits.
d taxes.
e marketable permits.

16 Policies to achieve allocative efficiency when there are external benefits include

a intellectual property rights.
b subsidies.
c below-cost provision.
d all of the above.
e none of the above.

17 A battery acid producer pollutes the water upstream from the nude swimmers belonging to the Polar Bear Club. If transactions costs are low, the quantity of pollution will be efficient

a only if Ronald Coase is a member of the Polar Bear Club.

b only if the distribution of costs and benefits is equal.

c only if water property rights are assigned to the producer.

d only if water property rights are assigned to the Polar Bear Club.

e if water property rights are assigned either to the producer or the Polar Bear Club.

18 Knowledge, as a factor of production,

a displays diminishing marginal productivity.

b creates external costs.

c has costs totalling those paid to the patent holder.

d is encouraged by intellectual property rights.

e is all of the above.

19 The income elasticity of demand for a better environment is

a negative.

b zero.

c positive.

d trendy.

e impossible to know without additional information.

20 The production of too few goods with positive externalities is an example of

a market failure.

b government failure.

c producer sovereignty.

d consumer sovereignty.

e external costs.

21 Polluters are best informed about the marginal benefits of pollution and have an incentive to mislead regulators about those benefits. An emission charge set by the regulators will likely be too

a high, resulting in excessive pollution.

b high, resulting in excessive cleanup.

c low, resulting in excessive pollution.

d low, resulting in excessive cleanup.

e good to be true.

22 Refer to Table 21.1. If the fertilizer market is perfectly competitive and unregulated, output is

a 1.

b 2.

c 3.

d 4.

e 5,

TABLE **21.1** CHEMICAL FERTILIZER MARKET

Output (tonnes)	Marginal Private Benefit ($)	Marginal Social Benefit ($)	Marginal Private Cost ($)	Marginal Social Cost ($)
1	140	140	50	80
2	120	120	60	90
3	100	100	70	100
4	80	80	80	110
5	60	60	90	120

23 Refer to Table 21.1. Fertilizer has a marginal external

a cost of $100.

b benefit of $100.

c cost of $30.

d benefit of $30.

e cost of $0.

24 Refer to Table 21.1. The allocatively efficient output of fertilizer is

a 1.

b 2.

c 3.

d 4.

e 5.

25 In the past, the levels of chlorofluorocarbons (CFCs) in refrigerators and aerosols have been

a less than socially optimal due to external costs.

b less than socially optimal due to external benefits.

c more than socially optimal due to external costs.

d more than socially optimal due to external benefits.

e decreasing the earth's average temperature.

Short Answer Problems

1 Governments provide education for free, or at least at a price (tuition) much less than cost. What is the economic argument that supports this policy?

2 Explain how a tax can be used to achieve efficiency in the face of external costs.

3 The production of steel also produces pollution and thus generates an external cost. Suppose the government attempts to solve the problem by imposing a tax on steel producers (who also produce pollution). At the after-tax level of output, we observe that the original marginal social cost curve is below the demand curve. Is the after-tax level of output efficient? If it is not, should steel production, and therefore pollution production, be increased or decreased?

4 Your roommate is an environmentalist who is appalled at the economic concept of an "efficient" level of pollution. She argues that since everyone agrees that pollution is "bad," society must work towards eliminating all pollution. How would you, as an economics major, convince her that it is not in society's best interests to eliminate all pollution?

5 What are the benefits and costs of creating intellectual property rights for the creation of new knowledge?

6 Two prairie pioneers, Jethro and Hortense, have adjacent fields. Because they get along so well and always work out any problems that arise, they have not bothered to put up a fence. Then one day Jethro buys a new pig, Babe. Babe sometimes wanders into Hortense's field and eats her corn. If Babe would only stay on Jethro's farm, he would eat valueless garbage. Suppose that Babe eats $500 worth of Hortense's corn per year (a negative externality imposed on Hortense) and that to build a fence between the farms costs $300. No property rights to keep animals off the fields have been established yet.
   a If the property right is given to Jethro so Babe can continue to wander, will Hortense build a fence? Explain.
   b If, instead, the property right is given to Hortense, so that she can charge Jethro for the corn Babe eats, will Jethro build a fence? Explain.
   c Explain how this example illustrates the Coase theorem.

7 The first two columns of Table 21.2 give the demand schedule for education in Hicksville, while the third column gives the marginal private cost. In Hicksville, unlike the textbook example of education, marginal cost increases with the quantity of students. Since education generates external benefits, marginal social benefit given in the last column is greater than marginal private benefit.

TABLE **21.2**

Quantity (number of students)	Marginal Private Benefit ($)	Marginal Private Cost ($)	Marginal Social Benefit ($)
100	500	200	800
200	400	250	700
300	300	300	600
400	200	350	500
500	100	400	400
600	0	450	300

   a Represent the data in Table 21.2 graphically.
   b What equilibrium price and quantity would result if the market for education is unregulated?
   c What is the allocatively efficient quantity of students in Hicksville?

8 In an attempt to address the inefficient level of education in Hicksville, the town council has decided to subsidize schooling. The council offers $200 to each student who buys a year of education.
   a Draw the new marginal private benefit curve, which includes the subsidy, on your graph and label it MPB_1.
   b What are the approximate new equilibrium price and quantity?

9 The Hicksville town council increases the subsidy to $400.
   a Draw another marginal private benefit curve, which includes the subsidy, on your graph and label it MPB_2.
   b What are the approximate corresponding equilibrium price and quantity?
   c What level of subsidy will achieve the efficient quantity of education?

10 Lever Sisters Company produces Flatulost, a popular room deodorizer. Unfortunately, the production process releases sulfur dioxide into the atmosphere. The marginal private cost (*MPC*) to Lever Sisters of producing Flatulost is

$$MPC = 1Q_S.$$

The marginal social cost (*MSC*) is

$$MSC = 3/2 Q_S.$$

The demand curve for Flatulost (there are no external benefits) is

$$P = 12 - 1/2 Q_D.$$

Q_S is the quantity of Flatulost supplied, P is the price of Flatulost in dollars, and Q_D is the quantity demanded.

a In an unregulated market, what is the equilibrium quantity of Flatulost? the equilibrium price?

b To achieve allocative efficiency, what should be the equilibrium quantity of Flatulost? the equilibrium price?

c Compare the unregulated market quantity and price with the allocatively efficient quantity and price.

d The government wants to impose a tax on Flatulost to achieve the allocatively efficient quantity of output. What should the tax be?

ANSWERS

True/False/Uncertain and Explain

1 F $MSC = MPC +$ externality. (485–486)

2 T $MSC = MPC +$ externality. (485–486)

3 T Property rights would allow recovery of (external) costs. (480–482)

◑ 4 F External benefits affect MSB, not MSC. (489–490)

5 T Where MPC (instead of MSC) intersects demand. (477–478)

6 U True if transactions costs are low; false otherwise. (482–483)

7 F Quantity where $MSB = MSC$ of pollution. (485–487)

8 T Intellectual property rights overcome positive externality problem of knowledge. (490–491)

9 F Permits overcome the need for regulators to know. (484–485)

10 F All countries have dominant strategy of polluting. (487–488)

Multiple-Choice

1 e Falls on third party. (477)

◑ 2 b Vertical distance between MSC and MPC at $Q = 6$. (485–486)

3 d Where MPC intersects demand. (485–486)

4 b Where MSC intersects demand. (485–486)

5 d Draw graph. Don't know if positive, negative, or any externality. (489–490)

6 d Cost falls on third party. (477)

7 e Failure to achieve allocative efficiency. (477–478)

8 b Where MC intersects demand. (489–490)

9 c Where MC intersects MSB. (489–490)

◑ 10 d Shift MC down by vertical distance between MSB and demand. (489–490)

11 c Public interest to achieve allocative efficiency. (418–419, 457)

12 e Definition. (477)

◑ 13 a MPC shifts up by vertical distance equal to external cost per unit. (485–486)

14 b Outcomes of market failure. (477–478)

15 b Patents correct problems of positive externalities. (483–487)

16 d All move output to where $MSB = MSC$. (489–491)

17 e This is the Coase theorem. (480–483)

18 d No ↓ marginal productivity; creates external benefits; patent monopoly → loss from restricted use. (488–491)

19 c Better environment is normal good so $\eta_y > 0$. (478–479)

20 a Markets fail to produce the allocatively efficient quantity of goods with positive externalities. (477–478)

21 c True MB greater than that reported, so true MB curve above reported curve. (483–485)

22 d Where $MPB = MPC = 80$. (485–486)

23 c $MSC - MPC$ is constant in this example. (485–486)

24 c Where $MSB = MSC$. (485–486)

25 c Market overproduction of good with external costs. (485–486)

Short Answer Problems

1 Government subsidizes education heavily. The economic argument is that education generates external benefits. In particular, when individuals are educated, society at large receives benefits beyond the private benefits that accrue to those choosing how much education to obtain.

2 The existence of external costs means that producers do not take into account all costs when deciding how much to produce. If a tax is levied that is exactly the amount of the external cost, the cost will no longer be external. As a result, the producer will take it into account and thus be induced to produce the efficient quantity.

3 Since the marginal social cost curve is below the demand curve at the after-tax output, marginal social cost is less than marginal benefit. This means that the tax has been set too high; it has been set at a level in excess of the external cost. As a result, the after-tax level of steel production will be less than the efficient level. The level of steel production and pollution production

should be increased by decreasing the amount of the tax.

4 We all want to eliminate pollution, *ceteris paribus*, but every action, including reducing pollution, has a cost. Once again, the key concept underlying the economic argument is opportunity cost. What is the opportunity cost of reducing pollution, or, what does society have to give up to achieve a pollution-free environment?

Small reductions in pollution are relatively inexpensive—eliminating lead from gasoline and paint, conserving energy to reduce output from coal-fired electrical plants, etc. But to eliminate all pollution would mean eliminating all cars and airplanes, outlawing all power except solar and hydroelectric power, shutting down most factories, etc. The cost of eliminating *all* pollution is enormous, and that additional cost is far greater than the additional benefits from further reductions in pollution. Therefore some level of pollution is efficient. Pollution is part of the opportunity cost of the benefits we receive from driving or flying instead of walking, from enjoying the comfort of air conditioning in hot weather, and from enjoying goods produced in factories. The efficient level of pollution balances the marginal social cost of the pollution against the marginal social benefit of the production and consumption associated with that level of pollution.

5 Intellectual property rights create incentives for individuals to create new knowledge by granting the inventor a limited monopoly to benefit from the application of her idea. Without the property right, anyone could freely use the idea and there would be little profit to the inventor. The limited monopoly, although necessary as an incentive to produce knowledge, has a social cost—the restriction of knowledge-based output below the efficient, competitive quantity.

6 a Hortense will build a fence. Although the fence costs $300 per year, it saves her the $500 in lost corn that Babe would otherwise eat.

b Jethro will build a fence. The $300 per year is less than the $500 per year he would now have to pay Hortense for Babe's wanderings.

c The Coase theorem states that if transactions costs are low and property rights are established, there are no externalities and an efficient outcome occurs regardless of who is assigned the property right. Because Jethro and Hortense can work out their problems amicably, transactions

costs are low. The outcome of building a fence eliminates the negative externality of the wandering pig and occurs regardless of which pioneer is assigned the property right. The outcome is efficient because, for this one decision, the $300 cost to society of the fence is less than the $500 cost of consumed corn.

7 a Figure 21.4 is a graphical representation of the data in Table 21.2. The demand for education is given by the marginal private benefit curve (labelled *MPB*), the marginal private cost curve is labelled *MPC* and the marginal social benefit curve is labelled *MSB*. Ignore the other curves for now.

FIGURE **21.4**

b In an unregulated market, equilibrium price and quantity are determined by the intersection of the *MPB* and *MPC* curves. Thus the equilibrium price would be $300 and the equilibrium quantity is 300 students.

c Since there are no external costs, the efficient quantity is determined by the intersection of the *MPC* and *MSB* curves. This implies that allocative efficiency is attained at a quantity of 500 students.

8 a The subsidy increases the marginal private benefit to each student by the amount of the subsidy, $200. The new *MPB* curve, labelled MPB_1, is included in Fig. 21.4.

b The new equilibrium after the $200 subsidy is at the intersection of the *MPC* and MPB_1 curves. The price of a unit of education will be approximately $370 and there will be approximately 430 students.

9 a With a subsidy of $400 per student, the *MPB* curve will shift to MPB_2 in Fig. 21.4.

b With this subsidy the equilibrium will be at the intersection of the *MPC* and MPB_2 curves. The corresponding price of a unit of education will be approximately $430 and the number of students will be approximately 570.

c In order to achieve an efficient outcome, the subsidy must make the *MPB* curve coincide with the *MSB* curve. This requires a subsidy of $300 per student.

10 a In an unregulated market, the equilibrium quantity would be determined by the intersection of the supply (*MPC*) and demand curves. In equilibrium, $Q_S = Q_D = Q^*$. Setting the *MPC* equation equal to the demand equation yields

$$1Q^* = 12 - 1/2Q^*$$
$$3/2Q^* = 12$$
$$Q^* = 8$$

To solve for the equilibrium price (P^*), substitute Q^* into the demand (or into the *MPC*) equation.

$$P^* = 12 - 1/2Q^*$$
$$P^* = 12 - 1/2 (8)$$
$$P^* = 8$$

b In order to achieve allocative efficiency, *MSC* must equal marginal social benefit (*MSB*). Since there are no external benefits, the demand curve is also the *MSB* curve. In equilibrium, $Q_S = Q_D = Q^*$. To find the equilibrium quantity, set the *MSC* equation equal to the demand equation.

$$3/2Q^* = 12 - 1/2Q^*$$
$$2Q^* = 12$$
$$Q^* = 6$$

To solve for the equilibrium price (P^*), substitute Q^* into the demand (or into the *MSC*) equation.

$$P^* = 12 - 1/2Q^*$$
$$P^* = 12 - 1/2 (6)$$
$$P^* = 9$$

c Compared with the allocatively efficient outcomes, the unregulated market produces too much Flatulost (8 units versus 6) and the product sells at too low a price ($8 versus $9).

d The tax should be equal to the cost differential (*MSC* – *MPC*) at the optimum output of 6 units. Since the *MSC* curve = $1.5 \times MPC$ curve, the tax should be 50 percent.

PROBLEM

The Canadian Radio-television and Telecommunications Commission (CRTC) is holding public hearings on renewing the licence of Cretin's Choice Cable TV Company. You have been hired to help the CRTC evaluate the contradictory claims made by different interest groups in testimony to the commission. Figure P4.1 shows the best available information about costs and revenues for Cretin's Choice.

FIGURE **P4.1**

a   On the basis of Fig. P4.1, explain why there is market failure and a potential role for government regulation.
b   Cretin's Choice would like to maximize its profits. Identify the firm's profit-maximizing rule and explain the outcome (price, quantity, economic profit, consumer's surplus, deadweight loss) on Fig. P4.1.

c   Consumer groups are pushing for a regulatory rule that maximizes consumer surplus. Identify the rule and explain the outcome (price, quantity, economic profit, consumer's surplus) on Fig. P4.1. If the CRTC adopts the rule, what options might you suggest that would keep the cable company in business?
d   Any CRTC regulation rule has to appear to meet the public interest goal of maximum allocative efficiency. Identify the rule (other than marginal cost pricing) that comes closest to achieving this goal and explain the outcome (price, quantity, economic profit, consumer's surplus, deadweight loss) on Fig. P4.1.
e   While Cretin's Choice wants maximum profits, it recognizes the CRTC's need to *appear* to use the regulatory rule in part **d**. What argument can you expect to hear from Cretin's Choice? Use Fig. P4.1 to explain.
f   If, despite your advice to the contrary, the CRTC accepts the industry argument in part **e**, what theory of regulation is supported?
g   After years of the type of regulation in part **f**, the CRTC deregulates Cretin's Choice's market. If rates of return increase, what theory of regulation is supported?

MIDTERM EXAMINATION

You should allocate 32 minutes for this examination (16 questions, 2 minutes per question). For each question, choose the one *best* answer.

1 Refer to Fig. P4.2. Producer surplus lost from the tax (not including tax paid) is equal to triangle

a *abc.*
b *dbc.*
c *dac.*
d *dij.*
e *gdi.*

FIGURE **P4.2**

2 Refer to Fig. P4.2. Consumer surplus lost from the tax (not including tax paid) is equal to triangle

a *abc.*
b *dbc.*
c *dac.*
d *dij.*
e *gdi.*

3 Total surplus is given by the sum of

a the gain from trade accruing to consumers and the gain from trade accruing to producers.
b the gain from regulation and the gain from anti-combine laws.
c revenues received by firms and government subsidies.
d consumer payments and producer profit.
e none of the above.

4 Consider the natural monopoly in Fig. P4.3. Producer surplus is a maximum when quantity is

a Q_0 and price is P_3.
b Q_1 and price is P_1.
c Q_1 and price is P_4.
d Q_2 and price is P_2.
e Q_3 and price is P_0.

FIGURE **P4.3**

5 The inequality in the distribution of wealth is

a less than the inequality in the distribution of income.
b decreased by the existence of assortative mating.
c a better measure of the inequality in the distribution of economic resources than is the inequality in the distribution of income.
d even greater if we look at the distribution of wealth among the richest 1 percent of all families.
e all of the above.

6 The demand for government intervention in a market depends on

a consumer surplus per buyer.
b number of buyers.
c producer surplus per firm.
d number of firms.
e all of the above.

7 Consider the Lorenz curves in Fig. P4.4. Which point indicates that the richest 20 percent of families earn 60 percent of the income?

a *a*
b *b*
c *c*
d *d*
e none of the above

FIGURE **P4.4**

8 Refer to Fig. P4.5. The unregulated outcome in the paper market is

a quantity = 40, price = 11.
b quantity = 40, price = 13.
c quantity = 50, price = 12.
d quantity = 50, price = 14.
e quantity = 60, price = 13.

FIGURE **P4.5**

9 Refer to Fig. P4.5. A tax of _____ per tonne is necessary to achieve the efficient output of _____ tonnes of paper.

a $14; 50
b $14; 30
c $13; 40
d $2; 50
e $2; 40

10 The public interest theory predicts that the political process seeks to minimize

a producer surplus.
b consumer surplus.
c total surplus.
d deadweight loss.
e allocative efficiency.

11 The factor of production least likely to display diminishing marginal productivity is

a land.
b labour.
c capital.
d entrepreneurship.
e knowledge.

12 According to the Coase theorem, if transactions costs are low and property rights exist,

a negative externalities cause deadweight losses.
b positive externalities cause deadweight losses.
c private transactions are efficient.
d public transactions are efficient.
e the efficient level of pollution will be zero.

13 If the marginal tax rate decreases as income increases, the income tax is defined as

a progressive.
b proportional.
c negative.
d regressive.
e redistributive.

14 Which of the following is *not* part of an individual's true wealth?

a stock of assets
b flow of earnings
c human capital
d physical assets
e financial assets

15 The *total benefit* of a given level of provision of a public good can be obtained by

a adding the marginal benefit of each level of provision up to the given level.
b adding the marginal benefit of each level of provision and then subtracting the marginal cost of each level of provision.
c adding the net benefit of each level of provision up to the given level.
d multiplying net benefit by the quantity of the public good provided.
e none of the above methods.

16 Voters are asked to vote for either proposition *A* or proposition *B*. Proposition *A* will win if it

a is closer to allocative efficiency.
b is supported by bureaucrats.
c is preferred by the median voter.
d generates greater social benefits than social costs.
e generates the fewest negative externalities.

ANSWERS

Problem

a Market failure is the inability of an unregulated market to achieve allocative efficiency. Cretin's Choice is a natural monopoly with economies of scale. While only a monopoly can achieve the economies of scale, in the absence of regulation, it will restrict output, increase price, and create a deadweight efficiency loss.

b The profit-maximizing rule is to choose the quantity of output where $MC = MR$ and charge the highest possible price. On Fig. P4.1, price is *b*, quantity is *k*, economic profit is *bcgf*, consumer's surplus is *abf*, and deadweight loss is *fhp*.

c The marginal cost pricing rule (set price equal to MC) maximizes consumer surplus. On Fig. P4.1, price is *e*, quantity is *q*, loss per unit is *op*, and consumer's surplus is *aep*. The firm is making a loss and will not voluntarily stay in business. You could suggest that the company be allowed to price discriminate or that it receive a government subsidy (financed by taxes that would create a deadweight loss elsewhere).

d An average cost pricing rule sets price equal to ATC. On Fig. P4.1, price is *d*, quantity is *n*, economic profit is zero, consumer's surplus is *adl*, and deadweight loss is *lmp*. If this deadweight loss is less than the deadweight loss associated with subsidizing the marginal cost pricing rule in part **c**, then the average cost price rule comes closest to achieving allocative efficiency.

e Cretin's Choice will argue that their costs are much higher than those reflected in the ATC curve of Fig. P4.1. The company will inflate its costs and argue that its real ATC curve is higher and just tangent to the demand curve at point *f*. If the CRTC accepts this argument and applies the average cost pricing rule, the regulated price and outcome will be the same as the monopolist's own profit-maximizing rule in part **b**.

f If the CRTC accepts the industry argument in part **e**, the capture theory of regulation is supported.

g If, after deregulation, rates of return increase, the public interest theory of regulation is supported.

Midterm Examination

1 a See text discussion. (427–429)

2 b See text discussion. (427–429)

3 a Consumer surplus plus producer surplus. (455–456)

4 c Private monopoly outcome. (459–462)

5 d Reverse **a, b** true. Wealth distribution does not capture human capital resources so **c** false. (437–438)

6 e See text discussion. (456–457)

7 d Moving from 80 percent to 100 percent of families (richest 20 percent) moves income from 40 percent to 100 percent of total (60 percent). (437–438)

8 c Where $D = MSB$ intersects MPC. (485–486)

9 e $2 per tonne tax (vertical distance between MPC and MSC) makes firm's MC equal to MSC. Output where $D = MSB$ intersects MSC. (485–486)

10 d Or maximize allocative efficiency. (457–458)

11 e Because of positive externalities. (488–489)

12 c There are no externalities. Level of pollution where $MSB = MSC$. (482–483)

13 d Definition. (443–444)

14 b Flow of earnings is *income* from individual's stock of wealth. (437–438)

15 a **b–d** involve irrelevant costs. (420–422)

16 c 50 percent of votes plus 1. (426–427)

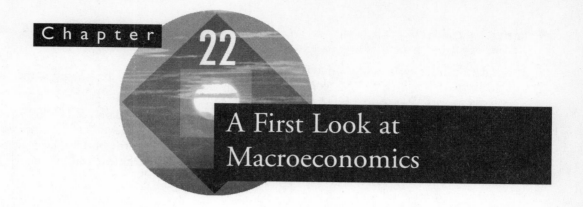

KEY CONCEPTS

Origins and Issues of Macroeconomics

Modern macroeconomics was born during the **Great Depression.**

regardless of long term consequences

◆ Keynes' focus was the short-term problems of the depression, which he thought were caused by too little spending → need for ↑ government spending. ⟹ *But it too could trigger inflation & a ↓ long-term growth rate*

↓ *economic growth & deficits*

◆ Once out of depression, long-term problems of inflation, etc. become central → government spending must be moderated. The events of the 1960s/1970s showed the importance of these long-term problems. ⟹ *↑ inflation, ↓ economic growth, ↑ Unemployment* *↑ or ABOVE*

◆ Recently, macroeconomics has merged the short-term and long-term issues in a broad study of unemployment, economic growth, inflation, and deficits. Our goal is to understand these theories. *& policies* *B/c long & short term most successfully studied together.*

① Jobs and Unemployment

Each year in Canada, many jobs are created and destroyed. Average net effect is 200,000 new jobs, but when production ↓ → more jobs destroyed than created, and vice versa when production ↑. *↓ available*

◆ Unemployment occurs when qualified workers seeking jobs cannot find any. *→ 4 week period*

• **Unemployment rate** is percentage of labour force unemployed. **Labour force** is sum of unemployed and employed.

• Measured unemployment is flawed due to exclusion of discouraged workers and part-time workers who desire full-time work. *considered employed.*

✱Fig 22.1 - Pg 504. Unemployment in Canada

✱ Based on Fig 22.1

◆ Unemployment fluctuated greatly in Canadian history, with peaks occurring in 1930s, early 1980s, and early 1990s, general upward trend since World War II. *war is good for economy 1.2%)* *1982 recession* *(1945)* *(1933) Great Depression @ 19.3%.*

◆ Canadian unemployment moves with U.S. unemployment, but recently has risen to higher levels. *Fig 22.2 - Pg 505.*

◆ Costs of unemployment are lost output of unemployed, deterioration of job prospects, increased crime, and social problems. *→ lost production & lost incomes* *→ education out of date.* *↓ theft, illegal work* *↓ theft, alcoholism, depression, suicide, domestic violence, fear, frustration, lose self-esteem*

② Economic Growth

Economic growth is ↑ in economy's capacity to produce goods and services, measured by ↑ in real *gross* domestic product (real GDP).

◆ **Real GDP** is the value of total production, *(aggregate)* measured in the prices of a single year. *(1986 prices)* *to eliminate influence of inflation & see how much production has grown from year to year.* *✱ Real GDP - does not include total production of underground economy.*

◆ **Potential GDP** is real GDP when labour, capital, land, and entrepreneurial ability are fully employed. *Long-term economic growth is measured by Pot. GDP.* *✱ Fig 22.3*

◆ Economic growth in Canadian history has two features. *✱ Fig 22.3*

• Long-term economic growth, as measured by potential GDP, grew rapidly in the 1960s, but much less rapidly since then due to a productivity slowdown. *1930's & 1960's* *— a slowdown in growth rate of output per person b/c of energy price shocks,*

• There are also **business cycles**, the periodic but irregular fluctuation of real GDP around potential. *GDP.* *structural change & rapid inflation* *eg. when real GDP < pot. GDP, & vice-versa → it means resources are underused (labour is unemployed & capital underutilized)*

◆ Each cycle is irregular, but has two turning points (a *peak* and a *trough*), and two phases (a **recession** when real GDP decreases for two or more periods, and an **expansion** when real GDP increases). *1990-1991.* *GDP is relative* *starts as trough & ends as peak* *begins* *— peak = upper turning point, where expansion ends & recession begins* *— trough = lower turning pt, where recession ends & recovery begins*

✱ Fig 22.3 - Pg 506. Economic Growth in Canada
✱ Fig 22.4 - Pg 507 - Business Cycle

and we have a current account surplus, this tends to create expansionary pressures on real GDP. On the other hand, as the economy expands, Canadians tend to buy more imported goods, pushing the current account towards a deficit.

3 The inflation rate is calculated as the percentage change in prices using the formula

$$\text{Inflation rate} = \frac{\text{Current year's price level} - \text{Last year's price level}}{\text{Last year's price level}} \times 100.$$

For example, the average 1995 price level was 133.5, and the average 1994 price level was 130.7, allowing us to calculate the inflation rate for 1995:

$$\text{Inflation rate} = \frac{133.5 - 130.7}{130.7} \times 100 = 2.1\%.$$

4 Inflation creates problems because it creates unpredictable changes in the value of money. The *value of money* is the quantity of goods and services that can be bought with a given amount of money. When an economy experiences inflation, the value of money falls—you cannot buy as many goods with a dollar this year as you could last year.

To illustrate this point, consider the data in Table 22.1 on the price of a chocolate bar in Canada over the last 46 years:[1]

TABLE **22.1**

Year	Price of Chocolate Bar (¢)	Number of Bars $1 Buys
1950	10	10.00
1966	15	6.67
1976	30	3.33
1986	75	1.33
1996	100	1.00

The table shows us the strong cumulative impact of inflation over this time period, as well as the result that the value of a dollar has fallen enormously over this time period—it buys about 1/10th as many chocolate bars as it did in 1950. When your grandfather tells you "a dollar ain't worth what it used to be," he's telling the truth!

We will return in Chapter 34 to the value of money in more detail.

SELF-TEST

True/False/Uncertain and Explain

1 Higher economic growth is good for an economy.

2 If Canada sells more to the rest of the world than it buys from the rest of the world, Canada will have an international deficit.

3 Canadian unemployment is virtually identical to U.S. unemployment.

4 Discouraged workers are counted as unemployed but probably should not be.

5 In Canada, fiscal policy is implemented by the federal government.

6 In the recession phase of a business cycle, the unemployment rate is rising.

7 A government budget deficit will create problems for the government.

8 Macroeconomics focuses only on short-term problems such as unemployment.

9 If the price level was 130 in 1998, and 110 in 1997, the inflation rate in 1998 was 20 percent.

---

[1] *Source:* Statistics Canada, *The Consumer Price Index,* with calculations and extrapolation from 1989 by H. King.

10 Since inflation is costly, getting rid of it is always a good idea.

Multiple-Choice

1 An example of fiscal policy is changing the
a interest rate.
b money supply.
c exchange rate.
d tax rates.
e all of the above.

2 If the inflation rate is positive, the price level in an economy is
a falling rapidly.
b rising.
c constant.
d falling slowly.
e zero.

3 Most of the time since 1970, the current account
a deficit has been large.
b surplus has been large.
c deficit has been small.
d surplus has been small.
e has had alternating surpluses and deficits.

4 Which of the following statements about modern macroeconomics is correct?
a It was born during the 1960s/1970s.
b It initially focused on short-term problems.
c It focuses only on short-term problems.
d It now merges both short-term and long-term problems.
e Both **b** and **d**.

5 In comparison to the U.S. unemployment rate, the Canadian unemployment rate moves
a independently of the U.S. rate.
b with the U.S. rate, but at a lower level recently.
c in the opposite direction of the U.S. rate.
d with the U.S. rate, but at a higher level recently.
e with the U.S. rate, and at the same level.

6 An unpredictable inflation causes problems because
a it leads to a rise in the variability of the business cycle.
b the stock market falls in value.
c the value of money starts rising.
d resources are diverted from productive activities to tax evasion.
e resources are diverted from productive activities to forecasting inflation.

7 The costs of unemployment include all of the following *except*
a workers quit and go to university.
b child abuse increases.
c lost job prospects.
d crime increases.
e suicide increases.

8 Deficits are a problem
a if they are caused by economic growth.
b only if they are international deficits, not government budget deficits.
c only if they are government budget deficits, not international deficits.
d only when they are caused by borrowing for consumption purposes.
e only when they are caused by borrowing to buy profitable assets.

9 Which of the following statements about long-term economic problems is *true*?
a Keynes ignored them.
b Keynes said they could be cured by increased government spending.
c Economists consider them much less important than short-term problems.
d They include inflation and slow economic growth.
e All of the above.

10 Comparing Canada's economic growth with the major industrial economies' growth shows that
a Canada experienced a slowdown in productivity, but they did not.
b Canada and the United States experienced a slowdown in productivity, but Japan and Germany did not.
c Canada did not experience the slowdown in productivity that the others did.
d Canada always had a lower level of productivity and economic growth.
e All four countries experienced a slowdown in productivity at about the same time.

11 Which one of the following is *not* a policy challenge?

a lowering unemployment
b stabilizing the business cycle
c keeping inflation low
d stopping economic growth
e lowering government deficits

12 Increasing potential GDP is

a always beneficial since living standards rise.
b always too costly since pollution and resource depletion rise.
c beneficial only if pollution rises at 5 percent a year.
d beneficial if the benefits of rising living standards outweigh the costs of higher pollution, etc.
e none of the above.

13 In which of the following years was the unemployment rate in Canada almost 20 percent?

a 1982
b 1976
c 1959
d 1933
e 1926

14 In a country with a population of 20 million, there are 9 million employed and 1 million unemployed. What is the labour force?

a 20 million
b 10 million
c 9 million
d 8 million
e 1 million

15 In a country with a population of 20 million, there are 9 million employed and 1 million unemployed. What is the unemployment rate?

a 11 percent
b 10 percent
c 8 percent
d 5 percent
e 1 percent

16 Which of the following will *increase* the Canadian current account deficit?

a Japan buys wheat from farmers in Canada.
b Japan buys wheat from farmers in Australia.
c Japan buys Canada Savings Bonds.
d Canada buys Toyotas from Japan.
e Canada sells coal to Japan.

17 Which of the following politicians is talking about the business cycle?

a "Canadian unemployment is falling due to the upturn in the economy."
b "Crime rates increase every spring as the school year ends."
c "An average of 200,000 new jobs are created each year in Canada."
d "More capital investment will create more jobs."
e All of the above.

18 Which of the following statements about Canada's inflation rate is false?

a It is currently lower than that of other industrial countries.
b It was low in the 1960s.
c It rose in the 1970s.
d It fell in the 1980s due to the actions of the Bank of Canada.
e Historically, it has always been higher than that of other industrial countries until recently.

19 Including discouraged workers in the measured unemployment rate would

a not change the measured unemployment rate.
b lower the measured unemployment rate.
c lower the labour force.
d raise the measured unemployment rate only if there are no part-time workers.
e raise the measured unemployment rate.

20 Real GDP is defined as the value of all

a goods produced in an economy in a year.
b goods and services produced in an economy in a year.
c final goods produced in an economy in a year.
d final goods and services produced in an economy in a year.
e final goods and services produced in an economy in a year, controlling for the level of inflation.

21 If a price index was 128 at the end of 1987 and 136 at the end of 1988, what was the rate of inflation for 1988?

a 4.2 percent
b 5.9 percent
c 6.25 percent
d 8 percent
e 9.4 percent

22 If the price index in 1997 is equal to 130, and the inflation rate between 1997 and 1998 is 5 percent, then the price index in 1998 is equal to

a 136.5.
b 135.
c 125.
d 123.5.
e 105.

23 An unpredictable inflation is

a costly because the higher inflation will cause unemployment.
b costly because people shift resources from production to predicting inflation.
c not costly because people do not alter their behaviour.
d costly because of the lost output that results.
e none of the above.

24 The government deficit will rise if

a we buy more from other countries than we sell to them.
b we sell more to other countries than we buy from them.
c government revenues rise.
d unemployment rises.
e the baby boomers continue to run the country.

25 Which of the following gives the correct order of the sequence of business cycle phases?

a expansion, peak, recession, trough
b expansion, peak, trough, deviation
c expansion, trough, recession, peak
d expansion, recession, trough, peak
e expansion, deviation, recession, trough

Short Answer Problems

1 What are the economic costs of unemployment?

2 Go to the Statistics Canada World Wide Web site (**http://www.statcan.ca/**) or the Statistics Canada publication *The Consumer Price Index*, and find out the price level in December of the most recent year available, as well as the previous year, and calculate the inflation rate over that year.

3 What is meant by the value of money? Why does the value of money fall when there is inflation?

4 The federal government gives full-time students a tax credit per month of studies. In 1980, Tracy received this credit, which was worth $50 per month, whereas in 1992 Jennifer received a credit worth $60 per month. In 1980, the price level was 62.3, and in 1992 it was 130. Is value of the tax credit money worth more to Jennifer or Tracy? (Ignore any changes in tax codes, etc.)

5 What is the current account? What has its recent history been like?

6 What is happening to real GDP compared to potential GDP, and to the unemployment rate during each of the four parts of the business cycle?

7 Workers and managers in the ABC Company have negotiated a wage agreement under the expectation that the rate of inflation will be zero over the period of the contract. In order to protect the workers against unpredictable inflation, however, the contract states that at the end of each year, the wage rate will increase by the same percentage as the consumer price index (CPI). At the beginning of the contract the CPI is 214 and the wage rate is set at $10 an hour. At the end of the first year the CPI is 225, and at the end of the second year the CPI is 234. What will the new wage rate become at the end of the first year? the second year?

8 Consider the following information about an economy: Population—25 million, employment—10 million, unemployment—1 million.

a What is the labour force in this economy?
b What is the unemployment rate?

9 Consider the following data on unemployment and the growth rate of real GDP from the country of Dazedland:

Year	Percentage Change in Real GDP	Unemployment Rate
1	2.0	7.0
2	3.0	6.0
3	1.0	7.8
4	0.0	9.0
5	–2.0	11.5
6	–0.3	9.5
7	3.0	6.5
8	1.5	7.5

a Identify the peaks and troughs of the business cycle for this economy.

b In what years is this economy in recession?

c What is the relation between unemployment and the business cycle for this economy?

10 Is more economic growth good or bad for a society?

ANSWERS

True/False/Uncertain and Explain

1 U It depends on the benefits versus the costs of the higher growth. (510)

2 F Sales > purchases → international *surplus*. (513–514)

3 F Canadian and U.S. unemployment move together, but recently Canadian unemployment > U.S. unemployment. (504–505)

4 F They are not counted as unemployed, but probably should be. (503)

5 T It chooses spending, taxation, and deficit → fiscal policy. (515)

6 T As economy moves in recession, real GDP growth becomes negative, some workers become unemployed. (507–508)

7 U It depends whether or not the government borrows to ↑ consumption (bad) or ↑ investment (good). (514)

8 F Recently macroeconomics has merged the short-term and long-term issues into a broad study. (502)

9 F Inflation = $((130 - 110)/110) \times 100 = 18.2\%$. (511)

10 U Inflation is costly, but so is getting rid of it → ↑ unemployment. It depends on the relative size of the costs. (512–513)

Multiple-Choice

1 d a and b are monetary policy, c is neither. (515)

2 b Positive inflation → current price level − past price level > 0 by definition. (511)

3 a See Text Fig. 22.10. (514)

4 e It was born during the Great Depression, when it focused on short-term problems, but recently it has merged studies of both. (502)

5 d See Text Fig. 22.2 and its discussion. (504–505)

6 e Forecasting inflation becomes important because unpredictable inflation → unpredictable winners and losers because the value of money *falls*. (512)

7 a This is not costly to society. (505)

8 d Both types of deficits can be problems, if they are for consumption, because they do not generate profits/income to help repay the resulting debts. a is irrelevant. (514)

9 d Keynes did worry about them, noting they could be caused by too much government spending. Economists now study them and short-term problems together. (502)

10 e See Text Fig. 22.5—all four countries had a substantial ↓ in their growth rates around 1970. (508)

11 d Raising economic growth is a policy challenge. (515)

12 d To decide, must weigh both costs and benefits and see which is higher. (510)

13 d During the Great Depression of the 1930s. (504)

14 b Labour force = unemployed + employed. (503)

15 b Unemployment rate = unemployed/labour force = 1/10. (503)

16 d a and e lower the deficit, b and c are irrelevant. (514)

17 a Upturn → expansion → unemployment falls. b is irrelevant, c is the average over the cycle, d is growth in potential GDP. (507)

18 e Historically, it was about the same as other countries until recently. (511–513)

19 e It would add extra unemployed workers to the measured rate. (503)

20 e Definition. (506)

21 c 6.25% = $((136 - 128)/128) \times 100$. (511)

22 a Solve by inverting formula inflation rate = $((P_{1998} - P_{1997})/P_{1997}) \times 100$. (511)

23 b It is costly because it makes economy like giant casino, so people try to predict inflation instead of producing goods and services. (512)

24 d a, b, e are irrelevant, while c lowers deficit. Unemployment ↑ → more government payments and less tax revenues. (514)

25 a Definition. (507–508)

Short Answer Problems

1 The biggest cost of unemployment is the lost output and income. When workers are unemployed for long periods of time, their skills and abilities deteriorate, and so do their job prospects. In addition, there are the costs of higher crime and more social problems.

2 You should have used the following formula:

$$\text{Inflation rate} = \frac{\text{Current year's price level} - \text{Last year's price level}}{\text{Last year's price level}} \times 100.$$

3 The value of money is the quantity of goods and services that can be purchased with one unit of money. Since inflation means that prices are rising on average, it means that one unit of money will buy less. Thus the value of money falls when there is inflation.

⊘4 There are two ways to answer this question. First, between 1980 and 1992 the tax credit has risen in value by 20 percent (= 10/50 × 100), while the price level has risen by 109 percent (= ((130 − 62.3) × 100). Clearly prices have risen faster than the dollar value of the credit, lowering the value of this money, so Jennifer gains less from it. Second, you could calculate the purchasing power of the tax credit in terms of how many goods it can purchase (remember the price index measures the cost of a typical family's purchases). For Tracy the credit purchased 0.8 of a typical family's purchases (= 50/62.3), whereas for Jennifer it purchased 0.46 (= 60/130). Clearly Tracy gained more from the credit.

5 The current account includes our exports minus our imports and also takes interest payments paid to and received from the rest of the world into account. As Text Fig. 22.10 shows, Canada's current account has fluctuated since 1960, but since the late 1980s it has been persistently around 4 percent of GDP.

6 During the recession phase of the business cycle, the rate of growth of real GDP slows down and becomes negative, and real GDP falls below potential GDP. During this phase the unemployment rate is rising. At the trough, real GDP reaches its lowest point below potential GDP, and the unemployment rate is at its highest point over the cycle. The trough is a turning point between the recession phase and the expansion phase during which the rate of growth of real GDP increases and the unemployment rate falls. At the end of an expansion, the economy reaches the peak of the business cycle. The peak is characterized by real GDP at its highest point above potential GDP and the rate of unemployment is at its lowest point over the business cycle.

⊘7 In order to determine the new wage rate at the end of the first year we must determine the percentage increase in the CPI and apply that percentage change to the initial wage rate of $10 an hour. The percentage change in the CPI is ((225 − 214)/214) × 100, or 5.1 percent. Therefore the new wage rate at the end of the first year will be $10.00 × 1.051 = $10.51. During the second year, the increase in the CPI is 4 percent. Thus the new wage rate at the end of the second year will be $10.51 × 1.04 = $10.93.

8 a The labour force is 11 million, the sum of employment and unemployment.
b The unemployment rate is 9.1 percent, the number of unemployed as a percentage of the labour force.

9 a Peaks occur at turning points in real GDP when it is rising, year 4. Troughs occur at turning points in real GDP when it is negative, year 6.
b The economy is in recession when the growth rate of real GDP is negative, years 5 and 6.
c There is a rough inverse relationship between the two variables—when real GDP is rising, the unemployment rate is falling (between years 1 and 2), and when real GDP is falling, the unemployment rate is rising (between years 4 and 5).

10 There is no correct answer to this question, since it depends on the balance of the costs versus the benefits of more growth—it is a normative question. However, a society would need to weigh the costs (lost consumption because of resources devoted to growth rather than consumption, more rapid resource depletion, more environmental pollution, and an increase in the pace of economic change) against the benefit (an increase in consumption possibilities of individuals and governments) and make a judgment.

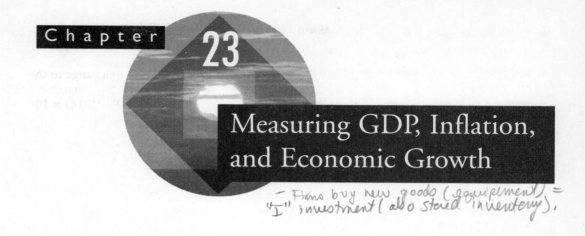

Chapter 23

Measuring GDP, Inflation, and Economic Growth

- Firms buy new goods (equipement) = "I" investment (also stored inventory).

KEY CONCEPTS

Gross Domestic Product

Gross domestic product (GDP) is value of total production of goods and services in a year, and is a **flow** (quantity per unit of time). A **stock** is a quantity at a point in time.

- Key stock is **capital** (plant, equipment, buildings, and inventories used to produce goods and services). *→ Final goods → inventories·*

  - **Investment** (*I*) = purchase of new plant, equipment, buildings, and ↑ inventories → Δcapital stock = **net investment**. *→ amount by which capital ↑.*

    Investment ↑ capital stock *Fig 23.1 pg 526*

  - **Gross investment** = net investment + replacing depreciated capital. *(or net = gross - depreciated)*
  - **Depreciation** = ↓ stock of capital because of wear and tear. *(a.k.a. capital consumption).*

- Another key stock is **wealth** (value of all things people own), and Δwealth = saving. *- Saving adds to wealth.*

  - **Saving** (*S*) = after-tax income − consumption. *← amt. of income left over after C*
  - **Consumption expenditure** (*C*) = amount of after-tax income spent on consumption goods and services. *amt spent on goods + services* *= pot GDP influenced by capital stock growth* *= real GDP influenced by investment*

The flows of investment and saving interact with flows of income and consumption in the *circular flow* to determine total production = aggregate income = aggregate expenditure. *← GDP measured by this flow*

Fig 23.2 528

- There are four economic sectors (firms, households, governments, rest of world) operating in three key markets (goods markets, factor markets, financial markets).

- Households sell factor services to firms in return for income → total income of households = aggregate income (*Y*). *→ labour, interest, etc.*

- Firms sell to households in markets for goods. ⇒ Consumption "C" expenditure is the payment that households make for goods.

- Households place their *S* in financial markets → *which is* borrowed by firms (to finance *I*), by governments (to cover budget deficits), and by rest of the world. *saving* *→banks* *investment* *for their deficits.*

- Firms produce goods and services and sell them:
  - *C* to households, *Consumption exp = goods & service*
  - *I* to other firms, *investment = equipement etc.*
  - **government expenditure** (*G*) to governments, *→ Gov't buys goods & services from firms.*
  - **net exports** (*NX*) = exports (*X*) − imports (*M*) to rest of world. *→ Gov't exp. (G)*

- Governments purchase goods and services, collect taxes from households and firms, give them *(households)* transfer payments (**net taxes** (*T*)) = taxes − subsidies), and borrow. *welfare* *→ to pay for G* *from households (Banks - savings).* *→ money for bormers, etc. hospitals.*

- The rest of the world buys our exports and sells us imports, and borrows and lends to us in financial markets. *(banks)*

Circular flow shows how to value GDP.

- Firms' production of goods and services is purchased by economic decision makers (production = expenditure).

- Money earned by sales is used to pay incomes, rents, profits, etc. (expenditure = income).

- Result: income = production = expenditure.

- This equality → basic equation:
  $Y = C + I + G + NX$.

Circular flow can also help us to understand how *I* is financed by national saving + borrowing from rest of world. *S + Gov't S (T−G) ∴ nat. S = S + (T−G)*

- Household income is spent on $C + T + S$ → $Y = C + S + T$ → household saving = $(Y − T) − C$ = after-tax income − consumption.

- Government saving = $T − G$ (if $T > G$, → spending government can lend some of its surplus, etc.). *→ money collected* *to rest of world*

◆ **National saving** = $S + (T - G)$ is available for investment purposes. *→ or to lend to world.*

◆ If foreigners sell Canadians more goods than they buy from us $(M > X)$, *deficit* we must borrow this amount from them to finance it *→ + we able to pay.* → part of their savings flows to us for investment purposes.

◆ Result: I = national saving + borrowing from rest of world = $S + (T - G) - (X - M)$. *→Investment → S+(T-G)* *(X-M).*

◆ This can be rewritten as $I + G + X = S + T + M$, or **injections** (expenditure that did not originate with households) = **leakages** (income that is not spent on domestically produced goods).

Measuring Canadian GDP

Statistics Canada measures GDP two ways based on income = production = expenditure equality: *Expenditure app. & Factor Incomes app.*

◆ *Expenditure approach* measures $C + I + G + NX$. *personal C ↙ ↘ Business I.* *Fig 23.1 Pg 531.*

◆ Items not measured in GDP include

- **intermediate goods and services** (bought by firms from each other and used as inputs in production), *→ if counted would be "double-counting"*
- used goods, *→ already counted as part of GDP in the year it was first produced.*
- financial securities. *(Bonds, stocks) - b/c they are only pieces of paper.*

◆ *Factor incomes approach* adds up all incomes paid from firms to households, and makes adjustments. *& Fig 23.2 Pg 533.*

- **Net domestic income at factor cost** = wages, etc. + profits + interest/investment income + farm income + nonfarm unincorporated business income. *3 is not GDP, need more adjustments. (from factor cost to market price)*
- Net domestic product at market prices = net *← after subtracting depreciation* domestic income + indirect taxes – subsidies. *GST + PST*
- GDP = net domestic product + depreciation. *put together expend. & factor incomes (also called capital & through we get (above) consumption)*

◆ To value production of an industry/firm, use value added of each sector, where **value added** = value of firms' output – value of intermediate goods bought from other firms. *avoid double counting by adding final product* *∴ Agg expend = Agg. Income = GDP. use Agg Income & Agg. expend. to measure GDP.*

The Price Level and Inflation

There are two price indexes used to measure the price level: *① CPI ② GDP deflater.*

◆ **Consumer Price Index (CPI)** measures current cost of typical urban family's *base*-period basket of consumer goods and services relative to base-period cost =

$$\text{CPI} = \frac{\text{Current-period's value of basket}}{\text{Base-period's value of basket}} \times 100.$$

→ Fig 23.3 pg 536 *↳ measures basket of goods.*

GDP changes b/c of ① prices change ② change in volume of goods & services produced } = change in Real GDP.

◆ **GDP deflator** measures current cost of *current*-period basket of all produced goods and services relative to base-period cost = *(current yr)*

$$\frac{\text{Nominal GDP}}{\text{Real GDP}} \times 100. \quad \text{Fig 23.4 - Pg 537}$$

GDP deflater ↳ (base yr) ↳ measures all goods.

- **Nominal GDP** is measured using current prices *uses expenditure approach* → includes impact of inflation and changes in quantity of goods and services.
- **Real GDP** is measured using base prices → shows only quantity of goods and services.

◆ Price indexes are imperfect measures of inflation because of *(& over-state inflation)*

- new goods of higher quality *and* prices replacing old goods, *→NEW GOODS BIAS.*
- quality improvements creating some part of price rises in existing goods and services, *→ QUALITY CHANGE BIAS.*
- consumers changing consumption basket towards cheaper goods not reflected in *fixed* price index basket. *→SUBSTITUTION BIAS* *- CPI & GDP deflater overestimate inflation rate by .1 to 1.0 percentage points a year.*

How Is Real GDP Used?

Real GDP is used to make international comparisons and assess economic welfare over time.

◆ Comparing real GDP per capita between countries can be troublesome due to price variation → correcting for this often gives different results. *∴ must be based on same goods & in same currency.*

◆ Real GDP as a measure of economic welfare is flawed because of two factors: *↑ purchasing power parity.*

- It does not include some items that ↑ economic welfare—quality improvements, household production, underground economy, leisure time, health and life expectancy, political freedoms.
- It does include some items that ↓ economic welfare—expenditures fighting crime, depletion of resources, pollution.

HELPFUL HINTS

1 Studying the circular flow and the national accounts may seem boring, but it is useful for several reasons. First, they provide crucial equalities that are the starting point for our economic model—studying this material will help you pass the course! Second, many current debates involve the tradeoff of economic growth and environmental damage. Understanding what GDP does and does not measure is crucial to this debate. Third, in macroeconomics we study

how several markets operate simultaneously in a joint, interrelated equilibrium—the circular flow gives us our first taste of this interrelation.

2 There are several key equations in this chapter. The first of these key equations can be understood by carefully examining the circular flow. The circular flow shows a stylized view of the economy, which the equations attempt to measure. In macroeconomics we are interested in understanding what affects GDP, and we start in this chapter by seeing how to measure production (GDP). However, we cannot directly measure production that easily. Examining the circular flow helps us to measure it indirectly. In the circular flow, production is purchased by the four economic decision makers (measured by expenditure), and the money earned from this is used to pay incomes. Production can be measured in three different ways, all of which are equivalent: Income = Expenditure = Value of production (GDP).

3 This equation and the circular flow give rise to four crucial identity equations:

i $Y = C + I + G + X - M$ ← *expenditure approach (to measure GDP)*

Equation **i** reflects the expenditure approach to measuring GDP. It tells us that GDP is equal to the total amount of spending on domestic output in the economy by households, firms, government, and foreigners. Imports are subtracted because they are not domestically produced.

ii $Y = C + S + T$

All income accrues to households that own the factors of production. Equation **ii** indicates that income must be spent on goods and services (C) or spent as net taxes (T) or saved (S). Saving is defined as disposable income ($Y - T$) minus consumption expenditure (C).

Combining equations **i** and **ii**:

$$C + I + G + X - M = C + S + T$$

which can be rewritten as:

iii $I + G + X = S + T + M$

This equation indicates that injections into the circular flow ($I + G + X$) equal leakages from the circular flow ($S + T + M$). This is necessary to create equilibrium.

Finally, we can rewrite **iii** to see how investment is financed:

iv $I = S - (G - T) - (X - M)$

investment

This equation states that the amount financial markets will provide for firm borrowing equals household saving minus the amount needed to finance the government deficit minus the amount needed to finance a net export surplus.

4 Be sure to distinguish carefully between intermediate goods and investment goods. Both are typically goods sold by one firm to another, but they differ in terms of their use. Intermediate goods are goods that are processed and then resold, while investment goods are final goods. Also note that the national income accounts include purchases of residential housing as investment because housing, like business capital stock, provides a continuous stream of value over time.

5 Note the difference between government spending on goods and services (G) and government transfer payments. Both involve payments by the government, but transfer payments are not payments for currently produced goods and services. Instead, they are simply a flow of money, just like taxes. Think of transfer payments as negative taxes. We define net taxes (T) as taxes minus transfer payments.

6 A price index for the current year is computed as the ratio of the value of a basket of goods in the current year to the value of the *same* basket of goods in a base year, multiplied by 100. It calculates the cost of purchasing the same choice of goods in two different years. There are two major differences between the price indexes presented in this chapter.

a Kinds of goods included in the basket. The goods in the basket used to calculate the Consumer Price Index are purchased by a typical urban Canadian family. The goods in the basket used to calculate the GDP deflator, on the other hand, are all the goods and services included in GDP. The GDP deflator basket includes capital goods.

b Which basket year is used. The CPI basket is a collection of commodities purchased in the *base* year. The GDP deflator basket is the collection of goods purchased in the *current* year. Thus the CPI uses a fixed basket of goods (as long as the base year is fixed), while the basket of goods used to compute the GDP deflator changes each year.

7 It is very important to understand the difference between real and nominal GDP. Nominal GDP is the value, *in current prices*, of the output of final goods and services in the economy in a year. Real GDP evaluates those final goods and services *in the prices prevailing in a base year*.

Nominal GDP can rise from one year to the next either because prices rise or because the output of goods and services rises. A rise in real GDP, however, means that the output of goods and services has risen. Consider, for example, a simple economy that produces only pizzas. In most cases, we are more interested in real GDP —the number of pizzas we can eat!

SELF-TEST

True/False/Uncertain and Explain

1 The payment of wages to households for their labour services is an example of a real flow from firms to households.

2 A higher government deficit lowers investment, other things being equal.

3 Net investment gives the net addition to the capital stock.

4 If GDP is equal to consumption expenditure plus gross investment plus government purchases of goods and services, then exports must equal imports.

5 If two economies have the same real GDP per person, then the standard of living is the same in each economy.

6 In the aggregate economy, income is equal to expenditure and to GDP.

7 If you are interested in knowing whether the economy is producing a greater amount of output, you would want to look at real GDP rather than nominal GDP.

8 Goods that are produced this year but not sold this year, do not add to this year's GDP.

9 The GDP deflator is calculated as real GDP divided by nominal GDP, multiplied by 100.

10 If there were only households and firms and no government, market price and factor cost would be equal for any good.

Multiple-Choice

1 Consider the data in Table 23.1. What is the GDP deflator in 1997?

a 250
b 200
c 160
d 125
e 88.9

TABLE **23.1**

Year	Nominal GDP	Real GDP	GDP Deflator (1991 = 100)
1991	125	125	100
1997	250	200	
1998	275		122.22

2 Use the data in Table 23.1. What is real GDP in 1998?

a 336.2
b 275
c 225
d 220
e 110

3 The difference between the value of a firm's production and value of intermediate goods bought from other firms is

a net exports.
b investment in inventories.
c net taxes.
d transfer payments.
e value added.

4 Investment is financed by

a $C + I + G + NX.$
b $C + S + T.$
c $S + T + M.$
d $S + (T - G) + (X - M).$
e $S + (T - G) - (X - M).$

5 Which of the following is an example of a real flow from households to firms?

a goods and services
b factors of production
c payments for goods and services
d payments for factors of production
e loans

6 From the data in Table 23.2, compute nominal GDP in the current year.

a $197
b $208
c $209
d $226
e It cannot be calculated given the data.

TABLE **23.2**

Item	Price ($) Base	Current	Quantity Base	Current
Rubber ducks	1.00	1.25	100	100
Beach towels	9.00	6.00	12	14

7 Table 23.2 gives price and quantity data for an economy with only two consumption goods: rubber ducks and beach towels. What is the Consumer Price Index for the current year?

a 112
b 105.6
c 100.5
d 100
e 94.7

8 The underground economy is all economic activity that

a produces intermediate goods or services.
b is not taxed.
c is legal in itself but is illegally unreported, or is illegal.
d has negative social value.
e is conducted underground.

9 To obtain the factor cost of a good from its market price

a add indirect taxes and subtract subsidies.
b subtract indirect taxes and add subsidies.
c subtract both indirect taxes and subsidies.
d add both indirect taxes and subsidies.
e subtract depreciation.

10 The value of a firm's output minus the value of intermediate goods purchased is

a net exports.
b value added.
c net profit.
d indirect production.
e capital consumption.

11 Given that pollution is a by-product of some production processes,

a GDP accountants adjust GDP downward.
b GDP accountants adjust GDP upward.
c GDP accountants do not adjust GDP unless pollution is a serious problem, as in the former East Germany.
d GDP tends to overstate economic welfare.
e GDP tends to understate economic welfare.

12 Which of the following is an example of a leakage from the circular flow of income?

a exports
b investment
c saving
d subsidies
e government expenditures

13 For the aggregate economy, income equals

a expenditure, but these are not generally equal to GDP.
b GDP, but expenditure is generally less than these.
c expenditure equals GDP.
d expenditure equals GDP only if there is no government or foreign sectors.
e expenditure equals GDP only if there is no depreciation.

14 Interest plus miscellaneous investment income is a component of which approach to measuring GDP?

a factor incomes approach
b expenditure approach
c injections approach
d output approach
e opportunity cost approach

15 Which of the following is *not* a reason for GDP incorrectly measuring the value of total output?

a crime
b nonmarket activities
c the underground economy
d capital consumption
e externalities such as pollution

16 Which of the following is *false*?

a $Y = C + I + G + M - X$
b $I + G + X = S + T + M$
c $Y = C + S + T$
d $Y + M = C + I + G + X$
e $Y = C + I + G + NX$

17 The capital stock does *not* include the

a house owned by the Smith family.
b Smith family holdings of stock in the Smith Pickle Company.
c pickle factory building owned by the Smith family.
d pickle packing machine in the pickle factory building owned by the Smith family.
e pickle inventories in the pickle factory building owned by the Smith family.

18 From the data in Table 23.3, what is net investment?

a $160
b $240
c $400
d $500
e −$160

TABLE **23.3**

Amount	Item ($)
Wages, salaries, and supplementary labour income	800
Farmers' income	80
Government purchases of goods and services	240
Capital consumption	240
Gross private domestic investment	400
Personal income taxes net of transfer payments	140
Indirect taxes	120
Net exports	80
Consumption expenditures	640
Interest and miscellaneous investment income	100

19 From Table 23.3, what additional data are needed to compute net domestic income at factor cost?

a income of nonfarm unincorporated businesses
b the statistical discrepancy
c corporate profits
d depreciation
e both a and c

20 From the data in Table 23.3, what is after-tax income?

a $260
b $500
c $640
d $1,100
e $1,220

21 Real GDP

a overestimates welfare because of the existence of the underground economy.
b is an accurate measure of welfare.
c corrects nominal GDP with purchasing power parity prices.
d overestimates welfare because of the existence of pollution.
e overestimates welfare because it implies economists provide useful services.

22 Saving can be measured as income minus

a taxes.
b transfer payments.
c taxes minus consumption expenditure.
d net taxes minus consumption expenditure.
e net taxes plus subsidies.

23 Consider the data in Table 23.4. What is current nominal GDP?

a 192,000
b 189,900
c 95,000
d 93,000
e none of the above

TABLE **23.4** There are only two goods in this economy.

	Price ($)		Quantity	
	Base Year	Current Year	Base Year	Current Year
Bread	1.00	2.10	70,000	75,000
Computer disks	1.00	1.80	25,000	18,000

24 Consider the data in Table 23.4. What is current real GDP?

a 192,000
b 189,900
c 95,000
d 93,000
e none of the above

25 Consider the data in Table 23.4. What is the current value of the GDP deflator?

a 206
b 204
c 200
d 49
e none of the above

Short Answer Problems

1 How can we measure Gross Domestic *Product* by using either the expenditure or the incomes approach, when neither of these approaches actually measures production?

2 Suppose nominal GDP rises by 75 percent between year 1 and year 2.
 a If the average level of prices has also risen by 75 percent between year 1 and year 2, what has happened to real GDP?

b If the average level of prices has risen by less than 75 percent between year 1 and year 2, has real GDP increased or decreased?

3 What productive activities are *not* measured and thus are not included in GDP? Is this a serious problem?

4 Economic analysts who studied the former Soviet economy noted in the late 1980s that the Soviet Union produced many natural resources that it did not sell on the world market, but turned into consumption and investment goods instead. Calculations showed that the market value of the Soviet natural resources on the world market was greater than the market value of the Soviet processed goods.
 a What can you say about the value added of these goods?
 b Many politicians in Canada argue that we would be better off if we did not sell our unprocessed resources, but worked to process the goods first instead (for example, this is often argued about log shipments out of British Columbia). Was the former Soviet Union made better off by processing its resources? Is it always better to process goods before exporting them?

5 Use the data for an imaginary economy given in Table 23.5 to compute the following:

TABLE **23.5**

Amount	Item (billions of $)
Consumption expenditure (C)	600
Taxes (TX)	400
Transfer payments (TR)	250
Exports (X)	240
Imports (M)	220
Government spending on goods and services (G)	200
Gross investment (I)	150
Depreciation (Depr)	60

a GDP
b net investment
c net exports
d after-tax income
e saving
f total leakages from and total injections into the circular flow of income. Are they equal?
g the value of each of the three sources of financing for investment

6 Use the data for the same imaginary economy given in Table 23.6 to compute:

TABLE **23.6**

Amount	Item (billions of $)
Wages, salaries, and supplementary labour income	550
Indirect taxes	120
Subsidies	20
Farmers' income	20
Corporate profits	80
Interest and miscellaneous investment income	90
Depreciation	60
Income of nonfarm unincorporated businesses	70

a net domestic income at factor cost
b net domestic product at market prices
c GDP

7 Table 23.7 gives data for an economy in which there are three consumption goods: bananas, coconuts, and grapes.

TABLE **23.7**

Goods	Quantity in Basket	Base Period Price ($)	Base Period Expenditure ($)	Current Period Price ($)	Current Period Expenditure ($)
Bananas	120	6		8	
Coconuts	60	8		10	
Grapes	40	10		9	

a Complete the table by computing expenditures for the base period and for the same quantity of each good in the current period.
b What is the value of the basket of consumption goods in the base period? in the current period?
c What is the Consumer Price Index for the current period?

8 Table 23.8 gives data for an economy in which there are three final goods included in GDP: pizzas, beer, and CDs.
a Complete the table by computing expenditure on each good evaluated at base period prices.
b What is the value of nominal GDP in the current period?
c What is the value of real GDP in the current period?
d What is the GDP deflator in the current period?

TABLE **23.8**

Goods	Quantity in Basket	Current Period Price ($)	Current Period Expenditure ($)	Base Period Price ($)	Base Period Expenditure ($)
Pizza	110	8	880	6	
Beer	50	10	500	8	
CDs	50	9	450	10	

9 Table 23.9 gives data for an imaginary economy.

TABLE **23.9**

Year	Nominal GDP	Real GDP	GDP Deflator
1995	3,055		94
1996		3,170	100
1997	3,410	3,280	
1998		3,500	108

a Complete Table 23.9.
b What is the base year for the GDP deflator?

10 Figure 23.1 shows the circular flow for Mars. All amounts are in thousands of dollars.

FIGURE **23.1**

Firms' Borrowing

Use Fig. 23.1 to calculate for Mars:
a GDP
b aggregate expenditure
c investment
d aggregate income
e household saving
f government borrowing or saving
g foreign borrowing or saving
h firms' borrowing

ANSWERS

True/False/Uncertain and Explain

1 **F** It is example of money flow in payment for real flow. (527)

2 **T** $\uparrow$ deficit $\rightarrow$ $\downarrow$ $(T - G)$ $\rightarrow$ $\downarrow$ $I = [S + (T - G) - (X - M)]$. (530)

3 **T** Net investment nets out depreciation (replacement of worn-out capital), leaving only new capital additions. (526)

4 **T** $Y = C + I + G + NX \rightarrow$ if $Y = C + I + G$ $\rightarrow NX = 0 \rightarrow X = M$. (530)

5 **U** Real GDP is imperfect measure of standard of living, answer depends on factors such as pollution, underground economy, etc. (541–543)

6 **T** From circular flow, firm production is sold (expenditure) and earnings used to pay out incomes. (529–530)

7 **T** Real GDP measures amount of goods and services, while nominal measures current dollar value and includes inflation's impact. (537)

8 **F** GDP measures production in current year. (528)

9 **F** GDP deflator = ((nominal GDP)/(real GDP)) × 100. (537)

10 **T** Market price = factor cost + taxes – subsidies. (533)

Multiple-Choice

1 **d** GDP deflator = ((nominal GDP)/(real GDP)) × 100. (537)

2 **c** Real GDP = ((nominal GDP)/(GDP deflator)) × 100. (537)

3 **e** Definition. (534)

4 **e** Definition. (530)

5 **b** **a** is in opposite direction, others are money flows. (528)

6 **c** Nominal GDP = sum of dollar value (= current price × current quantity) of all goods. (537)

7 **e** CPI = ((sum of current prices × base quantities)/(sum of base prices × base quantities)) × 100. (536)

8 **c** Definition. (542)

9 **b** Market price = factor cost + indirect taxes – subsidies. (533)

10 **b** Definition. (534)

11 **d** No such adjustment occurs, so GDP overstates economic welfare. (543)

12 **c** Definition $\rightarrow$ money taken out of circular flow of spending. (530)

13 **c** Expenditure = money earned by sales of produced goods $\rightarrow$ it is used to pay incomes (including profits). (529–530)

14 **a** Definition. (532)

15 **d** This is depreciation and is part of GDP. (541–543)

16 **a** $Y = C + I + G + \underline{X - M}$. (529–530)

17 **b** This is not capital, it is financial asset. (526)

18 **a** Net investment = gross investment – capital consumption. (526)

19 **e** Table lists other three components of factor incomes. (532–534)

20 **e** $Y = C + I + G + NX = 640 + 400 + 240 + 80$ = 1,360, $T = 140$, $Y - T = 1,360 - 140 =$ 1,220. (529–534)

21 **d** **a** is backwards, **b** is not true, **c** and **e** are nonsense. (541–543)

22 **d** From $S = (Y - T) - C$. (529)

23 **b** Nominal GDP = sum of current expenditures on all goods. (537)

24 **d** Real GDP = sum of current quantities at base prices. (537–538)

25 **b** GDP deflator = ((nominal GDP)/(real GDP)) × 100. (537–538)

Short Answer Problems

1 The analysis of the circular flow showed that firms produce goods and services (what we wish to measure), sell them (what the expenditure approach measures), and then use the proceeds to pay for factor incomes, rents, profits, etc. (what the incomes approach measures). Therefore expenditure = production = income.

2 a Real GDP is unchanged. The increased value of goods and services is only because of increased prices.

b The fact that prices have risen less in proportion to the increase in nominal GDP means that real GDP has increased.

3 Activities that produce goods and services that are not included in GDP are criminal activities, production in the underground economy, and nonmarket activities. The first of these is not reported because the activities themselves are illegal. The second refers to goods and services that are legal but are not reported to circumvent taxes or government regulations. The third includes productive activities that households perform for themselves. Because they do not hire someone else to mow the lawn or wash the car, it is not included in GDP. The seriousness of the problem depends on the actual size of activity. The underground economy is usually estimated as about 1 to 5 percent of the Canadian economy.

4 a The value added was negative, since the value of produced goods was less than the value of intermediate products.

b If we use the measure of real GDP, the former Soviet Union was not made better off—the action of processing lowered real GDP compared to just selling the resources on the world market. Clearly, it is *not* always better to process goods before export, it may lower GDP.

5 a GDP = $C + I + G + (X - M)$ = \$970 billion.
b Net $I = I - Depr$ = \$90 billion.
c $NX = X - M$ = \$20 billion.
d After-tax income = $GDP + TR - TX$ = \$820 billion.
e Saving = after-tax income - C = \$220 billion.
f Total leakages = $(TX - TR) + M + S$ = \$590 billion. Total injections = $I + G + X$ = \$590 billion. So, total leakages = total injections.
g $I = S + (T - G) + (M - X)$ or 150 = 220 + (150 - 200) + (220 - 240). Saving contributes \$220 billion, the government budget deficit reduces investment by \$50 billion, and the net export surplus reduces investment by \$20 billion.

6 a Net domestic income at factor cost = wages, salaries, and supplementary labour income + interest and miscellaneous investment income + corporate profits + farmers' income + income of nonfarm unincorporated business = \$810 billion.
b Net domestic product at market prices = net domestic product at factor cost + indirect taxes - subsidies = \$910 billion.
c GDP = net domestic product at market prices + depreciation = \$970 billion.

7 a Table 23.7 is completed here as Table 23.7 Solution. Note that the base-period quantities are evaluated at current prices to find the value of quantities in the current period.

TABLE **23.7** SOLUTION

Goods	Quantity in Basket	Base Period Price (\$)	Base Period Expenditure (\$)	Current Period Price (\$)	Current Period Expenditure (\$)
Bananas	120	6	720	8	960
Coconuts	60	8	480	10	600
Grapes	40	10	400	9	360

b The value of the basket of consumption goods in the base period is the sum of the expenditures in that period: \$1,600. The value of the basket of consumption goods in the current period is obtained as the sum of the values of quantities in that period: \$1,920.
c The consumer price index is the ratio of the value of quantities in the current period to the base period expenditure, times 100:
CPI = (1,920/1,600) × 100 = 120.

8 a Table 23.8 is completed here as Table 23.8 Solution. Base-period expenditure for each item is obtained by evaluating the current period quantity at the base-year price.

TABLE **23.8** SOLUTION

Goods	Quantity in Basket	Current Period Price (\$)	Current Period Expenditure (\$)	Base Period Price (\$)	Base Period Expenditure (\$)
Pizza	110	8	880	6	660
Beer	50	10	500	8	400
CDs	50	9	450	10	500

b The value of nominal GDP in the current period is the sum of expenditures in the current period: \$1,830.
c The value of real GDP in the current period is the sum of the current-period quantities evaluated at base period prices; in other words, what the expenditures would have been at base-year prices: \$1,560.
d The GDP deflator for the current period is the ratio of nominal GDP to real GDP, times 100:
GDP deflator = (1,830/1,560) × 100 = 117.3.

9 a Table 23.9 is completed here as Table 23.9 Solution. The following equation is used: GDP deflator = (nominal GDP/real GDP) × 100.

TABLE **23.9** SOLUTION

Year	Nominal GDP	Real GDP	GDP Deflator
1995	3,055	3,250	94
1996	3,170	3,170	100
1997	3,410	3,280	104
1998	3,780	3,500	108

b The base year is 1996 – GDP deflator is 100.

10 a GDP can be calculated from how households spend their income: $Y = C + S + T = 50 + 30 + 15 = \$95,000$.

b Aggregate expenditure = GDP = $95,000.

c Investment is the only missing component of aggregate expenditure, and can be deduced from the equation $Y = C + I + G + NX$ or $95 = 50 + I + 16 + 2$, implying $I = \$27,000$. (Note that the components of aggregate expenditure must all flow through the goods market.)

d Aggregate income paid to households must equal aggregate expenditure earned by firms, so it equals $95,000.

e Household saving goes from households to financial markets, and equals $30,000.

f Government borrowing or saving = $T - G = 15 - 16 = -\$1,000$, borrowing.

g From examining the goods market, foreign borrowing or saving = $X - M = \$2,000$ of borrowing.

h Firms' borrowing comes from the fact saving = firms' borrowing + government borrowing + foreign borrowing, or $30 = $ firms' borrowing + $1 + 2$, so that firms' borrowing = $27,000.

PROBLEM

a Consider the following data for the economy of Autoland for 1997 and 1998. Calculate the value of nominal GDP for each year.

TABLE **P5.1**   1997

Item	Amount (billions of $)
Government purchases of goods and services	60
Government transfer payments	30
Income taxes	80
Wages, etc., paid to labour	200
Export earnings	30
Consumption expenditure	180
Import payments	25
Net investment expenditure	15
Depreciation	5

TABLE **P5.2**   1998

Item	Amount (billions of $)
Wages, etc., paid to labour	200
Indirect taxes	20
Profits	20
Subsidies	5
Interest and miscellaneous investment income	5
Depreciation	10
Farmers' income	10
Income of nonfarm unincorporated business	10

b Using your data from **a**, complete the following table:

TABLE **P5.3**

Year	Nominal GDP (billions of $)	Price Level	Real GDP (billions of 1986 $)
1997		132.5	
1998		140.0	

c Calculate the inflation rate, the growth rate in real GDP, and the growth rate in nominal GDP over this time period.

MIDTERM EXAMINATION

You should allocate 16 minutes for this examination (8 questions, 2 minutes per question). For each question, choose the one *best* answer.

1 Which of the following would be counted as unemployed in Canada?

a Doris only works five hours a week but is looking for a full-time job.

b Kanhaya has stopped looking for work since he was unable to find a suitable job during a two-month search.

c Sharon is a college student with no job.

d Maurice is working in his garden while looking for work.

e Taylor is a homemaker.

2 A business cycle is the

a rise of real GDP for more than 2 periods.

b fall of real GDP for more than 2 periods.

c irregular fluctuation of potential GDP around real GDP.

d rise in the economic potential to produce goods and services.

e irregular fluctuation of real GDP around potential GDP.

3 Macroeconomic policy challenges include

a keeping the deficit high if borrowing is for consumption.

b stabilizing the business cycle.

c stabilizing inflation at the current level.

d all of the above.

e none of the above.

4 If a price index was 150 at the end of 1997 and 165 at the end of 1998, what was the rate of inflation for 1998?

a 15 percent

b 9.1 percent

c 10 percent

d 50 percent

e 65 percent

5 Which of the following is *not* a part of the factor incomes approach to GDP?

a net exports

b wages, salaries, and supplementary labour income

c corporate profits

d farmers' income

e income of nonfarm unincorporated businesses

6 In the circular flow, the flows of investment and saving interact with the flows of income and consumption to determine

a total production.

b aggregate income.

c aggregate expenditure.

d all of the above.

e none of the above.

7 Which of the following is *not* an example of investment in the expenditure approach to measuring GDP? General Motors

a buys a new auto stamping machine.

b adds 500 new cars to inventories.

c buys Canadian government bonds.

d builds another assembly plant.

e replaces some worn-out stamping machines.

8 The technique used to calculate the CPI implicitly assumes that consumers buy

a relatively more of goods with relative prices that are rising.

b relatively fewer goods with relative prices that are rising.

c the same relative quantities of goods as in a base year.

d goods and services whose quality improves at the rate of growth of real income.

e more computers and CD players and fewer black-and-white TVs.

ANSWERS

Problem

a For 1997, calculate nominal GDP as the sum of $C + I + G + NX$. For G, you must use only purchases of goods and services, and you need to calculate gross investment (= net investment + depreciation, or $20 billion) as well as net exports (= exports – imports, or $5 billion). Thus nominal GDP = 180 + 20 + 60 + 5 = $265 billion for 1997.

For 1998, you need to use the incomes approach. First, calculate net domestic income at factor cost = wages, etc. + profits + interest and miscellaneous investment income + farmers' income + income of nonfarm unincorporated business = 200 + 20 + 5 + 10 + 10 = $245 billion. Next, to get net domestic product you must add indirect taxes and subtract subsidies from net domestic income, or 245 + 20 – 5 = $260 billion. Finally, to get gross domestic product, you must add depreciation to net domestic product, or 260 + 10 = $270 billion for 1998.

b Table P5.3 is completed below as Table P5.3 Solution, using the fact real GDP = nominal GDP divided by the price level.

TABLE **P5.3** SOLUTION

Year	Nominal GDP (billions of $)	Price Level	Real GDP (billions of 1986 $)
1997	265	132.5	200.0
1998	270	140.0	192.9

c The inflation rate is equal to

$$5.7\% = \frac{140.0 - 132.5}{132.5} \times 100$$

The growth rate of real GDP is equal to

$$-3.6\% = \frac{192.9 - 200}{200} \times 100$$

The growth rate of nominal GDP is equal to

$$1.9\% = \frac{270 - 265}{265} \times 100$$

Midterm Examination

1 d Doris is employed part time, Kanhaya is not looking for work → discouraged worker, Sharon and Taylor are out of labour force. (503)

2 e Definition. (507)

3 b It should be reducing the deficit and keeping inflation low. (515)

4 c 10% = ((165 − 150)/150) × 100. (511)

5 a It is part of expenditure approach. (532)

6 d Expenditure = money earned by sales of produced goods → it is used to pay incomes (including profits). (529–530)

7 c This is purchase of financial assets, not capital stock. (526)

8 c Because it assumes same basket of goods used for years being compared. (536–537)

Chapter 24

Aggregate Demand and Aggregate Supply

KEY CONCEPTS

This chapter introduces the fundamental model of **aggregate demand** (*AD*) and aggregate supply (*AS*).

real GDP = Y = C + I + G + X - M.

Aggregate Demand → higher the price level means, the smaller the quantity of real GDP demanded!

Quantity of real GDP demanded is total amount of final goods and services produced in Canada that economic agents plan to buy → depends on price level, expectations, fiscal/monetary policy, and world economy.

Fig 24.1 pg 55?

◆ *AD* is total quantity real GDP (*Y*) demanded at given price level (*P*). — *higher prices = smaller GDP demanded*

◆ ↑ in *P* → ↓ level *AD*, represented by movement up along *AD* curve because of
  ↓ downward curve

  • *wealth effect*—as ↑ *P* → ↓ value of some assets → ↓ spending. *∴ ↑P = you are less wealthy ∴ can't buy much* → *money is worth less*

  • *substitution effects*—as ↑ *P*, people substitute *↑ in M ? / ↓ in X $* towards relatively cheaper foreign goods (↓ *NX*) *X - M* and buying next year (↓ *C* and *I*). — *think prices will be cheaper in future, so wait to buy.*

◆ Changes in other factors → *shift* of *AD* curve. *↑ influence demand (other things besides prices that)*

  • If ↑ expectations of future income, future inflation, future profits → ↑ *AD*. *b/c a) have more money b) cheaper today c) investment*
  gov't

  • If **fiscal policy** ↑ taxes or ↓ government purchases → ↓ *AD*. — *less money to spend.*
  Bank of Canada

  • If **monetary policy** ↓ interest rates or ↑ money supply → ↑ *AD*. — *have more money to spend.*

  • If ↑ exchange rate or ↓ foreign income → ↓ *AD*.

Fig 24.2 - Pg 557

Aggregate Supply

Aggregate quantity of goods and services supplied is sum of quantities of final goods and services produced by all firms in economy = real GDP.
— *measured by real GDP.*

- AS = relationship between the quantity of real GDP supplied & the price level (GDP deflator) (& this relationship depends on time frames - Long run & Short run)

◆ *AS* is total quantity *Y* supplied at given *P*, and depends on time frame → two separate *AS* concepts: short-run (*SAS*) and long-run (*LAS*).
  Fig 24.3 - Pg 558

◆ **Long-run aggregate supply** (*LAS*) is relationship between quantity of real GDP supplied and price level when real GDP = potential (all labour, land, capital, and entrepreneurial ability are fully employed). *↓LAS movement = b/c pot. GDP is independent of price level.*

  • *LAS* curve is vertical at potential GDP. *(always)*

  • ↑ *P* → equivalent percentage ↑ factor prices *↓ real level* → real wages remain constant → no Δ employment → no Δ quantity supplied *Y*. *(GDP)*
  Fig 24.4 - Pg 559

◆ **Short-run aggregate supply** (*SAS*) is relationship between quantity of real GDP supplied and price level when wages and other factor prices are held constant.
  - full employment when pot GDP = real GDP.

  • *SAS* curve is upward sloping.

  • ↑ *P* → ↑ employment → ↑ quantity supplied *Y*.
  Fig 24.5 - Pg 560

◆ *LAS* shifts when potential GDP changes:
  b/c ↓

  • Δ aggregate labour hours. *(growth of labour hrs)*
  growth

  • Δ productivity due to Δ capital stock, Δ human capital, Δ technology. *↓ b/c of change in pot. GDP*

◆ *SAS* shifts along with *LAS* if it shifts, but also shifts if Δ factor prices. → *money wage rate* *∴ ↑ money wage rate & factor prices ↓ SAS.*

◆ Changes in factor prices do not shift *LAS* since no change in underlying supply variables.
  Fig 24.6 - Pg 562 *↓ ↑ in labour hours & ↑ in productivity ∴ ↑ pot. GDP (which ↑ LAS & ↑ SAS)*

AD–AS Equilibrium

There are two different types of macroeconomic equilibriums—long-run equilibrium is state towards which economy is heading, short-run equilibrium occurs at each point in time along path to long-run equilibrium.

↓ Δ in money wage rate ↓ SAS ↓ leaves LAS unchanged

◆ **Short-run equilibrium** occurs where *AD = SAS*, with *P* adjusting to achieve equilibrium.
  Fig 24.7 - Pg 563

[handwritten: ✱Fig 24.8 - Pg 524]

◆ This equilibrium may occur at

- **full-employment equilibrium**—$AD = SAS$ along LAS, real GDP = potential,
- **below full-employment equilibrium**—$AD = SAS$ left of LAS, real GDP < potential by amount of **recessionary gap**,
- **above full-employment equilibrium**—$AD = SAS$ right of LAS, real GDP > potential by amount of **inflationary gap**.

◆ Economy fluctuates in short run because of fluctuations in AD and AS.

- If ↑ AD so Y > potential, economy does not stay in above-full equilibrium → upward pressures on wages shift SAS left towards long-run equilibrium.
- If ↑ factor prices so SAS left and Y < potential → **stagflation** results (↑ P, ↓ Y) → slow adjustment back to long-run equilibrium via ↓ factor prices (SAS right) or government intervention (AD right).

[handwritten: ✱Fig 24.9 - Pg 546 & Fig 24.10 - Pg 567]

Growth, Inflation, and Cycles in the Canadian Economy

◆ Levels of Y and P have changed dramatically over time in Canadian economy, but with three features: *[handwritten: Long term growth, Inflation, Business cycle]*

- Growth in Y results from LAS shifting right on average, due to ↑ in underlying supply variables. *[handwritten: → labour force growth, capital, technological change]*
- Growth in Y is not steady, but goes in cycles because AD and SAS do not shift at same pace.
- Persistent inflation occurs when AD grows faster than LAS. *[handwritten: aggreg. demand ↑ at a faster rate]* *[handwritten: MAJOR SOURCE: ✱ growth rate of quantity of money]*

◆ In 1970s, ↑ inflation and ↓ growth due to massive ↑ oil prices, and ↑ quantity of money.

◆ Central banks responded by restraining AD → *[handwritten: policy actions]* deep recession in 1981–1982.

◆ Through 1980s, steady growth and inflation as LAS shifts to the right.

◆ In 1991, ↓ AD → recession. Since then, slow growth and low inflation.

H E L P F U L   H I N T S

1 The aggregate demand and aggregate supply model introduced in this chapter (and developed in detail throughout this book) is an insightful method of analysing complex macroeconomic events. In order to help yourself sort out these complex events, it will be helpful if *you always draw a graph*—even if it is a small graph in the margin of a multiple-choice question. Graphs are powerful and effective tools for analysing economic events, and you should become familiar with using them as soon as possible.

2 When using these graphs, there are two factors that often confuse students:

a Sometimes graphs are based on explicit numerical or algebraic models, in which case the intercepts, slopes, sizes of shifts, etc., have explicit values. Often these numbers are based on real-world values, but sometimes they are just "made-up" numbers that the instructor has picked to illustrate the point (although they are still economically logical). Avoid the common problem of getting caught up in the exact values of the numbers. Concentrate on the basic economic results—for example, a rise in AD leads to a rise in the price level and real GDP.

b One common mistake students make is failing to *distinguish between a shift in a curve versus a movement along a curve*. This distinction is crucial in understanding the factors that influence AD and AS, and you can be sure that your instructor will test you on it! The slope of the AD curve reflects the impact of a change in the price level on aggregate demand. A change in the price level produces a *movement along* the AD curve. A change in one of the factors affecting the AD curve other than price is reflected by a *shift* in the entire AD curve. In a similar manner, a change in price produces a movement along the SAS or the LAS curve and does not lead to a shift in the curve.

3 A change in price will not shift the AD or the AS curves. To cement the previous point, consider Fig. 24.1. The initial long-run equilibrium is at the point *a*.

Let us examine what happens in our model when there is a fall in expected future income and profits (such as happened in the recent recession). This leads to a fall in consumption and investment, and a fall in aggregate demand, shown as the shift from AD_0 to AD_1.

We can best understand what happens next by imagining that the curve AD_0 can be peeled off the page, that it no longer exists—after all, the factors that created it no longer exist! This leaves us with the curves SAS_0 and AD_1, and with a price level of P_0. There is a surplus of goods and services (the quantity of real GDP supplied is equal to Y_0 [at *a*] greater than the quantity of real GDP demanded of Y_c [at c]), so that firms find their inventories piling up. In this case, they cut prices to try and sell output, which leads to a fall in price. This fall in price eliminates the surplus in two ways. First, price falls, firms supply fewer goods and services: a movement along the *SAS* curve from a to b. (Be careful, the price change does NOT shift the *SAS* curve.) Second, the fall in price leads to a rise in the quantity demanded: a movement along AD_1 from c to b. (Note there is no shift in the *AD* curve as price changes.)

FIGURE **24.1**

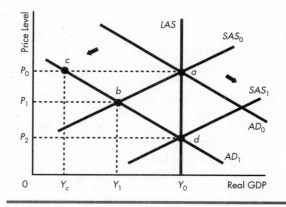

The end result is the new below full-employment equilibrium at b, with a lower price level and a lower level of real GDP.

4   In Fig. 24.1, the point b is a short-run below full-employment equilibrium, but it is not a long-run equilibrium since $Y_1 < Y_0$ (potential). There are two possible adjustments back from Y_1 to Y_0. First, the government or central bank could intervene with an expansionary fiscal or monetary policy, raising AD from AD_1 back to AD_0—the economy will move back to a full-employment, long-run equilibrium at a with $Y = Y_0$ (potential). Second, if the government does nothing, then the unemployment at b will lead to downward pressures on wages and other factor prices (although this can be very slow). As wages fall, the *SAS* curve shifts slowly right, eventually reaching SAS_1, with a full-employment, long-run equilibrium at d with $Y = Y_0$ (potential).

5   On the supply side, a crucial (and often hard to understand) distinction occurs between suppliers' behaviour in the short run and the long run. The short run and long run are not lengths of calendar time, but are defined in terms of whether or not factor prices change. In the short run, the prices of factors of production do not change; in the long run, they do change.

To see what this implies for the supply decision, consider what happens when the price level rises. In the short run, factor prices stay unchanged. As a result, per unit revenues are rising, while per unit costs are unchanged. Therefore profit-maximizing firms react by hiring more factors of production and supplying more real GDP as the price level rises—the **short-run aggregate supply curve** is upward sloping.

In the long run, factor prices adjust by the same amount as the price level, which means that the costs of each unit of production have risen by the same percentage as the revenue. These two effects offset each other, and firms do not change their supply decision as the price level rises—the **long-run aggregate supply curve** is vertical.

This distinction between the short run and the long run also applies to the influences that affect the short-run and long-run aggregate supply curves. Since prices of factors of production are held constant for the short-run aggregate supply curve but not for the long-run aggregate supply curve, a change in the prices of factors of production will shift *SAS* but not *LAS*.

SELF-TEST

True/False/Uncertain and Explain

1   An increase in the foreign exchange value of the dollar will increase aggregate demand in Canada.

2   A shift to the right in the aggregate demand curve leads to a rise in the price level, which in turn shifts the short-run aggregate supply curve to the right.

3 If the aggregate demand curve and the short-run aggregate supply curve both shift to the right at the same time, then the price level rises.

4 An increase in the expected rate of inflation will decrease aggregate demand.

5 As the price level increases, the aggregate quantity of goods and services supplied increases.

6 An economy is initially in short-run equilibrium and then expected future profits decrease. The new short-run equilibrium will be a below full-employment equilibrium.

7 Increases in long-run aggregate supply are the main force generating the underlying tendency of real GDP to expand over time.

8 Any factor that shifts the short-run aggregate supply curve to the right will also shift the long-run aggregate supply curve to the right.

9 If there is a significant technological advance (other things remaining unchanged), the long-run aggregate supply curve will shift to the right but the short-run aggregate supply curve will not shift.

10 If the economy is in an above full-employment equilibrium, the long-run aggregate supply curve will shift to the right until the economy is in a full-employment equilibrium.

Multiple-Choice

1 The fact that the short-run aggregate supply and aggregate demand curves do not shift at a fixed, steady pace explains why we observe

a persistent inflation.
b business cycles.
c economic growth.
d large government budget deficits.
e persistent unemployment.

2 We observe an increase in the price level and a decrease in real GDP. Which of the following is a possible explanation?

a The expectation of future profits has increased.
b The expectation of future income has increased.
c The price of raw materials has increased.
d The stock of capital has increased.
e The money supply has increased.

3 A technological improvement will shift

a both *SAS* and *AD* to the right.
b both *SAS* and *LAS* to the left.
c *SAS* to the right but leave *LAS* unchanged.
d *LAS* to the right but leave *SAS* unchanged.
e both *SAS* and *LAS* to the right.

4 An increase in wages will shift

a both *SAS* and *LAS* to the right.
b both *SAS* and *LAS* to the left.
c *SAS* to the left, but leave *LAS* unchanged.
d *LAS* to the right, but leave *SAS* unchanged.
e *SAS* to the right, but leave *LAS* unchanged.

5 Which of the following is a reason for the downward slope of the aggregate demand curve?

a the wealth effect
b the substitution effects
c the expected inflation effect
d the nominal balance effect
e both **a** and **b**

6 Short-run equilibrium always occurs when the

a economy is at full employment.
b economy is below full employment.
c economy is above full employment.
d quantity of real GDP demanded equals the quantity of real GDP supplied.
e *AD* curve intersects the *LAS* curve.

7 Consider the economy represented in Table 24.1. In short-run equilibrium, the price level is _____ and the level of real GDP is _____ billion 1986 dollars.

a 120; 600
b 120; 500
c 125; 550
d 130; 600
e 130; 500

TABLE **24.1**

Price Level	Aggregate Demand	Short-Run Aggregate Supply (billions of 1986 $)	Long-Run Aggregate Supply
100	800	300	600
110	700	400	600
120	600	500	600
130	500	600	600
140	400	700	600

8 Consider the economy represented in Table 24.1. The economy is in a (an)

a full-employment equilibrium and factor prices will not change.
b above full-employment equilibrium, and factor prices will rise.
c above full-employment equilibrium, and factor prices will fall.
d below full-employment equilibrium, and factor prices will fall.
e below full-employment equilibrium, and factor prices will rise.

9 Consider the economy represented in Table 24.1. There is

a an inflationary gap equal to $100 billion.
b an inflationary gap equal to $50 billion.
c a recessionary gap equal to $50 billion.
d a recessionary gap equal to $100 billion.
e no gap, the economy is at full employment.

10 Which of the following will cause the aggregate demand curve to shift to the right?

a an increase in interest rates (at a given price level)
b an increase in expected inflation
c an increase in taxes
d a decrease in the price level
e an increase in the price level

11 The economy cannot remain at a level of real GDP above long-run aggregate supply (*LAS*) because prices of factors of production will

a fall, shifting *LAS* right.
b fall, shifting *SAS* right.
c rise, shifting *LAS* left.
d rise, shifting *SAS* left.
e rise, shifting *SAS* right.

12 Consider Fig. 24.2. Which graph illustrates what happens when government spending rises?

a (a)
b (b)
c (c)
d (d)
e none of the above

FIGURE **24.2**

13 Consider Fig. 24.2. Which graph illustrates what happens when the money supply falls?

a (a)
b (b)
c (c)
d (d)
e none of the above

14 Consider Fig. 24.2. Which graph illustrates what happens when expected future income rises?

a (a)
b (b)
c (c)
d (d)
e none of the above

15 Consider Fig. 24.2. Which graph illustrates what happens when factor prices fall?

a (a)
b (b)
c (c)
d (d)
e both (a) and (b)

16 *Persistent* inflation is caused by

a shifts to the right in aggregate demand.
b shifts to the right in short-run aggregate supply.
c the tendency for long-run aggregate supply to rise faster than aggregate demand.
d shifts to the right in short-run aggregate supply accompanied by shifts to the left in aggregate demand.
e the tendency for aggregate demand to rise faster than long-run aggregate supply.

17 Consider an economy starting from a position of full employment. Which of the following changes does *not* occur as a result of a fall in aggregate demand?

a The price level falls.
b The level of real GDP falls in the short run.
c A recessionary gap arises.
d Factor prices will fall in the long run, shifting the short-run aggregate supply curve to the right.
e The long-run aggregate supply curve shifts left to create the new long-run equilibrium.

18 If wages fall, then

a *AD* shifts to the right.
b firms hire less labour.
c *LAS* shifts to the right.
d *SAS* shifts to the right.
e both **c** and **d**.

19 Potential GDP is the level of real GDP at which

a aggregate demand equals short-run aggregate supply.
b there is full employment.
c there is a recessionary gap.
d there is over full employment.
e prices are sure to rise.

20 Short-run aggregate supply is the relationship between the price level and the quantity of real GDP supplied, holding constant

a only the wage rate.
b the quantities of factors of production.
c the level of government spending.
d the price level.
e the prices of factors of production.

21 If prices of factors of production remain constant, an increase in aggregate demand will cause a(n)

a increase in the price level and an increase in real GDP.
b increase in the price level and a decrease in real GDP.
c decrease in the price level and an increase in real GDP.
d decrease in the price level and a decrease in real GDP.
e increase in the price level, but no change in real GDP.

22 Which of the graphs in Fig. 24.3 illustrates a below full-employment equilibrium?

a (a)
b (b)
c (c)
d (d)
e both (c) and (d)

FIGURE **24.3**

(a)   **(b)**

(c)   **(d)**

23 Which of the graphs in Fig. 24.3 illustrates an above full-employment equilibrium?

a (a)
b (b)
c (c)
d (d)
e both (c) and (d)

24 If real GDP is greater than potential GDP, then the economy is

a not in short-run equilibrium.
b in a full-employment equilibrium.
c in an above full-employment equilibrium.
d in a below full-employment equilibrium.
e in long-run equilibrium.

25 Which one of the following newspaper quotations describes a movement along a *SAS* curve?

a "The fall in consumer spending may lead to a recession."
b "The rise in consumer spending is expected to lead to inflation, without any increase in real GDP."
c "Recent higher wage settlements are expected to cause higher inflation this year."
d "Growth has been unusually high the last few years due to more women entering the workforce."
e "The recent tornadoes destroyed many factories in Calgary and Edmonton."

Short Answer Problems

I The substitution effects imply that an increase in the price level will lead to a decrease in the aggregate quantity of goods and services demanded. Explain.

2 Why is the *LAS* curve vertical?

3 Why is the *SAS* curve positively sloped?

4 What are the most important factors in explaining the steady and persistent increases in the price level over time in Canada?

5 Suppose the economy is initially in long-run equilibrium. Graphically illustrate the short-run effects of an increase in wages. What happens to the price level and the level of real GDP?

6 Consider an economy that is in above full-employment equilibrium due to an increase in *AD*. Prices of factors of production have not changed. With the help of a graph, discuss how the economy returns to long-run equilibrium, with no government intervention.

7 Suppose that the economy is initially in long-run equilibrium. Next, suppose that investors' confidence in the future falls (they expect future profits to fall).

a Explain (with the aid of a graph) what this shock does to *AD*, the price level, real GDP, and *AS* in the short run.
b Suppose that the government does not take any action and that investor confidence stays low. What kind of adjustments occur in the long run? Explain what happens to the price level, real GDP, *AD,* and *AS* during this adjustment, illustrating the changes on your graph.

8 With the aid of a graph, illustrate the case of an economy that has persistent inflation and positive economic growth over a three-year period.

9 Consider an economy where economists have estimated that last year's real GDP was $600 billion, equal to potential GDP. The price level was 120. Suppose that this year the economists estimate that potential GDP has risen by 10 percent. However, *actual* real GDP has fallen by 5 percent, while the price level has also fallen by 5 percent.

Draw an *AD–AS* graph that shows last year's equilibrium, as well as last year's aggregate demand, aggregate supply (short-run and long-run), price level, and real GDP level. Next, given the information above, show what has happened to the price level and the level of real GDP this year (show this year's equilibrium), plus what has happened to aggregate demand, short-run aggregate supply, and long-run aggregate supply since last year.

10 In 1996, the Saguenay region of Quebec suffered some of the worst floods in memory, with many roads, towns, and buildings destroyed. Several observers, especially those in the construction industry, argued that the rebuilding of the destroyed capital stock would strongly stimulate the local economy.

a Assuming that the economy was originally in long-run equilibrium, explain with the aid of graphs what has happened and will happen over the next few years to the price level, real GDP, *LAS*, *SAS*, and *AD* in the local economy.
b Some observers implied the local economy was better off, in a purely economic sense, as a result of the floods and the resulting rebuilding process. Do you agree?

ANSWERS

True/False/Uncertain and Explain

1 F ↑ value of dollar makes Canadian exports more expensive and imports cheaper → ↓ demand Canadian goods. (557)

2 F ↑ in P → movement along SAS curve, not shift in it. (565–566)

3 U It depends on relative size of two shifts—try drawing a graph. (565–566)

4 F If individuals expect ↑ inflation rate, they will spend more today to avoid higher future prices. (556)

5 U Answer is **T** if it is short-run, and **F** if it is long-run. (561)

6 U It depends on where initial equilibrium is and on size of fall in AD that results from ↓ future profits—try drawing a graph or two. (565–566)

7 T ↑ population, ↑ capital stock, ↑ human capital, and new technology shift LAS right over time. (568)

8 F Changes in factor prices shift only SAS and not LAS. (561–562)

9 F Anything that shifts LAS also shifts SAS. (562)

10 F SAS shifts in this type of situation, not LAS. (566)

Multiple-Choice

1 b Sometimes curves shift left (creating recession) and sometimes right (creating boom). (568–569)

2 c Answers **a**, **b**, and **e** ↑ AD → ↑ real GDP, while **d** shifts LAS right, → ↑ real GDP. **c** shifts SAS left → ↑ P, ↓ real GDP. (565–566)

3 e Technological improvements → labour is more productive → ↑ in quantity supplied in both short and long run. (562)

4 c Wages are held constant along given SAS; if wages ↑, production is less at every price level → SAS shifts left. (561–562)

5 e **c** shifts AD curve, and **d** doesn't exist. (556)

6 d Short-run equilibrium always occurs where $AD = SAS$; equilibrium *may* occur at answers **a**–**c** and **e**, but it doesn't always occur there. (563)

7 c Short-run equilibrium occurs where $AD = SAS$, which occurs at $P = 125$ and real GDP = 550—halfway between $P = 120$ and $P = 130$. (563)

8 d Real GDP = 550 billion < potential GDP of 600 billion → below full-employment equilibrium → unemployed factors eventually offer to work for less. (563–564)

9 c Actual real GDP = 550 billion, which is 50 billion less than potential GDP of 600 billion. (564)

10 b Answers **a** and **c** cause it to shift to left, while **d** and **e** are movements along AD curve. (556–557)

11 d Above long-run aggregate supply, extra demand for factors → ↑ their prices → ↑ cost of production → shifting SAS left. (566)

12 c ↑ in government spending → ↑ aggregate spending, shifting AD right. (556–557)

13 d ↓ in money supply → ↓ aggregate spending, shifting AD left. (556–557)

14 c ↑ in expected future income → ↑ in household consumption, shifting AD right. (556–557)

15 a When factor prices ↓, firms produce more at every price level shifting SAS right. (562)

16 e Combination of these shifts → shortages → ↑ P. **a**, **b** and **c** *may* → ↑ P, while **d** → P ↓. (565)

17 e ↓ in AD creates recession, → ↓ factor prices, shifting SAS right, pushing economy back to LAS. (565–566)

18 d If wages fall, cost of production falls, firms hire more labour, supply more goods and services, represented by (only) SAS shifting right. (567)

19 b Definition. (558)

20 e Short run is defined as time period within which factor prices are constant. (559)

21 a AD ↑ → shortages → ↑ prices → ↑ aggregate quantity supplied in short run, so P ↑ and real GDP ↑. (565–566)

22 a Below full-employment equilibrium occurs when $AD = SAS$ to left of LAS. (563–565)

23 e Above full-employment equilibrium occurs when $AD = SAS$ to right of LAS. (563–565)

24 c Equilibrium is with $AD = SAS$; if this is > LAS → above full-employment equilibrium. (563–565)

25 a ↓ consumer spending → shift left in AD → movement down a SAS curve in short-run → ↓ P and ↓ Y. (559–560)

Short Answer Problems

1 There are two substitution effects. First, if the prices of domestic goods rise and foreign prices remain constant, domestic goods become relatively more expensive, and so households will buy fewer domestic goods and more foreign goods. This means that there will be a decrease in the quantity of real GDP demanded. Thus, an increase in the price level (the prices of domestic goods) will lead to a decrease in the aggregate quantity of (domestic) goods and services demanded.

Second, if the prices of current goods rise and future prices remain constant, current goods become relatively more expensive, and so households will defer buying goods until the future. This means that there will again be a decrease in the quantity of real GDP demanded.

2 Long-run aggregate supply is the level of real GDP supplied when each firm in the economy is producing at its capacity output and there is full employment. Since this level of real GDP is independent of the price level, the long-run aggregate supply curve is vertical. This is the level of real GDP attained when prices of factors of production are free to adjust so as to clear factor markets.

3 The short-run aggregate supply curve is positively sloped because it holds prices of factors of production constant. When the price level rises, firms see the prices of their output (revenues) rising, but the prices of their input (costs) remain unchanged. Each firm is then induced to increase output and so aggregate output increases.

4 The price level can rise as the result of either an increase in aggregate demand or as the result of a decrease in aggregate supply. Both of these forces have contributed to periods of a rising price level. The steady and persistent increases in the price level, however, have been the result of a tendency for aggregate demand to rise faster than aggregate supply.

5 In Fig. 24.4, the economy is initially at point *a* on the SAS_0 curve. An increase in wages will shift the SAS curve leftward to SAS_1. At the new equilibrium, point *b*, the price level has risen and the level of real GDP has decreased.

FIGURE **24.4**

6 In Fig. 24.5 shown here, the increase in *AD* from AD_0 to AD_1 results in the above full-employment equilibrium at point *b* and causes the price level to increase. Since wages have not changed, the real cost of labour to firms has fallen, and thus, output is stimulated as indicated by the movement along the SAS_0 curve from point *a* to point *b*. Furthermore, the purchasing power of workers' wages has fallen. Eventually, workers will demand higher wages and firms will be willing to pay them. In a similar way, other prices of factors of production will rise as well. This long-run rise in prices of factors of production will shift the SAS curve left, which results in a new equilibrium. There will continue to be pressure for wages and other prices of factors of production to rise until the SAS curve shifts all the way to SAS_1, where the purchasing power of wages and other prices of factors of production has been restored and the economy is again at full employment, point *c*.

FIGURE **24.5**

7 a Lower investor confidence leads to lower aggregate spending, shifting the *AD* curve left in Fig. 24.6 to AD_1. This fall in aggregate demand creates a surplus at the original price level, leading to firms cutting prices, which leads to a fall in quantity produced, represented by the movement along SAS_0 to the new equilibrium at point *b*, leading to a lower level of real GDP.

b The economy is in a below full-employment equilibrium, and eventually unemployed factors start offering to work for lower factor prices, which shifts the *SAS* curve right to SAS_1, raising aggregate supply, lowering prices even more, and leading to a new long-run equilibrium at point *c*, with a higher level of real GDP than at point *b*. There is no shift in *AD*.

FIGURE **24.6**

8 In order to have these two events, long-run aggregate supply is growing (shifting rightward), and aggregate demand is shifting rightward as well, but at a faster pace. Figure 24.7 illustrates such a case, with the points *a, b,* and *c* showing the three years. (The *SAS* curves have been omitted from the graph for simplicity.)

FIGURE **24.7**

⌀ 9 Figure 24.8 shows the original full-employment equilibrium, at last year's equilibrium price level of 120 and income level of 600.

FIGURE **24.8**

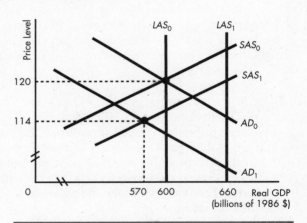

For the current year, the *LAS* curve has shifted right to LAS_1, a value of 660, and the *SAS* curve shifts with it to SAS_1, all else equal. The new short-run equilibrium must be along the intersection of SAS_1 and an *AD* curve. Since prices are 5 percent lower at 114, and real GDP is 5 percent lower at 570, the new *AD* curve must have shifted left as shown.

10 a Figure 24.9 shows the original long-run equilibrium at Y_0 and P_0.

FIGURE **24.9**

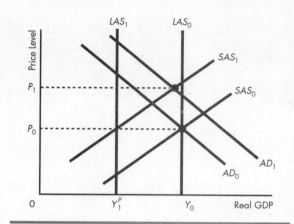

The destruction of towns, roads, etc. is a destruction of the capital stock, which would lower potential GDP, and shift the *LAS* curve left to LAS_1 as shown (shifting the *SAS* curve left as well). The resulting rebuilding would stimulate investment demand, and raise *AD* (perhaps dramatically) to AD_1. The result in the short run would be an increase in the price level to P_1, although the net effect on real GDP would be uncertain. Over the next few years, the shortage of labour and other factors (e.g., raw materials for rebuilding) would tend to bid up wages, creating inflationary pressures due to a leftward shift in the *SAS* curve. This would be countered somewhat by the shift rightward in the *LAS* curve as the new investment results in the capital stock returning towards its original value. The long-run result would tend to be a return to the original level of GDP, but with a higher price level.

b The region is worse off—higher inflation, and in the short run a lower level of potential GDP and probably a lower level of real GDP.

Aggregate Demand and the Multiplier

KEY CONCEPTS

Components of aggregate expenditure are consumption (C), investment (I), government expenditures (G), and exports (X) – imports (M).

◆ **Aggregate planned expenditure** (AE) = planned C + planned I + planned G + planned X – planned M.

Consumption Expenditure and Saving

◆ Consumption and saving depend on **disposable income** (YD = income + transfers – taxes).

- **Consumption function** shows ↑ YD → ↑ consumption.
- **Saving function** shows ↑ YD → ↑ saving, with $\Delta C + \Delta S = \Delta YD$.

◆ At low levels of YD, $C > YD$ and $S < 0$ (dissaving occurs).

◆ ↑ YD by $1 → ↑ C and ↑ S, but rises in C and S are less than $1.

- **Marginal propensity to consume** (MPC) = fraction of ΔYD that is consumed = $\Delta C/\Delta YD$ = slope of consumption function.
- **Marginal propensity to save** (MPS) = fraction of ΔYD that is saved = $\Delta S/\Delta YD$ = slope of saving function.
- $MPC + MPS = 1$.

◆ Consumption and saving are a function of real GDP since ↑ real GDP → ↑ YD.

- ↑ Y by $1 → ↑ net taxes → ↑ YD by less than $1.
- **Marginal tax rate** = $\Delta T/\Delta Y$.

- *Marginal propensity to consume out of real GDP* = $MPC \times (1 -$ marginal tax rate) = slope of consumption expenditure out of real GDP.

Investment and Government Expenditures

◆ Investment is determined by real interest rate and expected real profit rate.

- **Real interest rate** = loan interest rate – expected inflation rate.
- ↑ real interest rate → ↓ I.
- ↑ expected real profit rate → ↑ I.

◆ Government expenditures of goods and services are independent of real GDP.

Exports and Imports

◆ Canada's exports are influenced by

- international prices—↑ foreign prices or ↓ foreign exchange rate → ↑ exports.
- international trade agreements—more international trade → ↑ exports.
- real GDP in rest of world—↑ GDP → ↑ X.

◆ Canada's imports are influenced by

- international prices—↑ foreign prices relative to Canadian prices or ↓ foreign exchange rate → ↓ imports.
- international trade agreements—more international trade → ↑ imports.
- real GDP in Canada—↑ GDP → ↑ M.

◆ **Import function** is relationship between imports and real GDP.

- **Marginal propensity to import** is fraction of ΔY spent on imports = $\Delta M/\Delta Y$ = slope of import function.
- Other variables shift import function.

Equilibrium Expenditure and Real GDP

Aggregate expenditure plans interact to determine Y, and AE is influenced by Y.

◆ AE can be represented by graph or schedule. $\uparrow Y \rightarrow \uparrow AE$.

◆ Aggregate expenditure has two parts:

  • **Autonomous expenditure** = part of AE that does *not* vary with income.
  • **Induced expenditure** = part of AE that *does* vary with income.

◆ Actual aggregate expenditure may not equal planned expenditure if level of real GDP is not consistent with plans.

◆ **Equilibrium expenditure** occurs when AE = real GDP.

  • On graph this occurs when AE curve crosses 45° line.
  • If real GDP is above equilibrium value, AE < real GDP. Firms cannot sell all their production → ↑ unplanned inventories → firms ↓ production → ↓ real GDP until equilibrium occurs.
  • If real GDP below equilibrium value, AE > real GDP. Firms sell all their production and more → unplanned ↓ inventories → firms ↑ production to restore inventories → ↑ real GDP until equilibrium occurs.

The Multiplier

Multiplier is amount by which change in autonomous expenditure is multiplied to determine change in equilibrium expenditure and real GDP.

◆ ↑ autonomous expenditure → primary effect of ↑ aggregate planned expenditure → ↑ real GDP → further (secondary) ↑ in aggregate planned expenditure (e.g. ↑ consumption) → ↑ real GDP even more, etc.

◆ Secondary induced effects → total Δ real GDP > initial Δ autonomous expenditure.

◆ Multiplier = (Δ real GDP)/(Δ autonomous expenditure) = 1/(1 − slope of AE function) > 1 because of induced effects.

  • Higher slope of AE function → larger induced effects → larger multiplier.
  • Slope of AE function is higher if ↑ MPC (= b) or ↓ marginal tax rate (= t) or ↓ marginal propensity to import (= m).

◆ Recessions and depressions begin with expenditure fluctuations magnified by multiplier effect.

The Multiplier, Real GDP, and the Price Level

Aggregate demand curve shows relationship between real GDP demanded and price level, other things remaining the same, and can be derived from AE curve.

◆ AE curve shows relationship between AE and real GDP, other things remaining the same.

◆ ↑ price level → shifts AE curve downward, lowers equilibrium real GDP, shown by movement up and to left on AD curve.

◆ Δ nonprice variables → both AE and AD curve shift.

  • ↑ I → ↑ AE curve → shift right in AD curve by $\Delta I \times$ multiplier.

Real-world multipliers are smaller than those discussed above because of changes in price level.

◆ In short run, ↑ AE → ↑ price level → lowers AE some, offsetting ↑ Y somewhat → multiplier is smaller.

◆ In long run, vertical LAS → large enough ↑ price level so ↓ AE totally offsets initial rise → multiplier = 0.

Mathematical Note to Chapter 25: The Algebra of the Multiplier

◆ Aggregate planned expenditure (AE) = sum of components planned levels → $AE = C + I + G + X - M$ (1).

  • Consumption = autonomous consumption (a) + induced →
    $C = a + bYD = a + b(Y - T)$
    $= a + b(1 - t)Y$ (2).
  • Imports depend on real GDP → $M = mY$ (3).

◆ Substitute (2) and (3) into (1):
  $AE = a + b(1 - t)Y + I + G + X - mY$.

  • or: $AE = [a + I + G + X] + [b(1 - t) - m]Y$,
  • or: $AE = a + eY$, where A = autonomous expenditure and e is slope of AE curve.

◆ Equilibrium occurs when $Y = AE$ along the 45° line → $Y = A + eY$ → $Y - eY = A$ → $(1 - e)Y = A$ → $Y = A/(1 - e)$ in equilibrium.

◆ If $\Delta A \rightarrow \Delta Y = \Delta A/(1 - e) \rightarrow$
  multiplier $= \dfrac{\Delta Y}{\Delta A} = \dfrac{1}{1 - e}$.

HELPFUL HINTS

1 Chapter 24 introduced us to the basic *AD–AS* model, and showed us some of its usefulness in exploring the economy. The next two parts of the text return to aggregate demand (Chapters 25–29) and aggregate supply (Chapters 30–32) in order to explore in detail their composition, and the crucial variables that affect them. In Chapters 25 and 26 we learn the details of the goods and services market (the *AE* function) and fiscal policy. In Chapters 27 and 28 we learn the details of the financial sector and monetary policy. Chapter 29 unites the goods and services sector with the financial sector, exploring their interaction to complete our understanding of aggregate demand.

2 Aggregate demand is the relationship between the price level and the quantity of goods and services demanded; in other words, it is the relationship between the price level and the level of planned aggregate expenditure. One purpose of this chapter is to help you better understand the behaviour of planned aggregate expenditure by separating and examining its individual components. In particular, consumption expenditure, investment, and net exports—the three components of private aggregate expenditure—will be examined. As you put the discussion of this chapter and the next in perspective, remember that the ultimate objective is a more complete understanding of aggregate demand (and what shifts it), which combines these expenditure components with government expenditure on goods and services. This understanding of the components such as consumption will help you in later chapters to understand the potential causes of past and future recessions.

Be sure you are able to distinguish the *AD* curve from the *AE* curve—they are based on different thought experiments. Each *AE* curve holds constant the price level, and represents only a single point on an *AD* curve, while the *AD* curve allows the price level to vary. Changing the price level will shift the *AE* curve, but create a movement along the *AD* curve.

3 Unplanned changes in inventory are an important part of the story of how equilibrium expenditure is achieved, and how it changes in the face of a shock. To help you see how this works, suppose that you were running a retail store—for example, selling CDs or dresses.

Based on your normal sales and the costs versus benefits of holding inventories, you would have a target optimal planned inventory of perhaps 200 dresses. Each week you might sell an average of 40 dresses, and also reorder 40 dresses from the manufacturer who supplies you. In this simple example, production of 40 dresses equals the sales (planned expenditure) of 40 dresses on average, with week to week fluctuations depending on the weather, etc.

Next, suppose that there is a change in planned expenditures by consumers that leads to a fall in your sales to only 30 dresses a week. Initially, you are still ordering 40 dresses a week because you think that this is just a temporary fluctuation that will eventually reverse itself. However, after a few weeks there has been no reversal, and you find that your inventory of dresses in the store has had an unplanned rise. You react to this by cutting your orders to your supplier in order to shrink your inventory. In turn, the dress manufacturer cuts production, and may lay off workers, etc.—the fall in planned expenditures by consumers has led to a fall in real GDP.

There are two real-world complications to this simple story. First, while initially the text holds constant the price level, in the real world (and at the end of the chapter), prices do some adjusting. For example, our dress shop might cut prices to try and move excess inventory and raise sales.

Second, there are many industries where firms cannot hold inventories, and must adjust production or prices instantly when sales fall. Most service industries fall into this category— consider the example of a law firm. A law firm cannot maintain an inventory of legal briefs. Instead, it reacts to changes in the demand for its services by an immediate change in production. As a result, lawyers and others in various service industries have frequent periods of low workloads, followed by frequent periods of high workloads—in a sense, the inventory adjustment occurs by an adjustment of the hours of work.

4 This chapter distinguishes between *autonomous* expenditure and *induced* expenditure. Autonomous expenditure is independent of changes in real GDP, whereas induced expenditure will vary as real GDP varies. In general, a change in autonomous expenditures creates a change in real GDP, which in turn creates a change in induced expenditure. As the flow graph in Fig. 25.1 illustrates, these changes are at the heart of the multiplier effect.

FIGURE **25.1**

(It is important to realize, however, that even though autonomous expenditure may be independent of changes in real GDP, it will not be independent of changes in other variables, for example, the price level.)

5 The induced effects from changes in real GDP are critical in determining the size of the multiplier, and depend on the slope of the aggregate expenditure (*AE*) curve. It is thus important to understand the relationship between the slope of the *AE* function and its three main influences: the marginal propensity to consume (out of disposable income), the marginal propensity to import, and the marginal tax rate.

Consider the increase in spending domestic goods and services that results from a one-dollar increase in real GDP. (You can see the following arguments illustrated in Fig. 25.1.) Only consumption and imports have induced components. Furthermore, any increase in imports must be subtracted from the increase in consumption expenditure since we only measure expenditure on *domestic* goods and services. The slope of the *AE* function is equal to the marginal propensity to consume *out of real GDP* (so that we control for taxes) minus the marginal propensity to import.

6 The concept of the multiplier is very important. It is a result of the interaction of the various components of aggregate expenditure. In particular, an initial increase in autonomous expenditure will increase real GDP directly, but

that is not the end of the story. That initial increase in real GDP will generate an increase in *induced* expenditure, which further increases real GDP, and thus induces further increases in expenditure. The total effect on real GDP will be larger than the initial increase in autonomous expenditure because there is induced expenditure. You should become thoroughly familiar with both the intuition and the mathematics behind the multiplier.

The stabilizing effect of income taxes can also be noted here. The higher the income tax rate, the lower the slope of the *AE* function and therefore the lower the multiplier. This automatic stabilizer effect works by reducing the second round induced effects in the multiplier process. As Fig. 25.1 illustrates, when real GDP rises, higher taxes mean less of a rise in disposable income, and therefore smaller purchases of domestic goods and services and smaller increases in induced expenditure.

7 The multiplier shows the change in equilibrium expenditure, and the change in equilibrium real GDP, price level held constant—it shows the shift rightward or leftward in the *AD* curve. However, normally the price level will change in face of a shift in the *AD* curve, with the size of the change depending on the *AS* curve. In the short run, the change in the price level creates an opposite change in aggregate expenditure, that somewhat offsets the initial change in aggregate expenditure, so that the total change in real GDP is less than the initial shift in *AD* would indicate. In the long run, this offsetting effect is 100 percent.

S E L F - T E S T

True/False/Uncertain and Explain

1 An increase in the price level will shift the aggregate expenditure curve upward.

2 When aggregate planned expenditure exceeds real GDP, inventories will rise more than planned.

3 Equilibrium expenditure occurs when aggregate planned expenditure equals real GDP.

4 If the level of GDP in the rest of the world declines but GDP remains unchanged in Canada, we would expect Canadian net exports to decline.

5 The sum of the marginal propensity to consume and the marginal propensity to save is equal to 1.

6 A change in disposable income will shift the consumption function.

7 If the slope of the *AE* function is 0.75, the multiplier is equal to 3.

8 An increase in autonomous expenditure of $1 million will generate an increase in equilibrium real GDP of more than $1 million.

9 The higher the marginal propensity to consume out of real GDP and the higher the marginal propensity to import, the higher is the multiplier.

10 A rise in the real rate of interest and in the expected real profit rate will lead to a rise in investment expenditure.

Multiple-Choice

1 An increase in the price level will

a shift the *AE* curve up and increase equilibrium expenditure.

b shift the *AE* curve up and decrease equilibrium expenditure.

c shift the *AE* curve down and increase equilibrium expenditure.

d shift the *AE* curve down and decrease equilibrium expenditure.

e have no impact on the *AE* curve.

2 A fall in the price level will

a increase aggregate expenditure and thus produce a movement along the aggregate demand curve.

b increase aggregate expenditure and thus produce a rightward shift in the aggregate demand curve.

c increase aggregate expenditure and thus produce a leftward shift in the aggregate demand curve.

d have no effect on aggregate expenditure.

e increase aggregate expenditure, but produce no effect on the aggregate demand curve.

3 The aggregate expenditure curve shows the relationship between aggregate planned expenditure and

a disposable income.

b real GDP.

c the interest rate.

d consumption expenditure.

e the price level.

4 If unplanned inventories rise, aggregate planned expenditure is

a greater than real GDP and firms will increase output.

b greater than real GDP and firms will decrease output.

c less than real GDP and firms will increase output.

d less than real GDP and firms will decrease output.

e less than real GDP and firms will decrease investment.

5 Which of the following quotations illustrates the idea of the multiplier?

a "The new stadium will generate $200 million in spinoff spending."

b "Higher expected profits are leading to higher investment spending by business, and will lead to higher consumer spending."

c "The projected cuts in government jobs will hurt the local retail industry."

d "Taking the grain elevator out of our small town will destroy 300 jobs."

e All of the above.

6 Which of the following would increase Canada's exports?

a a decrease in the prices of goods and services in the rest of the world

b an increase in Canadian real GDP

c an increase in the level of GDP in the rest of the world

d an increase in the foreign exchange value of the dollar

e a decrease in the level of real GDP in the rest of the world

7 Which of the following would lead to an increase in the amount of investment, other things remaining the same?

a an increase in real interest rates
b an increase in the expected inflation rate
c a decrease in the expected future profit rate
d an increase in loan interest rates
e a decrease in the expected inflation rate

8 The fraction of the last dollar of disposable income saved is called the marginal

a propensity to consume.
b propensity to save.
c propensity to dispose.
d tax rate.
e propensity to import.

9 Which of the following would increase Canadian imports from the rest of the world?

a an increase in the prices of goods and services in the rest of the world
b a decrease in Canadian real GDP
c an increase in the level of GDP in the rest of the world
d an increase in the foreign exchange value of the dollar
e a decrease in the foreign exchange value of the dollar

10 If $AE = 50 + 0.6Y$ and $Y = 200$ then unplanned inventory

a increases are 75.
b increases are 30.
c decreases are 75.
d decreases are 30.
e changes are 0 and equilibrium exists.

11 Consumption is a stable function of real GDP because

a the MPC out of disposable income equals one.
b net taxes are not a function of real GDP.
c the MPC out of real GDP equals zero.
d net taxes are an unstable function of real GDP, but this is countered by the fact that consumption is an unstable function of disposable income.
e net taxes are a stable function of real GDP.

⊜12 Consider Fig. 25.2. The equation of the consumption function in this figure is

a $C = 200 + 0.8\,YD$.
b $C = 200 + 800\,YD$.
c $C = 200 + 0.75\,YD$.
d $C = 200 + 0.25\,YD$.
e $C = 200 + 200\,YD$.

FIGURE **25.2**

⊜ 13 If the saving function is $S = -25 + 0.4\,YD$, then the consumption function is

a indeterminate without further information.
b $C = -25 + 0.4\,YD$.
c $C = 25 - 0.4\,YD$.
d $C = 25 + 0.6\,YD$.
e $C = 25 - 0.4\,YD$.

⊜ 14 Consider Fact 25.1. What is the equation for the aggregate expenditure function of this economy?

a $AE = 16 + 0.7\,Y$
b $AE = 36 - 0.7\,Y$
c $AE = 26 + 0.8\,Y$
d $AE = 36 + 0.9\,Y$
e $AE = 36 + 0.7\,Y$

FACT **25.1**

The economy of Beverly Hills has a consumption function of $C = 10 + 0.8Y$, investment equal to 6, government purchases equal to 10, exports equal to 10, and an import function of $M = 0.1Y$.

⊜ 15 Consider Fact 25.1. What is equilibrium real GDP in this economy?

a 36
b 120
c 130
d 360
e none of the above

16 In Fig. 25.3, the marginal propensity to consume out of real GDP is

a 0.3.
b 0.6.
c 0.9.
d 1.0.
e none of the above.

FIGURE **25.3**

17 In Fig. 25.3, autonomous aggregate expenditure is

a 10.
b 100.
c 150.
d 347.
e 375.

18 In Fig. 25.3, the marginal propensity to import is

a 0.
b 0.1.
c 0.25.
d 0.3.
e 0.6.

19 In Fig. 25.3, the multiplier is

a 0.25.
b 1.00.
c 1.60.
d 2.50.
e 10.

20 In Fig. 25.3, at the equilibrium level of real GDP, *induced* expenditure is

a 28.
b 150.
c 225.
d 347.
e 375.

21 Autonomous expenditure is *not* influenced by

a the interest rate.
b the foreign exchange rate.
c real GDP.
d the price level.
e any variable.

22 The slope of the *AE* curve is equal to

a the marginal propensity to consume out of real GDP minus the marginal propensity to import.
b the marginal propensity to consume.
c the marginal propensity to import.
d one minus the marginal propensity to import.
e the autonomous expenditure multiplier.

23 Which of the following will lead to an increase in the slope of the *AE* function?

a an increase in the marginal propensity to import
b an increase in the marginal tax rate
c a decrease in the marginal propensity to consume
d a decrease in the marginal propensity to save
e an increase in the marginal propensity to save

24 Suppose that, because of an increase in expected future profit, investment increases by $10 billion. If the multiplier is 2, the *AD* curve will

a shift to the right by the horizontal distance of $20 billion.
b shift to the right by a horizontal distance greater than $20 billion.
c shift to the right by a horizontal distance less than $20 billion.
d not be affected.
e shift upward by a vertical distance equal to $20 billion.

25 Suppose the multiplier is 2 and the short-run aggregate supply curve is positively sloped. Suppose further that, because of an increase in expected future profit, investment increases by $10 billion. Equilibrium real GDP will

a increase by $20 billion.
b increase by more than $20 billion.
c decrease by less than $20 billion.
d be unaffected.
e increase by less than $20 billion.

Short Answer Problems

1 Explain how studying the circular flow in Chapter 23 helps us to understand the multiplier process of Chapter 25.

2 Suppose aggregate planned expenditure is greater than real GDP. Explain the process by which equilibrium expenditure is achieved.

3 Define and explain what autonomous expenditure is, and what induced expenditure is, and what role each plays in the multiplier process.

4 Explain (without algebraic expressions) why the multiplier is larger if the marginal propensity to consume is higher.

5 Explain how the effects of price level changes on the *AE* curve will generate an *AD* curve.

6 Table 25.1 illustrates the consumption function for a household.

TABLE **25.1**

Disposable Income (1986 $)	Consumption Expenditure (1986 $)	Saving (1986 $)
0	3,000	
3,000	5,250	
6,000	7,500	
9,000	9,750	
12,000	12,000	
15,000	14,250	

  a Compute the household's saving at each level of disposable income by completing Table 25.1.
  b Compute the household's *MPC* and *MPS*.
  c From the information given and computed, draw the household's consumption and saving functions.
 ⊚ **d** Write out the equations of the consumption and saving functions.

7 Consider an economy with the following components of aggregate expenditure:

Consumption function: $C = 20 + 0.8Y$,
Investment function: $I = 30$,
Government expenditures: $G = 8$,
Export function: $X = 4$,
Import function: $M = 2 + 0.2Y$.
  a What is the marginal propensity to consume out of real GDP in this economy?
 ⊚ **b** What is the equation of the aggregate expenditure function in this economy?
  c What is the slope of the *AE* function?
  d Find this economy's equilibrium aggregate expenditure and real GDP by completing the columns of Table 25.2.

TABLE **25.2**

Y	C	I	G	X	M	AE
0						
30						
60						
90						
120						
150						
180						

 ⊚ **e** Using the equation of the aggregate function you derived in **d**, solve mathematically for the equilibrium aggregate expenditure and real GDP.
  f What is the multiplier for this economy?

8 Consider an economy with the following characteristics:

Autonomous part of consumption expenditure = $10 billion
Investment = $5 billion
Government expenditures of goods and services = $40 billion
Exports = $5 billion
Marginal propensity to consume (out of real GDP) = 0.64
Marginal propensity to import (out of real GDP) = 0.14

(Assume that the price level is constant.)
  a What is autonomous expenditure in this economy?
  b What is the slope of the *AE* function?
 ⊚ **c** What is the equation of the *AE* function?
  d Draw a graph containing the *AE* curve for this economy (label it AE_0) as well as a 45° line.
  e What is equilibrium expenditure?
  f What is induced expenditure in equilibrium?

9 Return to the economy of Short Answer Problem **8**. Now suppose that the government decides to increase its purchases of goods and services to $60 billion.
  a Using the graph from Short Answer Problem **8d**, draw the new *AE* curve and label it AE_1.
 ⊚ ⊙ **b** What is the new equilibrium expenditure? Solve for this value using both the graphical approach and the mathematical approach.
  c What is the multiplier?
  d What is the change in autonomous expenditure, induced expenditure, consumption, imports, and investment after this increase?

10 Now consider a new economy that is identical to the economy of Short Answer Problem **8** except that the marginal propensity to import is 0.24.

a What is the slope of the *AE* function in this economy?

⊚ **b** What is the new equation of the *AE* function?

c On a new graph, draw the new *AE* curve for this economy, as well as a 45° line. Label it *AE*$_2$.

d What is equilibrium expenditure?

e What is the multiplier?

ANSWERS

True/False/Uncertain and Explain

1 **F** ↑ in price level lowers *AE* through wealth effect, etc. (595–596)

2 **F** *AE* > real GDP → excess sales → ↓ inventories. (589–590)

3 **T** Definition. (588)

4 **T** If ↓ real GDP in rest of world, ↓ *X*, but no change in *M* → ↓ *NX* = *X* – *M*. (584–585)

5 **T** Last dollar of *YD* is either spent or saved. (580)

6 **F** Change in *YD* → movement along consumption function. (578–579)

⊙ **7** **F** Multiplier = 1/(1 – *e*) = 1/(1 – 0.75) = 1/0.25 = 4. (592)

8 **U** Depends on whether short run or long run, and on slope of *SAS* if short run. (595–598)

⊙ **9** **U** Multiplier = 1/(1 – *e*) → ↑*e* → ↑ multiplier, but *e* = *MPC* out of real GDP – marginal propensity to import, so it depends on the relative sizes of the two marginal propensities. (593–594)

10 **U** ↑ real rate of interest → ↓ investment, ↑ expected profits → ↑ investment, depends on relative strength of two effects. (583)

Multiple-Choice

1 **d** ↑ price level → ↓ aggregate expenditure due to the three effects → new equilibrium at lower real GDP = equilibrium expenditure. (595–596)

2 **a** ↓ price level → ↑ aggregate expenditure due to three effects → movement along *AD* curve. (595–596)

3 **b** Definition. (586)

⊙ **4** **d** If ↑ inventories → *AE* < real GDP → ↓ firms' sales → they ↓ production in response. (589–590)

5 **e** All of the choices discuss secondary, induced effects. (590–591)

6 **c** ↑ world real GDP → they buy more goods and services, including from Canada. **a**, **d**, **e**, all ↓ exports, **b** has no impact on exports. (584–585)

7 **b** This would ↓ real interest rates, other things remaining the same, → ↑ investment. Other answers ↓ investment. (583)

8 **b** Definition. (580)

9 **d** This makes foreign goods cheaper. **a**, **b**, **e** ↓ imports, **c** has no impact. (584–585)

⊙ **10** **b** *Y* = 200 → *AE* = 50 + 0.6(200) = 170. Unplanned inventories = *Y* – *AE* = +30. (589–590)

11 **e** This makes relationship between *YD* and real GDP stable. (581)

⊚ **12** **c** Intercept = 200, slope = Δ*C*/Δ*YD*, and from *YD* = 0 to *YD* = 800, slope = +600/+800 = 0.75. (606–607)

⊚ **13** **d** *C* = *YD* – *S* = *YD* – (–25 + 0.4*YD*) = 25 + 0.6*YD*. (606–607)

⊚ **14** **e** *AE* = 10 + 0.8*Y* + 6 + 10 + 10 – 0.1*Y* = 36 + 0.7*Y*. (606–607)

⊚ **15** **b** Solve *Y** = 36 + 0.7*Y** → *Y**(1 – 0.7) = 36 → *Y** = 36/0.3 = 120. (606–607)

16 **c** *MPC* out of real GDP = slope of consumption function = Δ*C*/Δ*Y* = 90/100 = 0.9. (581)

17 **c** Intercept of *AE* function. (588)

⊙ **18** **d** Marginal propensity to import = *MPC* out of real GDP – slope of *AE* curve = 0.9 – 0.6 = 0.3, where the slope of *AE* curve = Δ*AE*/Δ*Y* = 225/375. (588–590)

19 **d** Multiplier = 1/(1 – *e*) = 1/(1 – 0.6) = 1/0.4 = 2.5. (592)

20 **c** Induced = aggregate – autonomous = 375 – 150 = 225. (588–590)

21 **c** Definition. (588)

22 **a** Definition. (592)

⊙ **23** **d** This raises *MPC* and *e*. Others lower *e*. (593–594)

24 **a** Multiplier effect raises *AE* and *Y* by 2 times original Δ autonomous expenditure → shift right by same amount in *AD* curve. (596–597)

25 **e** Multiplier effect of Question 24 is reduced by ↑ price level due to positively sloped *SAS* curve. (598)

Short Answer Problems

1 The circular flow shows us that firms produce goods and services, sell them on the market to consumers, investors, governments, and the rest of the world, and use the money earned to pay factors of production, who in turn buy goods and services. The circular flow thus shows us the secondary, induced effects of the multiplier process in action. An initial increase in autonomous expenditure means more sales for firms, which means more factor income, which means more consumption expenditure, etc.

2 If aggregate planned expenditure is greater than real GDP, inventories will fall more than planned, and firms will increase output to replenish those depleted inventories. As a result, real GDP increases. This procedure will continue as long as real GDP is less than aggregate planned expenditure. Thus it will stop only when equilibrium is attained—when real GDP is equal to aggregate planned expenditure.

3 Autonomous expenditure is the part of aggregate expenditure that does *not* vary with real GDP, but varies as a result of changes in other variables such as the real interest rate. Induced expenditure is the part of aggregate expenditure that does vary with real GDP. The multiplier process starts out with a change in autonomous expenditure that changes aggregate expenditure, which in turn changes real GDP. This change in real GDP creates secondary effects by changing induced expenditure in the same direction, which in turn changes aggregate expenditure and real GDP, leading to a total effect that is a multiple of the initial change in autonomous expenditure.

4 Any initial stimulus to autonomous expenditure will generate a direct increase in real GDP. The basic idea of the multiplier is that this initial increase in real GDP will generate further increases in real GDP as increases in consumption expenditure are *induced*. At each round of the multiplier process, the increase in spending, and thus the further increase in real GDP, are partially determined by the marginal propensity to consume. Since a larger marginal propensity to consume means a larger increase in real GDP at each round, the total increase in real GDP will also be greater. Thus the multiplier will be larger if the marginal propensity to consume is larger.

5 The aggregate demand curve illustrates the relationship between the price level and aggregate expenditures. The aggregate expenditure diagram shows the level of equilibrium expenditure *holding the price level constant*. If the price level changes, the *AE* curve will shift and a new level of equilibrium expenditure will result. Thus, for each price level, there is a different level of equilibrium expenditure. These combinations of price level

and corresponding aggregate expenditure are points on the aggregate demand curve. For example, if the price level rises, autonomous expenditure will decline, and the *AE* curve will shift down. This will lead to a decrease in equilibrium expenditure. Since an increase in the price level is associated with a reduction in equilibrium expenditure, the *AD* curve is negatively sloped.

6 The answers to **a** are shown in Table 25.1 Solution, where saving = $YD - C$.

TABLE **25.1** SOLUTION

Disposable Income (1986 $)	Consumption Expenditure (1986 $)	Saving (1986 $)
0	3,000	−3,000
3,000	5,250	−2,250
6,000	7,500	−1,500
9,000	9,750	−750
12,000	12,000	0
15,000	14,250	+750

b The *MPC* = change in consumption/change in disposable income. Using the first two entries in the table, we can see that change in consumption is 2,250, and the change in disposable income is 3,000, so that the *MPC* = 0.75 = 2,250/3,000. The *MPS* = change in saving/change in disposable income. Using the first two entries in the table, we can see that change in saving is +750, and the change in disposable income is 3,000, so that the *MPS* = 0.25 = 750/3,000. Using any other two adjacent entries in the table will yield the same result.

c The consumption function is shown in Fig. 25.4, and the saving function is illustrated in Fig. 25.5.

FIGURE **25.4**

FIGURE **25.5**

@ **d** The equation of the consumption function is based on an intercept of 3,000 and the slope (*MPC*) of 0.75. $C = 3,000 + 0.75\,YD$. Similarly, for the saving function, $S = -3,000 + 0.25\,YD$.

7 a From the consumption function equation we know this is $0.8 = \Delta C/\Delta Y$.

@ **b** Substitute the various equations into $AE = C + I + G + X - M$: $AE = 20 + 0.8\,Y + 30 + 8 + 2 - 0.2\,Y = 60 + 0.6\,Y$.

c The slope of the *AE* function comes from the equation and equals $\Delta AE/\Delta Y = 0.6$, or can also be calculated from *MPC* out of real GDP – marginal propensity to import $= 0.8 - 0.2$.

d The answer is presented in Table 25.2 Solution below. The table is constructed by substituting the various values of *Y* into the equations. Note that equilibrium occurs when $AE = Y$ at a value of 150.

TABLE **25.2** SOLUTION

Y	C	I	G	X	M	AE
0	20	30	8	4	2	60
30	44	30	8	4	8	78
60	68	30	8	4	14	96
90	92	30	8	4	20	114
120	116	30	8	4	26	132
150	140	30	8	4	32	150
180	164	30	8	4	38	168

@ **e** Equilibrium occurs when

$Y = AE$, or
$Y^* = 60 + 0.6\,Y^*$, or
$Y^*(1 - 0.6) = Y^*(0.4) = 60$, or
$Y^* = 60/0.4 = 150$.

f The multiplier $= 1/(1 - \text{slope of } AE \text{ function}) = 1/(1 - 0.6) = 1/0.4 = 2.5$.

8 a Autonomous expenditure is the sum of the autonomous part of consumption expenditure, investment, government purchases of goods and services, and exports. This sum is $60 billion.

b The slope of the *AE* function is equal to the *MPC* to consume out of real GDP minus the marginal propensity to import $= 0.64 - 0.14 = 0.50$.

@ **c** The equation is of the form $AE = A + eY$, where *A* is autonomous expenditure and *e* is the slope of the *AE* function. In this case, the equation is $AE = 60 + 0.5\,Y$, where units are billions of dollars.

d See the curve labelled AE_0 in Fig. 25.6. The curve was drawn by noting that the amount of autonomous expenditure ($60 billion) gives the vertical intercept and that the slope of the *AE* function is 0.5.

FIGURE **25.6**

e Equilibrium expenditure can be solved one of two ways. Equilibrium expenditure occurs at the intersection of the AE_0 curve and the 45° line. Equilibrium expenditure is $120 billion. Secondly, it can be calculated by solving the $AE = Y$ equation:

$Y^* = 60 + 0.5\,Y^*$, or
$Y^*(1 - 0.5) = 60$, or
$Y^* = 60/0.5 = 120$.

f Induced expenditure = total expenditure – autonomous expenditure $= 120 - 60 = 60$ in this case.

9 a See the curve labelled AE_1 in Fig. 25.6. The new curve reflects the fact that autonomous expenditure increases by $20 billion but the slope of the *AE* function remains unchanged.

@⊙ **b** The new equilibrium expenditure is $160 billion. This is given by the intersection of the AE_1 curve with the 45° line, or by solving the new equilibrium condition:

$Y^* = 80 + 0.5Y^*$, or
$Y^*(1 - 0.5) = 80$, or
$Y^* = 80/0.5 = 160$.

c Since a $20 billion increase in autonomous expenditure generated a $40 billion increase in equilibrium expenditure, the multiplier is 2. This, of course, can be obtained by using the formula that the multiplier $= 1/(1 - e)$ where e is the slope of the AE function.

d The total change in real GDP is $40 billion. First, we can note that the change in autonomous expenditure is just the change in government purchases of +$20 billion, and we can further note:

Δ total expenditure $= \Delta$ autonomous expenditure $+ \Delta$ induced expenditure, or

+$40 billion = +$20 billion + $20 billion

so that the change in induced expenditure is also $20 billion.

   Second, the marginal propensity to consume out of real GDP is 0.64, so the change in consumption is 0.64 times $40 billion, or $25.6 billion. The change in imports is the marginal propensity to import out of real GDP (0.14) times $40 billion, or $5.6 billion. Investment is autonomous, and is therefore not affected by the change in real GDP.

10 a Using the same analysis as in Short Answer Problem **8b**, we find that the slope of the AE function is 0.4 in this economy.

 ⓔ **b** The equation is of the form $AE = A + eY$, where A is autonomous expenditure and e is the slope of the AE function. In this case, the equation is $AE = 60 + 0.4Y$, where units are billions of dollars.

c See Fig. 25.7 shown here. The AE curve, AE_2 was constructed by noting that the amount of autonomous expenditure continued to be $60 billion but that the slope of the AE function is 0.4, less than for the economy of Short Answer Problem **8**. Therefore AE_2 is flatter than AE_1 with equilibrium coming at the level where the autonomous expenditure of $60 billion times the multiplier of 5/3 equals $100 billion.

FIGURE **25.7**

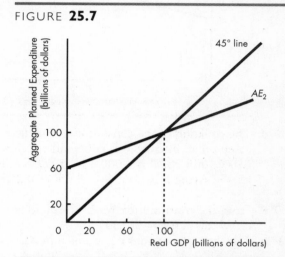

d Equilibrium expenditure is $100 billion, given by the intersection of AE_2 and the 45° line. It can also be found by using the mathematical approach used in Short Answer Problem **8**.

e The multiplier is given by the formula: $1/(1 - e) = 1/(1 - 0.4) = 1/0.6 = 1.67$ in this case.

26

Fiscal Policy

KEY CONCEPTS

Government Budgets

The **federal budget** is annual statement of revenue and outlays of government of Canada (**provincial budget** is for provincial governments).

- One purpose is to finance government activities, other is to use budget to achieve macroeconomic policy objectives (**fiscal policy**).

- Fiscal policy is made by government and Parliament, in consultation with bureaucrats, provincial governments, and business and consumer groups.

- Typical budget outlines budgetary revenues and outlays, and deficit/surplus.

- Budgetary revenues come from personal income taxes (largest source), corporate income taxes, indirect taxes (such as GST), and investment income.

- Budgetary outlays include transfer payments, expenditures on goods and services, debt interest payments, and contingency reserve.

- Budget balance = revenues – outlays.

  - Revenues > outlays → **budget surplus**.
  - Revenues < outlays → **budget deficit**.
  - Revenues = outlays → **balanced budget**.

- Federal budget has been in deficit since 1974, and deficit grew in early 1980s and has remained high since.

  - ↓ income tax revenues in late 1970s due to tax cuts.
  - Total outlays ↑ and ↓ with business cycle, but also ↑ over this period as ↑ interest payments steadily.

- **Government debt** = total borrowing by governments = sum of past deficits – sum of past surpluses.

  - Persistent deficit → ↑ borrowing → ↑ interest payments → ↑ deficit, etc.

- Canada's budget deficit is similar to that of other industrial nations.

- Cutting size of deficit is difficult politically, but concrete plans are now in place to do so.

- Provincial government outlays are almost as large as federal, and they are focused on hospitals, schools, and colleges/universities.

  - They tend to fluctuate with federal outlays.
  - Less fiscal policy at provincial level.

Fiscal Policy Multipliers

- Fiscal policy actions can either be

  - **automatic**—triggered by state of economy,
  - **discretionary**—initiated by act of Parliament → involves Δ government spending and Δ taxes.

- **Induced taxes** vary as Y varies (measured by marginal tax rate (t)), while **autonomous taxes** (T_a) do not.

- Government changes expenditures, taxes, and transfers to attempt to smooth out business cycle fluctuations.

- **Government expenditures multiplier** = (Δ real GDP)/(Δ government expenditures) = $1/(1 - e) > 1$ because initial ↑ government expenditures → ↑ real GDP → secondary, induced effects.

- **Autonomous tax multiplier** = (Δ real GDP)/(Δ taxes) < 0. *negative*

- ↑ taxes → ↓ disposable income → ↓ consumption → ↓ aggregate expenditure and real GDP → secondary, induced effects.
- Since some of tax change affects saving, Δ consumption = $MPC \times \Delta$ taxes → autonomous tax multiplier = $-MPC/(1 - e)$.

◆ Autonomous transfers multiplier = $MPC/(1 - e)$ since transfers are negative taxes.

◆ **Balanced budget multiplier** shows Δ real GDP after simultaneous Δ government expenditures = Δ autonomous taxes, and is positive.

◆ ↓ multiplier in recent years as ↑ marginal tax rate and marginal propensity to import.

◆ Multipliers for provincial spending are low because of high provincial marginal propensity to import → little discretionary provincial fiscal policy.

◆ Taxes and transfer payments act like automatic stabilizers → reduce fluctuations in aggregate expenditure two ways:

- ↓ induced taxes and ↑ transfer payments in a recession → ↑ YD → ↑ spending automatically.
- Induced taxes and transfer payments ↑ marginal tax rate → smaller MPC to consume out of real GDP → smaller secondary, induced effects → smaller multiplier.

◆ Budget deficits fluctuate with business cycle due to cyclical fluctuations in net taxes.

- **Cyclical deficit** is present only if real GDP < potential.
- **Structural deficit** would exist even if real GDP = potential.
- Actual deficit = cyclical + structural.

Fiscal Policy in the Short Run and the Long Run

Price level adjustments can change outcome of fiscal policy.

◆ **Expansionary fiscal policy** (↑ government expenditures or ↓ taxes) → rightward shift AD curve by amount = multiplier × policy change.

◆ **Contractionary fiscal policy** (↓ government expenditures or ↑ taxes) → leftward shift AD curve.

◆ In short run, expansionary policy still has positive but reduced effects because ↑ AD → ↑ price level → ↓ AE, movement along AD, partially offsetting initial effect.

◆ If real GDP at potential, expansionary policy → ↑ AD → ↑ price level → ↓ AE, movement up along AD, fully offsetting initial effect.

◆ Fiscal policy also has effects on AS:

- government purchases of capital goods → ↑ AS,
- ↓ taxes → ↑ incentives to work and save → ↑ supply labour and capital → ↑ AS.

◆ Government budget deficits may place a burden on future generations if

- government debt is bought by foreigners who must be repaid out of higher future taxes,
- current deficits → ↓ current investment → ↓ growth.

Mathematical Note to Chapter 26: The Algebra of Fiscal Multipliers

◆ Aggregate planned expenditure (AE) = $C + I + G + X - M$ (1).

- Taxes = autonomous + induced → $T = T_a + tY$.
- Consumption depends on disposable income → $C = a + b(Y - T) = a - bT_a + b(1 - t)Y$ (2).
- Imports (M) = mY (3).

◆ Substitute (2) and (3) into (1): $AE = a - bT_a + b(1 - t)Y + I + G + X - mY$.

- Or: $AE = [a - bT_a + I + G + X] + [b(1 - t) - m]Y$,
- Or: $AE = a + eY$, where A = autonomous expenditure and e is slope of AE curve.

◆ Equilibrium occurs when $Y = AE$ along the 45° line → $Y = A + eY$ → $Y - eY = A$ → $(1 - e)Y = A$ → $Y = A/(1 - e)$ in equilibrium.

◆ Δ government expenditures affects A directly ($\Delta A = \Delta G$) → $\Delta Y = \Delta G/(1 - e)$ → government expenditures multiplier = $\dfrac{\Delta Y}{\Delta G} = \dfrac{1}{1 - e}$.

◆ Δ autonomous taxes affects A indirectly ($\Delta A = -b\Delta T_a$) → $\Delta Y = -b\Delta T_a/(1 - e)$ → government expenditures multiplier = $\dfrac{\Delta Y}{\Delta T_a} = \dfrac{-b}{1 - e}$.

◆ For balanced budget multiplier, $\Delta G = \Delta T_a$ → $\Delta Y = \Delta G/(1 - e) - b\Delta T_a/(1 - e)$ → $\Delta Y = (1 - b)\Delta T_a/(1 - e)$ → balanced budget multiplier = $\dfrac{1 - b}{1 - e}$.

HELPFUL HINTS

1 It is crucial to distinguish between two types of autonomous shocks. One type adds to the instability of the economy; it includes changes in autonomous consumption, investment, and exports. The other type is usually a planned shock that will (hopefully) reduce the instability of the economy; it includes fiscal policy—changes in government spending and taxes. Because both shocks work through the same multiplier process, the same process that creates the instability is also available to reduce the instability.

2 As a college or university student, you are aware of the impact on your education of government spending cuts in aid of deficit reduction. Colleges and universities get as much as 80 percent of their revenue from provincial governments, who in turn receive bloc funding from the federal government, funding targeted for spending on education, health, and social services.

   As part of deficit reduction attempts, the federal government has recently been cutting the size of these intergovernmental transfers, with even bigger cuts forecast in the future. As Text Fig. 26.4 shows, these transfers are an important part of the provinces' revenues. The result is that the provinces must cut their own spending if they wish to keep their deficits under control. In many provinces health-care spending has been cut, as well as post-secondary spending. This has led to higher tuition fees (up 17 percent in one year in Saskatchewan), and more crowded classrooms.

3 Helpful Hint 5 in Chapter 23 emphasized the difference between government expenditure on goods and services, and government transfer payments. The difference is crucial once again in understanding why the government expenditures multiplier ($= 1/(1 - e)$) is larger than the autonomous transfers multiplier ($= MPC/(1 - e)$).

   A $1 increase in government purchases of goods and services directly raises autonomous expenditure by $1 in the first round of the multiplier. However, a $1 increase in spending on autonomous transfer payments raises consumers disposable income by $1, and some of this is saved, so that only $1 × MPC is consumed, and autonomous expenditure rises by < $1 in the first round of the multiplier.

SELF-TEST

True/False/Uncertain and Explain

1 Raising government spending and lowering transfer payments at the same time will raise the level of real GDP.

2 If the price level is variable, a rise in government purchases will *never* lead to a rise in real GDP.

3 The federal deficit is the total amount of borrowing that the federal government has undertaken.

4 It is only government purchases of goods and services, not transfer payments, that are crucial in analysing the federal deficit.

5 An increase in transfer payments matched by an increase in taxes will lead to an increase in real GDP equal to the size of the increase in transfer payments.

6 A government starts out with a balanced budget. In the next year, the percentage growth in outlays is higher than the percentage growth in revenues. It will now have a deficit.

7 A cut in autonomous taxes of $1 million will generate an increase in equilibrium real GDP of more than $1 million.

8 Taxes and transfer payments that vary as income varies act as automatic stabilizers in the economy.

9 An increase in government purchases will shift the *AE* curve upward and thus the *AD* curve to the right.

10 The transfer payment multiplier is smaller than the government expenditures multiplier.

Multiple-Choice

1 If the marginal propensity to consume out of real GDP is 0.6, and the marginal propensity to import is 0.1, then the government expenditure multiplier is

a 3.33.
b 2.5.
c 2.
d 1.67.
e impossible to calculate without further information.

2 In recent years in Canada, the multiplier has been

a falling because of a gradual increase in the marginal propensity to import.
b falling because of a gradual decrease in the marginal propensity to import.
c rising because of a gradual increase in the marginal propensity to import.
d rising because of a gradual decrease in the marginal propensity to import.
e fluctuating around a constant level of 1.25.

3 Suppose the model of investment expenditure was changed so that investment consisted of autonomous investment *plus* a portion that was positively related to the level of real GDP. The

a slope of the *AE* function would become larger.
b multiplier would become larger.
c multiplier would become smaller.
d slope of the *AE* function would become smaller.
e both a and b.

4 Which of the following is the formula for the tax function?

a $G = G_a + gY$
b $M = mY$
c $T = T_a + tY$
d $T = 1/(1 - e)$
e none of the above

5 Which of the following quotations correctly refers to the effects of fiscal policy in the *long run*?

a "The rise in taxes will lower real GDP."
b "The rise in taxes will raise prices only."
c "A change in the budget has no impact on real GDP unless it changes aggregate supply."
d "A change in the budget has no impact on real GDP."
e All of the above.

6 Which of the following statements is *true*? Provincial government outlays

a are small and irrelevant to the economy.
b are an important source of fiscal policy.
c have high multipliers.
d are focused on transfer payments to individuals, such as unemployment insurance.
e tend to fluctuate with federal outlays.

7 Which of the following happens automatically if the economy goes into a recession?

a Only government outlays rise.
b Only net taxes rise.
c The deficit rises.
d The deficit falls.
e Both government outlays and net taxes rise, and the deficit stays the same.

8 Which of the following would *not* increase the budget deficit?

a an increase in interest on the government debt
b an increase in government purchases of goods and services
c an increase in government transfer payments
d an increase in indirect business taxes
e a decrease in government investment income

9 During an expansion, tax revenue

a and government outlays decline.
b declines and government outlays increase.
c increases and government outlays decline.
d and government outlays increase.
e stays constant and government outlays increase.

10 Consider an economy where the marginal propensity to consume is 0.875, the marginal tax rate is 20 percent, and the marginal propensity to import out of real GDP is 0.10. In this economy what is the transfer payments multiplier?

a 2.50
b −2.50
c 2.1875
d −2.1875
e .3125

11 Consider an economy after the marginal propensity to consume is 0.875, the marginal tax rate is 20 percent, and the marginal propensity to import out of real GDP is 0.10. In this economy what is the balanced budget multiplier?

a 2.50
b −2.50
c 2.1875
d −2.1875
e .3125

12 The budget deficit grew after 1974 because

a government purchases of goods and services rose, while tax revenues remained constant.
b government purchases of goods and services remained constant, while tax revenues fell.
c debt interest payments rose, while tax revenues remained constant.
d debt interest payments rose, while tax revenues fell.
e none of the above.

13 Currently the country of Ricardia has a budget plan that entails constant government outlays equal to $100 billion and a tax scheme that is related positively to real GDP by the following equation: Taxes = $25 billion + 0.1 (real GDP). If the structural deficit is $10 billion, what is potential GDP in this economy?

a $65 billion
b $75 billion
c $650 billion
d $750 billion
e $850 billion

14 Federal fiscal policy is influenced by

a government bureaucrats.
b provincial governments.
c Parliament.
d business and consumer groups.
e all of the above.

15 The cyclical deficit

a is present only if real GDP is greater than potential.
b would exist even if real GDP equals potential.
c equals the structural deficit plus the actual deficit.
d stabilizes the economy.
e is none of the above.

16 If the slope of the *AE* function is 0.6, and the government desires to shift the *AD* curve rightward by $5 billion, the correct change in government expenditures is

a $2 billion.
b $2.5 billion.
c $3 billion.
d $7.5 billion.
e $8.33 billion.

17 Which of the following is a burden that a government deficit might impose on future generations?

a higher taxes for future Canadians to repay government debt owed to domestic lenders
b higher taxes for future Canadians to repay government debt owed to foreign lenders
c lower growth because of lower investment
d a and c
e b and c

18 Which of the following statements about expansionary fiscal policy is *false*?

a It may have no long-run impact on real GDP.
b It can offset fluctuations in aggregate expenditure and aggregate demand.
c The *AD* curve shifts rightward by an amount = multiplier × policy change.
d It never has an impact on aggregate supply.
e It usually raises the price level.

19 If a tax cut increases potential GDP, the long-run tax multiplier must be

a larger than 1.0.
b between 0 and 1.0.
c larger than 0.
d 0.
e negative.

20 Consider Fact 26.1. The price level in New Estevan is

a 1000.

b 280.

c −280.

d none of the above.

e impossible to calculate with the available information.

FACT **26.1**

Consider the following equations representing the expenditure components for the closed economy of New Estevan:

Consumption: $C = 2,000 + 0.6(Y - T) - 3P$

Investment: $I = 1,400$

Government expenditures: $G = 2,000$

Net taxes: $T = 0.6Y$

Government debt interest payments: $= 0$

Aggregate supply is vertical at potential GDP: $Y = 6,000$

where P is the price level.

---

21 Consider Fact 26.1. In long-run equilibrium, the government budget balance is

a a surplus of 400.

b a surplus of 1600.

c a deficit of 1600.

d a deficit of 1400.

e none of the above.

22 Consider Fact 26.1. The long-run multiplier for this economy is

a 2.5.

b 1.7.

c 1.3.

d 0.6.

e 0.

23 Consider Fact 26.1. If government spending increases to 4,000, *ceteris paribus*, then the new equilibrium real GDP is

a 11,000.

b 9,400.

c 8,600.

d 7,200.

e 6,000.

24 Consider Fact 26.1. If government spending increases to 4,000, *ceteris paribus*, then in the new equilibrium the new government budget balance is a

a surplus of 2,600.

b surplus of 1,640.

c surplus of 1,160.

d surplus of 320.

e deficit of 400.

25 Consider Fact 26.1. If government spending increases to 4,000, *ceteris paribus*, then in the new equilibrium the new price level will be

a 85.

b 288.

c 320.

d 643.

e 947.

Short Answer Problems

1 What changes in the components of the government budget since 1974 are the principal causes of continuing large government deficits?

2 During the summer of 1995, Saskatchewan had a provincial election. A central plank of the Saskatchewan Liberal Party's election strategy was a promise to cut taxes dramatically, stating that this would create 50,000 new jobs (about 10 percent of the labour force) over the next 5 years. Critics claimed that this policy would have only a small effect in Saskatchewan, that most of the new jobs from the tax cuts would show up in other provinces.

a What economic concept underlies the Liberals' promise?

b What economic concept underlies the critics' argument?

c The Liberals lost the election, so we do not get to see if the tax cuts would have had the promised effect, but what do you think would have happened?

3 Suppose you are visiting the town of Elbow, Saskatchewan, which is suffering a depressed economy due to low wheat prices. You spend $100 on accommodation and another $100 golfing and dining at the excellent local golf club.

a What factors will influence how much extra real GDP will be generated within Elbow by your $200 of expenditure? (Treat Elbow as if it were a separate economy.)

b What does your answer imply for the argument made by the Elbow town council that the Saskatchewan government should shift a government department to the town in order to stimulate the town's economy?

4 Explain why the multiplier of an expansionary fiscal policy is smaller once we consider the aggregate supply curve. What happens if there are incentive effects on *AS*?

5 Explain whether or not the following events will shift the *AE* curve and/or the *AD* curve and briefly explain why. (For each case, assume that the other variables are not changing.)
a a rise in the price level
b a rise in expected future profits for businesses
c a tax cut
d an increase in government expenditures

6 How might a deficit be a burden on future generations of Canadians?

ⓔ ⓓ **7** You may wish to review the mathematical notes to Chapters 25 and 26 before doing this problem. Consider the expenditure functions for the following economy:

Consumption: $C = 4,000 + 0.7(Y - T) - 20P$
Investment: $I = 2,000$
Government: $G = 5,000$
Exports: $X = 400$
Imports: $M = 0.1Y$
Taxes: $T = 2,000$

where *P* is the price level.

a What is the equation of the aggregate expenditure function? What is autonomous expenditure in this economy? What is the slope of the *AE* function?
b Assume that the price level is equal to 100. Calculate equilibrium real GDP, consumption, and imports.
c If the price level is now equal to 200, what is the new equilibrium real GDP?
d Using your information from **b** and **c**, sketch the AD curve for this economy.
e Calculate the government expenditures multiplier, the autonomous tax multiplier, the transfer payments multiplier, and the balanced budget multiplier for this economy.
f Suppose that the price level is equal to 100, and that government purchases increase by 2,000. What is the resulting change in real GDP demanded, holding constant the price level? Suppose that the change in real GDP demanded raises the price level by 100. What is the overall

change in real GDP from the two effects? What is the multiplier after the two effects have worked through the economy? Why is your answer different from **e**?

8 As finance minister for the government of Canada, your crack team of economists has estimated the economy's aggregate expenditure function to be

$$AE = 5,000 + 0.75Y$$

(price level held constant), and have estimated the *MPC* to be 0.9. All figures are in billions of dollars. You are confident that this is correct, since you threatened to exile the economists to Inuvik should they err. You have decided that in order to get re-elected next year, you need to raise real GDP by $200 billion.
a If you decide to change only government purchases, how much change is required to accomplish your goal?
b If you decide to change only autonomous taxes, how much change is required to accomplish your goal?
c If you decide to use a balance budget change in government purchases *and* autonomous taxes, how much should you change them to accomplish your goal?
d Having selected method **c**, you find that the increase in real GDP is less than $200 billion, jeopardizing your chance for re-election. Before you exile the poor economists to Inuvik, is there any excuse for their mistake? (In other words, what went wrong?)

9 Suppose that the economy is in equilibrium at the point where the *AD* curve crosses the *SAS* curve. (Assume that the economy stays in the short run for the rest of this question.) Suppose that the government raises taxes dramatically.
a Initially, assume the price level is held constant. Carefully explain what happens to aggregate expenditure, aggregate demand, and real GDP as a result of this autonomous shock. Draw a two-part graph as part of your answer, showing aggregate expenditure and the 45° line on the top, and the *AD–SAS* curves on the bottom.
ⓓ **b** What happens to the levels of the components of aggregate expenditure after this shock?
c Next, show on the graph from **a** what happens when the price level changes. Explain the overall effect on aggregate expenditure, aggregate demand, short-run aggregate supply, the price level, and real GDP from the combined effects of the shock and the resulting change in the price level.

10 In the economy of Paridisio, government outlays are related to the level of real GDP by the formula: Outlays = 500 − 0.6 Y, while tax revenues are related to the level of real GDP by the formula: Taxes = 100 + 0.2 Y.

a Complete Table 26.1.

TABLE **26.1**

Real GDP	Outlays	Revenues	Budget Balance
0			
100			
200			
300			
400			
500			
600			

b If potential GDP is 300, what is the structural deficit for Paridisio?

c If real GDP is currently 200, what are the values of the cyclical deficit, the structural deficit, and the actual deficit?

d Is the tax structure in this economy acting as an automatic stabilizer?

A N S W E R S

True/False/Uncertain and Explain

1 U It depends on sizes of each increase. (622)

2 F In short run, ↑ G → AD shifts right, and ↑ real GDP. (624–625)

3 F Deficit = outlays − revenues in current year. (611)

4 F Government spending on goods, transfer and interest payments are all part of outlays. (611)

5 F They exactly offset each other (Δ net taxes = 0), so Δ real GDP = 0. (618–620)

6 T If outlays grow faster than taxes → outlays > taxes next year → a deficit. (611)

7 U Depends on whether short run or long run, and on slope of SAS if short run. (624–626)

8 T If ↓ income → ↓ taxes + ↑ transfers → ↑ disposable income → ↑ aggregate expenditure → ↑ income, offsetting initial fall. (620–621)

9 T ↑ government purchases → ↑ autonomous expenditure → AE curve shifts upward → higher level of AD, same price level. (623–624)

10 T Since $MPC < 1$, government multiplier $[1/(1 − e)]$ > transfer multiplier $[MPC/(1 − e)]$. (620)

Multiple-Choice

1 c $e = MPC$ − marginal propensity to import = 0.5, multiplier = $1/(1 − e) = 1/(1 − 0.5)$ = 2.0. (616–617)

2 a ↑ marginal propensity to import → ↓ slope of the AE function → ↓ multiplier. (620)

⏺ 3 e New slope of the AE function = MPC + marginal propensity to invest − marginal propensity to import, and is higher → ↑ multiplier. (616–617)

4 c Definition. (634)

5 c In long run, changes in fiscal policy have an impact only if they change potential GDP (aggregate supply). (625–627)

6 e They have small multipliers and are not really used for fiscal policy, but they are almost as large as the federal government, and federal government does unemployment insurance. (614, 620)

7 c In recession, ↓ Y → ↓ taxes; ↑ spending on unemployment insurance, etc. → ↑ deficit. (621–622)

8 d This is ↑ revenue. (610–611)

9 c ↑ real GDP → ↑ tax revenue. ↓ unemployment → ↓ transfer payments. (620–621)

10 c $e = 0.875(1 − 0.2) − 0.1 = 0.6$. Transfers multiplier = $MPC/(1 − e) = 0.875/(1 − 0.6)$ = 2.1875. (621)

11 e $e = 0.6$ from **10**. Balanced budget multiplier = $(1 − MPC)/(1 − e) = (1 − 0.875)/(1 − 0.6)$ = 0.3125. (635)

12 d See text discussion. (611–613)

⏺ 13 c $10 billion = $G − T$ = $100 billion − $25 billion − 0.1 (potential GDP) → potential GDP = $(100 − 25 − 10)/0.1$ = $650 billion. (610)

14 e See text discussion. (622)

15 d Cyclical is present when real < potential, and acts like an automatic stabilizer. (622)

⏺ 16 a Government expenditures multiplier = $1/(1 − $ slope of AE function$) = 1/(1 − 0.6)$ = 2.5. Invert ΔY = multiplier × ΔG → ΔG = ΔY/multiplier = 5/2.5 = 2. (616–617)

17 e Borrowing → future interest payments to domestic and foreign lenders, but only foreign repayment hurts. Deficits may cause crowding out → ↓ investment. (613)

18 d If the government purchases capital goods, or if tax rates affect incentives, policy could affect *AS*. (623–626)

19 c Rightward shift *LAS* → ↑ real GDP, so multiplier is greater than zero, but cannot say by how much. (625–626)

20 b Equilibrium equation is $Y^* = 5400 + 0.24Y^* - 3P$. Substituting $Y^* = 6,000$ into this yields $P = 280$. (634–635)

21 b Balance = $G - T = 2,000 - 0.6(6,000) = -1,600$ (surplus of 1,600). (634–635)

22 e In long run, vertical *LAS* curve → multipliers = 0. (625–626)

23 e No change in vertical *LAS* → no change in Y^*. (625–626)

24 e Balance = $G - T = 4,000 - 0.6(6,000) = 400$. (634–635)

25 e Equilibrium equation is $Y^* = 7,400 + 0.24Y^* - 3P$. Substituting $Y^* = 6,000$ into this yields $P = 947$. (634–635)

Short Answer Problems

1 The deficit has risen because the level of government outlays as a percentage of GDP has risen, while taxes as a percentage of GDP fell during the late 1970s. The components of spending that have shown the most consistent growth are transfer payments and interest payments on government debt.

2 a The Liberals are counting on the autonomous tax multiplier to boost aggregate expenditure and create new jobs.

b The critics are arguing that most of the new expenditure would be on products from outside the province—they are arguing that the marginal propensity to import for a province is very high, so that the multipliers are very low.

c It is likely that fiscal policy multipliers are low for the provinces due to high marginal propensities to import. For your information, in Saskatchewan imports were about 62 percent (= 15.14 billion/24.28 billion) of provincial real GDP in 1995.[1]

3 a Your $200 will trigger a multiplier process—the owners of the factors of production at the golf course will spend their extra income, for example. This spending induces second round increases in consumption expenditure, leading to

a final change in real GDP in Elbow that is a multiple of $200. The size of the multiplier effect will be determined by two things. First, the larger the marginal propensity to consume in Elbow and the smaller the marginal propensity to import (from outside Elbow), the larger the multiplier will be. In a small town, the marginal propensity to import from outside the town is likely to be quite high, making the multiplier much smaller. Second, the effect is smaller if the aggregate supply curve is steeper—the rise in aggregate demand gets reduced by a rise in the price level.

b Clearly, such a shift could stimulate the town's economy, since the annual increase in government spending will create multiplier effects. The usefulness of this endeavour is limited by the factors mentioned that might reduce the size of the multiplier. (This was actual government policy in Saskatchewan until the Conservatives were defeated, at least partially because of this policy.)

4 The multiplier tells us the size of the change in real GDP (the shift in the *AD* curve) relative to the size of an initial change in government expenditure or autonomous taxes, holding constant the price level. Once we consider the *AS* curve, we know the price level will rise as aggregate demand increases—the rise in the price level being higher, the steeper the *AS* curve. This rise in the price level lowers aggregate expenditure, shown by the movement up the *AD* curve, leading to a smaller rise in real GDP.

Incentive effects would potentially shift the *AS* curve rightward, increasing the value of the multiplier.

5 Any change that does not initiate as a change in real GDP will shift the *AE* curve. Therefore all four changes will shift the *AE* curve. Any change in autonomous expenditure that is not caused by a change in the price level will shift the *AD* curve. Therefore **a** involves a movement along an *AD* curve, while **b–d** involve shifts in the *AD* curve.

6 The burden of deficit depends on the extent to which government debt is owned by foreigners. Future generations will have to pay the higher interest payments on the increased government debt, but to the extent that they also receive those interest payments (if paid to domestic lenders), there is no net burden.

However, if part of the debt is owned by foreigners, Canadian taxpayers will make all the

---

[1] *Source:* Statistics Canada, *CANSIM* matrices D21425 and D31874 on the World Wide Web.

interest payments, but the part received by foreigners will be a net burden.

An additional burden to future generations would occur if the deficit crowds out investment. In this case, the capital stock inherited by future generations will be less than it would otherwise have been.

7 a The equation can be found totalling the components of aggregate expenditure:

$AE = 4,000 + 0.7(Y - 2,000) - 20P + 2,000 + 5,000 + 400 - 0.1Y$, or
$AE = 10,000 - 20P + 0.6Y$.

Autonomous expenditure, which does not depend on real GDP, is $10,000 + 20P$. The slope is 0.6.

b Substitute $P = 100$ into the AE function, and solve for $Y^* = AE$:

$Y^* = 10,000 - 20(100) + 0.6Y^*$, or
$Y^*(1 - 0.6) = 8,000$, or
$Y^* = 8,000/0.4 = 20,000$.

Equilibrium consumption equals $4,000 + 0.7(20,000 - 2,000) - 20(100) = 14,600$. Imports $= 0.1(20,000) = 2000$.

c Substitute $P = 200$ into the AE function from **a**:

$Y^* = 10,000 - 20(200) + 0.6Y^*$, or
$Y^*(0.4) = 6,000$, or
$Y^* = 6,000/0.4 = 15,000$.

d One point on the curve is $P = 100$, $Y = 20,000$ and another point is $P = 200$, $Y = 15,000$. This is illustrated in Fig. 26.1.

FIGURE **26.1**

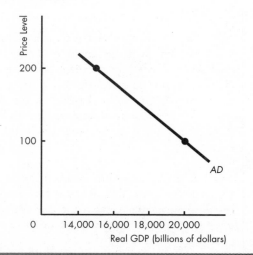

e The government expenditures multiplier $= 1/(1 - e) = 1/(1 - 0.6) = 2.5$.
The autonomous tax multiplier $= -MPC/(1 - e) = -0.7/(1 - 0.6) = -1.75$.

The transfer payments multiplier $= MPC/(1 - e) = 0.7/(1 - 0.6) = 1.75$.
The balanced budget multiplier
$= (1 - MPC)/(1 - e) = (1 - 0.7)/(1 - 0.6) = 0.3/0.4 = 0.75$.

f The change in real GDP demanded equals the change in government purchases times the government expenditures multiplier, or $2,000 \times 2.5 = 5,000$. If the price level rises by 100, then autonomous expenditure falls by 5,000, as we saw in **d**. This fall completely offsets the rise in real GDP due to the rise in government purchases of 2,000. Therefore the overall change in real GDP is equal to zero, and the multiplier is equal to zero. The answer is different here compared with part **e**, because the price level is allowed to adjust which leads to the offsetting effects.

8 a The government expenditures multiplier equals $1/(1 - e) = 1/(1 - 0.75) = 4$ in this case, so in order to raise real GDP by $200 billion you need government purchases by $50 billion $= $200/4$ billion.

b The autonomous tax multiplier equals $-MPC/(1 - e) = -0.9/(1 - 0.75) = -3.6$ in this case, so in order to raise real GDP by $200 billion you need to *lower* taxes by $55.6 billion $= $200/3.6$ billion.

c The balanced budget multiplier equals $(1 - MPC)/(1 - e) = (1 - 0.9)/(1 - 0.75) = 0.4$, so you would need to increase government purchases and taxes by $200/0.4 = $500 billion each in order to raise real GDP by $200 billion.

d The multiplier effects we have been analysing are based on the assumption that the price level is constant. In the real world, the stimulation of aggregate demand that you have carried out would raise the price level, which would lower aggregate expenditure, and partially (or completely) offset the rise in real GDP from your policy.

9 a Figure 26.2 shows what happens to aggregate expenditure (top of the graph) and to aggregate demand and supply (bottom). As taxes rise, disposable income falls, and household consumption falls, leading to a fall in autonomous expenditure, shown by the shift downward in aggregate expenditure from AE_0 to AE_b. This fall leads to a fall in real GDP (holding constant the price level) from Y_0 to Y_b, with the new equilibrium at the point b, which is shown in the bottom graph as the shift left in the AD curve from AD_0 to AD_1.

FIGURE **26.2**

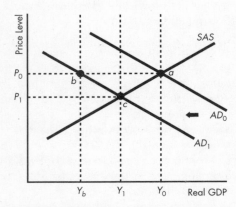

c At the original price level P_0, there is excess supply. This surplus leads to firms cutting their prices, leading to a fall in the price level. This fall gets rid of the excess supply, leading to a new equilibrium at the point c. The fall in the price level raises aggregate expenditure back up to the level AE_1, which also shows up as the movement along the curve AD_1 from b to c. The fall in the price level leads to a movement along the SAS curve from point a to point c. At the new equilibrium, the overall effect of the shock is a lower level of aggregate expenditure, a lower level of aggregate demand, a lower level of aggregate supply, a lower price level, and a lower level of real GDP.

10 a Table 26.1 is completed as Table 26.1 Solution below, using the two formulas plus the fact the budget balance = revenues – outlays.

TABLE **26.1**

Real GDP	Outlays	Revenues	Budget Balance
0	500	100	−400
100	440	140	−300
200	380	180	−200
300	320	220	−100
400	260	260	0
500	200	300	100
600	140	340	200

b Since the fall in real GDP equals the fall in aggregate expenditure, we know that the five components of aggregate expenditure have fallen in value. Since government spending, investment, and exports are autonomous, they are unchanged. Consumption will have fallen for two reasons—the fall in autonomous expenditure that initiated the changes, plus a fall in induced consumption due to the fall in real GDP. Imports will have fallen due to the fall in real GDP.

b The structural deficit is the deficit that would exist with the existing budget structure at potential GDP, and is equal to a deficit of 100.

c The structural deficit is still 100, the actual deficit is 200 at real GDP of 200, and the cyclical deficit = actual − structural = 100.

d Yes it is, since as real GDP falls, tax revenues fall and outlays rise, creating upward pressure on aggregate expenditure.

Money, Banking, and Interest Rates

What Is Money?

Money is something acceptable as a **means of payment** → method of settling a debt.

◆ Money has three functions—medium of exchange, unit of account, store of value.

◆ Medium of exchange—accepted in exchange for goods and services.

- Better than **barter** (direct exchange of goods for goods) → avoids double coincidence of wants.
- Money reduces costs of transactions.

◆ Unit of account—agreed measure for prices.

- Simpler to keep track of prices in terms of one good (money).
- Unit of account function for future transactions → standard for deferred payments.

◆ Store of value—exchangeable at a later date.

- Underpins medium of exchange function.
- Weakened by inflation.

◆ Money has four forms—commodity, convertible paper, fiat, deposit.

◆ Commodity money was first form.

- Valuable in its own right for production or consumption.
- Suffers from problems of cheating on its value, and opportunity cost of its use.

◆ Convertible paper money is paper claim to commodity that is used as means of payments.

- Initially 100 percent backed by gold.
- Eventually only fractionally backed.

◆ Fiat money is intrinsically worthless, backed only by government declaration.

- **Currency** is notes and coins we use today.

◆ **Deposit money** is deposits at financial institutions.

◆ Money today is currency + deposits, with two measures:

- **M1**—currency outside banks + demand deposits at banks.
- **M2+**—M1 + personal savings deposits + nonpersonal notice deposits + all deposits at near banks.

◆ Currency plus some deposits are means of payments: other deposits are not, but have **liquidity** (quickly convertible into means of payments).

◆ Deposits are money, but cheques are only an instruction to bank.

◆ Debit cards are like cheques, while credit cards are ID cards for loans → neither is money.

Depository Institutions

Depository institutions take deposits from households and firms, and make loans to others.

◆ Three main types are **chartered banks** (chartered under Bank Act), **credit unions** and caisses populaires, **trust and mortgage loan companies**.

◆ Bank's balance sheet shows its assets, liabilities, and net worth. Liabilities + net worth = assets.

◆ Banks aim to maximize net worth by lending out deposits.

- Must be prudent about risk to avoid crises.
- Banks keep **reserves** (cash + deposits at Bank of Canada) to meet cash withdrawals.

- Banks divide other assets into very short-term liquid assets, longer-term investment securities, and loans.

◆ Depository institutions make money by borrowing at low rates and lending at high rates → in return they provide four main economic services:

- create liquid assets
- minimize cost of borrowing funds
- minimize cost of monitoring borrowers
- pool and therefore reduce risks

How Banks Create Money

Depository institutions create money (deposits) by making loans.

◆ Banks create money when they lend out excess reserves.

- **Reserve ratio** = reserves/total deposits.
- **Desired reserve ratio** = ratio banks wish to hold.
- **Excess reserves** = actual reserves − desired reserves.

◆ If a bank gets new deposit → excess reserves.

- Bank loans out excess reserves.
- Borrower spends loan → recipient of money deposits it at new bank.
- New bank has excess reserves → further steps in deposit multiplier process.

◆ Total Δ deposits = deposit multiplier × initial Δ reserves → **deposit multiplier** = Δ deposits/Δ reserves = 1/desired reserve ratio > 1.

◆ Actual deposit multiplier reduced because some loan money held back as cash.

The Demand for Money

People chose an inventory of money based on four factors—price level, interest rate, real GDP, financial innovation.

◆ People hold money for its buying power.

- Select amount of nominal money to achieve desired real money = nominal/price level.
- ↑ price level → equivalent ↑ in nominal money demanded → no change in real money demanded.

◆ Interest rate = opportunity cost of holding money.

- ↑ interest rate → ↓ in quantity of real money demanded.

- Demand for money curve (*MD*) is relationship between quantity of real money demanded and interest rate, other things remaining the same

◆ ↑ real GDP → rightward shift *MD* curve.

◆ Recent financial innovations tend to ↓ demand M1 and ↑ demand M2+.

Interest Rate Determination

People divide their wealth between bonds and money.

◆ Bond prices are inversely related to interest rates → values are jointly determined.

◆ Interest rates are determined where quantity of real money demanded = quantity supplied.

HELPFUL HINTS

1 What is money? In one sense, whatever meets the functions of money is money. For example, cigarettes are well documented as fulfilling the functions of money in prisoner-of-war camps and similar situations. However, you should be able to answer this question on several levels. First, at the level of general definition: money is a medium of exchange. Second, at the level of classification: chequable deposits are money but savings deposits are not. Third, at the level of specific definitions: M1, M2, M2+, and M3 are official definitions of money.

2 As we work through the text, notice the important role of changes in interest rates and the exchange rate in creating shifts in aggregate demand and business cycle shocks. Chapters 27 and 28 begin the process of learning what affects the values of the interest and exchange rates, showing that the money market plays a crucial role. Chapter 27 explains the demand for money, and part of the supply of money. The latter is determined by the actions of the Bank of Canada (Chapter 28) and the deposit creation process. An important concept in this chapter is the deposit multiplier process by which banks create money. Become thoroughly familiar with this process.

There are two fundamental facts that allow banks to create money. First, one of the liabilities of banks is money: chequable deposits. Banks create money by creating new chequable deposits. Second, banks hold fractional reserves. This means that when a bank receives a deposit, it only holds part of it as reserves and loans the rest. Note that the bank is not indulging in a scam—it is still maintaining assets (reserves plus loans) to match its liabilities (deposits). When that loan is spent, at least part of the proceeds will likely be deposited in another bank, creating a new deposit (money).

The deposit multiplier process follows from this last fact: banks make loans when they receive new deposits; these loans are spent and then return to another bank, creating another new deposit. The process then repeats itself, adding more deposits (but in progressively smaller amounts) in each round. Practise going through examples until the process becomes second nature.

3 To clarify how the deposit multiplier process works, turn to Text Fig. 27.2. We will examine the balance sheets (also known as T-accounts) for the first two banks in the multiplier process. In your analysis, note that at every step the change in liabilities must be matched by an equivalent change in assets. All figures are in thousands.

The initial deposit by Art of $100 at Art's Bank creates the changes in its T-account shown in Table 27.1(a). This deposit leaves the bank with $100 extra reserves, but they desire only $25 extra reserves (= 25 percent of the new deposits of $100). Art's Bank therefore lends the excess reserves to Amy, crediting her account with an extra $75, shown in part (b) of Table 27.1. Amy spends her money buying a copy-shop franchise from Barb, leading to the withdrawal of $75 shown in part (c) of Table 27.1. (Barb deposits this money at Barb's Bank, discussed below.) The final (net) position of Art's Bank is shown in part (d) of Table 27.1. Note that the initial deposit has led to $100 in new deposits for Art's Bank, $25 in new reserves, and $75 in new loans.

The entire process starts anew with the deposit by Barb of the $75 she got from Amy for the franchise. This deposit in Barb's Bank is shown in part (a) of Table 27.2. Barb's Bank now has $75 in actual reserves, but only desires to hold $18.25 in reserves (= 25 percent of the $75 in new deposits), leaving Barb's Bank with $56.25 in excess reserves. These excess reserves are lent to Bob. His account is credited with the $56.25, as shown in part (b) of Table 27.2. In turn, Bob uses his money to pay off a loan from Carl, leading to the withdrawal shown in part (c) of Table 27.2. (Carl will deposit this money, leading to the further expansions shown in Text Fig. 27.2, but we will examine only these two

banks.) The final position of Barb's Bank is shown in part (d) of Table 27.2. Note that they have $75 in new deposits, $18.25 in new reserves, and $56.25 in new loans.

TABLE **27.1** ART'S BANK

(a) Initial New Deposit of $100

Assets		Liabilities	
Reserves	+$100	Deposits	+$100

(b) Loan Creation of $75

Assets		Liabilities	
Loans	+$75	Deposits	+$75

(c) Withdrawal of Loan Money

Assets		Liabilities	
Reserves	−$75	Deposits	−$75

(d) Final Position

Assets		Liabilities	
Reserves	+$25	Deposits	+$100
Loans	+$75		
	+$100		

TABLE **27.2** BARB'S BANK

(a) Initial New Deposit of $75

Assets		Liabilities	
Reserves	+$75.00	Deposits	+$75.00

(b) Loan Creation of $56.25

Assets		Liabilities	
Loans	+$56.25	Deposits	+$56.25

(c) Withdrawal of Loan Money

Assets		Liabilities	
Reserves	−$56.25	Deposits	−$56.25

(d) Final Position

Assets		Liabilities	
Reserves	+$18.75	Deposits	+$75.00
Loans	+$56.25		
	+$75.00		

The crucial point that drives this multiplier process is the desire of the banks to make profits, by turning reserves, which earn no revenues, into loans, which earn revenues.

4 A crucial aspect to the multiplier process is the size of the final changes. Given the assumptions of how banks act, the deposit multiplier can be calculated. The multiplier process stops when banks have lent out all of their excess reserves, so all reserves held are desired. This implies original change in reserves = final desired change in reserves = desired reserve ratio × change in deposits, or:

Δ reserves = desired reserve ratio × Δ deposits.

This can be rewritten to yield the deposit multiplier:

$$\text{Deposits multiplier} = \frac{\Delta \text{ in deposits}}{\Delta \text{ in reserves}}$$

$$= \frac{1}{\text{desired reserve ratio}}$$

As discussed in the text, real-world deposit multipliers will differ from the deposit multiplier.

5 Ordinary use of the term *money* does not capture some of the important distinctions that are made in economics. In order to avoid confusion regarding the concept of the demand for money, it is important that these distinctions be clear.

For example, we often talk about our income as the amount of *money* we make over a certain period of time. In this context, we are speaking of money as a flow—a quantity received over some period of time.

On the other hand, when we talk about how much *money* we have in our chequing accounts or in our wallets at a certain point in time, we are speaking of money as a stock—a quantity at a point in time. The distinction between these two concepts is very important.

To avoid potential confusion, economists rarely use the term *money* when referring to a flow. Instead, they use less ambiguous alternative terms like income or wage. In this chapter, *money* always refers to a *stock*. When we talk about the demand for *money* we are talking about the desire to hold a *stock of money* and not spend it. (However, it *is* being held for future spending purposes.)

6 It is crucial to distinguish between real and nominal money. *Nominal money* is the actual dollars held as cash and demand deposits. *Real money* is the measure of the purchasing power of nominal money—how many goods and services it can buy. You only hold nominal money for purchases, so it is the real balances that you care about.

Therefore if the average price level rises, and all else stays the same (especially your desired real spending), you will want the same amount of real balances as before. In order to achieve this, you will need a rise in nominal money equivalent to the rise in the average price level.

7 The inverse relationship between the price of a perpetuity and the interest rate can be easily summarized in the following simple formula:

$$\text{Interest rate} = \frac{\text{annual payment}}{\text{price of asset}} \times 100.$$

SELF-TEST

True/False/Uncertain and Explain

1 If the price level increases, there will be an increase in the quantity of real money people will want to hold.

2 If interest rates rise, the quantity of real money demanded is likely to decrease.

3 Individual households are generally better at pooling risk than are depository institutions.

4 If a depositor withdraws currency from a bank, that bank's reserve ratio declines.

5 If households or firms have more money than they want to hold, they will buy financial assets. This will cause the prices of financial assets to rise and the interest rates earned on those assets to fall.

6 In our modern economy, credit cards are money.

7 Money is anything that is generally acceptable as a medium of exchange.

8 Bank reserves consist of cash in the bank's vault plus its deposits at the Bank of Canada.

9 The deposit multiplier is equal to 1 divided by the desired reserve ratio.

10 A notice deposit at a chartered bank is an example of money.

Multiple-Choice

1 Consider Fact 27.1. Based on the Bank of Speedy Creek's initial balance sheet, what is their desired reserve ratio?

a 4 percent
b 8 percent
c 12.5 percent
d 25 percent
e 40 percent

FACT **27.1**

The Bank of Speedy Creek has chosen the following initial balance sheet:

Assets		Liabilities	
Reserves	$40	Deposits	$500
Loans	$460		
	$500		

Frodo Baggins comes along and deposits a 10 dollar bill.

---

2 Consider Fact 27.1. After Frodo's deposit, but before any other actions have occurred, the total amount of money in the economy has

a stayed the same, with its components unchanged.
b stayed the same, with currency falling and deposits rising.
c fallen, with currency falling and deposits staying the same.
d risen, with currency unchanged and deposits rising.
e fallen, with currency falling and deposits unchanged.

3 Consider Fact 27.1. After Frodo's deposit, but before any other actions have occurred, the Bank of Speedy Creek will have excess reserves of

a zero.
b $9.00.
c $9.20.
d $10.00.
e $40.00.

4 Consider Fact 27.1. After Frodo's deposit, given that the bank is profit seeking, how many more loans will it make?

a zero
b $9.00
c $9.20
d $10.00
e $40.00

5 Consider Fact 27.1. After Frodo's deposit, and after the bank has lent the amount it wishes to lend, and after all withdrawals of borrowed money have occurred, the total amount of reserves in the Bank of Speedy Creek will be $_____, the total amount of loans will be $_____, and the total amount of deposits will be $_____

a 40.80; 469.20; 510.00.
b 40.00; 460.00; 500.00.
c 50.00; 470.00; 520.00.
d 41.00; 469.00; 510.00.
e 42.50; 467.50; 510.00.

6 Consider Fact 27.1. If all the banks in the banking system had the same desired reserve ratio as the Bank of Speedy Creek, what would be the total change in deposits within the system resulting from Frodo's initial deposit?

a $125.00
b $100.00
c $80.00
d $40.00
e $12.50

7 Which of the following is *not* a function of money?

a medium of exchange
b measure of liquidity
c standard of deferred payment
d store of value
e unit of account

8 When a contract specifies future payment of a certain number of dollars for services rendered, money is functioning as a

a medium of exchange.
b measure of liquidity.
c commodity money.
d store of value.
e standard of deferred payment.

9 Canadian currency today is an example of

a fiat money.
b commodity money.
c convertible paper money.
d private debt money.
e fractionally backed gold-convertible money.

10 If all banks hold 100 percent reserves, what is the deposit multiplier?

a 0
b 1
c 10
d 100
e infinite

11 Which of the following is a component of M2+ but *not* of M1?

a currency
b personal demand deposits at chartered banks
c personal savings deposits at chartered banks
d personal savings deposits at trust companies
e both c and d

12 Which of the following is most liquid?

a demand deposits
b real estate
c government bonds
d savings deposits
e cheques

13 Consider Fig. 27.1. Which of the following best describes the response of this household to an increase in their annual income?

a movement from *a* to *f*
b movement from *a* to *c*
c movement from *e* to *a*
d movement from *b* to *a*
e none of the above

FIGURE **27.1** THE DEMAND FOR REAL MONEY BALANCES BY AN INDIVIDUAL HOUSEHOLD

14 Consider Fig. 27.1. Which of the following best describes the response of this household to a fall in the market price of bonds?

a movement from *a* to *b*
b movement from *a* to *c*
c movement from *a* to *f*
d movement from *a* to *e*
e movement from *e* to *a*

15 If the rate of interest is above the equilibrium rate of interest, how is equilibrium achieved in the money market?

a People buy goods to get rid of excess money, lowering the price of goods, and lowering the rate of interest.
b People sell goods to get rid of excess money, lowering the price of goods, and lowering the rate of interest.
c People sell bonds to get rid of excess money, lowering the price of bonds, and lowering the rate of interest.
d People sell bonds to get rid of excess money, raising the price of bonds, and lowering the rate of interest.
e People buy bonds to get rid of excess money, raising the price of bonds, and lowering the rate of interest.

16 If households and firms find that their holdings of real money are less than desired, they will

a sell financial assets, which will cause interest rates to rise.

b sell financial assets, which will cause interest rates to fall.

c buy financial assets, which will cause interest rates to rise.

d buy financial assets, which will cause interest rates to fall.

e buy goods, which will cause the price level to rise.

17 Which of the following is *not* a store of value?

a credit cards

b demand deposits

c term deposits

d other chequable deposits

e savings deposits

18 Money market equilibrium occurs

a when interest rates are constant.

b when the level of real GDP is constant.

c when money supply equals money demand.

d only under a fixed exchange rate.

e when both **a** and **b** are true.

19 If the prices of goods and services were stated in terms of kilograms of salt, then salt is a

a unit of account.

b standard of deferred payment.

c store of value.

d quasi-money.

e medium of exchange.

20 Which of the following is a *disadvantage* of a commodity money?

a It is valued for its own sake.

b Its value as money is much greater than its value as a commodity.

c The commodity could be used in other ways, if it was not used as a medium of exchange.

d It has little intrinsic value.

e It is not bulky to carry around.

21 A chequable deposit in a depository institution is an example of

a commodity money.

b fiat money.

c convertible paper money.

d deposit money.

e public debt money.

22 Which of the following is a liability of a chartered bank?

a vault cash

b loans

c securities

d demand deposits

e its deposits at the Bank of Canada

23 Which of the following will cause the demand curve for real money to shift to the left?

a an increase in real GDP

b a decrease in interest rates

c the expanded use of credit cards

d an increase in the quantity of money supplied

e an increase in the price level

24 Real money is equal to nominal money

a divided by real GDP.

b minus real GDP.

c divided by the price level.

d minus the price level.

e divided by velocity.

25 Which of the following is money?

a a chequable deposit

b a blank cheque

c a credit card

d a term deposit

e a Canada Savings Bond

Short Answer Problems

1 Banks can no longer issue their own paper money, but can create money by creating deposit money by crediting people's deposits. Since there is no paper money deposited to back up this creation, is this created money real? Is it acceptable in society? Why or why not?

2 Explain why credit cards are not money.

3 Carefully explain how and why banks create new money during the deposit multiplier process.

4 Why do people care about the quantity of real money they hold rather than the quantity of nominal money?

5 Suppose an individual sells $1,000 worth of government securities to the Bank of Canada and deposits the proceeds ($1,000) in Bank 1. Note that this new deposit initially increases the quantity of money by $1,000. (In the next chapter we will see how such a new deposit arises.) Assume that the desired reserve ratio for all banks is 20 percent (0.2). There is no currency drain. Table 27.3 gives information for the first round of the money expansion process that will be generated by this new deposit.

a Follow the first six rounds of the money creation process by completing Table 27.3.

TABLE **27.3** MONEY CREATION PROCESS— NO CURRENCY DRAIN

Bank Number	New Deposits	New Loans	New Reserves	Increase in Deposits	Cumulative Increase in Deposits
1	1,000	800	200	1,000	1,000
2					
3					
4					
5					
6					

b What is the total increase in the quantity of money after six rounds?

c What is the deposit multiplier?

d After all rounds have been completed, what will the total increase in deposits be?

6 For the first two banks in Short Answer Problem 5, show their balance sheets for each stage of the process (initial deposit, loan creation, borrower's withdrawal, final position).

7 For the entire banking system in Short Answer Problem 5, what do the final balance sheet changes look like? (Assume that banks have only reserves, loans, and deposits.)

8 The chartered banks in Gondor have the following assets and liabilities (none is missing from the list except as indicated):

Currency reserves	$20 million
Reserves held at the Bank of Gondor	$10 million
Loans	?
Securities	$25 million
Demand deposits	$150 million
Notice deposits	$600 million

a Construct the balance sheet for the entire banking system in Gondor. What is the amount of loans in this system?

b Assuming that the banks have freely chosen their reserves, what is the desired reserve ratio in this system? What is the deposit multiplier?

9 Consider a perpetuity with an annual payment of $100. What is the interest rate on this financial asset, if its price is

a $1,000?

b $900?

c $1,100?

10 Show on a graph and briefly explain what each of the following will do (in sequence) to the demand for real money (defined as M1) and therefore the equilibrium interest rate. Assume that the real money supply remains constant.

a The price level rises.

b There is a financial innovation (the widespread adoption of electronic funds transfers) that reduces the need to use chequing accounts.

c Real GDP falls during a recession.

ANSWERS

True/False/Uncertain and Explain

1 F Real money demand independent of price level. (649)

2 T ↑ interest rate → ↑ opportunity cost of holding money → ↓ quantity money demanded. (649)

3 F Large size allows them to pool risk. (646)

4 T Withdrawal → ↓ reserves = ↓ deposits → ↓ reserve/deposit ratio—do a balance sheet. (646)

5 T Agents substitute towards bonds → ↑ bond demand → ↑ bond price → ↓ bond interest rate. (653)

6 F Credit cards are form of ID used to make short-term loans. (642–643)

7 T Basic function of money. (638)

8 T Definition. (644)

9 T Definition. (648)

10 U Depends on definition of money → notice accounts not part of M1, but part of M2+. (643)

Multiple-Choice

1 b Desired reserve ratio = chosen reserves/deposits = 40/500 = 0.08. (646)

2 b ↓ currency as deposit made = ↑ deposits. (647)

3 c Excess = actual ($50) – desired ($40.80 = 0.08 × $510). (647)

4 c Banks will lend the amount of excess reserves. (647)

⊚◑ **5 a** Work through balance sheet changes as shown in Helpful Hint 3. (647–648)

◑ **6 a** Δ deposits = (1/(desired reserve ratio)) × Δ reserves = (1/0.08) × $10 = $125. (648)

7 b See text discussion. (638–639)

8 e Definition. (638–639)

9 a Definition. (639–641)

10 b Multiplier = 1/(desired reserve ratio) = 1/1 = 1. (648)

11 e Definition. (641)

12 a Most readily changed into currency. (643)

13 e $a \rightarrow f$, $e \rightarrow a$ are falls in income, others are Δ interest rates. (650–651)

14 a ↓ price of bonds → ↑ interest rates. $a \rightarrow f$, $a \rightarrow e$, $e \rightarrow a$, are income changes, $a \rightarrow c$ is fall in interest rates. (650–651)

◑ **15 e** If rate of interest > equilibrium → too much money → buy bonds → ↑ price of bonds → ↓ interest rates since price of bonds and interest rates inversely related. (653)

16 a They substitute money for bonds, extra sales → ↓ price of bonds → ↑ interest rates. (653)

17 a Credit cards cannot necessarily be used for purchases in the future, the credit card company could refuse to honour your card. (642–643)

18 c Definition. (653)

19 a Definition. (638–639)

20 c It has an opportunity cost when used as money. (639)

21 d Definition. (641)

22 d Others are all assets = claims on someone else. (644)

23 c Financial innovation means people use less money. (650–651)

24 c Definition. (649)

25 a Definition. (642–643)

Short Answer Problems

1 This created money is real because it is backed by the assets of the bank, which consist of the bank's reserves, loans, and holdings of securities. Deposit money is generally accepted in society (you can buy goods, pay debts, etc., with it) because people know that the banks will provide currency upon demand.

2 A credit card is not money, but rather a mechanism for borrowing money, which must be repaid. Repayment takes place when the credit card bill is paid by cheque.

3 Banks create money by making new loans. When banks get a new deposit, this leaves them with excess reserves. Their desire to make profits (maximize net worth) leads banks to lend out the excess reserves, creating a matching deposit, which is new money. When the proceeds of these loans are spent, the person receiving the money will deposit much of it in a bank deposit, which is also new money.

4 Nominal money is simply the number of dollars, while real money is a measure of what money will buy. Real money will fall if the price level rises, and if the number of dollars is constant. What matters to people is the quantity of goods and services that money will buy, not the number of dollars. If the price level rises by 10 percent, people will want to hold 10 percent more dollars (given a constant real income and interest rates) in order to retain the same purchasing power.

5 a Table 27.3 is completed here as Table 27.3 Solution. Note that 80 percent of each new deposit will be lent and 20 percent will be held as reserves. When a new loan is deposited in the next bank, it becomes a new deposit.

TABLE **27.3** SOLUTION

Bank Number	New Deposits	New Loans	New Reserves	Increase in Deposits	Cumulative Increase in Deposits
1	1,000	800	200	1,000	1,000
2	800	640	160	800	1,800
3	640	512	128	640	2,440
4	512	410	102	512	2,952
5	410	328	82	410	3,362
6	328	262	66	328	3,690

b After six rounds, the total (cumulative) increase in the quantity of money is $3,690 (the last number of Table 27.3 Solution).

c The deposit multiplier in this case is equal to 1/(desired reserve ratio). Since the desired reserve ratio is 0.2, the deposit multiplier is 5.

d The total increase in money will be $5,000 after all rounds are completed. This is obtained by multiplying the initial increase in deposits ($1,000) by the deposit multiplier (5).

6 Bank 1's balance sheets are shown in Table 27.4, and Bank 2's are shown in Table 27.5.

TABLE **27.4** BANK 1

(a) Initial New Deposit of $1,000

Assets		Liabilities	
Reserves	+$1,000	Deposits	+$1,000

(b) Loan Creation of $800

Assets		Liabilities	
Loans	+$800	Deposits	+$800

(c) Withdrawal of Loan Money

Assets		Liabilities	
Reserves	−$800	Deposits	−$800

(d) Final Position

Assets		Liabilities	
Reserves	+$200	Deposits	+$1,000
Loans	+$800		
	+$1,000		

TABLE **27.5** BANK 2

(a) Initial New Deposit of $800

Assets		Liabilities	
Reserves	+$800	Deposits	+$800

(b) Loan Creation of $640

Assets		Liabilities	
Loans	+$640	Deposits	+$640

(c) Withdrawal of Loan Money

Assets		Liabilities	
Reserves	−$640	Deposits	−$640

(d) Final Position

Assets		Liabilities	
Reserves	+$160	Deposits	+$800
Loans	+$640		
	+$800		

7 The total change in reserves in the system must be equal to the initial new reserves of +$1,000. Total new deposits have been calculated as +$5,000. For the balance sheet to balance therefore, loans must be +$4,000, and the balance sheet is as shown in Table 27.6.

TABLE **27.6**

Assets		Liabilities	
Reserves	+$1,000	Deposits	+$5,000
Loans	+$4,000		
	+$5,000		

8 a The balance sheet is shown in Table 27.7 (all values are in millions). Since assets must equal liabilities in the balance sheet, loans = $750 − $30 − $25 = $695.

TABLE **27.7**

Assets		Liabilities	
Reserves	+$30	Demand Deposits	+$150
Securities	+$25	Notice Deposits	+$600
Loans	+$695		+$750
	+$750		

b The desired reserve ratio = desired reserves/deposits = 30/750 = 0.04. The deposit multiplier = 1/(desired reserve ratio) = 1/0.04 = 25.

9 The interest rate on a perpetuity is obtained using the formula from Helpful Hint 7:

a $r = \dfrac{100}{1,000} \times 100 = 10$ percent

b $r = \dfrac{100}{900} \times 100 = 11.11$ percent

c $r = \dfrac{100}{1,100} \times 100 = 9.09$ percent

10 a A change in the price level will have no impact on real money demand, and therefore no impact on the equilibrium interest rate. In Fig. 27.2, demand for real money remains at MD_0, and the interest rate remains at r_0.

b This financial innovation would reduce the need to use chequing accounts, which are part of M1. Therefore the demand for real money falls to MD_1, and the equilibrium interest rate falls to r_1 in Fig. 27.2.

c The fall in real GDP lowers the demand for real money to MD_2, and the equilibrium interest rate falls to r_2 in Fig. 27.2.

FIGURE **27.2**

Monetary Policy

The Bank of Canada

The **Bank of Canada** is Canada's **central bank.** It supervises financial institutions and conducts monetary policy.

◆ **Monetary policy** attempts to control inflation and business cycle by Δ money supply, exchange rate, and interest rates.

◆ Canada's central bank is somewhat subordinate to the federal government.

- An independent central bank determines monetary policy with no government interference. Possible advantage—central bank can better stand up to short-term pressures.
- A subordinate central bank must follow government directions, but can still have significant power.

◆ Bank of Canada balance sheet shows

- liabilities = Bank of Canada notes + deposits (reserves) of chartered banks + government deposits,
- assets = government securities + loans to banks,
- **monetary base** = Bank of Canada notes + bank reserves + coins in circulation.

◆ Monetary policy is difficult because current tools create delayed, future effects → need to try to predict economy's future course.

◆ **Monetary policy indicators** are current features of economy that help predict future course. Main indicator one is **overnight loans rate** (interest rate on loans banks make to each other).

◆ Bank of Canada attempts to Δ bank reserves → Δ overnight rate → Δ quantity of money, etc., by manipulating four main policy tools:

- Δ required reserve ratio—minimum reserves banks must hold (currently = 0). = most pref tools.
- Δ **bank rate**—the rate it lends to chartered banks. ↑ bank rate → ↑ costs of borrowing reserves → ↑ reserves held by banks → ↓ loans to public. ↑ banker's deposit rate = rate earned by banks' deposits at Bank of Canada → ↑ overnight loans rates.
- **Open market operations**—buying/selling government bonds, which Δ monetary base with further effects.
- **Government deposit shifting**—transferring government funds between Bank of Canada and chartered bank deposits. If shift deposits out of Bank of Canada into chartered banks, chartered banks get more deposits and more reserves → more loans and money created.

Controlling the Money Supply

The major policy tool of the Bank is an open market operation.

◆ Bank of Canada carries out open market operations with banks or public → same essential outcome.

◆ Bank of Canada buys government bonds → ↑ chartered bank reserves = ↑ excess reserves → ↑ lending → loans used to make payments → ↑ new deposits elsewhere and ↑ currency held by public.

- The new deposits → ↑ chartered bank reserves → ↑ desired reserves and ↑ excess reserves.
- The excess reserves are used to make new loans → further second round or multiplier effects.
- Overall result is ↑ currency (**currency drain**) and ↑ deposits = money supply.

- *Bank of Canada buying government bonds → ↑ money supply.*

◆ Bank of Canada sells government bonds → ↓ chartered bank reserves → loans called in → ↓ deposits → further second round effects → ↓ money supply.

- *Bank of Canada selling government bonds → ↓ money supply.*

◆ **Money multiplier** = amount Δ monetary base (*MB*) is multiplied by to get resulting Δ in quantity of money = $\Delta M / \Delta MB$.

◆ Size of Δ money supply depends on size of second round effects, which are larger if

- currency drain is smaller.
- desired reserve ratio is smaller.

Influencing Interest Rates and the Exchange Rate

Changes in real money supply (*MS*) → Δ interest rates (*r*) and Δ prices of financial assets.

◆ ↑ *MS* → excess money holdings → people buy financial assets → ↑ price of financial assets → ↓ interest rates.

◆ ↓ *MS* → shortage of money → people sell financial assets → ↓ price of financial assets → ↑ interest rates.

◆ Monetary policy also influences the **exchange rate** (price at which Canadian dollar exchanges for another currency).

- ↑ *MS* → ↓ *r* → ↓ demand for Canadian dollar → ↓ exchange rate.
- ↓ *MS* → ↑ *r* → ↑ demand for Canadian dollar → ↑ exchange rate.

Ripple Effects of Monetary Policy

The quantity of money affects aggregate demand and therefore real GDP and price level through several channels.

◆ Open market operations: buying bonds → ↑ *MS* → ↓ *r* which

- ↓ exchange rate → ↑ net exports → ↑ *AD*.
- ↑ consumption and investment → ↑ *AD*.

◆ Historical evidence:

- Actual Canadian interest rates move inversely with Δ*MB*.
- ↑ interest rate gap between Canada and United States → ↑ pressure on exchange rate.

Money in the AD-AS Model

◆ In the *AD–AS* model, Δ *MS* → Δ *AD*.

- With unemployment, ↑ *MS* → ↑ *AD* → ↑ real GDP and price level.
- With full employment, ↑ *MS* → ↑ *AD* → ↑ price level only.
- With inflationary pressure, ↓ *MS* → ↓ *AD* → reduces pressure.

◆ **Quantity theory of money** predicts ↑ money supply → ↑ price level by same percentage.

◆ Quantity theory starts with definition of **velocity of circulation** ($V = PY/M$) → **equation of exchange** ($MV = PY$).

- Assumes velocity and potential GDP are unaffected by Δ money supply.
- Then, in long run → $\Delta P = (V/Y)\Delta M$ → $\Delta P/P = \Delta M/M$.

◆ Historical evidence suggests money growth rate strongly influences inflation, but in short run other *AD–AS* factors are crucial.

The Bank of Canada in Action

◆ Strong ↓ pressure on money growth rates in early 1980s → ↑ *r* sharply → created recession, slowed inflation.

- Similar policy in late 1980s → ↓ inflation some more, but contributed to 1990–1991 recession.

◆ Economic agents attempt to profit by predicting actions of the Bank → *r* may change before Δ *MS*.

HELPFUL HINTS

I Open market operations are the most important policy tools of the Bank of Canada, and it is important to understand how they affect the quantity of money. To understand the effect of open market operations on the monetary base and thus the quantity of money, remember that one liability of the Bank of Canada is banks' deposits at the Bank of Canada that serve as bank reserves. These deposits combined with currency in circulation (the other major liability of the Bank of Canada) constitute the monetary base. The largest class of assets on the books of the Bank of Canada is its holdings of government securities. Finally, recall that if total assets increase, due to the conventions of double entry bookkeeping, total liabilities must increase by the same amount.

An open market purchase of government securities is an increase in the assets of the Bank of Canada (government securities) paid for by an increase in its liabilities, principally an increase in the deposits of banks at the Bank of Canada. This increase in liabilities of the Bank of Canada is an increase in the monetary base, which will have a multiplied effect on the quantity of money.

2 Here are some further notes on open market operations:

a To remember whether an open market purchase will lead to a decrease or an increase in money, think of open market operations as an exchange of government securities for cash. For example, think of an open market purchase as the Bank of Canada acquiring government securities by giving cash to the public. This increases the money supply.

Be careful to avoid making a very common error when working through open market operations. When the Bank of Canada buys or sells securities, chartered bank reserves at the Bank of Canada change. Many students automatically place the changed bank reserves at the Bank of Canada under assets in the Bank's balance sheet, because they are an asset on the chartered bank balance sheet. However, this is an error—the reserves are a deposit at the Bank of Canada, and therefore a *liability* to the Bank.

b Remember that government securities are assets to the Bank of Canada just as they are to members of the public who hold them. They are liabilities of the government of Canada.

c Government securities are traded in two markets: the primary market in which the treasury sells newly issued government securities, and the secondary market in which government securities previously purchased in the primary market are bought and sold. This secondary market is the open market in which *open market* operations take place.

d To understand how an open market operation changes interest rates, consider the changes in the banking sector. For example, an open market purchase of government securities (which will increase the money supply) leaves the banking sector with excess reserves. Profit-seeking banks attempt to lend these excess reserves. At the original interest rate, loan demand (borrowing) equalled loan supply. To convince economic agents to borrow more money, banks must lower interest rates. The result is that as the money supply increases, interest rates fall. Therefore we can see intuitively how an open market purchase leads directly to lower interest rates.

e The text does not work through an open market sale, so for the extra practice let us try one. Suppose that the Bank of Canada wishes to lower the money supply and decides to lower the monetary base by $100 million. It decides to do so by selling $100 million worth of securities to the Royal Bank. The Royal Bank pays for the securities out of its reserves held at the Bank of Canada. Table 28.1 below shows the changes in the two balance sheets. Note that the Royal Bank now has a fall in its reserves, and if desired reserves are too low, must call in some loans to raise reserves. This action will trigger a fall in deposits and the overall money supply, as desired by the Bank of Canada.

TABLE **28.1**

Bank of Canada

Assets		Liabilities	
Securities	−100	Deposits (reserves) of Royal Bank	−100

Royal Bank

Assets		Liabilities	
Reserves	−100		
Securities	+100		
	0		

3 An important equation in this chapter is the equation of exchange:

Quantity of money × Velocity of circulation = Price level × Real GDP.

This equation simply says that the quantity of money times the average number of times each dollar is spent (equalling total expenditure) is equal to the dollar value of the goods and services on which it was spent. The equation is always true by definition—it is an identity. If we further assume that the velocity of circulation and potential GDP are independent of the quantity of money, we get the quantity theory of money. These assumptions imply that when the quantity of money increases by 10 percent, the price level must increase by 10 percent in order to maintain equality between the two sides of the equation.

4 We can also explore the link between velocity and money demand. Recall that in equilibrium, real money supply (M/P) equals real money demand

(*MD*). Substituting this into our definition of velocity yields the following relationship between velocity and real money demand.

$$V = \frac{PY}{M} = \frac{Y}{\left(\frac{M}{P}\right)} = \frac{Y}{MD}$$

Velocity and real money demand are inversely related. *If velocity is not constant,* higher interest rates lead to lower money demand (agents conserve on money holdings) and higher velocity (agents carry out more transactions to make up for lower money holdings).

S E L F - T E S T

True/False/Uncertain and Explain

1 If real GDP is increasing and the real money supply is increasing, then interest rates will also be increasing.

2 An increase in the quantity of money shifts the aggregate demand curve to the right.

3 An increase in the quantity of money will cause the price level to rise, but will leave real GDP unchanged.

4 A rise in the money supply will lower the exchange rate.

5 If the quantity of money is $50 billion and nominal GDP is $200 billion, the velocity of circulation is 1/4.

6 Historical evidence for Canada as well as international evidence shows a very close correspondence between money and the price level.

7 If the Bank of Canada wants to lower interest rates, it should sell government securities in the open market.

8 The Bank of Canada is an independent central bank.

9 If the Bank of Canada sells government securities in the open market, chartered bank reserves will increase.

10 The higher the banks' desired reserve ratio, the larger is the money multiplier.

Multiple-Choice

1 Which of the balance sheets in Table 28.2 shows the initial impact on the banking sector of an open market purchase by the Bank of Canada of $100 worth of government securities from the banking sector?
a (a)
b (b)
c (c)
d (d)
e none of the above

TABLE **28.2** CHARTERED BANKS' BALANCE SHEETS

(a)

Assets	Liabilities
Reserves +100	
Securities −100	

(b)

Assets	Liabilities
Reserves −100	
Securities +100	

(c)

Assets	Liabilities
Reserves +100	Deposits +100

(d)

Assets	Liabilities
	Deposits +100
	Securities −100

2 Which of the balance sheets in Table 28.2 shows the initial impact on the banking sector of an open market purchase by the Bank of Canada of $100 worth of government securities from a private individual?

a (a)
b (b)
c (c)
d (d)
e none of the above

3 Which of the balance sheets in Table 28.2 shows the initial impact on the banking sector of an open market sale by the Bank of Canada of $100 worth of government securities to a private individual?

a (a)
b (b)
c (c)
d (d)
e none of the above

4 Which of the balance sheets in Table 28.2 shows the initial impact on the banking sector of an open market sale by the Bank of Canada of $100 worth of government securities to a bank?

a (a)
b (b)
c (c)
d (d)
e none of the above

5 Which of the following statements is *false*, given the empirical evidence on the quantity theory of money?

a The only cause of inflation is higher growth rates of money.
b Internationally, inflation and high growth rates of money are positively correlated among high-inflation countries.
c Internationally, inflation and high growth rates of money are positively correlated among low-inflation countries.
d A major cause of inflation is higher growth rates of money.
e As the growth rate of money rose through the 1960s, inflation rose too.

6 According to the quantity theory, which of the following would raise the price level?

a the discovery of a hoard of 1930s currency in someone's barn
b the decision by several banks to call in 20 percent of their loans
c a massive fire in the vaults of the Bank of Montreal that destroys several million dollars in uninsured reserves
d **a** and **b** would raise the price level
e **b** and **c** would raise the price level

7 Which of the following would *not* affect the size of the monetary base?

a A bank exchanges government securities for a deposit at the Bank of Canada.
b A bank exchanges vault cash for a deposit at the Bank of Canada.
c The Bank of Canada buys government securities from a bank.
d The Bank of Canada buys government securities from someone other than a bank.
e The Bank of Canada sells government securities to a bank.

8 Which of the following is one of the main policy tools of the Bank of Canada?

a prime rate
b exchange rate
c currency ratio
d bankers' deposit rate
e **b** and **d**

9 The bank rate is the interest rate

a banks charge their very best loan customers.
b banks pay on term deposits.
c the Bank of Canada pays on reserves held by banks.
d the Bank of Canada charges when it lends reserves to banks.
e received for holding Government of Canada Treasury bills.

10 The quantity theory of money begins with the equation of exchange—$MV = PY$—and then adds the assumptions that

a velocity varies inversely with the rate of interest, and the price level is independent of the level of the money supply.

b velocity and the price level are independent of the level of the money supply.

c potential GDP and the money supply are independent of the price level.

d potential GDP and the price level are independent of the level of the money supply.

e velocity and potential GDP are independent of the level of the money supply.

11 The bank rate is an effective signal of monetary policy because it is

a a measure of the cost of borrowing to replenish reserves.

b useful for predicting monetary policy.

c equal to the prime rate.

d a rough approximation of the value of the money multiplier.

e **a** and **b**.

12 Why is the exchange rate a key monetary variable?

a It is one of the four main policy tools.

b It is a key policy objective.

c It is a barometer of monetary policy.

d It shows how much the monetary base must be multiplied in order to measure the resulting increase in the money supply.

e It is part of the channel by which a change in money supply affects aggregate demand.

13 Examining Canadian historical evidence on the relation between money supply growth and inflation reveals that

a on average, the quantity of money grows faster than inflation.

b variations in the growth rate of the quantity of money are correlated with variations in the inflation rate.

c during World War II and its aftermath, there was a break in the relationship between money growth and inflation.

d during the years since 1950, inflation has been less volatile than money supply growth.

e all of the above.

14 In a situation of unemployment, an increase in the money supply will lead to a

a rise in real GDP and the price level.

b rise in real GDP, but a fall in the price level.

c rise in real GDP, but no change in the price level.

d rise in the price level, but no change in real GDP.

e fall in the price level and real GDP.

15 According to the quantity theory of money,

a V/M is constant.

b Y/M is constant.

c Y/P is constant.

d M/P is constant.

e M/V is constant.

16 The monetary expansion process continues until

a required reserves are eliminated.

b the Bank of Canada eliminates required reserves.

c the discount rate is lower than the prime rate.

d the prime rate is lower than the discount rate.

e excess reserves are eliminated.

17 In an expansionary open market operation, the Bank of Canada

a sells government bonds, which decreases bank reserves, leading to a decrease in lending, leading to a decrease in the money supply.

b sells government bonds, which decreases bank reserves, leading to a decrease in lending, leading to an increase in the money supply.

c sells government bonds, which decreases bank reserves, leading to an increase in lending, leading to an increase in the money supply.

d buys government bonds, which increases bank reserves, leading to an increase in lending, leading to a decrease in the money supply.

e buys government bonds, which increases bank reserves, leading to an increase in lending, leading to an increase in the money supply.

18 An expansionary monetary policy will

a raise interest rates and lower the exchange rate.

b have no impact on interest rates, but raise the exchange rate.

c have no impact on interest rates nor on the exchange rate.

d lower interest rates and raise the exchange rate.

e lower interest rates and the exchange rate.

19 If the price level is 2, real GDP is $100 billion, and the quantity of money is $40 billion, what is the velocity of circulation?

a 2.5
b 4.0
c 5.0
d 10.0
e 50.0

20 According to the quantity theory of money, an increase in the quantity of money will lead to an increase in the price level

a but have no effect on real GDP or the velocity of circulation.
b as well as increasing both real GDP and the velocity of circulation.
c as well as increasing real GDP but decreasing the velocity of circulation.
d as well as decreasing real GDP but increasing the velocity of circulation.
e but have no effect on real GDP while decreasing velocity.

@ **21** The higher the interest rate, the

a lower the quantity of money demanded, and the higher is the velocity of circulation.
b lower the quantity of money demanded, and the lower is the velocity of circulation.
c higher the quantity of money demanded, and the higher is the velocity of circulation.
d higher the quantity of money demanded, and the lower is the velocity of circulation.
e higher the quantity of money demanded, but the money supply remains unaffected.

22 Suppose there is an increase in the tendency for loans to return to banks in the form of new deposits and reserves; in other words, there is a *decrease* in the currency drain. Select the best statement.

a The deposit multiplier will decrease.
b The deposit multiplier will increase.
c The money multiplier will decrease.
d The money multiplier will stay constant.
e The money multiplier will increase.

23 The money multiplier will increase if either the fraction of deposits that households and firms want to hold as currency

a increases or the desired reserve ratio increases.
b decreases or the desired reserve ratio decreases.
c decreases or the desired reserve ratio increases.
d increases or the desired reserve ratio decreases.
e none of the above.

24 If the Bank of Canada buys government securities in the open market, the supply curve of real money will shift to the

a left, and the interest rate will rise.
b left, and the interest rate will fall.
c right, and the interest rate will rise.
d right, and the interest rate will remain constant as money demand will shift to the right as well.
e none of the above.

25 Which of the Bank of Canada's policy tools is the most important?

a choosing exchange rate regimes
b setting reserve requirements
c changing the bank rate
d paying for the government's deficit
e open market operations

Short Answer Problems

1 Often the Bank of Canada uses monetary policy to raise interest rates, in order to offset downward pressure on the exchange rate. Explain briefly but carefully how this works.

2 How does an open market purchase of government securities lead to an increase in the monetary base?

3 What role does the size of the currency drain play in the size of the money multiplier?

4 The market for money is initially in equilibrium when the Bank of Canada increases the supply of money. Explain the adjustment to a new equilibrium interest rate.

5 According to the quantity theory of money, what is the effect of an increase in the quantity of money? What assumptions of the theory are crucial for this effect to occur? Why?

6 Figure 28.1 illustrates the current equilibrium in the money market where *MD* is the demand curve for real money and *MS* is the supply curve for real money.

a Suppose that the Bank of Canada wants to stimulate aggregate expenditure by lowering the interest rate to 6 percent. By how much must the Bank of Canada increase the nominal money supply if the price level is 2?

FIGURE **28.1**

b Having determined the amount by which the Bank of Canada must increase the nominal supply of money, we now want to determine the open market operation that will be necessary if the money multiplier is 4. Will the Bank of Canada need to buy or sell government securities in the open market and in what amount? (Assume the Bank of Canada deals directly with chartered banks.)

7 Consider the following balance sheets for the Bank of Canada and the Bank of Speedy Creek:

TABLE **28.3**

Bank of Speedy Creek

Assets		Liabilities	
Reserves	60	Deposits	1,000
Securities	100		
Loans	840		
	1,000		

Bank of Canada

Assets		Liabilities	
Government securities	9,000	Bank of Canada notes	10,000
Loans to banks	500	Ch. banks' deposits	1,000
Other net assets	2,000	Government deposits	500
	11,500		11,500

a The Bank of Speedy Creek has chosen this balance sheet position—what is their desired reserve ratio? Explain.

b Suppose that the Bank of Canada buys all $100 of securities from the Bank of Speedy Creek. Show what happens to the balance sheets of the Bank of Speedy Creek and the Bank of Canada as a result of this action, explaining as you go. What does this action do to the monetary base?

c What will the Bank of Speedy Creek do next? Assuming no currency drain, what does this action do to the overall level of deposits in the banking sector? (Calculate the size of the deposit multiplier as part of your answer.)

d Explain what this open market operation does to the money supply and interest rates.

8 Suppose there is a decrease in the quantity of money. Using an aggregate demand—aggregate supply model, show what happens to the price level and the level of real GDP in the short run and in the long run.

9 We observe an economy in which the price level is 1.5, real GDP is $240 billion, and the money supply is $60 billion.
a What is the velocity of circulation?
b According to the quantity theory of money, what will be the result of an increase in the quantity of money to $80 billion?

10 Given the following data from the Canadian economy, graph the money market, showing the initial equilibrium in 1988 and the new equilibrium in 1989. Briefly explain why you decided *MD* and *MS* would be placed where you placed them in the graph.

Interest rate (1988) = 10.8 percent
Interest rate (1989) = 13.4 percent
Inflation rate (1988–1989) = 5.0 percent
Nominal money growth (1988–1989) = 4.6 percent
Real GDP growth (1988–1989) = 2.3 percent

A N S W E R S

True/False/Uncertain and Explain

◑ 1 U ↑ real GDP → *MD* shifts right. Since *MS* shifting right too, impact on *r* uncertain. (670–671)

2 T ↑ *MS* → ↓ *r* → ↓ exchange rate → ↑*NX*, *C*, *I* → *AD* shifts right. (674)

3 U True in long run, but in short run real GDP rises. (674–675)

4 **T** $\uparrow MS \rightarrow \downarrow r \rightarrow \downarrow$ demand for Canadian dollar $\rightarrow \downarrow$ exchange rate. (672–673)

5 **F** $V = PY/M = 200/50 = 4$. (676)

6 **F** There is some correspondence, but there are periods when there is virtually no correspondence. (676–678)

7 **F** Selling government bonds $\rightarrow \downarrow$ reserves $\rightarrow \downarrow$ loans and deposits $\rightarrow \downarrow MS \rightarrow \uparrow$ interest rates. (670–671)

8 **F** It is subordinate—see text discussion. (661)

9 **F** If securities are sold, people buy them with their deposits, $\rightarrow \downarrow$ reserves. (664)

10 **F** Desired reserve ratio $\uparrow \rightarrow$ more deposits kept back, less lent out, at each stage of money multiplier process. (667–669)

Multiple-Choice

1 **a** Bank of Canada credits banking sector's reserves at central bank and in return gets securities from banking sector. (666–667)

2 **c** Individual gets bank draft from Bank of Canada $\rightarrow$ deposited in his/her bank $\rightarrow$ Bank of Canada credits the reserves of his/her bank. (666–667)

3 **e** Open market sale would look like (c), except both values would be –100. (666–667)

4 **b** Bank gets $100 worth of securities, and pays for it with debit of its reserves held at Bank of Canada. (666–667)

5 **a** Empirical evidence reveals time periods when money growth fluctuates but inflation does not because velocity is not constant as assumed. (676–678)

6 **a** This money would $\uparrow$ spending and price level. **b** and **c** would $\downarrow$ money supply. (676)

7 **b** Others are all examples of open market operations. (662)

8 **d** Definition. (663–665)

9 **d** Definition. (664)

10 **e** See text discussion. (676)

11 **e** **a** is definition of bank rate, and **b** occurs because bank rate is barometer of open market operations. (664)

12 **e** $\Delta MS \rightarrow \Delta r \rightarrow \Delta$ demand for Canadian dollar $\rightarrow \Delta$ exchange rate $\rightarrow \Delta NX \rightarrow \Delta AD$. (671)

13 **e** See text discussion. (676–677)

14 **a** $\uparrow$ money supply $\rightarrow$ shift right in $AD \rightarrow \uparrow$ real GDP and price level if initial equilibrium is left of full employment (draw a graph). (674)

15 **d** Because theory assumes $Y/V (= M/P)$ is constant. (676)

16 **e** Until this occurs, banks will keep lending out excess reserves. (669)

17 **e** Buying bonds $\rightarrow \uparrow$ reserves to pay for them $\rightarrow \uparrow$ excess reserves $\rightarrow \uparrow$ lending to make profits $\rightarrow \uparrow$ spending and $\uparrow$ deposits $\rightarrow \uparrow$ money supply. (666–669)

18 **e** $\uparrow$ money supply $\rightarrow$ excess supply of money $\rightarrow$ excess demand for financial assets $\rightarrow \uparrow$ price of financial assets $\rightarrow \downarrow$ interest rates $\rightarrow \downarrow$ demand for Canadian dollar $\rightarrow \downarrow$ exchange rate. (671–673)

19 **c** $V = PY/M = 2(100)/(40) = 5$. (676)

20 **a** Due to assumption that neither is affected by Δ money supply. (676)

21 **a** $\uparrow$ interest rate $\rightarrow \uparrow$ opportunity cost of holding money $\rightarrow \downarrow$ money demand $\rightarrow \uparrow$ velocity since velocity $= Y/MD$. (676)

22 **e** Deposit multiplier does not depend on currency drain. Lower currency drain will result in more loan creation and more deposit (= money) creation at each stage of the multiplier. (668–669)

23 **b** Both decreases mean there is more reserves to create new loans at each stage of the multiplier process. (668–669)

24 **e** Buying bonds $\rightarrow \uparrow$ reserves $\rightarrow \uparrow$ deposits and money supply $\rightarrow$ excess supply of money $\rightarrow$ excess demand for financial assets $\rightarrow \uparrow$ price of financial assets $\rightarrow \downarrow$ interest rates. (670–671)

25 **e** See text discussion. (663–665)

Short Answer Problems

1 Raising interest rates will raise the interest rate gap between Canada and other countries, raising the demand for the Canadian dollar. This in turn will tend to raise the exchange rate, offsetting the initial downward pressure.

2 An open market purchase of government securities by the Bank of Canada increases the monetary base by increasing one of its components—banks' deposits at the Bank of Canada. The process depends on whether the securities are purchased from banks or from the nonbank public.

If the purchase is from banks, the process is direct—the Bank of Canada pays for the securities by crediting the bank's deposit at the Bank of Canada, which directly increases the monetary base. If the purchase is from the nonbank public, the Bank of Canada pays by writing cheques on itself which the sellers of the securities deposit in their banks. The banks, in turn, present the cheques to the Bank of Canada, which credits the banks' deposits at the

Bank of Canada. Thus in either case, the monetary base increases by the amount of the open market purchase.

3 During each round of the money multiplier process new loans are used for payments. Some of these payments are redeposited (triggering further loan and deposit expansion), and some are held back as currency. The higher the currency drain, the higher the amount held back, the smaller the amount redeposited, the smaller the amount available for further loan and deposit expansion, the smaller the overall deposit expansion, and the smaller the multiplier.

4 An increase in the supply of real money means that, at the current interest rate, the quantity of money supplied will be greater than the quantity of money demanded. Money holders will want to reduce their money holdings and will attempt to do so by buying financial assets. The increase in the demand for financial assets will cause the price of financial assets to rise and thus interest rates on financial assets to fall. As interest rates fall, the quantity of money demanded increases, which reduces the excess supply of money. This process continues until the interest rate has fallen sufficiently that the quantity of money demanded is the same as the quantity of money supplied.

5 According to the quantity theory of money, an increase in the quantity of money will cause the price level to increase by an equal percentage. The required assumptions are that velocity and potential GDP are independent of changes in the money supply, so that the change in the money supply affects only the price level.

6 a The current equilibrium interest rate is 8 percent and the Bank of Canada would like to increase the money supply sufficiently to lower the interest rate to 6 percent. Since the quantity of real money demanded at an interest rate of 6 percent is $70 billion, the Bank of Canada will want to increase the supply of real money by $10 billion: from $60 billion to $70 billion.

Real money is nominal money divided by the price level and the Bank of Canada only controls the supply of *nominal* money. Since the price level is 2, the supply of *nominal* money must rise by $20 billion in order to increase the supply of real money by $10 billion. Therefore the Bank of Canada will need to increase the *nominal* money supply by $20 billion.

b To increase the supply of money, the Bank of Canada will need to buy government securities in the open market that will increase bank reserves and the monetary base. Given the money multiplier is 4, if we want a total increase in money of $20 billion, we need a $5 billion increase in the monetary base. This requires an open market purchase of $5 billion in government securities.

7 a Desired reserve ratio = chosen reserves/deposits = 60/1,000 = 0.06 or 6%.

TABLE **28.4**

(a) Changes in Balance Sheets

Bank of Speedy Creek

Assets		Liabilities	
Reserves	+100	Deposits	0
Securities	−100		
Loans	0		
	0		

Bank of Canada

Assets		Liabilities	
Government securities	+100	Bank of Canada notes	0
Loans to banks	0	Ch. banks' deposits	+100
Other net assets	0	Government deposits	0
	+100		+100

(b) Positions After the Open Market Operation

Bank of Speedy Creek

Assets		Liabilities	
Reserves	160	Deposits	1,000
Securities	0		
Loans	840		
	1,000		

Bank of Canada

Assets		Liabilities	
Government securities	9,100	Bank of Canada notes	10,000
Loans to banks	500	Ch. banks' deposits	1,100
Other net assets	2,000	Government deposits	500
	11,600		11,600

b The Bank of Canada increases its securities by 100, and pays for this by increasing the Bank of Speedy Creek's deposits by 100, which is an increase in this bank's reserves by 100 (matching the fall in security holdings). The balance sheets in Table 28.4 show the changes, and then the new positions.

The increase in chartered banks' deposits of 100 will also increase the monetary base (= notes in circulation + chartered banks' deposits) by 100.

c The Bank of Speedy Creek now has excess reserves of 100, since deposits are unchanged by the operation. They will lend out these excess reserves, creating a multiplier process that will result in an increase in loans and deposits throughout the entire system. The deposit multiplier is 1/(desired reserve ratio) = 1/0.06 = 16.67, so that the total increase in deposits is 1,667.

d Clearly there is an increase in the money supply, which creates an excess supply of money at the original interest rate. People spend their excess supply of money on bonds, driving up the price of bonds, and therefore lowering interest rates.

8 The consequences of a decrease in the quantity of money are illustrated in Fig. 28.2. The economy is initially in long-run equilibrium at point *a*, the intersection of AD_0 and SAS_0 (and *LAS*). The price level is P_0 and GDP is at potential, Y^*. A decrease in the quantity of money will shift the *AD* curve to the left, from AD_0 to AD_1. The new short-run equilibrium is at point *b*. The price level falls to P_1 and real GDP falls to Y_1. In the long run, however, input prices will also fall, which will shift the *SAS* curve rightward, from SAS_0 to SAS_1. A new long-run equilibrium is achieved at point *c*. Thus, in the long run, the price level falls further to P_2, while real GDP returns to potential, Y^*.

FIGURE **28.2**

9 a The velocity of circulation is defined by

$$\text{Velocity of circulation} = \frac{\text{Price level} \times \text{Real GDP}}{\text{Quantity of money}}$$

With the values for the price level, real GDP, and the quantity of money given in this problem, we have

$$\text{Velocity of circulation} = \frac{1.5 \times 240}{60} = 6$$

b The quantity theory of money predicts that an increase in the quantity of money will cause an equal percentage increase in the price level. An increase in money from $60 billion to $80 billion is a one-third (33 percent) increase. Thus the quantity theory of money predicts that the price level will rise by a third (33 percent). Since the initial price level is 1.5, the predicted price level will be 2.0. (This can also be confirmed by using the equation of exchange.)

10 The initial 1988 equilibrium is indicated in Fig. 28.3 at the intersection of MD_{1988} and MS_{1988}, with an interest rate of 10.8 percent. The rise in real GDP from 1988 to 1989, *ceteris paribus*, will mean a rise in real money demanded, shown by the shift right from MD_{1988} to MD_{1989}. The inflation rate is higher than the growth rate of the nominal money supply, so that the real money supply shrinks by a small amount from 1988 to 1989, shown by the shift left from MS_{1988} to MS_{1989}. The net result of these two changes is a rise in the interest rate from 1988 to 1989.

FIGURE **28.3**

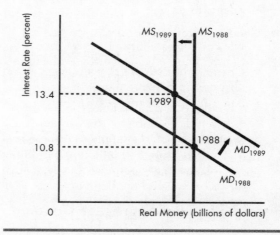

Fiscal and Monetary Interactions

Money, Interest, and Aggregate Demand

- Real GDP and the price level are determined by the interaction of *AD* and *AS*.

  - *AD* is determined by interaction of aggregate expenditure (fiscal policy) and money market (monetary policy).
  - Monetary and fiscal policy change aggregate expenditure directly and indirectly → ΔAD → Δ real GDP, Δ price level.

- This chapter explores how real GDP and interest rate are simultaneously determined.

- Money market equilibrium is where *MD* = *MS*.

  - *MD* is a function of *Y*.
  - $\Delta Y \rightarrow \Delta MD \rightarrow \Delta r$.
  - *r* depends on *Y*.

- Goods/services equilibrium is where *AE* = *Y*.

  - *AE* is a function of *I*, *C*, and *NX*.
  - Crucial is **investment demand curve**—relationship between *I* and *r*.
  - $\Delta r \rightarrow \Delta I (\Delta C, \Delta NX) \rightarrow \Delta AE \rightarrow \Delta Y$.
  - *Y* depends on *r*.

- There is only one value of *Y* and one value of *r* that give *simultaneous* or joint equilibrium in money market and goods/services market.

Fiscal Policy and Aggregate Demand

Expansionary fiscal policy is ↑ government purchases, ↑ transfer payments, or ↓ taxes to ↑*AD*, and has first and second round effects.

- First round effects: ↑ autonomous expenditure → ↑ aggregate expenditure → ↑ real GDP.

- Second round effects: ↑ real GDP → rightward shift *MD* → ↑ interest rate → ↓ investment → ↓ aggregate expenditure → smaller ↓ real GDP, *somewhat* offsetting first round ↑.

  - Tendency for expansionary fiscal policy to ↑*r* and ↓*I* is **crowding out** → usually only partial.
  - Expansionary fiscal policy may ↑ *I* (**crowding in**) if it ↑ expected future profits or ↑ profitability of current capital or ↓ taxes.
  - ↑*r* may cause **international crowding out** by ↑ exchange rate → ↓*NX*.

Monetary Policy and Aggregate Demand

Expansionary monetary policy is ↑ money supply to ↑*AD*, and has first round and second round effects.

- First round effects: ↑ money supply → ↓ interest rate → ↑ investment → ↑ autonomous expenditure → ↑ aggregate expenditure → ↑ real GDP.

- Second round effects: identical to second round fiscal policy effects.

- There is an exchange rate effect that augments the monetary policy—overall ↓ interest rate → ↓ demand Canadian dollar → ↓ exchange rate → ↑ net exports.

The Relative Effectiveness of Policies

- Fiscal policy is more powerful if less crowding out, which occurs if

  - Money demand *responsive* to interest rates ($\Delta MD \rightarrow$ small Δr).
  - Investment demand *unresponsive* to interest rates (given $\Delta r \rightarrow$ small Δ investment).

◆ Monetary policy is more powerful if

- Money demand *unresponsive* to interest rates ($\Delta MS \rightarrow$ large Δr).
- Investment demand *responsive* to interest rates (given $\Delta r \rightarrow$ large Δ investment).

◆ The Keynesian–monetarist controversy of the 1950s centred around whether fiscal policy or monetary policy was more effective:

- **Keynesians** believed economy was inherently unstable, fiscal policy more effective, due to little crowding out.
- **Monetarists** believed economy was inherently stable, monetary policy more effective, due to lots of crowding out.
- Empirical evidence → both policies effective.

Real GDP, the Price Level, and Interest Rates

Monetary and fiscal policy shift *AD*, price level constant.

◆ In the full *AD–AS* model, ↑ aggregate demand → ↑ price level → ↓ real money supply → ↑ interest rates → ↓ in quantity of real GDP demanded → smaller rise in real GDP than in partial model.

- If originally in unemployment equilibrium → overall ↑ both real GDP and price level.
- If originally in full-employment equilibrium → overall ↑ price level only.

Policy Coordination and Conflict

Government and Bank of Canada can work together to achieve common goals (**policy coordination**), or pursue conflicting goals (**policy conflict**).

◆ Monetary and fiscal policy both alter *AD*, but have opposite effects on interest and exchange rates.

- Expansionary fiscal policy ↑ *r* and ↑ exchange rate → ↓ *C, I, NX*.
- Expansionary monetary policy ↓ *r* and ↓ exchange rate → ↑ *C, I, NX*.
- Coordination allows ↑ *AD* with desired Δr by correctly mixing monetary and fiscal policy.

◆ One crucial conflict is about financing deficit.

- If government borrows from Bank of Canada, it avoids interest costs, but ↑ *MS* → inflationary pressures.
- Only small part of deficits financed by Bank of Canada.

HELPFUL HINTS

1 Chapters 25 and 26 examined the goods and services markets in isolation by using the aggregate expenditure model and assuming that the interest rate was given. When the interest rate changed, aggregate expenditure changed, resulting in a new (flow) equilibrium level of real GDP.

Similarly, Chapter 28 examined the money market in isolation by using the money supply and money demand model and assuming that the level of real GDP was given. When the level of real GDP changed, the demand for real money changed, resulting in a new (stock) equilibrium. The equilibrium value of real GDP was determined assuming a value for the interest rate and the equilibrium interest rate was determined assuming a value for real GDP.

This chapter puts the two models of these markets together and simultaneously determines equilibrium real GDP and the equilibrium interest rate. When the level of real GDP and the interest rate yield a simultaneous equilibrium in both the market for goods and services and the market for money, we have a *stock* and *flow equilibrium.*

Examining the simultaneous equilibrium reveals important *second round* effects of fiscal and monetary policy that did not appear in the partial analysis of earlier chapters. One example of these second round effects is crowding out. Because of crowding out, the fiscal policy multipliers in the full model are smaller than the multipliers examined in the partial model of Chapter 26.

2 The major focus of this chapter is on how an initial change in monetary or fiscal policy is transmitted through the economy to its eventual effect on aggregate demand—channels of monetary or fiscal policy. The graphical analysis presented in the text is of great value in studying these channels.

The economy initially starts out in equilibrium, then either monetary or fiscal policy throws a market out of equilibrium. As this market changes and moves towards a new equilibrium, changes are triggered in other markets. Eventually a new, simultaneous equilibrium is achieved in all markets.

It is helpful to augment the graphical analysis with simple "arrow diagrams" that show the *sequence* of changes as the economy adjusts to an initial policy change. For example, the interest rate transmission channel of monetary policy is represented by the following arrow diagram:

i) **First round:**

$$\uparrow M \rightarrow \uparrow MS$$
$$\uparrow MS \rightarrow \downarrow r \text{ (link 1)}$$
$$\downarrow r \rightarrow \uparrow I \text{ (link 2)}$$
$$\uparrow I \rightarrow \uparrow AE$$
$$\uparrow AE \rightarrow \uparrow \text{ real GDP}$$

Second round:

$$\uparrow \text{real GDP} \rightarrow \uparrow MD$$
$$\uparrow MD \rightarrow \uparrow r$$
$$\uparrow r \rightarrow \downarrow I$$
$$\downarrow I \rightarrow \downarrow AE$$
$$\downarrow AE \rightarrow \downarrow \text{ real GDP}$$

This diagram indicates that an expansionary monetary policy (an open market purchase of government securities by the Bank of Canada) will cause the quantity of money to increase ($\uparrow M$), which leads to an increase in the real supply of money ($\uparrow MS$). This in turn will result in a fall in the interest rate ($\downarrow r$) that will increase investment ($\uparrow I$), which is a part of aggregate expenditure ($\uparrow AE$). This will cause real GDP to begin increasing ($\uparrow$ real GDP), the end of the first round effects.

However, the rise in real GDP causes second round effects—the higher real GDP leads to a rightward shift in the demand for real money ($\uparrow MD$). The increase in the demand for real money will cause the interest rate ($\uparrow r$) to rise and thus investment ($\downarrow I$) and aggregate expenditure ($\downarrow AE$) will decrease, which will lead to a fall in real GDP ($\downarrow$ real GDP). This crowding out effect offsets somewhat the initial changes, but the economy still eventually converges to a new stock and flow equilibrium. (Ignore link 1 and link 2 in the arrow diagram for the moment.)

An arrow diagram can be a convenient way of summarizing the more detailed graphical analysis. Arrow diagrams can also be useful to reveal effects that can weaken or strengthen the ability of policy to change aggregate demand.

3   The transmission channel of fiscal policy (for example, an increase in government purchases of goods and services), is represented by the following arrow diagram:

ii) **First round:**

$$\uparrow G \rightarrow \uparrow AE$$
$$\uparrow AE \rightarrow \uparrow \text{ real GDP}$$

Second round:

$$\uparrow \text{real GDP} \rightarrow \uparrow MD$$
$$\uparrow MD \rightarrow \uparrow r \text{ (link 1)}$$
$$\uparrow r \rightarrow \downarrow I \text{ (link 2)}$$
$$\downarrow I \rightarrow \downarrow AE$$
$$\downarrow AE \rightarrow \downarrow \text{ real GDP}$$

The amount of government purchases on goods and services is represented by G. Otherwise the notation is the same as used above. (Once again, ignore link 1 and link 2.)

4   The text indicates that the strength of the effect of a change in the money supply on aggregate demand depends on the responsiveness of the demand for real money to changes in the interest rate and the responsiveness of investment demand to changes in the interest rate.

The arrow diagram given by i) illustrates how these factors affect the strength of monetary policy. The link between the increase in the supply of real money and the subsequent fall in the interest rate is indicated as link 1. If the demand for real money is very sensitive to interest rate changes (the MD curve is very flat or interest elastic), then this link is quite weak—a given increase in the supply of real money will have only a small effect on the interest rate. This in turn means a relatively small effect on investment. Link 2 captures the effect of a change in the interest rate on investment. If investment is very sensitive to interest rate changes (the investment demand curve is very flat or interest elastic), then this link is quite strong—a given fall in the interest rate will have a very large effect on investment.

We can also examine the factors that determine the strength of the effect of fiscal policy on aggregate demand. Links 1 and 2 of ii) are the relevant links; indeed they are the same as links 1 and 2 for monetary policy. If the demand for real money is very sensitive to interest rate changes (the MD curve is very flat), then link 1 is quite weak, the amount of crowding out is small, and fiscal policy is strong. Similarly, if investment is very sensitive to interest rate changes (the investment demand curve is very flat), then link 2 is quite strong, the amount of crowding out is large, and fiscal policy is weak.

Thus links 1 and 2 are critical in the transmission process and the focus of the Keynesian–monetarist controversy. It is interesting to think about the extreme Keynesian and monetarist positions in terms of these links. The existence of a liquidity trap (horizontal MD curve assumed by an extreme Keynesian) makes monetary policy ineffective because it completely breaks link 1—an increase in the supply of real money will have no effect on the interest rate. It also makes fiscal policy very strong, because there is no crowding out (a rise in real GDP has no impact on interest rates and investment).

The existence of a vertical investment demand curve (assumed by an extreme Keynesian) makes monetary policy ineffective because it completely breaks link 2. Similarly, the existence of a horizontal investment demand curve or a vertical *MD* curve (assumed by an extreme monetarist) implies complete crowding out and therefore ineffective fiscal policy.

Note that the same effects that create a strong fiscal policy create a weak monetary policy, and vice versa.

5   The effect of changes in monetary policy or fiscal policy on the exchange rate are very important in economies with large foreign sectors such as Canada. Changes in interest rates change the demand for the Canadian dollar in the same direction. This in turn causes an appreciation in the Canadian dollar if the interest rate rises, and a depreciation in the exchange rate if the interest rate falls. However, there is a crucial difference between fiscal and monetary policy for this effect, because of the fact the two policies have opposite effects on interest rates.

An expansionary fiscal policy will *raise* interest rates, *raising* the exchange rate, *lowering* net exports, thus *offsetting* the expansionary policy. However, an expansionary monetary policy *lowers* interest rates, *lowering* the exchange rate, *raising* net exports, thus *augmenting* the expansionary policy.

S E L F - T E S T

True/False/Uncertain and Explain

1   In the full *AD–AS* model, an expansionary monetary policy leads only to a rise in price, not a rise in real GDP.

2   Crowding in is more powerful than crowding out.

3   If aggregate demand is increased by an increase in the money supply, interest rates fall and investment increases.

4   If aggregate demand is increased by an increase in government purchases of goods and services, interest rates fall and investment increases.

5   An increase in the rate of interest will cause the investment demand curve to shift leftward.

6   An increase in the money supply will cause the interest rate to rise.

7   An increase in the money supply will cause the exchange rate to rise.

8   Other things equal, a change in the money supply will have a larger effect on aggregate planned expenditure the more responsive is investment demand to the interest rate.

9   Crowding out will be greater if the investment demand curve is very steep.

10   An increase in government purchases of goods and services eventually will shift the demand curve for real money rightward, increasing the interest rate.

Multiple-Choice

1 Which of the following best describes an expansionary fiscal policy? Aggregate expenditure

a rises, leading to a rise in real GDP, leading to a rise in money demand, leading to a fall in the rate of interest, leading to a further rise in real GDP.

b rises, leading to a rise in real GDP, leading to a rise in money supply, leading to a fall in the rate of interest, leading to a further rise in real GDP.

c falls, leading to a rise in real GDP, leading to a rise in money demand, leading to a fall in the rate of interest, leading to a further rise in real GDP.

d rises, leading to a fall in real GDP, leading to a rise in money demand, leading to a fall in the rate of interest, leading to a partially offsetting rise in real GDP.

e rises, leading to a rise in real GDP, leading to a rise in money demand, leading to a rise in the rate of interest, leading to a partially offsetting fall in real GDP.

2 Other things remaining the same, which of the following sequences of events moderate the effect of expansionary monetary policy on aggregate demand? Interest rates

a decrease, Canadian dollar depreciates, prices of exports fall, and prices of imports rise.

b increase, Canadian dollar appreciates, prices of exports rise, and prices of imports fall.

c decrease, Canadian dollar appreciates, prices of exports rise, and prices of imports fall.

d increase, Canadian dollar depreciates, prices of exports fall, and prices of imports rise.

e decrease, investment demand rises, aggregate expenditure rises, real GDP rises, and demand for real money rises.

3 Crowding in refers to the tendency for an increase in government purchases of goods and services to

a induce a rise in money demand, leading to a rise in interest rates and a fall in investment.

b induce a fall in money demand, leading to a fall in interest rates and a rise in investment.

c induce an increase in the money supply.

d raise interest rates, which leads to a rise in the exchange rate, leading to a fall in net exports.

e raise profit expectations in the private sector, leading to a rise in investment demand.

4 In the full *AD–AS* model, changes in aggregate demand because of fiscal and monetary policy have smaller effects on real GDP because the resulting rise in the price level increases interest rates that lower

a investment.

b net exports.

c consumption.

d all of the above.

e none of the above.

5 Coordinating fiscal and monetary policy is better for the economy because it

a allows cheap financing of the deficit.

b allows the desired change in interest rates by appropriately mixing monetary and fiscal policy.

c has the opposite effects on the interest rate and the exchange rate.

d all of the above.

e none of the above.

6 In the full *AD–AS* model, changes in the price level imply

a the real-world fiscal policy multiplier is smaller because the price level moves in the opposite direction of the change in real GDP.

b monetary policy is no longer useful.

c fiscal policy is no longer useful.

d the real-world fiscal policy multiplier is smaller because the price level moves in the same direction as the change in real GDP.

e b and c.

7 Consider the full *AD–AS* model with unemployment. After an expansionary monetary policy has increased aggregate demand, real GDP

a falls overall because of the rise in the price level.

b rises even more because of the rise in the price level.

c is not affected by the rise in the price level.

d does not change overall because of the rise in the price level.

e rises, but by a smaller amount because of the rise in the price level.

8 Counting the first and second round effects, the impact of a contractionary fiscal policy is to decrease real GDP,

a reduce the interest rate, and reduce investment.

b reduce the interest rate, and increase investment.

c increase the interest rate, and reduce investment.

d increase the interest rate, and increase investment.

e none of the above.

9 Counting the first and second round effects, the impact of a contractionary monetary policy is to decrease real GDP,

a reduce the interest rate, and reduce investment.
b reduce the interest rate, and increase investment.
c increase the interest rate, and reduce investment.
d increase the interest rate, and increase investment.
e none of the above.

10 A decrease in the money supply will initially cause investment to

a increase and aggregate planned expenditure to increase.
b increase and aggregate planned expenditure to decrease.
c decrease and aggregate actual expenditure to increase.
d decrease and aggregate planned expenditure to decrease.
e increase and aggregate actual expenditure to increase.

11 Consider Fig. 29.1. Why is the situation depicted *not* a stock and flow equilibrium?

a The level of aggregate planned spending is inconsistent with the interest rate.
b The money market and the goods market are not individually in equilibrium.
c The expenditure equilibrium occurs at a different level of real GDP than the level of real GDP assumed when the demand curve is drawn for real money.
d The level of investment in part (c) is inconsistent with the level of investment in part (b).
e Aggregate expenditure is greater than aggregate supply.

12 Suppose Fig. 29.1 depicts the actual current position of an economy. In stock and flow equilibrium, real GDP will be

a less than $800 billion and the interest rate will be higher than 4 percent.
b less than $800 billion and the interest rate will be lower than 4 percent.
c more than $800 billion and the interest rate will be higher than 4 percent.
d more than $800 billion and the interest rate will be lower than 4 percent.
e none of the above.

13 An increase in the money supply will eventually lead to an increase in real GDP, which will shift the demand curve for real money to the

a left, causing the interest rate to fall.
b left, causing the interest rate to rise.
c right, causing the interest rate to fall.
d right, causing the interest rate to rise.
e right, causing the money supply to rise.

14 Monetary policy will have the *smallest* effect on aggregate demand when the sensitivity of the demand curve for real money to the interest rate is

a large and the sensitivity of the investment demand curve to the interest rate is large.
b large and the sensitivity of the investment demand curve to the interest rate is small.
c small and the sensitivity of the consumption function to the interest rate is large.
d small and the sensitivity of the investment demand curve to the interest rate is small.
e small and the sensitivity of the consumption function to the interest rate is small.

FIGURE **29.1**

(a)

(b)

(c)

15 Consider an economy where the demand for real money is very sensitive to changes in the interest rate. The problem with monetary policy in this economy is that

a there will be a high level of crowding out.

b monetary policy will create changes in the exchange rate that offset the monetary policy.

c a change in the interest rate creates only a small change in investment demand.

d a change in the money supply creates too large a change in the interest rate.

e a change in the money supply creates only a small change in the interest rate.

16 Overall, a tax cut will

a increase aggregate planned expenditure by causing disposable income to increase.

b increase aggregate planned expenditure by causing the interest rate to fall.

c decrease aggregate planned expenditure by causing disposable income to fall.

d decrease aggregate planned expenditure by causing the interest rate to rise.

e increase aggregate planned expenditure by causing investment to rise.

17 Statistical evidence from a variety of historical and national experiences suggests that

a fiscal policy affects aggregate demand and monetary policy does not.

b monetary policy affects aggregate demand and fiscal policy does not.

c both fiscal policy and monetary policy affect aggregate demand.

d neither fiscal policy nor monetary policy affect aggregate demand.

e fiscal policy affected aggregate demand only during the Great Depression of the 1930s.

18 Aggregate demand can be increased by increasing the money supply (expansionary monetary policy) or by increasing government purchases of goods and services (expansionary fiscal policy). Which of the following is a correct comparison?

a The interest rate will rise under the monetary policy and fall under the fiscal policy, while consumption will increase under both.

b The interest rate will fall under the monetary policy and rise under the fiscal policy, while consumption will increase under both.

c Consumption will rise under the monetary policy and fall under the fiscal policy, while the interest rate will increase under both.

d Consumption will rise under the monetary policy and fall under the fiscal policy, while the interest rate will decrease under both.

e Consumption will fall under both the monetary policy and fiscal policy, while the interest rate will increase under both.

19 A tax cut will cause

a a decrease in the interest rate, which will lead to a decrease in the exchange rate.

b a decrease in the interest rate, which will lead to an increase in the exchange rate.

c an increase in the interest rate, which will lead to a decrease in the exchange rate.

d an increase in the interest rate, which will lead to an increase in the exchange rate.

e no change in the interest rate.

20 A Keynesian belives the economy is inherently

a unstable, and fiscal policy is more important than monetary policy.

b unstable, and monetary policy is more important than fiscal policy.

c stable, and fiscal policy is more important than monetary policy.

d stable, and monetary policy is more important than fiscal policy.

e stable, and crowding out is strong.

21 The extreme monetarist position has a

a horizontal investment demand curve and a horizontal demand curve for real money.

b horizontal investment demand curve and a vertical demand curve for real money.

c vertical investment demand curve and a horizontal demand curve for real money.

d vertical investment demand curve and a vertical demand curve for real money.

e vertical investment demand curve and a horizontal supply curve for real money.

22 A change in interest rates will affect aggregate demand through which one of the following changes?

a a shift of the investment demand curve and movement along the aggregate expenditure curve

b a shift of the demand for real money curve and the investment demand curve

c a shift of the investment demand curve and the aggregate expenditure function

d movements along both the investment demand and the aggregate expenditure curves

e a movement along the investment demand curve and a shift of the aggregate expenditure curve

23 An increase in aggregate demand brought about by fiscal policy changes can be offset by the

a crowding out effect.

b exchange rate effect.

c expenditure effect.

d consumption effect.

e a and **b**.

24 If the supply of money increases, bond prices are most likely to

a fall as the interest rate rises.

b rise as the interest rate rises.

c fall as the interest rate falls.

d rise as the interest rate falls.

e stay constant.

25 If the aggregate supply curve was vertical, expansionary fiscal policy would cause all of the following *except*

a an increase in investment.

b an increase in the demand for real money.

c an increase in interest rates.

d an increase in the price level.

e a decrease in investment.

Short Answer Problems

1 Trace the main steps following an increase in the supply of real money, price level held constant.

2 Why does an increase in the supply of real money have a smaller effect on aggregate planned expenditure if the demand for real money is very sensitive to changes in the interest rate?

3 Explain how an increase in the money supply leads to an increase in aggregate planned expenditure through a change in the exchange rate.

4 How does crowding out take place?

5 Consider an economy that has real GDP less than potential, and needs an expansionary policy. Evaluate an expansionary fiscal policy versus an expansionary monetary policy, based on the following four considerations:

a the empirical evidence on the relative effectiveness of each policy,

b the impacts of each on investment,

c the impacts of each on potential GDP,

d the impacts of each on the deficit.

6 Figure 29.2 depicts an economy. Note that MD_0 corresponds to real GDP = $400 billion, MD_1 corresponds to real GDP = $500 billion, and MD_2 corresponds to real GDP = $600 billion.

a What are the equilibrium values for real GDP, the interest rate, and investment?

b Is this a stock and flow equilibrium? Why or why not?

FIGURE **29.2**

7 Consider again the economy depicted by Fig. 29.2. Suppose that the Bank of Canada increases the supply of real money from $300 billion to $400 billion.

a What is the initial effect on the interest rate?

b What effect will this have on investment?

c As a result of this change in investment, what happens to equilibrium GDP? Why will this level of GDP not be achieved?

d What are the interest rate, investment, and real GDP at the new stock and flow equilibrium?

e Show the new stock and flow equilibrium on Fig. 29.2.

8 Figure 29.3 depicts an economy. Note that MD_0 corresponds to real GDP = $400 billion, MD_1 corresponds to real GDP = $500 billion, and MD_2 corresponds to real GDP = $600 billion. Suppose that the government increases its purchase of goods and services by $100 billion.

a What is the initial full multiplier effect on real GDP? Why will the economy not remain at this level of real GDP?

b As a result of this full multiplier effect on real GDP, what happens to the demand curve for real money and to the interest rate?

c What are the interest rate, investment, and real GDP at the new stock and flow equilibrium? How much investment is crowded out? What are the differences in the effects of monetary policy and fiscal policy illustrated by Short Answer Problems **7** and **8**?

d Show the new stock and flow equilibrium on Fig. 29.3.

9 Suppose that as a result of the increase in real GDP in Short Answer Problem **8**, firms' expectations of future profits increase.

a What happens to investment demand as a result? What is this called?

b What will be the first and second round results of this rise in firms' profit expectations? Specifically, what happens to *AE, I, MD, r,* and real GDP? (A written explanation is sufficient.)

10 Why will more crowding out take place if investment demand is very sensitive to interest rate changes?

ANSWERS

True/False/Uncertain and Explain

❂1 **U** Depends on whether originally unemployment or full-employment equilibrium. (702–703)

2 **U** Depends on relative strength of each effect, which is unknown. (695)

3 **T** $\uparrow MS \rightarrow \downarrow r \rightarrow \uparrow I \rightarrow$ more aggregate expenditure $\rightarrow AD$ shifts rightward. (702)

4 **F** $\uparrow G \rightarrow \uparrow$ real GDP $\rightarrow \uparrow MD \rightarrow \uparrow r \rightarrow \downarrow I$. (695)

5 **F** $\uparrow r \rightarrow$ movement along *ID* curve. (694)

6 **F** $\uparrow MS \rightarrow$ excess supply of money $\rightarrow \uparrow$ demand for bonds $\rightarrow \uparrow$ price of bonds $\rightarrow \downarrow$ interest rates. (698)

❂7 **F** $\uparrow MS \rightarrow \downarrow r \rightarrow \downarrow$ demand for Canadian assets $\rightarrow \downarrow$ demand for Canadian dollar $\rightarrow \downarrow$ exchange rate. (699)

8 **T** ΔMS works by $\Delta r \rightarrow \Delta ID \rightarrow \Delta AE$, so if impact of *r* on *ID* is larger, impact of ΔMS on *AE* is larger. (700)

9 **F** Steep investment demand curve is not responsive to $\uparrow r$. Crowding out creates $\uparrow r$, and smaller impact of $\uparrow r$, smaller crowding out. (699)

FIGURE **29.3**

10 T $\uparrow G \rightarrow \uparrow$ real GDP $\rightarrow MD$ shifts rightward $\rightarrow \uparrow$ supply of bonds $\rightarrow \downarrow$ price of bonds $\rightarrow \uparrow r$. (694)

Multiple-Choice

1 e $\uparrow G \rightarrow \uparrow AE \rightarrow \uparrow$ real GDP $\rightarrow \uparrow MD \rightarrow \uparrow r \rightarrow \downarrow I \rightarrow \downarrow AE \rightarrow \downarrow$ real GDP. (692–694)

2 e This $\uparrow MD \rightarrow \uparrow r \rightarrow \downarrow$ investment $\rightarrow \downarrow AE \rightarrow \downarrow$ real GDP, moderating the rise in real GDP. (697–699)

3 e Definition. (695)

4 d $\uparrow$ price level $\rightarrow \uparrow r \rightarrow \uparrow$ cost of borrowing $\rightarrow \downarrow C$ and I; $\uparrow r \rightarrow \uparrow$ demand for Canadian dollar $\rightarrow \uparrow$ exchange rate $\rightarrow \downarrow NX$. (702)

5 b Monetary and fiscal policy have opposite effects on interest rates $\rightarrow$ using both at same time in different strengths means can get Δr at desired level. (704–705)

6 d Δ price level $\rightarrow \Delta$ real money supply $\rightarrow \Delta r \rightarrow \Delta$ investment demand and aggregate expenditure that offset original changes due to policy. (702–703)

7 e Shift rightward in AD curve $\rightarrow$ excess demand for goods/services $\rightarrow \uparrow$ price level $\rightarrow \uparrow r \rightarrow \downarrow$ aggregate expenditure. (702)

8 b $\downarrow$ real GDP $\rightarrow \downarrow$ money demand $\rightarrow \downarrow$ interest rate $\rightarrow \uparrow$ investment. (692–695)

9 c $\downarrow$ real GDP $\rightarrow \downarrow$ money demand $\rightarrow \downarrow$ interest rate somewhat offsetting original rise $\rightarrow \uparrow$ investment but not enough to overcome initial $\downarrow$ investment. (696–699)

10 d $\downarrow$ money supply $\rightarrow \uparrow$ interest rate $\rightarrow \downarrow$ planned investment $\rightarrow \downarrow$ planned aggregate expenditure. (698–699)

11 c The higher equilibrium real GDP will shift money demand $\rightarrow$ current money demand is inconsistent. (690–691)

12 a The current real GDP of $800 billion will raise money demand $\rightarrow \uparrow$ interest rate $\rightarrow \downarrow$ investment $\rightarrow \downarrow$ aggregate expenditure $\rightarrow \downarrow$ equilibrium real GDP. (690–691)

13 d Money demand depends positively on real GDP, and higher real GDP $\rightarrow \uparrow$ supply of bonds $\rightarrow \downarrow$ price of bonds $\rightarrow \uparrow$ interest rate. (698–699)

14 b Sensitive $MD \rightarrow \Delta MS \rightarrow$ small Δr, and insensitive $ID \rightarrow \Delta r \rightarrow$ small Δ investment. (700)

15 e Because with sensitive money demand, Δ interest rate needed to get money market in equilibrium after Δ money supply is small. (700)

16 a $\downarrow$ taxes $\rightarrow \uparrow$ disposable income $(Y - T) \rightarrow \uparrow$ consumption $\rightarrow \uparrow$ aggregate planned expenditure. (692–695)

17 c See text discussion. (701)

18 b Under both, $\uparrow$ real GDP $\rightarrow \uparrow$ consumption. Under fiscal policy crowding out $\rightarrow \uparrow$ interest rate. Under monetary policy, $\uparrow$ money supply $\rightarrow \downarrow$ interest rate. (704)

19 d Tax cut $\rightarrow \uparrow$ real GDP $\rightarrow \uparrow$ money demand $\rightarrow \uparrow$ interest rate $\rightarrow \uparrow$ demand for Canadian financial assets $\rightarrow \uparrow$ demand for dollar $\rightarrow \uparrow$ exchange rate. (695)

20 a See text discussion. (700–701)

21 b See text discussion. (700–701)

22 e By definition of ID curve $\rightarrow \Delta$ autonomous expenditure. (692–694)

23 e $\uparrow$ real GDP $\rightarrow \uparrow$ money demand $\rightarrow \uparrow r \rightarrow \uparrow$ exchange rate, $\downarrow$ investment. (695)

24 d $\uparrow MS \rightarrow$ excess supply of money $\rightarrow$ spent on bonds $\rightarrow \uparrow$ bond prices, $\downarrow r$. (696–697)

25 a Expansionary policy creates crowding out ($\downarrow I$). (695)

Short Answer Problems

1 An increase in the supply of real money
— will shift the supply curve of real money rightward and lower the interest rate;
— the lower interest rate will cause investment to increase;
— the increase in investment means that aggregate planned expenditure increases;
— the increase in aggregate planned expenditure means that equilibrium GDP is higher and that at the current level of real GDP, inventories are being depleted more rapidly than planned;
— as inventories fall more rapidly than planned, real GDP begins to rise (towards the new equilibrium);
— rising real GDP causes the demand curve for real money to shift rightward causing the interest rate to rise;
— the higher interest rate will cause investment to decrease;
— the decrease in investment means that aggregate planned expenditure decreases;
— the decrease in aggregate planned expenditure means that equilibrium GDP is lower;
— as actual real GDP increases and equilibrium GDP decreases, they will converge at a new stock and flow equilibrium.

2 If the demand for real money is very sensitive to changes in the interest rate, the demand curve for real money is very flat. Thus when the money supply increases and the supply curve for real money shifts rightward, the resulting change in the equilibrium interest rate will be small.

Ceteris paribus, a small interest rate change will lead to a small change in investment and a small change in aggregate planned expenditure.

3 An increase in the real supply of money will shift the supply curve of real money rightward and lower the interest rate. The lower interest rate (relative to interest rates in other countries) will cause people to want to sell low-interest Canadian financial assets and buy relatively high-interest foreign financial assets. Therefore the demand for dollars decreases and the demand for foreign currencies increases, which results in a lower exchange rate relative to foreign currencies. This fall in the exchange rate will cause net exports to increase as foreigners can now buy Canadian goods for less (in terms of their currencies) and Canadians must pay more (in dollars) for foreign goods. The increase in net exports is an increase in aggregate planned expenditure.

4 Crowding out is the tendency for expansionary fiscal policy to cause the interest rate to rise and thus investment to decline. Expansionary fiscal policy "crowds out" investment. The increase in the interest rate is a consequence of the fact that the increase in real GDP that occurs as a consequence of an increase in government expenditure on goods and services, for example, will cause the demand curve for real money to shift rightward. Thus the equilibrium interest rate will rise.

5 a The empirical evidence is that both policies work with a fair degree of strength, so you could pick either.
b An expansionary fiscal policy raises interest rates, and therefore will lower investment, while an expansionary monetary policy lowers interest rates and will raise investment. On these grounds, you would tend to pick monetary policy.
c The fiscal policy lowers investment, which means in the long run less capital stock and less growth of potential GDP, while the monetary policy has the opposite effect. On these grounds, you would tend to pick monetary policy.
d Expansionary fiscal policy usually means some combination of more spending and lower taxes, which leads to a higher deficit. Expansionary monetary policy has no impact on the deficit, so you would tend to pick it.

6 a The equilibrium value for real GDP is at the intersection of the AE_0 curve and the 45° line—$400 billion. The equilibrium value for the interest rate is 5 percent, since the relevant MD curve is MD_0 when real GDP is $400 billion. At an interest rate of 5 percent, investment is $100 billion (part b).
b This is a stock and flow equilibrium because equilibrium real GDP is $400 billion when the interest rate is 5 percent (flow equilibrium) and the equilibrium interest rate is 5 percent when real GDP is $400 billion (stock equilibrium). In other words, it is a stock and flow equilibrium because the values of real GDP and the interest rate that give stock equilibrium and flow equilibrium are the same.

7 a The initial effect of an increase in the supply of real money from $300 billion to $400 billion is to lower the interest rate from 5 percent to 3 percent.
b The fall in the interest rate from 5 percent to 3 percent will increase investment from $100 billion to $200 billion.
c Equilibrium GDP will increase from $400 billion to $600 billion. This level of GDP will not be achieved because, as real GDP begins to rise above $400 billion, the money demand curve will start shifting rightward and the interest rate will begin to rise. This will cause investment and thus the AE curve to shift back down somewhat.
d In the new stock and flow equilibrium we must have a single real GDP and interest rate combination that (given the new money supply) leaves both the money market and the market for goods in equilibrium. This occurs at an interest rate of 4 percent and real GDP of $500 billion. Investment will be $150 billion.
e The new stock and flow equilibrium is shown in Fig. 29.2 Solution. Note that the relevant demand curve for real money is MD_1, which is drawn assuming real GDP = $500 billion. MS_0 has shifted to MS_1, I_0 has shifted to I_1, and AE_0 has shifted to AE_1.

8 a The full multiplier effect of an increase in government purchases of $100 billion is to increase equilibrium GDP by $200 billion ($100 billion × $1/(1 -$ slope of AE function))—from $400 billion to $600 billion. This is not a stock and flow equilibrium. The economy will not remain here (indeed it would likely never attain this level) because as real GDP increases, the demand curve for real money will shift rightward, raising the interest rate, which reduces investment, aggregate planned expenditure, and equilibrium real GDP.
b If the full multiplier effect on real GDP (from $400 billion to $600 billion) took place, the

FIGURE **29.2** SOLUTION

FIGURE **29.3** SOLUTION

demand curve for real money would shift from MD_0 to MD_2, causing the interest rate to rise from 5 percent to 7 percent.

c In the new stock and flow equilibrium the interest rate is 6 percent and real GDP is $500 billion. Only this combination of interest rate and real GDP gives both a stock (money market) and flow (goods market) equilibrium. Investment has fallen to $50 billion from $100 billion, so $50 billion of investment is crowded out.

   Both the expansionary monetary policy of Short Answer Problem 7 and the expansionary fiscal policy of Short Answer Problem 8 have the same effect on real GDP. The monetary policy, however, reduced the interest rate and increased investment, while the fiscal policy increased the interest rate and reduced investment.

d Note the new stock and flow equilibrium is shown in Fig. 29.3 Solution. Note that the relevant demand curve for real money is MD_1 which is drawn assuming real GDP = $500 billion. AE_0 has shifted to AE_1, and I_0 has shifted to I_1.

9 a The higher profit expectations leads firms to raise their investment demand. This is called crowding in.

  b The higher investment demand leads to a rise in autonomous expenditure, which in turn leads to a rise in aggregate expenditure, which in turn raises real GDP (the first round effects). The higher real GDP leads to the second round effects—real money demand rises as a result of the higher real GDP, leading to higher interest rates, which in turn lead to lower investment demand, lowering aggregate expenditure and lower real GDP, which somewhat crowds out the first round effects.

10 If investment demand is very sensitive to changes in the interest rate, the investment demand curve is very flat. Therefore the increase in the interest rate that initiates the crowding out effect will induce large decrease in investment spending, which means large crowding out.

PROBLEM

The Canadian economy is originally in a full-employment equilibrium. Suppose that the U.S. economy goes into recession, and at the same time expectations of future profits fall.

a Holding constant the price level, carefully explain (and show on a graph) what these changes do to aggregate expenditure and aggregate demand. Explain what happens to each component of aggregate expenditure and real GDP.

b Next, show on your graph and explain what happens to aggregate expenditure and aggregate demand in the short run when the price level adjusts.

The Bank of Canada decides to redress the economy's problems by carrying out an expansionary monetary policy.

c Give an example of the type of open market operation the Bank of Canada would carry out in such a circumstance. Show what happens to the balance sheets of the Bank of Canada and the banking sector as a result of the initial impacts of the operation. What is the overall impact of such an operation on chartered bank reserves, loans, deposit, and the money supply?

d Explain what this policy will do to the real money supply, money demand, the interest rate, investment, net exports, and aggregate expenditure, holding constant the price level.

e Next, with the price level adjusting, explain what this policy does to aggregate demand and aggregate supply, and real GDP.

f Does the quantity theory of money hold in this economy?

MIDTERM EXAMINATION

You should allocate 48 minutes for this examination (24 questions, 2 minutes per question). For each question, choose the *best* answer.

1 We observe an increase in the price level and an increase in real GDP. A possible explanation is that the

a money supply has fallen.
b expectation of future income has decreased.
c price of raw materials has increased.
d stock of capital has increased.
e expectation of future profits has increased.

2 The aggregate demand curve (*AD*) illustrates that, as the price level falls, the

a quantity of real GDP demanded increases.
b quantity of real GDP demanded decreases.
c quantity of nominal GDP demanded increases.
d quantity of nominal GDP demanded decreases.
e value of assets fall.

FIGURE **P6.1**

3 The changes represented in Fig. P6.1 must

a not occur in the real world, because *AD* and *SAS* cannot change at the same time.
b lead to an inflationary gap.
c lead to a recessionary gap.
d create inflation.
e none of the above.

4 Long-run aggregate supply will increase for all of the following reasons *except*

a a fall in wages.
b a rise in human capital.
c the introduction of new technology.
d more aggregate labour hours.
e more capital stock.

5 The consumption function shows the relationship between consumption expenditure and

a the interest rate.
b the price level.
c disposable income.
d saving.
e nominal income.

6 If real GDP is less than aggregate planned expenditure, then

a aggregate planned expenditure will increase.
b real GDP will increase.
c the price level must fall to restore equilibrium.
d imports must be too large.
e both **a** and **b** are true

7 In a recent study, the University of Underfunded argued that it created four times as many jobs as people it hired directly. This argument illustrates the idea of

a the marginal propensity to consume.
b the multiplier.
c government spending.
d the tax multiplier.
e universities wasting taxpayers' dollars.

8 Suppose that, because of an increase in expected future profit, investment increases by $10 billion. Which of the following would *reduce* the effect of this increase in autonomous expenditure on equilibrium real GDP?

a an increase in the marginal propensity to consume
b a decrease in the marginal propensity to import
c a decrease in the marginal tax rate
d a steeper aggregate supply curve
e a flatter aggregate supply curve

9 If the slope of the *AE* function is 0.75, what is the autonomous tax multiplier?

a 0.57
b 1.50
c 2.00
d 4.00
e impossible to calculate without further information

10 Which of the following is *not* a source of budgetary revenues?

a personal income taxes
b transfer payments
c corporate income taxes
d indirect taxes
e investment income

11 The presence of induced taxes means

a fiscal policy multipliers are made stronger.
b discretionary fiscal policy is eliminated.
c there is always a structural deficit.
d there is always a cyclical deficit.
e fluctuations in aggregate expenditure are reduced.

12 Figure P6.2 illustrates an economy initially in equilibrium at point *a*. If government purchases increase, in the long run the economy will move to the intersection of

a AD_1 and SAS_1, where wage rates and the price level are higher and output is constant at $500 billion.
b AD_1 and SAS_1, where the price level is higher and output has risen to $620 billion.
c AD_0 and SAS_1, where wage rates are higher and output rises to $620 billion.
d AD_0 and SAS_1, where wage rates are higher and output falls to $380 billion.
e AD_1 and SAS_0, where the price level is higher and output rises to $620 billion.

FIGURE **P6.2**

13 Consider the following data on the economy of Adanac:

Currency reserves of private banks	$ 5 billion
Currency in circulation	15 billion
Demand deposits of banks	40 billion
Demand deposits of other financial institutions	50 billion
Personal savings deposits at other financial institutions	125 billion
Nonpersonal notice deposits at banks	200 billion

What is the value of M1 and the value of M2+ in this economy in billions of dollars?

a 105; 230
b 110; 235
c 55; 430
d 55; 230
e 60; 430

14 A bank can create money by

a selling some of its investment securities.
b increasing its reserves.
c lending its excess reserves.
d printing more cheques.
e converting reserves into securities.

15 The amount of real money people want to hold will increase if either real income increases or the

a price level increases.
b price level decreases.
c interest rate increases.
d interest rate decreases.
e price of bonds falls.

16 Which of the following statements about depository institutions is *false*?

a They aim to maximize net worth without other considerations.
b They take deposits from households and firms, and lend to other households and firms.
c They minimize the cost of borrowing.
d They pool and reduce risk.
e They hold a variety of assets, not just loans.

17 According to the quantity theory of money, a decrease in the quantity of money will cause

a both the price level and real GDP to decline in the short run, but, in the long run, only the price level will fall as real GDP returns to its initial level.
b both the price level and real GDP to increase in the short run, but, in the long run, only the price level will rise as real GDP returns to its initial level.
c the price level to fall in the short run, but, in the long run, the price level will return to its initial level.
d the price level to fall and real GDP to rise in both the short run and the long run.
e the price level to fall and real GDP to fall in both the short run and the long run.

18 An open market purchase of government securities by the Bank of Canada will

a increase bank reserves and thus increase the monetary base.
b decrease bank reserves and thus decrease the monetary base.
c increase bank reserves and thus decrease the monetary base.
d decrease bank reserves and thus increase the monetary base.
e decrease bank reserves but increase the money supply if banks have excess reserves.

19 An attempt to simulate the economy by using the Bank Rate would work by

a lowering the bank rate, resulting in more excess reserves, resulting in more loans, resulting in more deposits and money.
b raising the bank rate, resulting in more excess reserves, resulting in more loans, resulting in more deposits and money.
c raising the bank rate, resulting in less excess reserves, resulting in less loans, resulting in less deposits and money.
d lowering the bank rate, resulting in less excess reserves, resulting in less loans, resulting in less deposits and money.
e lowering the bank rate, resulting in more excess reserves, resulting in more loans, resulting in less deposits and money.

20 Which of the following quotations *correctly* describes the impact of monetary policy on the economy?

a "House sales are down lots, due to the higher money growth."

b "The extra money pumped into the economy by the central bank is creating less exports."

c "The tightening of money growth is helping sell goods abroad."

d "Businesses are investing more, now that monetary policy has become less expansionary."

e "The extra money pumped into the economy by the central bank is creating more jobs."

21 International crowding out refers to the tendency for an increase in government purchases of goods and services to induce a

a fall in interest rates, leading to a fall in the exchange rate, leading to an increase in net exports.

b fall in interest rates, leading to a withdrawal of foreign funds from Canada.

c rise in interest rates, leading to a fall in the exchange rate, leading to an increase in net exports.

d rise in interest rates, leading to a rise in the exchange rate, leading to an increase in net exports.

e rise in interest rates, leading to a rise in the exchange rate, leading to a fall in net exports.

22 An expansionary monetary policy will lead to a fall in interest rates, which will lead to a

a rise in the demand for the dollar, leading to a rise in the exchange rate, which leads to a fall in net exports.

b rise in the demand for the dollar, leading to a rise in the exchange rate, which leads to a rise in net exports.

c rise in the demand for the dollar, leading to a fall in the exchange rate, which leads to a rise in net exports.

d fall in the demand for the dollar, leading to a fall in the exchange rate, which leads to a rise in net exports.

e fall in the demand for the dollar, leading to a fall in the exchange rate, which leads to a fall in net exports.

23 There will be no crowding out if

a the demand for real money is totally unresponsive to changes in the price level.

b the supply of real money is totally unresponsive to changes in the interest rate.

c investment is very responsive to changes in the interest rate.

d investment is totally unresponsive to changes in real GDP.

e the demand for real money is totally unresponsive to changes in real GDP.

24 The Bank of Canada and the government have a potential conflict about the government borrowing from the Bank of Canada because the borrowing will

a raise money demand and raise interest rates, lowering investment too much.

b raise money demand and raise interest rates, which puts too much upward pressure on aggregate demand.

c lower the money supply and raise interest rates, lowering investment too much.

d raise the money supply, creating deflationary pressures.

e raise the money supply, creating inflationary pressures.

ANSWERS

Problem

a The U.S. recession leads to a fall in their imports of Canadian goods, which means a fall in our exports.

The lower profit expectations lead to a fall in investment demand. Both factors lead to a fall in aggregate planned expenditure, represented by a shift downward in the *AE* curve to AE_b in Fig. P6.3. The fall in aggregate expenditure leads to a rise in inventories, which leads to firms lowering production, leading to a fall in real GDP that is a multiple of the initial fall in aggregate expenditure. The fall in real GDP leads to a fall in real money demand that leads to a fall in interest rates, leading to a rise in aggregate expenditure. However, overall aggregate expenditure is lower—the new equilibrium is at *b*, compared with the original equilibrium at *a*. The shift down in aggregate expenditure is also shown as a shift leftward in aggregate demand in part (b) of the graph.

Consumption is lower because of the fall in real GDP. Investment has two conflicting effects, and may be higher or lower. Government purchases are unchanged. Exports are lower because of the shock, and imports are also lower because of the fall in real GDP.

FIGURE **P6.3**

(a)

(b)

b   After the shock, at the original price level aggregate demand is less than aggregate supply ($Y_b < Y_0$). This surplus leads to a fall in the price level. This in turn leads to a decrease in the real quantity supplied in the short run (the movement from a' to c'), as well as a rise in the real money supply, which leads to a fall in the interest rate, a rise in investment and aggregate expenditure (from AE_b to AE_1), and a movement along the aggregate demand curve from b' to c'.

c   The Bank of Canada wants to raise the money supply, and will do so by purchasing government securities. If, for example, they buy these securities directly from the chartered banks, they will pay for them by crediting the chartered banks' deposits at the Bank of Canada (which are reserves). The result of such a purchase is shown in Table P6.1.

TABLE **P6.1**

Bank of Canada		Chartered Banks	
Assets	**Liabilities**	**Assets**	**Liabilities**
Government securities (+)	Bank deposits (+)	Reserves (+)	
		Government securities (−)	

This operation will lead to a deposit multiplier effect, leading to more reserves, more loans, more deposits, and a higher money supply.

d   The higher nominal money supply will lead to a higher real money supply, price level held constant. This in turn creates a surplus of money, which leads to a rise in the demand for financial assets, which leads to a rise in the price of these assets, which leads to a fall in the interest rate. The lower interest rate leads to a rise in investment demand and aggregate expenditure, as well as a fall in the demand for Canadian dollars and therefore a fall in the value of the Canadian dollar and a rise in net exports and aggregate expenditure.

e   The higher aggregate expenditure translates into a shift rightward in the aggregate demand curve, which leads to a rise in the price level, which triggers a movement along the short-run aggregate supply curve, leading to a rise in real GDP.

f   No, it does not because one of the crucial assumptions of the quantity theory does not hold—since the economy is in the short run, real GDP is not independent of changes in the money supply.

Midterm Examination

1   e   Answer e shifts AD right, $\rightarrow \uparrow P$ and real GDP. **a** and **b** shift AD left, while **c** shifts SAS left $\rightarrow \downarrow Y$, and **d** shifts LAS right $\rightarrow \downarrow P$. (565–566)

2   a AD curve is downward sloping due to three effects. It is real GDP by definition, not nominal, and asset values $\uparrow$ here. (554–555)

3   e   These changes can occur. Whether or not there is gap cannot be determined without LAS curve. (563–564)

4   a   Changes in wages change SAS only, not LAS. (561–562)

5   c   Definition. (578–579)

6 e Firms' sales > production → ↓ inventories → ↑ production. New equilibrium has higher real GDP = higher AE. (589–590)

7 b University spending creates multiplier effects. (590–591)

8 d This → more ΔP, less ΔY. All others make effect larger. (598)

9 e Autonomous tax multiplier = $MPC/(1 - e)$ → we need to know MPC. (619)

10 b Outlay. (610)

11 e Induced taxes act as automatic stabilizer. Multipliers are weaker, can still do discretionary policy, and there may or may not be a cyclical/structural deficit depending on other factors. (620–621)

12 a In the long run, wage rates fully adjust to higher price level, and economy stays at potential GDP of $500 billion. (625–626)

13 c M1 = currency in circulation + banks' demand deposits, M2+ = M1 + (personal savings and nonpersonal notice deposits at banks) + deposits at other financial institutions. (641)

14 c Lending its reserves is done by crediting borrowers' deposits, creating more deposits = more money. (646)

15 d Real money demand is not affected by Δ price level, ↓ price of bonds → ↑ interest rate, which lowers real money demand. (649–650)

16 a They must also balance off risk considerations. (644)

17 a In long run, real GDP is independent of Δ money supply. (676)

18 a Bank of Canada pays for securities by crediting banks' reserves, which are part of monetary base. (666–667)

19 a ↓ bank rate → ↓ cost of borrowing from central bank → ↓ desired reserves → excess reserves → ↑ loans, etc. (663–664)

20 e ↑ MS → ↓ r → ↑ C (so **a** wrong), ↑ I (so **d** wrong), ↑ NX (so **b** and **c** wrong) → ↑ AD → more jobs. (671–673)

21 e Definition. (695)

22 d ↓ interest rates → Canadian assets less desirable → ↓ demand for these assets and for Canadian dollars → ↓ exchange rate, etc. (699)

23 e Because then Δ real GDP due to fiscal policy has no impact on real money demand or on interest rates. (699)

24 e If government borrows from Bank of Canada, the Bank prints money to give to government → ↑ money supply → ↑ AD, creating inflation. (704–705)

30

Long-Run and Short-Run Aggregate Supply

KEY CONCEPTS

Labour Productivity and Real GDP

Labour productivity is total output per person employed.

◆ Derived from aggregate **production function** (*PF*), which shows quantity real GDP produced as quantity of labour employed varies, given capital stock and technology.

◆ Properties of *PF*

- Slope = **marginal product of labour** = Δ real GDP per hour additional labour.
- ↓ marginal product as ↑ labour used (**diminishing marginal product of labour**) because of constant capital stock.

◆ The *PF* shifts up (**economic growth**) if

- ↑ capital stock → more machines or human capital.
- technological change → invention of new technology, and innovation of making it work.

◆ Growth is variable because of fluctuations in investment and pace of technological innovations.

◆ Canada's 1995 production function is about 40 percent higher than the 1976 one.

The Demand for Labour

Quantity of labour demanded = number of labour hours hired by all firms in economy.

◆ **Demand for labour** (*LD*)—quantity of labour demanded at each real wage rate.

◆ **Real wage rate** is wage per hour in constant dollars = **money wage rate** (in current dollars)/price level.

◆ Firms hire labour as long as the marginal product of labour > real wage rate. Since ↓ marginal product of labour as ↑ labour hired→ *LD* slopes downward.

◆ Δ in real wage can be due to Δ money wage or Δ price level.

◆ Demand for labour curve shifts rightward if ↑ marginal product of labour due to ↑ capital stock or ↑ technology.

◆ Canadian demand for labour generally shifts rightward over time, but slowed down in the 1990s.

The Supply of Labour

Quantity of labour supplied = number of hours labour services households supply to firms.

◆ **Supply of labour** (*LS*)—quantity of labour supplied at each real wage rate.

◆ ↑ real wage rate→ ↑ quantity labour supplied because of

- Permanent ↑ hours of those working, as long as substitution effect (↑ real wage rate → ↑ opportunity cost of not working) > income effect (↑ real wage rate → ↑ demand leisure).
- ↑ **labour force participation rate** (proportion of those working or seeking it) as new higher real wage > **reservation wage** (wage required to make a person participate) of more people.
- Temporary ↑ hours of those working (intertemporal substitution), due to temporarily higher real wages.

Long-Run Aggregate Supply

Long-run aggregate supply is relationship between quantity of real GDP supplied and price level when real GDP = potential GDP. **Long-run aggregate supply curve** (*LAS*) graphs this relationship.

◆ Long-run equilibrium in labour market at real wage where $LD = LS \rightarrow$ unemployment at natural rate.

◆ *LD* and *LS* shift in long run because of changes in underlying forces, but over time $\Delta LD > \Delta LS > 0 \rightarrow \uparrow$ quantity of labour employed and real wage.

◆ When price level changes, money wage rate also changes to keep real wage rate at the level that makes $LD = LS \rightarrow$ employment is unchanged $\rightarrow$ *LAS* vertical at potential GDP.

◆ *LAS* shifts rightward if $\uparrow$ labour productivity ($\uparrow$ real wage) or $\uparrow$ labour supply ($\downarrow$ real wage).

◆ 1990s $\uparrow$ labour supply $\rightarrow \uparrow$ real GDP, but real wage stagnant.

Short-Run Aggregate Supply

Short-run aggregate supply is relationship between quantity of real GDP supplied and price level when money wage and all other influences remain constant. **Short-run aggregate supply curve** (*SAS*) graphs this relationship.

◆ With fixed money wage in short run, real wage rate changes as price level changes $\rightarrow$ labour demand changes.

◆ It is assumed employment is set by firms choosing how much to hire given real wage $\rightarrow$ *LD* may not equal *LS*.

◆ As a result, in short run, $\uparrow$ price level $\rightarrow \downarrow$ real wage rate $\rightarrow \uparrow$ labour demand $\rightarrow \uparrow$ employment $\rightarrow \uparrow$ real GDP produced $\rightarrow$ *SAS* upward sloping.

◆ *SAS* shifts rightward with *LAS* if $\uparrow$ potential GDP.

◆ *SAS* shifts rightward by itself if $\downarrow$ money wages.

◆ If ΔAD in short run $\rightarrow$ movement along *SAS* curve, Δ price level and real GDP.

H E L P F U L   H I N T S

I   The purpose of this chapter is to deepen our understanding of aggregate supply: the relationship between the price level and the quantity of real GDP supplied. Chapter 24 introduced the basic *AD–AS* model, and showed some of its usefulness in exploring the economy. The next part of the text examined aggregate demand in detail (Chapters 25–29), while this part (Chapters 30–32) examines aggregate supply in detail in order to explore its composition, and the variables that affect it. As we will see in the following part (Chapters 33–36), aggregate supply is a crucial variable in understanding macroeconomic problems and policy.

2   Our work at understanding aggregate supply is broken down into two constituent issues—the aggregate production function and the labour market.

The first issue is—how is the quantity of real GDP supplied determined in general? When the capital stock and the state of technology are given, the maximum amount of real GDP that can be produced depends on the quantity of labour employed. This relationship between employment and the quantity of real GDP supplied is captured by the aggregate production function.

To understand the determination of the quantity of real GDP supplied, it is necessary to pursue the second issue—how is the level of employment determined? The answer—in the labour market. The demand for labour is determined by firms, and the supply of labour is determined by households. If money wages continuously adjust to clear the labour market, the level of employment will always be the equilibrium level with full employment. If, on the other hand, money wages are fixed in the short run, the level of employment can deviate from its equilibrium level.

Since our interest is in aggregate supply, we want to know how the quantity of real GDP varies as the price level varies. This brings us to a third issue—how do changes in the price level affect employment and thereby real GDP? It turns out that if money wages continuously adjust, the level of employment, and thus the quantity of real GDP supplied, is independent of the price level. Whatever the price level, the wage rate will adjust so that the unique equilibrium level of employment is achieved. This implies a long-run aggregate supply curve that is vertical at potential GDP.

On the other hand, if wages are constant, the level of employment, and thus the quantity of real GDP supplied, depends on the actual value of the price level relative to the expected value of the price level. If the price level turns out to be equal to its expected value, the equilibrium level of employment (full employment) results. If the price level is higher than expected, the level of employment turns out to be higher than the equilibrium value and thus real GDP supplied will be larger than potential GDP. If the price level is lower than expected, employment will be less than equilibrium and real GDP supplied will be less than potential GDP. This implies a positively sloped short-run aggregate supply curve.

3 To understand why the amount of labour hired occurs at the level where the marginal product of labour (MP_L) equals the real wage rate, put yourself in the place of a firm hiring labour. The firm will hire more labour only if profits rise. In order for profits to rise, the extra labour must generate additional revenue that is greater than or equal to its additional cost. This requires that the price of output times the extra output generated by the hiring be greater than or equal to the money wage rate:

$$(P \times MP_L) > W$$

Therefore firms will hire labour until the extra revenue from the last unit hired is equal to the extra cost:

$$(P \times MP_L) = W$$

Dividing both sides of this equality by the price level yields the final condition that determines the demand for labour:

$$MP_L = W/P$$

4 The following arrow diagram is helpful in understanding why the short-run aggregate supply curve is positively sloped. It shows the sequence of events that link a change in the price level with the subsequent change in the quantity of real GDP supplied. Let P = the price level, W/P = the real wage rate, L = the quantity of labour employed, and Y = the quantity of real GDP supplied. If money wages are fixed we have:

$$\uparrow P \rightarrow \downarrow (W/P) \rightarrow \uparrow L \rightarrow \uparrow Y$$

If the money wage rate is constant, an increase in the price level ($\uparrow P$) will cause the real wage rate to fall ($\downarrow (W/P)$). At the lower real wage rate, firms will want to hire more labour ($\uparrow L$), which implies an increase in the quantity of real GDP supplied ($\uparrow Y$). Thus the short-run aggregate supply curve is positively sloped.

If money wages continuously adjust, an increase in the price level will have no effect on the quantity of real GDP supplied because the real wage rate will not fall.

SELF-TEST

True/False/Uncertain and Explain

1 If an economy is producing at levels above its long-run aggregate supply, we would expect wages to rise.

2 A fall in the price level will lead to a rise in unemployment.

3 An economy is initially in macroeconomic equilibrium and then expected future profits decrease. The new equilibrium real GDP will be lower.

4 If the real wage rate falls, the substitution effect implies that households will increase the time spent working.

5 If the real wage rate is currently high relative to what it is expected to be in the future, workers will tend to supply less labour now and more in the future.

6 The diminishing marginal product of labour implies that the demand for labour curve is negatively sloped.

7 As the real wage rate rises, the quantity of labour demanded decreases, other things remaining constant.

8 After an increase in the price level, the real wage rate will be unchanged.

9 If the marginal product of each unit of labour increases, the demand for labour curve shifts to the right.

10 If the money wage rate and the price level both rise by 10 percent, the quantity of labour demanded will increase.

Multiple-Choice

1 The aggregate production function shows

a how much real GDP changes as the capital stock changes, all else remaining the same.

b how much real GDP changes as the price level changes, all else remaining the same.

c how much labour demand changes as the real wage rate changes, all else remaining the same.

d how much labour demand changes as the money wage rate changes, all else remaining the same.

e none of the above.

2 Which one of the following quotations describes a rightward shift in the labour demand curve?

a "Recent higher wage rates have led to more leisure being consumed."

b "The recent lower price level has induced people to work more hours."

c "The recent higher real wage rate has induced people to work more hours."

d "The recent high investment in capital equipment has raised hiring by firms."

e "Adding extra workers leads to lower productivity of each additional worker."

3 Which one of the following quotations describes a movement along a labour supply curve?

a "Recent higher wage rates have led to more leisure being consumed."

b "The recent lower price level has induced people to work more hours."

c "The recent higher real wage rate has induced people to work more hours."

d All of the above.

e None of the above.

4 Which one of the following quotations describes a movement along a long-run aggregate supply curve?

a "The recent higher price levels have lowered production in the country."

b "The recent higher price levels have raised production in the country."

c "The recent higher price levels have led to compensating rises in wages, with no changes in labour hired or production."

d "The recent lower price levels have led to lower production in the country."

e None of the above.

5 Which one of the following quotations describes a shift rightward in a short-run aggregate supply curve?

a "The recent higher price levels have lowered production in the country."

b "The recent higher price levels have raised production in the country."

c "The recent higher price levels have led to compensating rises in wages, with no changes in labour hired or production."

d "The recent lower price levels have led to lower production in the country."

e None of the above.

6 Which one of the following variables is *not* held constant in deriving the short-run aggregate supply curve?

a the level of wages

b raw material prices

c climate

d price level

e technology

7 If tacos sell for $2 each at the Burning Belly Taco Stand, and the wage rate of a taco-maker is $60 per day, the real wage rate for the Burning Belly manager is

a 2 tacos per day.

b $60 per day.

c 120 tacos per day.

d $2 per day.

e 30 tacos per day.

8 Initially, tacos sell for $2 each at the Burning Belly Taco Stand, and the wage rate of a taco-maker is $60 per day. Suppose that the price of a taco rises to $2.50 after a *National Inquisitor* story linking tacos to baldness cures. The profit-maximizing Burning Belly manager will

a employ more taco-makers because the real wage rate has risen to $2.50 per day.

b employ fewer taco-makers because the real wage rate has risen to $2.50 per day.

c employ the same number of taco-makers because the wage rate is unchanged.

d employ more taco-makers because the real wage rate has fallen to 24 tacos per day.

e start advertising "I'm the owner, but I'm a customer too."

9 The labour demand curve is

a positively sloped and shifts when there is a change in the capital stock.

b positively sloped and shifts when there is a change in the quantity of labour employed.

c negatively sloped and shifts when there is a change in the capital stock.

d negatively sloped and shifts when there is a change in the quantity of labour employed.

e negatively sloped and shifts when there is a change in the real wage rate.

10 Which of the following would shift the aggregate production function upward?

a a decrease in the stock of capital

b a fall in the real wage rate

c an increase in labour employed

d an increase in the price level

e a technological advance

11 The demand for labour curve shows that, holding other things constant, as the

a price level increases, the quantity of labour demanded decreases.

b real wage rate increases, the quantity of labour demanded increases.

c money wage rate increases, the quantity of labour demanded decreases.

d money wage rate increases, the quantity of labour demanded increases.

e real wage rate increases, the quantity of labour demanded decreases.

12 In the long run, an increase in real GDP implies that

a potential GDP has increased.

b aggregate demand has increased.

c the economy has moved up its short-run aggregate supply curve.

d the price level has increased.

e real wages have fallen.

13 In the long run, an increase in the price level will cause the

a real wage rate to fall and increase employment.

b real wage rate to fall and decrease employment.

c money wage rate to rise by the same proportion and increase employment.

d money wage rate to rise by the same proportion and leave employment unchanged.

e money wage rate to rise by the same proportion and decrease employment.

14 Why is the demand for labour curve negatively sloped?

a At lower wage rates, workers do not work as hard and so firms must hire more of them.

b The marginal product of labour declines as labour input increases.

c As technology advances, less labour is required to produce a given output.

d As the price of output rises, firms will want to hire less labour.

e As the marginal product of labour increases, fewer workers are needed.

15 Figure 30.1 depicts the labour market. The price level, measured by the GDP deflator, is 150. What is the money wage rate in equilibrium?

a $8

b $12

c $15

d $18

e $24

FIGURE **30.1**

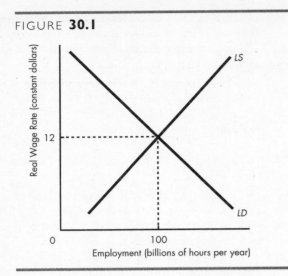

16 Refer to Fig. 30.1 and assume that when the money wage was set, the GDP deflator was expected to remain constant at 150. If the GDP deflator actually turns out to be 200 in the short run, the real wage rate will be

a $9, and employment will be less than 100 billion hours per year.

b $9, and employment will be more than 100 billion hours per year.

c $24, and employment will be less than 100 billion hours per year.

d $24, and employment will be more than 100 billion hours per year.

e $6, and employment will be more than 100 billion hours per year.

17 The aggregate supply curve is vertical at full-employment real GDP if

a the real wage rate adjusts continually so as to leave the labour market always in equilibrium.

b the money wage rate is fixed but the real wage rate changes because of changes in the price level.

c employment is determined by the quantity of labour demanded.

d employment is determined by the quantity of labour supplied.

e employment is determined by the money usage.

18 In the short run, if the price level falls, the real wage rate will be

a lower than the equilibrium real wage rate, and employment will fall.

b lower than the equilibrium real wage rate, and employment will rise.

c higher than the equilibrium real wage rate, and employment will fall.

d higher than the equilibrium real wage rate, and employment will rise.

e equal to the equilibrium real wage rate, and employment will stay constant.

19 In the long run, if the price level falls, the real wage rate will be

a less than the equilibrium real wage rate, and employment will fall.

b less than the equilibrium real wage rate, and employment will rise.

c higher than the equilibrium real wage rate, and employment will fall.

d higher than the equilibrium real wage rate, and employment will rise.

e equal to the equilibrium real wage rate, and employment will stay constant.

20 If the money wage rate is $12 per hour and the GDP deflator is 150, what is the real wage rate per hour?

a $18

b $15

c $12

d $8

e $6

21 The demand for labour and the supply of labour are both increasing over time, but the demand for labour is increasing at a faster rate. Over time we expect to see the

a real wage rate rising and employment falling.

b real wage rate and employment rising.

c real wage rate falling and employment rising.

d real wage rate and employment falling.

e long-run aggregate supply curve shifting left.

22 An increase in the capital stock will _____ the aggregate production function and _____ the demand for labour curve.

a increase; leave constant

b decrease; leave constant

c increase; increase

d decrease; increase

e leave constant; leave constant

23 A profit-maximizing firm will hire additional units of labour up to the point at which

a workers are no longer willing to work.
b the marginal product of labour is zero.
c the marginal product of labour is a maximum.
d the marginal product of labour is equal to the real wage.
e the marginal product of labour is equal to the money wage.

24 In the short run, employment is determined by the

a quantity of labour demanded at the actual real wage rate.
b quantity of labour supplied at the actual real wage rate.
c intersection of the demand for labour and supply of labour curves.
d intersection of the aggregate demand and aggregate supply curves.
e price level.

25 Which of the following is *not* a reason for a positively sloped supply of labour curve?

a intertemporal substitution of labour
b entrance into the labour force only if the real wage is at least as high as the reservation wage
c income effect of a change in the real wage
d substitution effect of a change in the real wage
e exit from the labour force only if the real wage is lower than the reservation wage

Short Answer Problems

1 Explain why the labour force participation rate increases as the real wage rate increases. Why does this help explain the positive slope of the labour supply curve?

2 Suppose the price level increases unexpectedly. In the long run, what will happen to the money wage rate, the real wage rate, employment, and real GDP?

3 Suppose the price level increases unexpectedly. In the short run, what will happen to the money wage rate, the real wage rate, employment, and real GDP?

4 "Fluctuations in aggregate demand cannot affect real GDP or employment." Discuss the validity of this statement.

5 What determines the demand for labour in the short run?

6 Table 30.1 gives information about the aggregate production function for a rather small economy, where L = units of labour per day and Y = units of output per day (real GDP).

TABLE **30.1** AGGREGATE PRODUCTION FUNCTION

L	Y	MP$_L$
0	0	
1	8	
2	15	
3	21	
4	26	
5	30	
6	33	

a Complete the last column of Table 30.1 by computing the marginal product of labour (MP_L). Remember to place the marginal product halfway between the two rows.
b How much labour will be demanded if the money wage rate is $6 and the GDP deflator is 150?
c Draw a graph of the demand for labour.

7 Table 30.2 gives the supply of labour schedule for the economy of Short Answer Problem **6**.

TABLE **30.2** SUPPLY OF LABOUR

Real Wage Rate	Quantity of Labour Supplied
8	7.5
7	6.5
6	5.5
5	4.5
4	3.5
3	2.5

a On the graph from Short Answer Problem **6c**, draw the supply of labour curve.
b What is the equilibrium real wage rate?
c What is the equilibrium level of employment?
d What is the level of output at this level of employment?

8 Suppose the economy presented in Short Answer Problems **6** and **7** is in the long run.
a If the GDP deflator is 100, what is the equilibrium money wage rate, the level of employment, and the level of output?
b If the GDP deflator is 80, what is the equilibrium money wage rate, the level of employment, and the level of output?

c If the GDP deflator is 120, what is the equilibrium money wage rate, the level of employment, and the level of output?

d Draw the long-run aggregate supply curve for this economy.

9 Now suppose the economy of Short Answer Problems **6** and **7** is characterized by a fixed money wage, set at $4.50. Use the short-run model to answer the following questions.

a If the actual value of the GDP deflator is 100, what is the real wage rate, the level of employment, and the level of output?

b If the actual value of the GDP deflator is 82, what is the real wage rate, the level of employment, and the level of output?

c If the actual value of the GDP deflator is 128, what is the real wage rate, the level of employment, and the level of output?

d On the graph from Short Answer Problem **8d**, indicate three points on the short-run aggregate supply curve for this sticky wage economy. Draw part of that curve by connecting the points.

🕐10 Now suppose that a technological advance gives a new aggregate production function summarized in Table 30.3.

TABLE **30.3** NEW AGGREGATE PRODUCTION FUNCTION

L	Y	MP_L
0	0	
1	10	
2	19	
3	27	
4	34	
5	40	
6	45	

a Complete the last column of Table 30.3 by computing the marginal product of labour. Remember to place the marginal product halfway between the two rows.

b On the graph from Short Answer Problems **6c** and **7a**, draw the new demand for labour curve.

c In the long run, what will be the new equilibrium real wage rate, level of employment, and level of output? (The supply of labour curve is unchanged.)

d What happened to the *SAS* and *LAS* curves?

ANSWERS

True/False/Uncertain and Explain

1 T Economy will be in above full-employment equilibrium → extra demand for labour → ↑ wages. (727)

2 U It depends on whether money wages constant. (726–730)

3 U ↓ in expected future profits shifts *AD* left, but impact on real GDP depends if long run or short run. (726–730)

4 F ↓ real wage rate → ↓ opportunity cost of leisure → ↑ leisure via the substitution effect. (723)

5 F High current real wage rate → high current return to working → more labour supplied. (724)

6 T If hire more labour, diminishing marginal product → ↓ marginal product. Therefore firms will hire more labour only if ↓ real wage rate. (721)

7 T Definition of labour demand curve. (720)

8 U Depends if short run or long run. (726–730)

9 T ↑ marginal product → ↑ output per worker → ↑ number desired at a constant real wage rate. (722)

10 F Real wage rate = (money wage rate/price level) × 100 is unchanged → quantity of labour demanded unchanged. (720)

Multiple-Choice

1 e Definition: how much real GDP changes as the labour hired changes. (717)

2 d This leads to higher productivity and more labour demand. **a, b,** and **c** are *LS* effect, **e** movement along curve. (722)

3 d See text discussion → note that ↓ price level → ↑ real wage rate. (723–724)

4 c No Δ employment → no Δ production → vertical *LAS*. (730–731)

5 e **a** is nonsense, **b, c,** and **d** are movements along curves. (731)

6 d All others are by definition. (729–730)

7 e Real wage rate = money wage rate/price of good = $60/$2 = 30. (720)

8 d Real wage = $60/$2.50 = 24 < 30 → hire more labour since cheaper. (720)

9 c Negatively sloped due to diminishing marginal product. **d** and **e** → movements along the curve. (722)

10 e Technological advance → ↑ productivity of labour. (718)

11 e Demand for labour depends inversely on real wage rate. (720)

12 a Fluctuations in real GDP due to Δ *LAS*. (727)

13 d Money wage rises because flexible, real wage stays the same → no Δ employment. (726–727)

14 b Diminishing marginal product creates downward-sloping labour demand curve. (720)

15 d Real wage set where *LD* = *LS* at $12, money wage = real wage × price level/100. (720)

◑ 16 b Actual real wage = money wage/price level × 100, and lower real wage → more labour demanded. (728–729)

17 a Vertical *AS* → *LAS* → real wage adjusts. (726–729)

18 c Lower actual price level → higher real wage (since money wage constant) → ↓ labour demanded. (728–729)

19 e Money wage adjust to any price level changes → real wage constant → no change in labour hired. (726–727)

20 d Real wage = money wage/price level × 100. (720)

◑ 21 b Draw a graph. (727–728)

22 c ↑ capital stock → ↑ output at each unit of labour, and ↑ marginal productivity → labour demand shifts right. (718, 722)

◑ 23 d Here profits maximized. (720)

24 a Firms select labour hired given actual real wage rate. (728–729)

25 c This effect tends to create negatively sloped labour supply curve. (723–724)

Short Answer Problems

1 Individuals have a reservation wage below which they will not supply labour. If the real wage rate is below an individual's reservation wage, she will not even enter the labour force. As the real wage rate rises, it will exceed the reservation wages of an increasingly larger group of people, thus the labour force increases relative to the size of the working age population; the labour force participation rate increases.

As this rate increases, more individuals offer to supply labour, thus the quantity of labour supplied increases. Because the original impetus was an increasing real wage rate, the real wage rate and the quantity of labour supplied are positively related.

2 In the long run, an increase in the price level will, at the current money wage rate, reduce the real wage rate. A fall in the real wage rate means that the labour market is now characterized by excess demand for labour; at the lower real wage rate, the quantity of labour demanded exceeds the quantity of labour supplied. Since the wage rate is flexible, the money wage rate will rise until the labour market is again in equilibrium; it will rise until the real wage rate has returned to its previous level. In the long run, employment stays at its original level as does real GDP.

3 In the short run, an increase in the price level will, at the constant money wage rate, reduce the real wage rate. Because the money wage rate does not adjust in the short run, this lower real wage rate will remain and, since the level of employment is determined by the demand for labour, the level of employment will increase. This implies that the quantity of real GDP supplied will increase via the aggregate production function.

4 This statement is valid in the long run, when the *LAS* curve is vertical. In this case, fluctuations in *AD* create changes in the price level, but there are no changes in employment or production. However, this statement is not valid in the short run, when the *SAS* curve is upward sloping. Then, fluctuations in *AD* create changes in real wages, employment, and production.

5 The demand for labour is set where the real wage rate equals the marginal product of labour. The marginal product of labour is affected by the capital stock, and the technology. In the short run, the money wage is constant, so that the real wage varies as the price level varies. Therefore in the short run the demand for labour is affected by the price level, capital stock, and level of technology.

6 a Completed Table 30.1 is shown here as Table 30.1 Solution. The marginal product of labour is the additional output produced by an additional unit of labour.

TABLE **30.1** SOLUTION

L	Y	MP$_L$
0	0	
		8
1	8	
		7
2	15	
		6
3	21	
		5
4	26	
		4
5	30	
		3
6	33	

b The real wage rate is computed as follows: Real wage rate = Money wage rate × 100/GDP deflator.

In our case, the money wage rate is $6 per unit and the GDP deflator is 150. Therefore the real wage is $4. Since a profit-maximizing firm will hire labour until the marginal product of labour is equal to the *real* wage rate, we can see that the quantity of labour demanded at a real wage rate of $4 is 4.5 units.

c The graph of the demand curve for labour (labelled LD_0) is given in Fig. 30.2. The demand curve for labour is the same as the marginal product of labour curve (see Table 30.1 Solution).

FIGURE **30.2**

7 a Figure 30.2 illustrates the supply curve of labour (labelled *LS*) on the same graph with the LD_1 curve from Short Answer Problem **6**.

b The equilibrium real wage rate is $4.50 since the quantity of labour demanded and supplied are both equal to 4 units per day. This can be seen from the graph or the tables.

c The equilibrium level of employment is 4 units.

d From the aggregate production function in Table 30.1, we can see that 4 units of labour will yield 26 units of output per day.

8 Regardless of the value of the GDP deflator, in the long run, the equilibrium *real* wage rate is $4.50, the level of employment is 4 units per day, and the level of output is 26 units per day. If we know the real wage rate and the GDP deflator, the money wage rate can be found as follows:

Money wage rate = real wage rate × GDP deflator/100.

a If the GDP deflator is 100, a real wage rate of $4.50 implies a money wage rate of $4.50.

b If the GDP deflator is 80, a real wage rate of $4.50 suggests a money wage rate of $3.60.

c If the GDP deflator is 120, a real wage rate of $4.50 suggests a money wage rate of $5.40.

d The long-run aggregate supply curve (labelled *LAS*) is given in Fig. 30.3. Parts **a**, **b**, and **c** indicate that at every price level output is 26 units per day.

FIGURE **30.3**

9 a If the actual value of the GDP deflator is 100, since the money wage rate is fixed at $4.50, the real wage rate is $4.50. This implies that employment is 4 units and output is 26 units.

b If the actual value of the GDP deflator is 82, since the money wage rate is fixed at $4.50, the real wage rate is $5.50 (4.5/82 × 100 = 5.5). Employment is determined by the demand for labour which, at a real wage of $5.50, is 3 units per day. This suggests (from Table 30.1) that output is 21 units per day.

c If the actual value of the GDP deflator is 128, since the money wage rate is fixed at $4.50, the real wage rate is $3.50. Employment is determined by the demand for labour and is 5 units per day. From Table 30.1, this implies a daily output of 30 units.

d Figure 30.3 indicates three points on the short-run aggregate supply curve in the sticky wage economy: point *a* corresponds to output = 26, GDP deflator = 100; point *b* corresponds to output = 21, GDP deflator = 82; point *c* corresponds to output = 30, GDP deflator = 128. The points are connected to give a portion of the short-run aggregate supply curve (labelled *SAS*).

⊘ **10 a** Completed Table 30.3 is shown here as Table 30.3 Solution. Note that the marginal product of each unit of labour has increased as a result of the technological advance.

TABLE **30.3** SOLUTION

L	Y	MP_L
0	0	
		10
1	10	
		9
2	19	
		8
3	27	
		7
4	34	
		6
5	40	
		5
6	45	

b Figure 30.2 gives the graph. Notice that the new labour demand curve, LD_1, lies to the right of LD_0.

c It can be seen from Fig. 30.2 or Tables 30.2 and 30.3 that the quantity of labour demanded equals the quantity of labour supplied at a real wage rate of $5.50. The level of employment is now 5 units of labour per day, which implies an output of 40 units per day (from Table 30.3).

d The *LAS* shifts right from 26 to 40, and the *SAS* curve moves with it.

Employment, Wages, and Unemployment

KEY CONCEPTS

Employment and Wages

Real GDP and employment are positively linked: more of one usually means more of the other.

◆ Statistics Canada surveys households to estimate job status:

- **Working-age population** = number of people 15 years and over.
- Divided into those in **labour force** (employed + unemployed) and those not in labour force.
- Employed = those with full-time and part-time jobs.
- Unemployed = without work, actively seeking within last 4 weeks, waiting to be called back after layoff, or waiting to start new job within 4 weeks.
- Some part-time workers are involuntary → want a full-time job.

◆ Statistics Canada looks at four labour market indicators:

- **Unemployment rate** = percentage of labour force who are unemployed.
- **Involuntary part-time rate** = percentage of labour force who are part-time but want full-time.
- **Labour force participation rate** = percentage of working-age population who are in labour force.
- **Employment-to-population ratio** = percentage of working-age population with jobs.

◆ In Canada since 1960,

- ↑ unemployment rate in recessions.
- involuntary part-time rate has upward trend, and ↑ in recessions.

- labour force participation rate has strong upward trend, but ↓ also in recessions because of **discouraged workers** → people who temporarily leave labour force in a recession.
- ↑ employment-to-population ratio overall (many new jobs created), but also ↓ in recessions.
- participation rates for men ↓ and women ↑ (strongly) over this period.

◆ To see quantity of labour employed, and control for part-time versus full-time, need to examine **aggregate hours** = total hours worked. Has upward trend, ↓ recessions. ↓ hours per worker until earlier 1990s, with faster falls in recessions.

◆ **Real wage rate** = quantity of goods an hour's work can buy = **money wage rate** (dollars per hour)/price level.

◆ Manufacturing wages fell strongly in early 1980s, with slow recovery, while total labour compensation in all sectors has upward trend, but fell in 1993 and 1994 due to productivity slowdown.

Unemployment and Full Employment

◆ People become unemployed when they

- are laid-off → **job losers**.
- voluntarily quit → **job leavers**.
- enter (**entrants**) or re-enter (**re-entrants**) the labour force.

◆ People end unemployment when they are hired, recalled, or withdraw from the labour force.

◆ Primary source of unemployment is job loss → fluctuates strongly with business cycle.

◆ There is a wide range of duration of unemployment → half are unemployed over 14 weeks.

- Unemployment rate higher for younger people.
- Types of unemployment:
  - **frictional** (due to normal turnover, people searching for good job matches) → influenced by the baby boomers, unemployment insurance generosity.
  - **structural** (job losses in industries/regions declining due to technological change) → high around 1980.
  - **seasonal** (number of jobs decreases in certain seasons) → rises in Atlantic provinces in winter.
  - **cyclical** (due to economic slowdowns) → fluctuates with the cycle.
- **Natural rate of unemployment**—only frictional, structural, and seasonal unemployment occurring, or no cyclical unemployment. Actual unemployment rate fluctuates around the natural rate, as real GDP fluctuates around potential GDP.
- **Full employment** occurs when unemployment rate = natural rate.

Explaining Employment and Wage Rates

- **Labour demand curve** (downward sloping) shows quantity of labour firms plan to hire at each real wage.
- **Labour supply curve** (upward sloping) shows quantity of labour households plan to supply at each real wage.
- Equilibrium in the labour market when quantity demanded = quantity supplied.
- Since 1960, $\Delta LD > \Delta LS > 0$ due to growing labour productivity and growing working-age population → ↑ real wages and employment.
- There have also been large changes in the structure of labour market → services industry has had employment and wages growing faster than manufacturing.

Explaining Unemployment

Three reasons for unemployment—job search, job rationing, sticky wages.

- **Job search** unemployment occurs when people take time to find jobs while unemployed.
  - Constant change in labour market → always job search, source of frictional, structural, and cyclical unemployment.
  - When structural change high or economy in recession, job search high.

- ↑ job search if ↑ proportion of working-age population, if ↑ unemployment compensation, or if technological change or globalization increase structural change.

- **Job rationing** is paying a wage that creates an excess supply of labour and frictional unemployment → three reasons:
  - Firms pay **efficiency wages** → higher wages designed to maximize profits by ↑ work effort, ↓ labour turnover rate, and ↑ quality of labour.
  - **Insider–outsider theory** argues insiders (those with jobs) may stop firms from lowering wages to hire outsiders (unemployed).
  - Minimum wages keep wages too high for some workers.

- Money wages are stickier than prices, so actual real wage changes slower than equilibrium real wage → excess supply of labour when labour demand falls → temporary rise in cyclical unemployment.

HELPFUL HINTS

1 In a dynamic economy, not all unemployment is inefficient. There are economic benefits of frictional unemployment both to the individual and to society. Younger workers typically experience periods of unemployment as they try to find jobs that match their skills and interest. The benefit of the resulting frictional unemployment is a more satisfying and productive work life. Society benefits because the frictional unemployment that accompanies such a job-search process allows workers to find jobs in which they are more productive. As a result, the total production of goods and services in the economy rises. (Compare this with the case for most graduates in the Republic of China. They are assigned jobs upon graduation, with very little personal input about type of job or location.)

Structurally unemployed workers are not going to get a new job without retraining or relocation. This means a much greater cost to the worker and to society—for example, structurally unemployed workers are typically unemployed for much longer time periods. These workers bear the brunt of the cost of restructuring industries in our economy, although society gains from the shift to the new industries.

2 When economists use the term "full employment," or equivalent "the natural rate of unemployment," this does not mean that everyone has a job. Rather, it means that the only unemployment is frictional, structural, and seasonal—there is no cyclical unemployment. (Note this implies the natural rate is higher in the winter time!)

It is possible for the actual rate of unemployment to be less than the natural rate of unemployment. This is the same as saying that it is possible for the level of employment to exceed full employment. In these situations, people are spending too little time searching for jobs, and therefore less productive job matches are being made.

3 As the text explains, there are four different *types* of unemployment, but defining these types does not *explain* them. Three basic explanations of unemployment help us to see where the types of unemployment come from.

Frictional unemployment comes from job search (there is always job search in the economy because of changes in the fortunes of individual firms, people searching for good matches), and from job rationing leading to a wage above the equilibrium wage, with queuing for jobs as a result. It is often the result of a downturn in one firm.

Structural unemployment comes from excessive job search in times of structural change because of globalization or technological change. It is due to a downturn in a specific industry or region.

Seasonal unemployment is due to job search in specific seasons when certain types of jobs do not exist.

Cyclical unemployment comes from a rise in job search during a recession, when a fall in the demand for labour has led to too high a real wage (because of a sticky money wage), and fewer jobs compared to the number of searchers. It is due to a general downturn in the entire economy.

SELF-TEST

True/False/Uncertain and Explain

1 If there is an increase in the pace of labour turnover, the unemployment rate will rise.

2 Being unemployed for a few months after graduating from university hurts the graduate.

3 A decline in the number of jobs in the automobile sector matched by an equal rise in the number of jobs in the banking sector will not alter the unemployment rate.

4 At full employment, there is no unemployment.

5 Bill has just graduated from high school and is looking for his first job. Bill is frictionally unemployed.

6 Job rationing keeps real wages too high and creates cyclical unemployment.

7 The employment-to-population ratio is the percentage of working-age population who are in the labour force.

8 Equilibrium in the labour market is when labour demand equals labour supply and unemployment is zero.

9 If the employment-to-population ratio rises, unemployment falls.

10 If the number of discouraged workers falls, the employment-to-population ratio will fall.

Multiple-Choice

1 Which of the following events would raise cyclical unemployment?

a money wages become stickier

b a rise in unemployment insurance benefits

c a rise in the pace of technological change

d a rise in both job destruction and job creation

e all of the above

2 One possible cause of unemployment is

a flexible wages lead to too many fluctuations in real wages.

b flexible wages lead to too few fluctuations in real wages.

c sticky wages lead to too many fluctuations in real wages.

d job search leads to technological change.

e outsiders will not allow firms to hire insiders if it means lower wages.

3 Which of the following is *not* a possible explanation for unemployment?

a job search

b efficiency wages

c insiders and outsiders

d sticky wages

e part-time searches

4 Unemployment will increase if there is an increase in the number of people

a entering retirement.

b withdrawing from the labour force.

c recalled from layoffs.

d leaving jobs to go to school.

e leaving school to find jobs.

5 Which of the following would be considered structurally unemployed?

a a Saskatchewan farmer who has lost her farm and is unemployed until retrained

b a Nova Scotia fishery worker who is searching for a better job closer to home

c a steelworker who is laid off but who expects to be called back soon

d an office worker who has lost her job because of a general slowdown in economic activity

e none of the above

6 Which of the following would be considered cyclically unemployed?

a a Saskatchewan farmer who has lost her farm and is unemployed until retrained

b a Nova Scotia fishery worker who is searching for a better job closer to home

c a steelworker who is laid off but who expects to be called back soon

d an office worker who has lost her job because of a general slowdown in economic activity

e none of the above

7 Which of the following would be considered frictionally unemployed? A steelworker who

a loses her job because of technological change.

b is laid off but expects to be called back soon.

c gives up her job because she retires.

d decides to leave the labour force and become a full-time ballet student.

e becomes discouraged and stops looking for a job.

8 If the economy is at full employment, then the

a entire population is employed.

b entire labour force is employed.

c only unemployment is frictional unemployment plus discouraged workers.

d unemployment rate is less than 3 percent.

e only unemployment is frictional, structural, and seasonal unemployment.

9 Including discouraged workers in the measured unemployment rate would

a not change the actual rate.

b lower the measured unemployment rate.

c raise the natural rate of unemployment.

d raise the full employment rate.

e raise the measured unemployment rate.

10 The natural rate of unemployment is

a the rate at which unemployment equals 0 percent.

b the same as cyclical unemployment.

c the rate at which cyclical unemployment equals 6 percent.

d the rate at which cyclical unemployment equals 0 percent.

e none of the above.

11 The demand for labour and the supply of labour are both increasing over time, but the demand for labour is increasing at a faster rate. Over time, therefore we expect to see the

a real wage rate rising and employment falling.
b real wage rate rising and employment rising.
c real wage rate falling and employment rising.
d real wage rate falling and employment falling.
e long-run aggregate supply curve shifting left.

12 If the number of discouraged workers rises, all else unchanged, then the

a unemployment rate will rise.
b employment-to-population ratio will fall.
c labour force participation rate will rise.
d labour force participation rate will fall.
e both a and c.

13 In a country with a working-age population of 20 million, 13 million are employed, 1.5 million are unemployed, and where 1 million of the employed are working part-time, half of whom wish to work full-time, the size of the labour force is

a 20 million.
b 15.5 million.
c 14.5 million.
d 13 million.
e 11.5 million.

14 In a country with a working-age population of 20 million, 13 million are employed, 1.5 million are unemployed, and where 1 million of the employed are working part-time, half of whom wish to work full-time, the size of the labour force participation rate is

a 75.5 percent.
b 72.5 percent.
c 65 percent.
d 57.5 percent.
e none of the above.

15 In a country with a working-age population of 20 million, 13 million are employed, 1.5 million are unemployed, and where 1 million of the employed are working part-time, half of whom wish to work full-time. The unemployment rate is

a 10 percent.
b 10.3 percent.
c 11.5 percent.
d 15.4 percent.
e none of the above.

16 Which of the following quotations describes job search unemployment?

a "Wages are so good at the factory, they always have enough applicants to pick whomever they want for the job."
b "Professors with tenured jobs are refusing to take pay cuts to help hire new professors."
c "Wages have failed to fall in the current economic downturn, creating extra unemployment."
d "People are taking too long to find jobs, because unemployment insurance is so generous."
e All of the above.

17 In a recession, what is the largest source of the rise in unemployment?

a job leavers
b job losers
c new entrants to the labour force
d re-entrants to the labour force
e involuntary part-time workers

18 In a recession, typically

a unemployment rises.
b participation rates fall.
c employment-to-population ratios fall.
d all of the above.
e none of the above.

19 Which of the following would be counted as unemployed in Canada?

a Doris only works five hours a week but is looking for a full-time job.
b Kanhaya has stopped looking for work since he was unable to find a suitable job during a two-month search.
c Sharon is a college student with no job.
d Maurice has been laid off from his job for 20 weeks but expects to be called back soon.
e Bogdan has been laid off from his job but does not expect to be called back, and is not looking.

20 Cyclical unemployment is caused by

a efficiency wages.
b insiders.
c the minimum wage.
d sticky money wages.
e all of the above.

21 In the past 20 years in the labour market

a real wages have fallen in all industries.

b real wages have risen in all industries.

c employment has fallen strongly, creating more unemployment.

d labour demand growth was negative.

e none of the above.

22 Job search unemployment rises if

a the proportion of working-age population rises.

b unemployment compensation becomes more generous.

c globalization rises.

d all of the above.

e none of the above.

23 In the long run, a decrease in labour demand causes the real wage rate to _____ and employment to _____ .

a stay constant; fall

b stay constant; stay constant

c fall; stay constant

d fall; fall

e fall; rise

24 In the short run, a decrease in labour demand causes the real wage rate to _____ and employment to _____.

a stay constant; fall

b stay constant; stay constant

c fall; stay constant

d fall; fall

e fall; rise

25 An efficiency wage refers to wages

a paid below the equilibrium wage rate in order to increase the firm's efficiency.

b set to generate the efficient level of employment.

c paid above the equilibrium wage rate in order to increase worker productivity.

d being too high because of sticky money wages.

e being too high because of insiders stopping firms from lowering them.

Short Answer Problems

1 Explain why an economy does not have zero percent unemployment when it has full employment.

2 Consider the following information about an economy: working-age population—20 million; full-time employment—8 million; part-time employment—2 million (1 million of whom wish they had full-time jobs); unemployment— 1 million.

a What is the labour force in this economy? What is the labour force participation rate?

b What is the unemployment rate?

c What is the involuntary part-time rate?

d What is the employment-to-population ratio?

e If 0.6 million of those unemployed are frictionally, structurally, and seasonally unemployed, what is the natural rate of unemployment?

f What is the amount of cyclical unemployment?

⊘3 Consider the labour demand and supply schedules for an economy in Table 31.1.

TABLE **31.1**

Real Wage Rate (constant dollars per hour)	Labour Demand (millions of workers)	Labour Supply (millions of workers)
3	32	8
4	28	12
5	24	16
6	20	20
7	16	24
8	12	28
9	8	32

a If the natural rate of unemployment is 10 percent, calculate the labour force and the number unemployed in equilibrium.

b Suppose that labour demand falls by 4 million workers at each wage rate. If wages are sticky, calculate the resulting cyclical unemployment and total unemployment rate after the change.

4 In Chapter 22 we learned about the costs of unemployment. Are they more severe for frictional or structural unemployment?

5 Explain the difference between cyclical and structural unemployment. How would you tell a cyclically unemployed person from a structurally unemployed person?

⊘6 Explain what recent unemployment insurance reforms might do to the four types of unemployment. Are these reforms a good idea from the unemployment viewpoint?

7 Examine each of the following changes in John Carter's labour market activity, and explain whether they are unemployment, employment, or out of the labour force. If they are unemployment, which of the four types of unemployment are they?

a John graduates from Barsoom High and starts looking for a job.

b John has no luck finding the full-time job he wants and takes a part-time job working cleaning out the canals.

c Canal-cleaning doesn't work out for John because of unforeseen allergies, so he quits.

d Discouraged by the lack of work, John stops looking and stays home watching his favourite soap opera, "As Mars Turns."

e John sees an advertisement on TV for the Barsoom Swordfighter School, and enrols to get his B.S.F.

f John graduates at the top of his class and joins up with Princess Dejah Thoris's guard.

g An inventor at Barsoom University comes up with a new laser personal defence system, and the Princess disbands her guard—John spends a long time looking for work.

h John gets a job cleaning up after the sandstorms, but once the wet season comes along, he is laid off.

i John sees an advertisement seeking someone to help explore the ruins of the lost city of Rhiannon and signs up as security—the six-armed tribes are particularly ferocious there.

8 "The theory of job rationing tells us firms and insiders keep real wages too high and therefore create extra unemployment. Real wages should be forced downward to create more employment." Discuss this statement.

⊘ 9 Consider the data from 1995 in Table 31.2 on Canada as a whole and Newfoundland specifically.[1]

TABLE **31.2**

Economy	Labour Force Participation Rate	Unemployment Rate	Employment-to-Population Ratio
Canada	64.8	9.5	58.6
Newfoundland	53.1	18.3	43.3

Newfoundland has twice the unemployment of Canada, as well as a radically lower employment-to-population ratio and labour force participation rate. By examining these, can you get any insight into the impact of such a high unemployment rate on the labour market in Newfoundland? Why is the gap in the employment-to-population ratio (15.3 points) so much bigger than the unemployment gap (8.8 points)?

10 Go to Statistics Canada's website (**http://www.statcan.ca/**), or their publication *Perspectives on Labour and Income*, or their catalogue on *The Labour Force Survey* and find the current unemployment rate, the current employment-to-population ratio and the current labour force participation rate for your province and for Canada as a whole. How do they differ? Can you identify any conditions in your province that would create this difference?

ANSWERS

True/False/Uncertain and Explain

1 T There will be higher flows in and out of labour force → more job search unemployment. (744–745)

2 U It depends on whether time unemployed → better job. (746)

3 F Workers retrain/relocate → ↑ structural unemployment. (746–747)

4 F Full employment → frictional, structural, and seasonal unemployment. (748)

5 T Searching for jobs = frictionally unemployed. (746–747)

6 F It creates frictional unemployment, since it is independent of the cycle. (754–755)

7 F Percentage with jobs. (740)

8 F Even in equilibrium there is natural unemployment. (748)

⊘ 9 U True if participation falls or does not rise by much, otherwise false. (740–741)

10 F This will only change labour force participation. (741)

Multiple-Choice

1 a Last three raise frictional or structural unemployment, but if money wages adjust slower, cyclical unemployment is larger and lasts longer. (748)

2 c Flexible wages → correct number of fluctuations always. Sticky wages → too many fluctuations. Job search caused *by* technological change, **e** is backward. (755)

---

[1] *Source:* Statistics Canada, *Labour Force Survey*, various issues, or Statistics Canada's website (**http://www.statcan.ca/**).

3 e   They are employed while searching. (753–755)

4 e   Others all lower unemployment. (744–745)

5 a   Structural unemployment includes having wrong skills. Others are frictional or cyclical unemployment. (746–747)

6 d   Cyclical unemployment is due to economy-wide slowdowns. (746–747)

7 b   a is structural, rest are not officially unemployed. (746–747)

8 e   Definition. (748)

9 e   It would add extra unemployed workers to the measured rate. (741)

10 d   Definition. (748)

11 b   Draw a graph. (750–751)

12 d   Discouraged workers were unemployed, but stop looking and exit labour force, so unemployment rate ↓, labour force participation ↓, employment-to-population ratio unchanged. (741)

13 c   Employed + unemployed. (740)

14 b   Labour force/working-age population = 14.5/20 = 72.5 percent. (740)

15 b   Unemployed/labour force = 1.5/14.5 = 10.3 percent. (740)

16 d   a and b are job rationing, c is cyclical. (753–754)

17 b   See text discussion. (744–745)

18 d   See text discussion. (740–742)

19 d   Doris is employed, Kanhaya must be looking for work, Sharon is out of labour force, Bogdan does not expect to be called back. (739)

20 d   When recession lowers demand for labour, wages fail to fall → ↑ unemployment. (748)

21 e   See text discussion. (742–743)

22 d   See text discussion. (753–754)

23 d   Wages adjust fully → draw a graph. (749–751)

24 a   Wages do not adjust in short-run → draw a graph. (755)

25 c   Definition. (754)

Short Answer Problems

1   An economy always has some unemployment, that of people searching for jobs—frictional, structural, and seasonal unemployment. We define full unemployment as when there is only frictional, structural, and seasonal unemployment.

2 a   The labour force is 11 million, the sum of employment and unemployment. The labour force participation rate = percentage of working-age population who are in the labour force = 11/20 or 55 percent.

b   The unemployment rate is 9.1 percent, the number of unemployed as a percentage of the labour force.

c   It is 9.1 percent, the percentage of the labour force who are part-time and want full-time.

d   It is 50 percent, percentage of working-age population with a job.

e   The natural rate of unemployment is frictional plus structural plus seasonal unemployment. In our case, it is the rate of unemployment if unemployment were only 0.6 million. Thus the natural rate of unemployment is 5.45 percent.

f   Cyclical unemployment is actual unemployment minus natural unemployment, or 0.4 million.

3 a   Equilibrium is when $LD = LS$ at 20 million workers employed. In equilibrium, all unemployment is natural.
Unemployment rate = unemployed/(unemployed + employed), or
$0.10 = $ unemployed/(unemployed + 20), or
$0.10 \times$ (unemployed + 20) = unemployed, or
$0.1 \times$ (unemployed) + 2 = unemployed, or
$2 = 0.9 \times$ (unemployed), or
unemployed = 2/0.9 = 2.22 million.
Labour force = employed + unemployed
           = 22.22 million.

b   If wages are sticky, then they will stay at the equilibrium value of $6. Demand is now 4 million lower at that value, so there are only 16 million workers employed out of a labour force of 22.22 million, for an unemployment rate of 28 percent = $(6.22/22.22) \times 100$. The extra unemployment caused by the fall in labour demand is 4 million, the amount of cyclical unemployment.

4   The costs of unemployment include the lost output of the unemployed, and the deterioration of skills and abilities; in other words, human capital erodes. In addition, there are the social costs of higher crime and a loss of human dignity. These costs will be higher for structural unemployment because it lasts longer.

5   Cyclical unemployment is caused by a downturn in the economy, when there is a fall in demand for all products. Structural unemployment is caused by structural changes in a specific industry or region, and there is a fall in demand for a certain type of labour whose skills are no longer desired.

Cyclical unemployment will end when the economy turns up. Structural unemployment will end when the workers retrain or move.

6 The recent reforms reduce the compensation while unemployed, reduce the total period you can get compensation, and make it more difficult to get compensation if you quit or are fired for "just cause." As a result, people will be quicker to take a job when offered one, since the value of further search is now lower due to the lower compensation—this will reduce frictional unemployment for sure, but will not create new jobs under seasonal, structural, or cyclical. However, presumably workers under these four types will be more likely to take a low-wage or different job because of the lower unemployment compensation, if they can find one, reducing these types of unemployment (least effect on cyclical). As well, people who quit jobs have a harder time getting coverage so will be less likely to quit; frictional unemployment will be lower for this reason.

These reforms will reduce natural unemployment, which may be good. However, people will be less able to spend time searching for the optimal job match and will settle for "inappropriate" jobs more frequently, which is not optimal from society's viewpoint. It is hard to say if the previous levels were too generous or not without further information.

7 a He is an entrant, and is frictionally unemployed.
 b He is now employed, although he is also involuntarily part-time.
 c He is a job leaver, and is frictionally unemployed.
 d He is a discouraged worker, but technically out of the labour force.
 e He is still out of the labour force.
 f He is employed.
 g He is structurally unemployed.
 h He is initially employed, but then is seasonally unemployed.
 i He is employed again.

8 Yes, firms and insiders keep real wages too high, but the result is higher productivity in each case. Forcing down real wages might create more employment, but it would also create lower productivity and lower real GDP. It is not clear that this is desirable.

9 The higher unemployment rate has pushed many workers out of the labour force—they have become discouraged workers and are not even attempting to find work. The bigger gap in the employment-to-population ratio reflects this, because it includes the formally unemployed, and the discouraged workers.

10 The answer to this question will depend on the time period in question, and what is happening in your province, but differences might reflect structural change in your province's key industries (e.g., automobile manufacturing, tourism, fisheries, agriculture, oil, forestry, etc.), or differential migration rates (e.g., in British Columbia), or different business cycles, etc.

32

Investment, Capital, and Interest

KEY CONCEPTS

Capital and Interest

◆ The economy's **capital stock** is quantity of plant, equipment, buildings, and inventories.

- **Gross investment** = purchases of new capital stock.
- **Depreciation** = wearing out and scrapping of existing capital.
- **Net investment** = Δ capital stock = gross investment − depreciation.

◆ In Canada, net investment is positive every year (capital stock grows fairly steadily), but fluctuates strongly with the business cycle → gross investment does too.

◆ Canada's investment as a percentage of GDP is lower than the developing countries, and was lower than the industrial countries until recently.

◆ The return on capital is the long-term **real interest rate** (= nominal interest rate − inflation rate).

◆ World real interest rates tend to move together.

◆ Real interest rates were low in the 1970s, rose sharply to a peak in 1985 at 9 percent, fell down in the late 1980s to around 6 percent, and increased in the 1990s to 9 percent again.

Investment

Business investment is influenced by expected profit rate and real interest rate → invest if expected profit rate > real interest rate.

◆ ↑ expected profit rate → ↑ investment.

- Expected profit rate ↑ in an expansion, ↓ in a recession due to fluctuations in sales.

- Advances in technology → eventually higher profits.

◆ Opportunity cost of capital funds = real interest rate. Includes direct borrowing costs, or forgone income from using retained earnings.

◆ **Investment demand** is relationship between level of investment and real interest rate.

- Investment demand curve (*ID*) slopes downward.
- ↑ expected profit rate → rightward shift *ID*.
- Fluctuations in expected profit rate main source of fluctuations in *ID*.

◆ Canadian *ID* curve shifted rightward in 1980s, shifted leftward 1990 due to ↓ expected profit rate, rightward again afterwards.

Saving and Consumption Expenditure

Investment is financed by national saving (private + government) and international borrowing.

◆ Households allocate disposable income (*YD*) between saving (*S*) and consumption expenditure (*C*):

- ↑ real interest rate → ↑ opportunity cost of consumption → ↓ *C*, ↑ *S* (↓ borrowing).
- ↑ disposable income → ↑ *C* and *S*.
- ↑ purchasing power of net assets (real value of assets − debts) due to ↓ price level → ↑ *C*, ↓ *S* (↑ borrowing).
- ↑ expected future income → ↑ *C*, ↓ *S* (↑ borrowing).

◆ Crucial variables are *YD* (short run → Chapter 25) and real interest rate (long run).

◆ **Consumption demand** (*CD*) is relationship between consumption expenditure and real interest rate → downward sloping.

◆ **Saving supply** (*SS*) is relationship between saving and real interest rate → upward sloping.

◆ Δ other variables *shift CD* and *SS* curves.

◆ ↑ purchasing power of net assets or expected future income → *CD* shifts rightward and *SS* leftward.

◆ ↑ *YD* → both curves shift rightward, strength of each effect measured by marginal propensities.

- **Marginal propensity to consume** (*MPC*) = fraction of a change in disposable income that is consumed = $\Delta C / \Delta Y$.
- **Marginal propensity to save** (*MPS*) = fraction of change in disposable income saved = $\Delta S / \Delta Y$.
- *MPC* > *MPS*.

◆ For Canada,

- Big ↑ real interest rate has small impact on *CD* and *SS*,
- Both have shifted strongly rightward due to ↑ disposable income.

Long-Run Equilibrium in the Global Economy

Real interest rate is determined in world capital market. Capital is very mobile, unlike labour, and responds quickly to eliminate interest rate differentials.

◆ Real interest rate determined by equilibrium in the world capital market, where world *ID* = world *SS*, with interest rate adjusting to achieve equilibrium.

◆ Global fiscal policy affects real interest rate and investment:

- For the global (closed) economy, $I = S + (T - G)$.
- Net government budget surplus → ↑ *S* → ↓ real interest rate → ↑ *I*.
- Opposite effect for a government deficit → ↑ *r* and crowds out *I*.

◆ In early 1970s, huge ↑ price of oil → ↑ income of oil-exporting nations → ↑ world saving → little change in investment demand → ↓ real interest rate.

◆ Through late 1970s to mid-1980s, growth in investment demand, but little growth in saving as ↑ government deficits offset ↑ in national saving → real interest rates back ↑.

◆ In late 1980s, ↓ real interest rate as saving grew faster than investment demand, as ↓ productivity growth (slow investment demand growth) → ↓ expected future income → ↑ saving growth.

Net Exports, Investment, and Fiscal Policy

Canada's national investment, consumption, and government purchases have no impact on world real interest rate, but do determine net exports and net lending/borrowing with rest of world.

◆ If exports > imports → foreigners must borrow from us to pay the difference.

◆ If imports > exports → we must borrow from foreigners.

◆ For Canada, $I = S + (T - G) - (X - M)$ → borrowing from the rest of the world helps finance our investment.

◆ In Canadian capital market, world real interest rate is given, and if at that rate *ID* > (*SS* + government saving) → we borrow difference from rest of the world (net exports < 0).

◆ If *ID* < (*SS* + government saving) → we lend to the rest of the world, net exports > 0.

◆ Exchange rate adjusts to make net exports adjust to the required level.

◆ **Real exchange rate** = opportunity cost of foreign-made goods in terms of Canadian-made goods.

- ↑ real exchange rate → ↑ cost of Canadian goods to foreigners, ↓ cost of foreign goods to Canadians → ↓ net exports.

◆ If ↑ (*C* + *I* + *G*) relative to potential GDP → ↑ real exchange rate, ↓ net exports, ↑ net international borrowing.

◆ If ↑ government budget deficit → ↓ national saving → gap between *SS* and *ID* higher → ↑ net exports, ↑ borrowing from rest of world or ↓ lending to rest of world.

◆ Higher government deficits can create worries about repayment → lenders require a risk premium on top of world real interest rate.

H E L P F U L   H I N T S

1 In this chapter, we examine consumption and saving in a different manner than in Chapter 25. Chapter 25 emphasized the role of disposable income in influencing consumption and saving, and did not discuss the real interest rate, purchasing power of net assets, or expected future income—we implicitly held them constant throughout the analysis. As a result, the consumption and saving functions of that

chapter were drawn with consumption and saving solely as a function of disposable income.

In this chapter, we allow all four variables to influence consumption and saving. However, the crucial role is played by the real rate of interest, so now when we graph consumption demand and saving supply, the real rate of interest is on the vertical axis, and changes in disposable income (and purchasing power of net assets and expected future income) create shifts in the variables. We are still talking about the same decision, but when we draw the graphs in this chapter compared to Chapter 25, we are carrying out a different thought experiment, and holding constant different variables.

2 In Chapter 27, the rate of interest was determined in the money market. In this chapter, the rate of interest is determined in the world capital market. Why does this difference exist? Does monetary policy work in this model?

The model of Chapter 27 did have a bond (or capital) market indirectly built into it, because money demand was jointly determined with bond (capital) demand and supply. In the more complex model here, the two are integrated, and changes in world capital markets affect money demand.

The model of Chapter 27 determined the short-term interest rate, which is strongly but not exclusively influenced by monetary policy. The model of this chapter determines the long-term interest rate, which is less influenced by domestic interest rates, and more so by world rates. The exact relationship between the short-term and long-term rates is something we will have to leave for another course in economics!

SELF-TEST

True/False/Uncertain and Explain

1 The Canadian capital stock fluctuates quite strongly from year to year.

2 An increase in disposable income will raise consumption demand, lower saving supply, and raise the real interest rate.

3 Global fiscal policy has no effect on the real interest rate, it is determined where $ID = SS$.

4 If our exports are higher than our imports, foreigners must borrow from us to pay the difference.

5 Higher world government deficits raise the amount of private saving.

6 The higher a household's expected future income, the greater is its consumption expenditure today.

7 Firms will invest in a project if the expected profit rate is greater than the real interest rate.

8 For the domestic economy, if ID does not equal SS plus government saving, the real interest rate will adjust to create equilibrium.

9 An increase in the expected profit rate will shift the investment demand curve leftward.

10 If the expected inflation rate increases and the nominal rate of interest increases, then the real rate of interest has increased.

Multiple-Choice

1 The most important factor explaining the fluctuations in investment demand is fluctuations in

a   real interest rate.
b   expected profit rate.
c   depreciation.
d   expected inflation.
e   interest rates.

2 Which of the following would shift consumption demand leftward?

a an increase in current disposable income
b an increase in future expected income
c a decrease in current disposable income
d an increase in the real interest rate
e a decrease in the real interest rate

3 The investment demand curve shows the relationship between the level of investment and

a disposable income.
b real GDP.
c expected future profit.
d the real interest rate.
e the expected inflation rate.

4 Which of the following would cause a household to increase the amount it saved?

a a decrease in current disposable income
b an increase in expected future income
c an increase in net taxes
d a decrease in expected future income
e none of the above

5 Gross investment is

a additions to the capital stock.
b net investment – depreciation.
c the quantity of plant, equipment, and inventories.
d the financial assets held by firms.
e net investment + depreciation.

6 If a firm pays for investment spending out of retained profits,

a this is cheaper than borrowing the funds.
b it still pays for the funds because of the new taxes created.
c the opportunity cost is zero.
d it still pays an opportunity cost, since the funds are now lost to shareholders.
e it still has to pay an opportunity cost, since shareholders could have lent the money out.

7 An increase in expected future income shifts the consumption demand curve _____ and the saving supply curve _____.

a not at all; not at all
b leftward; leftward
c rightward; rightward
d rightward; leftward
e leftward; rightward

8 An increase in disposable income shifts the consumption demand curve _____ and the saving supply curve _____.

a not at all; not at all
b leftward; leftward
c rightward; rightward
d rightward; leftward
e leftward; rightward

9 Canada's investment as a percentage of GDP has been

a steady from year to year.
b higher than most developing countries.
c shrinking over the last 20 years.
d lower than most industrial countries, but recently has closed the gap.
e higher than most industrial countries, but has recently closed the gap.

10 Which of the following newspaper quotations describes a situation where Canada would end up with lower investment?

a "A rise in the U.S. government budget deficit is forcing up world interest rates."
b "World lenders are worried about Canada's government budget deficit."
c "The booming developing nations are dramatically raising their spending on new investment projects."
d All of the above.
e None of the above.

11 Consider Fig. 32.1. If currently the expected profit rate is normal, and the real rate of interest is 6 percent, then planned investment is _____ billion 1986 dollars.

a 10
b 20
c 30
d 40
e 50

FIGURE **32.1** I_b is with a normal expected profit rate.

12 Consider Fig. 32.1. Currently the expected profit rate is normal, and the real rate of interest is 6 percent. If the real interest rate falls, all else remaining the same, a *possible* new level of investment is _____ billion 1986 dollars.

a 40
b 30
c 20
d 10
e all of the above

13 Consider Fig. 32.1. Currently the expected profit rate is normal, and the real rate of interest is 6 percent. If the expected profit rate falls, all else remaining the same, a *possible* new level of investment is _____ billion 1986 dollars.

a 50
b 40
c 30
d 20
e all of the above

14 In Canada over the business cycle,

a net investment fluctuates strongly with the cycle.
b gross investment fluctuates strongly in an opposite manner to the cycle.
c the capital stock fluctuates strongly with the cycle.
d depreciation fluctuates strongly with the cycle.
e all of the above.

15 Consumption demand is most strongly affected by

a disposable income and the real rate of interest.
b the expected profit rate and the real rate of interest.
c purchasing power of net assets and expected future income.
d purchasing power of net assets and disposable income.
e the real exchange rate and the real interest rate.

16 Consider Fig. 32.2. If this represents the world capital market, the equilibrium saving and investment would be

a higher than 60 billion constant dollars if net exports are positive.
b lower than 60 billion constant dollars if net exports are positive.
c lower than 60 billion constant dollars if net exports are negative.
d 60 billion constant dollars.
e not determinable unless we know whether or not there is a global government budget surplus or deficit.

FIGURE **32.2**

17 Consider Fig.32.2. If this was the capital market for one country (with a balanced government budget), and the world interest rate is equal to 9 percent, then this country has net exports equal to _____ billion constant dollars.

a +80
b +65
c +15
d –65
e –80

18 Real interest rates around the world

a tend to move inversely with the world business cycle.
b tend to move together.
c have fluctuated in a small range around 6 percent since 1970.
d all of the above.
e none of the above.

19 A higher government budget surplus leads to a

a rise in national saving.
b rise in net exports.
c rise in lending to the rest of the world.
d no change in the domestic real interest rate.
e all of the above.

20 In Canada's economy, the real interest rate is determined by

a national investment.
b national saving.
c government budget deficit/surplus.
d all of the above.
e none of the above.

21 Which of the following newspaper quotations best describes a movement along the *CD* curve?

a "Large falls in consumer borrowing rates are expected to strongly stimulate spending."

b "Consumer confidence in the future is at an all-time low, dragging down spending."

c "The Bank of Canada is worried that the price level might actually fall this year, depressing consumer spending."

d "The government is being urged to cut income taxes to try and stimulate the economy."

e All of the above.

22 The real exchange rate is the

a opportunity cost of foreign-made goods in terms of Canadian-made goods.

b rate at which the real interest rate is calculated world-wide.

c level of the exchange rate that would make net exports equal to zero.

d rate of the exchange rate that would make the government budget balance.

e none of the above.

23 The reason the growth in the capital stock does not include depreciation is because it is

a already included in gross investment.

b not expenditure on capital equipment.

c just expenditure to replace worn-out capital equipment.

d just expenditure on new capital equipment.

e too hard to measure.

24 In the global economy, $I =$

a $S + (T - G)$.

b $S + (T - G) - (X - M)$.

c $S + (T - G) + (X - M)$.

d $S + (G - T)$.

e $S + (G - T) - (X - M)$.

25 In the Canadian economy, $I =$

a $S + (T - G)$.

b $S + (T - G) - (X - M)$.

c $S + (T - G) + (X - M)$.

d $S + (G - T)$.

e $S + (G - T) - (X - M)$.

Short Answer Problems

I In Chapter 25, we saw the "Paradox of Thrift"—how a rise in saving would lead to a fall in aggregate expenditure and a fall in the level of equilibrium real GDP. In this chapter, a rise in saving will lead to a fall in the real rate of interest, a rise in the amount of investment, a rise in the capital stock, and therefore a rise in potential GDP. Can you explain why we get this different result?

2 Table 32.1 gives the expected profit rates for four individual investment projects under consideration by a firm. Project *A* might be building a new factory and project *B* might be buying a new machine. For the sake of simplicity, suppose that each project costs $1 million. What will be the amount of investment by this firm if the real interest rate is

a 13 percent?

b 10 percent?

c 7 percent?

d 3 percent?

TABLE **32.1**   INVESTMENT PROJECTS

Project	Expected Profit Rate (%)
A	4
B	12
C	8
D	6

3 Consider Table 32.2, which shows the consumption choices of the Greystoke household for different combinations of income and the real interest rate.

TABLE **32.2**   Consumption in thousands of constant dollars

	Real Interest Rate = 5%	Real Interest Rate = 6%	Real Interest Rate = 7%
Disposable Income = 5,000	6,000	5,000	4,000
Disposable Income = 6,000	6,600	5,600	4,600
Disposable Income = 7,000	7,200	6,200	5,200

a Fill in Table 32.3 below with the Greystoke household saving amounts.

TABLE **32.3**   Saving in thousands of constant dollars

	Real Interest Rate = 5%	Real Interest Rate = 6%	Real Interest Rate = 7%
Disposable Income = 5,000			
Disposable Income = 6,000			
Disposable Income = 7,000			

b If the real interest rate is 5 percent, what is the *MPC* and the *MPS*?

c From the information given and computed, draw the household's consumption demand and saving supply curves.

4 It is often argued in the press that the risk of separation hurts Canada by making foreign investors fear there is a chance Canadian bonds will not repaid, leading to a requirement for a risk premium on world capital markets. With the aid of a graph of the Canadian capital market, and assuming we are net borrowers, explain what this factor does to Canadian interest rates, investment demand, saving supply, and long-term economic prospects. Is the press argument correct?

5 Consider the Canadian capital market. After an especially brilliant speech by the prime minister, people decide that (a) expected future income is higher than they previously thought, (b) expected future profits are higher than they previously thought, and (c) the risk of separation is lower than they previously thought. Show what the net effect of these changes are on Canadian consumer demand, saving supply, real interest rates, and net exports. Assume that initially Canada is a net borrower from the rest of the world.

6 a Consider the values of consumption expenditure, investment, taxes, and government expenditure for the (isolated) economy of Opar shown in Table 32.4. Real GDP is constant at its potential level of 100 million opals, the government expenditure is constant at a level of 12 million opals, and the government deficit is constant at 2 million opals. All expenditure values are in millions of opals.

TABLE **32.4**

Real Interest Rate (% per year)	Consumption Expenditure	Investment	Saving	Saving + Government Saving
3	75	22		
4	70	18		
5	65	14		
6	60	10		
7	55	6		
8	50	2		

Calculate saving and fill in the final two columns of Table 32.4. What is the real interest rate in equilibrium in Opar?

b Consider next the values of consumption expenditure, investment, taxes, and government expenditure for the (isolated) economy of Pellucidar, shown in Table 32.5. Real GDP is constant at its potential level of 120 million opals, the government expenditure is constant at a level of 15 million opals, and the government deficit is constant at 4 million opals. All expenditure values are in millions of opals.

TABLE **32.5**

Real Interest Rate (% per year)	Consumption Expenditure	Investment	Saving	Saving + Government Saving
3	100	32		
4	95	28		
5	90	24		
6	85	20		
7	80	16		
8	75	12		

Calculate saving and fill in the final two columns of Table 32.5. What is the real interest rate in equilibrium in Pellucidar?

7 An enterprising adventurer builds a machine that drills through the earth, and connects Opar to Pellucidar. International trade and capital markets open up.

a Fill in Table 32.6 for total *world* expenditures, and calculate the world real interest rate in the new equilibrium. All expenditure values are in millions of opals.

TABLE **32.6**

Real Interest Rate (% per year)	Consumption Expenditure	Investment	Saving	Saving + Government Saving
3	175	54		
4				
5				
6				
7				
8				

b For Opar after world trade, what is the level of saving, investment, net exports, and international lending or borrowing?

c For Pellucidar after world trade, what is the level of saving, investment, net exports, and international lending or borrowing?

8 Technological innovation raises productivity in Canada, all else remaining the same. With the aid of a graph of Canada's capital market, explain what this does to Canadian real interest rates, the level of saving, investment, consumption demand, and net exports. Assume we are initially neither a net borrower nor a net lender.

9 The country of X elects a new prime minister, who promptly and unexpectedly cuts all taxes in half, leaving constant the level of government spending. Explain with the aid of a graph of the domestic capital market what this does to the domestic real rate of interest, saving, investment, net exports, and international borrowing and lending. Assume X is initially neither a net borrower nor a net lender.

10 In Chapters 27 and 28, interest rates were determined in the money market, with monetary policy having a strong influence. In this chapter, interest rates are determined in the world capital market. Can you explain why we have this different result?

A N S W E R S

True/False/Uncertain and Explain

1 F Investment fluctuates, but this is such a small portion of capital stock that the latter is fairly steady. (763)

2 F It will raise both *CD* and *SS*. (772–773)

3 F It is determined where *ID* = (*SS* + global government saving). (776–777)

4 T See text discussion. (779)

5 T Higher government deficits → ↓ *SS* + government saving → ↑ real interest rate → ↑ saving. (776–777)

6 T Households save less (or borrow) to spend part of future income today. (770)

7 T Then return on capital > cost. (766)

8 F In domestic economy, real interest rate set by world rate → *ID* does not need to equal *S* + government saving because economy can borrow from rest of world. (779)

9 F ↑ expected profit rate → ↑ in *ID* to take advantage of higher future profits. (766)

10 U Real rate = nominal rate − expected inflation, so it depends on relative size of increases. (764)

Multiple-Choice

1 b See text discussion. (767)

2 c d and e are movements along the function, a and b shift it rightward. (772–773)

3 d Definition. (766)

4 d a, b, c, lower saving. (770–773)

5 e Definition. (763)

6 e Funds could have been lent out to other firms. (766)

7 d Households will try to spend some of future income now, by ↓ saving or ↑ borrowing. (773)

8 c Because *MPC* and *MPS* are both positive. (772–773)

9 d See text discussion. (764)

10 d a shifts world saving leftward, c shifts world *ID* rightward, b raises the risk premium, → ↑ real interest rate faced by Canada → ↓ investment demand. (777–779)

11 c Where 6 percent crosses I_b. (767)

12 a Must be below 6 percent on I_b. (767)

13 d Where 6 percent crosses I_a. (767)

14 a See text discussion. (763)

15 a See text discussion. (774–775)

16 e Intersection of *SS* + government saving and *ID*. (775–776)

17 b Balanced budget, only *SS* and *ID* matter. At 9 percent, *SS* > *ID* by 65 billion → excess savings are loaned to the rest of the world, who use them to buy this country's products → net exports > 0 by the difference. (779)

18 b Due to mobile capital. (779)

19 e Surplus gets added to national saving → *SS* + government saving shifts rightward at fixed world real interest rate, allowing for more world lending and therefore more net exports. (779)

20 e Determined by world rate + risk premium. (779)

21 a Others are all shifts in the curve. (771–773)

22 a Definition. (780)

23 c No new capital stock. (763)

24 a From the circular flow, given net exports = 0 for the world economy. (776)

25 b From the circular flow, given net exports → 0. (779)

Short Answer Problems

1 In Chapter 25, the short-run fixed-price aggregate expenditure model gets a different result for two reasons. First, it assumes that investment is unchanged. However, in this chapter, the rise in saving lowers the real rate of interest, raising investment expenditure, which offsets the fall in aggregate expenditure from the lower consumption. Second, the model of Chapter 25 is actually dealing with the quantity of real GDP demanded, while the model of this chapter deals with potential GDP.

2 The firm will undertake each project for which the rate of return exceeds the real interest rate.

a If the real interest rate is 13 percent, investment by the firm will be zero since none of the projects has a rate of return that exceeds 13 percent.

b If the real interest rate is 10 percent, investment by the firm will be $1 million because project B is profitable.

c If the real interest rate is 7 percent, investment by the firm will be $2 million since both projects B and C are profitable at that lower interest rate.

d If the real interest rate is 3 percent, investment by the firm will be $4 million because the interest rate is now low enough that all four investment projects are profitable.

3 a Table 32.3 Solution shows the correct values, calculated by noting that Saving + Consumption = Disposable Income.

TABLE **32.3** SOLUTION
Saving in thousands of constant dollars

	Real Interest Rate = 5%	Real Interest Rate = 6%	Real Interest Rate = 7%
Disposable Income = 5,000	−1,000	0	+1,000
Disposable Income = 6,000	−600	+400	+1,400
Disposable Income = 7,000	−200	+800	+1,800

b $MPC = \Delta C/\Delta Y = +600/+1,000 = 0.6.$
$MPS = \Delta S/\Delta Y = +400/+1,000 = 0.4.$

c The graphs are shown in Fig. 32.3. CD_0 and SS_0 are drawn for a disposable income of 5,000, CD_1 and SS_1 are drawn for a disposable income of 6,000, and CD_2 and SS_2 are drawn for a disposable income of 7,000.

FIGURE **32.3**

(a)

(b)

4 Figure 32.4 shows the Canadian market, with the world real interest rate below the domestic equilibrium at r_0, creating a need for net borrowing = negative net exports. The presence of the risk premium means Canada faces a higher interest rate, such as $r_p > r_0$. This lowers investment demand, raises saving supply (the movement along the curves), reduces the gap of needed net borrowing, and makes the negative net exports closer to zero. Since consumer demand = disposable income − saving supply, consumer demand is lower as a result of this factor. The lower investment created by the higher interest rates will create a lower capital stock, and lower growth and real GDP over time. The press is correct, if there is such a premium.

FIGURE **32.4**

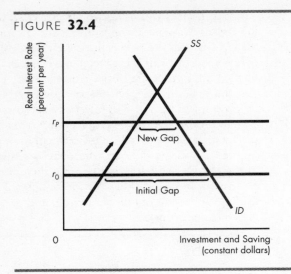

of 12 million opals. Government saving = –2 million opals. All expenditure values are in millions of opals.

TABLE **32.4** SOLUTION

Real Interest Rate (% per year)	Consumption Expenditure	Investment	Saving	Saving + Government Saving
3	75	22	15	13
4	70	18	20	18
5	65	14	25	23
6	60	10	30	28
7	55	6	35	33
8	50	2	40	38

Equilibrium occurs when investment equals saving + government saving at an interest rate of 4 percent.

b Table 32.5 Solution is filled in below, using the same methodology as in **a**. Equilibrium occurs at an interest rate of 6 percent. All expenditure values are in millions of opals.

5 Figure 32.5 shows the effects of the changes. The higher expected future income raises consumer demand and lowers saving supply to SS_1, the higher expected profit rate raises investment demand to ID_1, and the lower risk of separation lowers the risk premium required to borrow on the world market, lowering the interest rate from r_0 to r_1. The fall in the interest rate creates a movement along the new curves that reinforces the shifts, leading to a larger gap (and more international borrowing and lower net exports— they become more negative), less saving (and therefore more consumption) and more investment.

TABLE **32.5** SOLUTION

Real Interest Rate (% per year)	Consumption Expenditure	Investment	Saving	Saving + Government Saving
3	100	32	9	5
4	95	28	14	10
5	90	24	19	15
6	85	20	24	20
7	80	16	29	25
8	75	12	34	30

FIGURE **32.5**

7 a The second and third columns in Table 32.6 Solution are calculated by adding together consumption expenditure in each country at each real interest rate, etc. The rest of the table is calculated using the same methodology from Short Answer Problem **6**, but now potential world GDP of 220 million is used. All expenditure values are in millions of opals.

6 a Table 32.4 Solution is filled in below. Saving is calculated using the fact that $S = Y - C - T$, where income is constant at 100 million opals, and taxes are 10 million opals given the deficit of 2 million opals and government expenditure

TABLE **32.6** SOLUTION

Real Interest Rate (% per year)	Consumption Expenditure	Investment	Saving	Saving + Government Saving
3	175	54	24	18
4	165	46	34	28
5	155	38	44	38
6	145	30	54	48
7	135	22	64	58
8	125	14	74	68

The world real interest rate will be where investment equals saving + government saving, at 5 percent.

b At this interest rate in Opar, saving is 25 million opals, investment is 14 million opals, saving + government saving is 23 million opals, leaving a surplus of 9 million opals that are lent to the world market, which are matched by an equivalent net export of 9 million opals.

c At this interest rate in Pellucidar, saving is 19 million opals, investment is 24 million opals, saving + government saving is 15 million opals, leaving a deficit of 9 million opals that are borrowed from the world market, which are matched by an equivalent net export of –9 million opals.

8 The rise in productivity will increase the expected profit rate, raising investment demand to ID_1 in Fig. 32.6. At the fixed world interest rate, a gap between domestic saving and investment now arises, that is financed by international borrowing, leading to negative net exports. There is no change in the real interest rate, saving or consumption, since none of the variables that affect them change.

FIGURE **32.6**

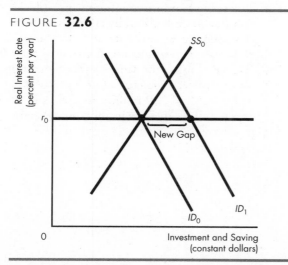

9 The cut in taxes will have two effects. First, it lowers government saving, shifting the SS curve to SS_1. Second, the rise in the deficit probably makes investors think that repayment is less likely, leading to a rise in the required risk premium, raising the real interest rate faced by this country. This rise will lower investment demand some, and raise saving some, partially or totally offsetting the fall in government saving. Figure 32.7 shows the case where the net effect of the change is a fall in saving (and therefore a rise in consumption), the creation of a gap leading to net international lending, and negative net exports.

FIGURE **32.7**

10 There are two reasons. First, the money market in Chapters 27 and 28 actually jointly determines equilibrium in the money market *and* the bond (capital) market—it is possible to work out a relation between the markets, where both effects work. Second, the market in Chapters 27 and 28 is for short-term bonds, while this chapter emphasizes long-term results. Monetary policy can have an immediate effect on interest rates in the short run, whereas in the long run the world factors we have examined here are dominant.

Chapter 33

Economic Growth

KEY CONCEPTS

Long-Term Growth Trends

Growth in potential GDP occurs due to ↑ population and ↑ potential GDP per person (↑ living standards).

◆ Canada's growth high in earlier part of century, ↓ between World Wars, ↑ until 1973, slower since then.

◆ Internationally, since 1960, Canada has been catching up to the United States, but Japan and other Asian countries have been catching up to both countries.

The Sources of Economic Growth

◆ Growth requires essential preconditions → most basic is an appropriate *incentive* system.

◆ Three institutions are crucial:

- Markets—prices send signals that create incentives, and enable people to specialize, trade, save, and invest.
- Property rights—if clearly established and enforced, give people assurance their income and savings will not be confiscated.
- Monetary exchange—facilitates transactions.

◆ Incentive system allows people to specialize and trade → more goods/services for same labour → ↑ real GDP per person.

◆ This source of growth eventually runs its course. For further growth to continue need

- saving and investment in new capital → ↑ capital per worker → ↑ productivity,
- growth in human capital → ↑ productivity (by learning and repetitively doing tasks),

- discovery of new technologies.

◆ Rapid changes in technology create rapid growth.

Growth Accounting

Growth accounting calculates how much of economic growth is due to growth of labour and capital or to technological change.

◆ **Productivity** (real GDP per hour of work) determines how much income an hour of labour can earn.

◆ Productivity growth comes from growth in capital per hour of labour and technological change (which includes human capital).

◆ **Productivity function** (*PF*) is relationship between real GDP per hour of labour and capital per hour of labour, holding constant technology.

- ↑ capital per hour of labour → ↑ real GDP per hour of labour (movement along *PF* function).
- Technological change → ↑ real GDP per hour of labour (upward shift of *PF* function).
- ↑ one input, other inputs held constant → ↑ output at a diminishing rate → **law of diminishing returns**.

◆ *One-third rule* says, on average, one percent ↑ capital per hour of labour (with no change in technology) → one-third of one percent ↑ output per hour of labour.

◆ Can use this rule to calculate contribution of capital growth to real GDP growth, and to study reasons for changes in productivity growth:

- 1965–1973 → high productivity growth due to high technological change.
- 1973–1988 → lower productivity growth due to slowdown in impact of technological change.

- 1988–1995 → lower productivity growth due to negligible impact of technological change.

◆ Three factors were responsible for ↓ contribution of technological change after 1973:

- Energy price shocks → ↓ usefulness of energy-inefficient capital, introduction of new energy-efficient technology that did not increase labour productivity.
- Environmental protection → new laws and regulations requiring new capital that did not contribute to real GDP (although they contributed to quality of life).
- Changes in composition of output → many traditional industries had declines in labour inputs, and new high-technology industries had increases in labour inputs. Aggregate measures of productivity can be misleading in this situation.

Growth Theory

Causes of economic growth complex because of interaction of population growth, technological change, saving, and investment.

◆ Three main theories of economic growth.

◆ **Classical growth theory** comes from late eighteenth century, a time of high population growth, and argues population growth is determined by level of income per person.

- Advances in technology → ↑ demand for labour and real wage rate → ↑ quantity of labour supplied.
- Since real wage rate > **subsistence real wage rate** (minimum needed to maintain life), population grows → ↑ labour supply → real wage rate back to subsistence rate → workers' income has not increased.
- In reality, population growth moderates.
- Modern population growth theory argues that as ↑ real wage rate → ↑ opportunity cost of women's time and of children → ↓ birth rate.

◆ **Neoclassical growth theory** says population growth rate determines economic growth, not vice versa.

- Key variable is growth rate of capital stock → set by demand for and supply of capital.
- Demand for capital from investment decision, supply of capital from saving decision.
- Ongoing *exogenous* technological advances → ↑ productivity of capital → ↑ demand for capital → ↑ capital per person and real interest rate.

- ↑ real interest rate → real interest rate > **rate of time preference** (target real interest rate savers wish to achieve) → ↑ saving → ↑ supply of capital → (↑ capital per person → ↑ real GDP per person) → ↓ real interest rate until = rate of time preference, growth stops.
- Neoclassical growth theory predicts growth rates and income levels per person in different countries should converge, but doesn't happen.

◆ **New growth theory** attempts to overcome this shortcoming by explaining technological changes as a profit-maximizing *endogenous* choice.

- New discoveries come about because people seek (temporary) profits that come from them, but once made, discoveries are copied and benefits dispersed through economy, *without* diminishing returns.
- Result is that knowledge is a special kind of capital that is not subject to diminishing returns → demand for knowledge capital is flat.
- Inventions → ↑ rate of return to knowledge capital until > rate of time preference, ↑ capital per person and real GDP growth.
- Rate of return > rate of time preference → ↑ saving and capital per person and real GDP growth with *no automatic slowdown* because return to capital does not diminish.

Achieving Faster Growth

Faster growth comes from ↑ capital per hour of work or ↑ technological advances.

◆ Miracle economies of Asia achieved high growth from very high saving rates, high rate of investment in human capital, and learning-by-doing in high-technology industries.

◆ Growth theory's main suggestions for increasing economic growth rates:

- Stimulate saving by tax incentives.
- Subsidize research and development by patents or direct public funding.
- Target high-technology industries for public research funds.
- Encourage international trade to take advantage of dynamic comparative advantage → being first into a new field, with ability to produce at lower opportunity cost.

HELPFUL HINTS

1 Economic growth, especially growth in potential GDP per person, is a powerful force in raising living standards. Countries become rich by achieving high rates of growth in per person GDP and maintaining them over a long period of time. The role of compounding of income can create startling effects in this regard. We can see this, and get some idea of the importance of understanding growth, by examining the post-1973 productivity slowdown. Growth between 1947 and 1973 was 3.2 percent per year, but after 1973 only 1.8 percent per year. This means that between 1973 and 1995, real GDP per person rose by about 48 percent ($= ((1.018)^2 - 1) \times 100$). However, if economic growth had continued at the pre-1973 rate of 3.2 percent, real GDP per person would have risen by about 100 percent ($= ((1.032)^2 - 1) \times 100$). Even the worst recession over this time period only lowered real GDP per person by about 5 percent. Curing the productivity slowdown would clearly have a big payoff!

2 The key to understanding the different theories of growth is understanding the role of "the law of diminishing returns" in each theory. This law states that adding more of one input, other inputs held constant, eventually leads to a situation of diminishing returns to adding extra inputs.

In neoclassical theory, the discovery of a new technology leads to an increase in the return on capital, and an increase in the demand for capital, and an increase in the amount of capital used. In turn, the fact that the return for capital is above the rate of time preference leads to an increase in saving, and an increase in the supply of capital, and a further increase in the amount of capital used. However, the increase in capital eventually leads to diminishing returns. As an example, we might think of the introduction of new and more powerful computers. As the number of computers increases, holding constant the number of workers, the extra output of the nth computer will not be as high as the productivity of the first computer. Eventually, the productivity of the extra capital must fall (the capital demand curve is downward sloping), and economic growth automatically slows down.

New growth theory has a different idea of technology and capital, with no diminishing returns, and no slow down in economic growth.

New growth theory examines "knowledge capital," a concept of technology that is not embodied so much in capital, but in ideas. These might include new management techniques, or new processes of production, such as the assembly line that can be copied from business to business without encountering diminishing returns. As an example, consider the introduction of new and better software (such as the first word processing package). As more copies of the software are introduced into different businesses around the country, we do not run into diminishing returns, at least not until the entire country has access to the new knowledge. Even then, new software will be continually developed and introduced without diminishing returns (the knowledge capital demand curve is flat), and economic growth need not automatically slow down.

SELF-TEST

True/False/Uncertain and Explain

1 Canada's recent growth slowdown is quite unusual in Canadian history.

2 When a country adopts a better technology, its productivity function will shift upward.

3 Rapid changes in technology create growth without need for new capital.

4 Growth theory argues economic growth will eventually slow down because the return to capital begins to diminish as the amount of capital increases.

5 High economic growth has typically been accompanied by high saving rates.

6 Classical growth theory argues that economic growth eventually leads to a smaller population growth rate.

7 Specialization is the crucial source of current growth.

8 Other countries are catching up with Canada's real GDP per person.

9 Neoclassical growth theory requires ongoing technological change to get ongoing economic growth.

10 The slowdown in productivity growth after 1973 was due to a slowdown in the growth of capital per hour of labour, with a constant rate of technological change.

Multiple-Choice

1 Which of the following is *not* a source of economic growth?

a   rising stock market prices
b   better educated workers
c   growing stock of capital equipment
d   an appropriate incentive system
e   advances in technology

2 Suppose that productivity increased 24 percent last year. Capital per hour of work increased by 12 percent as well. The increase in capital was responsible for

a   all of the increase in productivity.
b   5/6 of the increase in productivity.
c   1/2 of the increase in productivity.
d   1/3 of the increase in productivity.
e   1/6 of the increase in productivity.

3 Suppose that productivity increased 24 percent last year. Capital per hour of work increased by 12 percent as well. An increase in technology was responsible for

a   all of the increase in productivity.
b   5/6 of the increase in productivity.
c   1/2 of the increase in productivity.
d   1/3 of the increase in productivity.
e   1/6 of the increase in productivity.

4 In the neoclassical growth theory, if the real interest rate exceeds the rate of time preference, then

a   the real interest rate will eventually decline.
b   capital per hour of work will increase.
c   real GDP per hour of work will increase.
d   all of the above.
e   only **b** and **c**.

5 In new growth theory, if the real interest rate exceeds the rate of time preference, then

a   the real interest rate will eventually decline.
b   capital per hour of work will increase.
c   real GDP per hour of work will increase.
d   all of the above.
e   only **b** and **c**.

6 Which theory of economic growth concludes that growth always slows down unless there are new technological inventions?

a   classical theory
b   neoclassical theory
c   new growth theory
d   all of the theories
e   none of the theories

7 Which theory of economic growth concludes that technological advances increase the demand for capital?

a   classical theory
b   neoclassical theory
c   new theory
d   all of the theories
e   none of the theories

8 Canada's growth slowed down since 1973 mostly because of

a   higher population pressures.
b   lower amounts of saving.
c   diminishing returns.
d   slowdowns in technological change.
e   too rapid increases in technological change.

9 Markets are an essential precondition to growth because

a they suffer from diminishing returns.

b they allow countries to benefit from dynamic comparative advantage.

c prices send signals that create incentives.

d people have an assurance that their income and savings will not be confiscated.

e all of the above.

10 The miracle economies of Asia achieved higher growth by

a very high saving rates.

b high rates of investment in human capital.

c learning-by-doing in high-technology industries.

d all of the above.

e none of the above.

11 If there were significant technological advances last year, and the capital stock per hour of work grew by 9 percent, then

a the real rate of interest must have fallen.

b economic growth would have been significantly less than 3 percent.

c economic growth would have been significantly more than 3 percent.

d economic growth would have been about 3 percent.

e both **a** and **c**.

12 Which of the following is a suggestion for increasing Canadian economic growth rates?

a Stimulate saving by taxing consumption.

b Reduce the time period for patents to increase replication.

c Put less public research funds into universities.

d Protect infant industries to take advantage of dynamic comparative advantage.

e None of the above.

13 Compared to the growth in other countries, Canada has been

a falling behind most other countries.

b dramatically catching up to and passing other countries.

c worsening versus the United States, but doing better versus other countries.

d doing as well or better than most countries except certain Asian countries.

e none of the above.

14 One of the reasons technological change slowed down after 1973 was the

a energy-inefficiency of the new capital stock.

b lack of changes in the composition of output.

c one-third rule.

d law of diminishing returns.

e introduction of new environmental protection laws and regulations.

15 A technological advance leads to

a only a movement along the productivity function, and an increase in real GDP per person.

b only a movement along the productivity function, and a decrease in real GDP per person.

c a fall in the real rate of interest, and an increase in real GDP per person.

d a shift upward in the productivity function, and a movement along the productivity function.

e an increase in capital per hour of labour, and only a movement along the productivity function.

16 A good incentive system

a leads to specialization and trade, with higher GDP per person.

b is all that is needed to have continuous growth.

c solves the problem of diminishing returns.

d has no role for government.

e can have the real interest rate above the rate of time preference for an extended period of time.

17 Incentives are important in the new growth theory because they

a imply there are no diminishing returns.

b lead to higher rates of saving.

c imply that economic growth does *not* lead to population growth.

d create dynamic comparative advantage.

e lead to profit-seeking searches for new discoveries.

18 In the classical growth theory, economic growth eventually stops after a technological advance because of

a diminishing returns.

b knowledge capital being easily replicated.

c the real rate of interest falling back down to the rate of time preference.

d the real wage rate becoming too high.

e high population growth resulting from the increase in real wages.

19 Knowledge capital is different from ordinary capital because

a it can be replicated without diminishing returns.

b its demand curve is flat.

c it does not lead to an automatic slowdown in growth.

d all of the above.

e none of the above.

20 The law of diminishing returns

a holds only for knowledge capital.

b states that if capital increases by 1 percent, real GDP increases by about 1/3 of a percent.

c states that if capital increases by 1 percent, real GDP increases by about 3 percent.

d holds only for capital.

e does not hold for knowledge capital.

21 The basic sources of economic growth include

a saving and investment in new capital.

b investment in human capital.

c discoveries of new techniques.

d discoveries of new management processes.

e all of the above.

22 Which of the following statements about Canada's long-term growth trends is *false*?

a Economic growth has tended to be steady, except for the business cycle.

b Economic growth shows periods of slow and high growth.

c Economic growth has been slow since 1973.

d Economic growth has been generally faster in Japan than in Canada.

e African countries have fallen further behind Canada in recent years.

23 The rate of time preference is the

a target real interest rate savers wish to achieve.

b nominal rate of interest minus expected inflation.

c marginal productivity of capital.

d minimum needed to maintain life.

e saving rate that leads to continuous growth.

24 The capital demand curve is flat in the new growth theory because

a the productivity of capital diminishes as more capital is employed per hour of labour.

b technological advances occur frequently due to profit-seeking activities.

c discoveries can be replicated without diminishing their marginal productivity.

d the rate of time preference is constant.

e population growth in response to high wages lowers the real wage rate.

25 The key difference between neoclassical growth theory and new growth theory is that

a capital is not subject to diminishing returns under new growth theory.

b capital is subject to diminishing returns under new growth theory.

c increases in technology lead to increases in population that drive workers' incomes back down to the subsistence level in neoclassical theory.

d technological advances are exogenous in new growth theory.

e the one-third rule only holds in the neoclassical growth theory.

Short Answer Problems

1 Explain briefly why an appropriate incentive system is a precondition to growth.

2 Explain why this source of growth eventually runs its course.

3 Explain what happens in classical growth theory when advances in technology increase the real wage rate.

4 Some economists speculate that the Asian miracle economies have achieved such fast growth at least partially due to their adeptness at replicating new technology. Explain how and why this replicating is such a good source of growth.

5 Paul Krugman has argued that the Asian miracle economies growth is mostly due to the mobilization of capital and labour resources that were previously underutilized, and that therefore North American worries that these countries will catch up to and surpass Canada and the United States are unfounded. Assuming his argument is true, explain why this argument implies that these worries are unfounded.

6 Use the concept of a productivity function to explain why an increase in the amount of capital per worker will lead to economic growth.

7 You are given the data in Table 33.1 on the economy of Erehwon where the one-third rule holds, and the labour supply and population is unchanging over these three years. Do the calculations needed to show the contributions of changes in capital per worker (as a fraction of the total change) and technological change to productivity, and fill in the rest of the table.

TABLE **33.1**

Year	1998	1999	2000
Capital per hour of work	125	150	200
Productivity	35	40	44.4
Contribution of capital	—		
Contribution of technological change	—		

8 On a graph, sketch the productivity functions from Short Answer Problem 7 for the three years, showing the production points for each of the three years.

9 Consider the following productivity function:

TABLE **33.2**

Capital per Hour of Work	Real GDP per Hour of Work
100	60
120	64
156	70

The economy is originally producing 60 units of real GDP per hour of work in year 1.

a Does this productivity function meet the one-third rule?

b Graph this function, and the current point of production. Suppose that there is a technological advance that increases real GDP per hour of work by 20 percent, holding constant the capital per hour of work. Show the impact of this change on your graph.

c In year 2, real GDP per hour of work is now 84 units. Show this point on your graph. How much (if any) of the increase in real GDP was due to the technological advance, and how much (if any) was due to an increase in the capital per hour of work?

⊘10 Some commentators have argued that Japan has had a higher growth rate than countries like Canada or the United States because the Japanese care more about the future and less about present consumption, reflected in a lower rate of time preference. Explain within the context of growth theory whether or not this argument seems likely to be true.

ANSWERS

True/False/Uncertain and Explain

1 **F** Growth also slowed down between World Wars. (789)

2 **T** Technological advance → ↑ productivity, capital per worker unchanged. (795)

3 **F** Rapid technological change is embodied in new human and physical capital. (795–796)

4 **U** Depends on which theory → **T** if neoclassical, **F** if new growth. (799–806)

5 **T** See discussion of miracle economies. (807)

6 **F** Economic growth → ↑ real wage rate → ↑ population growth. (800–801)

7 **F** It is the initial source of growth, but once specialization is high, growth slows down. (792)

8 **U** Some countries are (Asian), some are not (African and Central and South American). (791)

⊘9 **T** A technological advance → ↑ demand for capital → ↑ capital per person → ↑ economic growth. Real rate of interest > rate of time preference → ↑ supply of capital → more economic growth, but real rate of interest down due to diminishing returns → growth eventually stops, unless there is more technological change. (802–803)

10 **F** Due to slowdown in technological change → see text discussion. (796–797)

Multiple-Choice

1 **a** This has no impact on productivity, others ↑ it. (792–793)

⊘2 **e** By one-third rule, capital ↑ 12 percent → real GDP per hour of work ↑ 4 percent, or 1/6 of increase in productivity. (796–797)

⊘3 **b** From 2, 5/6 is left over for technology. (796–797)

4 **d** If real rate of interest > rate of time preference → saving → ↑ supply of capital right → capital per hour of work → (and real GDP per hour of work ↑), ↓ real rate of interest → since capital demand curve downward sloping (draw a graph). (802–803)

⊘5 **e** If real rate of interest > rate of time preference → ↑ saving → supply of capital right → ↑ capital per hour of work (and ↑ real GDP per hour of work), but no change in real rate of interest since capital demand curve flat (draw a graph). (804–806)

⊘6 **b** Due to diminishing returns to capital (downward-sloping capital demand curve). (802–803)

7 d All conclude technological advances → ↑ productivity of capital. (799–806)

8 d See text discussion. (798–799)

9 c Incentives to specialize, trade, save, and invest. (792)

10 d See text discussion. (806–807)

11 c One-third rule says capital growth → real GDP per hour of labour of about 3 percent, but technological growth must add more to this. (795–796)

12 a **b** would lower return to and number of inventions, **c** would lower research and number of inventions, and trade should be encouraged. (806–807)

13 d See text discussion. (790–791)

14 e See text discussion. (798)

15 d Technological advance → shift up in *PF*, and ↑ productivity of capital → ↑ demand for capital → movement along *PF*. (795)

16 a It eventually no longer contributes to growth, does not solve diminishing returns, government is needed to allocate property rights, and has little to do with real rate of interest. (792)

17 e This makes technological change endogenous, and continuous. (804)

18 e This ↓ real wages. (800–801)

19 d **a** due to its nature, which implies **b**, which in turn implies **c**—see text discussion. (804–806)

20 e Holds for ordinary capital and labour, but not knowledge capital. (804)

21 e See text discussion. (792–793)

22 a Growth rates have fluctuated. (789–791)

23 a Definition. (802)

24 c Therefore as ↑ capital stock, real rate of interest does not diminish. (804–805)

25 a Due to the different nature of knowledge capital. (804)

Short Answer Problems

1 The incentive system includes markets to send signals and enable people to specialize, trade, save and invest (all of which increase growth), property rights to ensure income and savings are not confiscated and hence encourage people to work and save, and monetary exchange to facilitate transactions and encourage trade.

2 This source creates growth by increasing specialization. Eventually the level of specialization is so high, there is little left to be gained from further specialization.

3 Technology advances imply increases in the demand for labour, and the real wage rate. As the real wage rate goes up, the rate of population growth increases, leading to an increase in the supply of labour, leading to a decrease in the real wage rate back down to the subsistence wage rate, so workers are no better off than at the beginning.

4 Knowledge capital can be replicated without running into diminishing returns, so that the real rate of interest rises after the replication, which in turn brings more saving, and more supply of capital, and therefore capital per hour of work can increase without limit, implying that growth can increase without limit.

5 If the growth is due to increasing the amounts of capital and labour, then eventually these countries will run into diminishing returns to each of these inputs, which means that the rises in productivity will slow down, meaning that economic growth will also slow down.

6 The productivity function illustrates how per person output increases as the per person stock of capital increases, given the state of technology. If the amount of capital per worker increases, then the productivity of workers is increasing more rapidly, which means that per person output is increasing more rapidly; that is to say, there is faster economic growth. This is illustrated graphically by more rapid movements up along the graph of the productivity function.

7 Table 33.1 is reproduced below as Table 33.1 Solution, with the calculations in place.

TABLE **33.1** SOLUTION

Year	1998	1999	2000
Capital per hour of work	125	150	200
Productivity	35	40	44.4
Contribution of capital	—	46.6%	100%
Contribution of technological change	—	53.4%	0

The percentage change in capital from 1998 to 1999 was 20 percent ((25/125) × 100), implying a resulting percentage change in productivity of 6.67 percent. The total change in productivity was 14.3 percent ((5/35) × 100), leaving 7.63 percent due to technological change. Capital's contribution was (6.67/14.3) × 100 = 46.6 percent, and technology's contribution was 53.4 percent.

The percentage change in capital from 1999 to 2000 was 33 percent ((50/150) × 100), implying a resulting percentage change in productivity of 11 percent. The total change in productivity was 11 percent $((4.4/40) \times 100)$, leaving no contribution due to technological change. Capital's contribution was 100 percent.

8 The graphs are shown in Fig. 33.1. Note that from Table 33.1 the three yearly points must be where shown, and given our result about technological change in 1999 and 2000, the shift in 1999 and no shift in 2000 must be so.

FIGURE **33.1**

FIGURE **33.2**

9 a Between 100 and 120, the percentage change in capital per hour is $(20/100) \times 100 = 20$ percent, while the percentage change in real GDP per hour is $(4/60) \times 100 = 6.67$ percent. One-third of 20 percent is 6.67 percent. Between 120 and 156, the percentage change in capital per hour is $(36/120) \times 100 = 30$ percent, while the percentage change in real GDP per hour is $(6/64) \times 100 = 9.4$ percent. One-third of 30 percent is 10 percent, a little bit higher than 9.4 percent. The one-third rule roughly holds.

b Figure 33.2 shows the original productivity function as PF_0, with the three points from the table graphed on it, with the current production point marked as Year 1. A 20 percent increase in productivity would lead to a shift upwards in the productivity function to PF_1, shown in Table 33.3, and graphed as PF_1, with the new production point marked as Year 2.

c The point is labelled as Year 2 on the graph. We can see that the increase in real GDP per hour of work from 60 to 84 units is broken down into two components. The technological change is shown as the movement from the point Year 1 to the point *a*, a total change of 12 units or 50 percent $(= (12/24) \times 100)$ of the total change. The increase in capital per hour must be from 100 to 156 units to get production up to 84 units, and is shown as the movement from the point *a* to the point Year 2. This is a total change of 12 units or 50 percent $(= (12/24) \times 100)$ of the total change.

10 The lower the rate of time preference, the more willing is a person or country to forgo current consumption and save for the future. This means that, if Japan has a lower rate of time preference, in any given situation, the higher will be Japan's saving rate. This in turn means the higher is the increase in the supply of capital in Japan in any situation. Therefore in general Japan will have a higher capital stock per person than Canada, and it will generally be increasing each year at a higher rate, which in turn leads to a higher growth rate of real GDP per person in Japan than in Canada. Thus this argument seems to be true.

TABLE **33.3**

Capital per Hour of Work	Real GDP per Hour of Work
100	72
120	76.8
156	84

PROBLEM

You have been hired as a special advisor to the prime minister, based on your outstanding marks in macroeconomics. The cabinet is considering a new policy of dramatically and unexpectedly shrinking the size of the government budget deficit to zero in a few years. The prime minister needs you to sort out conflicting claims about the effect of this proposed policy on the economy. The Finance Minister, a former punk singer, Slash T. O. Thebone, is pushing for a massive cut in the deficit, arguing that this will stimulate investment and economic growth, reduce real interest rates, and boost the economy. The Social Services Minister, a former union leader, Ima Sof Tie, argues that such an unexpected policy would lead to a strong and sharp recession, with a fall in real GDP and a rise in unemployment, which she argues will hurt the economy. The prime minister wants to know the following:

a Will the proposed policy create a recession? What will happen to real GDP, the price level, unemployment and employment in the short run? Is Minister Tie correct?

b What will the proposed policy do to the economy in the long run? Specifically, what will it do to the real rate of interest, consumption demand, saving supply, investment, net exports, and potential GDP in the long run? Is Minister Thebone correct?

c Which argument is correct? What do you recommend?

Please note that the prime minister knows some economics, but hates graphs (he had a bad experience in an exam in university), so just a verbal answer is called for.

MIDTERM EXAMINATION

You should allocate 32 minutes for this examination (16 questions, 2 minutes per question). For each question, choose the one *best* answer.

1 An increase in the real rate of interest shifts the consumption demand curve _____ and the saving supply curve _____.

a not at all; not at all
b leftward; leftward
c rightward; rightward
d rightward; leftward
e leftward; rightward

2 Which of the following events would lower the world real interest rate?

a a rise in expected future income
b a fall in expected future profits
c advances in technology
d a rise in expected future profits
e a fall in world disposable income

3 On October 9, 1996, the Canadian finance minister revealed that efforts to shrink the government budget deficit were proceeding well ahead of the announced plan. As a result, that same day the real interest rates on Canadian long-term bonds fell significantly. This fall would be shown on a graph of the Canadian capital market as a

a shift rightward in the *SS* curve.
b shift leftward in the *SS* curve.
c fall in the world interest rate.
d fall in the risk premium paid by Canadians on top of the world interest rate.
e shift rightward in the *ID* curve.

4 If the price level increases, then in the short run real GDP supplied will

a   remain unchanged but, in the long run, real GDP supplied will increase.

b   increase and, in the long run, real GDP supplied will increase.

c   increase but, in the long run, real GDP supplied will remain unchanged.

d   decrease but, in the long run, real GDP supplied will increase.

e   decrease and, in the long run, real GDP supplied will decrease.

5 Given that the use of all other factor inputs are held constant, a diminishing marginal product of labour might best be described as when the total number of hours worked in the economy

a   increases and total output increases.

b   increases and total output increases at a decreasing rate.

c   increases and total output decreases.

d   decreases and total output increases.

e   increases and total output increases at an increasing rate.

6 Which of the following would be considered seasonally unemployed?

a   a Saskatchewan farmer who has lost her farm and is unemployed until retrained

b   a Nova Scotia fishery worker who is laid off during the winter

c   a steelworker who is laid off but who expects to be called back soon

d   an office worker who has lost her job because of a general slowdown in economic activity

e   none of the above

7 In a country with a working-age population of 20 million, 13 million are employed, 1.5 million are unemployed, and 1 million of the employed are working part-time, half of whom wish to work full-time. The size of the employment-to-population ratio is

a   72.5 percent.

b   65 percent.

c   75.5 percent.

d   57.5 percent.

e   none of the above.

8 In a country with a working-age population of 20 million, 13 million are employed, 1.5 million are unemployed, and 1 million of the employed are working part-time, half of whom wish to work full-time. The size of the involuntary part-time ratio is

a   3.4 percent.

b   3.8 percent.

c   2.5 percent.

d   5 percent.

e   none of the above.

9 Which of the following quotations describes job rationing unemployment?

a   "Wages are so good at the factory, they always have enough applicants to pick whomever they want for the job."

b   "Professors with tenured jobs are taking pay cuts to help hire new professors."

c   "Wages have failed to fall in the current economic downturn, creating extra unemployment."

d   "People are taking too long to find jobs, because unemployment insurance is so generous."

e   All of the above.

FIGURE **P7.1** I_b is with a normal expected profit rate.

10 Consider Fig. P7.1. Currently the expected profit rate is normal, and the real rate of interest is 6 percent. If the real interest rate falls and the expected profit rate falls, all else remaining the same, a *possible* new level of investment is _____ billion 1986 dollars.

a   40

b   30

c   20

d   40 or 30

e   20 or 10

11 Which one of the following quotations describes a movement along the labour demand curve?

a "Recent higher wage rates have led to more leisure being consumed."

b "The recent lower price level has induced people to work more hours."

c "The recent higher real wage rate has induced people to work more hours."

d "The recent high investment in capital equipment has raised hiring by firms."

e None of the above.

12 Which one of the following quotations describes a shift rightward in a *LAS* curve?

a "The recent higher price levels have lowered production in the country."

b "The recent higher price levels have raised production in the country."

c "The recent higher price levels have led to compensating rises in wages, so that there have been no changes in labour hired or production."

d "The recent lower price levels have led to lower production in the country."

e None of the above.

13 Which theory of economic growth concludes that in the long run, people do not benefit from growth?

a classical theory

b neoclassical theory

c new growth theory

d all of the theories

e none of the theories

14 The key difference between neoclassical growth theory and classical growth theory is that

a capital is not subject to diminishing returns under classical growth theory.

b capital is subject to diminishing returns under classical growth theory.

c increases in technology lead to increases in population that drive workers' incomes back down to the subsistence level in classical theory.

d technological advances are exogenous in classical growth theory.

e the one-third rule only holds in the neoclassical growth theory.

15 Suppose that productivity has increased by 15 percent over last year. Capital per hour of work increased by 9 percent as well. The increase in capital was responsible for

a all of the increase in productivity.

b 4/5 of the increase in productivity.

c 1/3 of the increase in productivity.

d 3/5 of the increase in productivity.

e 1/5 of the increase in productivity.

16 Suppose that productivity has increased by 15 percent over last year. Capital per hour of work increased by 9 percent as well. An increase in technology was responsible for

a all of the increase in productivity.

b 4/5 of the increase in productivity.

c 1/3 of the increase in productivity.

d 3/5 of the increase in productivity.

e 1/5 of the increase in productivity.

ANSWERS

Problem

a A dramatic fall in the deficit would involve either a large cut in government expenditures, or a large rise in taxes, leading to a fall in disposable income and consumption expenditure. In either case, in the short run this would be an unexpected fall in aggregate demand. This fall in aggregate demand leads to a fall in the price level, and since wages would not have incorporated this unexpected change, real wages will turn out to be too high. Employment would fall due to the too-high real wages, leading to a fall in production, and a fall in real GDP in the short run. Sticky wages would mean that this situation was in place for some time period, so that we would have cyclical unemployment for some time period. Therefore Minister Tie is correct.

b We know that a lower government deficit is the same as more government saving, so that total national saving rises. (Since we are in the long run, we can assume that real GDP is back to the old potential level, so that there is no shift in consumer demand or saving supply due to a change in disposable income.) Finally, the lower deficit should reduce the fear among international lenders of defaulting on our loans, so that the risk premium we pay should fall, reducing the interest rate we pay to borrow internationally.

The result of this policy is a reduction in the real rate of interest, which will increase investment demand, and decrease private saving (and therefore increase private consumption demand). The net effect of more government saving and less private saving on national saving is unclear. The rise in investment demand will tend to make the gap between investment demand and national saving larger, requiring more international borrowing (which implies lower net exports). However, in the long run the rise in investment demand will create a higher growth rate of the capital stock, leading to a higher level of potential GDP. Minister Thebone is correct too!

c   Both ministers are correct. In the short run, the policy will create a recession, and raise unemployment. In the long run, the policy will lower real interest rates, and raise growth. Your personal recommendation should be based on an evaluation of the relative costs of the recession versus the growth, something we will return to in Chapter 36.

Midterm Examination

1   a   Movement along each curve. (771)

❷2   b   a and e shifts *SS* left, c and d shifts *ID* right → ↑ real rate of interest, while b shifts *ID* leftward. (777–778)

❸3   d   Risk premiums respond to worries about repayment, these will be lessened. No Δ *SS* curve, because this is just new information about something that has already happened. (781)

4   c   *SAS* upward sloping, *LAS* vertical at potential GDP. (726–730)

5   b   Definition. (718)

6   b   Job not available in winter. (747–748)

7   b   Employed/working-age population = 13/20 = 65 percent. (740)

8   a   Involuntarily part-time/labour force = .5/14.5 = 3.4 percent. (740)

9   a   This describes efficiency wages, a form of job rationing. (754–755)

10   d   New investment curve is I_a, with the interest rate < 6 percent → must be at or above the investment level of 20 billion dollars on I_a. (767)

11   e   a, b, c are *LS* effect, d shift in curve. (720, 722)

12   e   a is nonsense, b, c, and d are movements along curves. (727)

13   a   In long run, technological advances → ↑ demand for labour → ↑ real wages → ↑ population → ↓ real wages. (799–801)

14   c   In neoclassical theory, population growth is not driven by economic growth. In both theories, capital is subject to diminishing returns, technology is exogenous, and the one-third rule holds. (799–803)

❂15   e   By one-third rule, capital ↑ 9 percent → real GDP per hour of work ↑ 3 percent, or 1/5 of increase in productivity. (796–797)

❂16   b   From 3, 12 percent or 4/5 due to technology. (796–797)

The Business Cycle

KEY CONCEPTS

Cycle Impulses and Mechanisms

There are different theories of the business cycle, emphasizing different outside initiating *impulses*, and different cycle mechanisms → but all theories emphasize the role of investment.

◆ In an expansion, investment is high and capital stock ↑ quickly → ↑ capital per hour of labour → diminishing returns to capital → ↓ profit rate → ↓ investment eventually → recession begins.

◆ In a recession, investment low and capital stock ↑ slowly or not at all → ↓ capital per hour of labour → ↑ marginal product of capital → ↑ profit rate → ↑ investment eventually → recession ends.

Aggregate Demand Theories of the Business Cycle

Three *AD* theories of the business cycle.

◆ **Keynesian theory of the business cycle** regards volatile expectations as main cycle source.

◆ Keynesian impulse is Δ expected future sales/profits → Δ demand for capital and investment.

◆ Expectations are volatile because crucial events are unknown, impossible to forecast, and have large effects when they change.

◆ Keynesian cycle mechanism has two aspects:

  • Initial change in investment has a multiplier effect → strong shifts in *AD* curve.

  • Due to downward-rigid money wages, *SAS* curve is assumed nearly horizontal to left of potential GDP. ↓ *AD* → unemployment equilibrium with no natural restoration to full employment until ↑ expectations.

  • Above full employment, wages very flexible and *LAS* curve vertical → prices adjust quickly, economy stays near full employment.

◆ **Monetarist theory of the business cycle** regards Δ money stock as main source of the cycle.

◆ Impulse in monetarist theory is Δ growth rate of the money supply by the Bank of Canada.

◆ Monetarist cycle mechanism is

  • ↓ money growth → ↑ interest rates → ↑ exchange rate → ↓ investment demand and exports → multiplier effect → *AD* leftward.

  • *SAS* curve upward sloping → ↓ *AD* → ↓ both real GDP and price level.

  • Money wage only temporarily sticky → unemployment equilibrium → ↓ money wage rate → *SAS* adjusts rightward → ↓ price level, ↑ real GDP toward full-employment equilibrium.

◆ *Rational expectations theories of cycle* claim money wages set by **rational expectation** of price level (forecast based on all available information).

  • **New classical theory of the business cycle** regards unanticipated fluctuations in *AD* as main source of cycle.

  • **New Keynesian theory of the business cycle** regards unanticipated *and* anticipated fluctuations in *AD* as sources of the cycle.

◆ In new classical theory

  • Unanticipated ↓ *AD* → ↓ price level → ↑ real wage since money wage constant → ↑ unemployment.

- Money wages adjust quickly because of unemployment → *SAS* shifts rightward, economy moves back to full employment.
- Anticipated change *AD* fully built into flexible money wages so *SAS* adjusts instantly → no change employment or real GDP, just in price level.
- Since economy adjusts quickly towards full employment on its own → little need for government policy.

◆ In new Keynesian theory

- Initial effects of ↓ *AD* the same, but money wages are assumed sticky because of long-term nature of most wage contracts → money wages adjust slowly in face of the shock, *SAS* curve adjusts slowly.
- If anticipated change in *AD* → current wages built on past expectations because of long-term contracts → money wages cannot adjust to anticipated change → it affects both real GDP and employment.
- Economy adjusts slowly towards full employment → need for government policy.

Real Business Cycle Theory

Real business cycle (RBC) theory regards random fluctuations in productivity as main source of the cycle.

◆ Key impulse is Δ pace of technological change → Δ growth rate of productivity.

◆ Key assumption of a strong *intertemporal substitution effect*—when current real wage or current real interest rate temporarily high, people ↑ labour supply strongly, and vice versa.

◆ Assumed money wage rate adjusts freely → unemployment always at natural rate → only *LAS* matters.

◆ RBC recession starts with technological change → some existing capital obsolete → temporary fall in productivity.

- This fall → ↓ demand for labour and capital → ↓ real rate of interest → ↓ labour supply (but by less than ↓ labour demand) → small ↓ real wage rate, large ↓ employment.
- ↓ investment demand → ↓ *AD*, and ↓ employment → ↓ aggregate supply → ↓ real GDP, Δ price level can be up or down.

◆ Δ *AD* affects price level only, not real variables.

◆ Critics of RBC theory argue

- money wages are sticky,

- intertemporal substitution is too weak to account for big Δ employment,
- technological shocks are *caused by AD* fluctuations.

◆ Defenders of RBC theory argue that

- it is consistent with facts (explains both growth *and* cycles) and microeconomic theory.
- technological change Δ *AD*, not reverse.
- cycle is efficient, no role for government policy.

The 1990–1991 Recession

◆ Primary causes:

- Bank of Canada's price stability policy → ↓ money growth → ↑ real interest rates.
- U.S. recession → ↓ exports.
- Canada–United States Free Trade Agreement → increasing uncertainty → ↓ investment.

◆ The first two causes → *AD* shifting leftward, while the third → both *AD* and *SAS* shifting leftward → ↑ price level and ↓ real GDP.

◆ In labour market, ↑ real wage rates, ↓ employment and ↑ unemployment.

◆ This suggests money wages rose too much, because of unanticipated slowdown in inflation.

The Great Depression

Great Depression had ↓ real GDP of 30 percent, ↑ unemployment from 2.9 percent to 20 percent.

◆ Primary cause of Great Depression was ↑ uncertainty and pessimism → ↓ investment and ↓ consumer spending → stock market crash → worsening uncertainty and pessimism.

◆ These unexpected shocks → ↓ in *AD* more than shift in *SAS* → ↓ real GDP and ↓ price level.

◆ Depression prolonged by further unexpected shifts left in *AD*:

- Collapse of the financial system in the United States → collapse of the money supply → ↑ real interest rates → further ↓ investment.
- International tariff war → collapse of international trade.

◆ One view argues collapse in spending due mostly to pessimism and uncertainty, other view argues collapse of money supply was crucial.

◆ Great Depression unlikely to occur again due to the presence of Bank of Canada acting as a lender of last resort, deposit insurance, a higher government presence, and multi-income families.

HELPFUL HINTS

1 This chapter should be very rewarding to those who have expended the effort to understand the previous chapters, because it introduces no new analytical structure. Instead, the power of the fully developed aggregate demand and aggregate supply model is demonstrated by analysing some interesting macroeconomic episodes, including the Great Depression. You should be pleased that you have mastered this powerful analytical tool.

2 As you examine various macroeconomic episodes, focus on these key factors: Are changes primarily in aggregate demand, aggregate supply, or both? As you follow the various changes, be sure you understand what is going on in the labour market that underlies the goods and services market. It is this market that will tell you what is happening to the key variables of employment and unemployment.

3 This chapter contains competing theories that are used to explain real-world events. There is no dispute over the facts such as the level of prices or real GDP. The disputes centre around what changes in the economy created the facts, and touches on what government policies might affect the economy.

   To help you remember and understand these theories, consider Table 34.1. It highlights the similarities and differences between the theories, and it helps to highlight how radically different real business cycle theory is.

   Theories differ based on two primary factors: the source of the cycle (*AD* versus *AS*), and the responsiveness of the labour market (sticky versus flexible wages). Be sure you can catalogue and understand these theories.

   Remember, these are theories, *not* statements of facts, and their explanations could be incorrect. Only proper empirical investigation over time will cast light on their validity.

SELF-TEST

True/False/Uncertain and Explain

1 A recession today is likely to be much less severe than during the 1930s because the government sector is much larger today.

2 Most fluctuations in real GDP are the best possible responses of the economy to the uneven pace of technological change.

3 The reduction in the growth rate of the money supply by the Bank of Canada in 1988 and 1989 was generally anticipated by households and firms.

4 The unemployment of the 1990 recession could have been avoided by an expansionary monetary or fiscal policy.

5 In order for the RBC theory to explain the behaviour of the labour market (real wages and employment), it must assume that the natural rate of unemployment rises in a recession.

6 The stock market crash of 1929 was the cause of the Great Depression.

TABLE **34.1**

Labour Market Structure		Theory	Primary Source of the Cycle
Wages are sticky	U above natural rate for long time periods	Keynesian and New Keynesian	AD Shocks
Wages are flexible	U above natural rate for short time periods	New classical and Monetarist	
	U = natural rate always	Real business cycle	AS Shocks

7 Unanticipated falls in aggregate demand cause recessions only in new Keynesian theory, not in new classical theory.

8 During the early stages of a recession, interest rates tend to fall but later they typically rise.

9 A fall in aggregate demand will cause a recession.

10 Monetarists and real business cycle theorists tend to believe that wages are flexible and adjust quickly.

Multiple-Choice

1 During the Great Depression, which was caused by an aggregate
a supply shock, the rate of inflation increased.
b supply shock, the rate of inflation decreased.
c demand shock, the rate of inflation increased.
d demand shock, the rate of inflation decreased.
e demand shock, the rate of inflation became negative.

2 The cause of the 1990 recession was an aggregate
a supply shock, accompanied by a rightward shift in aggregate demand.
b supply shock, accompanied by a leftward shift in aggregate demand.
c demand shock alone.
d demand shock, accompanied by a rightward shift in aggregate supply.
e supply shock alone.

3 Once the Great Depression started, aggregate demand was expected to
a fall, but it did not fall as rapidly as expected.
b fall, but it fell faster than expected.
c rise, but it actually fell.
d rise, which it did due to an increase in the money supply.
e rise, but it rose less than expected.

4 An increase in aggregate demand causes GDP to increase by the least amount in the
a Keynesian theory.
b monetarist theory.
c new Keynesian theory.
d new classical theory.
e real business cycle theory.

5 If the Bank of Canada unexpectedly decreases the money supply during a recession,
a nothing will happen since the recession is already occurring.
b the recession will tend to deepen, as the higher interest rates discourage investment.
c the recession will tend to deepen, because the value of the Canadian dollar will fall.
d the recession will be stopped, as the higher interest rates encourage more saving.
e interest rates will fall, since the change in the money supply was unexpected.

6 In which theory of the business cycle is government policy likely to be *most* effective?
a Keynesian
b monetarist
c new classical
d new Keynesian
e real business cycle

7 The Great Depression was prolonged by
a a massive fall in confidence following the stock market crash.
b extended bank failures in the United States leading to a large fall in the money supply.
c structural reorganizing of the economy.
d governments increasing their spending and cutting taxes.
e a and b.

8 According to Friedman and Schwartz, the Great Depression was caused by
a the stock market crash of 1929.
b a fall in the real money supply leading to higher interest rates and lower investment.
c a rise in the money supply leading to higher inflation.
d falls in business and consumer confidence.
e imports falling.

9 Consider Fig. 34.1. Which graph(s) represent(s) an economy that is recovering from a recession without any government involvement?

a (a)
b (b)
c (c)
d (d)
e (b) and (d)

FIGURE **34.1**

(a)

(b)

(c)

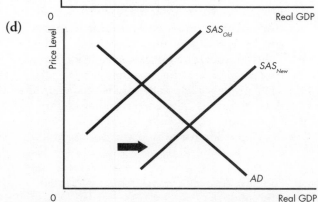

(d)

10 In Fig. 34.1, which graph(s) represent(s) an economy where the government is helping it recover from a recession?

a (a)
b (b)
c (c)
d (b) and (a)
e none of the graphs

11 In Fig. 34.1, which graph(s) represent(s) an economy entering a recession due to falling consumer and investor expectations?

a (a)
b (b)
c (c)
d (b) and (d)
e none of the graphs

12 In Fig. 34.1, which graph(s) represent(s) an economy entering a recession due to a negative productivity shock?

a (a)
b (b)
c (c)
d (b) and (d)
e none of the graphs

13 If the intertemporal substitution effect is weak, then the RBC theory of the business cycle would have problems explaining

a how to get a large fall in employment in a recession.
b how a recession begins.
c why aggregate demand falls in a recession.
d the automatic adjustment to full employment.
e what creates technological change.

14 Which of the following news quotes *best* describes a *Keynesian* view of a recession?

a "Rapid computerization is creating obsolete workers and higher unemployment."
b "The unexpectedly tight fiscal policy is lowering spending and creating unemployment."
c "The promised anti-inflationary policy of the Bank of Canada is lowering spending as promised."
d "The promised cuts in government spending have helped lower consumer spending and created unemployment."
e "Businesses are very worried about future sales and have lowered their purchases of capital equipment."

15 Which of the following news quotes *best* describes a *new classical* view of a recession?

a "Rapid computerization is creating obsolete workers and higher unemployment."

b "The unexpectedly tight fiscal policy is lowering spending and creating unemployment."

c "The promised anti-inflationary policy of the Bank of Canada is lowering spending as promised."

d "The promised cuts in government spending have helped lower consumer spending and created unemployment."

e "Businesses are very worried about future sales and have lowered their purchases of capital equipment."

16 The intertemporal substitution effect states that

a in a recession, investment is low and the capital stock rises slowly, leading to a rising marginal product of capital.

b money wages are based on a rational expectation of the price level.

c a fall in productivity leads to a fall in the demand for capital, and a fall in the real interest rate.

d when current real wages and real interest rates are high, people decrease their labour supply strongly.

e when current real wages and real interest rates are high, people increase their labour supply strongly.

17 Recessions tend to begin when

a consumption expenditure decreases.

b investment decreases.

c investment increases.

d government purchases decrease.

e net exports decrease.

18 The initial cause of the Great Depression was

a a dramatic increase in the prices of raw materials during 1929.

b a fall in the money supply during 1929.

c a fall in investment and consumer spending because of uncertainty about the future.

d the stock market crash of 1929.

e b and c.

19 What is the key impulse in the Keynesian theory of the business cycle?

a changes in expected future sales and profits

b changes in the money supply

c unanticipated changes in aggregate demand

d anticipated changes in aggregate demand

e changes in the pace of technological change

20 According to the real business cycle theorists, the increase in the unemployment rate during a recession is due to an increase in the

a deviation of the rate of unemployment from the natural rate of unemployment resulting from a real wage rate that is too high to clear the labour market.

b deviation of the rate of unemployment from the natural rate of unemployment resulting from an increase in job market turnover.

c natural rate of unemployment resulting from a real wage that is too high to clear the labour market.

d natural rate of unemployment resulting from an increase in job market turnover.

e rate of new entries into the labour market.

21 Typically in a recession, investment

a is low at the start, but eventually rises as the recession ends.

b is high at the start, but eventually falls as the recession ends.

c has the same pattern as in an expansion.

d is constant.

e moves around, but with no distinct pattern.

22 During the 1990 recession, the real wage rate

a fell and employment fell.

b fell and employment rose.

c stayed constant and employment fell.

d rose and employment rose.

e rose and employment fell.

23 During the Great Depression, the money wage rate

a rose and the real wage rate remained about the same.

b rose and the real wage rate rose.

c fell and the real wage rate remained about the same.

d fell and the real wage rate rose.

e fell and the real wage rate fell.

24 Which of the following news quotes *best* describes a *real business cycle* view of a recession?

a "Rapid computerization is creating obsolete workers and higher unemployment."

b "The unexpectedly tight fiscal policy is lowering spending and creating unemployment."

c "The promised anti-inflationary policy of the Bank of Canada is lowering spending as promised."

d "The promised cuts in government spending have helped lower consumer spending and created unemployment."

e "Businesses are very worried about future sales and have lowered their purchases of capital equipment."

25 Multi-income families reduce the probability of another Great Depression by

a reducing the probability of everyone in the family being simultaneously unemployed.

b investing more in the economy.

c paying more taxes.

d increasing fluctuations in consumption.

e none of the above.

Short Answer Problems

1 What was the cause of the 1990 recession? What was the cause of the Great Depression?

2 What is the basic controversy among economists about the behaviour of the labour market during recession? Why is the controversy important for designing an appropriate anti-recessionary economic policy?

3 List the four important features of the Canadian economy that make severe depression less likely today.

4 How do government transfer payments in Canada help to reduce the severity of a recession caused by an unexpected decrease in aggregate demand?

5 Suppose that you have been selected to be the economic advisor to the prime minister, based on your sterling performance in macroeconomics. You have been asked to evaluate the new Keynesian theory of the business cycle, and the real business cycle theory of the business cycle, and to explain what they argue should be the optimal government policy in the face of a recession.

a What does each theory argue is the likely cause of a recession, and why?

b What does each theory argue is the best response to a recession? Why do the two theories differ? That is, what crucial differences in their approach to the economy leads to the different policy conclusions?

c The prime minister wants to know which theory you think is better, and why?

6 a If an individual was politically conservative and tended to distrust the government, which theory or theories of the business cycle do you think they would support?

b If an individual was politically leftist and tended to trust the government, which theory or theories of the business cycle do you think they would support?

7 Table 34.2 gives data for a hypothetical economy in years 1 and 2.

TABLE **34.2**

	Year 1	Year 2
Real GDP (billions of dollars)	500	450
Price level (GDP deflator)	100	105

a If the real business cycle theory is true, what happened to aggregate demand and aggregate supply in this economy?

b If the new Keynesian theory is true, what happened to aggregate demand and aggregate supply in this economy?

8 Consider the labour market in the economy from Short Answer Problem 7.

a If the real business cycle theory is true, what happened in the labour market? Is the unemployment natural or not?

b If the new Keynesian theory is true, what happened in the labour market? Is the unemployment natural or not?

9 Consider the economy from Short Answer Problem 7 again.

a Suppose instead that you knew that the expected price level in year 1 was 100 and that in year 2 it was 110, would this allow you to decide which theory was correct?

b Suppose instead that you knew that the expected price level in year 1 was 100 and that in year 2 it was 105, would this allow you to decide which theory was correct?

10 Some economists argue that real business cycle theory is false because it is unable to explain the events of the Great Depression, especially the events in the labour market. Briefly evaluate this argument.

A N S W E R S

True/False/Uncertain and Explain

1 T Larger government sector → larger automatic stabilizers. (837)

2 U Depends on whether RBC theory is correct. (831–832)

3 F It was unanticipated → unexpectedly low inflation → recession. (832)

4 U Depends if sticky wage or flexible wage theories true. (832–834)

5 **T** All unemployment natural in RBC theory. (828–830)

6 **F** It was a symptom of uncertainty about future that was initial cause. (836)

7 **F** In both theories, unanticipated fall → wages set too high → unemployment and recession. (825–827)

8 **F** Reverse occurs. (821)

9 **U** **F** if RBC theory correct, **T** if others correct. (822–832)

10 **T** They believe in flexible wage theory. (826, 829)

Multiple-Choice

1 **e** ↓ consumer and investor confidence → shift leftward in *AD* so severe → ↓ price level. (835)

2 **b** ↓ consumer and investor confidence → shift leftward in *AD*, and ↑ wages plus restructuring → shift leftward in *SAS*. (832–833)

3 **b** See text discussion. (835)

4 **e** Vertical *SAS* curve. (822–832)

5 **b** ↓ real money supply → ↑ interest rates → ↓ investment demand → ↓ aggregate demand. (832)

6 **a** Flat *SAS* curve → biggest swings in *Y* for a given Δ*AD*. (822–832)

7 **e** See text discussion. (835–836)

8 **b** They argue that monetary forces are most important. (835–836)

9 **d** Recession → unemployment → ↓ real wages → shift rightward in *SAS*. (826–827)

10 **b** Expansionary policy → shift rightward in *AD*. (826–827)

11 **c** ↓ expectations → ↓ consumption and investment → shift leftward in *AD*. (826–827)

12 **e** In RBC theory, negative productivity shock shifts *LAS*, there is no *SAS*. (830–831)

13 **a** Intertemporal substitution → Δ current real wage or real interest rate → big Δ labour supply. (829–830)

14 **e** Key impulse in Keynesian theory is Δ expected sales/profits. (822–823)

15 **b** Key impulse in new classical theory is unexpected change in *AD*. (825–826)

16 **e** Definition. (829–830)

17 **b** See text discussion. (821)

18 **c** See text discussion. (835)

19 **a** See text discussion. (822)

20 **d** All unemployment is natural, and real wage rate is always correct. (829–830)

21 **a** See text discussion. (821)

22 **e** See text discussion. (834)

23 **c** See text discussion. (835)

24 **a** Key impulse is Δ pace of technological change. (828)

25 **a** This leads to smaller ↓ consumer confidence when one member becomes unemployed. (837)

Short Answer Problems

1 The cause of the 1990 recession was an unanticipated reduction in the rate of growth of aggregate demand. This was the result of the Bank of Canada decision to reduce the rate of growth of the money supply, the U.S. recession lowering exports, and uncertainty lowering investment. Thus the aggregate demand curve did not shift rightward by as much as expected—it actually shifted down.

The major cause of the Great Depression was an unanticipated fall in aggregate demand, which was the consequence of reduced investment and reduced consumer expenditure (especially on durable goods) due to uncertainty and pessimism. For several years (1930–1932), aggregate demand fell by more than expected. This caused real GDP to fall and the rate of inflation to fall.

2 Economists disagree about the speed with which the money wage rate adjusts to clear the labour market. Some economists (Keynesians and new Keynesians) believe that money wages are sticky and adjust only slowly. As a consequence, when a recession occurs, the real wage does not fall sufficiently to clear the labour market in the short run and thus there is an excess supply of labour (unemployment). Other economists (monetarists, new classical theorists, and real business cycle theorists) believe that wages are flexible. According to monetarists and new classical theorists, any recession is temporary in nature, because wages adjust downward quickly and the *SAS* shifts rightward, moving the economy towards full employment. According to RBC theorists, when a recession occurs, real wages adjust instantly. Any increase in unemployment is thus interpreted as an increase in natural unemployment.

These issues have significant implications for the design of an appropriate policy as a response to recession. If the Keynesians and new Keynesians are correct, then it may be useful to consider expansionary monetary or fiscal policies to counteract recession. If the others are correct, since the short-run aggregate supply adjusts quickly, or only the vertical *LAS* is relevant, expansionary monetary or fiscal policy will simply increase the rate of inflation and have no effect on real GDP or unemployment.

3 The four important features of the Canadian economy that make severe depression less likely today are: (1) bank deposits are insured; (2) the Bank of Canada is prepared to be the "lender of last resort"; (3) taxes and government spending play a stabilizing role; and (4) multi-income families are more economically secure.

4   When a recession arises, unemployment increases and disposable income declines. This decline in disposable income leads to a reduction in consumption expenditure, which has a multiplied negative effect on real GDP. Transfer payments, however, reduce these secondary effects of a recession by reducing the amount by which disposable income falls. As incomes fall and unemployment increases, government transfer payments increase in the form of higher unemployment benefits or other welfare payments. As a result, the fall in disposable income is reduced and the decline in consumption is less.

5 a   The new Keynesian theory argues the likely source of a recession is a negative shock to aggregate demand, most likely due to unanticipated, and possibly anticipated, changes in one or more of the underlying variables. The RBC theory argues that the key impulse is a change in the pace of technological change, leading to a negative shock to the *LAS*.

  b   The new Keynesian theory also argues that money wages are sticky, so that the labour market and the *SAS* adjust slowly—the economy is in the recession for some time period unless the government increases *AD*. The RBC theory argues that the labour market has already adjusted instantly, and output is at potential GDP. Any government policy will affect *AD*, but have no impact on real variables, so no policy should be carried out.

  The crucial difference is due to the impulse variable that starts the recession—in one case it is an *AD* variable and can be counteracted by increasing *AD*, and in the other case it is a *LAS* variable, and increasing *AD* has no beneficial effect.

  c   This is a personal choice, but should be based on an argument as to which impulse variable seems most likely to be correct to you.

6 a   The monetarist, new classical, and RBC theories all argue government intervention to offset the business cycle is unneeded—a conservative person is most likely to support one of these.

  b   The Keynesian and new Keynesian theories all argue that government intervention can offset the business cycle, so a leftist is more likely to support one of these.

7 a   Since real GDP has fallen, the *LAS* curve must have shifted left, since the only *AS* curve is a vertical *LAS* in a RBC world. For the price level

to have risen, it must be the case that either the *AD* curve rose, or fell so little that in combination with the *LAS* curve shift the price level has risen.

  b   In order to get both the price level rising, and real GDP falling, it must be the case that the *SAS* curve shifted leftward by more than the shift rightward in the *AD* curve (if there was one), indicating that people anticipated a rise in *AD* (leading to a rise in wages and a shift left in the *SAS*), but the actual rise was less than anticipated.

8 a   A real business cycle recession starts with a temporary fall in productivity, which leads to a fall in the marginal product of capital, and a fall in the demand for capital (and therefore a fall in the real interest rate), a fall in the demand for investment, and a shift leftward in the *AD* curve. In addition, there is a fall in the demand for labour because of the fall in productivity, and a shift leftward in the supply of labour because of the lower real interest rate. These two shifts lead to a fall in employment and a shift leftward in the *LAS* curve. All the unemployment is natural.

  b   In the new Keynesian labour market, money wages are based on wrong expectations, so that real wages are too high since the rise in money wages is more than the rise in the price level. Labour supply is greater than labour demand, creating the unemployment. All the extra unemployment is cyclical, not natural.

◑9 a   Since the actual price level was lower than the expected price level, the fall in real GDP must have been due to an increase in aggregate demand that was less than expected. Therefore actual real GDP must be less than potential GDP—the new Keynesian theory is most likely to be correct.

  b   Since the actual price level is equal to the expected price level, then actual real GDP must equal potential GDP—the RBC theory is most likely to be correct.

10   In the Great Depression, the real wage rate stayed roughly constant, but the level of unemployment rose from about 3 percent to about 20 percent. If the RBC theory is correct, all of this unemployment is natural. This would require either an enormous negative productivity shock, or a huge intertemporal substitution effect in response to a large fall in the real rate of interest. The real interest rate actually rose during the Great Depression, due to the large fall in the money supply. It would seem unlikely that the RBC theory can explain the behaviour of the labour market in the Great Depression.

Inflation

KEY CONCEPTS

Inflation and the Price Level

Inflation is when price level (P) is rising and money is losing value.

◆ It is average of prices, and an ongoing process, not just one-time change.

◆ Inflation rate = annual percentage change in
$$P = \frac{P_1 - P_0}{P_0} \times 100.$$

Demand-Pull Inflation

Demand-pull inflation arises from increasing aggregate demand.

◆ Main sources are ↑ money supply, ↑ government purchases, ↑ exports → *AD* shifts right → in short run, with no Δ potential GDP or money wage rate → ↑ P (inflation), ↑ Y, ↓ unemployment to below natural rate.

◆ Unemployment less than natural rate → labour shortage → ↑ wages and costs → *SAS* shifts left → ↑ prices even more, real GDP back to original level.

◆ If *AD* shifts right again, and wages rise again, a *price-wage spiral* may result.

◆ Canada had demand-pull inflation in late 1960s, early 1970s, triggered by ↑ exports to United States, ↑ Canadian government expenditures and money growth.

Cost-Push Inflation

Cost-push inflation arises from decreasing aggregate supply, due to increase in costs.

◆ Main sources are ↑ money wage rates and ↑ money prices of raw materials → firms decrease production → *SAS* shifts leftward → ↑ price level, ↓ real GDP (**stagflation**).

◆ If government or Bank of Canada shifts *AD* rightward in response → ↑ prices again → input owners raise prices again → a cost-price spiral may result.

◆ If there is no government or Bank response → economy remains below full employment.

◆ Canada had strong cost-push inflation in 1970s due to ↑ price of oil.

Effects of Inflation

Firms and households make economic decisions based on forecasts of inflation.

◆ Incorrect forecasts in labour markets → costly departures from full employment and income redistribution.

 • If inflation > anticipated → wages set too low → employers gain, workers lose income, but firm has trouble keeping workers as a result → ↑ other costs.

 • If inflation < anticipated → wages set too high → employers lose, workers gain income, but firm lays off workers as a result → ↑ unemployment.

◆ Incorrect forecasts in capital markets → incorrect borrowing/lending and income redistribution.

- If inflation > anticipated → interest rates set too low → borrowers gain at expense of lenders, but both wished to have made different decisions.
- If inflation < anticipated → interest rates set too high → lenders gain at expense of borrowers, but both wished to have made different decisions.

◆ People forecast inflation in different ways, including hiring economists, who make best possible forecast based on all relevant information → a **rational expectation**.

◆ If ↑ AD correctly anticipated → money wages adjust to keep up with anticipated inflation → SAS shifts leftward as ↑ AD → Δ price level only, no Δ real GDP or employment → actual inflation = expected inflation.

◆ If ↑ AD more than expected → ↑ money wage only to reflect expected part → SAS leftward by less than if fully expected → new short-run below-full employment equilibrium to right of potential GDP → eventually ↑ money wages and SAS leftward again.

◆ If ↑ AD less than expected → ↑ money wage to reflect expected change → SAS leftward by more than if correctly expected → new short-run below-full employment equilibrium to left of potential GDP → eventually ↓ money wages and SAS rightward.

◆ Anticipated inflation is costly, ↑ costs as ↑ inflation:

- "Bootleather costs"—as ↑ inflation → ↓ value of money → people spend money more frequently → ↑ velocity of circulation → ↑ transactions costs.
- Other transactions costs—people use less efficient alternatives to money (foreign exchange, barter).
- ↓ potential GDP due to higher transactions costs.
- ↓ long-term growth due to inflation–tax interaction reducing return to saving, inflation uncertainty reducing investment, and diversion of resources into avoiding costs of inflation.

Inflation and Unemployment: The Phillips Curve

Phillips curve shows relationship between inflation and unemployment.

◆ **Short-run Phillips curve** ($SRPC$) shows relationship between inflation and unemployment for a given expected inflation rate and a given natural rate of unemployment. It is negatively sloped.

◆ In short run, if actual inflation > expected → AD curve shifts right further than expected, movement along SAS, real GDP > potential, unemployment < natural rate → movement up and left along $SRPC$.

◆ **Long-run Phillips curve** ($LRPC$) shows relationship between inflation and unemployment when actual inflation = expected. It is vertical at the natural rate of unemployment.

◆ If actual inflation = expected → AD curve shifts right as expected, real GDP = potential, unemployment = natural rate.

◆ If ↓ expected inflation rate → $SRPC$ shifts downward, and vice versa.

◆ If ↑ natural unemployment rate → both $LRPC$ and $SRPC$ shift rightward.

Interest Rates and Inflation

A large part of changes in nominal rate of interest are due to changes in expected inflation.

◆ Nominal interest rate = real rate + expected inflation.

◆ Demand and supply forces determine equilibrium real interest rate → nominal rate determined by this plus expected inflation → real rate independent of expected inflation.

◆ ↑ expected inflation → ↑ nominal interest rate by equivalent amount, keeping real rate of interest constant.

◆ Canada and other countries show positive relationship between nominal interest rate and inflation rate. Average Canadian real interest rate steady at about 3.5 percent.

HELPFUL HINTS

1   This chapter is complex and important because it finalizes the development of the complete modern macroeconomic model. This is the basic model generally used by macroeconomists as they analyse the economy. It has proven to be a very powerful tool for analysis.

2 An important concept introduced in this chapter is that of a *rational expectation*—the best possible forecast based on all relevant information. Text Fig. 35.7 applies this concept to forecasting the price level. We know the *actual* price level is found in the short run at the intersection of the *AD* curve and the *SAS* curve, and in the long run at the intersection of the *AD* curve and the *LAS* curve. Thus in Fig. 35.7, when *AD* is expected to rise to AD_1, the best *forecast* of the new price level (the forecast most likely to be correct) is at the intersection of AD_1 and *LAS*, yielding a wage demand that in turn leads to SAS_1.

Note that the rational expectation of the price level will be at the intersection of the *expected* aggregate demand curve and the *expected short-run* aggregate supply curve in the short run, and the *expected long-run* aggregate supply curve in the long run. The *actual* equilibrium, which determines the *actual* price level, is at the intersection of the *actual* aggregate demand curve and the *actual short-run* aggregate supply curve.

3 An important implication of the assumption people forecast using rational expectations is that the consequences of any macroeconomic event (a monetary or fiscal policy) depend on expectations. The effect on the price level and real GDP of a given increase in the money supply will be different for different price level expectations. The position of the short-run aggregate supply curve depends on the expected price level, which in turn depends on the expected policy, and thus so does the macroeconomic equilibrium. Depending on whether the actual level of policy is anticipated or unanticipated, different outcomes will occur.

For example, a given increase in the money supply can result in an increase in real GDP, no change in real GDP, or even a reduction in real GDP depending solely on the expected policy. An increase in real GDP will result if the increase in aggregate demand is not anticipated (or underanticipated); no change in real GDP will result if the increase in aggregate demand is correctly anticipated; and reduction in real GDP will result if the increase in aggregate demand is less than anticipated (overanticipated).

4 An alternative method of studying inflation and unemployment uses the Phillips curve. Consider an unexpected rise in the inflation rate in this setting (triggered by an unexpected rise in aggregate demand). In the short run, there is a movement along the short-run Phillips curve, leading to a fall in unemployment to a level below the natural rate (equivalently, there is a movement along the short-run aggregate supply curve triggered by a fall in the real wage, leading to more employment and higher real GDP above the natural rate). In the long run, inflation expectations adjust upward (real wages rise), leading to an upward shift in the short-run Phillips curve and a rise in unemployment back to the natural rate at a point back on the long-run Phillips curve (employment falls and real GDP falls as short-run aggregate supply shifts leftward).

5 Students (and politicians and commentators!) are often confused by the fact that sometimes a fall in the growth rate of the money supply leads to a *rise* in the interest rate, and sometimes it leads to a *fall* in the interest rate. The key to understanding this difference is to focus on the time frame—short or long run. Figure 35.1 illustrates the changes in the nominal rate of interest over time when the growth rate of the money supply is lowered. Initially, the rate of interest is r_0, and then there is an unanticipated fall in the growth rate of the money supply at time T*, which leads to an unexpectedly low level of the real money supply. As we saw in Chapter 29, in the short run this will lead to a rise in the rate of interest (to the level r_1), which in turn leads to a fall in investment demand and aggregate demand. If this is unexpected, it leads to lower inflation and lower real GDP. In the long run, once economic agents realize that the lower inflation is going to remain in place, they lower their forecast of inflation, which in turn lowers the nominal rate of interest to a level such as r_2.

FIGURE **35.1**

SELF-TEST

True/False/Uncertain and Explain

1 When inflation is unanticipated, people do not change their behaviour, which means it has no negative effects on nor does it hurt the economy.

2 The Phillips curve shows that if there is a rise in the inflation rate, unemployment will fall.

3 Stagflation occurs when real GDP falls and the price level rises.

4 The inflation resulting from expansionary monetary policy is an example of cost-push inflation.

5 During a period with zero expected inflation, the (nominal) interest rate is 5 percent. If the expected rate of inflation rises to 6 percent, the interest rate will rise to 11 percent.

6 If people expect aggregate demand to increase but it does not, the price level will rise and real GDP will decrease.

7 If the price level at the beginning of 1994 is 120 and the price level at the beginning of 1995 is 130, the rate of inflation is 8.3 percent.

8 If an increase in aggregate demand is correctly anticipated, inflation will not occur.

9 If there is an increase in the rate of inflation, employers will gain at the expense of workers.

10 The long-run Phillips curve shows a tradeoff between inflation and unemployment.

Multiple-Choice

1 Which of the following business quotes illustrates costs associated with an anticipated inflation?

a "The bank is losing money on its loans, given the current rate of interest."
b "Wage increases were low last year, but I am having trouble keeping workers."
c "I find I have to send invoices out to customers twice a month now, because of the higher inflation."
d "The low inflation rate means my borrowing costs are too high."
e None of the above.

2 The short-run Phillips curve shows the relationship between

a the price level and real GDP in the short run.
b the price level and unemployment in the short run.
c unemployment and real GDP in the short run.
d inflation and unemployment, when inflation expectations can change.
e inflation and unemployment, when inflation expectations do not change.

3 Demand-pull inflation occurs when

a aggregate demand increases.
b aggregate supply decreases.
c input costs rise.
d people incorrectly forecast inflation.
e unemployment is above the natural rate.

4 If the rate of inflation is lower than anticipated,

a lenders will gain at the expense of borrowers, and workers will gain at the expense of employers.
b borrowers will gain at the expense of lenders, and workers will gain at the expense of employers.
c lenders will gain at the expense of borrowers, and employers will gain at the expense of workers.
d borrowers will gain at the expense of lenders, and employers will gain at the expense of workers.
e lenders will gain at the expense of borrowers, and whether employers or workers will gain is uncertain.

5 In an economy with the price level greater than expected and output above the natural rate, which of the following is a possible explanation, *ceteris paribus*?

a Potential real GDP has increased by more than expected.

b Potential real GDP has increased by less than expected.

c Aggregate demand has decreased by more than expected.

d Aggregate demand has increased by less than expected.

e Aggregate demand has increased by more than expected.

6 In an economy with the price level less than expected and output below the natural rate, which of the following is a possible explanation, *ceteris paribus*?

a Potential real GDP has increased by more than expected.

b Potential real GDP has increased by less than expected.

c Aggregate demand has decreased by more than expected.

d Aggregate demand has decreased by less than expected.

e Aggregate demand has increased by more than expected.

7 Suppose that initially the nominal rate of interest is 8 percent and the expected rate of inflation is 5 percent. If the expected rate of inflation increases to 8 percent, what will the new nominal rate of interest be?

a 3 percent

b 8 percent

c 11 percent

d 13 percent

e 16 percent

8 A correctly anticipated increase in the rate of growth of the money supply will cause nominal interest rates to

a fall and real interest rates to fall.

b fall and leave real interest rates unchanged.

c rise and real interest rates to rise.

d rise and leave real interest rates unchanged.

e rise and real interest rates to fall.

9 If the actual price level is higher than the expected price level, then real GDP

a must be above potential real GDP.

b must be below potential real GDP.

c must be equal to potential real GDP.

d can be above, below, or equal to potential real GDP depending on the position of the aggregate demand curve.

e can be above or equal to potential real GDP depending on the position of the aggregate demand curve.

10 Suppose aggregate demand increases by less than anticipated, *ceteris paribus*. This will result in a

a rise in inflation and real GDP falling below potential real GDP.

b rise in inflation and real GDP rising above potential real GDP.

c fall in inflation and real GDP falling below potential real GDP.

d fall in inflation and real GDP rising above potential real GDP.

e fall in inflation and real GDP staying at potential real GDP.

11 Figure 35.2 illustrates an economy initially in equilibrium at point *a*. What would cause the short-run aggregate supply curve to shift from SAS_0 to SAS_1?

a a rise in the price of oil

b an increase in the price level

c an increase in the marginal product of labour

d an increase in the demand for money

e a decrease in wages

FIGURE **35.2**

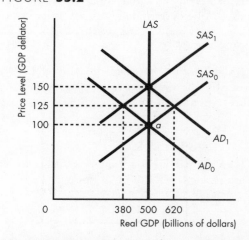

12 If the *AD* curve in Fig. 35.2 is correctly expected to shift from AD_0 to AD_1, what will be the new equilibrium real GDP and price level?

a $380 billion and price level = 125
b $500 billion and price level = 150
c $500 billion and price level = 100
d $620 billion and price level = 125
e $500 billion and price level = 125

13 If the *AD* curve in Fig. 35.2 is expected to shift from AD_0 to AD_1 but, in fact, remains at AD_0, what will be the new equilibrium real GDP and price level?

a $380 billion and price level = 100
b $500 billion and price level = 150
c $500 billion and price level = 100
d $620 billion and price level = 125
e $380 billion and price level = 125

14 If the *AD* curve in Fig. 35.2 is expected to remain at AD_0 but, in fact, shifts to AD_1, what will be the new equilibrium real GDP and price level?

a $380 billion and price level = 125
b $500 billion and price level = 150
c $500 billion and price level = 100
d $620 billion and price level = 125
e $500 billion and price level = 125

15 Figure 35.3 illustrates an economy's Phillips curves. What is the natural rate of unemployment?

a 9 percent
b 6 percent
c 4 percent
d depends on the actual inflation rate
e cannot be determined without more information

FIGURE **35.3**

16 Figure 35.3 illustrates an economy's Phillips curves. What is the expected inflation rate?

a 9 percent
b 4 percent
c 2 percent
d depends on the actual inflation rate
e cannot be determined without more information

17 Figure 35.3 illustrates an economy's Phillips curves. If the current inflation rate is 4 percent, what is the current unemployment rate?

a 9 percent
b 6 percent
c 4 percent
d 3 percent
e cannot be determined without more information

18 A rise in the price level due to a rise in the price of oil

a will create a stagflation in the short run.
b will trigger a price-wage spiral.
c may trigger a price-wage spiral.
d a and b.
e a and c.

19 A fully anticipated increase in the rate of inflation

a is not costly because contracts can be adjusted.
b benefits both workers and employers.
c is costly because it increases the value of money.
d is costly because it encourages an increase in the frequency of transactions that people undertake.
e is costly because it redistributes from lender to borrower.

20 Which of the following is *not* true of a rational expectation forecast?

a It uses all available information.
b It can often be wrong.
c It is always correct.
d It is the best possible forecast.
e Sometimes economic agents purchase their forecasts from specialists.

21 Which of the following would cause the aggregate demand curve to keep shifting rightward year after year?

a a one-time tax cut
b a one-time increase in government purchases of goods and services
c inflation
d excess wage demands
e a positive rate of growth in the quantity of money

22 The current year's price level is 180, and the rate of inflation over the past year has been 20 percent. What was last year's price level?

a 100
b 144
c 150
d 160
e 216

23 The price level is expected to fall because of an expected fall in aggregate demand. If aggregate demand remains unchanged, then the actual price level will

a stay the same and real GDP will stay the same.
b fall and real GDP will decrease.
c rise and real GDP will increase.
d rise and real GDP will decrease.
e fall and real GDP will increase.

24 If the rate of inflation is lower than expected, borrowers

a and lenders both lose.
b and lenders both gain.
c gain but lenders lose.
d lose but lenders gain.
e lose but lenders are just as well off.

25 If the rate of inflation is lower than expected, then

a expectations could not be rational expectations.
b real GDP will be less than potential real GDP.
c the real interest rate will be lower than expected.
d the real wage rate will be lower than expected.
e the money wage rate will be higher than expected.

Short Answer Problems

1 What will happen to the price level and real GDP if the government increases its purchases of goods and services and that increase is not anticipated (the price level is not expected to change)?

2 Explain how the events in Short Answer Problem 1 could lead to a price-wage spiral.

3 What is the relationship between the expected rate of inflation and interest rates?

4 Explain carefully the difference between the short-run Phillips curve and the long-run Phillips curve.

5 Sometimes politicians or other commentators make the following type of statement: "Unemployment is a more serious economic and social problem than inflation. Increasing inflation by a small amount in order to lower unemployment is therefore worthwhile." Briefly evaluate this statement.

6 Why does inflation start? Why does it persist?

7 Table 35.1 gives the initial actual aggregate demand and short-run aggregate supply schedules for an economy in which the expected price level is 80, and potential real GDP is 500.

a What is actual real GDP and the actual price level?

TABLE **35.1** AGGREGATE DEMAND AND SUPPLY

Price Level	Real GDP Demanded	Real GDP Supplied
60	600	400
80	500	500
100	400	600
120	300	700
140	200	700

b In year 1 the economy is in the equilibrium characterized in a. It is *expected* that in year 2, aggregate demand will be as given in Table 35.2. (Assume that the long-run aggregate supply curve is not expected to shift, and does not shift.) What is the *vertical* amount of the expected shift in the aggregate demand curve when real GDP is $500 billion?

TABLE **35.2** AGGREGATE DEMAND AND SUPPLY

Price Level	Real GDP Demanded	Real GDP Supplied
60	800	
80	700	
100	600	
120	500	
140	400	

c What is the (long-run) rational expectation of the price level for year 2?

d The expected shift in aggregate demand will cause the short-run aggregate supply (*SAS*) curve to shift. What will the new *SAS* curve be? For each price level, give the new values of real GDP supplied in the last column of Table 35.2.

8 a Suppose aggregate demand does *not* change but remains as it is in Table 35.1. What will real GDP and the price level be in year 2?

b Calculate the expected and actual inflation rates, and compare them.

9 When the rate of inflation is expected to be zero, Jennifer wants to lend money if the interest rate is at least 5 percent, and Pat wants to borrow money if the interest rate is 5 percent or less. Thus they make a loan agreement at a 5 percent rate of interest if they expect zero inflation.

a If they both expect a rate of inflation of 4 percent over the period of the loan, what interest rate will they agree to?

b If they both expect a rate of *deflation* of 2 percent over the period of the loan, what interest rate will they agree to?

c Suppose Jennifer expects the rate of inflation to be 4 percent, and Pat expects it to be 6 percent. Will they be able to work out a loan agreement? If so, what interest rate will they agree to?

d Suppose that Pat and Jennifer both expect a rate of inflation of 4 percent, and have agreed to the interest rate from your answer to **a**, and a loan of $100 for one year has occurred. Instead of an inflation rate of 4 percent, an actual rate of 9 percent occurs. Who gains, who loses, and how much?

10 The country of Colditz has an expected inflation rate of 8 percent, and its recent inflation and unemployment history is summarized in Table 35.3. Originally both unemployment and inflation are each 8 percent.

TABLE **35.3**

Inflation (% per year)	Unemployment (%)
12	4
10	6
8	8
6	10
4	12

a What is Colditz's natural rate of unemployment?

b Draw a diagram of Colditz's short-run and long-run Phillips curves.

c If inflation unexpectedly rises to 12 percent per year, explain what happens to unemployment.

d Return to the original situation. If the expected inflation rate rises to 10 percent, and the actual inflation rate rises to 10 percent, explain and show on your graph what happens, *ceteris paribus*, to inflation and unemployment.

ANSWERS

True/False/Uncertain and Explain

1 F It makes payments from long-term contracts unpredictable, hurting one side or other. (854)

2 U True if short run, false if long run. (858–860)

3 T Definition. (852)

4 F Cost-push inflation is due to ↑ factor prices. (849–850)

5 T Because lenders demand compensation for inflation. (862–863)

6 T If expected ↑ aggregate demand → ↑ wage demands → leftward shift *SAS* curve, but no Δ *AD* curve → stagflation. (856)

7 T Inflation rate = $((P_1 - P_0)/P_0) \times 100 = ((130 - 120)/120) \times 100 = 8.3$. (848)

8 F *AD* shifts rightward, *SAS* shifts leftward due to higher wage demands → price level rises. (855–856)

9 U True if unanticipated, false if anticipated. (854)

10 F It is vertical at the natural rate of unemployment. (860)

Multiple-Choice

1 c Example of higher transactions costs → others are unanticipated inflation costs. (856–857)

2 e Definition. (858–859)

3 a Definition. (849)

4 a Because interest rates and wage rates too high given actual inflation rate. (854)

5 e Draw a graph. (855–856)

6 c Draw a graph. (855–856)

7 c Initially, real rate = 8 − 5 = 3 percent. New nominal rate = real rate + expected inflation = 3 + 8 = 11 percent. (862)

8 d ↑ growth rate of money supply → ↑ inflation rate → ↑ nominal rate by same amount (since anticipated) → no change in real rate. (855–856)

9 a Because actual price level = expected when *SAS* crosses *LAS*, and equilibrium occurs when *AD* = *SAS* —try drawing a graph. (855–856)

10 a Because actual price level = expected when *SAS* crosses *LAS*, and equilibrium occurs when *AD* = *SAS* —try drawing a graph. (856)

11 a ↑ price of crucial input → ↑ costs of production → shift left in *SAS*. (851–852)

⏱ 12   b   Expected P found from intersection of EAD $= AD_1$, and actual SAS is set here → new equilibrium where actual AD and SAS cross. (855–856)

⏱ 13   e   Expected P found from intersection of EAD $= AD_1$, and actual SAS is set here → new equilibrium where actual AD and SAS cross. (855–856)

⏱ 14   d   Expected P found from intersection of EAD $= AD_0$, and actual SAS is set here → new equilibrium where actual AD and SAS cross. (855–856)

15   a $LRPC$ is at natural rate. (858–860)

16   c   Expected inflation rate is where $SRPC$ crosses $LRPC$. (858–860)

17   c   Found by reading off the $SRPC$. (858–860)

18   e   ↑ price of oil → shift left in SAS curve → cost-push inflation (stagflation), which *may* trigger price-wage spiral *if* government raises aggregate demand. (851–852)

19   d   Higher inflation ↓ value of money → people ↓ money holdings → ↑ transactions. (856–857)

20   c   It is correct on *average*. (855)

21   e   **a** and **b** have one-time effects, **c** is caused by ΔAD and **d** is a supply-side effect. (849)

⏱ 22   c   Invert formula: inflation rate $= ((P_1 - P_0)/P_0)$ $\times 100$. (848)

23   e   ↓ expected price level → shift right SAS → new equilibrium to the right of LAS along original AD curve. (855–856)

24   d   Because interest rate turns out to be too high given actual inflation. (854)

⏱ 25   b   Equilibrium to left of where $SAS = LAS$. Rational expectations can be wrong, real wage rate and real interest rate will be higher than expected, and money wage will be equal to expected. (854–856)

Short Answer Problems

1   An increase in government purchases of goods and services will shift the aggregate demand curve to the right. If the price level is not expected to change, the short-run aggregate supply curve remains unchanged, and the increase in aggregate demand will cause the price level to rise and real GDP to increase.

2   The higher price level leads to demands for higher wages, which push up the costs of production and shift the SAS curve leftward, leading to a further rise in the price level and a fall in real GDP. A price-wage spiral could result *if* the government once again raises the level of their purchases or if the government continues to run a deficit (financed by printing money),

then AD will continue to shift rightward, triggering leftward shifts in SAS, leading to the price-wage spiral.

3   When the rate of inflation is expected to rise, the nominal interest rate will also rise to compensate for the increased rate at which the purchasing power of money is eroding. The essential point is that lenders and borrowers are interested in the quantity of goods and services that a unit of money will buy. Lenders will insist on the higher interest rate, to compensate for the loss of purchasing power of money, and borrowers will agree because they realize that the dollars they repay will buy fewer goods and services.

4   The short-run Phillips curve is constructed assuming that the expected inflation rate is constant, and is therefore downward sloping. As a result, if there is a rise in the inflation rate (and therefore a fall in real wages), there will be a fall in unemployment to a rate below the natural rate. The long-run Phillips curve is constructed assuming that the expected inflation rate adjusts fully to reflect changes in the actual inflation rate, and is therefore vertical at the natural rate of unemployment. If there is a rise in the actual inflation rate, there is an equivalent rise in the expected inflation rate (so that the real wage rate stays constant), and the rate of unemployment stays constant at the natural rate.

5   Partially this statement is a value judgment, based on the tradeoff of a higher cost to society from the higher inflation versus the gain to society from a lower inflation rate. In this case, we would need to evaluate the costs of inflation versus the costs of unemployment. However, there is also a problem with this statement. In the short run, such a tradeoff does exist, represented by the downward-sloping short-run Phillips curve. In the long run, there is no such tradeoff. As a result, a higher inflation rate will lead to a lower unemployment rate in the short run, but eventually inflation expectations will rise, represented by a shift upward in the short-run Phillips curve, and unemployment will return to the natural rate. Therefore in the long run, increasing inflation will have no impact on the unemployment rate, but will increase the costs to society that come from the higher inflation.

6   Inflation is a rise in the price level, and starts with either a shift rightward in the AD curve due to an increase in the money supply, government spending, or exports (demand-pull inflation), or with a shift leftward in the AS

curve due to an increase in wages or raw materials prices (cost-push inflation). However, the rise in the price level in either case can only persist if a price-wage spiral results from the initial shock. A price-wage spiral starts when increases in aggregate demand and shifts leftward in *AS* chase each other up the long-run aggregate supply curve.

7 a Actual real GDP and the actual price level are determined by the intersection of the aggregate demand curve and the short-run aggregate supply curve. Real GDP is $500 billion and the price level is 80, because at a price level of 80, the quantity of real GDP demanded equals the quantity of real GDP supplied ($500 billion).

b The price level associated with $500 billion of real GDP demanded for the original aggregate demand curve (Table 35.1) is 80. The price level associated with $500 billion of real GDP demanded for the new expected aggregate demand curve (Table 35.2) is 120. Therefore the aggregate demand curve is expected to shift upward by 40.

c The rational expectation of the price level is given by the intersection of the expected aggregate demand curve (Table 35.2) and the expected long-run aggregate supply curve. Long-run aggregate supply is equal to $500 billion and is not expected to change. Since the price level associated with $500 billion of real GDP demanded is 120, the rational expectation of the price level is 120.

d The quantities of real GDP supplied for the new *SAS* curve are shown in completed Table 35.2 Solution. The original expected price level is 80. From part **b** we know that the new expected price level is 120, which implies that the *SAS* curve shifts up by 40. Thus at each quantity of real GDP supplied, the price level on the new *SAS* curve is 40 points higher than on the original *SAS* curve (Table 35.1).

For example, real GDP supplied of $500 billion now requires a price level of 120 rather than 80. Similarly, real GDP supplied of $400 billion now requires a price level of 100 rather than 60. [*Note:* The values in parentheses in this table are inferred by extrapolation rather than calculated from Table 35.1.]

TABLE 35.2 SOLUTION
AGGREGATE DEMAND AND SUPPLY

Price Level	Real GDP Demanded	Real GDP Supplied
60	800	(200)
80	700	(300)
100	600	400
120	500	500
140	400	600

8 a The new macroeconomic equilibrium in year 2 will occur at the intersection of the actual *AD* curve and the relevant *SAS* curve. Since the *AD* curve was expected to shift, the relevant *SAS* curve is the one associated with the expected price level of 120 (the *SAS* curve completed in Table 35.2 Solution). But the *AD* curve did not actually shift, thus the *AD* curve is given in Table 35.1. The intersection of these curves is at real GDP equal to $400 billion and price level equal to 100. When the price level is 100, the quantity of real GDP demanded is equal to the quantity of real GDP supplied at $400 billion.

b Expected inflation is 50 percent = $((120 - 80)/80) \times 100$, more than actual inflation of 25 percent = $((100 - 80)/80) \times 100$.

9 a Since both Jennifer and Pat expect the rate of inflation to be 4 percent, they expect the value of money to decrease by 4 percent. Thus they will agree to a 9 percent rate of interest to offset this, leaving a 5 percent real rate of interest paid after accounting for inflation.

b If both Jennifer and Pat expect a rate of deflation of 2 percent, they expect the value of money to increase by 2 percent. By the same logic as above, they will agree to a 3 percent rate of interest.

c If Jennifer expects a 4 percent rate of inflation, she will want to lend only if the interest rate is at least 9 percent. Pat expects a 6 percent rate of inflation and will borrow if the rate of interest is 11 percent or less. Thus Jennifer and Pat could agree on any interest rate between 9 and 11 percent.

d From **a**, we know that they will agree to an interest rate of 9 percent, meaning Pat repays $109. Jennifer expects a real gain of $5 (she can buy 5 percent more goods), after accounting for the 4 percent inflation. However, the actual 9 percent inflation raises the price of goods by 9 percent, so that her $109 after one year buys only the same amount of goods as the $100 did originally. She has therefore lost $5, and Pat has gained the $5, due to the real interest rate of zero.

10 a The natural rate of unemployment is the rate of unemployment that occurs when the actual rate of inflation equals the expected rate of inflation—in this case, the natural rate of unemployment is 8 percent.

   b See Fig. 35.4. The long-run Phillips curve is vertical at the natural rate of unemployment. The current short-run curve is $SRPC_0$ (ignore the other short-run curve for the moment).

FIGURE **35.4**

c In this case, the relevant short-run Phillips curve is $SRPC_0$, the curve for an expected inflation rate of 8 percent. From the curve (or Table 35.3), it can be seen that with inflation equal to 12 percent, unemployment is 4 percent at the point *a*.

d A rise in the expected inflation rate will shift the short-run Phillips curve to a new curve, with the new curve crossing the long-run Phillips curve at the new expected inflation rate of 10 percent. (The actual shape of the curve is not clear without further information, so it has been assumed that the new curve is parallel to the old curve.) If the actual inflation rate is 10 percent, then the unemployment rate will be 8 percent, at the natural rate, at the point *b*.

Macroeconomic Policy Challenges

Policy Goals

Five main macroeconomic goals.

◆ *Achieving highest sustainable rate of potential GDP growth* can dramatically improve real GDP per person.

◆ *Smoothing out avoidable business fluctuations* can reduce lost output and bottleneck costs.

◆ *Maintaining unemployment at the natural rate* reduces losses from high unemployment and bottleneck costs of too low unemployment, but it is difficult to estimate natural rate.

◆ *Maintaining low inflation* avoids transactions costs and costs of unpredictable inflation.

◆ *Lowering current account deficit* to its efficient level reduces unnecessary borrowing costs.

◆ The goals of ↑ real GDP growth, smoothing business cycle, and keeping unemployment at natural rate are complementary → concentrating on real GDP growth is one core policy target, and inflation is the other.

◆ Real GDP growth goal conflicts with the inflation goal in the short run.

Policy Tools and Performance

Federal government uses **fiscal policy** (Δ tax rates, benefit rates, and government expenditures), and Bank of Canada uses **monetary policy** (Δ money supply and interest rates) to achieve macroeconomic policy goals.

◆ Fiscal policy expansionary under Trudeau and contractionary under Mulroney → followed a cycle similar to business cycle.

◆ Monetary policy expansionary in late 1970s and anti-inflationary in early 1980s, and again in 1989.

Long-Term Growth Policy

Long-term growth comes from accumulation of physical and human capital, and new technology → government policy can affect these somewhat.

◆ National saving = private saving + government saving.

  • Private saving risen since 1970, but rising government dissaving has meant national saving has fluctuated around 17 percent.
  • ↓ government deficits → ↓ government dissaving → ↑ national saving.
  • ↓ specific taxes, ↓ inflation rate → ↑ private saving.

◆ Social returns to human capital > private returns → government wishes to ↑ investment in human capital → subsidizes schooling.

◆ Investments in new technologies ↑ growth strongly due to lack of diminishing returns, spillovers → governments fund and provide tax incentives for research and development.

Business Cycle and Unemployment Policy

◆ Three alternative policies to stabilize business cycle, and minimize cyclical unemployment:

  • **Fixed-rule policy** is independent of state of the economy, such as always balancing budget.
  • **Feedback-rule policy** specifies responses to changes in state of economy, such as cutting tax rates in a recession.

- **Discretionary policy** responds to state of economy in unique manner—learning from past mistakes in similar situations.

◆ Fixed and feedback rules react differently to aggregate demand shocks.

◆ Suppose ↓ AD → recession.

- **Monetarist** advocates fixed rule of doing nothing → recession eventually ends when ↑ AD again (temporary shock), or SAS shifts right as wages fall (permanent shock).
- **Keynesian activist** advocates feedback rule of expansionary fiscal and monetary policy to try to *counter* swings in AD → return economy to full employment quickly.
- Economy stays in recession longer under fixed rule.

◆ In theory, feedback rules seem superior, but some economists argue that in practice flawed because they

- require greater knowledge of potential GDP than currently available.
- operate with time lags, making precise decisions difficult.
- introduce unpredictability into long-term contracting since feedback rule must be inferred.

◆ Fourth argument against feedback rules is they fail in face of aggregate supply shocks, such as productivity slowdowns emphasized by RBC theory.

- Feedback rule raises AD → further rises in the price level, output unchanged.
- Fixed rule does nothing → no further rises in price level, output unchanged.

◆ Governments can also try to reduce natural rate of unemployment, by ↓ unemployment compensation and minimum wage, or reducing regional differences in unemployment.

Inflation Policy

◆ Cost-push inflation arises from ↑ in factor prices shifting SAS leftward.

- Feedback rule raises AD → further rises in the price level, output back to full employment. This *accommodates* the inflation, encouraging further rises in factor prices.
- Fixed rule does nothing → no further rises in price level, eventually factor prices and SAS return to original levels.

◆ In theory, inflation can be tamed by reducing the growth of aggregate demand in a credible and predictable manner → reducing expectations and wage demands without creating recession.

◆ In practice, anti-inflationary policy → recession.

◆ Economic agents do not always believe an announced anti-inflationary policy because in the past announced policies have been abandoned → do not revise expectations downward → recession results when actual AD less than expected.

◆ Bank of Canada suffers from **time-inconsistency problem**—anti-inflationary plans look bad when viewed at a later time period, and are abandoned.

Current Account Policy

Reducing fluctuations in cycle reduces fluctuations in current account, but it still could be too high at potential GDP.

◆ ↓ AD would cut deficit, but create conflicts.

◆ ↓ interest rates → dollar depreciates → ↑ net exports, ↓ deficit, but also ↑ money supply and price level, which offset effect of depreciation.

◆ ↑ tariffs and quotas is often suggested to ↑ net exports, but in fact ↓ imports → foreigners cannot buy as much from us → ↓ exports too.

◆ Current account balance = (private saving – investment) + (taxes – government expenditures) → cutting government deficit would tend to restore current account balance.

H E L P F U L   H I N T S

1 In this chapter, only a few new concepts are introduced, and the model developed in previous chapters is used to analyse the effects of policy. This represents a payoff for all the effort required to master that model.

However, this chapter asks the most important macroeconomic question—can the government and the Bank of Canada carry out successful fiscal and monetary policies to reduce the problems of the business cycle?

2 There are numerous complications that arise in real-world use of the aggregate demand and aggregate supply models to make policy decisions. In previous chapters these were simplified to maximize learning. Now, a more realistic perspective of problems that confront a

policy maker is given. Among the most important problems is the inability to predict the *magnitude* or the *timing* of factors that affect aggregate demand or aggregate supply.

a Our macroeconomic model is a good guide to the *qualitative* effects of changes in factors that affect aggregate demand and aggregate supply. For example, we know that an increase in the money supply will shift the aggregate demand curve rightward. When conducting policy, however, qualitative knowledge is not sufficient. We must also have *quantitative* knowledge. We must know *how much* a given increase in the money supply will increase aggregate demand.

While we may have an understanding of the direction of the effect, knowledge of the magnitude of the effect is much more difficult to obtain and much more limited. This reduces the potential for policy to be used to "fine tune" the economy.

b In addition to direction and magnitude, we must also know *timing*. The full effect on aggregate demand of policy changes made today will not be immediate. Much, if not most, of that effect will occur only with considerable time lags. Thus it is important that policy makers be able to predict these time lags in order to be confident that the future effect of a policy change made today will be appropriate when the effect actually occurs.

Unfortunately, that is extremely difficult. Lags are often long and vary in length. This makes them unpredictable. As a result, policy makers may initiate a policy today which, when it has its effect sometime in the future, turns out to shift aggregate demand in the "wrong" direction because circumstances have changed. In such a case, policy will actually turn out to be destabilizing and therefore worse than doing nothing at all.

Consider the following analogy of the goal of driving a car from your house to the house of a friend. The policy goal is to get the car from here to there. To make this simple, consider a single policy tool: the steering wheel. If you want the car to turn right, you turn the steering wheel clockwise. To turn left, you turn the steering wheel counterclockwise. Note that the direction in which the steering wheel turns is important, but so is the magnitude of the turn in order that the car can change direction without accident. Most of us can steer a car rather well because there is essentially no lag between the time we turn the steering wheel and the turning of the front wheels of the car. Now, consider how the task would be complicated if there is a time lag of one minute. In this case, a

much better prediction of where the car will be one minute hence is required. Consider how the task would be complicated further if there is not only a time lag but the length of that time lag is variable, and thus unpredictable. You might choose to stay home (a fixed policy).

In the real world, cars do not operate with this type of lag. However, a large ship at sea typically operates with this length of lag. This can make piloting a ship very difficult.

3 This chapter presents two opposing views of the usefulness of countercyclical policy. These views come partially from differing assumptions about one crucial factor—the speed with which the private sector reacts to macroeconomic shocks relative to the speed with which the government sector reacts.

The advocates of fixed rules (real business cycle theorists, monetarists, new classical theorists) believe on the whole that the private sector reacts quickly—people have rational expectations, process new information quickly because there are economic incentives to do so, sign flexible wage contracts that allow wages to react quickly to changes in the price level. They also believe that the government sector reacts slowly because of lags in recognizing problems, implementing policy, and carrying out policy. Fixed-rule advocates therefore arrive logically at the conclusion that feedback rules are doomed at best to impotence, and at worse can harm the economy.

The advocates of feedback rules (Keynesians, new Keynesian theorists) believe that the private sector reacts slowly—people sign long-term contracts that prevent wages from reacting quickly to changes in the price level. They also believe that the government sector can react more quickly than the private sector and, therefore arrive logically at the conclusion that feedback rules can make the economy better off by speeding up the recovery from recession.

As of yet, no clear-cut empirical evidence favours either viewpoint.

4 Many students (and policy makers!) fall into the trap of thinking that it is obvious that feedback rules must be better than fixed rules, since theoretically feedback rules seem to be able to do everything fixed rules can, plus more. Do not fall into this trap! There are many problems with the actual implementation of feedback rules in the real world: they require very good knowledge of the economy (for example, the level of full employment); they introduce unpredictability into the economy; they can generate *bigger*

fluctuations in aggregate demand, due to the lags mentioned previously; they do not work for aggregate supply shocks. These reasons make it far from obvious that feedback rules are better than fixed rules.

S E L F - T E S T

True/False/Uncertain and Explain

1 Aggregate supply shocks are more frequent than aggregate demand shocks.

2 The use of feedback rules cannot make the business cycle worse.

3 A current account deficit can be cut without affecting other policy goals by raising the money supply.

4 One of the goals of economic policy is to reduce the unemployment rate below its natural rate.

5 In Canada, fiscal policy is implemented by the federal government.

6 The use of a feedback rule rather than a fixed rule increases the likelihood of cost-push inflation.

7 Increasing private saving and the government deficit will increase the economic growth rate.

8 Recent Canadian monetary experience suggests that anti-inflationary monetary policy does not work.

9 Cost-push inflation cannot persist unless it is accommodated by the central bank.

10 A feedback policy rule is superior to a fixed rule.

Multiple-Choice

1 Which of the following is *true*? Monetary policy affects the economy
a immediately, and fiscal policy affects it immediately.
b immediately, and fiscal policy does not affect it at all.
c immediately, and fiscal policy affects it after a lag.
d after a lag, and fiscal policy affects it immediately.
e after a lag, and fiscal policy affects it after a lag.

2 An economy is initially in full-employment equilibrium when a drought occurs. This is an aggregate _____ shock and a _____ rule will raise inflation with no impact on real GDP.
a demand; fixed
b supply; fixed
c demand; discretionary
d demand; feedback
e supply; feedback

3 An economy is initially in full-employment equilibrium when consumer confidence falls. This is an aggregate _____ shock and a _____ rule will raise real GDP back to its original value.
a demand; fixed
b demand; feedback
c supply; monetary
d demand; fiscal
e supply; fixed

4 Which of the following is an example of a fixed policy rule?
a Wear your boots if it snows.
b Leave your boots home if it does not snow.
c Wear your boots every day.
d Take your boots off in the house if they are wet.
e Listen to the weather forecast and then decide whether to wear your boots.

5 Time inconsistency is

a maintaining a steady growth of nominal GDP.

b maintaining the same policy that you planned to carry out at an earlier date.

c the problem that arises with feedback rules due to time lags in implementing policies.

d carrying out the same policy regardless of the state of the economy.

e when a plan that originally looked good, looks bad when the time comes around to carry it out.

6 Which of the following is an argument *for* a feedback rule?

a Feedback rules require greater knowledge of the natural rate than we have.

b Feedback rules introduce unpredictability.

c Aggregate supply shocks cause most economic fluctuations.

d Aggregate demand shocks cause most economic fluctuations.

e Feedback rules generate bigger fluctuations in aggregate demand.

7 Over the 1980s in Canada, fiscal policy featured

a constantly rising deficits.

b constantly falling deficits.

c an expansionary policy.

d a somewhat contractionary policy.

e a and c.

8 Over the 1980s in Canada, monetary policy featured

a rising growth of M2+.

b falling growth of M2+.

c rising inflation.

d zero inflation.

e a cycle in the growth of M2+ that tended to counter fiscal policy.

9 Cost-push inflation is best met by a(n)

a fixed rule.

b feedback rule.

c discretionary policy.

d political business cycle.

e socialist approach.

10 Taming inflation is difficult because

a the Bank of Canada is too independent.

b the Phillips curve shows that unemployment always rises when inflation falls.

c the natural rate of inflation is equal to 6 percent.

d surprise anti-inflationary policies work well.

e of time inconsistency.

11 In practice, inflation reduction

a worked in 1982 without any unemployment resulting.

b worked in 1990 without any unemployment resulting.

c never worked.

d worked well due to time inconsistency.

e none of the above.

12 Fighting inflation through the use of contractionary policy is

a generally endorsed by politicians in election years.

b generally unpopular with politicians in election years.

c a zero-cost way to reduce inflation.

d always easily accepted by workers.

e an example of a fixed rule.

13 Attempting to lower a current account deficit by lowering interest rates will not work because

a lowering interest rates raises spending and the current account deficit.

b lowering interest rates raises the money supply and the price level, leading to an offsetting fall in net exports.

c changing interest rates has no impact on the current account deficit.

d lowering interest rates raises private saving and therefore raises the current account deficit.

e lowering interest rates raises the government deficit and therefore raises the current account deficit.

14 The best way to cut a current account deficit is to

a lower aggregate demand.

b raise private investment.

c raise the government deficit.

d lower the government deficit.

e raise tariffs and quotas.

15 Fixed-rule monetary policies are intended to

a bring long-run inflationary pressures under control.

b counteract temporary increases in aggregate demand.

c counteract temporary decreases in real output.

d offset supply shocks.

e keep real GDP growth high.

16 Economists who favour fixed rules over feedback rules argue that policy lags are

a shorter than the forecast horizon and that potential GDP is known reasonably well.

b shorter than the forecast horizon and that potential GDP is not known.

c longer than the forecast horizon and that potential GDP is known reasonably well.

d longer than the forecast horizon and that potential GDP is not known.

e equal to the forecast horizon and that full-employment real GDP is constant.

17 If the Bank of Canada announces its intention to reduce the rate of growth of the money supply, but it lacks credibility, the short-run Phillips curve will

a shift leftward.

b shift rightward.

c not move.

d become vertical.

e become flatter.

18 If the Bank of Canada announces its intention to slow the rate of growth of the money supply, and has full credibility, the short-run Phillips curve will

a quickly shift leftward.

b quickly shift rightward.

c not shift.

d become horizontal.

e **a** and **d**.

19 Which of the following is one of the two core macroeconomic policy targets?

a unemployment constant at 6 percent

b steady growth in real GDP

c steady growth in nominal GDP

d a flexible exchange rate

e inflation at the natural rate

20 If the marginal tax rate _____, the returns to saving ____.

a rises; are unchanged

b falls; fall

c falls; rise

d falls; are unchanged

e rises; rise

21 Which of the following is *not* a long-term growth determinant that can be influenced by government policy?

a national saving

b investment in human capital

c investment in consumer durables

d investment in new technologies

e government deficits

22 From 1970 to 1995, national saving averaged

a 10 percent.

b 15 percent.

c 17 percent.

d 25 percent.

e 30 percent.

23 According to real business cycle theories,

a any decline in real GDP is a decline in long-run real GDP.

b wages are flexible but labour market equilibrium does not necessarily imply full employment.

c fluctuations in aggregate demand change long-run real GDP.

d fluctuations in aggregate demand cannot affect the price level.

e feedback rules are best.

24 A fixed rule for monetary policy

a requires considerable knowledge of how changes in the money supply affect the economy.

b would be impossible for the Bank of Canada to achieve.

c generates bigger fluctuations in aggregate demand.

d would result in constant real GDP.

e minimizes the threat of cost-push inflation.

25 Government deficits tend to lower economic growth because they

a lower aggregate demand.

b increase private investment and lower private saving.

c are a time-inconsistent policy.

d lower expenditure on research and development.

e crowd out national saving by using up some of private saving.

Short Answer Problems

1 The Bank of Bohemia is attempting to lower inflation in Bohemia from 8 percent, but the policy is leading to higher real interest rates and real wage rates.

a What do the high real interest rates and real wage rates indicate about expectations and this policy?

b Some business observers are objecting to this policy, arguing that the high real interest rates are choking off investment and future growth. Comment on the validity of this argument.

2 The prime minister of Bohemia has made the following statement: "We are reducing government expenditure to reduce the deficit and create more jobs." How can this be true? Won't reducing government expenditure reduce aggregate demand and create unemployment?

3 Distinguish between a fixed rule and a feedback rule.

4 The purpose of policy is to stabilize. How can feedback rules result in even greater variability in aggregate demand?

5 If the Bank of Canada announced its intention to reduce the rate of inflation by reducing the rate of growth of the money supply, expected inflation would decline accordingly, and thus a reduction in the actual rate of inflation could be achieved without a recession. Why does this not seem to be the case?

6 Assume that the Bank of Canada knows exactly how much and when the aggregate demand curve will shift, both in the absence of monetary policy and when the Bank of Canada changes the money supply.

In this environment, compare the effects on real GDP and the price level of a temporary decline in aggregate demand that returns gradually to its previous level over several periods under fixed and feedback policy rules. Assume the economy is initially at long-run real GDP and that long-run real GDP is constant. Illustrate each of the following rules on a separate graph.

a First, assume that the Bank of Canada follows the fixed rule: Hold the money supply constant.

b Now, assume that the Bank of Canada follows the feedback rule: Increase the money supply whenever aggregate demand falls and decrease the money supply whenever aggregate demand rises.

7 Consider an economy that experiences a temporary increase in aggregate demand. The Bank of Canada follows a feedback rule similar to the one given in Short Answer Problem **6b**, but now we assume that the Bank of Canada does *not* have perfect knowledge of how much and when aggregate demand will shift.

In year 1, the economy is in macroeconomic equilibrium at long-run real GDP, but, as the year ends, there is a burst of optimism about the future, which initiates a (temporary) rise in aggregate demand. As a result, in year 2, real GDP increases and the rate of unemployment falls below its natural rate. Given its feedback rule, the Bank of Canada reduces the money supply "to keep the economy from overheating." The effect on aggregate demand, however, takes place only after a time lag of one year. In year 3, this burst of optimism returns to its previous level and thus so does aggregate demand. In addition, the monetary policy implemented in year 2 finally has its effect on aggregate demand in year 3. Analyse the behaviour of real GDP and the price level using three graphs: one each for years 1, 2, and 3. Assume that all changes in aggregate demand are unanticipated and that long-run real GDP is constant. Did a feedback monetary policy rule stabilize aggregate demand?

8 Assume that real business cycle theories are correct. There is a fall in long-run real GDP due to droughts on the Prairies. First, graph the effect on real GDP and the price level if the Bank of Canada follows the fixed rule: Hold the money supply constant. Then, on the same graph, illustrate the effect on real GDP and the price level if the Bank of Canada follows the feedback rule: Increase the money supply whenever real GDP falls and decrease the money supply whenever real GDP rises.

◑ 9 Consider a central bank that decides to start an anti-inflationary policy. Figure 36.1 shows the initial state of the economy (point *a*) and the expected state next period (point *b*). The bank decides to carry out a gradual policy of inflation reduction. In year 1, it will reduce the growth in *AD* to 5 percent; in year 2 it will reduce the growth in *AD* to 2.5 percent. If the policy is unexpected initially, show on the graph what will occur over the next few years.

FIGURE **36.1**

10 You are an economic advisor to the governor of the Bank of Canada. Recently the economy has slid into a recession—unemployment has risen from 7 percent to 11 percent, the price level has risen from 125 to 135, and real GDP has fallen from 200 billion 1986 dollars to 180 billion 1986 dollars. Two other advisors are attempting to persuade the governor of the validity of their arguments. Ms. F. Ixed argues that this is a *LAS* shock, with full-employment real GDP falling and the natural rate of unemployment rising. Therefore she insists, the optimal policy is to do nothing. Mr. F. E. Edback argues that this recession is due to an unexpectedly low *AD*, and that the optimal policy is to carry out an expansionary monetary policy.

a The governor, Jane Raven, has asked you to draw an *AS–AD* graph for each argument, to test its veracity. No explanation is necessary other than to indicate where the original and new equilibriums are. Are both arguments theoretically possible?

b Ms. Ixed also argues that even if it is an *AD* shock that has caused the current recession, using a feedback policy will just make the economy worse. She argues that timing lags in the implementation of monetary policy mean that the stimulation to aggregate demand will come too late to do any good and will just do harm. Explain and illustrate her argument on the graph you have drawn for Mr. Edback's explanation of the recession.

c Governor Raven wants your advice. Should she order an expansionary monetary policy? Why or why not?

ANSWERS

True/False/Uncertain and Explain

1 U There is no strong economic evidence either way. (882)

2 F If there are timing lags → feedback policy can arrive too late → makes cycle worse. (881–882)

3 F ↑ money supply → ↓ interest rates → ↓ exchange rate → ↑ net exports and ↓ current account deficit, but Δ interest rates and exchange rate → ↑*AD*, with impacts on price level, etc. (888)

4 F One goal is to keep unemployment at natural rate. (871)

5 T It chooses spending, taxation, and deficit → fiscal policy. (873)

6 T Feedback rules accommodate wage increases. (884–885)

7 U Depends on relative sizes, because growth is affected by national saving = private saving + government saving. (876)

8 F Inflation was lowered both in 1982–1985 and in 1990–1992, at the cost of ↑ unemployment. (887–888)

9 T If not accommodated ↑ unemployment → ↓ factor prices → *SAS* shifts rightward → price level returns to original level. (884–885)

10 U It depends on which theory you think is best. (881–882)

Multiple-Choice

1 e Due to policy lags and a short forecast horizon. (881–882)

2 e Drought → *LAS* shifts leftward. Raising *AD* (feedback rule) has no impact on real GDP. (882–883)

3 b ↓ consumer confidence → ↓ consumption → shift leftward in *AD*. A feedback rule will raise *AD* and counter shock. (879–880)

4 c Same choice regardless of circumstances. (878)

5 e Definition. (887–888)

6 d Others are reasons *against* feedback rules. (878–881)

7 d See text discussion. (873–874)

8 e See text discussion. (874–875)

9 a Keeping *AD* constant does not accommodate inflation and reduces chances of future cost-push inflation. (884–886)

10 e Time inconsistency → actual anti-inflationary policies are not always carried out → hard to promise credibly to reduce inflation → expectations do not fall easily → unemployment results when anti-inflationary policy is carried out. (887–888)

11 e In both 1982 and 1990, unemployment resulted due to time inconsistency, but inflation was reduced. (887–888)

12 b Because it generally means unemployment, which voters weigh as being more important than inflation fighting. (887–888)

13 b See text discussion. (888–889)

14 d Since current account balance = (private saving − investment) + (taxes − government expenditures). (889)

15 a They ignore short-run pressures. (884–885)

16 d Therefore policy arrives too late, and is often incorrect. (878–882)

17 c Expectations will not change. (886–888)

18 a As inflation expectations are reduced. (886–888)

19 b See text discussion. (871–872)

20 c Lower marginal tax rate → more after-tax earnings from saving. (876–877)

21 c See text discussion. (876–877)

22 c See text discussion. (876)

23 a Because aggregate supply curves are all vertical at long-run real GDP. (882–883)

24 e Because it would not accommodate cost-push inflation, reducing likelihood of future cost-push inflation. (881)

25 e Since national saving = private saving + government saving. (876)

Short Answer Problems

1 a The fact that real interest rates and real wage rates have shot up indicate that this is an unexpected policy—if it was expected and working, the rates would be constant.

   b The higher real interest rates will indeed lower investment, meaning a lower capital stock and less growth of potential GDP in the long run. However, the lower inflation will also raise growth, as we saw in Chapter 35. The net effect is probably less growth in the short run, and more growth in the long run, once real interest rates come back down.

2 Indeed, in the short run, reducing government expenditures will reduce aggregate demand and create unemployment. However, in the long run, the lower government deficit will raise national saving, raise economic growth, and presumably create more jobs.

3 A fixed rule specifies an action that will be pursued regardless of the state of the economy, whereas a feedback rule specifies actions that may change depending on the state of the economy.

4 Policy actions, for example, an open market operation, will affect aggregate demand only after a time lag. This means that a policy action that is taken today will have its intended effect sometime in the future. Therefore it is necessary for policy makers to forecast the state of the economy for a year or two to be confident that the effect of the policy action taken today will be appropriate when the effect occurs. This is very difficult to do since the lags are long (one to two years) and unpredictable. As a result, policy makers face a very good chance that the policy action taken today will have a future effect opposite to what originally seemed appropriate; in other words, policy could destabilize rather than stabilize aggregate demand.

5 The problem is that expected inflation may not decline as a result of the announcement by the Bank of Canada. There may be a credibility problem because expectations are much more strongly affected by the Bank's record of actions than by its announcement to take action. If people do not believe the Bank of Canada, they will not adjust expectations. Then if the Bank of Canada carries out the policy, a recession will result in spite of the fact that an announcement was made. In addition, sticky wages could slow down the adjustment of the labour market.

6 a The behaviour of real GDP and the price level under the fixed rule is illustrated in Fig. 36.2(a). The economy is initially at point a on the aggregate demand curve AD_0: the price level is P_0, and real GDP is at its long-run value denoted Y_0. The temporary decline in aggregate demand shifts the aggregate demand curve downward to AD_1.

   Since the money supply is held constant under the fixed rule, the new equilibrium is at point b: the price level has fallen to P_1, and real GDP has fallen to Y_1. The economy is in recession. As the aggregate demand curve gradually returns to AD_0, the price level gradually rises to P_0 and real GDP gradually returns to Y_0.

FIGURE **36.2**

(a)

(b)

b The behaviour of real GDP and the price level under the feedback rule is illustrated in Fig. 36.2(b). Once again the economy is initially at point a on the aggregate demand curve AD_0. The temporary decline in aggregate demand temporarily shifts the aggregate demand curve to AD_1. Given the Bank of Canada's feedback rule, it will increase the money supply sufficiently to shift the AD_1 curve back to AD_0. Thus the Bank of Canada offsets the decline in aggregate demand and equilibrium remains at point a: the price level remains at P_0 and real GDP remains at Y_0.

As the temporary causes of the decline in aggregate demand dissipate, the aggregate demand curve will begin gradually shifting upward. The Bank of Canada will then decrease the money supply just enough to offset these shifts. As a result, the aggregate demand curve will remain at AD_0 and equilibrium will remain at point a. In these circumstances, the feedback rule is superior to the fixed rule—the recession is shorter in duration.

7 The state of the economy in years 1, 2, and 3 is illustrated in Fig. 36.3, parts (a), (b), and (c), respectively. The initial equilibrium (point a) in year 1 is illustrated in part (a). The economy is producing at long-run real GDP (Y_1) and the price level is P_1.

In year 2, the aggregate demand curve shifts to AD_2 in part (b) because of the burst of optimism. The Bank of Canada also reduces the money supply, but there is no immediate effect on aggregate demand. Therefore the equilibrium in year 2 occurs at the intersection of the AD_2 and SAS curves; at point b in part (b). Real GDP has risen to Y_2, which is above long-run real GDP, and the price level has risen to P_2.

In year 3, there are two effects on aggregate demand. First, the burst of optimism expires, pushing the aggregate demand curve back from AD_2 to AD_1. But, in addition, the Bank of

Canada's reduction in the money supply initiated in year 2 finally has its effect on aggregate demand in year 3. As a result, the aggregate demand curve shifts all the way down to AD_3, and the new equilibrium is at point c in part (c). The price level has fallen to P_3, and real GDP has fallen to Y_3, which is below its long-run value. The Bank of Canada's feedback policy in year 2 has caused a recession in year 3 even though it looked like the right policy when it was implemented. Note that if the Bank of Canada had been following a fixed rule it would not have changed the money supply in year 2 and as a result, in year 3, the equilibrium would have been at point a and real GDP would have been at capacity. Because of imperfect knowledge on the part of the Bank of Canada and the delayed effect of policy changes, the feedback rule has resulted in destabilizing aggregate demand; policy has increased the *variability* of aggregate demand.

FIGURE **36.3**

(a)

(b)

(c)

8 The effects on real GDP and the price level are illustrated in Fig. 36.4. Because we *assume* that real business cycle theories are correct, the only aggregate supply curve is the potential GDP curve. The economy is initially in equilibrium at the intersection of the AD_0 and LAS_0 curves, point *a*. Real GDP is Y_0, and the price level is P_0. Then long-run real GDP falls, and the aggregate supply curve shifts leftward from LAS_0 to LAS_1.

If the Bank of Canada follows the fixed policy rule, it will hold the money supply constant, and the aggregate demand curve will remain at AD_0. Thus the new equilibrium is at point *b*: real GDP will fall to Y_1 (the new capacity), and the price level will have risen to P_1. If, on the other hand, the Bank of Canada follows the feedback rule, the fall in real GDP will lead the Bank of Canada to increase the money supply, which will shift the aggregate demand curve rightward from AD_0 to AD_1. Note that monetary policy will have no effect on long-run real GDP and thus no effect on the (long-run) aggregate supply curve. Therefore, under the feedback policy rule, the new equilibrium is at point *c*: real GDP has remained at Y_1, but the price level has risen to P_2. The consequence of a feedback rule is a larger increase in the price level (higher inflation) with no effect on real GDP.

FIGURE **36.4**

9 The anti-inflationary policy is illustrated in Fig. 36.1 Solution. It will reduce the growth of aggregate demand to a (vertical) distance of 5 percent, at AD_1. However, the actual SAS will be based on the expected inflation rate of 10 percent, and therefore SAS_1 is the relevant curve, yielding an equilibrium in year 1 at the point *c*, with a fall in real GDP, and a rise in inflation of (say) 7.5 percent, less than expected.

In year 2, the central bank allows aggregate demand to rise a further 2.5 percent, or a vertical rise to 107.625 (105×102.5), crossing the potential GDP curve at the point *d*, where AD_2 and LAS cross. The actual impact on the economy depends on how much adjustment of expectations occurs. If the policy is now credible, and if wages can adjust sufficiently, there will be a fall in the short-run aggregate supply curve to SAS_2, and the equilibrium will be at the point *d*, with a very small inflation, and with real GDP back to the natural rate.

FIGURE **36.1** SOLUTION

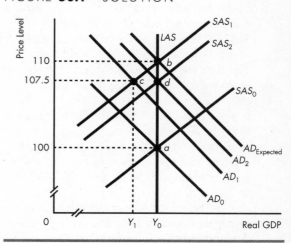

10 a Ms. Ixed's argument is shown in Fig. 36.5(a), and Mr. Edback's in Fig. 36.5(b). The original equilibrium is at point *a*, and the new equilibrium is at point *b*. As the graphs show, both arguments are theoretically possible.

FIGURE **36.5**

(a)

Real GDP (billions of 1986 dollars)

(b)

Real GDP (billions of 1986 dollars)

b She is arguing that the stimulation to aggregate demand (shown as the shift from AD_0 to AD_1) arrives after wages start to adjust downward (shown by SAS_1 shifting to SAS_0). Therefore the new equilibrium is at the point c, with the economy overheating due to the expansionary monetary policy.

c Which policy you pick is a matter of choice. However, your choice should be based on an economic argument. You would support a feedback rule if you thought (a) it was an AD shock, and (b) the central bank could successively and quickly implement the appropriate stimulation. You would pick a fixed rule of doing nothing if you thought (a) it was an AS shock, or (b) even if it was an AD shock, the Bank of Canada reacts too slowly or incorrectly when carrying out the policy.

PROBLEM

You have been hired as an economic consultant for the premier of the country of Nova Caledonia. The economy of Nova Caledonia is experiencing a recession, reflected in the data in Table P8.1.

TABLE **P8.1**

	Year 1	Year 2
Price Level (GDP deflator)	125	130
Real GDP (billions of constant dollars)	200	190
Real wages (billions of constant dollars)	15.00	15.45
Employment (billions of hours)	100	90
Unemployment (%)	8	11

One set of advisors (new Keynesians) have told the premier that the recession has been caused by an unexpected fall in aggregate demand (due to an unexpected fall in exports), combined with sticky wages (inflation was expected to remain constant at 7 percent).

a Explain briefly to the premier what these advisors think is happening to the market for goods and services (draw an *AD–AS* graph as part of your answer), and in the labour market (just describe what is going on, do not draw a graph).

Another set of advisors (real business cycle theorists) have argued that the above events are due solely to an aggregate supply shock, driven by technological change.

b Explain briefly to the premier what these advisors think is happening to the market for goods and services (draw an *AD–AS* graph as part of your answer), and in the labour market (just describe what is going on, do not draw a graph of the labour market).

c After this explanation, and your sorry admission that there is no clear consensus on which view is correct, the premier wants to know what happens if
i he believes the new Keynesian argument, and follows the appropriate policy, *but* the real business cycle argument turns out to be correct, or if
ii he believes the real business cycle argument, and follows the appropriate policy, *but* the Keynesian argument turns out to be correct.

d The premier has decided to pick an expansionary policy, but cannot decide between raising government spending, or cutting taxes. He wishes to know which policy is better if he is concerned about economic growth as well as the business cycle.

MIDTERM EXAMINATION

You should allocate 24 minutes for this examination (12 questions, 2 minutes per question). For each question, choose the one *best* answer.

1 A rise in the natural rate of unemployment is shown as a

a rightward shift in the long-run Phillips curve.
b leftward shift in the long-run Phillips curve.
c rightward shift in the short-run Phillips curve.
d leftward shift in both the short-run and long-run Phillips curves.
e rightward shift in both the short-run and long-run Phillips curves.

2 Suppose OPEC unexpectedly collapses, leading to a fall in the price of oil. This is a positive aggregate supply shock. As a result, the price level will

a rise and real GDP will increase.
b rise and real GDP will decrease.
c fall and real GDP will increase.
d fall and real GDP will decrease.
e rise and real GDP will stay the same.

3 Figure P8.1 illustrates an economy initially in macroeconomic equilibrium at point *a*. If the money supply is expected to increase by 50 percent, what is the rational expectation of the price level?

a 100
b 120
c 130
d 150
e We cannot tell without more information on wage negotiations.

FIGURE **P8.1**

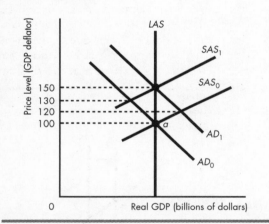

4 An increase in expected inflation raises the nominal interest rate because

a borrowers require compensation for the inflation eroding the value of money.
b lenders require compensation for the inflation eroding the value of money.
c the inflation creates higher transactions costs.
d the real rate of interest rises by an amount equal to the increase in expected inflation.
e none of the above.

5 The supporters of sticky wage theories attributed the rise in unemployment during the 1990 recession to a(n)

a increase in the natural rate of unemployment.
b sharp fall in real wages.
c increase in labour force participation.
d rise in real wages.
e rise in structural unemployment.

6 How did monetary policy affect interest rates during the Great Depression?

a High real interest rates resulted from a decrease in the money supply.
b Low real interest rates resulted from a decrease in the money supply.
c High real interest rates resulted from an increase in the money supply.
d Low real interest rates resulted from an increase in the money supply.
e High real interest rates resulted from the positive inflation.

7 What is the key impulse in the new Keynesian theory of the business cycle?

a changes in expected future sales and profits
b changes in the money supply
c unanticipated changes in aggregate demand
d anticipated changes in aggregate demand
e changes in the pace of technological change

8 What is the key impulse in the RBC theory of the business cycle?

a changes in expected future sales and profits
b changes in the money supply
c unanticipated changes in aggregate demand
d anticipated changes in aggregate demand
e changes in the pace of technological change

9 According to real business cycle theories, if the Bank of Canada increases the money supply when real GDP declines, real GDP

a will increase, but only temporarily.
b will increase permanently.
c and the price level will both be unaffected.
d will be unaffected, but the price level will rise.
e will fall due to the inefficiencies introduced into production as a result.

10 Which of the following supports the claim that feedback rules exaggerate fluctuations in aggregate demand? Policy makers

a use the wrong feedback rules to achieve their goals.

b must take actions today that will not have their effects until well into the future.

c do not really want to stabilize the economy.

d try to make their policies unpredictable.

e have enough knowledge of the economy.

11 If one of your professors was to cancel your final exam unexpectedly the morning you were scheduled to write it, this would be an example of

a your lucky day.

b a time-inconsistent policy.

c a feedback-rule policy.

d a discretionary policy.

e a time-consistent policy.

12 To _____ government saving, the government deficit must _____.

a decrease; fall

b decrease; be zero

c increase; be zero

d increase; fall

e increase; rise

FIGURE **P8.2**

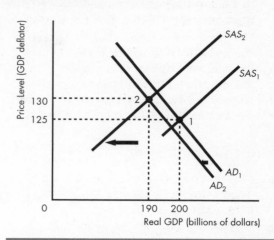

ANSWERS

Problem

a The new Keynesian graph of the market for goods and services is shown in Fig. P8.2. Note the fall in aggregate demand combined with the shift leftward in aggregate supply (due to the rising wages).

The labour market has rising real wages, falling employment and rising unemployment, implying that the real wage is too high (nominal wages were based on the expected inflation of 7 percent, but since *AD* was unexpectedly low, the actual inflation is only 4 percent, creating high real wages), creating unemployment above the natural rate.

b The real business cycle graph of the market for goods and services is shown in Fig. P8.3. Note that aggregate demand is assumed constant, and that a shift leftward in aggregate supply causes all the changes. This shift is due to a fall in productivity, due to the technological change, which lowers the demand for labour and capital (lowering the real interest rate). There is also a fall in the supply of labour, due to the lower real interest rate, creating a big fall in labour hired, and therefore a shift leftward in the *LAS* curve.

FIGURE **P8.3**

c i According to the new Keynesian theory, the right policy is to stimulate aggregate demand by an expansionary policy, attempting to raise the price level, lower real wages, raise employment and real GDP. If, however, the real business cycle theory is correct, this stimulation of aggregate demand will just lead to extra inflation, with its costs, with no change in real GDP.

ii   According to the real business cycle theory, the correct policy is to do nothing. If, however, the Keynesian theory is correct, this will result in the recession lasting longer than necessary.

d   Both policies will raise the deficit, lowering national saving (= private saving + government saving), which lowers economic growth. However, cutting taxes on savings might raise private saving, and counter this effect.

Midterm Examination

1   e   *LRPC* is vertical at new higher natural rate, and *SRPC* shifts with it since it crosses *LRPC* at natural rate. (860–861)

2   c   This will lead to a fall in the cost of production and a rightward shift in *SAS*. (851–852)

3   d   ↑ money supply by 50 percent → ↑ *AD* by 50 percent vertically → new expected equilibrium where AD_1 crosses *LAS* curve. (855–856)

4   b   Borrowers are paying the money, so are happy if its value erodes, the higher transactions costs do not affect interest rates, and the real rate is set independently of inflation. (862)

5   d   Unexpectedly low inflation → unexpectedly high real wages → sticky wage unemployment. (834)

6   a   Banking failures → ↓ real money supply → ↑ nominal interest rates, which combined with negative inflation → higher real interest rates. (836–837)

7   c   Anticipated changes are not as important— see text discussion. (825)

8   e   See text discussion. (828)

9   d   Because *LAS* is vertical. (882–883)

10   b   Therefore fluctuations in *AD* are exaggerated. (881–882)

11   b   Changing a pre-announced plan (the exam) at a later time-period. (887–888)

12   d   Because government saving = taxes − expenditures = − government deficit. (876)

Chapter 37

Trading with the World

KEY CONCEPTS

Patterns and Trends in International Trade

◆ **Imports** are goods and services we buy from other countries, **exports** are what we sell to them.

- **Balance of trade** = value of exports – value of imports.
- If balance of trade > 0 → **net exporter**.
- If balance of trade < 0 → **net importer**.

◆ Canada's major export and import is motor vehicles.

◆ Trade includes trade in services, such as tourism → American vacationing in Banff is Canadian export.

◆ Our major trading partner is the United States.

Opportunity Cost and Comparative Advantage

Countries can produce anywhere on or inside production possibilities frontier (PPF).

◆ Slope of PPF = Δ y-axis variable/Δ x-axis variable = opportunity cost of one more x-axis variable.

◆ A country has **comparative advantage** in production of good for which it has lowest opportunity cost.

Gains from Trade

A country gains from trading by buying goods from other countries with lower opportunity costs and selling to other countries goods for which it has lowest opportunity cost.

◆ The post-trade price is between initial pre-trade opportunity costs of the two countries → buyer gains from price lower than their opportunity cost, seller gains from opportunity cost higher than their opportunity cost.

◆ Countries pay for their imports with their exports → the value of exports = the value of imports (in the absence of international borrowing).

◆ *Both* countries gain by specializing in production of goods in which they have a comparative advantage and trading for other goods → can therefore *consume outside* the PPF.

- Since post-trade prices different than pre-trade opportunity costs, production levels adjust → countries produce more of their exported good, less of imported good.

◆ Country has **absolute advantage** in all goods if it has higher productivity → can produce given output of all goods with less workers.

◆ Even with absolute advantage, if opportunity costs diverge between countries → everyone has comparative advantage in something and can gain from trade.

Gains from Trade in Reality

◆ Most trade can be explained by comparative advantage → but much trade is trade in similar goods, due to

- Diversified tastes → demand for many (similar) products.
- Economies of scale → cheapest way to make many products is specialization and trade.

◆ Increasing our imports benefits us and the exporting nation, but can create *adjustment costs* → lost jobs/wages for those in import-competing industries → leads to government intervention.

Trade Restrictions

Governments restrict trade to protect domestic industries → **protectionism**.

- Two methods of restriction—tariffs and nontariff barriers.

- Canada has always had tariffs, but they have ↓ since 1930s, under **General Agreement on Tariffs and Trade**, an international agreement to limit government trade restriction.

  - North American Free Trade Agreement with the United States and Mexico further ↓ barriers.

- **Tariffs** are taxes on imported goods → ↑ imported price → ↓ imports → ↑ domestic production → net losses to importing country because opportunity cost of domestic production > original import price.

- Tariffs → less imports in home country → exporters in foreign country sell fewer goods → ↓ income → ↓ foreign country imports = home country exports → no change in balance of trade (if there is no international borrowing).

- When tariffs ↑ lots in the 1930s → world trade collapsed.

- **Nontariff barriers** restrict supply of imports.

  - **Quotas** set import quantity restriction, with quota licences distributed by home country.
  - **Voluntary export restraints** (VERs) set export quantity restrictions, with foreign distributors having export licences.

- Quotas/VERs → ↓ import supply → ↑ domestic price → ↑ domestic production.

  - ↑ import prices → owning quotas profitable.
  - Quotas and tariffs have similar effects on price and quantity, difference is who gains profit = selling price − import price.

The Case Against Protection

Trade restrictions are used despite losses of gains from trade for three somewhat credible reasons.

- Protecting strategic industries achieves national security → but hard to identify which industries are strategic.

- Protecting **infant industries** allows them to mature and allows learning-by-doing spillovers. These seem unlikely in reality.

- Foreign companies may **dump** their products on world markets at prices less than cost in order to gain global monopoly.

  - But dumping is very hard to detect since costs are hard to determine.
  - **Countervailing duties** are tariffs imposed to discourage subsidized foreign companies.

- A country may restrict trade for the following less credible reasons:

  - to save jobs in import-competing industries → but free trade creates jobs elsewhere,
  - to compete with cheap foreign labour → but what counts is wages and productivity (comparative advantage),
  - to bring diversity and stability → but economic size provides this,
  - to penalize lax environmental standards → but trade and economic growth work better,
  - to prevent rich countries from exploiting developing countries → but this ignores comparative advantage.

- Major reason for trade restriction is to protect groups/industries that suffer disproportionately under freer trade.

  - Net gains from trade are positive, but there are losers in import-competing industries.
  - Some (incomplete) compensation of losers occurs from unemployment insurance.

The Canada–United States Free Trade Agreement

- Despite protectionism pressures, Canada has free trade agreement with the United States and Mexico, which involves

  - reducing common tariffs to zero in phases,
  - reducing nontariff barriers,
  - freer trade in energy and services,
  - future negotiations on subsidies,
  - a dispute-settling mechanism.

- Total effects of the agreement are unknown at the moment, but they do include

  - large ↑ in total volume of trade.
  - significant changes in some sectors → large adjustment costs.

HELPFUL HINTS

1 This chapter applies the fundamental concepts of opportunity cost and comparative advantage discussed in Chapter 3 to the problem of trade between nations. The basic principles are the same for trade between individuals in the same country and between individuals in different countries.

Many people involved in debates about trade seem confused by the concept of comparative advantage, partially because they implicitly consider *absolute advantage* as the sole reason for trade. A country has an absolute advantage if it can produce all goods using less inputs than another country. However, such a country can still gain from trade. Consider California and Saskatchewan. California has a better climate and, with widespread irrigation, has an absolute advantage in the production of all agricultural products. Indeed, California frequently has more than one harvest a year! This would seem to imply that California has no need to trade with Saskatchewan. Saskatchewan, however, has a *comparative advantage* in the production of wheat. Therefore California will specialize in fruits and trade them for wheat. California could easily grow its own wheat, but the opportunity cost would be too high—the lost fruit crops. By specializing and trading, both California and Saskatchewan can gain.

2 One of the most crucial results of this chapter is to understand that both countries can gain from trade. This gain occurs because the post-trade price is between the two countries' pre-trade opportunity costs. We can see this illustrated in Text Fig. 37.6, where the equilibrium price of a car is 3 tonnes of grain, between the pre-trade opportunity costs of 1 tonne and 9 tonnes.

Students are often puzzled by where to put the price when working through these types of examples. How did the authors come up with the value of 3? In a sense, it is an arbitrary value, one they just plucked out of a hat. Given the logic of voluntary trade, it must be between the two pre-trade values of 1 and 9. However, by redrawing the export supply and the import demand curves with different slopes, the authors might have arrived at a value of 6 tonnes. This would have been equally logical, and equally valid.

In the real world, the strength of the demand for specific products by the consumers of each country will determine the slopes of the export supply and import demand curves, and determine just where the equilibrium price is set. In your examples, you will either be able to pick where you want the price to be (given that it must be between the two pre-trade opportunity costs), or you will be given some specific information telling you where the price is.

3 One of the important things we learn about the economic effects of trade restrictions is that a tariff and a quota are the same. A voluntary export restraint (VER) is also a quota, but it is a quota imposed by the exporting country rather than by the importing country.

All trade restrictions raise the domestic price of the imported goods and reduce the volume and value of imports. They also reduce the value of exports by the same amount as the reduction in the value of imports. The increase in price that results from each trade restriction produces a gap between the domestic price of the imported good and the foreign supply price of the good.

The difference between the alternative trade restrictions lies in which party captures this excess. In the case of a tariff, the government receives the tariff revenue. In the case of a quota imposed by the importing country, domestic importers who have been awarded a licence to import capture this excess through increased profit. When a VER is imposed, the excess is captured by foreign exporters who have been awarded licences to export by their government.

4 The major point of this chapter is that gains from free trade can be considerable. Why then do countries have such a strong tendency to impose trade restrictions? The key is that while free trade creates overall benefits to the economy as a whole, there are both winners and losers. The winners gain more in total than the losers lose, but the latter tend to be concentrated in a few industries.

Given this concentration, free trade will be resisted by some acting on the basis of rational self-interest. Even though only a small minority benefit while the overwhelming majority will be hurt, it is not surprising to see trade restrictions implemented. The cost of a given trade restriction to *each* of the majority will be individually quite small, while the benefit to *each* of the few will be individually large. Thus the minority will have a significant incentive to see that restriction takes place, while the majority will have little incentive to expend time and energy in resisting trade restriction.

5 To understand the source of pressures for trade restrictions, let us summarize those who win and lose from trade restrictions.

Under the three forms of restrictions (tariffs, quotas, and VERs) *consumers* lose, because the price of the imported good rises. *Domestic producers* of the imported good and their factors of production gain from all three, because the price of the imported good rises. *Foreign producers* and their factors of production lose under all three schemes, because their export sales fall. Under quotas and VERs, the *holders of import licences* gain from buying low and selling high (they may be foreign or domestic). *Government* gains tariff revenue under tariffs and, potentially, votes under other schemes.

Given this list, it is hardly surprising that the main supporters of trade restrictions are domestic producers and their factors of production.

S E L F - T E S T

True/False/Uncertain and Explain

1 Elected governments are slow to reduce trade restrictions because there would be many fewer losers than gainers.

2 Japan is dumping steel if it sells it in Japan at a lower price than it sells it in Canada.

3 If a country has an absolute advantage, it will not benefit from trade.

4 Countries may exchange similar goods with each other due to economies of scale in the face of diversified tastes.

5 When governments impose tariffs, they are increasing their country's gain from trade.

6 Trading according to comparative advantage allows all trading countries to consume outside their PPF.

7 If country A must give up 3 units of Y to produce 1 unit of X and B must give up 4 units of Y to produce 1 unit of X, then A has a comparative advantage in the production of X.

8 A tariff on a good will raise its price and reduce the quantity traded.

9 A quota will cause the price of the imported good to fall.

10 When a Canadian citizen stays in a hotel in France, Canada is exporting a service.

Multiple-Choice

1 Consider Table 37.1. Under free trade, the international price of donut holes would be $____ per hundred donut holes, and _____ million holes would be exchanged.
a 0.75; 6
b 1.00; 3
c 1.25; 4
d 1.25; 5
e 1.50; 4

TABLE **37.1** INTERNATIONAL TRADE IN DONUT HOLES

International Price (dollars per 100 holes)	Glazeland's Export Supply of Holes (millions)	Snorfleland's Import Demand for Holes (millions)
0.50	1	10
0.75	2	8
1.00	3	6
1.25	4	4
1.50	5	2
1.75	6	0

2 Consider Table 37.1. Snorfleland's donut hole producers manage to convince their government that there is a need to protect the domestic industry from Glazeland's cheap imports. (They argue that holes are a crucial food group.) In response, Snorfleland's government sets an import quota of 3 million donut holes. The resulting price of a donut hole in Snorfleland will be $_____ per hundred holes, and domestic production of donut holes will _____.

a 0.75; fall
b 0.75; rise
c 1.25; remain unchanged
d 1.38; rise
e 1.38; remain unchanged

3 Consider Table 37.1. Starting from the free-trade equilibrium, Glazeland's donut hole exporters convince their government that making donut holes is a way of life being threatened by the cruel vagaries of the international market and, therefore deserves to be subsidized. Glazeland's government responds by subsidizing donut hole production by $0.25 per hundred holes. The resulting *international price* will be approximately $_____ per hundred holes, and the quantity traded will be _____ million donut holes.

a 1.00; 4
b 1.00; 5
c 1.12; 4
d 1.12; 4.5
e 1.50; 5

4 Consider Table 37.1. Glazeland's government has subsidized donut hole production by $0.25 per hundred holes. Snorfleland's domestic producers have responded by filing a suit with the government that domestic production has been hurt by the unfair subsidy. Snorfleland's government responds by charging a countervailing duty on Glazeland donut holes of $0.25 per hundred holes. The *domestic* price in Snorfleland after the net effects of the subsidy and the countervailing duty will be $_____ per hundred holes, and Snorfleland will import _____ million holes.

a 1.00; 4
b 1.00; 5
c 1.12; 4
d 1.12; 5
e 1.25; 4

5 Refer to Fig. 37.1. The opportunity cost of 1 beer in Partyland is _____, and the opportunity cost of 1 beer in Cowabunga is _____.

a dependent on where on the PPF we measure it; dependent on where on the PPF we measure it
b 100 pizzas; 25 pizzas
c 3 pizzas; 1 pizza
d 1 pizza; 1 pizza
e 1 pizza; 1/3 pizza

FIGURE **37.1** PARTYLAND AND COWABUNGA—PPF FOR BEER AND PIZZA

6 Refer to Fig. 37.1. The opportunity cost of 1 pizza in Partyland is _____, and the opportunity cost of 1 pizza in Cowabunga is _____.

a dependent on where on the PPF we measure it; dependent on where on the PPF we measure it
b 100 beers; 25 beers
c 3 beers; 1 beer
d 1 beer; 1 beer
e 1 beer; 3 beers

7 Refer to Fig. 37.1. If trade occurs between Partyland and Cowabunga,

a there will be a lot of drunk turtles.
b Partyland will supply both pizza and beer, because it has a comparative advantage in both.
c Cowabunga will supply both pizza and beer, because it has a comparative advantage in both.
d Partyland will supply pizza, and Cowabunga will supply beer.
e Partyland will supply beer, and Cowabunga will supply pizza.

8 Refer to Fig. 37.1. If trade occurs between Partyland and Cowabunga, the trade price for beer will be

a 1 beer for 1 pizza.
b 1 beer for 1/3 pizza.
c 1 beer for 3 pizzas.
d somewhere between 1 beer for 1 pizza and 1 beer for 3 pizzas.
e somewhere between 1 beer for 1 pizza and 1 beer for 1/3 pizza.

9 If Canada has imposed an import quota of one million pairs of shoes per year, an increase in the domestic demand for shoes will result in

a no change in the domestic prices of shoes, but an increase in the quantity of shoes imported.
b no change in the domestic prices of shoes or in the quantity of shoes imported.
c a rise in the domestic prices of shoes and in the quantity of shoes imported.
d a rise in the domestic prices of shoes and no change in the quantity of shoes imported.
e a rise in the domestic prices of shoes and an uncertain change in the quantity of shoes imported, depending on whether the increase in demand is greater than one million pairs or not.

10 When a *voluntary export restraint* agreement is reached, the gap between the domestic import price and the export price is captured by

a consumers in the importing country.
b the person with the right to import the good.
c the government of the importing country.
d foreign exporters.
e the domestic producers of the good.

11 The implementation of the Canada–United States Free Trade Agreement has revealed that

a Canada has been severely damaged by the agreement.
b Canada has been helped enormously by the agreement.
c free trade does not work.
d all losers from free trade will be compensated.
e there has been a large rise in the volume of international trade, benefiting consumers, but at the cost of a high rate of job destruction in the late 1980s and early 1990s.

12 If we import more than we export, then

a we will be unable to buy as many foreign goods as we desire.
b we will make loans to foreigners to enable them to buy our goods.
c we will have to finance the difference by borrowing from foreigners.
d our patterns of trade, including the direction of exports and imports, will be different than if exports equal imports.
e c and d.

13 If country *A* has an absolute advantage in the production of everything,

a no trade will take place because country *A* will have a comparative advantage in everything.
b no trade will take place because no country will have a comparative advantage in anything.
c trade will probably take place, and all countries will gain.
d trade will probably take place, but country *A* will not gain.
e trade will probably take place, but country *A* will be the only one to gain.

14 Which of the following is *not* an argument for protectionism?

a to protect strategic industries
b to save jobs in import-competing industries
c to gain a comparative advantage
d to allow infant industries to grow
e to prevent rich nations from exploiting poor nations

15 International trade based on comparative advantage allows each country to consume

a more of the goods it exports, but less of the goods it imports than without trade.
b more of the goods it imports, but less of the goods it exports than without trade.
c more of the goods it exports and imports than without trade.
d less of the goods it exports and imports than without trade.
e either **a** or **b**, depending on the price of the goods.

16 A tariff on good *X* which is imported by country *A* will cause the

a demand curve for *X* in country *A* to shift upward.

b demand curve for *X* in country *A* to shift downward.

c supply curve of *X* in country *A* to shift upward.

d supply curve of *X* in country *A* to shift downward.

e demand and the supply curve of *X* in country *A* to shift upward.

17 When a *quota* is imposed, the gap between the domestic price and the export price is captured by

a consumers in the importing country.

b the domestic producers of the good.

c the government of the importing country.

d foreign exporters.

e the person with the right to import the good.

18 Which of the following is a Canadian service export?

a A Canadian buys dinner while travelling in Switzerland.

b A Swiss buys a dinner while travelling in Canada.

c A Canadian buys a clock made in Switzerland.

d A Swiss buys a computer made in Canada.

e **a** and **b**.

19 Which of the following statements about international trade is *true*?

a Tariffs will increase jobs in our export industries.

b Quotas are better than tariffs because they do not raise prices.

c Tariffs are needed to allow us to compete with cheap foreign labour.

d No one gains from free trade between a poor country and a rich country.

e VERs raise prices as much as equivalent tariffs do.

20 In country *A*, 1 unit of capital and 1 unit of labour are required to produce 1 unit of *X*, and 2 units of capital and 2 units of labour are required to produce 1 unit of *Y*. What is the opportunity cost of good *X*?

a the price of 1 unit of capital plus the price of 1 unit of labour

b 1 unit of capital and 1 unit of labour

c 2 units of capital and 2 units of labour

d 1/2 unit of *Y*

e 2 units of *Y*

21 When a *tariff* is imposed, the gap between the domestic price and the export price is captured by

a consumers in the importing country.

b the person with the right to import the good.

c the domestic producers of the good.

d foreign exporters.

e the government of the importing country.

22 Country *A* and country *B* are currently engaging in free trade. Country *A* imports good *X* from country *B* and exports *Y* to *B*. If country *A* imposes a *quota* on *X*, country *A*'s *X*-producing industry will

a expand, and its *Y*-producing industry will contract.

b expand, and its *Y*-producing industry will expand.

c contract, and its *Y*-producing industry will contract.

d contract, and its *Y*-producing industry will expand.

e expand, and its *Y*-producing industry will be unchanged.

23 The imposition by country *A* of a tariff on imported goods from country *B* will increase the price consumers pay for imported goods and

a reduce the volume of imports and the volume of exports.

b reduce the volume of imports and increase the volume of exports.

c reduce the volume of imports and leave the volume of exports unchanged.

d will not affect either the volume of imports or the volume of exports.

e increase the volume of imports but decrease the volume of exports.

24 Which of the following is *most* responsible for significant reduction in trade restrictions since World War II?

a the Smoot–Hawley Act

b the voluntary exports restraint agreement between the United States and Japan

c the United Nations

d the General Agreement on Tariffs and Trade

e the Canada–United States Free Trade Agreement

25 Country A imports good X from country B and exports Y to B. Why would country A prefer arranging a voluntary export restraint rather than a quota on X?

a to not hurt country B's imports
b to prevent country B from retaliating by restricting country A's exports
c to keep the domestic price of X low
d to increase government revenue
e to help domestic producers

Short Answer Problems

I Why can *both* parties involved in trade gain?

2 How does a tariff on a particular imported good affect the domestic price of the good, the export price, the quantity imported, and the quantity of the good produced domestically?

3 How does a tariff on imports affect the exports of the country?

4 It is often argued by union leaders that tariffs are needed to protect domestic jobs. In light of your answers to Short Answer Problems **2** and **3**, evaluate this argument.

5 Consider a simple world in which there are two countries, Atlantis and Beltran, each producing food and cloth. The PPF for each country is given in Table 37.2.
a Assuming a constant opportunity cost in each country, complete the table.
b What is the opportunity cost of food in Atlantis? of cloth?
c What is the opportunity cost of food in Beltran? of cloth?
d Draw the PPFs on separate graphs.

TABLE **37.2** ATLANTIS AND BELTRAN—PPF FOR FOOD AND CLOTH

Atlantis		Beltran	
Food (units)	Cloth (units)	Food (units)	Cloth (units)
0	500	0	800
200	400	100	600
400		200	
600		300	
800		400	
1,000		—	—

6 Suppose that Atlantis and Beltran engage in trade.
a In which good will each country specialize?
b If 1 unit of food trades for 1 unit of cloth, what will happen to the production of each good in each country?
c If 1 unit of food trades for 1 unit of cloth, draw the consumption possibility frontiers for each country on the corresponding graph from Short Answer Problem 5.
d Before trade, if Atlantis consumed 600 units of food, the most cloth it could consume was 200 units. After trade, how many units of cloth can be consumed if 600 units of food are consumed?

7 Continue the analysis of Atlantis and Beltran trading at the rate of 1 unit of food for 1 unit of cloth.
a If Atlantis consumes 600 units of food and 400 units of cloth, how much food and cloth will be consumed by Beltran?
b Given the consumption quantities and the production quantities from Short Answer Problem **6b**, how much food and cloth will Atlantis and Beltran import and export?

8 Figure 37.2 gives the import demand curve for shirts for country A, labelled D, and the export supply curve of shirts for country B, labelled S.
a What is the price of a shirt under free trade?
b How many shirts will be imported by country A?

FIGURE **37.2**

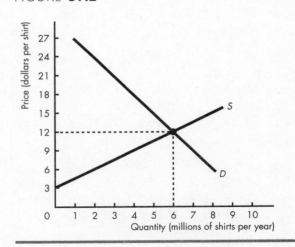

9 Suppose the shirtmakers in country A of Short Answer Problem **8** are concerned about foreign competition and, as a result, the government of country A imposes a tariff of $9 per shirt.

a What will happen to the price of a shirt in country *A*?

b What is the price the exporter will actually receive?

c How many shirts will be imported by country *A*?

d What is the revenue from the tariff? Who captures it?

10 Suppose that instead of a tariff, country *A* imposes a quota of 4 million shirts per year.

a What will be the price of a shirt in country *A*?

b What price will the exporter actually receive?

c How many shirts will be imported by country *A*?

d What is the difference between the total amount paid by consumers and the total amount received by exporters—the "excess profit"? Who captures it?

ANSWERS

True/False/Uncertain and Explain

1 F They will be slow because losers' losses are individually much greater than winners' gains. (922)

2 F Dumping would be selling in Canada at lower price than in Japan. (919)

3 U If comparative advantage exists → gains from trade exist. (910)

4 T Diversified tastes → many products demanded. Economies of scale → cheaper method of production, but requires specialization and trade. (911–912)

5 F Trade restrictions reduce gains from trade → cost of purchasing export < current benefit → lost gains from trade. (914–916)

6 T Countries will specialize and trade to consume outside PPF. (908–909)

7 T *A* has a lower opportunity cost $(3Y < 4Y =$ lost *Y* per unit of gained *X*). (905–906)

8 T Tariff → shift up in export supply curve → ↑ price and ↓ quantity traded. (914–915)

9 F Quota ↓ supply → ↑ price. (916–917)

10 F Canada is importing (using) a service. (903)

Multiple-Choice

1 c Equilibrium is where export supply = import demand. (914)

2 d Equilibrium is where quota = import demand → ↑ price. Higher domestic price → ↑ domestic production. (916–917)

3 d Subsidy ↑ Glazeland's export supply by 1 million at each price → new equilibrium where new supply = old demand. (916–917)

4 e In addition to the change from **3**, tariff → ↓ export supply by 1 million, exactly offsetting the subsidy. (914)

5 e Opportunity cost of 1 more beer = lost pizza. For Partyland, going from 0 beer to 25 beers costs 25 pizzas → one for one. Do same calculation for Cowabunga. (905–906)

6 e Same type of calculation as in **5**. (905–906)

7 d Each specializes in where they have comparative advantage (lowest opportunity cost). (906)

8 e Trade price is between the opportunity costs in each country at the pre-trade equilibrium. (907)

9 d Quota → fixed maximum import quantity. Therefore if ↑ demand → ↑ price. (916–917)

10 d Because they have right to export. (917)

11 e See text discussion. (923–924)

12 c Necessary in order to get foreign exchange. General patterns of trade unchanged, once we have enough dollars. (904)

13 c Absolute advantage in everything → comparative advantage in only some goods. (910)

14 c See text discussion. (918–921)

15 c Consumption possibilities frontier is outside PPF. (908–909)

16 c Tariff → ↑ domestic price = export price + tariff → shift upward of supply curve. (914–915)

17 e Under quota, domestic government allocates the licence to import. (916–917)

18 b **a** and **c** → import, **d** → export of a good. (903)

19 e Tariffs ↓ exports and jobs in export industries, quotas restrict supply → ↑ prices, cheap foreign labour doesn't necessarily hurt us, poor and rich countries can have comparative advantage and gain from trade. VERs restrict supply and raise prices just like tariffs. (914–917)

20 d Inputs required to make one *X* could make 1/2 *Y*. (905–906)

21 e They collect tariff revenue = import price – export price. (914–915)

22 a Quota → ↓ imports → ↑ domestic price of X → ↑ domestic production. ↓ imports = ↓ B's exports → ↓ its income → ↓ its imports → ↓ A's exports → ↓ Y production in A. (916–917)

23 a Tariff → ↑ domestic price of imports → ↓ imports → ↑ domestic production. ↓ imports = ↓ B's exports → ↓ its income → ↓ its imports → ↓ A's exports → ↓ export production in A. (914–919)

24 d See text discussion. (912–913)

25 b Under a VER → exporting country gains excess revenue → less likely to retaliate, since hurt less. (916–917)

Short Answer Problems

1 For two potential trading partners to be willing to trade, they must have different comparative advantages; that is, different opportunity costs. Then they will trade and both parties will gain. If the parties do not trade, each will face its own opportunity costs. A price at which trade takes place must be somewhere between the opportunity costs of the two traders. This means that the party with the lower opportunity cost of the good in question will gain because it will receive a price above its opportunity cost. Similarly, the party with the higher opportunity cost will gain because it will pay a price below its opportunity cost.

2 A tariff on an imported good will *raise its price to domestic consumers* as the export supply curve shifts upward. The export price is determined by the original export supply curve. As the domestic price of the good rises, the quantity of the good demanded falls, and thus the relevant point on the original export supply curve is at a lower quantity and a *lower export price*. This lower quantity means that the quantity imported falls. The rise in the domestic price will also lead to an *increase in the quantity of the good supplied domestically*.

3 When country A imposes a tariff on its imports of good X, not only does the volume of imports shrink, but the volume of exports of Y to country B will shrink by the same amount. Thus a balance of trade is maintained. As indicated in the answer to Short Answer Problem 2, the export price of good X received by country B and the quantity exported falls when a tariff is imposed. This fall in the price and the quantity exported means that the income of country B has fallen. This implies that the quantity of Y

(A's export) demanded by country B will fall and thus A's exports decline.

4 This argument has some partial truth to it. As Short Answer Problem 2 shows, the tariff will lead an increase in domestic production of the protected good, which will lead to an increase in jobs in that industry. However, as Short Answer Problem 3 shows, the same tariff will reduce foreign income, and reduce foreign purchases of our goods, reducing our exports and our export production, reducing jobs in the export industry. The net effect on jobs in unclear, but is definitely not large.

5 a Completed Table 37.2 is shown here as Table 37.2 Solution. The values in the table are calculated using the opportunity cost of each good in each country. See **b** and **c** below.

TABLE **37.2** SOLUTION
ATLANTIS AND BELTRAN—PPF FOR FOOD AND CLOTH

Atlantis		Beltran	
Food (units)	Cloth (units)	Food (units)	Cloth (units)
0	500	0	800
200	400	100	600
400	300	200	400
600	200	300	200
800	100	400	0
1,000	0	—	—

b To increase the output (consumption) of food by 200 units, cloth production (consumption) falls by 100 units in Atlantis. Thus the opportunity cost of a unit of food is 1/2 unit of cloth. This opportunity cost is constant as are all others in this problem, for simplicity. Similarly, the opportunity cost of cloth in Atlantis is 2 units of food.

c In Beltran a 100-unit increase in the production (consumption) of food requires a reduction in the output (consumption) of cloth of 200 units. Thus the opportunity cost of food is 2 units of cloth. Similarly the opportunity cost of cloth in Beltran is 1/2 units of food.

d Figure 37.3(a) and (b) illustrate the production possibility frontiers for Atlantis and Beltran, respectively labelled PPF$_A$ and PPF$_B$. The rest of the diagram is discussed in the solutions to Short Answer Problems **7** and **8**.

FIGURE **37.3**

(a)   **(b)**

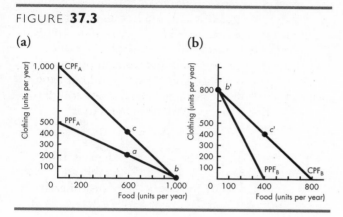

6 a We see from the solution to Short Answer Problems **5b** and **c** that Atlantis has a lower opportunity cost (1/2 unit of cloth) in the production of food. Therefore Atlantis will specialize in the production of food. Beltran, with the lower opportunity cost for cloth (1/2 unit of food), will specialize in cloth.

b Each country will want to produce every unit of the good in which they specialize as long as the amount they receive in trade exceeds their opportunity cost. For Atlantis, the opportunity cost of a unit of food is 1/2 unit of cloth, but it can obtain 1 unit of cloth in trade. Because the opportunity cost is constant, Atlantis will totally specialize by producing all of the food it can: 1,000 units per year, point *b* in Fig. 37.3(a). Similarly, in Beltran, the opportunity cost of a unit of cloth is 1/2 unit of food but a unit of cloth will trade for 1 unit of food. Since the opportunity cost is constant, Beltran will totally specialize in the production of cloth and will produce 800 units per year, point *b'* in Fig. 37.3(b).

c The consumption possibility frontiers for Atlantis and Beltran, labelled CPF$_A$ and CPF$_B$, are illustrated in Fig. 37.3(a) and (b), respectively. These frontiers are straight lines that indicate all the combinations of food and cloth that can be consumed with trade. The position and slope of the consumption possibility frontier for an economy depend on the terms of trade between the goods (one for one in this example) and the production point of the economy.

The consumption possibility frontier for Atlantis (CPF$_A$), for example, is obtained by starting at point *b* on PPF$_A$, the production point, and examining possible trades. For example, if Atlantis traded 400 units of the food it produces for 400 units of cloth, it would be able to consume 600 units of food (1,000 units produced minus 400 units traded) and 400 units of cloth, which is represented by point *c*.

d If Atlantis consumes 600 units of food, trade allows consumption of cloth to be 400 units, 200 units more than possible without trade. The maximum amount of cloth that can be consumed without trade is given by the production possibility frontier. If food consumption is 600 units, this is indicated by point *a* on PPF$_A$. The maximum amount of cloth consumption for any level of food consumption with trade is given by the consumption possibility frontier. If food consumption is 600 units, this is indicated by point *c* on CPF$_A$.

7 a Since Atlantis produces 1,000 units of food per year (point *b* on PPF$_A$), to consume 600 units of food and 400 units of cloth (point *c* on CPF$_A$) it must trade 400 units of food for 400 units of cloth. This means that Beltran has traded 400 units of cloth for 400 units of food. Since Beltran produces 800 units of cloth, this suggests that Beltran must consume 400 units of food and 400 units of cloth (point *c'* on CPF$_B$).

b Atlantis exports 400 units of food per year and imports 400 units of cloth. Beltran exports 400 units of cloth per year and imports 400 units of food.

8 a The price of a shirt under free trade will occur at the intersection of country *A*'s import demand curve for shirts and country *B*'s export supply curve for shirts. This occurs at a price of $12 per shirt.

b Country *A* will import 6 million shirts per year.

9 a The effect of the $9 per shirt tariff is to shift the export supply curve (*S*) upward by $9. This is shown as a shift from *S* to *S'* in Fig. 37.2 Solution. The price is now determined by the intersection of the *D* curve, which is unaffected by the tariff, and the *S'* curve. The new price of a shirt is $18.

FIGURE **37.2** SOLUTION

---

b Of this $18, $9 is the tariff, so the exporter only receives the remaining $9.

c Country *A* will now import only 4 million shirts per year.

d The tariff revenue is $9 (the tariff per shirt) × 4 million (the number of shirts imported), which is $36 million. This money is received by the government of country *A*.

10 a The quota restricts the quantity that can be imported to 4 million shirts per year regardless of the price and is represented by a vertical line in Fig. 37.4 (which corresponds to Fig. 37.2). The market for shirts will thus clear at a price of $18 per shirt.

FIGURE **37.4**

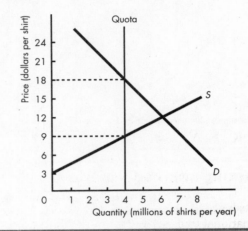

---

b This $18 price is received by the people who are given the right to import shirts under the quota. The amount received by the exporter is $9, given by the height of the *S* curve at a quantity of 4 million shirts per year.

c Country *A* will import 4 million shirts per year, the quota limit.

d The "excess profit" is $9 per shirt (the $18 received by the importer minus the $9 received by the exporter) × 4 million shirts, which is $36 million. This is captured by the importers who have been rewarded by the government of country *A* because they have been given the right to import under the quota. This is essentially a right to make an "excess profit."

The Balance of Payments and the Dollar

KEY CONCEPTS

Financing International Trade

The **balance of payments accounts** measure Canada's international transactions.

◆ **Current account**—net exports + net interest payments + net transfers.

◆ **Capital account**—foreign investment in Canada – Canadian investment abroad.

◆ **Official settlements account**—net changes in Canada's **official international reserves** (government's holdings of foreign currency) → if ↑ official reserves, official settlement balance is negative.

◆ Current account balance + capital account balance + official settlements balance = 0. To pay a current account deficit we must borrow from abroad or ↓ official reserves.

◆ Starting in early 1980s, a large current account deficit (and capital account surplus) emerged, but both had disappeared by 1996.

◆ A country that in current year is borrowing more from rest of world than it is lending is a **net borrower**.

- **Net lender** lends more to rest of world than it borrows.
- **Debtor nation** has borrowed more than lent to rest of world over its history.
- **Creditor nation** has lent more to rest of world than it has borrowed.
- Being a net borrower is not a problem if it is to finance investment that generates higher income to pay debts.

◆ Current account balance (*CAB*) is primarily determined by net exports (*NX*).

◆ Circular flow (Chapter 23) showed injections = withdrawals:

- $I + G + X = S + T + M$ or,
- Net exports = **private sector surplus** $(S - I)$ + **government sector surplus** $(T - G)$.
- Domestic and international sectors' deficits/surpluses are related → *NX* and *CAB* can change only if government sector surplus or private sector surplus change.
- Up to 1981, Canada's current account deficit (→ international borrowing) was for investment, but between 1981 and 1988 it was for consumption, since then for investment again.

The Exchange Rate

Foreigners and Canadians swap dollars for foreign currency in the **foreign exchange market**.

◆ **Foreign exchange rate** = price at which one currency exchanges for another → number of U.S. cents per Canadian dollar.

◆ **Currency depreciation** is ↓ in value of dollar in terms of another currency, **currency appreciation** is ↑.

◆ The Canadian dollar has fluctuated lots versus U.S. dollar since 1975 → due to fluctuations in demand and supply for Canadian dollar.

◆ The quantity of Canadian dollars demanded in the foreign exchange market = amount traders plan to buy at a given price → a *derived demand* based on demand for Canadian exports and Canadian assets.

◆ ↓ exchange rate → ↑ quantity demanded of Canadian dollars (movement down to the right along demand curve), because

- exports become cheaper for foreigners → ↑ demand for exports → ↑ demand for dollars.
- ↑ expected profits from buying Canadian dollars and holding them until they appreciate → ↑ demand.

◆ The demand curve shifts *rightward* if

- ↑ **Canadian interest rate differential** (Canadian interest rate − foreign interest rate) → ↑ demand for Canadian assets.
- ↑ expected future exchange rate → ↑ expected profits from buying Canadian dollars and holding them until they appreciate → ↑ demand.

◆ Quantity of Canadian dollars supplied in foreign exchange market = amount traders plan to sell at a given price in order to buy other currencies to buy imports and foreign assets.

◆ ↑ exchange rate → ↑ quantity supplied of Canadian dollars (movement up to the right along supply curve), because

- imports become cheaper for Canadians → ↑ demand for imports → ↑ demand for foreign currency → ↑ supply Canadian dollars.
- ↑ expected profits from buying foreign currency and holding it until it appreciates → ↑ demand for foreign currency = ↑ supply Canadian dollars.

◆ The supply curve shifts *leftward* if

- ↑ Canadian interest rate differential (Canadian interest rate − foreign interest rate) → ↓ demand for foreign assets → ↓ demand for foreign currency = ↓ supply of Canadian dollar.
- ↑ expected future exchange rate → ↓ expected profits from selling Canadian dollars and buying foreign currency and holding it until Canadian dollar depreciates → ↓ supply of Canadian dollar.

◆ Market equilibrium determined by demand and supply, with exchange rate adjusting as required.

◆ Exchange rate is often volatile, because supply and demand often move together, creating big swings in value of exchange rate.

- Between 1986 and 1991, the Canadian dollar rose dramatically in value, mostly because people expected it to rise → ↑ demand for Canadian dollar, ↓ supply of Canadian dollar.
- Between 1991 and 1995, opposite effect occurred.

◆ Expectations of Δ exchange rate are due to the forces of **purchasing power parity** (two currencies have the same value or purchasing power) and **interest rate parity** (two currencies earn the same interest rate, adjusted for expected depreciation).

◆ If purchasing power parity does not hold, and Canadian dollar is more valuable than the U.S. dollar for purchases → people expect it to depreciate → ↓ demand for Canadian dollar, ↑ supply → it does depreciate.

◆ Interest rate parity almost always holds (adjusted for risk), but if returns are higher in Canada, ↑ demand for Canadian dollar instantly → quick ↑ exchange rate.

◆ Bank of Canada can affect exchange rate two ways:

- Use monetary policy to Δ interest rates → Δ exchange rate.
- Buy or sell Canadian dollars directly. Buying dollars → ↑ demand → ↑ exchange rate.

◆ Such interventions Δ official international reserves:

- Buying Canadian dollars requires selling foreign currency → ↓ official reserves.
- This limits amount of intervention.

HELPFUL HINTS

1 There is an important difference between trade within a single country and trade between countries—currency. Individuals trading in the same country use the same currency, and trade is straightforward. International trade is complicated by the fact that individuals in different countries use different currencies. A Japanese selling goods will want payment in Japanese yen, but a Canadian buyer will likely be holding only Canadian dollars. This chapter addresses this trade complication by looking at the balance of payments of a country, as well as the relation of the balance of payments to the foreign exchange rate.

2 It is important to understand foreign exchange rates as prices determined by supply and demand. They are prices of currency determined in markets for currency. The demand for Canadian dollars in the foreign exchange market arises from the desire on the part of foreigners to purchase Canadian goods and services (which requires dollars) and Canadian financial or real assets.

The supply of Canadian dollars is a special type of supply, because the offer to sell a Canadian dollar is equivalent to an offer to buy foreign currency. Therefore it depends on the desire of Canadians to buy foreign goods and services (which requires foreign currency), and to buy foreign assets. Remembering that the supply of Canadian dollars equals the demand for foreign currency will help you to understand many of the shifts in the supply of Canadian dollars.

3   The exchange rate is often volatile because supply and demand often shift in a reinforcing manner, since they are both affected by the same changes in expectations. These changes in expectations are driven by two forces: purchasing power parity and interest rate parity. Each of these is a version of the law of one price, which states anytime there is a discrepancy in the price of the same good in two markets, natural economic forces (unless restricted) will eliminate that discrepancy and establish a single price. Suppose that the price in market 1 rises relative to the price in market 2. Individuals will now buy in the market with the lower price and not in the market with the higher price. This increase in the demand in market 2 and decrease in demand in market 1 will cause the two prices to come together. This principle applies to international markets as well: natural market forces will result in a single world price for the same good.

Suppose that purchasing power parity does not hold. For example, suppose that the price of good A in Canada is $6, and in Japan 600 yen, and that the exchange rate is currently 120 yen per dollar. The dollar price of A in Japan is $5 (600 yen / 120 yen per dollar). People expect the demand for A in Canada to fall (= a fall in the demand for Canadian dollars), and the demand for A in Japan to rise (= supply of dollars rising), which would lead to the exchange rate depreciating towards 100 yen per dollar (the purchasing power parity level). Their expectations will lead to a fall in the demand for the Canadian dollar and a rise in the supply of the Canadian dollar, so that the exchange rate will depreciate even before the demand for A adjusts!

The law of one price also holds for the price of assets such as bonds. If we recall that bond prices are inversely related to interest rates, then we can see that interest rate parity is a version of the law of one price. For example, consider a situation where, taking into account the expected depreciation of the Canadian dollar,

the Canadian interest rate was higher than the U.S. rate (which implies the price of bonds is lower in Canada). Buyers would demand Canadian bonds, raising their price and lowering Canadian interest rates. In addition, they would be selling U.S. bonds, lowering their price and raising U.S. interest rates. These actions occur until the interest differential between the two countries has shrunk to a level where it just reflects the expected depreciation of the Canadian dollar—interest parity holds.

4   In Chapter 28, we saw how monetary policy influenced the economy via changes in the interest rate, and changes in the exchange rate. This chapter fills in the details of the latter channel. A change in the money supply leads to a change in the interest rate, which changes the demand and supply of the Canadian dollar, and therefore the exchange rate, and therefore net exports and aggregate demand, and therefore inflation, real GDP, and unemployment.

There is also another international effect that the Bank of Canada often worries about. Imported goods play an important role in the production process, so that a depreciation of the Canadian dollar will raise the cost of production (Canadian dollar price of imports = foreign price/exchange rate). This in turn can create cost-push inflation. The Bank of Canada often works to offset temporary fluctuations in the exchange rate, or to smooth permanent changes in the exchange rate, in order to reduce fluctuations in the price level.

SELF-TEST

True/False/Uncertain and Explain

1   A rise in Canadian interest rates will lead to a rise in the demand for the Canadian dollar.

2   The demand and supply of the Canadian dollar tend to move independently of each other.

3   Countries with currencies that are expected to appreciate will have higher interest rates than countries with currencies that are expected to depreciate.

4 If the yen price of the dollar is 100 yen per dollar and the price of a traded good is $10 in Canada, purchasing power parity implies that the price in Japan will be 1,000 yen.

5 There can be no such thing as a balance of payments surplus/deficit, because by definition a *balance* of payments must always *balance*.

6 A larger government sector deficit leads to a higher current account deficit.

7 If the exchange rate between the Canadian dollar and the Japanese yen changes from 130 yen per dollar to 140 yen per dollar, the Canadian dollar has appreciated.

8 If the foreign exchange value of the dollar is expected to rise, the demand for dollars increases.

9 If a nation is a net borrower from the rest of the world, it will be a debtor nation.

10 If a country has a large government budget deficit and the private sector deficit is small, the balance of trade deficit will be large.

Multiple-Choice

1 If the Bank of Canada wishes to raise the exchange rate, it should

a lower interest rates.
b raise the money supply.
c buy foreign exchange.
d sell Canadian dollars.
e buy Canadian dollars.

2 Which of the following quotations best describes the purchasing power parity effect in action?

a "The recent high Canadian interest rate has raised the demand for the Canadian dollar."
b "The market feeling is that the Canadian dollar is overvalued and will likely depreciate."
c "The price of bananas is the same in Canada and the United States, adjusting for the exchange rate."
d "The expected depreciation of the Canadian dollar is currently lowering demand for it."
e None of the above.

3 If you think that the exchange rate will depreciate over the next month, you can make money by

a buying Canadian dollars.
b buying U.S. dollars.
c selling Canadian dollars.
d selling U.S. dollars.
e b and c.

4 Consider Table 38.1. Between 1994 and 1995, the Canadian dollar has _____ versus the mark and _____ versus the yen.

a appreciated; depreciated
b appreciated; appreciated
c depreciated; depreciated
d depreciated; appreciated
e none of the above

TABLE **38.1**

Currency	1994 Exchange Rate	1995 Exchange Rate
German Mark	2 marks/dollar	3 marks/dollar
Japanese Yen	120 yen/dollar	90 yen/dollar

5 Consider Table 38.1. Between 1994 and 1995, the yen

a must have depreciated in value versus the mark.
b must have appreciated in value versus the mark.
c may or may not have appreciated in value versus the mark.
d will have appreciated in value versus the mark if the mark has a higher weight in the Canadian trade index.
e will have appreciated in value versus the mark if the mark has a lower weight in the Canadian trade index.

6 Which of the following statements is *true*? A high and persistent current account deficit implies Canada is a

a net borrower.
b net lender.
c debtor nation.
d creditor nation.
e a and c.

7 $NX =$

a $C + I + G.$
b $(S + I) - (T + G).$
c $(G - T) + (I - S).$
d $(S - I) + (G - T).$
e none of the above.

8 The Bank of Canada cannot just set the exchange rate at any level it desires because

a such intervention violates international law.
b the foreign exchange market is unregulated.
c this would make Canada a debtor nation.
d this would require constant changes in international reserves.
e interest rate parity forbids it.

9 Which of the following is one of the balance of payments accounts?

a current account
b borrowing account
c official lending account
d net interest account
e public account

10 Suppose Canada initially has all balance of payments accounts in balance (no surplus or deficit). Then Canadian firms increase their imports from Japan, financing that increase by borrowing from Japan. There will now be a current account

a surplus and a capital account surplus.
b surplus and a capital account deficit.
c deficit and a capital account surplus.
d deficit and a capital account deficit.
e deficit and a capital account balance.

11 When would the exchange rate fall the most?

a When the supply and demand of dollars both increase.
b When the supply of dollars increases, and the demand decreases.
c When the supply of dollars decreases, and the demand increases.
d When the supply and demand of dollars both decrease.
e When there is intervention by the Bank of Canada.

12 The country of Mengia came into existence at the beginning of year 1. Given the information in Table 38.2, in year 4 Mengia is a

a net lender and a creditor nation.
b net lender and a debtor nation.
c net borrower and a creditor nation.
d net borrower and a debtor nation.
e net lender and neither a creditor nor a debtor nation.

TABLE **38.2**

Year	Borrowed from Rest of World (billions of dollars)	Loaned to Rest of World (billions of dollars)
I	60	20
2	60	40
3	60	60
4	60	80

13 Assuming that Mengia's official settlement account is always in balance, in which year or years in Table 38.2 did Mengia have a current account surplus?

a year 1
b year 2
c years 1, 2, and 3
d years 1 and 2
e year 4 only

14 If Mengia's official settlement balance was in deficit every year, for which year or years in Table 38.2 can you say for sure there was a current account surplus?

a year 1
b year 2
c years 2 and 3
d years 1 and 2
e years 3 and 4

15 Which of the following will shift the supply curve of dollars to the right?

a an increase occurs in the demand for foreign goods by Canadian citizens
b a decrease occurs in the demand for Canadian goods by foreigners
c the dollar is expected to appreciate next year
d U.S. interest rates rise
e none of the above

16 Suppose that the dollar–yen foreign exchange rate changes from 140 yen per dollar to 130 yen per dollar. Then the yen has

a depreciated against the dollar, and the dollar has appreciated against the yen.

b depreciated against the dollar, and the dollar has depreciated against the yen.

c appreciated against the dollar, and the dollar has appreciated against the yen.

d appreciated against the dollar, and the dollar has depreciated against the yen.

e neither appreciated nor depreciated, but the dollar has depreciated against the yen.

17 Which of the following will shift the demand curve for dollars to the right?

a an increase occurs in the demand for foreign goods by Canadian citizens

b a decrease occurs in the demand for Canadian goods by foreigners

c the dollar is expected to appreciate

d the dollar is expected to depreciate

e U.S. interest rates rise

18 If the interest rate in Canada is greater than the interest rate in Japan, interest rate parity implies that

a the inflation rate is higher in Japan.

b Japanese financial assets are poor investments.

c the yen is expected to depreciate against the dollar.

d the yen is expected to appreciate against the dollar.

e Canadian financial assets are poor investments.

19 The exchange rate is volatile because

a government intervention always make things worse.

b the demand curve is very flat.

c the demand curve is very steep.

d shifts in demand and supply are independent of each other.

e shifts in demand and supply are not independent of each other.

20 Suppose that a country's government expenditures are $400 billion, taxes (net of transfer payments) are $300 billion, saving is $300 billion, and investment is $250 billion. Net exports are in a

a surplus of $150 billion.

b surplus of $50 billion.

c deficit of $150 billion.

d deficit of $50 billion.

e deficit of $250 billion.

21 Suppose that a country's government expenditures are $400 billion, taxes (net of transfer payments) are $300 billion, saving is $300 billion, and investment is $250 billion. This country has a government budget

a surplus and a private sector surplus.

b surplus and a private sector deficit.

c deficit and a private sector surplus.

d deficit and a private sector deficit.

e surplus and a private sector balance.

22 The distinction between a debtor or creditor nation and a net borrower or net lender nation depends on

a the distinction between the level of saving in the economy and the saving rate.

b the distinction between the level of saving in the economy and the rate of borrowing.

c the distinction between the stock of investments and the flow of interest payments on those investments.

d the distinction between exports and imports.

e nothing really; they are the same.

23 If the current account is in deficit, and the capital account is also in deficit, then the change in official reserves is

a negative.

b positive.

c probably close to zero, but could be either negative or positive.

d zero.

e not affected.

24 Suppose the exchange rate between the Canadian dollar and the British pound is 0.5 pounds per dollar. If a radio sells for 38 pounds in Britain, what is the dollar price of the radio?

a $19

b $26

c $38

d $57

e $76

25 The market in which the currency of one country is exchanged for the currency of another is called the

a money market.

b capital market.

c foreign exchange market.

d forward exchange market.

e international trading market.

Short Answer Problems

1 What is the relationship between a country's trade deficit, its government budget deficit, and its private sector deficit?

2 What determines the value of the exchange rate?

3 What is purchasing power parity?

4 Why do changes in Canadian interest rates change the value of the exchange rate?

5 Over its lifetime as a country, Canada has tended to be a net borrower more than a net lender. Is this good or bad?

6 The international transactions of a country for a given year are reported in Table 38.3.

TABLE **38.3**

Transaction	Amount (billions of dollars)
Exports of goods and services	100
Imports of goods and services	130
Transfers to the rest of the world	20
Loans to the rest of the world	60
Loans from the rest of the world	?
Increases in official reserves	10
Net interest pyaments	0

a What is the amount of loans from the rest of the world?
b What is the current account balance?
c What is the capital account balance?
d What is the official settlements balance?

7 The information in Table 38.4 is for a country during a given year.

TABLE **38.4**

Variable	Amount (billions of dollars)
GDP	800
Net taxes	200
Government budget deficit	50
Consumption	500
Investment	150
Imports	150

a What is the level of government expenditure on goods and services?
b What is the private sector surplus or deficit?
c What is the value of exports?

d What is the balance of trade surplus or deficit?

8 Suppose that the exchange rate between the Canadian dollar and the German mark is 2 marks per dollar.
a What is the exchange rate in terms of dollars per mark?
b What is the price in dollars of a camera selling for 250 marks?
c What is the price in marks of a computer selling for 1,000 dollars?

9 Suppose that a personal computer sells for US$2,000 in the United States and C$3,000 in Canada.
a Where would you buy the personal computer if the exchange rate between the Canadian dollar and the U.S. dollar was US$0.80 per C$? Where would you resell it if you wanted to make a profit? (Ignore any taxes, tariffs, transportation costs, and differences in quality.)
b Does purchasing power parity hold?
c If many businesses acted like you, and if the exchange rate was flexible, what would happen to the value of the exchange rate? What would be the new equilibrium exchange rate that would make purchasing power parity hold for personal computers, if the U.S. dollar price and the Canadian dollar price stayed constant?

10 Go to the Government Documents Section of your library, or to the Bank of Canada *Review*, or to the Statistics Canada Website (http://www.statcan.ca/). Find data for the years 1985–1995 on the value of the exchange rate in terms of U.S. cents, as well as data on Canadian and U.S. interest rates (use the prime interest rate banks charge to their best businesses). Construct a table of the Canadian interest rate differential versus the exchange rate, and discuss what kind of relationship you find.

ANSWERS

True/False/Uncertain and Explain

1 T Other things remaining the same, this will ↑ interest rate differential. (938–939)
2 F They are both affected by expectations of the future value of the dollar → move together. (942–943)
3 F If expected to appreciate → ↑ earnings in foreign currency terms → ↑ demand for their bonds → ↓ interest rates until interest rate parity holds. (943)

4 T Under purchasing power parity, yen price identical in each country. $10 × 100 yen/\$ = 1,000 yen. (944)

⌾**5** F Overall flow of money in/out of country = sum of the three balances of payment must balance. Individual balances may be in deficit/surplus/balance. (932–933)

⌾**6** U Depends on reaction of private sector surplus/deficit. (934–936)

7 T Dollar is more valuable → takes more yen to buy one dollar. (937)

8 T ↑ foreign exchange value of dollar → ↑ foreign exchange value of dollar assets → ↑ demand for dollar assets. (939)

9 U May or may not be true. Net borrower → *current* net borrowing > 0. Debtor nation → sum of *all* net borrowing > 0. (934)

10 T Balance of trade (negative) = government balance (large negative) + private balance (small negative). (934–936)

Multiple-Choice

1 e This ↑ demand for Canadian dollars. **a** lowers demand, **b–d** raise supply. (944–945)

2 c Two currencies have same purchasing power. (944)

3 e You will wish to buy foreign currency, since it will rise in value, which also requires you to sell Canadian dollars. (939–941)

4 a It takes more marks to buy \$1 (↑ in value), and less yen (↓ in value). (937)

⌾**5** b 1994: 1/60 mark/yen = (2 marks/\$)/(120 yen/\$). 1995: 1/30 mark/yen = (3 marks/\$)/(90 yen/\$). Takes less marks in 1995 to buy 1 yen, so yen has depreciated. (937)

6 a High current account deficit → likely capital account surplus. It is unclear about debtor versus lender. (934)

7 e $(S − I) + (T − G)$ by definition. (935)

8 d Such intervention requires buying/selling Canadian dollars, which changes official reserves, which cannot occur forever. (944–945)

9 a Definition. (932)

⌾**10** c Imports > exports → current account deficit. Borrowing > lending → capital account surplus. (Think about which direction money is flowing.) (932–933)

11 b Draw a graph. (942–943)

12 b Current lending > borrowing → net lender. Sum of past borrowing > sum of lending → debtor nation. (934)

13 e Official settlements balance = 0 → current account surplus = capital account deficit → occurs only when lending > borrowing. (932–933)

⌾**14** e Since current account + capital account + official settlements account = 0, when official settlements is a deficit, to be sure current is a surplus, it must be the case that capital is 0 or a deficit. (932–933)

15 a ↑ demand for foreign currency → ↑ supply of Canadian dollars. (941)

16 d It takes less yen to buy dollar → dollar depreciates. Via inverse relationship, yen has appreciated. (937)

17 c **a** has no impact on demand, **b**, **d**, and **e** shift it leftward. (938–939)

⌾**18** d Therefore Canadian dollar expected to depreciate → interest rate in Canadian dollar terms is equal. (944)

19 e They are both affected by the same expectations. (942–943)

20 d Net exports = $(T − G) + (S − I) = 300 − 400 + 300 − 250 = −50$. (934–936)

21 c Government sector deficit = $T − G = 300 − 400 = −100$. Private sector surplus = $S − I = 300 − 250 = +50$. (934–936)

22 c Net lender → stock of investments rising. Debtor nation → negative flow of interest payments on investments. (934)

23 a Official settlements balance = −(capital account + current account) = surplus → change in official reserves < 0. (932)

24 e $76 = £38 × ($2 per £). (937)

25 c Definition. (937)

Short Answer Problems

1 The national income accounting identities allow us to show that a country's balance of trade deficit is equal to the sum of its government budget deficit and its private sector deficit.

2 The value of the exchange rate is determined by supply and demand. The supply of the Canadian dollar is changed by two things—changes in the Canadian interest rate differential and changes in the expected future exchange rate. The demand for the Canadian dollar is also changed by the same two things.

3 Purchasing power parity follows from arbitrage and the law of one price. It means that the value of money is the same in all countries. For example, if the exchange rate between the dollar and the yen is 120 yen per dollar, purchasing power parity says that a good that sells for 120 yen in Japan will sell for 1 dollar in Canada. Thus, the exchange rate is such that money (dollars or yen) has the same purchasing power in both countries.

4 A change in Canadian interest rates changes the desirability of Canadian bonds relative to foreign bonds. This in turn changes the demand and supply of the Canadian dollar, which will change the value of the exchange rate.

5 Being a net borrower is all right if the country is borrowing for investment purposes, and creating earnings to pay off what is owes. This has mostly been the case for Canada; so being a net borrower is good—it has allowed a resource-rich but capital-poor country like Canada to develop its resources.

6 a Current account balance + capital account balance + official settlements balance = 0, or (100 − 130 − 20) + (loans from rest of world − 60) + (−10) = 0, so loans from the rest of the world = 120.

b The current account balance is a $50 billion deficit: exports minus imports minus transfers to the rest of the world plus net interest payments to the rest of the world.

c The capital account balance is a surplus of $60 billion: loans from the rest of the world minus loans to the rest of the world.

d Because official reserves increased, the official settlements balance is −10.

7 a Since we know that the government budget deficit is $50 billion and net taxes are $200 billion, we can infer that government expenditure on goods and services is $250 billion.

b The private sector surplus or deficit is given by saving minus investment. Investment is given as $150 billion, but we must compute saving. Saving is equal to GDP minus taxes minus consumption: $100 billion. Thus there is a private sector deficit of $50 billion.

c We know that GDP is consumption plus investment plus government expenditure on goods and services plus net exports (exports minus imports). Since we know all these values except exports, we can obtain that value by solving for exports. The value of exports equals GDP plus imports minus consumption minus investment minus government expenditure on goods and services; the value of exports equals $50 billion.

d There is a balance of trade deficit of $100 billion. This can be obtained in two ways. First we can recognize that the balance of trade surplus or deficit is given by the value of exports ($50 billion) minus the value of imports ($150 billion). The alternative method is to recognize that the balance of trade deficit is equal to the sum of the government budget deficit ($50 billion) and the private sector deficit ($50 billion).

8 a If 1 dollar can be purchased for 2 marks, then the price of a mark is 1/2 dollar per mark.

b At an exchange rate of 2 marks per dollar, it takes 125 dollars to obtain the 250 marks needed to buy the camera.

c At an exchange rate of 2 marks per dollar, it takes 2,000 marks to obtain the 1,000 dollars needed to buy the computer.

9 a The Canadian computer costs US$2,400 = C$3,000 × US$0.80 per C$. Therefore it is profitable to buy it in the United States for US$2,000 and sell it in Canada for US$2,400.

b No, the two currencies do not have the same purchasing power.

c The extra demand for U.S. computers would tend to push up the demand for U.S. dollars, leading to an appreciation of the U.S. dollar (and a depreciation of the Canadian dollar). The value of the exchange rate that makes purchasing power parity hold would be the value A that solves US$2,000 = C$3,000 × US$$A$ per C$, which is a value of 0.667.

10 The data is listed in Table 38.5. Your data may be slightly different, due to rounding errors, etc., in your data source.

TABLE **38.5**

Year	Differential	U.S. $/C$
1985	0.7	0.732
1986	2.27	0.72
1987	1.31	0.754
1988	1.43	0.813
1989	2.45	0.845
1990	4.06	0.856
1991	1.55	0.873
1992	1.23	0.827
1993	−0.07	0.775
1994	−0.38	0.732
1995	−0.17	0.729

Source: Bank of Canada *Review,* various issues.

We can see that there is a rough positive relationship between the differential and the value of the exchange rate. As the differential rose through the middle of the time period, so did the value of the exchange rate, driven by an increase in the demand for Canadian dollars and a decrease in the supply of Canadian dollars. As the differential fell towards the end, so did the exchange rate. The relationship is not exact, but it does meet the rough predictions of our theories.

PROBLEM

You are an advisor to the prime minister, specializing in exchange rate considerations. The country is suffering from a crisis of nonconfidence on world markets, sparked by fears the country might dissolve, leading to a fall in the return on Canadian assets (for example, government debt might not be repaid by the new nations formed from Canada). A new poll is issued, suggesting that the probability of separation is higher than previously thought. Foreigners start a selloff of Canadian assets. (The Bank of Canada is operating under a rule of trying to stabilize the exchange rate.)

a Explain to the prime minister (with the aid of a graph showing the demand and supply of dollars) what this will imply for the value of the Canadian dollar, as well as for interest rates, the value of the monetary base and the money supply, and for the three balance of payments accounts.

b Another advisor to the prime minister has told her that the Bank of Canada should be ordered to raise the money supply to try and lower interest rates. What will this do to the value of the exchange rate and to foreign holdings of Canadian assets? Can the Bank of Canada do this and still maintain a managed exchange rate?

c The prime minister has received a phone call from the owner of the Big Importer Company, complaining that the change in the value of the Canadian dollar has hurt his ability to sell imported whatzits in Canada. With the aid of a graph of the market for whatzits in Canada (with the vertical axis measuring the price of whatzits in Canadian dollars), explain to the prime minister what has happened to the price and quantity imported in this market. What has happened to exports? to the balance of trade?

MIDTERM EXAMINATION

You should allocate 16 minutes for this examination (8 questions, 2 minutes per question). For each question, choose the one *best* answer.

1 The short-run adjustment costs in Canada associated with reducing the level of tariffs under a North American Free Trade Agreement will be borne principally by

a taxpayers, whose higher taxes provide the generous retraining programs.

b employers and workers in those sectors in which Canada has a comparative advantage.

c employers and workers in those sectors in which Canada has a comparative disadvantage.

d Canadian consumers of imported goods.

e Canadian producers of exported goods.

2 Country *A* and country *B* are currently engaged in free trade. Country *A* imports good *X* from country *B* and exports good *Y* to *B*. If country *A* imposes a *tariff* on *X*, country *A*'s *X*–producing industry will

a expand, and its *Y*-producing industry will contract.

b expand, and its *Y*-producing industry will expand.

c contract, and its *Y*-producing industry will contract.

d contract, and its *Y*-producing industry will expand.

e expand, and its *Y*-producing industry will be unchanged.

3 Suppose Musicland and Videoland produce two goods—CDs and videos. Musicland has a comparative advantage in the production of CDs if

a fewer videos must be given up to produce one unit of CDs than in Videoland.

b less labour is required to produce one unit of CDs than in Videoland.

c less capital is required to produce one unit of CDs than in Videoland.

d less labour and capital are required to produce one unit of CDs than in Videoland.

e fewer CDs must be given up to produce one unit of videos than in Videoland.

4 Suppose Musicland and Videoland produce two goods—CDs and videos—and Musicland has a comparative advantage in the production of CDs. If the countries trade, the price of CDs in terms of videos will be

a greater than the opportunity cost of CDs in Musicland and less than the opportunity cost of CDs in Videoland.

b less than the opportunity cost of CDs in Musicland and greater than the opportunity cost of CDs in Videoland.

c greater than the opportunity cost of CDs in both countries.

d less than the opportunity cost of CDs in both countries.

e dependent only on the relative size of each economy.

5 Which of the following quotations best describes the interest rate parity effect?

a "The recent high Canadian interest rate has raised the demand for the Canadian dollar."

b "The market feeling is that the Canadian dollar is overvalued and will likely appreciate."

c "The price of bananas is the same in Canada and the United States, adjusting for the exchange rate."

d "The expected appreciation of the Canadian dollar is currently lowering demand for it."

e None of the above.

6 Canada has a trade deficit when the

a value of Canadian exports of goods and services exceeds the value of Canadian imports of goods and services.

b value of Canadian exports of goods and services is exceeded by the value of Canadian imports of goods and services.

c value of Canadian exports of goods exceeds the value of Canadian imports of goods.

d value of Canadian exports of goods is exceeded by the value of Canadian imports of goods.

e current account balance is less than zero.

7 If Fullofland is currently a net lender and a debtor nation,

a it has loaned more capital than it borrowed abroad this year, but borrowed more than it loaned during its history.

b it has borrowed more capital than it loaned abroad this year and also borrowed more than it loaned during its history.

c it has loaned more capital than it borrowed abroad this year and has loaned more than it borrowed during its history.

d its accounting system must be in error if it shows this nation to be a net lender and a debtor nation at the same time.

e its debts must be currently growing.

8 Which of the following would cause the dollar to depreciate against the yen?

a an increase in the Canadian monetary supply

b an increase in interest rates in Canada

c a decrease in interest rates in Japan

d an increase in the expected future exchange rate

e a decrease in the current exchange rate

ANSWERS

Problem

a The fear of lower future returns leads to a fall in the demand for Canadian dollar assets, leading to a fall in the demand for Canadian dollars. In Fig. P9.1, this, in turn, leads to a fall in the value of the exchange rate from F_a to F_b. To keep it from falling even further, the Bank of Canada intervenes and buys Canadian dollars, supplying foreign exchange from official reserves. They also might shrink the money supply, which will tend to raise Canadian interest rates. (There are also potential supply effects not shown here.)

Foreigners are lending us less, so the capital account will move towards a smaller surplus or a deficit. The fall in the foreign exchange value of the Canadian dollar will lead to a rise in exports and a fall in imports (see part **c** below), so that the current account will move towards a surplus. Since the Bank of Canada is supplying foreign exchange, this is a decrease in reserves, or a movement towards a surplus.

FIGURE **P9.1**

b A lower interest rate would spark a further fall in the demand for the Canadian dollar, as foreigners buy fewer Canadian assets, given the lower return. This would tend to push down the Canadian dollar's value, which would conflict with the Bank of Canada's attempts to stabilize the exchange rate.

c The market for whatzits is shown in Fig. P9.2. The new, higher exchange rate acts like a tariff, and raises the Canadian dollar price of the imported whatzits, shown as the shift upward in the supply curve. This leads to a new equilibrium, with a higher price, and a lower quantity imported and sold.

The market for Canadian exports would be acting in an opposite manner, with lower prices and more exports. The higher exports and lower imports will mean the balance of trade (and hence the current account) is moving towards a surplus.

FIGURE **P9.2**

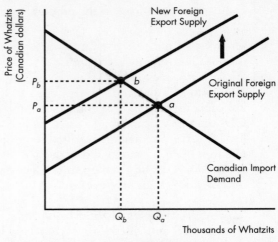

Midterm Examination

1 **c** Because U.S. or Mexican price lower $\rightarrow \downarrow$ domestic production. (921–922)

2 **a** Tariff $\rightarrow \uparrow$ domestic price of $X \rightarrow \downarrow$ imports $\rightarrow \uparrow$ domestic production. $\downarrow$ imports $= \downarrow$ B's exports $\rightarrow \downarrow$ its income $\rightarrow \downarrow$ its imports $\rightarrow \downarrow$ A's exports $\rightarrow \downarrow$ Y production in A. (914–916)

3 **a** Definition. (905–906)

4 **a** Trade will only occur between these two prices, otherwise one or both countries are worse off from trade and will not trade. (906–907)

5 **a** If two currencies do not have the same interest rate, market conditions will change the demand for assets and the dollar. (944)

6 **b** Definition of balance of trade. (932)

7 **a** Definitions of net lender and debtor nation. Debts are shrinking. (934)

8 **a** This $\downarrow$ interest rates $\rightarrow \downarrow$ demand for Canadian dollars. **b–d** $\uparrow$ demand, **e** move along, not a shift. (942–943)